THE NOSTRADAMUS ENCYCLOPEDIA

THE NOSTRADAMUS ENCYCLOPEDIA

The definitive reference guide to
the work and world of Nostradamus

PETER LEMESURIER

Thorsons
An Imprint of HarperCollins *Publishers*

Thorsons
An imprint of HarperCollins *Publishers*
77–85 Fulham Palace Road,
Hammersmith, London W6 8JB

Published in the UK by Thorsons 1998
1 3 5 7 9 10 8 6 4 2

DESIGNED AND PRODUCED BY
THE BRIDGEWATER BOOK COMPANY LTD

Picture research by Vanessa Fletcher

Peter Lemesurier asserts the moral right to be identified as the author of this work.

A catalogue record for this book is available
from the British Library.

ISBN 0 7225 3796 4

Printed and bound in Singapore by Tien Wah Press

CONTENTS

PREFACE

THIS ENCYCLOPEDIA is dedicated entirely to Nostradamus and his world. It is designed to present all the available information on the great French seer in easily accessible form, while also placing him in full context – not only biographically, but historically, culturally, and geographically, too.

But then this book is unique in many ways. Unlike most other treatments, it gives full details of the seer's family, friends, and associates, as well of his major contemporaries. It describes his hometown and tells the real story of his life, rather than the fanciful, romanticized one proffered by most of the existing accounts. It reveals his unsuspected but historically attested "other activities." And it presents for the first time astonishing new research that has at last revealed the secret of exactly how Nostradamus arrived at his predictions.

Even more to the point, the French texts (along with brief English paraphrases) of all the prophecies – except for the annual *Almanachs* – are reprinted in full and in the earliest available editions, while details are also given of their publishing history. Their language and literary characteristics are analyzed and their various sources and influences recorded, as are the reactions of Nostradamus's contemporaries. Summaries of the major interpretations of them are also included. A full Nostradamus dictionary and concordance – both unique to this volume – complement the text, and the book concludes with an all-important general index.

Cross-references to significant treatments elsewhere are given in parentheses, and people and places mentioned throughout may be referred to via the Indexes or in the general Gazetteer and Who's Who.

PART ONE

LIFE AND CAREER

Nostradamus in the context
of his times; his lifestory; his
career as physician, astrologer,
and mage; selected horographs.

NOSTRADAMUS IN CONTEXT

NOSTRADAMUS lived at a crucial time in European history. In France, it was the age of François I, Henri II, and the powerful Catherine de Médicis; in England, of Henry VIII and Elizabeth I; across the mighty Hapsburg Empire, of Charles V and Philip II, father of the Armada; in the vast lands to the south and east, of Suleiman the Magnificent and his marauding Ottoman armies.

Still lit by the glowing embers of the High Renaissance, it was a time both of optimistic world-exploration and of devastating internecine wars; both of scientific advance and of rampant plague; both of resplendent riches and of the direst poverty; both of intense and all-embracing scholarship and of the narrowest religious bigotry and persecution; both of nostalgia for a glowing classical past and of fears for an uncertain and possibly apocalyptic future.

Michel de Nostredame (Nostradamus), engraving by Léonard Gautier, first published c. 1600

In religion, after all, it was not only the era of Luther and Calvin, but also the heyday of the Catholic Jesuits and of the Inquisition – and, between them, these two implacably hostile wings of Christ's religion of love seemed determined to engineer the Apocalypse even before the century was out. Yet in scholarship it was also the age of Erasmus and the Scaligers; in literature of Ronsard and Rabelais, of Marot and Du Bellay; in music of Palestrina and Lassus, Tallis and Byrd; in painting and sculpture of Raphael and Titian, of Leonardo da Vinci and Michelangelo; in medicine and occultism of Paracelsus and John Dee. And in at least two of these spheres Nostradamus was, as we shall see, to earn his own illustrious place . . .

Born the year after Columbus set out on his last voyage of discovery, he was just four when Michelangelo started work on the ceiling of the Sistine Chapel, fifteen when Luther nailed his revolutionary theses to the church door at Wittenberg. It was in the year that he left college at Avignon, even while Magellan was striving to achieve the first circumnavigation of the globe, that Henry VIII met François I at the fabulous Field of the Cloth of Gold and, in the East, Suleiman ascended the Peacock Throne. Indeed, Suleiman's Ottoman hordes arrived before the very gates of Vienna in the self-same year as the twenty-five-year-old apothecary enrolled for his doctorate course at Montpellier, and even by the

The Catholic League (the violently extreme anti-Protestant faction) marches through the place de la Grève, Paris

time he finally started work as a licensed physician at Agen, the Emperor Charles V had only just managed to push them back again.

And so time passed. The young doctor fled, spent several years on the move, at length returned to his calling as an acknowledged plague-specialist, then retired from medicine to concentrate largely on prophecy, settling down with his new wife in Salon-de-Provence. That year of 1547 saw the deaths

Dr. John Dee, like Nostradamus a scholar and court astrologer – to Queen Elizabeth I

both of François I and of England's Henry VIII – and possibly, too, of the future seer's own father. Two years later came the publication in Lyon of a new Latin translation of the fourth-century Iamblichus's *De Mysteriis Aegyptiorum*, which broached the principles of theurgy, or the summoning up of gods and spirits. That fact, as we shall see, is no less relevant to the story of Nostradamus than it is to that of John Dee.

And so it was that the seer published the first of his series of annual *Almanachs* just as Palestrina, away in Italy, was starting work as Master of the Music at the Vatican. Almost contemporaneously with the appearance of the first of his collections of prophetic *Centuries*, Calvin suddenly started to make huge numbers of Protes-

tant converts throughout France. Within little more than a year of the *Propheties'* completion, France was in apparently terminal crisis, its King mortally wounded during a tournament, its forces largely converted into armies of wandering unemployed, its countryside consequently infested with robberbands, and its Catholics and Protestants at each other's throats. And by the time the seer died in 1566 – in the same year, as it happens, as the Emperor Suleiman – the land was racked with lawlessness and deprivation, and the gruesome Wars of Religion had begun that would rob it of about 1,600,000 of its citizens before the century had run its course.

The period, in short, was one of enormous energies, both constructive and destructive, and it was on the tensions between the two that men such as Nostradamus and his leading contemporaries fed and thrived. While some strong man, woman, or institution was in control, those energies could be focused and channeled, and all things seemed possible; but once that control was removed, all hell was liable to break loose.

As, indeed, it increasingly did.

France, after all, was as yet scarcely a nation. It was at best a patchwork kingdom. Aquitaine had been recovered from the English only in 1452. The Calais area was still in dispute. The independent kingdom of Provence had been acquired only in 1482. Lorraine, Franche-Comté, and Savoy were subjects of continual friction with the Holy Roman Empire to the east. And Brittany would not be formally annexed until as late as 1547.

At the purely local level, too, France was much more a community of coexisting fiefdoms than it was ever a united kingdom. Each local lord exercised seigneurial rights within his own domain and, within even that, local communities often had their own traditions and laws, which the King's officials were still hard put to research and codify. Weights and measures, for example, actually varied from district to district, as did the precise form of local government and administration. In the north, towns were generally run by councils under a mayor; in the south, where the ancient traditions of Rome were better preserved, they were run by senates composed of magistrates and headed by elected consuls. In the countryside, the peasants were subject to a bewildering variety of statuses varying from feudal retainership, via sharecropping, to limited freeholds – and indeed, often to more than one of them at once.

Nor was this administrative chaos particularly surprising, bearing in mind the state of communications throughout the kingdom at the time. To make no bones about it, these were virtually nonexistent. Certainly there was no general postal service. Except for the team of 120 royal couriers constantly posting back and forth on exclusive government business, anybody needing to send letters or packages inland (let alone abroad) was obliged to buy their way into the alternative courier-services run by powerful international bankers (notably the celebrated Medici of Florence) whose business – given the entirely unacceptable risks involved in transporting large quantities of gold and silver from place to place – depended largely on the forwarding of letters of credit.

Travel itself was in no better state. Engaging as it may be for us today to imagine Nostradamus flitting from place to place in some kind of horse-drawn carriage, such contrivances in fact did not come into use until the second half of the sixteenth century – and then only for royalty and the richest ladies within the great cities, or on the royal road from Paris to the royal residences in the Loire valley. Men, for their part, tended to shun them as a threat to their masculinity. Even Queen Catherine de Médicis, who later traveled the country ceaselessly in her despairing efforts to hold the disintegrating state together, never rode in anything more technologically advanced than a hand-borne litter, equipped though it may have been

Catherine de Médicis, vigorous Italian queen of Henri II and patron of Nostradamus

as a veritable office. That, indeed, was how she arrived in Salon to visit the seer in August 1564, in the course of her two-year peace-making publicity-tour of the kingdom with her son Charles IX. And her great contemporary Queen Elizabeth of England, after trying out the newfangled barrel-like contraption that had been specially built for her in around 1570, swore never again to repeat the experience.

But then none of this was particularly surprising. For the fact is that, except for those already mentioned, there were simply no roads for such vehicles to travel on in the first place. At best, the countryside was crisscrossed by a network of rough dirt tracks that became totally impassable whenever it rained – as it did with increasing frequency as the century wore on. All long-distance travel therefore had to be by litter or on horseback, and all long-distance goods carried on the backs of primitive trains of pack-horses. Unsurprisingly, therefore, not many of them were. Local communities remained largely self-sufficient, whether in food, clothes, or construction materials. Admittedly, there were regional specialties – silk from the southwest, perhaps, or general notions from the north – whose rarity lent them sufficient value to justify their importation to other regions. Books, too, were distributed in this way (see Book Printing and Publishing). But many such items fell into the category of "luxury goods," which only the richest could afford to buy – and in their case they were perfectly capable of organizing and paying for their own transportation, whether by sea or other means.

That said, however, *international* travel was in fact a good deal less complicated than it is today, even with the advent of the modern European Union. The concept of nationality in the modern sense had as yet barely arisen. Borders were virtually nonexistent. The first customhouse was not set up until 1544, and customs duties were not made a regular feature of royal revenue until twenty years later. The word *passeport*, similarly, seems not to have have been heard of much before 1539.

True, only the nobles and better-paid officials could afford to travel abroad anyway, but those who could were then perfectly entitled to travel in any country in western or northern Europe without let or hindrance – as indeed the children of the aristocracy were positively expected to do as the culminating part of their education.

Currencies, after all, were fully interchangeable. France admittedly had its own national coinage: during the first part of the century the golden crown (*ecu*) was valued at three pounds (*livres*), each of these being divided into shillings (*sous*) and pence (*deniers*). But English rose nobles and Spanish *ducats* and *pistoles* circulated just as freely, to say nothing of a host of smaller coins, with their relative values determined simply by the weight of metal they contained.

But all these manifestations of openness and integration were never more than the other side of the coin of chaos and division that was always equally present and ready to be tendered. The bewildering variety of pieces of gold and silver that continually passed from hand to grubby hand amid urban scenes of indescribable squalor may have helped to maintain the increasingly precarious health of the economy, but at the same time the very environment that it supported paradoxically invited in every kind of pestilence, social unrest, and political and religious agitation.

France in the sixteenth century, in short, was a kingdom of infinite diversity and contradiction, of chaos and internal stresses, always liable to fall apart at the seams. A great deal depended, as we have seen, upon the presence of a strong central authority – and François I and his vigorous and capable son Henri II duly supplied it. Still exercising the remnants of feudal power through powerful nobles who were themselves controlled largely through the awarding of offices and benefits, they strove ceaselessly to impose royal ordinances and edicts throughout the kingdom, thus eroding little by little the independent writ of local lords and communities. And to a large extent they were successful.

But fate was not on their side. From the 1520s, the subversive ideas of Lutheranism were already starting to make themselves felt within Catholic France, especially among the one-and-a-half million or so town-dwellers who made up around one-tenth of the population. By the 1530s the initial trickle of Protestant converts had become a flood, with Nostradamus's own stamping-grounds of Montpellier, Agen, and Lyon all local centers of Calvinism. From the 1520s, too, nature itself joined in, as the first of a whole series of plague-epidemics swept the country. And as if that was not enough, the late 1520s and

Europe at the time of Nostradamus

Dominions of Charles V
Ottoman Empire
Holy Roman Empire

1530s saw a distinct worsening of the weather, with severe agricultural crises resulting in 1529–30 and 1538–9, leading (as they would also repeatedly do later in the century) to widespread peasant penury, massdispossessions, migrations to the already bursting towns, and tens of thousands of deaths from starvation.

The link was quite specific, and so it soon became quite natural for those who thought about such things to see the change in the weather as a "sign of the times." As Nostradamus's illustrious younger contemporary Pierre de Ronsard was to put it some years later:

> Le Ciel qui a pleuré tout le long de l'année,
> Et Seine qui couroit d'une vague éfrenée,
> Et bestail et pasteurs largement ravissoit,
> De son malheur futur Paris avertissoit,
> Et sembloit que les eaux en leur rage profonde
> Voulussent renoyer une autre fois le monde.
> Cela nous predisoit que la terre, et les cieux
> Menaçoient nostre chef d'un mal prodigieux.[1]

And so it was perhaps not too much of a surprise when the real crisispoint did indeed come in 1559. That was the year when France, already devastated by a huge defeat at the hands of the Empire at St-Quentin two years before, saw both the sudden death of its King (expected by nobody, it seems, except Nostradamus and his Italian colleague Luca Gaurico) and the virtual disbandment of its armies. As we noted earlier, this last released onto an already saturated market a massive flood of unemployed soldiers, skilled in nothing but killing and looting, who (unlike their Spanish counterparts) had no New World to go and conquer – and this at a time when Catholics and Protestants were in the very throes of arming themselves to the teeth for a bloody confrontation.

The upshot was inevitable. As the psychically warped and constitutionally tubercular Valois princes died and succeeded each other in rapid succession, the Catholic Guises and Protestant Bourbon-Condés vied for power, squeezing out faithful old royal retainers such as High Constable Anne de Montmorency in the process, while the Queen Mother was forced into the unenviable role of trying frantically to steer a middle course for the sake of preserving the youthful monarchy and the integrity of the kingdom. Her constantly changing alliances, her endless travels, and reams of still-surviving diplomatic letters testify to the process.

Yet, despite her efforts, mere conflict rapidly turned into obsessive mutual slaughter, at the very same time as growing plague and famine were adding further thousands of deaths to the unholy mix. The kingdom was soon awash with blood, riddled with division, poisoned to the core with hatred. So dire did things become

Albrecht Dürer's
Horsemen of the Apocalypse

politically that the French Revolution came within a whisker of happening as early as 1588–9, rather than 200 years later. King Henri III was excommunicated and expelled from his capital. Rebels ruled much of the country. And if the beleaguered Catholics whose churches the Lutherans were increasingly sacking and looting could see in the signs of their age – and in Calvin the Antichrist – the familiar Plague, War, Famine, and Death that traditionally marked the onset of the dreaded Last Times, they were merely confirmed in that suspicion when the Protestants roped in thousands of mercenary German cavalry (the notorious *Reiter*) to lay waste whole swathes of eastern France, so adding to the scenario of doom the very Horsemen of the Apocalypse.

Later in this volume it will be shown how Nostradamus – himself a devout Catholic, despite some of his contemporaries' suspicions to the contrary – drew most of the details of his predictions from actual events, either long past, recently experienced, or even then in the making. In this case it is little wonder that many of his prophecies should seem, to modern eyes at least, so extraordinarily apocalyptic.

Well might Ronsard go on to write of those times:

> O toy historien, qui d'ancre non menteuse
> Escrits de nostre temps l'histoire monstrueuse,
> Raconte à nos enfants tout ce malheur fatal,
> Afin qu'en te lisant ils pleurent nostre mal
> Et qu'ils prennent exemple aux pechés de leurs peres,
> De peur de ne tomber en pareilles miseres.[2]

---

1 Discours des misères de ce temps (1562), 107–114:
The sky that all year long has wept and wept,
The Seine, whose flood has madly onward swept
O'erwhelming many a flock by shepherd led,
Warned Paris of catastrophe ahead,
As though the waters, raging on amain,
Were minded all the world to flood again.
All this forewarned us how both earth and sky
Hung o'er our heads untold calamity.

2 Discours des misères de ce temps (1562), 115–120:
Historian, in black ink that cannot fail
Of these our times to tell the monstrous tale,
Tell our descendants of our hapless fate,
That they may read, and weep for our estate,
And let them these their fathers' sins recall
Lest like misfortunes should themselves befall.

TABLE OF EVENTS 1500–70

1500

Population of Lyon *c.* 40,000.
Witch persecutions continue throughout century under influence of the *Malleus Maleficarum* of Institoris and Sprenger (1486).

Christopher Columbus makes landfall, 1502

1501

Twice as many religious works published in Paris as classical or humanist ones.
JUN. 28TH: **Nostradamus's father Jaume recorded as "merchant" at St-Rémy-de-Provence.**

1502

Christopher Columbus sets out on last voyage, exploring coasts of Honduras and Nicaragua.

1503

AUG. 18TH: Pope Alexander VI dies.
AUG. 18TH: Pope Pius III elected.
SEPT. 22ND: Pope Pius III dies.
NOV. 31ST: Pope Julius II elected.
DEC. 14TH: **Michel de Nostredame born at noon at St.-Rémy.**

1505

SEPT. 2ND: **Nostredame's father Jaume recorded as "notary" of St.-Rémy.**

1506

Christopher Columbus dies in poverty in Valladolid, Spain.
Work starts on the new St. Peter's Basilica, Rome.

1508

Michelangelo commissioned to paint ceiling of Sistine Chapel.

1509

Erasmus publishes *In Praise of Folly* against traditional academic theologians and clerics.
Rabelais becomes a Franciscan.

1510

Balboa joins expedition to Darien.
JUL. 8TH: **Nostredame's father Jaume recorded as "notary and merchant".**

1511

Medical faculty founded at University of Avignon.

1512

Lefèvre d'Étaples publishes new Latin edition of St. Paul.
NOV. 1ST: Michelangelo's ceiling of Sistine Chapel completed.
DEC. 21ST: Louis XII imposes conversion tax on Christianized Jews.

1513

FEB. 21ST: Pope Julius II dies.
MAR. 9TH: Giovanni de' Medici elected as Pope Leo X.
Balboa crosses Isthmus of Darien to Pacific Ocean.
Claude de Lorraine marries Antoinette de Bourbon.

1514

Artisans at Agen riot for a place on town council.

François I meets Henry VIII at the Field of the Cloth of Gold, 1520

1515

JAN.: Antoine Duprat appointed Chancellor.
15 JAN.: Louis XII dies: his twenty-year-old nephew François I succeeds.
MAR. 24TH: Alliance agreed between François I and Charles of Hapsburg: France partially defaults.
MAY: François I levies 8,000 Gascons and Basques, plus 23,000 German *Landsknechts* to reinforce his armies for an attack on Charles of Hapsburg's Swiss infantry in Italy.
SEPT.: France victorious in Italy at Battle of Marignano.
French population *c.* sixteen million: civil service numbers 4,041 (one per 3,950 of population).

1516

AUG.: Concordat of Bologna abolishes episcopal elections and provides for royal appointment (though papal spiritual investment) of bishops and abbots.
NOV. 29TH: Treaty of perpetual peace

signed with Swiss cantons, bribed never again to participate in wars involving France.

Erasmus publishes his *Novum Instrumentum*, Latin translation of scriptures.

François I jails three actors who criticize the Court.

1517

Balboa imprisoned and executed.

Ottomans take Cairo.

OCT. 31ST: Martin Luther denounces Roman Catholic indulgences in his "95 theses" at Wittenberg.

Nostredame's father Jaume recorded as "notary and scribe."

1518

Hernando Cortés sets out for Mexico.

JUL.: Nostredame's brother Bertrand baptized.

1519

Charles I of Hapsburg and Spain becomes Holy Roman Emperor Charles V, lord of Germany, the Netherlands, much of Italy and Spain, and most of South America.

AUG. 13TH: Nostredame's father Jaume calls himself "noble" while deputizing for a real one.

Nostredame starts his studies at Avignon.

Claude de Seyssel's *La Grande Monarchie de France* sets theoretical bounds to royal power.

First of many edicts lays down maximum inn-charges.

French Catholic religious reformers visit Strasbourg and Basle to observe Lutheran reform in action.

Leonardo da Vinci dies in retirement at Amboise.

1520

Anne de Montmorency becomes chief royal valet de chambre.

APR. 6TH: Raphael dies.

François I wrestles Henry VIII to ground at "Field of Cloth of Gold" meeting near Calais.

Plague sweeps the country.

AUG. 23RD: Emperor Charles V crowned.

Plague arrives in Avignon: university suspended; students leave.

Suleiman the Magnificent succeeds to Ottoman Empire.

1521

JAN.: Luther excommunicated.

Pope Leo X entitles Henry VIII of England "Defender of the Faith" for his defense of Catholic sacraments against Luther.

APR. 15TH: Sorbonne condemns 104 Lutheran propositions.

Lefèvre d'Étaples harassed for his reformist religious writings.

Ottomans take Belgrade.

Protestants so call themselves for the first time.

Cortés captures Mexico City.

Nostredame starts nine years of wandering and herbal research.

Ferdinand Magellan killed by Philippine natives.

First war against Charles V begins.

François I increases taxes to pay for wars.

Guillaume Briçonnet, Bishop of Meaux, starts religious reform movement.

DEC. 1ST: Pope Leo X dies.

1522

JAN. 9TH: Pope Adrian VI elected.

FEB. 19TH: "Jean de Nostredame" baptized.

APR. 27TH: With over 3,000 Swiss mercenaries killed at La Bicocca, France loses most of its possessions in Italy.

Henry VIII declares war on France.

François I raises money by selling offices.

Taille (general tax) reaches three million pounds annually.

Magellan's sole surviving ship returns to Seville after first global circumnavigation.

Montmorency appointed Marshal of France and Governor of Languedoc.

Ottomans capture Rhodes.

France wracked with pestilence.

1523

Freezing weather ruins crops in France.

APR. 27TH: Nostredame's brother Antoine baptized at St.-Rémy.

François I first takes up permanent residence in Paris.

Images of Virgin Mary destroyed at Paris and Meaux.

SEPT. 14TH: Pope Adrian VI dies.

NOV. 19TH: Pope Clement VII elected.

The disastrous Battle of Pavia, 1525, during which the cream of French chivalry was destroyed and François I and his two sons were taken prisoner. Painting by Gherardo Poli.

1524

JUL. 7TH: Charles de Bourbon invades southeast France for Charles V, taking Aix and nearly Marseille.

AUG. 27TH: François I lays siege to Pavia with a force of 30,000.

François makes first of many attempts to shorten legal proceedings.

Lefèvre d'Étaples publishes French translation of New Testament.

Taille increased to nearly six million pounds.

Pierre de Ronsard born at La Poissonière, Vendôme.

Rabelais transfers to Benedictines.

1525

FEB. 25TH: François defeated and captured at Pavia and most of French knightly class slain.

MAY: Captive François I moved from Italy to Madrid, and there falls ill.

Plague throughout the south: disease epidemics sweep the country.

OCT. 3RD: Paris Parlement scotches Bishop of Meaux's efforts at Church reform, issuing arrest-warrants that result in exile, execution, and imprisonment.

Adam de Craponne born.

Jules César Scaliger arrives from Italy to settle at Agen.

1526

JAN. 14TH: Treaty signed with Charles V freeing François I in exchange for his two sons, affiancing him to Eleanor, the Emperor's sister, ceding Burgundy and Italy, restoring Charles de Bourbon, and promising an army and fleet for an Imperial anti-Turkish crusade.

MAR. 17TH: François I freed.

AUG. 29TH: Ottomans wipe out Hungarian Christian army at Battle of Mohacs.

SEPT. 12TH: Ottomans sack Buda (Budapest).

Pizarro starts exploring northwest coast of South America.

Anti-Imperial League of Cognac signed up to by France, Pope Clement VII, Venice, various Italian states, and Henry VIII of England.

Paracelsus becomes lecturer in medicine at Basel.

Suleiman the Magnificent nearly takes Vienna.

1527

MAY 5TH: Charles de Bourbon sacks Rome for France, with the Pope a virtual prisoner in the Castel Sant'Angelo until December.

Henri D'Albret marries Marguerite d'Angoulême.

JUN. 5TH: Paracelsus starts work as lecturer at Basel, controversially throwing open his lectures to all.

JUN. 24TH: Paracelsus publicly burns the works of Galen and Avicenna in front of university of Basel.

1528

May 1st: French forces lay siege to Naples, but later surrender: of 39,000 men, only about 4,000 return safe and sound.

Clément Marot appointed court poet.

François I starts to extend and refurbish the Château de Fontainebleau.

Great Tower of the Louvre collapses.

Particularly severe plague throughout the south.

Statue of Virgin Mary beheaded in Paris.

Rabelais starts period of studies at Bordeaux, Toulouse, Orléans, and Paris.

1529

Period of cold, wet weather, agricultural crisis, and famine begins.

AUG. 3RD: Treaty of Cambrai removes all French possessions in Italy, as well as Artois and Flanders, re-affiances François I to Eleanor, Charles V's sister, and saddles France with 290,000–500,000 golden crowns war-damages.

Grand Robeyne at Lyon: famine-inspired popular revolt.

Paracelsus starts tour of Europe.

SEPT. TO OCT.: Ottomans besiege Vienna.

OCT. 23RD: Nostredame, now a qualified apothecary, enrols in the Montpellier medical faculty.

1530

Period of cold, wet weather, agricultural crisis, and famine continues.

Subsistence crises plus overpopulation start to upset previous equilibrium, and peasant world starts to disintegrate.

Inflation takes off in wake of climatic and agricultural crises: standard of living starts to fall.

MAR.: Ransom for the two royal princes François and Henri (paid for by a huge national levy) discharged on Spanish frontier, and princes and Eleanor exchanged.

Erasmus's *De civilitate morum puerilium* defines courtly behavior.

François I installs first chairs of Latin, Greek, and Hebrew in new Collège des Trois Langues, later Collège de France.

SEPT. 17TH: Rabelais leaves monastic life and enrols at Montpellier to study for medical degree.

Lefèvre d'Étaples publishes French translation of Old Testament.

Pizarro conquers Peru.

Six years of European peace begin.

1531

MAR.: German Lutheran states form defensive league against Charles V.

Diane de Poitiers widowed.

Severe famine in Lyon: disease sweeps the country.

First legislation to control grain exports in time of need.

François I embarks on three-year progress through France (including Marseille, for the wedding of his son Henri).

Juan Luis Vives publishes *De Disciplinis*, textbook on humanist education.

Normal weather returns.

Rabelais leaves Montpellier.

Turks threaten Austria and western Mediterranean.

Ottoman raiders ravage the Mediterranean coast of Europe westward as far as Nice for the next ten years.

1532

Attempts begin to reform tolls on roads and rivers.

Six months' drought.

Rabelais, doctor in Lyon, publishes *Pantagruel* (fabulous novel and allegorical textbook on humanist education) under pseudonym ALCOFRIBAS NASIER.

Vienna saved from Ottomans (just) by Charles V.

Rabelais writes to Erasmus complaining of Scaliger's venomous diatribes against him.

1533

Dauphin Henri marries Catherine de' Medici (later de Médicis) at Marseille.

Nostredame living at Agen.

Disease sweeps the country.

François I welcomed at Lyon as another Alexander the Great.

Rabelais publishes *Pantagrueline prognostication*.

1534

JUL.: Seven provincial infantry legions formed totaling 42,000, nearly one-third of them arquebusiers.

AUG. 15TH: Jesuit order founded by Ignatius Loyola to reinforce and purify Christian faith and practice.

AUG. 17TH–18TH: Antipapist placards posted at Amboise, Paris, Tours, Orléans, and Blois, attacking the Roman Catholic Mass.

Henry VIII of England breaks with Rome, declares himself Supreme Head of Church of England and suppresses the monasteries.

Henry VIII of England, patron of English Protestantism after breaking with Rome in 1534

Grande Aumone established at Lyon: the poor issued with certificates as part of poverty-relief program and municipal orphanages set up.

John Calvin starts writing *Institution of the Christian Religion*.

Michelangelo (sixty) completes decoration

of tomb of Giuliano and Lorenzo de' Medici and, commissioned to paint Last Judgment in Rome, befriends poetess Vittoria Colonna.

SEPT. 25TH: Pope Clement VII dies.

OCT. 13TH: Pope Paul III elected.

Ottomans attack Persia.

Rabelais publishes *Gargantua*.

Sorbonne tries to curtail curriculum of Collège de France – without success.

1535

JAN. 13TH: All printing banned and bookstores closed in reaction to subversive religious literature.

JAN. 21ST: François I takes part in massive ritual procession to reaffirm Roman Catholicism.

JAN. 23RD: Book trade placed under Parlement's supervision.

JAN. 29TH: Edict published announcing François's intention to exterminate Lutheranism: a year of terror grips major cities.

JAN.: Thirty-five Protestants burned in Paris.

JUN.: Charles V attacks Turks at Tunis.

JUL. 9TH: Chancellor Duprat dies: Pierre Poyet succeeds.

JUL.: Edict of Coucy offers amnesty to Protestants and allows recanting religious exiles to return.

Edict of Joinville reforms Aix Parlement after Parisian model and curtails powers of regional Governor.

Montmorency withdraws from Court.

Ottomans take Tunis.

Pizarro founds Lima, Peru.

Poet Clément Marot flees France.

Dec.: Rabelais petitions Pope to absolve him from "apostasy."

Venetian Ambassador notes that "there is nobody in France, however poor, who cannot read and write."

1536

FEB.: French launch surprise attack on Savoy and Piedmont.

Henry VIII commences Dissolution of English monasteries.

JUL. 2ND: Charles V declares war on France.

JUL. 12TH: Erasmus dies.

François Rabelais, doctor, novelist, and fellow-student of Nostradamus

AUG. 10TH: Dauphin François dies: his younger brother Henri (eighteen), the future Henri II, succeeds to the office and becomes heir apparent.

Jacques Lefèvre, French religious reformer, dies.

John Calvin, banished to Geneva, publishes *Institution of the Christian Religion*.

1537

JAN. 15TH: François I lays claim to Flanders.

Castiglione's *Book of the Courtier* published in French translation.

First of many measures taken to forbid printers to publish books without a royal *privilège*, or to publish religious books without a license from the Sorbonne.

François I defines powers of Provost Marshals (national police force) as covering treason, theft, begging, vagabondage, and brigandage.

Adam de Craponne's father dies while on commercial visit to Middle East.

MAY 22ND: Rabelais receives doctorate at Montpellier.

JUL. 31ST: Truce signed on the Somme.

OCT.: Montmorency starts new military campaign in Italy.

Marot returns to France after abjuring Protestantism.

Ottomans overrun Algeria.

1538

Further period of cold, wet weather, agricultural crisis, and famine begins.

MAY: Rabelais practices medicine at Lyon and elsewhere in the south, then travels to Italy with French Ambassador Jean du Bellay.

JUN.: Official Persecution of Protestants resumes.

JUL. 14TH: New truce signed between François I and Charles V.

Pope Paul III removes Henry VIII's title as "Defender of the Faith."

Montmorency appointed Grand Constable of France.

Rabelais at Aigues Mortes for meeting between Charles V and François I.

Provost Marshals' jurisdiction extended to cover poaching, sacrilege, and counterfeiting.

1539

Period of cold, wet weather, agricultural crisis, and famine continues.

JAN.: Charles V welcomed in Paris during progress through France.

Lyon print-workers strike against poor food, too many low-paid apprentices, and too many holy-days.

Edict of Fontainebleau provides for hunting down of Protestant "blasphemers."

Edict of Villers-Cotterêts bans all "union" activity and abolishes Provençal as official language for administration.

Nostredame possibly at Bordeaux.

1540

Jesuit order officially constituted by Pope Paul III.

John Calvin publishes his *Treatise on the Supper*.

Normal weather returns.

Parlement of Aix pursues and burns hundreds of the Protestant Waldensian sect.

Scaliger's son Joseph-Juste born.

SEPT. 22ND: François I signs naturalization papers at Chambord for "nostre bien-aimé Jacques de Nostredame" and his brother Pierre. Nostredame's brother Bertrand

marries Thomime Rousse.

Society of Jesus (Jesuits) founded by St. Ignatius Loyola.

Start of prosecutions of Protestants at Paris, Lyon, Bordeaux, Toulouse, Agen, Albi, Nîmes, Montpellier, and elsewhere.

1541

Anne de Montmorency falls from King's favor.

Calvin publishes *Ecclesiastical Ordinances*.

First import duties imposed.

François I imposes new, reformed *gabelle* (salt tax).

John Calvin establishes his theocracy at Geneva.

Pizarro assassinated.

Seneschal of Lyon steps in to end printers' strike.

War resumes around Perpignan.

SEPT. 23RD: Paracelsus allegedly murdered at Salzburg.

John Calvin, whose conversion of huge numbers to Protestantism coincided with the first appearance of Nostradamus's *Centuries*

1542

Calvin publishes *Forms of Prayer and Church Chants*.

Congregation of Cardinals of the Holy Inquisition set up by Pope Paul III.

Huge taxes levied.

Luxembourg recovered from the Empire.

Marguerite de Navarre starts work on her *Heptaméron*.

Poyet in Bastille for alleged embezzlement.

Henri II, whose death in 1559 Nostradamus may have predicted

Jean de Tournes, former employee of Gryphius, sets up as publisher in Lyon.
Macé Bonhomme opens a bookstore (later a printing works) in Avignon.
Claimed date of the so-called prophecies of Orval, "found" there by Olivarius in 1792.
Religious refugees flee France for Geneva.
Sorbonne burns Calvin's *Institution of the Christian Religion*.

1543

MAY: Death of Copernicus and publication of *De Revolutionibus Orbium Coelestium* in Nuremberg.
Even higher taxes levied.
Hallmarks introduced for gold and silver goods.
Rabelais returns to France from Italy as official royal agent.
Sorbonne issues twenty-five articles of Catholic Faith.

1544

Poverty-relief program set up in Paris.
Salt warehouses established to enforce salt tax on compulsory salt purchases.
Sorbonne issues *Index* of sixty-five forbidden "heretical" books.
Three years of peace begin.
MAY: Nostredame studies the plague and its treatment at Marseille under Louis Serres.
JUL.: François de Bourbon launches new military campaign in Italy, but withdraws as both Charles V and Henri VIII invade France.

JUL. 24TH: Vitry-en-Perthois destroyed by Charles V.
SEPT. 18TH: New treaty signed assigning Piedmont and Savoy to Charles V and Burgundy to François I – and a bride to Charles d'Orléans.
First border customhouse set up.
Henri II suspends most Provost Marshals in favor of local magistrates.
Henry VIII captures Boulogne.
Rabelais publishes *Grande et brave pronostication nouvelle*.

1545

Council of Trent convenes at Trento to reform Catholic Church in face of rising Protestantism.
APRIL: Massive anti-Protestant bloodbath in Lubéron, Provence.
French intervene militarily to support Mary Queen of Scots in Scotland.
Anti-salt tax revolts in Périgord.
SEPT.: Charles d'Orléans dies of plague.
Nostredame's brother Jehan lawyer at Aix-en-Provence.
Michelangelo (seventy) appointed architect for completion of St. Peter's, Rome.

1546

Architect Pierre Lescot appointed to rebuild the Louvre: royal family moves to Palais des Tournelles, near the Bastille.
Peace of Ardres assigns two million pounds to Henry VIII for Boulogne.
APR. 26TH: Nostredame's brother Hector marries Anthonete Morguete.
Rabelais publishes *Tiers Livre*, then flees to Metz.
Nostredame summoned to Aix, and then to Salon, to fight the plague.

1547

French population *c.* seventeen million.
JAN. 28TH: Henri VIII of England dies. Edward VI succeeds.
FEB. 6TH: Document at St.-Rémy refers to the heirs of the (presumably late) Jaume de Nostredame.
MAR. 31ST: François I dies at fifty-three: his surviving son, Henri II, succeeds, aged twenty-eight.

Henri II appoints four secretaries of state and starts reorganizing national finances.
John Dee travels to Belgium as lecturer at Louvain, then to France (Reims).
Henri II visits Italy.
Nostredame's brother Jean becomes Solicitor, then Procureur (Attorney General) to the Parlement de Provence at Aix.
Nostredame summoned to Lyon to fight the plague.
Nicolas de Fail's *Propos rustiques* satirizes the increasing hordes of beggars.
Foundation of antiheretical *Chambre Ardente*, or "Burning Chamber," to prosecute Protestants within domain of Paris Parlement.
Flow of religious refugees from France to Geneva increases dramatically.
Anne de Montmorency appointed High Constable, Governor of Languedoc, and Head of the Council.
SEPT.: John Dee returns to Trinity College, Cambridge, as Second Praelector in Greek.
Jean Dorat becomes Principal of Collège de Coqueret, Paris, where he teaches and enthuses Ronsard, Baïf, and du Bellay in the later "Pléiade" principles.
Rabelais in Rome with Cardinal Jean du Bellay, Ambassador to Rome.
NOV. 11TH: Nostredame marries Anne Ponsarte or Ponsarde, known as Gemelle ("the Twin") at Salon.
DEC. 2ND: Hernando Cortés dies.

1548

Chancellor Poyet dies.
Parlement de Paris effectively bans mystery plays as unsuited to an unqualified public.
Nostredame sets off for Italy: reported in Venice, Genoa, and Savona.
Price of salt rises to pay for salt police and leasing of salt warehouses.
AUG: Salt tax revolt starts in Angoumois, routs royal forces and spreads to Bordeaux area, where rebels kill twenty, including the King's representative.
Bordeaux tax-revolt brutally put down by Montmorency, advancing from Piedmont, with hundreds of summary executions and harsh repression.

The nepotistic Pope Paul III with his nephews, by Titian. He removed Henry VIII's title as "Defender of the Faith" and died in 1549.

1549

Bordeaux Parlement and council restored, and salt tax abolished in Guyenne, as King backs down in face of dubious odds.

Four times as many classical and humanist works published in Paris as religious ones.

JUN. 16TH: Henri II officially welcomed to Paris as the "Gallic Hercules" and as Tiphys, pilot of the Argonauts, with two weeks of tournaments, mock sea-battles, and exemplary burnings of Protestants.

Nostredame's Italian trip continues.

Latin translation of Iamblichus's *De Mysteriis Aegyptiorum* newly published by de Tournes at Lyon.

Joachim du Bellay (cousin of Cardinal Jean) publishes, with Ronsard's help, his *Deffense et illustration de la langue francoyse*, advocating the revival of Greek and Latin words, the use of foreign and technical terms, and the creation of new ones.

NOV. 10TH: Pope Paul III dies.

NOV.: Henri II introduces *taillon* (supplementary tax) to pay soldiery, adding some one million pounds annually to general *taille*.

Marguerite de Navarre, French religious reformer, dies.

1550

First Nostradamian Almanac possibly published.

JAN. 1ST: Henri II triumphally welcomed in Rouen, once again as "Hercules."

Population of Lyon 70–80,000, with around 5,000 employed in silk industry: French urbanization around 10 percent.

Nostredame's brother Antoine official tax-collector at St.-Rémy.

FEB. 7TH: Pope Julius III elected.

MAR.: Henri II recovers Boulogne from England at half price (400,000 crowns).

Apr. 22nd: Edward de Vere, Earl of Oxford, born (possible author or part-author of Shakespeare).

Nostredame returns from Italy.

Henri II angrily withdraws French bishops from reconvened Council of Trent.

Deaths of Duke Claude of Guise and Jean, Cardinal of Lorraine: François, Duke of Guise, and Charles, Cardinal of Lorraine, succeed.

Peletier's *Dialogue de l'orthographie et de la prononciation françoyse* published in an effort to standardize French.

First Jesuit seminary founded in Paris.

Ronsard emerges as leader of *Pléiade* poets.

Ronsard: *Odes*.

1551

Second Almanac possibly published.

Palestrina appointed Master of Music at Vatican.

South wing of Louvre demolished by Lescot.

Nostredame's first child Madeleine born (?).

Rabelais receives two priestly benefices.

1552

JAN.: Treaty of Chambord allies German Protestant states with France.

Henri II borrows 450,000 pounds from French and Italian bankers.

Taille fixed at five million pounds.

War between France and the Empire resumes in spring, with Montmorency in Rhineland and François de Guise in Lorraine.

Adam de Craponne military architect at Court of Henri II.

MAR. 1ST: Rabelais's *Quart Livre* banned by Paris Parlement.

APR. 1ST: *Traité des fardemens* finished.

Henri II introduces *présidiaux* (new, second-level legal tribunals).

Joachim du Bellay publishes Book IV of Virgil's *Aeneid* in translation.

Almanac for 1553 published in Lyon under name of Nostradamus.

Madeleine one year old.

DEC. 26TH: Siege of Metz raised, thanks largely to Adam de Craponne's work on strengthening and maintaining the city walls.

Adam de Craponne in charge of restoring and repairing the walls of Metz.

Italian astrologer Luca Gaurico (Luc Gauric) warns Henri II against single combat in an enclosed space around his forty-first year, and has this and other prophecies printed.

Rabelais, now a parish priest, publishes his *Quart Livre*, allegorically attacking the Vatican: possibly imprisoned.

Ronsard publishes *Amours*.

1553

MAY: Montmorency loses Thérouanne to Charles V.

JUL. 6TH: Protestant Edward VI of England dies: Catholic Mary Tudor succeeds.

Calvin burns anabaptist Michael Servetus alive for heresy.

Jodelle's *Cléopatre captive* and *Eugene* performed at Court.

Madeleine two years old.

Almanac for 1554 published in Lyon.

Nostradamus supplies facetious Latin inscription for new public fountain at Salon.

Death of Rabelais.

Joachim du Bellay becomes secretary to his cousin Cardinal Jean in Rome.

1554

JAN.: French besieged in Siena.

APR. 1ST: Nostradamus reaches *Century* **I. 42.**

Apr. 13th (Good Friday): Jean-Aimé de Chavigny, former Mayor of Beaune and pupil of Jean Dorat, reportedly starts work as Nostradamus's secretary and amanuensis.

JUL.: Queen Mary of England marries Philip II of Spain, so making England a Hapsburg domain.

Henri II creates *sénéchaux* (Lieutenants General) to preside over legal and administrative matters throughout southern France.

Montmorency's spring offensive to take Brussels defeated by Emmanuel Philibert of Savoy.

Two-headed infant brought from Senas for Nostradamus to examine. Two-headed kid brought from Aurons for Nostradamus and his guests to examine, 1½ months after the two-headed infant: severe divisions in the kingdom adumbrated.

Almanac for 1555 published in Lyon. César born (?); Madeleine three.

SEPT.: Craponne starts engaging workers for his canal project and seeking finance for it (up to 8,775 crowns by 1569).

Ronsard: *Bocage*, after Anacreon.

Severe winter frosts stop work on Craponne's pilot canal.

1555

MAR. 23RD: Pope Julius III dies.

APR. 1ST: Besieged French garrison of Siena defeated, but allowed to leave.

APR. 9TH: Pope Marcellus II elected. Spring frosts delay work on Craponne's pilot canal.

Traité des fardemens **published by Volant, Lyon.**

APR. 30TH: Royal *privilége* **granted for first edition of** *Propheties.*

MAY 1ST: Pope Marcellus II dies.

MAY 4TH: First edition of *Propheties* **published by Macé Bonhomme of Lyon, as well as by Roux of Avignon.**

Calvin sends first Protestant ministers to France from Geneva: Protestant numbers start to grow dramatically, especially in the towns.

Queen Mary of England starts to persecute Protestants.

MAY 23RD: Pope Paul IV elected.

BETWEEN MAY 20TH AND JUL. 27TH: Nostradamus reported passing through Lyon on his way to visit the Court in Paris: expresses fears of decapitation before August 25th.

Aug. 15th: After a month's travel by royal post-horse, Nostradamus arrives in Paris to visit Queen Catherine de Médicis, lodging at the Auberge St.-Michel until fetched by High Constable Montmorency in person.

SEPT. 25TH: Peace of Augsburg establishes peace between German Protestants and Catholics.

OCT. 25TH: Charles V abdicates, leaving the Empire to his brother Ferdinand, and Spain and the Netherlands to his son Philip II.

Madeleine four; César one.

Recovered from an attack of gout, Nostradamus visits the Queen, who sends him on to examine the royal children at Blois and cast their horoscopes: he allegedly reports back that all her sons will be kings.

Ronsard publishes *Continuation des Amours* and starts to write his *Hymnes*.

1556

Almanac for 1556/7 published in Lyon.

FEB. 5TH: Gauric sends written reminder to Henri II to avoid single combat in an enclosed space around his forty-first year.

FEB. 15TH: Truce of Vaucelles signed for five years, leaving France with gains intact.

Orlando di Lasso, setter of poems by Ronsard, and subsidized by Catherine de Médicis, publishes first book of motets.

The group of writers surrounding Ronsard and du Bellay (including Jodelle) officially name themselves "la Pléiade" after the ancient Alexandrian poets, using du Bellay's *Deffense* as their manifesto.

Almanac for 1557 published in Lyon and Paris.

Bertrand de Nostredame starts building works at the Mas de Roussan. Charles born; Madeleine five; César two.

Date of inscription over doorway of house in Turin claiming that "Nostradamus stayed here."

First edition of *Propheties* **republished in Avignon.**

Traité des fardemens **published in Paris and Lyon.**

JUL. 27TH: Nostradamus signs document before Salon lawyer Laurent, investing 200 crowns in Adam de Craponne's canal.

AUG. 17TH: Permission of Aix Parlement given for Craponne's irrigation canal from Durance.

Jean Dorat appointed professor of Greek at Collège Royal, Paris.

1557

Almanac for 1557 republished in Paris.

Théodore de Béza publishes his *Droit des magistrats sur leurs sujets* from Geneva.

Index Librorum Prohibitorum (newly published from this year) forbids Catholics to read certain authors, including Luther.

Nostradamus not listed in new *Index Librorum Prohibitorum.*

Mary Tudor painted by Antonio Moro. She married Philip II of Spain in 1554.

MAR. 14TH: Nostradamus in middle of writing the dedicatory letter to completed collection of *Propheties*.

MAY: François de Guise marches south to conquer Naples.

Protestants demonstrate in the rue St.-Jacques, Paris.

MAY 13TH: First water from Durance reaches Salon via Craponne's pilot canal.

JUN. 7TH: Mary of England declares war on France at instigation of Philip II.

AUG. 2ND: Philip II's brilliant general Emmanuel Philibert of Savoy attacks French in St.-Quentin under Coligny with huge army.

AUG. 10TH: 3,000 dead and 6,000 taken prisoner (including Montmorency, his four sons, and Charles de Bourbon) during bungled attempt to relieve St.-Quentin: panic sweeps the country.

AUG. 27TH: St.-Quentin falls to Spaniards amid vast slaughter.

SEPT. 17TH: New truce signed between France and Empire.

NOV.: Emmanuel Philibert forced by problems of supply and finance to disband his army.

Italian translation of Almanac for 1558 published in Milan.

Almanac for 1558 published in Lyon.

Nostradamus's brother Antoine attorney for the town of St.-Rémy.

Menodotus's *Paraphrase de C. Galen* published by du Rosne, Lyon.

***Traité des fardemens* published in Antwerp.**

NOV. 3RD: André born; Madeleine six; César three; Charles one.

NOV. 13TH: Second edition of *Propheties* published by du Rosne, Lyon

1558

Almanac for 1558 published in Lyon.
Almanac for 1558 published in Antwerp.

JAN. 8TH: François de Guise, back from Italy, retakes Calais from the Empire.

APR.: Dauphin François (fourteen) marries Mary Queen of Scots (sixteen).

JUN. 22ND: François de Guise retakes Thionville.

JUN. 27TH: Nostradamus finishes dedicatory letter to Henri II to

Queen Elizabeth I by an unknown artist. She succeeded to the English throne in 1558.

accompany the completed thousand *Propheties*.

JUL. 28TH: François de Guise assembles defense force of 50,000 at Pierrepoint.

JUL.: Count Egmont defeats French at Gravelines and threatens Paris.

François de Guise recaptures Calais from English.

Protestants demonstrate in the Pré-aux-Clercs, Paris.

Nostradamus's brother Antoine one of three Consuls for St.-Rémy.

Menodotus's *Paraphrase de C. Galen* published by du Rosne, Lyon.

Last three *Centuries of Propheties* published by de Tournes, Lyon.

AUG. 21ST: Scaliger dies.

NOV. 17TH: Catholic Queen Mary of England dies: her Protestant sister Elizabeth succeeds.

Almanac for 1559 published in Lyon.
Pirated English translation of Almanac for 1559 published in London.

Anne born; Madeleine seven; César four; Charles two; André one.

1559

Two English translations of Almanac for 1559 published in London.

APR. 2ND–3RD: Henri II, needing to concentrate on growing religious crisis at home, signs Peace of Cateau Cambrésis, which affiances Philip II to his daughter Elisabeth de Valois and Emmanuel Philibert to his sister Marguerite de Valois, restores much captured territory on both sides, including St.-Quentin, and renders tens of thousands of

unemployable soldiers jobless and destitute: huge unemployment and social problems result.

APR.: Calvinists hold first national synod of French Reformed Churches in Paris.

APR. 20TH: Craponne's canal officially opened at Salon.

Edict of Écouen imposes death penalty on heretics.

Opening of Calvin's Genevan Academy.

Robber-gangs start to roam the countryside.

MAY: Salon already benefiting from Craponne's canal to the tune of 7,000–8,000 crowns.

JUN. 30TH: Henri II mortally wounded in tournament to celebrate wedding of Philip II of Spain to his daughter Elisabeth, and engagement of Emmanuel Philibert of Savoy to his sister Marguerite.

JUL. 10TH: Henri II dies from injuries received during tournament of 30th: his son François II succeeds at age fifteen: Guises (uncles of his wife Mary Stuart, Queen of Scots) take over: Montmorency ousted.

JUL. 14TH: Ordinance announces reductions in army numbers.

AUG. 18TH: Pope Paul IV dies.

SEPT. AND OCT.: Guises issue edicts for the destruction of Protestant houses and execution of Protestants.

OCT.: Emmanuel Philibert of Savoy stops off in Salon on his way home from his wedding in Paris.

DEC. 23RD: Clerk Councilor Anne Du Bourg burned in Paris for opposing persecution of Calvinists.

Almanac for 1560 published in Lyon and Paris.

Craponne collaborates with the Ravel brothers to extend his canal to Lançon and other towns.

Nostradamus's *Les Significations de l'Eclipse qui sera le 16 Septembre* . . . published in Paris.

English translation of *Les Significations de l'Eclipse* . . . published in London.

Madeleine eight; César five; Charles three; André two; Anne one.

Menodotus's *Paraphrase de C. Galen* published by du Rosne, Lyon.

Ronsard's *Meslanges* eulogizes nature and

condemns colonization of New World. Jean de Tournes appointed publisher to the King in Lyon.

Index Librorum Prohibitorum completed: Nostradamus still not listed.

DEC. 25TH: Pope Pius IV elected.

Dec.: Anne Du Bourg, Protestant magistrate, burned at the stake in Paris.

DEC.: Marguerite de Valois arrives at Salon in deep mourning to join her new husband Emmanuel Philibert of Savoy and is welcomed in words composed by Nostradamus: a consultation follows.

1560

Almanac for 1560 published in German.

MAR. 6TH: Protestant "Conspiracy of Amboise" to capture young King François and oust Guises brutally put down.

MAR.: Michel de l'Hôpital becomes Chancellor.

MAR.: Protestants hold second National Synod at Poitiers.

French population *c.* twenty million. Peasant revolts begin against payment of the Church's tithe in Guyenne, around Nîmes, and at Auch.

MAY 1ST: Anti-Protestant *Cabans* of Salon start attempts to find and burn local Protestants.

AUG. 21ST: Nobles meet at Fontainebleau to consider religious crisis.

SEPT. 22ND: Nostradamus invests

200 more crowns in Craponne's canal.

DEC. 5TH: François II dies: ten-year-old Charles IX succeeds; Catherine de Médicis appointed regent; Guises ousted; Estates General call for religious tolerance and Catholic reform.

Almanac for 1561 published.

Almanac for 1561 published in English.

Madeleine nine; César six; Charles four; André three; Anne two.

***Prophetie Merveilleuse* for 1560–8 published in Paris.**

***Traité des fardemens* published by Volant of Lyon.**

Joachim du Bellay, original propagandist of the Pléiade, dies.

Ronsard inspired to write poem of exhortation to his countrymen following St.-Quentin disaster, including pseudo-sonnet eulogizing Nostradamus.

1561

JAN. 22ND: Francis Bacon born.

MAR.: Montmorency reconciled to his adversary the Duke of Guise.

MAR.: Montmorency, the Duke of Guise, and the Marshal de St.-André withdraw from Court to form a Catholic "Triumvirate."

APR.: Students threaten to massacre Protestants at the Pré-aux-Clercs, Paris: Catholic attacks on Protestants countrywide.

Protestant troops assemble under Condé, especially at Orléans.

APR. **14TH: Nostradamus takes out a one-year lease on a house in the rue de la Servellerie, Avignon, for eighteen crowns, possibly to escape the *Caban* threat, but gives it up again a few weeks later.**

JUL.: Craponne promises to extend his canal to Arles and the Rhône.

Riot at Beauvais when bishop announces Calvinist communion.

SEPT. 21ST: Contract of Poissy obliges Church to subsidize the monarchy from the tithe.

Anonymous *Exhortation aux princes* urges official religious tolerance.

Calvin sends 142 Protestant pastors to France from Geneva.

Chancellor issues edict halting Protestant executions.

Estates General summoned.

Jesuits set up college at Tournon to fight Calvinism in Rhône valley.

Montmorency goes to Rome to pledge loyalty.

Ottomans take Tripoli.

Almanac for 1562 published in Paris and Lyon.

Diane born; Madeleine ten; César seven; Charles five; André four; Anne three.

Fourth edition of *Propheties* published by Regnault, Paris.

***Le Remede tres utile contre la peste* . . . published in Paris.**

Nostradamus, summoned to Turin, predicts a son for Emmanuel Philibert and Marguerite de Valois, and announces the former's death "when a nine precedes a seventh." Nostradamus writes to a M. de Moral in Paris, repaying a debt of two rose nobles and two crowns incurred while visiting the Court in 1555.

1562

Almanac for 1562 published in English.

JAN. 2ND: French prelates, sent for the first time to Council of Trent by Catherine de Médicis, present Catholic "Articles of Reformation."

The signing of the Treaty of Cateau-Cambrésis, 1559 (Sienese School)

JAN. 17TH: King's Council recognizes Protestant Church, permits Protestant freedom of conscience and freedom of private worship.

JAN.: Prisoners of conscience freed.

FEB. 4TH: Nostradamus sends horoscope and advice to the Canons of Orange, who have sought his help in tracing lost church treasures following an attack by Protestant iconoclasts.

FEB. 13TH: Nostradamus invests 100 more crowns in Craponne's canal.

MAR. 27TH: Duke of Guise attempts to kidnap King at Fontainebleau.

MAR.: Massacre of Vassy, often cited as start of Wars of Religion, sees Guise troops kill twenty-three illegally assembled Protestants and injure over ninety. Protestants seize several cities, though repulsed elsewhere.

8,000 Protestant troops assemble at Orléans: *Reiters* being recruited in Germany.

Period of cold, wet weather, agricultural crisis, and famine begins.

Ronsard addresses to Queen Catherine de Médicis his *Discours des misères de ce temps*, supporting the royalist, Catholic cause against the Protestants, citing corpse-strewn fields and rivers red with blood, and apparently commending Nostradamus's prophetic work.

MAY: Toulouse preachers urge atrocities against Protestants.

JUL. 13TH: Paris Parlement legalizes summary execution of Protestants.

Summer campaigns by Protestants succeed, including that in the Rhône valley.

Almanac for 1563 published in Italy. Almanac for 1563 published in Lyon and Avignon.

Madeleine eleven; César eight; Charles six; André five; Anne four; Diane one.

OCT. 26TH: Catholic siege of Rouen ends amid massacre, rape, and looting.

DEC. 19TH: Duc de Guise defeats Protestant army in Normandy: Montmorency and Condé both captured by the other side.

Antoine de Bourbon dies at siege of Rouen.

Blois, Bourges, Poitiers, and the Saône valley recovered from the Protestants. Harsh weather results in astronomical grain prices and widespread starvation, with disease epidemics in the north: false rumors spread fear of further religious persecution; massacres in several cities newly liberated from Protestants.

Prince Louis de Bourbon-Condé publishes pamphlet accusing Guises of controlling the King and Catherine de Médicis.

Treaty of Hampton Court surrenders Le Havre to Elizabeth I in exchange for 6,000 men and 100,000 crowns.

1563

Period of cold, wet weather, agricultural crisis, and famine continues.

FEB.: Duc de Guise assassinated by a Protestant.

MAR. 19TH: Edict of Amboise reduces Protestant places of worship, banning them entirely in the Paris area.

MAY: King's Council demands five million more pounds annually from the Church to pay for mercenaries hired to defeat Condé.

Catholic League emerges as political movement to defend the Faith.

Low wages hit workers hard.

Montmorency recaptures Le Havre from England, aided by Condé.

Reformist Catholic Council of Trent comes to an end.

Seven French bishops summoned to Rome to answer charges of heresy.

Ronsard attacked by Protestant critics for his support of Nostradamus.

English translation of Almanac for 1564 published in London.

Madeleine twelve; César nine; Charles seven; André six; Anne five; Diane two.

NOVEMBER: The young King Charles IX visits Ronsard at his abbey of St.-Cosme.

1564

FEB. 18TH: Michelangelo dies.

FEB. 26TH: Christopher Marlowe born. Normal weather returns.

APR. 26TH: William Shakspere of Stratford-on-Avon baptised.

Catherine de Médicis and Charles IX set out on two-year royal progress through France to reunite and pacify the kingdom, taking about 20,000 retainers, including the entire government.

Customs collection becomes part of regular royal border policy.

Jesuit college founded at Lyon.

JUL.: Municipal elections placed under royal control.

SEPT. 7TH: Jean de Tournes dies of plague.

SEPT. 24TH: Charles IX and Catherine de Médicis reach Avignon on their two-year royal progress through France.

OCT. 16TH: Royal progress overnights at St-Rémy.

OCT. 17TH: Charles IX and Catherine de Médicis reach Salon, the former reportedly announcing that he has "only come to see Nostradamus": the seer and his family entertained at the castle.

OCT. 17TH: The seer "spots" the future Henri IV (currently aged ten) among the royal retinue and prepares his horoscope.

Almanac for 1565 published in Lyon. Translation of Almanac for 1565 published in Genoa.

Madeleine thirteen; César ten; Charles eight; André seven; Anne six; Diane three.

NOV. OR DEC. (?): Nostradamus summoned to Arles for further consultation by Charles IX and the Queen: presented with 300 crowns and appointed Councilor and Physician in Ordinary to the King.

1565

Almanac for 1565 republished in Lyon.

JUN. TO JUL.: Duke of Alba proposes Franco-Spanish alliance against Protestants.

Alba marches to Netherlands from Italy with huge army to put down Protestant iconoclastic riots.

Almanac "for 1565 to 1570" published in Italian.

Almanac for 1566 published, predicting a "strange

transmigration" for July 1st.

Jeanne d'Albret makes Protestantism the state religion of Béarn.

Ottomans fail to take Malta.

Anne Ponsarde, Nostradamus's wife, invests 100 crowns in Craponne's canal.

Chavigny definitely at Salon.

Madeleine fourteen; César eleven; Charles nine; André eight; Anne seven; Diane four.

DEC. 9TH: Pope Pius IV dies.

DEC. 21ST: Nostradamus writes to the Queen in his capacity as Royal Councilor, assuring her of some great piece of good fortune presaging future peace for the kingdom.

Ronsard publishes his *Abrégé de l'art poétique français*.

1566

Low wages hit workers hard.

Ordinance of Moulins obliges every town to feed its own poor.

JAN. 7TH: Pope (St.) Pius V elected.

Almanac for 1566 published in Italian and English.

Almanac for 1567 published, with *Presage* for November apparently predicting Nostradamus's death.

Almanac for 1567 published in Italian and English.

English translation of Almanac for 1568 published in London.

Jun. 17th: Nostradamus draws up his will.

JUN. 20TH: Nostradamus adds a codicil to his will bequeathing his cornelian-set gold ring and astrolabe to César and two walnut chests and their contents to Madeleine.

End of Jun.: Nostradamus writes "Hic prope mors est" on copy of Stadius's *Ephemerides*.

Jul. 1st: Nostradamus tells Chavigny "You will not see me alive at sunrise."

JUL. 2ND: Nostradamus found dead and almost cold in his room: subsequently buried with full civic honors in church of Cordeliers.

SEPT. 4TH: Suleiman the Magnificent dies: Selim II succeeds.

DEC. 25TH: Jean de Chaumont, Bishop

of Aix, ceremonially quits office to join the Protestants.

Madeleine fifteen; César twelve; Charles ten; André nine; Anne eight; Diane five.

Half of Lyon's lawyers Protestant.

1567

Condé accuses King of unfairness to Protestant nobles and demands recall of Estates General.

Condé's Protestants nearly capture the royal family on their flight to Paris, but are held off by Swiss mercenaries.

SEPT. 29TH: Protestant and Catholic nobles give battle at Nîmes.

NOV. 10TH: Battle of St.-Denis breaks Condé's siege of Paris, but results in Montmorency's death.

Madeleine sixteen; César thirteen; Charles eleven; André ten; Anne nine; Diane six.

Traité des fardemens **published in Poitiers.**

1568

MAR.: Peace of Longjumeau ends Second War of Religion and reaffirms Edict of Amboise.

SEPT.: Third War of Religion begins near Poitou.

OCT.: Catholics defeat Protestants at Moncontour, but Paris still threatened. Condé and Coligny, reinforced by mercenaries, besiege Chartres.

Jeanne d'Albret, Queen of Navarre, with her son Henri, reinforces Protestant La Rochelle.

Fourth edition of *Propheties* published by Benoist Rigaud, Lyon.

Traité des fardemens **(ed. César) published in Paris.**

Madeleine seventeen; César fourteen; Charles twelve; André eleven; Anne ten; Diane seven.

1569

Death of Emmanuel Philibert of Savoy (see Nostradamus's prediction of 1561).

Prince Louis de Bourbon Condé killed at Battle of Jarnac.

Madeleine eighteen; César fifteen; Charles thirteen; André twelve; Anne eleven; Diane eight.

1570

Treaty of St.-Germain brings to an end the Third War of Religion.

Unemployment hits wage-laborers and wages fall.

Adam de Craponne in severe financial difficulties.

Madeleine nineteen; César sixteen; Charles fourteen; André thirteen; Anne twelve; Diane nine.

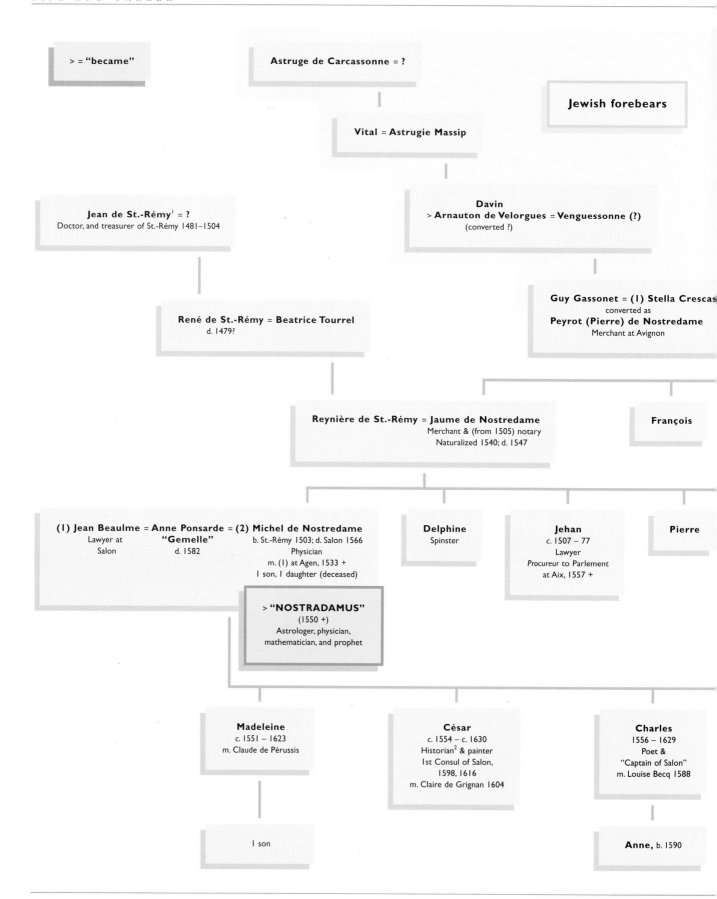

> = "became"

Astruge de Carcassonne = ?

Jewish forebears

Vital = Astrugie Massip

Jean de St.-Rémy[1] = ?
Doctor, and treasurer of St.-Rémy 1481–1504

Davin
> **Arnauton de Velorgues = Venguessonne (?)**
(converted ?)

René de St.-Rémy = Beatrice Tourrel
d. 1479?

Guy Gassonet = (1) **Stella Crescas**
converted as
Peyrot (Pierre) de Nostredame
Merchant at Avignon

Reynière de St.-Rémy = Jaume de Nostredame
Merchant & (from 1505) notary
Naturalized 1540; d. 1547

François

(1) **Jean Beaulme = Anne Ponsarde** = (2) **Michel de Nostredame**
Lawyer at   "**Gemelle**"   b. St.-Rémy 1503; d. Salon 1566
Salon   d. 1582   Physician
                                      m. (1) at Agen, 1533 +
                                      1 son, 1 daughter (deceased)

Delphine
Spinster

Jehan
c. 1507 – 77
Lawyer
Procureur to Parlement
at Aix, 1557 +

Pierre

> **"NOSTRADAMUS"**
(1550 +)
Astrologer, physician,
mathematician, and prophet

Madeleine
c. 1551 – 1623
m. Claude de Pérussis

César
c. 1554 – c. 1630
Historian[2] & painter
1st Consul of Salon,
1598, 1616
m. Claire de Grignan 1604

Charles
1556 – 1629
Poet &
"Captain of Salon"
m. Louise Becq 1588

1 son

Anne, b. 1590

THE NOSTRADAMUS FAMILY TREE

PRINCIPAL SOURCE: Leroy

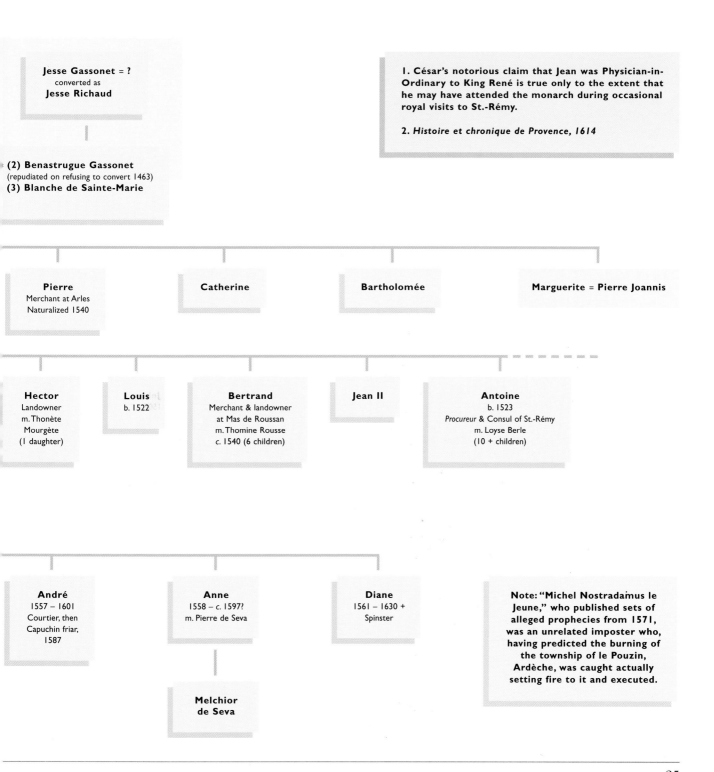

Jesse Gassonet = ?
converted as
Jesse Richaud

(2) Benastrugue Gassonet
(repudiated on refusing to convert 1463)
(3) Blanche de Sainte-Marie

1. César's notorious claim that Jean was Physician-in-Ordinary to King René is true only to the extent that he may have attended the monarch during occasional royal visits to St.-Rémy.

2. *Histoire et chronique de Provence, 1614*

Pierre
Merchant at Arles
Naturalized 1540

Catherine

Bartholomée

Marguerite = Pierre Joannis

Hector
Landowner
m. Thonète
Mourgète
(1 daughter)

Louis
b. 1522

Bertrand
Merchant & landowner
at Mas de Roussan
m. Thomine Rousse
c. 1540 (6 children)

Jean II

Antoine
b. 1523
Procureur & Consul of St.-Rémy
m. Loyse Berle
(10 + children)

André
1557 – 1601
Courtier, then
Capuchin friar,
1587

Anne
1558 – c. 1597?
m. Pierre de Seva

Diane
1561 – 1630 +
Spinster

Note: "Michel Nostradamus le Jeune," who published sets of alleged prophecies from 1571, was an unrelated imposter who, having predicted the burning of the township of le Pouzin, Ardèche, was caught actually setting fire to it and executed.

**Melchior
de Seva**

NOSTRADAMUS'S LIFESTORY

THE FIRST SON of a large family, Michel de Nostredame was born in St.-Rémy-de-Provence on December 14th, 1503, reportedly at noon. His alleged birthplace can still be seen (complete with obligatory municipal plaque) in the rue Hoche, hard against the ancient town ramparts. Whether the attribution is correct is a different matter. For all the carved decoration of the stone window-casement above the door, the house is remarkably small and humble, and there is a distinct suspicion that municipal pride and cultural overeagerness may have had rather more to do with its identification than actual historical fact.

Suitably old the now-dilapidated hovel may seem, but the child's father Jaume (i.e. James) de Nostredame was by that time a prosperous grainmerchant and would soon become a home-grown

lawyer into the bargain. Even had he inhabited this dark little alley in the first place, it seems likely that he would by then have acquired a much grander and more spacious home – though the common temptation to place it among the stylish townhouses of the place Favier (let alone in the magnificent residence of the Mistrals of Mondragon, now the Musée des Alpilles Pierre de Brun) must unfortunately be resisted.

The father himself was the son of a Jewish merchant by the name of Guy Gassonet who, on his conversion to Christianity in around 1463, seems to have taken from the then bishop the name Pierre, and from the day of his conversion (presumably July 2nd, Feast of the Visitation) the surname *de Nostredame* ("of Our Lady"). There even seems to have been some doubt, especially on the part of his new Christian wife (his determinedly unwavering Jewish one having by now been discarded), as to whether the name ought not to be *de Sainte-Marie*. But "de Nostredame" won out. And so their son Jaume would subsequently sign himself *Jacobus de nostra domina*, just as Michel in his turn would in due course sign himself *Michaletus de nostra domina*.

The family belonged (as the Nostradamus Family Tree reveals) to a tight-knit and continually intermarrying Jewish community with long roots that stretched back via Avignon and Carcassonne ever closer to the Spanish border. The tradition, therefore, that their ancestors were originally among the Spanish Jews (the so-called Marranos) who had fled Spain during the persecutions of the fourteenth and fifteenth centuries may well have more than a smidgin of truth about it. The later *Propheties* even seem, at X.96, to make veiled reference to the fact.

Certainly the succession of paternal Gassonets ('Little Gasson') and Venguessonnes ("Ben Guesson" or "son of Guesson") does seem to hint at the existence, somewhere in the as-yet unfathomed darkness beyond the known familytree, of a remote common ancestor, a Spanish Jew possibly known as Guasón ("Joker"). And if so, then the latter's presumed humorous streak (if such it was) was certainly to surface once again in the irrepressible young Michel.

**The claimed birthplace
of Nostradamus at
St.-Rémy-de-Provence**

NOTE: *Current knowledge of Nostradamus's life is based on a mixture of established fact, subsequent secondhand reports. and much later traditions of unknown attribution. The language of this section is carefully chosen to reflect these three categories of information.*

THE EARLY YEARS

Whether Jean, his maternal great-grandfather, appreciated this somewhat waggish demeanor may be doubted. He, after all, was seemingly charged with the serious business of instilling in the growing lad the rudiments of a broad education (certainly it is not easy to see where else he could have got it from). As a former Town Treasurer, the old gentleman was presumably competent to instruct him in mathematics – if, that is, he was not already too decrepit to embark on the task. As a respected physician whose heyday had coincided with the Italian High Renaissance, he was also well qualified to instruct the young Michel in Latin and Greek, as well as in astronomy and astrology (which were as yet inseparable), to say nothing of chemistry, medicine, and herbalism.

Wherever it came from, such early education as the boy received clearly found a ready response. It is evident from references in the eventual *Propheties* that he also took a lively interest, as a child of the Renaissance, in the plentiful classical antiquities of the area, and particularly in the ancient remains of the Roman city of Glanum, just south of the town. The extraordinary stone pillar left in the middle of the Romans' former stonequarry, partly for ritual purposes and partly to serve as a referencemarker (and known locally as *la Pyramide*); the almost perfectly preserved municipal arch and mausoleum of Sextus close by; the ruined city itself in its secluded valley among the hills – all these were later to be referred to repeatedly in the *Centuries* (see, for example, IV.27, X.29). So, too, was the former priory of St.-Paul-de-Mausole – i.e. "St. Paul's of the Mausoleum," which was better known subsequently as Vincent Van Gogh's asylum – which stands guard over the whole site (see VIII.34, IX.85). Indeed, whether merely as itself or as a geographical word-play on *Manus Solis* (the seemingly predicted last-Pope-but-two), the church and its name would come to resonate through the subsequent *Propheties* almost as a symbolic *leitmotif.*

And so it was that, by around the age of sixteen, the light-hearted but somewhat facetious youngster was ready to attend college at nearby Avignon for training in the classical *trivium* of grammar, rhetoric, and logic. Already noted for his biting wit, he reportedly soon became known, for good measure, as *le petit astrologue* – so serving notice, however unconsciously, of where his future fame might lie. The academic idyll was not to last, however. Toward the end of 1520 the plague swept in from the west, and the university at Avignon was temporarily disbanded. The students left, and Nostredame among them.

THE WANDERER

Now followed, by his own admission (*Proème, Traité des fardemens*), nine years not of renewed academia, but of constant wandering *par*

**The Roman arch and mausoleum
at ancient Glanum, which fascinated
the young Nostradamus**

plusieurs terres et pays, depuis l'an 1521 jusques à l'an 1529 . . . incessament courant, pour entendre et scavoir la source et origine des plantes[3] *et autres simples.*[4] It was from this moment, he added, that his medical vocation truly began.

No matter that, in the wake of Martin Luther's reforms, Europe was in growing religious turmoil. No matter that the Ottoman Turks were sweeping through the Mediterranean and deep into eastern Europe, or that France and the Holy Roman Empire were increasingly at each other's throats, with Imperial troops even invading Provence itself. No matter that the country was once more wracked by plague in 1525 and again in 1528. Indeed, the young Nostredame actually seems to have turned its advent to good account. In fine weather and (increasingly) in foul, he went about garnering the knowledge and experience of this and other diseases and their treatments that would later stand him in such excellent stead, to the point where (according to some sources) he was even able to qualify as an apothecary.

Had he, perhaps, read and studied the somewhat older Paracelsus, whose own current life all this so closely mirrored, and whose medical insights were later to find such striking echoes in his own? Possibly he had, but if so we shall probably never know. Certainly it seems unlikely that the two wandering healers' paths crossed at the time, or the Frenchman would surely have recorded the fact.

---

[3]   By a possibly Freudian slip, the word was originally printed *planetes.*

---

[4]   "through a number of lands and countries, from 1521 to 1529, constantly on the move in search of the understanding and knowledge of the sources and origins of plants and other medicinal herbs."

MEDICAL SCHOOL

"A doctor must be a traveler" – so insisted Paracelsus. But in 1526 the radical Swiss doctor, medical revolutionary, and alchemist suddenly settled down. On the strength of his evident experience, and to the horror of the medical establishment, he was actually appointed lecturer in medicine at Basel university. Three years later Nostredame was to execute a similar *volte-face*.

Why did the Frenchman decide to enter medical school now, rather than earlier?

There was an interesting (and, it has to be said, very practical) custom at the time whereby married sons or daughters might already claim their share of their paternal inheritance on reaching the age of twenty-five, rather than waiting for the father to die. By the same token, of course, they also effectively wrote themselves out of their father's will. Although unmarried at the time, Nostredame seems to have managed to take advantage of the ancient usage. Certainly he received 500 crowns as his share of the patrimony well before the death of his father, Jaume. Certainly, too, he no longer figured in the latter's will of 1534.

Could it be thanks to this sudden windfall and the consequent financial security, then, that the twenty-five-year-old healer finally decided to enroll for his doctorate at the famous Montpellier medical faculty in October of 1529? We cannot be certain. But we do have Nostredame's Latin enrollment entry, written and signed in his own hand.

NOSTRADAMUS'S ENROLLMENT

I, Mickey of Our Lady [it runs, with striking familiarity] of the nation of Provence, of the town of St.-Rémy, of the diocese of Avignon, have come to this university of Montpellier to study by the grace of God . . . and promise to observe the laws and statutes and privileges both laid down and to be laid down; I have paid its dues and choose as my patron and supervisor Antonio Romerio, this 23rd day of the month of October 1529, one thousand five hundred and twenty-nine, on the day above, 1529.

MICHALETUS DE NOSTRA DOMINA

On the evidence of this and Rabelais's later entry (see right) it looks as if each new student was expected to compose his own statement of intent to a set length of some sixty-five or seventy words, possibly as a kind of entrance test in classical literacy. Otherwise it is difficult to explain the obvious piece of schoolboy flattery at the end of the entry. It is also amusing to see how the "new boy" starts off as neatly as he can (even though he manages to go wrong as early as the second word), then gets progressively slapdash as the chore wears on.

All this seems engagingly human, at least.

Though originally a simple spinoff from the city's former role as a major importer of oriental herbs and spices, the medical faculty of Montpellier had a long and impressive history, boasting its own physic gardens and a distinguished staff of teachers. Then as now, consequently, it was *the* place to be for any aspiring young physician – and many an older one, too. Only the year after Nostredame's arrival, for example, the forty-year-old ex-monk François Rabelais – already a self-taught expert in theoretical medicine, as in a host of other disciplines – enrolled to take his own Bachelor's degree. Such was his prior learning, indeed, that he duly gained it only three months later.

But not, presumably, before the two almost equally self-willed and individualistic fellow medical students at Montpellier had got to know each other.

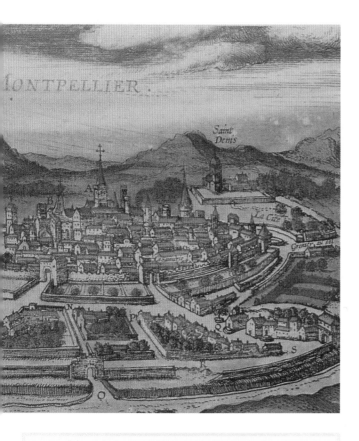

RABELAIS'S ENROLLMENT

**Rabelais's enrollment entry for the
Montpellier faculty, dated 1530**

THE YOUNG PHYSICIAN

It is traditional to suggest that this renewed bout of traveling was simply the result of Nostredame's chronic "ants-in-the-pants" syndrome. Others prefer to hang around his neck the convenient label of "wandering Jew." In fact, he was merely taking literally the instructions of the classical Hippocrates, on whose teachings (along with those of Galen) much of his instruction at Montpellier had been based (see Nostradamus the Physician). Every newly qualified doctor, Hippocrates had laid down, should set out to travel from town to town in search of experience and thus of "a reputation not merely as a doctor in name, but as a doctor in deed." From town to town, then, Nostredame may have wandered, but not this time for very long. For by 1533 he had set up as a doctor in the south-western town of Agen.

There was good reason for his decision. Agen had since 1525 been the home of an extraordinary, larger-than-life Renaissance character by the name of Jules César de l'Escalle (which he preferred to Latinize as Julius Caesar Scaliger – though, with unconscious irony, Nostradamus was later to refer to him as "Squaliger"). An Italian by the real name of Giulio Cesare della Scala, he had (by his own account, at least) been a courtier, studied painting under Dürer, fought as a soldier in Italy and The Netherlands, been knighted by the Emperor, and then attended university and qualified as a doctor. The eventual father of fifteen children, he had engaged in philosophical combat with Erasmus and would in due course do his best to destroy Rabelais and Girolamo Cardano as well. He was a noted biologist and botanist, too, as well as a poet, Latin grammarian, and literary critic. Now physician to Agen's bishop Antonio della Rovere, the fifty-year-old polymath and self-publicist evidently attracted the young Nostredame like a moth to a candle – and in more ways than one, at that.

Here, it seemed, was the Renaissance itself, in living flesh and blood. In the later seer's admiring words, Scaliger was a man *que je ne sçay si son ame seroit point le pere de l'eloquence Cicero, en la parfaite & supreme poësie un second Maro, en la doctrine de medicine deux Galiens, de qui je me tiens plus redeuable, que de personnaiges de ce monde.*[5]

And so Nostredame put down roots in Agen. He married, had two children. Yet all three were dead and gone again before they could even bequeath their names to posterity. Some epidemic was evidently to blame – possibly the plague. Shortly thereafter he was sued by his widow's family, perhaps for the return of her dowry.

---

[5]   ". . . whose soul, for all I know, is that father of eloquence, Cicero; in his perfect and supreme poetry another Virgil, in his medical teaching worth any two of Galen; and to whom I remain more indebted than to anybody else in this world." (*Traité des fardemens*, 1557 edition)

Whether Nostredame's time at Montpellier was as brief as Rabelais's is unknown. Certainly by around 1532 he would have gained his Doctor's degree. Tradition has it that he was then elected to the Faculty itself. There is no record of this at Montpellier, however – and in any case he did not stay long. Soon he was off on his travels again.

There is also a story to the effect that he was summoned to appear before the Inquisition of Toulouse, allegedly for telling a foundry worker that his casting of bronze images of the Virgin Mary was the work of the Devil: evidently the poker-faced Inquisitors, sniffing the gathering smoke of Protestant burnings and the growing smell of national fear that even moved Rabelais to recant at around this time, were unappreciative of the young Nostredame's austere Franciscan sympathies (see Nostradamus, the Bible, and the Church) or his characteristically caustic sense of humor. Others say that Scaliger, who quarreled with everybody, quarreled with him, too.

It does not seem at all unlikely.

Whatever the reason, Nostredame was soon on the move again – distraught, possibly, and looking for a new role in life. In his *Traité des fardemens et confitures* (1552) he mentions having practiced medicine in Bordeaux, Toulouse, Narbonne, and Carcassonne – though without saying when. He also claims to have treated the bishop of Carcassonne, whom he names as "Amanien de Foys." In fact, however, this must apply to a subsequent occasion, since not only was Amédée de Foix (the later Nostradamus was often oddly vague about names) appointed to the see much later, in 1552, but he never took up the post anyway. Instead, after a stay at Avignon, he was appointed to the see of Mâcon. It is probable, then, that the treatment took place at one or the other, and not at Carcassonne at all – and in any case not during the period under discussion.

The seer makes no mention at all, meanwhile, of rumored travels in the east of France, allegedly taking in Bar-le Duc and, in 1542, the abbey of Orval on the Luxembourg border, source of the highly dubious prophecies of the same name (q.v.). In the latter case this is not too surprising, since the whole area was racked by international disputes and wars at the time and was certainly no place for travelers.

THE PLAGUE DOCTOR

The most that can reliably be said is that by 1544 the wanderer had made it back to Provence, possibly by way of Vienne (which he describes as "Valence des Allobroges") – various prominent citizens of which he mentions by name in the *Traité*. Indeed, it is thanks to this book that we can now start to glean much more detailed information on what the future seer was really up to.

And his first reports concern his role in the 1544 plague outbreak at Marseille.

It was here, he says, that he was able to study the plague and its treatment under one of the outstanding physicians of the day, Louis Serres, whom he goes so far as to call "another Hippocrates" (the term, as we shall see, may well be therapeutically significant – though, as must by now be evident, he did also tend toward

Plague was rife in Provence in the mid-sixteenth century

descriptive generosity). Then, in 1546, he was urgently summoned to Aix-en-Provence to take control of another outbreak on his own account. His own report of the epidemic and his role in controlling it will be found under Nostradamus the Physician.

Evidently his efforts were seen as successful. Apocryphal reports speak of him being loaded with pensions and gifts, many of which he gave away – no doubt at least as much for lack of the means to carry them as out of any innate generosity. Soon he was being summoned to Salon, a day's ride to the west, where a similar outbreak had occurred. And it was here that he met his future second wife, Anne Ponsarde – otherwise spelled Ponsart(e) ("Ponsartia" in Latin) – whose husband, a rich Salon lawyer by the name of Jean Beaulme, had recently died.

If, then, as seems possible, Beaulme himself was one of the victims, Fortune's wheel had now performed a gratifying circle for the increasingly famous plague-doctor. At Agen, it was seemingly the plague that had deprived him of his first family; now, at Salon, it was the same plague that promised him a second one.

Before he could settle down with Anne however, there came another urgent summons. This time it was the city of Lyon that had been stricken. There, once again – and apparently for the last time – the miracle-worker performed his magic, much to the chagrin, it is said, of a local physician named Antoine Sarrazin. Actually his name was Philibert (Antoine, who may have been his grandson, would not even gain his baccalaureate at Montpellier until 1565).

Nostradamus writes of him in the final chapter of the *Traité* with much respect, using the Latin form *Phil. Sarracenus*, and describing him with characteristic exaggeration as *un notable personnaige de incomparable sçavoir . . . qui des miens premiers principes moy ja âgé l'avois instigué.*[6] Notable and knowledgeable or not, however, Sarrazin evidently felt his local reputation threatened by the unconventional outsider and reportedly sought to sabotage his efforts. In the end Nostredame was forced to insist that the authorities decide publicly between the two of them, and the issue was (it is said) finally decided when the onlookers started bawling "We want the savior of Aix!"

Reading between the lines of the *Traité*, it seems the "snubbed doctor" went off in a huff, resigned his position, and duly retired to the town of Villefranche, a little to the north. *Illi nec invideo,*[7] wrote Nostredame later, for whom the field was now clear to complete the job, aided by the able apothecary René le Pilierverd.

---

[6] "a notable personage of incomparable knowledge . . . whom in my latter years I had provoked with my basic principles."

[7] Latin: "Nor do I bear him any grudge."

SECOND MARRIAGE

Once again reportedly laden with gifts, Nostredame now returned to Salon and, on November 11th, 1547, was married to Anne Ponsarde in front of her own first cousin, the lawyer Étienne Hozier. Between them, the already rich young widow and the newly wealthy forty-three-year-old physician purchased a solid, respectable house in what was then the rue Ferreiroux (now, inevitably, the rue Nostradamus), a cul-de-sac leading from the place de la Poisonnerie (now the place de l'Ancienne Halle) to the town's inner northeastern ramparts, in the very shadow (in the evening, at least) of the castle on its rock.

And here Nostredame might have settled down at last to a renewed bout of married life.

ITALIAN JOURNEY

His first reaction, though, seems to have been quite the opposite. Some suggest that what bit him at this juncture was what they see as the old wanderlust, others that he just wanted one final fling. In fact, the true explanation probably lies much closer to the true nature of his ultimate quest.

For he now seems to have set out, in the wake both of Rabelais and of the new King Henri II himself, on an extended visit to Italy.

Various pieces of evidence point in this direction. There is the fact that the first of his six children was – surprisingly – not to be born until about four years later. There is the fact that – as various accounts suggest and the architecture tends to confirm – he seems to have insisted at the outset on adding an extra story to the house, complete with the observation-turret that was by now *de rigueur* for any self-respecting astrologer. (Self-evidently, it is extremely difficult to continue to live in a roofless house while it is being largely rebuilt.) Even more cogent, though, is the fact that Nostredame's presence was actually reported in several Italian cities.

As well as being spotted in Venice and Genoa during 1548, he is alleged to have visited Savona, where he met the celebrated apothecary Antonio Vigerchio, two of whose recipes for constipation he was later to append to his *Traité des fardemens et confitures* of 1552 (first published in 1555) – which may in many ways be regarded as the official journal of his trip and of the years immediately preceding it. Indeed, the collection of recipes and prescriptions for this book may well have been one of the incidental aims of the visit, which he presumably intended to finance by practicing medicine en route.

In Milan he seems to have picked up an account in Latin of a famous classical gastronomic orgy, a translation of which he was likewise to include in the *Traité*. Moreover, a subsequent inscription on a villa just outside Turin (then part of French Savoy) is reported as having once boasted visits by both Nostredame and the much earlier Dante (an equally inveterate wanderer) in the following enigmatic words:

> 1556
> NOSTRADAMUS A LOGE ICI
> OU IL HA LE PARADI,
> LENFER LE PURGATOIRE.
> JE MAPELLE LA VICTOIRE.
> QUI M'HONORE AURA LA GLOIRE.
> QUI ME MEPRISE AURA LA RUINE ENTIERE.[8]

More enthusiastic than literary, they were possibly inscribed when this house, too, was being either built or refurbished a few years after the actual event.

But why the sudden Italian trip? Why should a newly married physician of such eminence suddenly take off in this way, presumably leaving his wife to return temporarily to her family – even if he was proposing to profit from the experience by collecting recipes and prescriptions? Why – unless in order to prepare himself for what, in the event, was to be an entirely new career by consulting sources that were unavailable elsewhere?

But what sources? Here the word that springs immediately to mind is "Florence." Florence, after all, was the very powerhouse of the Renaissance. No scholar visiting Italy could possibly escape the lure of the city, any more than that of Rome. Every boy of noble birth – whether from France, England, or anywhere else – was expected to include it on his itinerary as part of the obligatory "grand tour" that marked the culmination of his education. But for Nostredame this was to be no mere grand tour. Almost certainly there were much deeper purposes afoot.

Nostradamus's original house at Salon (photographic reconstruction after Leroy)

---

8 Suggested crude translation:
Nostradamus rested here
Where did Paradise appear,
Hell and also Purgat'ry.
I am namèd Victory.
Who me honors famed shall be:
Who me scorns shall ruin see.

It was here, after all, that the great scholars employed by the Medici had for a century now been collecting, transcribing, and translating the ancient manuscripts of the long-lost Classical world. And not merely scientific and literary manuscripts. The initiative was at least as much esoteric and occult as it was exoteric and scientific. The whole point about Renaissance culture was that – unlike the jealous medieval Church that had contrived to enchain the European mind for so many centuries – it placed no taboo on any branch of knowledge, be it conventional or otherwise. That was why scholars such as John Dee, Paracelsus, and Nostredame felt so free to indulge themselves in studies of all types. Even the much later Isaac Newton was to delve at least as deeply and as extensively into esoteric subjects as into strictly scientific ones.

Thus, Marsilio Ficino (whom Nostradamus mentions specifically in the 1555 edition of the *Traité*) had translated not only Plato at the city's famous library of San Marco but also the *Corpus Hermeticum*, a compendium of ancient esoteric teachings allegedly handed down from Orpheus, Pythagoras, Plato, and the legendary Hermes Trismegistos himself. His pupil Pico della Mirandola (1463–94) had gone on to publish a book entitled *Nine Hundred Conclusions* (1486), in which he sought to reconcile Christianity, Judaism, and Islam in terms of the arcane Hebrew system of teachings known as the Cabala.

No wonder, then, that Nostredame was seemingly to spend at least the next year-and-a-half in Italy. And it is not difficult to imagine what he was up to.

For now he was determined to exploit what he perceived as his prophetic gift – *mon naturel instinct qui m'a esté donné par mes aiules*,[9] as he was later to describe it. But refining and perfecting this gift demanded a great deal of esoteric knowledge that was not easily available. Iamblichus's *De Mysteriis Aegyptiorum*, for example – the seminal Greek work on ritual theurgy (the summoning up of gods and spirits) – was no longer in print. However, Marsilio Ficino's Latin translation of it, published by Aldo Manuzio (pioneer of most modern punctuation conventions), had been in the Florentine library ever since 1497 – and it would be 1549 before Jean de Tournes of Lyon (perhaps encouraged by Nostredame himself: see Book Printing and Publishing) would finally bring out his own version of it in France.

There were other ancient magic books to be located and studied, too – and, if possible, acquired. There was Michael Psellus's important eleventh-century work *De Daemonibus* (also incorporated into Manuzio's book and available in Florence),[10] to which the subsequent *Propheties* were indeed to refer (I.42: see under Astrologer and Mage). There was the rare but preeminent *grimoire* known as the *Clavicula Salomonis* or Key of Solomon – a multilingual manual of magic that was allegedly composed by King Solomon himself and similarly devoted to such practices as theurgy. And no doubt there were other esoteric and magical tracts, most of which have since been lost.

mencent si bien a fleurir, mesmes despuis cent ans, quelque peu moyns, que la cité de Florence a produit une multitude de personnaiges tant scauantz en toute literature, que ie auserois affermer ce present siecle regner la uraye langue Attique, que nous ne soions beaucoup redeuables à noz predecesseurs de nousauoir laissé par escrit tant de monumentz. Si sommes, que par iceux nous comprenons leur temps, & cons020 la future iacture des lettres, qui pourra tant auenir comme par conflagration, ou inundation, ou par ignorante negligence a esté. I'ay uolué & reuolué possible non pas à suffisance tant de uielles librairies si ie pourrois trouuer aucun autheur digne de foy, qui feisse mention de la matiere que i'ay redigé par escrit non. Ie pense bien quilz en ont parlé, & ont usé de plusieurs sortes de distillations du temps mesmes de Hippocrates, que quand il parloit de roris cyriaci, ou de manna

Nostradamus acknowledges his debt to Florence in his *Traité des fardemens*

Certainly Nostredame finished up with his own collection of such works, for in his *Préface à César* (section 9)[11] he refers to having studied the *effrenées persuasions* of *celle occulte Philosophie* contained in *plusieurs volumes qui ont estés cachés par long siecles*[12] and admits to having subsequently burned them.

---

9   "my natural instinct bequeathed to me by my forefathers."

10   Jean de Tournes of Lyon was in due course to republish this, too.

11   See under The Major Prophecies.

12   "wild beliefs . . . that occult Philosophy . . . a number of volumes that have been hidden for long centuries."

A visit to Florence, then, was seemingly *de rigueur*, as was a subsequent journey to see the newly built splendors of Renaissance Rome, where he perhaps reencountered Rabelais, now secretary to the French Ambassador, Cardinal Jean du Bellay. He may even have been there for the enthronement of the new Pope Julius III in February 1550.

Now headed southward, Naples cannot have failed to attract him, either. Close nearby, after all, lay the cave of the ancient sybilline oracle whose national function he himself was increasingly determined to emulate on behalf of his own nation. And the fact that this was also where the preeminent Roman poet Virgil reportedly came to retire was merely the icing on the cake – for the often prophetic poetry of Virgil (it is quite clear from Nostradamus's verse) already exercised an enormous influence over him. The fact that it also came to be treated as a kind of state oracle cannot have escaped him, either.

But all this, if so, must have taken time. It is quite possible that fall was drawing on by now. What more natural, then, than to carry on southward with a view to crossing to Palermo and overwintering in Sicily? The island, after all, was the heart of the former *Magna Graecia*, or Greater Greece. In some ways it had been even more resplendently Greek than Greece itself. Certainly, with the Turks in control of southeastern Europe, it was the only piece of ancient Greece that was still easily accessible. And there, scattered across it, were the mighty remains of the ancient Greek temples – at Segesta, at Selinunte, at Agrigento, at Syracuse. Indeed, at the last two, the former temples of Athena were *still in use* – but now as temples to another Virgin Queen, the Virgin Mary (*Notre Dame!*), their elegant fluted pillars now joined together with clumsy curtain walls.

Might he not, then, be able to pick up clairvoyantly from the ancient stones some inkling of what, according to Iamblichus, used to go on within them? Might not the *genius loci* somehow impart to him the secrets of the ancient rites? It is easy to imagine something of the kind passing through the French occultist's mind – speculative though all such imaginings have unfortunately to remain. Nevertheless, the fact that some later reports indeed have him visiting Sicily is at least encouraging for the theory...

THE BUDDING PROPHET

It seems to have been around 1550 before Nostredame finally returned to his newly refurbished home and his no doubt impatient wife at Salon. Now at last family life could resume. Now at last, too, his true work could commence. Not only could he put the finishing touches to his long-planned *Traité des fardemens et confitures*, but he could embark on his series of annual *Almanachs* (see Nostradamus's Writings). And now, in recognition of his new status, he started for the first time to style himself "Nostradamus."

Publishing what was, in effect, a series of glorified annual weather-forecasts-cum-calendars, spiced with additional predictions for the *political and military* climate, may seem a superficial and unworthy occupation for a prophet of such eminence. Each *Almanach*, after all, was a small book in its own right and must have taken up a great deal of the valuable time of a man who was no youngster to start with. But matters meteorological were far from superficial at the time (see Nostradamus in Context and the Table of Events). Thousands were dying during the agricultural and social crises that were regularly sweeping France as a result of a rapidly deteriorating weatherpattern that has since been described in terms of a "Little Ice-Age," with freezing winters often followed by cold springs and unremittingly rainy summers.

Besides, the compilations were popular, earned him growing fame as a prophet (especially locally), and – by no means least of all – brought in a great deal of money.

The Sibyl of ancient Cumae

Romanticized 18th-century impression of Nostradamus

LEFT **Florence by Pianta della Catena. Nostradamus almost certainly visited the city's famous library on his Italian trip.**

THE IRRIGATOR

True, in the country around Salon the problem was often not too much water as too little of it. To the west lay a flat desert of gravel and pebbles known as the Désert de la Crau, which grew little beyond lizards and scorpions, snakes and birds of prey. Even Salon itself (the Roman *Castrum Salonense*) had originally been scarcely more than a fortress perched on a rock in the middle of a salt-marsh. To Nostradamus this must have been a matter of some concern – for numerous traditions assert that his prescriptions for controlling the plague (see Nostradamus the Physician) involved copious quantities of both fresh air and running water.

Both these prescriptions were pretty revolutionary, it has to be admitted, for an age that generally regarded the air as potentially malevolent and such "sexy" activities as washing and bathing as contrary to good religion.

Perhaps he had observed that large cities depending on wells for their water were more prone to the plague than more airy country towns that were fed by rivers and streams. The observation may have been correct, even if the assumed link was more suspect. But, at all events, running water does seem to have been something of an obsession with him. His prescriptions in the *Traité* constantly call for spring, rather than well, water.

Thus, in 1553, when the municipality constructed a new fountain in the town, it was Nostradamus who was called upon to compose the Latin inscription. This he did in characteristically facetious vein that was probably (and no doubt fortunately) lost on the town magistrates and consuls who had commissioned it:

SI HVMANO INGENIO PERPETVO
SALLONAE CIVIB. PARARI VINA POTVISSET
NON AMOENVM QVEM CERNITIS
FONTEM AQVARVM. S. P. Q. SALON. MAGNA
IMPENSA NON ADDVXISSET
DVCTA. N. PALAMEDE MARCO.
ET ANTON. PAVLO CONSS
M. NOSTRADAMVS
DIIS IMMORTALIBVS
OB SALONENSES
M.D.LIII

This might be freely translated as: "If unending human ingenuity had been up to the task of furnishing the citizens of Salon with a supply of wine, it would not have been necessary for the Senate and Magistrates of Salon to erect at great expense, under the consulship of Paul Antoine and Palamède Marc, this unlovely fountain that you see before you. Michel Nostradamus, on behalf of the people of Salon, 1553." Unfortunately the original fountain inscription is now lost.

But Nostradamus's interest in water and irrigation went much further than this. Before long he was teaming up with the young local architect and hydraulic engineer Adam de Craponne – fresh from his triumph in successfully reinforcing the walls of Metz against the vastly superior forces of the Emperor Charles V – to dig a network of canals to irrigate Salon's arid hinterland from the Durance River. In 1556 he invested 200 crowns in the project, in 1560 another 288, and in 1562 yet another hundred. Even after his death his widow Anne was to advance a hundred more. It is largely thanks to Craponne's project and its later imitators, in fact, that the area is now green and flowering and so full of canals that it actually boasts hydroelectric stations of its own.

Possibly the budding seer had foreseen all this. Yet he himself was scarcely to benefit from it. It would be 1559 before the full-scale canal eventually reached Salon, and well after his death before the network finally reached the sea in the south and Arles in the west, in the process watering the whole of the northern Crau.

Statue of Adam de Craponne, engineer, architect and canal-builder, in whose scheme to irrigate the Crau Nostradamus invested

THE MAGE OF SALON

In the meantime, however, Nostradamus, encouraged by various strange omens (see The Nostradamus Omens) was hard at work on his *magnum opus* – his planned series of a thousand verse-prophecies designed to foretell the entire future of the world. Already, in all probability, he had worked out most of the astronomical tables on which this would necessarily be based – a task that was Herculean enough in itself (see Astrologer and Mage). Now, having at last assembled his library of magical works and trained himself in the techniques involved, he could use them to refine and perfect his inherited gift of the "sight." The two approaches – the intellectual and the intuitive – he could subsequently hope to combine into a near-infallible tool for predicting the future. It then required only that he compose a four-line verse for each prediction.

His stated aim was to produce a volume consisting of ten books of one hundred such quatrains each. In acknowledgment of this basic structure, each book was to be called a *Centurie* (the term itself, as it happened, had nothing to do with periods of time). And the result would be the celebrated *Centuries* as we have them today (see Nostradamus's Writings and The Major Prophecies).

He would seem to have started work sometime during 1553. Certainly, by April 1st, 1554, he had (on the quatrain's own internal evidence) reached verse 42 of the first *Centurie* (see Astrologer and Mage). Yet there may have been problems along the way. For a start, the children were now beginning to arrive. Madeleine, the oldest, was admittedly already four, but César, the infant son to whom the prophecies would initially be dedicated, was still only one. Any nighttime noise from them must inevitably have disrupted the long nighttime séances that seem to have played such an important part in the process. Moreover, the arthritis that would later plague the seer may already have been setting in, rendering his writing increasingly illegible. To this possibility, indeed, may be due the fact that the long-awaited (though admittedly specialized) *Traité*, finished by its own admission in 1552, would seemingly have to wait another three years before a publisher could be found to take it on. At all events, no earlier copy seems to have survived.

What Nostradamus needed at this stage, in fact, was assistance, and it was here that his old philosophical and literary contacts seem to have come to his aid.

One of his great admirers at the time was the eminent Greek scholar Jean Dorat, recently appointed Principal of the Collège de Coqueret in Paris, who came from Limoges and so may first have encountered the young Nostredame during an earlier visit to Scaliger's "school of philosophers" at Agen. An inveterate encourager of young talent, he it was who, back in 1549, had so enthused various of his pupils and their friends in revitalizing the French language, especially with classical words and syntax, that two of them – Pierre de Ronsard and Joachim du Bellay (cousin of Rabelais's Cardinal in Rome) – helped to found a group of writers known as the Pléiade to bring the vision about (see Nostradamus's Language). Its influence was to prove immense, even affecting later foreign writers such as Francis Bacon and William Shakespeare.

Another of Dorat's pupils was Jean-Aimé de Chavigny, theologian, lawyer, and former magistrate at Beaune in Burgundy, who evidently caught his master's near-infatuation with the mage of Salon. The precise reason for this is not entirely clear, but it may initially have had something to do not only with Nostradamus's obvious eminence as a scholar but also with his distinctly original use of language (see Nostradamus's Language).

At all events, the bug bit deep. Before long, Chavigny was on his way to Salon to offer his services as the seer's secretary, amanuensis, and disciple. We may imagine that Nostradamus, possibly scenting the would-be magician, resisted at first, then gave in with a good grace. Chavigny, after all, was named after the biblical Beloved Disciple. Hopefully that at least was a good omen.

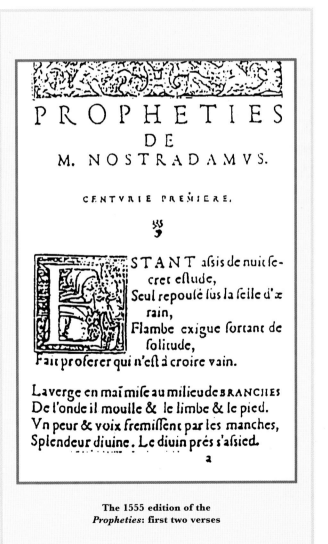

The 1555 edition of the *Propheties*: first two verses

THE *PROPHETIES*

Virtually no dates are known for Chavigny's stay in Salon, though he was certainly still there in 1565, and again at Nostradamus's death the following year, as well as for some time afterward. Various traditions, however, claim that he started work on Good Friday, 1554. And certainly it is true that from this point onward successful publications followed thick and fast.

Not only did Nostradamus's long-awaited *Traité des fardemens et confitures* now appear in print for the first time (with a dedication to his brother Jean, now Attorney General to the Parlement at Aix), but the *Propheties*, too, were soon proceeding apace. The *Préface à César* that served as the dedication to the first edition is dated March 1st, 1555 (see facsimile on p.125). By May 4th, thanks to the approval of the authorities and the professionalism of publisher Macé Bonhomme of Lyon, the book was already in print.

Notwithstanding the fact that it contained only the first 353 of the intended thousand verses (see Nostradamus's Writings), the beautifully printed volume's fame was immediate. And not only in Lyon. The regulation copy having been sent to the royal library in Paris, Nostradamus was at once summoned to attend Queen Catherine de Médicis herself by his friend the Duc de Tende. So urgent was the matter thought to be that the royal post-horse service was even put at his disposal, halving the expected two-months' journeytime.

SUMMONED TO COURT

Thus it was that sometime between July 14th and 27th, 1555, the already aging seer, no doubt either trotting or cantering uncomfortably from *relai* to *relai* on one of a group of pack-horses, was seen passing through Lyon, where he confessed to a premonition that he might be maltreated and even decapitated before August 25th. Nevertheless, he arrived in Paris safely enough on the 15th[13] (Feast of the Assumption of the Blessed Virgin Mary – *Notre Dame* again!). Finding that the Court had already left for its summer quarters at the castle of St.-Germain-en-Laye, he put up for the night at the Auberge St.-Michel (the name was presumably another good omen) – only to discover that he had run out of money and needed to borrow more to pay his bill. Scarcely had he settled up in the morning than he was collected (according to César's admittedly propagandist account) by the High Constable of France, the strangely named Anne de Montmorency himself, and whisked off to see the King. Most commentators not unreasonably assume that he also had a long consultation with the occult-obsessed Queen,

who had had him brought there in the first place. Afterward he was put up at the town residence of the Archbishop of Sens and presented with a hundred crowns each from the King and Queen in a velvet purse. Chavigny even suggests that he was appointed Royal Councilor.

Once ensconced in his palatial lodgings, however, he was stricken – possibly as a result of being plied with too much fine wine – with an attack of gout, which confined him to bed for nearly two weeks. Evidently he profited from the opportunity to charge good money for a whole series of consultations with the nobility. Following this, he was sent on to Blois to examine the royal children – and notably the future François II, Charles IX, and Henri III, then age eleven, five, and three respectively. Tradition has it that he was flabbergasted by their doom-laden astrological prospects and their weak, tubercular constitutions and, casting around for something positive to say, reported back to the Queen that "all your sons will be kings." Then, allegedly forewarned by a "lady of quality" that the religiously sensitive Justices of Paris were looking into his occult practices, he left in a hurry before either the Law could catch up with him or the Queen could add him to her permanent menagerie of leading magicians and astrologers (she had, after all, already "collected" the occultist scholar Gabriel Simeoni of Florence and the prominent astrologer Cosmo Ruggieri, even building for the latter an observatory at Chaumont).

CONTINUATIONS AND FRUSTRATIONS

And so it was that, probably by late autumn, the now-famous seer was back in Salon and able to resume work on his *Propheties*. By March 14th, 1557, he was partway through his planned dedicatory letter to the King, and by November had at least the next 289 verses ready for publication (see Nostradamus's Writings and Early Editions). In the atmosphere of national gloom and doom following the massive military disaster of St.-Quentin, the moment was judged right for an immediate, interim edition, and so its new publisher – Antoine du Rosne of Lyon – may perhaps be forgiven for having rushed and generally mangled the typesetting.

The seer then evidently carried on without a break, finishing the full thousand verses by June 27th, 1558. He even seems to have had some time to spare – for, in addition to the annual *Almanachs*, he managed in the meantime to bring out his free translation of Menodotus's *Paraphrase de C. Galen*, no doubt designed to show that the distinguished Graeco-Roman physician's medical outlook had, after all, been much closer to his own distinctly free way of thinking than his critics often realized.

At this point, however, there seems to have been a hitch. True, the much-respected Jean de Tournes of Lyon did publish the last three *Centuries* in the same year, while Barbe Regnault of Paris seems to have had the whole work in print in 1561. Yet thereafter, nothing. It was 1568, two years after the prophet's death, before

---

13 Most commentators take César's slightly ambiguous account to mean that the trip took place the following year, as Chavigny himself suggests, even though Nostradamus is known to have been in Salon on July 27th, 1556, signing a document before one Maître Laurent to invest 200 crowns in Craponne's canal. Again, Simeoni (see below) wrote to him from Court in February 1556 to express the hope that his visit to Paris *of the previous year* had been a success: the letter still survives.

the complete work again saw the light of day – and even then minus fifty-eight verses of the seventh *Century*.

Why? What had gone wrong? 1558, already a year of violent political and religious disputes, had admittedly seen a sudden onslaught on Nostradamus in the press, couched in the most vituperative of terms (see Criticisms and Reviews). But then the seer was used to such attacks, even if normally in less literary form. A more likely explanation might be some kind of publishing dispute. Possibly dissatisfied with du Rosne's rather crude and slapdash work, Nostradamus had decided to switch to a third publisher, one Benoist Rigaud of Lyon, for the final, complete edition. We may surmise that du Rosne had originally been sent the whole of the first seven *Centuries* for the second edition, but had been unable to find room for the last sixty verses (see Nostradamus's Writings, Early Editions and Book Printing and Publishing). Assuming that he had acquired the rights to the whole work, though, he had now objected to the change of publisher and refused to hand over the manuscript of the missing verses. Meanwhile Nostradamus and Chavigny had between them managed to mislay their own copy. And so Nostradamus and his publishers were stuck in an impasse.

CATASTROPHE

Even while the presumed dispute was still brewing, however, came a devastating hammerblow that set back the whole project even further. Under the terms of Henri II's new peace treaty with the Empire following the St.-Quentin disaster, Philip II of Spain (whose wife Mary of England had just died) was to marry Henri's daughter Elisabeth, while the brilliant Imperial general Emmanuel-Philibert, Duke of the newly independent Savoy, was to marry the King's sister Marguerite de Valois. The celebrations marking Philip's proxy-engagement and the duke's wedding began in Paris at the end of June, 1559.

With the Louvre currently being rebuilt, the obligatory tournament was held at the Palais des Tournelles (near the Bastille). In the course of it the King, determinedly riding out into the lists for a third time against the reluctant young Conte de Montgomery, captain of his Scottish guard, was mortally wounded in the brain by the latter's splintered lance. He died in agony eleven days later. In Ronsard's words: *Notre Prince au millieu de ses plaisirs est mort.*[14]

For France this was to prove a disaster of the first order, leading directly to half a century of instability, disintegration, and savage

Henri II is killed while jousting, June 30th, 1559, as apparently predicted in Nostradamus's verse I.35

14 *Elegie sur les troubles d'Amboise* (1560). Or, freely:
Our Prince amid his pleasures is undone.

conflict in which over a million-and-a-half would lose their lives. For Nostradamus it was both a triumph and a major setback: Catherine de Médicis and the Court, it seems, immediately jumped to the conclusion that the catastrophe was a fulfillment of Nostradamus's verse I.35, first published four years earlier (see facsimile p.105[15]). Indeed, some commentators suggest that the canny Queen had anticipated the outcome in advance and had even raised the verse during her earlier meeting with the seer at St.-Germain-en-Laye. There had, after all, been similar warnings by the Italian astrologer Luca Gaurico, better known in France as Luc Gauric: the King, he had twice written, should avoid "all single combat in an enclosed space, especially during his forty-first year."

GOOD AND BAD PUBLICITY

At all events, if Nostradamus and his prophecies had previously been famous, now they became all the rage. His publication of a further work designed to warn of the malign effects of the eclipse of September 16th that same year (see Early Editions) merely stirred the pot. Foreign ambassadors, quoting verses such as X.39 and X.55 from de Tournes' recently published edition (see The Major Prophecies), soon started sending home alarming reports.[16] The court of the new, sixteen-year-old King François II (who had quite recently married the only slightly older Mary Queen of Scots) was not merely in a state of chronic flux and uncertainty: it had fallen prey to rampant Nostradamania.

In 1560, meanwhile, Ronsard himself would include in an elegy on the *Troubles d'Amboise* (see "1560" in Table of Events) what amounted to a review of the *Propheties* in the form of a pseudo-sonnet that, on the whole, was remarkably favorable (see Criticisms and Reviews).

Yet there was a distinct downside to all this publicity for Nostradamus. The final edition of the *Propheties*, it will be recalled, included a dedicatory letter to King Henri II (see The Major Prophecies) wishing him "victory and felicity," and declaring in its valediction that he alone was worthy of the title of Christian King. In sanctioning its further issue now, therefore, not only could the seer be accused of failing to foresee the fact that King Henri would die before publication; he might even be accused of demeaning the new King François, too.

At this point, then, Nostradamus may have asked his new publisher, Benoist Rigaud, to substitute a new royal dedication. If so, Rigaud may well have refused unless the seer came up with the fifty-eight still-missing verses[17] (see Nostradamus's Writings). Du Rosne in turn may well have continued to refuse to supply them – if, indeed, he had not lost them by now. And so publication was effectively frozen, and would remain so until after the seer's death. To this we owe the fact that, even today, the seventh of Nostradamus's *Centuries* remains incomplete, despite the subsequent efforts of various well-meaning meddlers to complete them for him (see Forgeries and Fairy Tales).

NOSTRADAMUS THE ROYAL COUNCILOR

There was nothing to be done, then, but to continue with other work – notably the annual *Almanachs*, a work on treating the plague, and a treatise on astrology (see Early Editions). There was also a growing number of personal consultations for the aging seer to perform, some of them for very powerful people indeed. Fifty-one pieces of correspondence with such clients have recently been rediscovered.

As early as October of 1559, for example, Duke Emmanuel-Philibert himself rode into Salon, on his way home to Nice from the royal obsequies, and was joined in December by his wife, the late King's sister, borne in her litter at the head of a suitably funereal cortège of domestics and retainers. The town dignitaries welcomed her from a crimson dais – though most of their speeches had inevitably been written by Nostradamus himself as the town *savant*. Then they bore her on their own shoulders through the decorated streets to the castle on its rock. Summoned to attend them there, the seer is said to have been received most courteously and to have expatiated at some length on the alleged descent of the royal house of France from Francus, son of Hector of Troy – a theme, often referred to in the *Propheties*, that would also be taken up by Ronsard in his abortive epic poem *La Franciade* of 1572.

Stories are told of other consultations – for his friend the Duc de Tende, Governor of Provence, for the Conte de Crussol, for his regular cronies the Commandeur de Beynes and the Baron de la Garde, Admiral of the Eastern Fleet.

A further summons is said to have arrived from the Queen ordering him to Turin on behalf of Duke Emmanuel-Philibert, who wished to consult him about the future of both his shortly expected child and himself. Whether the increasingly crippled old seer ever made the journey, however, is extremely doubtful, even though his

---

[15] In an edited version of my own published translation for Piatkus Books this reads:
The younger lion shall surmount the old
On field of martial combat, man to man:
Twice challenged, thrice; eyes pierced in cage of gold,
Death shall come hard as only dying can.

[16] Possible translations of the two verses might read respectively:
The ill-wed eldest son a widow leaves
Nor any child, two Isles each other loathing,
Ere eighteen years his beardless chin achieves.
The next in line's the next to his betrothing.

They'll celebrate the ill-starred wedding morn
With deepest joy, yet ill shall come of it.
Husband and mother both shall Nora scorn.
Her Phoebus dead, how sad shall Nora sit!
They might also have quoted the verse-*presage* that the seer had already published in his *Almanach* for the same year, specifically for June (see *Presage* 40 under The Major Prophecies):
On each of sevenfold house shall death alight,
Hail, tempest, plague, and furious desecrators:
The Eastern King shall put the West to flight
And subjugate his former subjugators.

---

[17] Two verses seem to have resurfaced in the interim: possibly they were simply at the bottom of the last manuscript sheet that du Rosne *did* return.

alleged prediction of a son and of the Duke's death "when a nine precedes a seventh" may well have had some truth in it: the latter, certainly, died in 1569 – the year, as the prediction required, immediately before 1570.

In December 1561, following a Protestant riot and the sacking of their cathedral, the Canons of Orange, too, wrote to Nostradamus – this time to ask his help in locating their looted treasures. The seer replied by drawing up a horoscope (see Orange in the Gazetteer and Who's Who). This indicated that the culprits in fact belonged to their own number. They should be unmasked, wrote the seer, by reading aloud his letter of February 4th, 1562, in their assembly and watching the reactions of those present. Otherwise untold disasters would befall those concerned, not excluding death by plague.

Unfortunately no record survives of the outcome.

But then the citizens of Orange were not alone in suffering from the country's growing religious troubles at the time. The peasants, too, were getting caught up in them. Even in Salon the local Catholic peasantry – known as the *Cabans* on account of their gray winter cloaks – had started going on the rampage a year or so since. Incensed by the sound of children singing the latest, catchy Calvinist hymns, they had started trying to sniff out Protestants and if possible burn both them and their houses. Illogical as it may seem, Nostradamus was sometimes suspected of being one of them.

It was not just that he was an ancestral Jew, and thus thought of as somehow "different." He had studied at Montpellier, spent some years in Agen, and was in close touch with the printing industry in Lyon – and all three were known to be current hotbeds of Calvinism. His fairly long beard – a feature typical of the leading Protestants – cannot have helped either.

In 1561 Nostradamus (who by now had a wife and five children to protect, with a sixth either newly born or on the way) reacted by renting a house in Avignon for the duration. The general food situation being as increasingly critical as it was, however, the day was saved when harvest time supervened, the peasants returned to their holdings, and the seer was able to make over his lease to another.

The time had now come, he seems to have felt, to start tying up loose ends. He was not, after all, getting any younger. And so it was at around this juncture that he at last paid back the two rose nobles and two crowns that he had been forced to borrow from a Monsieur de Moral during his trip to Paris six years earlier. Possibly, too, it was at about this time that the seer, accepting that his *Propheties* were destined forever to remain incomplete, and were thus unlikely to be published in his lifetime, started work on his *Sixains* (see Nostradamus's Writings and The Major Prophecies). Since it was even less likely that they would ever be published, he could at last be more open and expansive, in particular citing actual dates for his predictions (see Dating and Sequencing the Prophecies). Had the author been some kind of forger he would, of course, have stuck as closely as possible to the seer's well-known style, vocabulary, and verse form. Given that he was Nostradamus, however, he was free to vary it at will. And so the resulting verses were not only much easier to understand than his earlier efforts, but more poetic, too.

And, exactly as the situation demanded, they turned out to number just fifty-eight.

Whatever happened, then, future generations would once again have the full thousand *Propheties*, just as he had always intended. His work was complete. And so it is supremely appropriate that it was at this very time that the crowning seal was placed upon it. For on October 17th, 1564, shortly after his publisher Jean de Tournes had died in Lyon of the plague, Queen Catherine de Médicis and her fourteen-year-old son, the new King Charles IX, arrived in Salon in the course of their two-year progress designed to pacify and reunite the kingdom, trailing some 20,000 nobles, domestics, troops, and retainers, including the unofficial royal harem and the entire government. The King, dressed in purple and adorned with silver jewelry, rode on horseback. The Queen – clad, as ever, in mourning – was borne in her customary litter.

Salon: the *cour d'honneur* of the Château de l'Empéri, where Nostradamus met the royal party in 1564

They arrived to find the town virtually empty. A local plague scare (no doubt connected with that in Lyon) had put almost everybody to flight. Evidently it had not occurred to them that, had there been the slightest whiff of truth in the rumor, neither Their Majesties nor the Court would have been seen for dust. At once, therefore, the King ordered his troops to round up the fugitives and return to attend the official welcome and supply the accustomed applause.

As ever, Nostradamus was called upon to do the honors. *Vir magnus belli, nulli pietate secundus,*[18] he declaimed, summoning up what still remained of his breath and his classical education, and apparently oblivious to the incongruity of the quotation. The consuls and magistrates tried to chip in, but tradition has it that the young King impatiently brushed them aside. "I have only come to see Nostradamus," he is alleged to have said.

Sporting a velvet hat and leaning heavily on a silver-embossed walking stick, the old seer, almost crippled now, lumbered painfully up the hill toward the castle by his monarch's side, the whole family trailing behind by royal command. Once in the *salle d'honneur*, he was formally welcomed by the King and his mother, who cooed lovingly over Diane, the youngest child. A long consultation followed.

Catherine de Médicis was obsessed by the occult and consulted Nostradamus on a number of occasions

THE SEER DISCOVERS A KING

Meanwhile, among the enormous retinue was eleven-year-old Henri, Prince de Béarn. Legend insists that the seer was so impressed with him that he asked to examine him and draw up his horoscope, sensing that he might turn out to be a future King of France and of Navarre, and a great one at that. Accordingly, the following morning he arranged to be present at the Prince's rising in his temporary lodgings, the house of Pierre Tronc de Coudoulet (who would shortly marry Nostradamus's nineteen-year-old niece Jeanne, daughter of his brother Bertrand). Before the attendants had a chance to cover the boy's nakedness with his shirt, he was able to tell everything that he needed to from the moles on his skin. The inheritance, Nostradamus confirmed, would be his.

Those present apparently either failed to grasp his drift or scoffed at the idea – which was just as well, since the suggestion was tantamount to treason. Anything of the kind, after all, would spell the end of the Valois dynasty over which the Queen presided.

But the boy remembered it. As the future Henri IV, he would

endlessly recall (it is said) how the attendants took so long putting on his shirt on that occasion that he feared an imminent whipping. The sight of the old man's stick cannot have helped, either.

Nor was that the end of the royal encounters. After visiting Aix, Marseille, Hyères, Toulon, and la Ste-Baume (the celebrated forest pilgrimage-cave sacred to Mary Magdalene, who is said to have spent her last days there), the vast royal cortège reached Arles, where it was apparently held up for two weeks by the Rhône in winter flood. Possibly for want of anything better to do, the King summoned Nostradamus for a further consultation.

Quite how the ailing old man managed to make it there is unknown. Even if Chavigny, his wife, and his daughter Madeleine (now fourteen) had managed to hoist him up onto a horse, he would presumably have been unable to dismount again for calls of nature – let alone remount – until he finally arrived. Possibly a litter was dispatched to collect him or he hired one. It is even possible that, thanks to the ancient Roman *Via Aurelia* that still ran straight most of the way to Arles beneath the very eyes of Montmorency's stronghold at Les Baux, some kind of wheeled transport might have been able to haul him across the flat, open *Crau*. For the weather had returned more or less to normal that year.

At all events, the required consultation duly took place, presumably in the palace of the Archbishop of Arles, who also owned the castle at Salon. Then came the crowning moment: Nostradamus was officially appointed Councilor and Physician-in-Ordinary to the King, "with all the rights, prerogatives, and honors appurtenant thereto." He was also awarded a pension to match and given a down payment of 300 crowns. At last, it seemed, he had made it.

It may have been on this occasion that the seer, no doubt under pressure to live up to his hosts' expectations, expressed his approval of a proposal to marry off Charles to Queen Elizabeth of England. In the event, the idea came to nothing: the Queen would reply in characteristic vein that "My Lord is too great for me, and yet too small." The seer's lingering influence may also have been behind similar, alternative marriage proposals in respect of the King's two younger brothers – both the future Henri III and

---

18 Latin: "Great man of war, second to none in piety."

Hercule-François, the scheming and unattractive Duke of Alençon (who would indeed go on to spend a year in England wooing the determined Virgin Queen, who nicknamed him "her Frog"). Whatever the truth of this, other pieces of advice were certainly now proffered, just as his new position demanded. At the end of 1565, for example, possibly panicked by the anticipated rejection of the original marriage proposal for Charles (it actually occurred in 1567), he sought to catch Queen Catherine on her arrival home from her grand tour with a letter assuring her that the forthcoming meeting of the Royal Council would bring peace throughout the kingdom, and wishing her long life, health, and prosperity.

There was no reply. Indeed, Nostradamus is nowhere referred to in the Queen's voluminous correspondence.

THE SEER PREDICTS HIS OWN DEATH

Of the blessings invoked by the seer, he himself was to enjoy only the last. Already plagued by arthritic pain and consequent insomnia, by 1566 he was dying of dropsy, though he still managed to write his *Almanach* for the following year, incorporating in it a *Presage* for November (see *Presage* 141 in The Major Prophecies) that seemingly foretold his own death:

> *Once back from embassy, and garnered in*
> *The kingly gift, all's done: his spirit sped,*
> *The dearest of his friends, his closest kin*
> *Beside the bed and bench shall find him dead.*

On June 17th he sent for the lawyer Joseph Roche to draw up his will, which left most of his property to his widow Anne Ponsarde, either absolutely or in trust. Three days later, possibly under filial pressure, he added a codicil, bequeathing his astrolabe and cornelian-encrusted gold ring to his son César and his two walnut chests and their contents to Madeleine, his oldest daughter. By the end of the month he was on the verge of suffocation, yet still determined not to take to his bed. In a copy of Stadius's *Ephemerides* for 1566 he managed to write *Hic prope mors est.*[19] Despite surgical intervention, his last hours were indeed at hand.

On the evening of July 1st, having received the Last Rites, he is said (prophet to the last) to have told Chavigny, "You will not see me alive at sunrise." In the morning he was found dead, his body barely cold, stretched on the floor in apparent fulfillment of *Presage* 141 (see above). It was July 2nd, Feast of the Visitation, sacred to Our Lady (*Notre Dame* again!).

Nostradamus was buried with full civic honors in the former chapel of the Franciscans at Salon, leaving behind him a wife, six children, an immortal body of prophecy, and a fortune of 3,444 crowns (see Last Will and Testament). His tombstone against the left-hand wall (now replaced by a copy in the west wall of the Chapel of Our Lady – *Notre Dame* again! – in Salon's Collégiale St.-

---

[19] Latin: "Death is close at hand."

**Self-portrait by César
Nostradamus**

Laurent) bore an epitaph written by his widow Anne and rendered into Latin by twelve-year-old César. In translation, it read:

> *Into the hands of Almighty God. The bones of the most illustrious Michel de Nostredame, alone judged worthy by all mortals to describe with near-divine pen the events of whole world under the influence of the stars. He lived 62 years, 6 months, 10 days and died at Salon in the year 1566. Begrudge him not his rest, you who come after. Anne Ponsarde, the Twin, of Salon wishes her husband true felicity.*

As for Anne herself, she survived him by sixteen years and was buried beside him in July 1585, just as she had wished. Their oldest son César would become a distinguished historian, poet, First Consul of Salon (twice), and amateur painter. His younger brother Charles would become a poet and a respected local figure, being dubbed "Captain of the town of Salon." The youngest brother, André, would become a courtier at Aix, but would then kill another man in a duel and be forced to spend the rest of his days as a Capuchin friar. As for the girls, Madeleine and her younger sister Anne would both marry, while Diane, the baby of the family who had so moved the Queen, would remain determinedly single.

But among them, the six children were to produce only three grandchildren, and of these (two sons of daughters, one daughter of a son) not one would perpetuate the name "Nostradamus."

Portrait of Nostradamus by his son César.
The legend reads: The Most Illustrious
Michael Nostradamus, Royal Councilor and
Physician, Prophet of France, and Pride of
His Country, in his 63rd Year.

PORTRAIT OF THE PROPHET

IN HIS *La Première Face du Janus François* of 1594, Nostradamus's long-time secretary and amanuensis, Jean-Aimé de Chavigny, offers a posthumous pen-portrait of his master. In translation, this reads:

He was of slightly less than average height, physically robust, lively, and vigorous. He had a broad, open brow, a straight, even nose, and gray eyes whose gaze was gentle, but which blazed when he was angry.[20] His countenance was both severe and smiling, so that his severity was seen to be tempered with great humanity. His cheeks were crimson, even in extreme old age, his beard was long and thick, and except in old age he was hale and hearty, with all his senses acute and quite unimpaired.

As for his mind, this was lively and sound, and easily able to understand anything it wished to. His judgment was refined, his memory admirable and reliable. He was taciturn by nature, thought much and spoke little, yet discoursed perfectly well as time and place demanded.

For the rest, he was alert, subject to sudden, instant rages, yet a patient worker. He slept only four or five hours a night. He praised and valued liberty of speech and was light-hearted by nature, as well as facetious, biting, and derisive.[21]

He approved the Ceremonies of the Roman Church and remained faithful to the Catholic faith and religion, holding that outside it there was no salvation. He gravely reproved those who, having withdrawn from its embrace, were prepared to let themselves be fed and watered by the easy-going freedoms of damnable foreign doctrines.[22] Their end, he asserted, would be evil and nasty.

Nor should I forget to mention that he was a keen practitioner of fasts, prayers, almsgiving, and austerities. He abhorred vice and castigated it severely. Indeed, I recall that when giving to the poor, to whom he was most generous and charitable, these words from Holy Scripture were constantly on his lips: "Love righteousness and hate iniquity."[23]

---

[20] This observation suggests that Chavigny himself may have been subject to that anger more than once.

---

[21] Once again, Chavigny's bald and unapologetic reporting of these rather less attractive facets of his master's character suggests that he himself may occasionally have been the butt of them.

---

[22] i.e. Lutheranism in particular.

---

[23] Either Nostradamus or Chavigny seems – not uncharacteristically of the former, at least – to have garbled the words of Hebrews 1:9: Chavigny's original text appears to recommend the making of friends and riches out of iniquity!

THE MANY FACES OF NOSTRADAMUS

Over the years Nostradamus was depicted in various guises – as the upholder of the truth, above a poem entitled "La Vérité" (LEFT), as physician (CENTER), and as prophet (RIGHT), accompanied by various airborne sigils

NOSTRADAMUS'S
LAST WILL AND TESTAMENT

SENSING the imminent approach of death, Nostradamus, stricken by gout, arthritis and severe dropsy, finally sent for Joseph Roche, lawyer, of Salon on June 17th, 1566, to draw up his will. The conventionally religious preamble ran as follows:

Maìstre Michel Nostradamus, docteur en medecine et astrophile de ladite ville de Sallon, conseiller et medecin ordinaire du Roy, estant en son bon entendement, encore qu'il ne soit pas en tout affaibly par son ancien aage et certaine maladie corporelle de laquelle il est à present detenu . . . comme bon vray chretien et fidelle, a recommandé son ame à Dieu le Createur, le priant que quand sera son bon playsir de l'appeler, que luy playse colloquer son ame au royaume eternel de Paradis . . .[24]

The document then went on to stipulate that the seer's remains be "taken for burial in the church of the convent of St. Francis of the said Salon, between the great door of the same and the altar of St. Martha, at the place where he has expressed the desire that a tomb or monument be made against the wall."[25] It was to be accompanied by four one-pound candles. Thirteen of the poor were immediately to be given six sous each. All funeral arrangements were to be at the discretion of the executors.

Bequests were made by him as follows:

• *To the Brothers*[26] *of St.-Pierre-des-Canons, one crown.*
• *To the Chapel of Our Lady of the White Penitents of Salon, one crown.*
• *To the Minor Brothers of the convent of St. Francis, two crowns.*
• *To his cousin Madeleine Besaudune, ten crowns, but only upon her marriage.*
• *To Mistress "Magdeleine Nostradamus," his daughter, six hundred golden crowns, and to each of his other daughters, Anne and Diane, five hundred golden crowns, upon their marriage.*
• *To Anne, "his beloved wife," four hundred golden crowns, but only all the while she remained a widow: should she remarry, the four hundred crowns to be repaid to his heirs. Also the use and habitation of such third part of the house as she should choose, to enjoy as long as she should live. Also his chests, bed, covers, sheets, and such other furniture and effects as went with the house, to be passed on to his heirs upon her death or remarriage. Also all her robes, clothes, rings, and jewels to enjoy at will.*
• *To his sons, all his remaining books and papers, to be packed into baskets and shut up in his room for the subsequent use of whichever of them turned out to be most apt to such studies.*
• *To César, his oldest son, the house, his gilded silver cup, and his large chairs made of wood and iron, the house to be at the common disposition of Anne, his wife, and his sons César, Charles, and André until their twenty-fifth birthdays, then to revert entirely to César, other than had already been specified in respect of his mother.*
• *To Charles and André, one hundred golden crowns each, to be paid on their twenty-fifth birthdays.*
• *To any further sons yet to be born, the same prerogatives as to the other sons his heirs, and to any further daughters the sum of one hundred crowns, or the same rights as the sons should these predecease them.*

Following this rather surprising last provision, César, Charles, and André "de Notredame" were named as sole heirs in turn, along with "the said Mistress Ponsarde," each to replace the other in the event of their dying without heirs. The children (the document continued) might marry only with the consent of their mother and nearest relatives, and in the event of all three sons' predecease, their inheritance would fall to the three daughters.

The inheritance, mainly comprising cash and credits, was to be invested with two or three solvent merchants "for honest gains and profits." The children's mother was to fulfill the role of guardian, and might sell no part of the household goods or chattels, destined as they were to be divided among Nostradamus's children once they came of age.

All profits from the investments might be used by her for her own use and for feeding and clothing the children, without the need for any rendering of accounts.

The heirs might claim no part of the inheritance until they reached the age of twenty-five,[27] nor might Nostradamus's brothers have anything to do with the handling of it. Instead, Anne Ponsarde was placed in sole charge.

The executors were named as "Pallamède Marc, squire, of Châteauneuf,[28] and sire Jacques, citizen, of Salon."

The seer's monetary assets, reckoned at 3,444 crowns and 10 sous,[29] were broken down into the following:

• *136 rose nobles*
• *101 simple ducats*
• *4 old crowns*
• *8 German florins*
• *1,419 crowns*
• *10 imperials*
• *17 marionettes*
• *8 half-crowns*
• *1 Louis XII crown*[30]
• *1,200 crown-pistollets*
• *2 golden lions in the form of old crowns*
• *a gold medallion worth two crowns*
• *3 Portuguese pieces of gold valued at 36 crowns*

---

[24] "Maître Michel Nostradamus, doctor of medicine and astrophile of the said town of Salon, Councilor and Physician-in-Ordinary to the King, being of sound mind, not yet enfeebled by his great age and the particular corporeal sickness by which he is presently afflicted . . . as a good, true, and faithful Christian, has commended his soul to God the Creator, praying that when it shall be His pleasure to call him, it may please Him to gather his soul to the eternal Kingdom of Paradise."

[25] Not, note, "*in the wall*," as certain more recent accounts would have it.

[26] Franciscan.

[27] Compare Nostradamus's own father's bequest to him under Nostradamus's Life Story.

[28] Former Consul of Salon, and one of Nostradamus's oldest cronies.

[29] i.e. around 10,000 pounds, or about $450,000 in modern money.

NOSTRADAMUS'S WILL

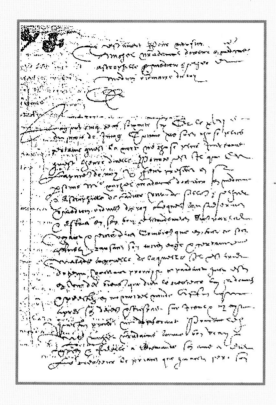

**The first page of
Nostradamus's will (lawyer's copy)**

**Last page of Nostradamus's will, bearing
his signature and those of his witnesses**

The cash was recorded as being stored in three coffers within the house, whose keys were assigned to (a) "Pallamède Marc, sire of Chasteauneuf," (b) "sire Martin Manson, Consul" and (c) "sire Jacques Suffren, citizen of the said Salon."

Against all this was to be set 1,600 crowns in debts.

The witnesses were listed as Joseph Reynaud, citizen; Martin Manson, consul; Jehan Allegret, treasurer; Pallamède Marc, squire and lord of Châteauneuf; Guillaume Giraud; Arnaud d'Amiranes; Jaumet Viguier, squire; and "Brother Vidal de Vidal, warden of the Convent of St. Francis of the said Salon." All duly signed their names except Joseph Reynaud, who could not write.

THE CODICIL

Three days later (perhaps as a result of pressure from the two oldest children, who sensed that they would be left with no personal memento of him) the old man arranged for a codicil to be added. This left his astrolabe and his great gold ring, inset with its stone of cornelian, to *César de Nostradamus, son fils bien-aymé*, and the two walnut chests in his study, along with their contents – namely his oldest daughter's clothes, rings, and jewels – to the same Madeleine absolutely and immediately upon his death.

This time the witnesses were listed as Jehan Allegret (who had signed previously); Jehan Giraud de Besson; and the three medics who were apparently tending Nostradamus at the time – namely Anthoine Paris, doctor of medicine; Guillem Eyraud, apothecary; and Gervais Bérard, surgeon, of Salon. Of these only Jehan de Giraud failed to sign.

And so it was that, in the very act of dying, Nostradamus once again contrived to bring together the three main branches of medicine that had for so long remained so determinedly apart (see Nostradamus the Physician).

---

30 Possibly a souvenir from his boyhood: King Louis died in 1515.

NOSTRADAMUS THE PHYSICIAN

B Y ALL ACCOUNTS, Nostradamus was a medical revolutionary. Indeed, the later the account, the more revolutionary
he becomes (see Books, Films, Videos, Disks, and Internet).
Thus, in Ward's account (1891) his plague treatment – and in
particular his by-now celebrated rose-pill remedy (see below) – is
merely described as "valuable." In Laver's (1942) he additionally
wields some kind of disinfectant powder. By the time of Cheetham
(1973) and her various imitators, the disease has started to be called
le charbon, and he is not only refusing to bleed his patients according
to custom but insisting on fresh air and clean water as well;[31] while
with the advent of Brennan (1992), Nostradamus has added to his
prescription clean bedding, moderate exercise, and a diet low in
animal fat.

All of which would be interesting, were it not for the fact that
none of the supplementary details mentioned seem to have been
recorded either by Nostradamus or by his immediate biographers.

What, then, is the truth of the matter?

Virtually all that we can be confident about is that
Nostradamus was firmly schooled and examined at Montpellier in
all the traditional methods. If anything, then, it was against these
that he rebelled. Yet they in turn are so often misrepresented in
modern literature on Nostradamus that it behoves us to start by
establishing just what they were.

THE CONTEMPORARY MEDICAL CANON
Instruction at Montpellier, as at other European medical schools of
the period, was based mainly on the teachings of the following:

1. Hippocrates	**4. Haly Abbas**
2. Aristotle	**5. Avicenna**
3. Galen	**6. Maimonides**

Of these, the writings of Aristotle and Galen especially were
approved by the Church, and any questioning of them was
regarded as heretical. This corpus of teaching, then, formed the
basis of contemporary medical practice.

Hippocrates (*c*.460–*c*.357 B.C.) was (and is) regarded as the
"Father of Medicine" and the founder of its code of ethics. A
native of the Greek island of Cos, he seems to have come of a long
line of physicians whose original allegiance had been to the cult of
the Greek Asklepios, god of healing. His approach was essentially
holistic, stressing nature's own healing powers, as assisted by a
healthy occupation, good diet, rest, fresh air, massage, and baths.
In a treatise entitled *On Air, Water, and Places* Hippocrates also
recognized the influence of climate on health. Nostradamus, in his
Traité des fardemens, specifically mentions the treatise on *Epidemics*
that is also attributed to Hippocrates.

Hippocrates's basic concept of health and disease, however, was
based on the humoric model of human physiology and tempera-
ment. This derived from the influential theory of the only slightly
earlier Empedocles of Agrigentum, Sicily, (495–435 B.C.), who
claimed that the whole universe was composed of the four
elements, Fire, Air, Earth, and Water. On this model, it was subsequently argued, the human organism, too, must be similarly
composed, and from this arose the doctrine of the four Humors –
namely Blood, Phlegm, Choler (or yellow bile), and Melancholy (or
black bile). The health of the entire organism, it was held,
depended upon all four of these being held in balance. In chapter
26 of his *Traité des fardemens et confitures* Nostradamus refers directly
to this dubious but highly influential concept, which still leaves its
cultural mark even today in our familiar terms "sanguine," "phleg-
matic," "choleric" and "melancholic" – to say nothing of other,
even more common expressions, such as "in a good humor."

**Bodily relationships with the four Humors
(engraving from L. Thurneysser's *Quinta essentia*, 1574)**

---

[31] This last notion may derive in part from Nostradamus's insistence in chapter 1 of
his *Traité des fardemens* that one of his prescriptions (that for a cosmetic sublimate) be
prepared using running, rather than well, water.

Aristotle and Plato: detail from *The School of Athens* in the Stanza della Segnatura, 1510–11, by Raphael. Aristotle played a fundamental part in the seer's medical education.

In order to maintain this precarious balancing act, Hippocrates's approach was essentially *homoeopathic*, with like allegedly curing like. To this end he recommended a selection of mild purgatives, hot drinks for use as perspirants and vegetable juices as diuretics. Emetics, astringents, and narcotics such as belladonna, mandragora, and opium might also be used sparingly (the last two being specifically mentioned by Nostradamus at IX.62). Bloodletting might also be performed, but only when strictly necessary.

Finally, the great physician of Cos recommended that every newly qualified doctor should travel from town to town "in order to gain a reputation not only as a doctor in name, but as a doctor in deed." If the records are to be believed (see Nostradamus's Lifestory), there seems to be no doubt that Nostradamus duly followed this precept to the letter.

Aristotle of Stagira, Macedonia, (384–322 B.C.), Plato's star pupil, in effect codified his master's philosophical teachings, while putting his own analytical spin on them. After a spell as tutor to the future Alexander the Great, he set up his celebrated Peripatetic School at the Athenian Lyceum, engaging there in much lecturing and scientific research. His particular interest was the collection and analysis of biological specimens, and it was his work on these that would lay the foundations for the sciences of comparative anatomy and embryology.

Unfortunately, though, his sheer authority in the scientific, philosophical, and cosmological spheres tended to discourage further investigation of his biology, especially when the Church, having originally opposed the Greek philosopher's teachings, belatedly switched to promoting them as virtual Holy Writ, thanks partly to the agitation of medieval thinkers such as Pierre Abelard. This attitude still prevailed at the time of Nostradamus and even beyond. Indeed, the later persecution of Galileo would rest heavily on it. It may safely be assumed, therefore, that Aristotelianism informed much of Nostradamus's thinking.

Galen (A.D. 129–*c*.199), or Claudius Galenus, is generally regarded as the founder of modern medicine. A Greek from Pergamum in Asia Minor, he used his experience of treating wounded gladiators at the local amphitheater to lay the basis for what is now known as experimental physiology. Transferring to Rome in A.D. 161, he quickly gained a wide reputation as a doctor (not least through his own arrogant self-advertisement) and was eventually appointed by the Emperor Marcus Aurelius as physician to his son Commodus. This gave him considerable authority, and he ruthlessly used it to such effect that for centuries afterward it was forbidden to question it.

Although Galen's theoretical approach was basically Hippocratic, he took the opposite, *allopathic* view of treatment, which has prevailed in orthodox medicine ever since. Symptoms were treated not with their like, in other words, but with their opposite. It was in this context, consequently, that the traditional armory of diets, massages, and drugs had now to be employed. As for Hippocrates's doctrine of the Humors, this was now reinforced with the doctrine of the *pneuma (*from the Greek word for "breath"), a subtle substance carried by the blood that was supposed to control the various body processes.

Fortunately, however, Galen left profuse and detailed written accounts of his many physiological experiments. With the liberating effect of the Renaissance, it thus eventually became possible to repeat and criticize them – and this would not only provide the basis for a great renewal of physiological knowledge specifically during Nostradamus's lifetime, but would at one and the same time sow the seeds of Galen's eventual theoretical downfall.

However, this last would take time. The initial tendency was to accept the new, critical, anatomical findings – as typified by Vesalius's *De humani corporis fabrica* of 1543, which demolished a good many of Galen's misconceptions – while at the same time still treating the actual writings of the great Greek physician more or less as Holy Writ. The tendency was not untypical of the Renaissance. But at least those writings could now be consulted in the original Greek, instead of in Latin translations of Hebrew translations of Arabic translations of Syriac translations . . .

Nostradamus himself joined in this process. Although his writings reveal vast respect for Galen – far more so than those of his Swiss contemporary Paracelsus, who on one occasion ceremonially burned Galen's works in front of the university at Basel – he nevertheless took pains, in his translation of Galen's *Paraphrase* of Menodotus's *Invitation to Medicine*[32] (allegedly based on both Latin and Greek originals), to emphasize that the great Greek physician's outlook had not been half as blinkered as his more recent disciples were wont to suggest. Menodotus, after all, had been one of the Alexandrian Empiricists, who had specifically emphasized practical rather than theoretical medicine and had advocated the use of a vast pharmacopoeia of tried and tested drugs without too much thought for the supposed principles underlying their operation. They worked, therefore they should be used: the approach, it has to be said, bears striking similarities to what we know of Nostradamus's own methodology, if his *Traité des fardemens* is to be regarded as typical.

Dedicated to two of Nostradamus's regular cronies, the Baron de la Garde and the Commandeur de Beynes, the *Paraphrase* is clearly an important pointer to Nostradamus's own medical thinking. In which case its underlying theme is revealing – namely that people, unlike animals, are supposed to think for themselves and not blindly to accept what is placed before them. And this, be it noted, in Galen's own words! As Nostradamus puts in in his dedication to the Commandeur de Beynes:

> *Suivès le droit sentier et voyez plaine,*
> *Que Galen puisse s'entendre en nostre langue . . .*[33]

Actually, this piece of veiled political point-scoring is somewhat arch and vastly overdone. Many of the words are in fact Nostradamus's, not Galen's, and the translation is not nearly as faithful or elegant as Erasmus's almost contemporary Latin version. Possibly this tells us something about how Nostradamus viewed translation – and consequently about how he in turn expected to be translated. Certainly his *Orus Apollo* (see Nostradamus's Writings) is little better in this regard.

As far as Galen is concerned, however, Nostradamus's respect for the great physician clearly remained unimpaired, even if he was more inclined to believe the great man himself than his much more restrictive latter-day disciples. And so the work commences with a short eulogy of Galen, allegedly translated from the Greek inscription on a statue to him:

> *Le temps estoit quand la terre engendra*
> *L'homme mortel par sa science infuse;*
> *Quand l'art iatrice Barbare parfondra*
> *Le grand Galen, qui lors estoit confuse*
> *Terre, immortelz nourrisoit quand, diffuse,*
> *Estoit sa fame et la porte damnable*
> *D'enfer vuidé par tout des mains qu'il use,*
> *Par sa doctrine iatrice tant louable.*[34]

Rabelais's edition of Hippocrates and Galen, published by Gryphius in 1532

---

[32] *Paraphrase de C. Galen sus l'exhortation de Menodote aux estudes des bonnes Artz, mesmement Medecine. Traduit de Latin en Françoys, par Michel Nostradamus* (Lyon, Antoine du Rosne, 1557).

---

[33] *Follow the path direct, and see full clear*
How Galen in our tongue can be conveyed . . .

---

[34] *Time was when Earth one mortal man infused*
With Galen's science and brought him forth to birth;
When savage healing arts, till then confused,
He did uproot as being of little worth.
Earth yet did bear immortals in those days
When his great fame the gates did burst apart
Of damnèd Hell, thanks to his healing ways,
His noble doctrine and physician's art.

We may safely assume, then, that Nostradamus observed and followed the teachings of Galen with considerable respect, and certainly no less than he did those of Hippocrates. Otherwise he would surely not have bothered either with the work itself or with its fulsome verse eulogy.

Haly Abbas or Ali ibn al Abbas, a Persian physician of the tenth century, is famed chiefly for compiling a comprehensive encyclopedia of medical knowledge up to that time known as the *Royal Book.*

Avicenna or Ibn Sina (980–1037), doctor to the Persian royal court, came to be known as the "Prince of Physicians." He was one of the first to introduce the teachings of Aristotle to the East. In his celebrated *Canon of Medicine* (which outdid and superseded earlier medical encyclopedias) he strove specifically to reconcile these with the teachings of Galen. Understandably, then, the book came to dominate instruction in the European and Asian medical schools

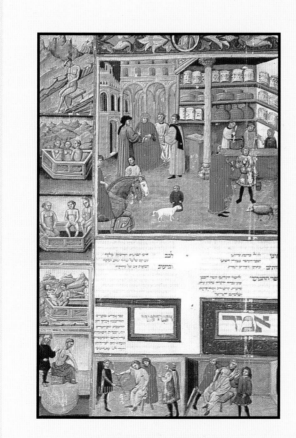

A page from the *Canon of Medicine* by Avicenna, which Nostradamus would have consulted at medical school in Montpellier

until the time of Nostradamus and beyond: despite Paracelsus's public burning of it in front of the University of Basel in 1527, along with the medical works of Galen, the seer's old faculty at Montpellier was still using it as late as 1650.

Moses Maimonides (1135–1204), a Jewish rabbi and Aristotelian philosopher, became physician to Saladin in Egypt after being expelled from Cordoba, and set up the Jewish college at Alexandria. Writing both in Arabic and in Hebrew, he produced in the latter the *Code of Maimonides.* This ethical dissertation is still highly regarded in Jewish medical circles – to which, of course, Nostradamus belonged, spiritually at least. Maimonides's career marked the end of empirical openness in Arabian medicine.

Such, then, were the teachings on which medical theory and treatment were based at the time of Nostradamus, and there is no reason to suppose that he rejected them to any large extent. On the other hand, his surviving medical writings are typically those of an apothecary rather than of a doctor, a fact that may suggest that his sympathies nevertheless lay with Menodotus and the Alexandrian Empiricists of the first three centuries of our era – whence, no doubt, the fact that he chose specifically to translate Galen's *Paraphrase* of Menodotus.

If so, then he was not alone. It was precisely at this time, as we have seen, that Andreas Vesalius (1514–64), the somewhat younger professor of anatomy at Padua, was using his own direct experience of dissection to throw Galen's doctrines into doubt. His contemporary Ambroise Paré (1510–90), surgeon to four kings of France, was using his own experience of tending wounded soldiers to reform both anatomical knowledge and medical treat-

Anatomical drawing by John Stephen of Kalkar for Vesalius's *De Humani Corporis Fabrica* of 1543

ment. Recognized to this day as the father of modern French surgery, he was wont to remark, "I dressed him: God healed him."

Others, too – including Columbus, Servetus, Fallopius, and Eustachio (both of these last two still commemorated in modern medical terminology) – were pushing well beyond the bounds formerly set by Galen. Profiting from the pioneering microbial ideas of the Roman Varro (116–27 B.C.), Girolamo Fracastoro, an expert on epidemic infection, was even theorizing, in his *De contagione et contagiosis morbis* of 1546, that diseases could be spread by invisible airborne or touch-transmitted particles.

And this, it will be recalled, was precisely the year in which Nostradamus was called to Aix to deal with the plague.

But it was the notorious Paracelsus (*c.*1493–1541), ten years Nostradamus's senior, who was possibly doing most to empiricize medicine and free it from its classical shackles at the time: not only did he insist (unusually) on medical hygiene and nature's own healing powers, but he made an enormous contribution to bringing a measure of rationality into diagnosis and treatment, as well as to replacing the traditional herbal remedies with new, chemical drugs.

If, then, Nostradamus was in any sense a medical revolutionary, he was merely acting in the spirit of the leading medical lights of his day. Possibly he himself was one of them. Certainly his writings suggest that his sympathies were with the reformers. Yet how far his medical practices reflected that fact is something that remains largely a closed book to us.

DIAGNOSTIC TECHNIQUES

But if such is the case where Nostradamus's medical philosophy and treatment are concerned, what of his diagnoses?

In the true spirit of Hippocrates, contemporary physicians attempted to treat the whole person, rather then merely the symptoms. At first glance this may seem quite enlightened, even laudable. Treating the symptoms, after all, amounts to treating effects, rather than causes, and there has to be more than a suspicion that many symptoms are really part of the natural healing process anyway. To the doctors of the day, therefore, allopathic treatment based on symptoms smacked more of the apothecary than of the true physician and was frowned on to such an extent that the earlier medical school of Salerno expressly forbade any commerce between doctors and apothecaries.

On the other hand, sixteenth-century physicians, for all their good intentions, were still dogged by the ancient idea that treating the whole person involved correcting the balance between the four theoretical Humors that were supposed to control the entire human organism – and, lacking any other evidence as to what the state of that balance might be, they resorted almost exclusively to two basic techniques. These were

1. examination of the urine,
2. astrology.

In case this approach should seem obtuse to the point of idiocy, it should be emphasized that contemporary doctors were not unaware of the obvious symptoms; they simply failed to make what to us would seem to be the obvious connection (as, indeed, Bach practitioners still do to this day) between symptoms and treatment.

1. EXAMINATION OF THE URINE

In the case of urinary diagnosis, we have it on Nostradamus's own authority that he himself practiced the technique – as, indeed, modern medicine still does today in certain contexts. In his *Traité des fardemens* he describes how, in some plague victims, *leurs urines*

Nostradamus combined an interest in astrology with medical practice

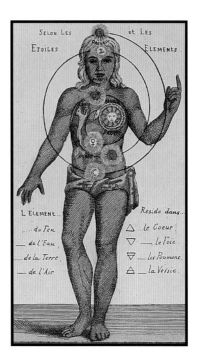

LEFT: **"Cosmic spiral" within the human body showing links with the elements**

Charts of the supposed astrological links with the human body, from *Les Tres Riches Heures du duc de Berry*

estoyent subtiles comme vin blanc.[35] The urine, after all, helps to reveal what is coming out of a patient, and thus, what is inside him or her, too. It was but a short step from this observation to the assumption that it also reflected, through its changing color, consistency, and content, the current balance of the supposed Humors.

2. ASTROLOGY

The use of astrological diagnosis is even better attested in Nostradamus's writings, and not least in his prescription for the Bishop of Béziers's gout of October 20th, 1559.[36] He himself confesses with some enthusiasm to being a *médecin astrophile* employing *astrologie judicielle et naturelle.* Indeed, it was his involvement in this aspect of medicine that was eventually to lead on quite naturally to his activities as a prophetic astrologer, even though to modern minds the combination of doctor and seer may seem a good deal odder, if not well-nigh incompatible.

Here it was not merely a case of drawing up a horoscope and then examining it with all the interpretational panoply of traditional astrology. Numerous surviving medieval charts also illustrate supposed links between the planets, the astrological houses or signs,

With us ther was a DOCTOUR of PHYSIK,
In al this world ne was ther noon him lyk
To speke of physik and of surgerye;
For he was grounded in astronomye . . .
Wel coude he fortunen the ascendent
Of his images for his pacient.
He knew the cause of everich maladye,
Were it of hoot or cold, or moiste, or drye,
And where engendred, and of what humour;
He was a verrey parfit practisour . . .
Ful redy hadde he his apothecaries,
To sende him drogges and his letuaries . . .
Wel knew he th'olde Esculapius,
And Deiscorides, and eek Rufus,
Old Ypocras, Haly, and Galien;
Serapion, Razis, and Avicen;
Averrois, Damascien, and Constantyn;
Bernard, and Gatesden, and Gilbertyn . . .

Description of a typical medieval physician, from the Prologue of Chaucer's *Canterbury Tales.* All three teachers mentioned in the last line were fourteenth-century precursors of Nostradamus at Montpellier.

and the parts of the body. To be sure, the various attributions differed widely, as might perhaps be expected of so arbitrary a system. But when to this was added a complicated system linking given conjunctions to specific Humors, it is easy to see how a physician might attempt to use the system to divine what was "really" amiss. To take just one example, conjunctions of the moon and Saturn were taken to indicate an excess of the "cold Humors" that might well indicate a tendency to apoplexy, paralysis, epilepsy, jaundice, or catalepsy. A variety of treatments might then be recommended for correcting the supposed condition – whether diet or rest, sleep or exercise, baths or emetics, purgatives or bleeding. This last was applied particularly by the majority of physicians who accepted the view of Erasistratus (*c.*300–260 B.C.), the so-called Father of Physiology, that it was really *plethora,* or an excess of blood, that was the main cause of disease – notwithstanding the Alexandrian physician's rejection both of the humoric theory and of blood-letting itself as debilitating to the patient.

The case of astrological diagnosis, meanwhile, does hint at one further notable aspect of contemporary practice – namely the extent to which, like ancient Babylonian medicine, it also laid great stress on *prognosis.* This fact, too, would have led on quite naturally to Nostradamus's subsequent role as a prophet. For, once again, there is every reason to conclude that he used such techniques, even though there is also plenty of evidence in his *Traité* (as noted above) that he normally supplemented them with the much more promising insights of the typical apothecary.

THE PLAGUE

Nostradamus's long-term interest in combating the plague was perhaps understandable, given (a) that he was an ancestral Jew, and (b) that Jews were widely held to be responsible for the disease. Indeed, it would seem that, thanks partly to his work in Marseille from 1544 under the celebrated Louis Serres, whom he describes as another Hippocrates, he eventually became an acknowledged expert on it. What, then, was his approach to the awful disease, and was it really as enlightened as a number of recent English-language commentators have asserted? Certainly it seems to have been unusually successful, if we are to believe the various accounts, or he would not have been in such great demand when various cities were afflicted.

It was in 1546, as he himself informs us in the *Traité des fardemens et confitures,* that *je feus esleu & stipendié de la cité d'Aix en Provence, ou par le senat & peuple je fus mis pour la conservation de la cité,*[37] and one has the distinct impression that this involved his being placed in overall charge of operations.

---

[35] "Their urine was as thin as white wine."

[36] See Gazetteer and Who's Who, under Béziers.

[37] "I was elected and hired by the city of Aix-en-Provence, where I was installed by the senate and people to save the city."

The Triumph of Death, 1503, depicting the Black Death – a forerunner of the plague that Nostradamus was to fight

Yet what did he actually do, once arrived from Marseille? Here our sole direct source of information is his own *Traité*, which describes in great detail the symptoms of the disease and the ways in which it was treated.

The outbreak, it seems, lasted all of nine months and was of unusual severity. So many died that the cemeteries were soon full to overflowing. Most patients became delirious by the second day and did not even last long enough to acquire the black patches (subcutaneous hemorrhages) that had given the disease its earlier name of the "Black Death." Their urine was "thin as white wine," and after their death much of the skin was seen to be sky-blue, with purple blood showing through it. Those who did acquire the black patches died quite suddenly, and their corpses were found to be positively covered with them.

As for the earlier stages of the disease, many had the famous *charbons* (not, as it happens, the name of the disease, but red carbuncles, or "small glowing coals") in front and behind, or even all over. Those who had these swellings (or buboes) on the backs of their bodies itched, but generally survived, whereas those who had them on their fronts died to a man or woman. Few of those who

had them behind the ears lasted as much as six days, especially during the earlier part of the outbreak.

Some with buboes in the armpits, or women whose breasts were affected, suffered nosebleeds that lasted day and night until they died. Pregnant women aborted, then died after four days, while their fetuses died forthwith, their bodies purple all over as though engorged with blood.

The disease (writes Nostradamus) was intensely infectious. Even approaching within five paces of a patient was sufficient to ensure infection, as was *merely being looked at by one*. The sole effective protection against the "bad and pestiferous air" of the disease (he continues) was continually to suck on a special type of rose-pill that he had had made up by a local apothecary, for which he duly supplies the prescription:

Prenés de la sieure ou le rament du boys de cyprés, he writes, *le plus verd que vous pourrés trouuer une once, de Iris de Florece six onces: de giroffles 3. onces: calami odorati 3. dragmes: ligni aloes 6. dragmes, faictes le tout mettre en poudre, qu'il ne s'esuente: & puis prenés des roses rouges incarnées trois ou quatre cets, qui soyent bien mondées toutes fraiches, & ceuillies auāt la rosee: & les ferés fort piller dedans un mortier de marbre, auec un piloir de bois: & les roses à demy pillées, mettés y dedens la poudre susdicte, & derechef le pillés fort, en l'arrousant un peu de suc de roses: & quand le tout sera bien meslé, faictes en de petites balottes plattes, faictes en la mode de trocisques & les faictes seicher à l'ombre, car elles sont de bonne odeur.*[38]

Quite what made this concoction so effective is open to question. Brennan claims that the calamus would have acted as a detoxicant and the cloves as a disinfectant. What *is* clear, though, is that Nostradamus personally was using it much as other doctors of the time used garlic – along with gloves, masks, and leather overgarments – in an attempt to protect themselves against the plague-infected air. In which case there is no reason (despite popular modern denials of the idea) to assume that he did not attire himself in similar garb.

What, then, are we to make of this extraordinary mixture of keen observation and apparent superstition? Certainly the more common form of bubonic plague was present, though in particularly virulent form. But the signs are that the intensely infectious pneumonic form of the disease – or even its catastrophic septicemic form – was there, too, if not actually prevalent.

No wonder, then, that Nostradamus reports total failure for all the treatments that he either attempted or sanctioned. He actually

---

[38] "Take the sawdust or shavings of cypress-wood, as green as you can find, one ounce; iris of Florence, six ounces; cloves, three ounces; sweet calamus, three drams; lignaloes, six drams. Pulverize the mixture and keep it airtight. Next, take some in-folded red roses, three or four hundred, clean, fresh, and culled before dewfall, and reduce them to powder in a marble mortar, using a wooden pestle. Then add some half-folded roses to the above powder and pound the mixture vigorously all over again, while sprinkling on it a little rose juice. When all the above has been mixed together thoroughly, fashion it into little flat pastilles as you would pills and let them dry in the shade. They will smell good."

details them. Not merely did they include stimulants and sung prayers (presumably to St. Roch of Montpellier among others, the patron saint of plague sufferers), but bleedings, too: *les seignés, les medicamens cordiaux, cantiques, ne autres*, he writes, *n'avoyent non plus d'efficace que rien*.[39] (So much, then, for the refusal to bleed his patients so often claimed of him by ill-informed modern commentators!) Indeed, the only effective plague remedy proved to be the rose-pill remedy detailed above – and then only in the closing stages of the outbreak.

None of which, it has to be said, sounds particularly enlightened. So what, if anything, was he up to behind the scenes that made his intervention so effective?

Here one can only guess at some kind of civic action. He had, after all, been employed by the municipality itself, and it is hardly likely that the regional capital's senate would have gone to such lengths to secure the services of a mere purveyor of pills. One has the distinct impression that he was given plenipotentiary powers to take action of a much more drastic kind. But of what kind?

It is at this point that we need to recall Nostradamus's training. He had, after all, been schooled not only in the somewhat hidebound doctrines of Galen but also in the much broader teachings of Hippocrates, who had stressed good diet, clean water, fresh air, and a healthy geographical situation as a basis for good health. This may have something to do with the fact that in the *Traité* – as though aware that urban squalor might indeed have something to do with encouraging the pestilence – he refers specifically to the fact that, while the plague was raging inside Aix, only good health was to be encountered in the countryside around. Moreover, the fact that Nostradamus also mentions the Hippocratic treatise on *Epidemics* in the same work is clear evidence that he was familiar with the teachings that it enshrined.

Cardinal Chigi heals plague victims in Rome, as Nostradamus tried to do at Aix-en-Provence in 1546

At Marseille, moreover, Nostradamus had studied under Louis Serres, whom he was to commend in the last chapter of the *Traité* specifically for his *perspicacité & sçavoir Hippocratique*[40] – which suggests fairly strongly that Serres turned to specifically Hippocratic insights and methods in his efforts to fight the plague.

Late impression of a medieval plague-doctor

Add to these points the fact that the unusual principles that evidently underlay his later work at Lyon reportedly upset the respected traditionalist physician Philibert Sarrazin, and that Nostradamus would later exhibit a remarkable interest in running water not unlike that of the ancient Romans, with their positive passion for civic hygiene and public sanitation, and the possibility starts to emerge that Nostradamus may well have attempted to improve the sanitation and public health of Aix, too. He admits in his account, after all, to throwing out all the infected bodies each morning. What, then, if he also threw out much else as well – the infected bedding, the kitchen garbage, the raw sewage that ran openly in the gutters – and used all the running water he could lay his hands on to wash down the streets and cleanse the private dwellings, too?

The result would almost certainly have been a reduction in the local rat population, and hence in the disease – even if possibly at the expense of the surrounding countryside.

Not that Nostradamus would necessarily have recognized the connection – even though his own ancestral scriptures seemed to point to it at I Samuel 5:6. Nor would any intuitive, prophetic foreknowledge that he may have had of the eventual discovery necessarily have helped him very much, since killing the rats would merely have caused more of their infected fleas to transfer themselves to human hosts.

Nevertheless, the possibility remains that Nostradamus may have done any, or all, of the things mentioned. If so, then this might explain his apparent success, to say nothing of the acclamation, fame, and riches with which he was subsequently to be rewarded.

Yet, for all that, the plague still lasted nine months – scarcely less, perhaps, than it would have lasted naturally. And of none of the more enlightened methods mooted, unfortunately, do we have any direct evidence.

---

[39] "Neither bleedings, stimulants, hymns nor anything else had any more effect than doing nothing at all."

[40] "Hippocratic perspicacity and knowledge."

ASTROLOGER AND MAGE

NOBODY who has studied the prophecies of Nostradamus at all seriously can help but be struck by the extraordinary frequency with which they seem to mirror almost exactly the major events not merely of classical history but of what to him was comparatively recent history too. So close are the similarities, indeed, as to give the impression that the "old fraud" was engaged in the unlikely exercise of attempting to claim retrospective credit for having predicted them.

In fact, of course, he was not. Not even his sternest critic would suggest that he was that stupid.

Nevertheless, the observation enshrines a vital clue as to how it was that the seer managed to produce not just a handful of prophecies of future events but over a thousand of them – and in less than ten years, at that.

But then Nostradamus had a whole sheaf of arrows to his predictive bow. They are listed here in the order in which we shall examine them:

1. **Judicial astrology**
2. **Traditional astrology**
3. **Aeonic astrology**
4. **Scrying and theurgy**

1. JUDICIAL ASTROLOGY

Judicial astrology is basically predictive astrology, and Nostradamus's contemporaries were no less familiar with it than he was. If proof of this were needed, one should look no further than the fact that Rabelais felt the need to parody it so unmercifully in his spoof *Prognostications* of 1533 and 1544 (see The Almanachs in Nostradamus's Writings). *Laisse-moi l'Astrologie divinatrice*, he had already made his fictional giant Gargantua write to his son Pantagruel,[41] *comme abuz et vanité.*[42]

In his *Préface à César* (see The Major Prophecies) Nostradamus admits specifically to revealing *quelques secretz de l'advenir accordés à l'astrologie judicielle, comme du passé*[43] (section 4 in the present edition), and in section 8 cites the Church's official approval of the practice. Quite why the Church should look more kindly on this particular form of occult science than on its other manifestations is not entirely clear, unless it should be that it was more strictly "astronomical" than traditional astrology, and less concerned with supposed esoteric planetary influences. Certainly the Church did not dissent from the seer's general claim of ecclesiastical blessing. His published works repeatedly contained in their official *privilèges* (see Book Printing and Publishing) the statement that they contained "nothing contrary to the Faith," and the clerical establishment never did anything to gainsay that claim. The most violent of printed criticisms would be leveled against Nostradamus

**Nostradamus contemplates
the significance of astrology
in making his predictions**

by his critics in around 1558 (see Criticisms and Reviews), yet irreligion was never among them. Nor, contrary to general opinion, was Nostradamus's name ever included in the Vatican's official *Index Librorum Prohibitorum*, banning Catholics from reading certain authors, which first appeared in 1557–9.

What, then, distinguishes judicial astrology – at least as Nostradamus understood it – from other forms of the art or science? The seer gives us several clues to the answer. The very fact that the above quotation ends with the mysterious phrase *comme du passé* is significant, suggesting as it does that *past events* actually had some role in the process. In section 10 of the *Préface*, too, he uses the enigmatic phrase *revolution tenant à la cause passée, presente & future,*[44] once again apparently bringing the past into the equation.

Elsewhere (in section 1 of the *Préface*, for example), he speaks of being guided *par Astronomiques revolutions*, and in section 14 refers specifically to the *dimension latitudinaire ou le grand Dieu eternel viendra parachever la revolution: ou les images celestes retourneront à se mouvoir.*[45] The punctuation, as so often in Nostradamus, is slightly eccentric – even (as here) in the original 1555 edition – but it starts to become clear

---

[41] *Pantagruel* (1532), chapter 8.

[42] Freely: "Spare me the malpractice and falsehood of divinatory astrology."

[43] Literally, "a few secrets of the future, harmonized with judicial astrology, as of the past."

[44] "holding circuit with past, present, and future developments."

that his predictions are to be thought of as in some way linked to the recurrence of certain previously determined planetary configurations, themselves linked to particular geographical latitudes. In section B.16 of the *Lettre à Henri II* he similarly claims to have *supputé et calculé les presentes propheties, le tout selon l'ordre de la chaisne qui contient sa revolution.*[46]

Now, until the time of Nostradamus, the term *revolution* as yet had none of its now-familiar political overtones. It was a strictly specialized, astrological term, of Latin derivation,[47] referring specifically to the return of a celestial body to its former position – and the notion of frequency was hence intimately bound up in it, too. It was precisely in this sense, for example, that Copernicus had recently used the very word in the title of his celebrated *De Revolutionibus Orbium Coelestium* of 1543: its subject was indeed the return of the planets to their former positions – even though in the German Pole's case it was used (presumably deliberately) as a double-edged term, covering not only the traditional notion of the astrological cycle, but also the ground-breaking new theory of the circumsolar orbit.

This was of course a sense unknown to the ancient Romans who had originally coined the term. Nevertheless, thanks to Copernicus, part of what was formerly astrology had now become astronomy, and as time went on the two would increasingly diverge.

Recent research has revealed that, in the wake of Copernicus, Nostradamus's version of judicial astrology, too, was far more astronomical than it was truly astrological. Not that Nostradamus spoke of circumsolar orbits. But his approach, nevertheless, was evidently likewise based not so much on supposed planetary influences as on the simple notion of *cyclic astronomical return.*

This, of course, helps to explain the evident similarities between known past events and the events that the seer predicts. Astrological influences and horoscopic mumbo-jumbo had little or nothing to do with it. No doubt that was why he felt able to be so rude about the traditional astrologers who were wont to criticize him, to the eternal puzzlement of his modern would-be astrological interpreters. In the words of my own translation of his Latin *LEGIS CANTIO CONTRA INEPTOS CRITICOS* (*Century* VI.100):

Think on this, reader, sagely as you may,
But shun my verse, you mob profane and shallow.
Star-gazers, snotty Philistines, away!
Let those more reverent my office hallow.[48]

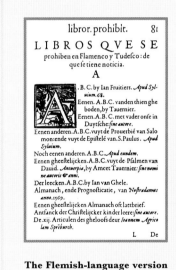

The Flemish-language version of Spain's *Index Librorum Prohibitorum* of 1583 bans Nostradamus's 1569 *Almanach*

Instead of traditional astrology, in fact, his technique simply demanded

(a) the identification of some significant past event,

(b) the determination of its latitude and of the planets' relative positions at the time (the sun and moon were traditionally counted as "planets" – i.e. "moving stars" – too),

(c) the identification and timing of some future occasion when the planets would be in similar relative positions, and

(d) the geographical siting of that event with reference to the difference in celestial latitude of the two astronomical "fixes."

No wonder that the seer's assistant Chavigny was subsequently to entitle his commentary and biography *La Premiere Face du Janus François* ("The First Face of the French Janus"): Janus, after all, was the Roman god with two faces, *who looked both forward and backward at once.*

The system, then, was indeed truly astronomical. Granted, it demanded a vast initial leap of faith – though one not untypical of Nostradamus's age. The astrological notion that the observable cycles of human existence may be in some way linked to equally observable celestial cycles may be a not unreasonable hypothesis, given the universe's evident basic unity and self-referential nature, yet it lacks scientific proof. Linked to the motions of sun and moon our lives may be, but more remote linkages, if they exist, are too faint to be detectable – as yet, at least.

That initial leap having been made, however, the rest was almost entirely scientific and mathematical. More traditional forms of astrology would intervene in the process only at the very beginning – when they might be involved in selecting which "planets" to concentrate on (for it goes without saying that the odds against the *entire planetary horoscope* ever repeating itself exactly are not merely astronomical, but virtually infinite) – and at the very end, when they could be used to assess the likely meanings of any differences between the two resulting charts.

---

[45] "the degree of latitude at which great God Eternal will complete the circuit where the celestial images will return to exert themselves."

[46] "reckoned and calculated the whole of the present prophecies according to the order of the chain which encompasses its circuit."

[47] From *revolvere*, "to roll back, return."

[48] Revised version of translation from Lemesurier: *Nostradamus: The Final Reckoning* (Piatkus, 1995).

If, then, such was indeed the basic technique used by Nostradamus, what evidence is there for it in his work, except for his specific statement to that effect? This can be listed fairly briefly:

❖ The already-established fact that the past events are constantly reflected in his predictions for the future, even to the names of the actual protagonists involved (Hannibal, Ahenobarbus, Nero etc.).

❖ The fact that the predicted future events constantly reflect precisely those types of event that most readily spring out at us from history – i.e. wars and battles, murders and disasters, rather than "good" events.

❖ The fact that the seer often cites particular clusters of planets and signs (normally at least three of them at a time), but never exact angles (see "rules" below).

❖ The fact that the seer often gives latitudes, but never longitudes – which is a necessary corollary of the technique (see "rules" below).[49]

❖ The fact that the datings and latitudes of major historical events, subjected to the technique, repeatedly confirm the places and datings for their recurrence as predicted by Nostradamus in those of his published prophecies that contain such information (see Sequence of Selected Horographs and Dating and Sequencing the Prophecies).

❖ The fact that the resulting predictions do not normally fall in chronological order – which (as we shall see) actually follows more or less automatically from the use of the technique.

True, there is always the question of Nostradamus's likely accuracy to consider. Even today, after all, published planetary ephemerides[50] rarely cover more than half a century or so. Any tables the seer used, he would therefore have had to assemble himself, largely from first principles. Indeed, we know that he had completed an Ephemeris of his own by 1553 at the latest: archival records at Salon reveal that his lawyer Hozier tried to withdraw it from publication by Brotot of Lyon in that year on the grounds of unacceptably poor printing. Possibly that was why it was the following year, when he was all of forty years old, before Nostradamus was able to settle down to writing his major *Prophecies*. Even then, his long-term tables probably contained no more than the dates on which the various "planets" changed signs.

But how accurate were those tables likely to be, even then? Like many astrologers of the day, Nostradamus may have added an observatory to his house (see Nostradamus's Life Story), yet this would have been no modern dome-and-telescope affair, but a simple turret-platform open to the sky. Indeed, the telescope would not be invented (officially, at least) until some forty-two years after his death. On the other hand, his published tables are quite accurate: the lunar positions in his 1566 *Almanach*, for example, are all within about two minutes of arc of the correct figures. Moreover,

Astronomers observing an eclipse, by Antoine Caron

he had a wide database to refer to, with horoscopes still surviving from Roman times about 1,500 years before. This would have enabled him to refine his figures to a very considerable degree. And it is always worth remembering that he was famed in his day not merely as an astrologer, but as a mathematician, too.

True, cumulative error would have been more liable to creep into the calculations where the faster-moving "inner planets" were concerned – the moon particularly – but with Mars completing one revolution about the sun only every two years, Jupiter every twelve, and Saturn every twenty-nine-and-a-half or so, his "perpetual calculations" might be expected to extend far into the future with a fair degree of accuracy – as, indeed, comparison of his proposed datings with modern astronomical data tends to confirm. In the light of this, though, we might expect his use of comparative horoscopy to concentrate on the outer planets as far as possible, with the moon least significant of all where timing is concerned.

---

49 He also repeatedly uses the term *climat* – from the Greek *klima*, "angle of slope or elevation of the sun" and thus "latitude" – whose use in this sense is still preserved in English in such expressions as "in sunnier climes." *See Préface à César* 2, 12; *Centuries* I.55, III.77; *Lettre à Henri II*, A.2.

50 Tables listing the daily positions of the sun, moon, and planets.

This brings us, then, to the precise "rules of the game" – as apparently applied by Nostradamus, at least. Inspection of the relevant astronomical tables, along with the prophecies themselves, suggests that these run as follows:

1. SELECT some major historical event, preferably from ancient times, large and dramatic enough to have an almost "archetypical" character about it (the very fact that it is still remembered itself serves as a partial guarantee of this), and whose location and date are known, even if only to the year.[51]

2. USING traditional astrological principles, select the date or period nearest to the event – *preferably during the month or so immediately preceding it* [52] – when the presence of at least four "planets" in their various houses[53] or signs[54] seems appropriate to the event. If the moon is one of them, increase this number to five, and in any case include at least one of the outer planets Mars, Jupiter, or Saturn, and normally the sun as well. The greater the number of planets (and especially of outer ones), the more specific the event's eventual recapitulation is likely to be.[55]

3. NOW, taking the four or more "planets" involved (hereinafter called the "operative planets"), search through the astronomical tables (preferably for noon) until the pattern of planets in houses or signs is repeated, and record the year and date. Here the most practical approach is usually to start with the outer planets and work inward. (*Note: exact angles and aspects are of no significance for the present exercise.*)

4. NEXT, look up the respective solar declinations at noon for the two occasions selected (i.e. the respective celestial latitudes of the sun) *to the nearest degree*, and work out how far to the south or north the latter declinations are from the former. Where (as is usual) a period of several days is involved, note the figure for the first *and* last days.

5. TAKING the latitude of the original event, apply to it the relative declinations – i.e. the latitude correction(s) – that you have just figured out, taking care to distinguish latitude north from latitude south. *This will give the predicted latitude or latitude band for the future event.*

6. SINCE the future date will probably refer in most cases to the *runup* to the future event, or even to its immediate aftermath, rather than to the event itself, regard the timing of the latter as subject to a tolerance of plus or minus at least one month – possibly even two.

7. SINCE the declination calculation is based only on the nearest degree, treat the future latitude as similarly subject to a tolerance of plus or minus one degree.

8. ONCE you have all the data for the future event, refer to the map to pinpoint its likely location (or locations), and use your intuition (as Nostradamus himself admitted to doing) to suggest the manner in which the original event is likely to be repeated.

9. FINALLY, if you are proposing to publish the results, frame your prediction in terms vague enough to cover a multitude of possible eventualities!

Comparison of the astrology of events from classical times with that of the major events predicted by Nostradamus leaves no room for doubt whatever that this was the primary method used by the seer (compare Sequence of Selected Horographs and Dating and Sequencing the Prophecies). The coincidences are far too frequent and too exact to permit any other explanation – let alone that of mere chance. Yet how inherently reliable is such a technique? Even if history is to some extent cyclic – as Nostradamus himself clearly believed – can it really be that its cycles reflect those going on in the heavens above to the extent suggested? If history and astrology are cyclic, in other words, is there some direct link between them?

Established science would certainly say "No," largely because it can conceive of no mechanism for the process. On the other hand, even established science cannot fly in the face of established facts. What, then, *are* the facts? Can the operation of the principle be demonstrated to an extent greater than that suggested by chance?

What is needed at this point, in other words, is evidence that particular ancient events have indeed been repeated in more recent times under the same astronomical configurations – and at the required latitude, too. Such evidence is no more easy to assemble than evidence to the contrary, largely because what the underlying theory predicts is that similar planetary configurations will produce similar events – *not* that similar events always occur under the same planetary configurations. Thus, while the natural tendency of anybody researching the question is to work from known events to astrology, the ideal method would involve working instead from astrology to known events – an extremely time-consuming process which, after all, took even Nostradamus himself half a lifetime.

---

51 The concluding sentence of section B.16 of the *Lettre à Henri II* tends to confirm that Nostradamus was quite happy to take the broader, year-based view.

52 The fact that both past and future astrological references are normally to the period immediately *before* the events offers an interesting sidelight on the ancient notion that astrology has to do with the *causes* of events, rather than with the events themselves.

53 Sequentially numbered, 30°-sectors of the heavens measured (in the northern hemisphere) anticlockwise from the eastern horizon at any given moment. The horoscopes of Nostradamus's day were much more concerned with houses than they were with signs, which had to be added to the basic template afterward. For a copy of one of Nostradamus's own horoscopes, see p.61.

54 30°-sectors of the heavens measured (in the northern hemisphere) anticlockwise from the position of the sun at the spring equinox, and still named after the constellations that originally appeared in them.

55 Even then, the resulting dates are not unique. Quadruple recapitulations involving two or more of Nostradamus's "outer" planets occur extremely rarely (around once per century or less on average), while those involving only one outer planet may occur more frequently (up to four times per century). Thus, conditions propitious for the "original" event will theoretically be repeated from time to time at different latitudes. Additional sources of insight are thus required (see below) if the precise results on any given occasion are to be successfully determined.

True, a dedicated computer program could nowadays perform the operation quickly and without difficulty. No doubt some enthusiast will in due course produce one. In the interim, however, the reader is invited to consider and compare the following pairs of *horographs*[56] – always bearing in mind that the slow-moving planets above the **thick line** were unknown to Nostradamus. (Uranus was discovered only in 1781, Neptune in 1846, and Pluto as recently as 1930.) "Operative planets" are **shown in red**, their "inoperative" counterparts **in black**.

The top chart on the right shows the planetary positions at the time of the celebrated Battle of Salamis of 480 B.C., when a small Greek fleet saved Athens by decisively defeating a vastly superior Persian one under the very eyes of Xerxes himself. The astrological situation for (say) June to July of that year, then, might perhaps be expected to repeat itself at the time of some equally unequal, nonterrestrial conflict with a surprising outcome, such as the Battle of Britain of 1940. But in fact it finds a quite different match. The period defined by the bottom chart is not that of the Battle of Britain, but that between June 4th and 21st, 1588, about a month before the departure of the huge Spanish Armada and its subsequent defeat by a much smaller number of English ships (ably assisted by the weather). Moreover, the difference between the two sets of declinations, applied to the latitude of the bay of Salamis, gives a latitude of 37° to 38°N – which corresponds to the bay of Cadiz and the port of Lisbon, where the Armada indeed assembled. (Compare, possibly, *Century* X.2.)

The English fleet engages the ships of the Spanish Armada, August 1588 – a possible "match" with Nostradamus's horoscopic chart for the Battle of Salamis

---

56 Simplified horoscopic charts showing only which "planets" are in which signs or houses at the time specified, and arranged so that they normally move conveniently from left to right.

BATTLE OF SALAMIS

These horoscopic charts compare planetary positions and show astrological "matches" between events from classical times and major events predicted by Nostradamus.

Horograph for June 13th, 480 B.C., to July 13th, 480 B.C.											
Pluto						★					
Neptune								★			
Uranus			★								
Saturn										★	
Jupiter	★										
Mars			★								
Venus					★						
Mercury			★								
Moon	★	★	★	★	★	★	★	★	★	★	★	★
Sun			★	★								

Solar noon declination to nearest degree: 23°N to 22°N
Geographical latitude: 38°N

Location: Bay of Salamis, just west of Athens, Greece
Event: Runup to battle of Salamis: defeat by small Greek fleet of huge Persian one, 480 B.C.

SPANISH ARMADA

Horograph for June 4th, 1588, to June 21st, 1588											
Pluto	★											
Neptune				★								
Uranus												★
Saturn		★										
Jupiter						★						
Mars			★									
Venus						★						
Mercury			★									
Moon	★	★	★	★	★	★	★					★
Sun			★	★								

Solar noon declination to nearest degree: 22°N to 23°N
Relative latitude: 1°S to 1°N   **Geographical latitude:** 37°N to 39°N

Possible location: Gulf of Cadiz to Lisbon
Event: Runup to Spanish Armada, sailing from Lisbon July 12th, 1588, destroyed from July 29th

Napoleon Bonaparte Crossing the Alps, by Jacques-Louis David. Napoleon's retreat from Moscow was a likely "match" with the massacre of the Teutoburger Wald in A.D. 9.

In the second pair of charts (right), the top one records the planetary positions for another major event – this time the grisly massacre of the Teutoburger Wald. This was arguably the most awful military disaster ever suffered by ancient Rome, when three entire Roman legions simply disappeared amid the German forests while on their march back to winter quarters in A.D. 9. Their dismembered and transfixed skeletons were not discovered until the following year. The chart for late August to late September of A.D. 9 (as ever, during the runup period) finds a remarkable match in the chart for late August to early September 1812. As it turns out, this marks with uncanny accuracy the runup to Napoleon's retreat from Moscow of that same year, during which the French army too was, in its turn, virtually wiped out. Moreover the mean latitude of the latter event works out at 56°N – well within the suggested tolerances for Moscow, at 55° 47'N. Opinions will differ, of course, over whether any or all of *Centuries* II.99, IV.75, IV.82, or IX.99 are the result of Nostradamus's own discovery of this particular "match."

It needs to be remembered, meanwhile, that sixteenth-century astrologers regarded the *houses* in which the planets found themselves as, if anything, even more auspicious than the *signs* (compare the copy of one of Nostradamus's horoscopes reprinted later in this section, for example). What mattered most of all, in other words, was the angle from which the planets looked down on the events concerned, rather than the mere names of the parts of the sky that they were currently occupying – which might quite easily be on the other side of the earth entirely at the time. Indeed, one can understand why an astrologer of that era, with his characteristic theory of planetary "influences," might think this coincidence of angles important when applying the current technique.

As it happens, however, planets that are in the same sign are by definition (according to one system, at least) in the same houses, too, once every two hours. Moreover, whenever the sun is one of them (as in all four cases above) any "match" between two separate events will necessarily also mean that all the planets involved are in the same houses at *roughly the same time.*

TEUTOBURGER WALD MASSACRE

Horograph for August 29th, A.D. 9, to September 22nd, A.D. 9												
	♑	♐	♒	♓	♌	♋	♎	♏	♍	♈	♒	♉
Pluto						★						
Neptune									★			
Uranus	★											
Saturn						★						
Jupiter				★								
Mars								★				
Venus					★							
Mercury						★						
Moon		★	★	★	★	★	★	★	★	★	★	★
Sun						★						

Solar noon declination to nearest degree: 9°N to 0°N
Geographical latitude: 52°N

Location: Teutoburger Wald, Germany
Event: Massacre and disappearance of three entire Roman legions in German forest, late A.D. 9

NAPOLEON'S RETREAT FROM MOSCOW

Horograph for: August 28th, 1812, to September 4th, 1812												
	♑	♐	♒	♓	♌	♋	♎	♏	♍	♈	♒	♉
Pluto											★	
Neptune									★			
Uranus								★				
Saturn										★		
Jupiter				★								
Mars					★							
Venus						★						
Mercury							★					
Moon		★	★	★	★							
Sun						★						

Solar noon declination to nearest degree: 10°N to 7°N
Relative latitude: 1°N to 7'N   **Geographical latitude:** 53°N to 59°N
(mean=56°N)

Possible location: Moscow (55° 45'N)
Event: Napoleon's retreat from Moscow and destruction of French army, October 19th to November 28th, 1812

Nevertheless, there are likely to be some occasions when planets that are in the same houses will not necessarily be in the same signs. This in no way diminishes the force of the argument, of course, since those planets will be presiding even more literally over the events involved, staring down on them from the self-same angle.

A truly stunning case in point is demonstrated by the pair of horographs on the right. This time the first of them (at the top) is for the runup to possibly the most world-shaking assassination of ancient times – namely that of Julius Caesar, which famously took place on the Ides (15th) of March, 44 B.C. Was there, then, some more recent event that closely mirrored that original, and which was presided over *from the same angle* by the same group of "planets"– the assassination of Abraham Lincoln, for example, or perhaps the fateful slaying of the Archduke Ferdinand in Sarajevo in 1914?

The bottom chart shows clearly that there was. But there is no match either with Lincoln or with the unfortunate Archduke. There is, however, a clear match with November 23rd to 29th, 1963 – *immediately after the assassination of President John F. Kennedy in Dallas on the 22nd*. In fact the match (unusually) was actually in preparation, with all the relevant planets correctly grouped, *some time before local midnight on the very day in question*.

During the period pinpointed, indeed, not only were the sun, Mercury, Venus, and Mars in the same houses at the same time (both charts are for around 11 a.m.), but in Kennedy's case all four of them were, with supreme irony, in the sign of Sagittarius, the Archer. As ever, too, the latitude is significant. The 1963 assassination is specifically marked out as taking place between latitudes 32° and 33°N – *precisely the latitude of Dallas, at 32° 47'N.*

President J. F. Kennedy, assassinated on November 22nd, 1963 in Dallas, Texas

Interpreters will naturally disagree over whether any or all of *Centuries* II.92, IV.49, or VI.37 apply at this point, while inveterate skeptics are naturally likely to find the whole thing altogether too much to stomach. Who, indeed, can really blame them?

Inevitably there will be dark mutterings about "stretching the dates," about "selectivity" and "mere chance."

Yet even finding three such matches *at the correct latitude* probably already threatens the possibility of this last – especially as several others of only marginally slighter impressiveness are not difficult to identify.

ASSASSINATION OF JULIUS CAESAR

Horograph for February 19th, 44 B.C. (*c.* 11a.m.) to February 20th, 44 B.C. (*c.* 11a.m.)											
Houses:	1	2	3	4	5	6	7	8	9	10	11	12
Pluto		★										
Neptune				★								
Uranus					★							
Saturn								★				
Jupiter									★			
Mars										★		
Venus										★		
Mercury										★		
Moon												★
Sun										★		

Solar noon declination to nearest degree: 11°S
Geographical latitude: 41° 54'N

Location: Rome
Event: Assassination of Julius Caesar, March 15th, 44 B.C.

ASSASSINATION OF JOHN F. KENNEDY

Horograph for November 23rd, 1963 (*c.* 11a.m.) to November 29th, 1963 (*c.* 11a.m.)											
Houses:	1	2	3	4	5	6	7	8	9	10	11	12
Pluto							★					
Neptune								★				
Uranus							★					
Saturn												★
Jupiter		★										
Mars										★		
Venus										★		
Mercury										★		
Moon	★	★	★									★
Sun										★		

Solar noon declination to nearest degree: 20°S to 21°S
Relative latitude: 9°S to 10°S   Geographical latitude: 33°N to 32°N

Possible location: Dallas, Texas (32° 47'N)
Event: Assassination of John F. Kennedy November 22nd, 1963

Among these are

Suicide of Nero, A.D. 68:   **Suicide of Hitler, 1945** (but interestingly predicted for several months "too early," and *in, or on the latitude of, Lisbon!*)[57]

Spartacus's slave revolt, 72–1 B.C.:   **French Revolution, 1789–92** (two separate matches, both tending to pinpoint southern rather than northern France – see Nostradamus and the French Revolution)

Athenian replacement of kings with tyrants, 1060 B.C.:   **Initial Russian Revolution, 1917** (apparently pinpointing the German war front)

Eruption of Vesuvius, A.D. 472, with ashes blown as far as Constantinople: **Chernobyl nuclear melt-down 1986** (with fallout predicted for farther south, as indeed occurred from week 2)

In the next section (Sequence of Selected Horographs) will be found a whole series of further proposed matches for the future whose sheer number (should they be fulfilled) would finally rule out "mere chance" as an adequate explanation. There would clearly be some hurried revision and reappraisal to be undertaken. Its parameters would have to include everything from supposed astrological "influences," via psychoastrology, to simple Jungian or Einsteinian synchronicity. An astrological version of Asimov's concept of "psychohistory," as broached in his celebrated *Foundation* trilogy, might even have to be invoked – a theory of global psychology that would not unreasonably require the resulting predictions to be more wrong about the actions of individuals than about those of people en masse. Certainly, as yet, nobody can be sure what the outcome of that reappraisal would be.

2. TRADITIONAL ASTROLOGY

As we noted earlier, traditional astrology – already an essential tool for Nostradamus's work as a doctor (see Nostradamus the Physician) – necessarily had a role in his initial selection of planets and signs (or houses) for the above technique. He also used it to compile the daily predictions for his annual *Almanachs* (see Nostradamus's Writings). Consequently we know that he made the following fairly conventional associations:

SATURN – *bad times generally*
JUPITER – *matters of authority, government, and religion*
MARS – *war, vengeance, and possibly pestilence*

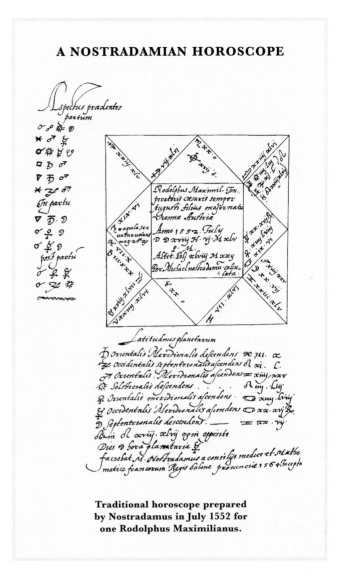

A NOSTRADAMIAN HOROSCOPE

Traditional horoscope prepared by Nostradamus in July 1552 for one Rodolphus Maximilianus.

In addition, it is conceivable that he also associated the following:

VENUS – *sexuality, love, and the sea*
MERCURY – *travel, communications, deviousness, and brigandage*

As for the various signs, he seems to have interpreted these, too, in more or less traditional terms.

It needs to be remembered, however, that Nostradamus was dealing here not with the birthcharts of individuals, but with the destinies of whole cities, regions, and nations. Just as in classical times nearly all of these had their own tutelary deities, so in the seer's own day many of them were still associated with the planets that were later named after those deities, as well as with the zodia-

---

[57] Intriguingly, on the presumed Nazi escape route to South America – but then individuals as self-willed as Hitler are much less likely to be swayed by the prevailing *Zeitgeist* than people en masse. Compare Asimov's psychohistory.

cal signs that were their "native territories." The seer associates Venice, "star of the sea," with Venus, for example, and Lyon (not unnaturally) with Leo and its "planet," the sun. (He also, incidentally, associates the sun with Christianity, and the moon with Islam.) Rome appears to be connected with Jupiter, France with the sign of Aries,[58] and Austria and Savoy with Libra – though there are hints that he also uses the word *Balance* to refer, via a running pun on the Latin *Libra* and *liber/libera/liberum* ("free"), to the "free world" or even (just possibly) the "land of the free" (compare IV.96, which seems to describe the subsequent American Revolution in precisely these terms). Later authorities additionally list Germany, Syria, Palestine, Poland, and Sweden as nations associated with Aries, and Africa, Scotland, and Holland with Scorpio.

In writing his *Propheties*, then, we may assume that Nostradamus looked in the first instance at the general planetary positions either during the runup to the selected event or in its immediate aftermath, then chose the precise period during which those that seemed most relevant to the event and its location were in the most appropriate signs. From this point on, however, the procedure was entirely mechanical.

Having at length discovered his "match," he would then have been faced with a future chart that differed from the original one in a number of respects. Not only would the "operative planets" be at slightly different angles within their signs, but the "inoperative" ones would be in different signs entirely. Thus he could now set to work on them with the traditional astrologer's apparatus of angles, oppositions, conjunctions, and other aspects and associations. Indeed, he quite often mentions conjunctions in particular. However, we do not know how he defined the concept. To him, as to certain modern astrologers, a "conjunction" may merely have meant the presence of two planets *within the same sign*; equally, it may have signified a difference in angle of as little as two or three degrees.

There is no evidence in the texts, though, that – for the purposes of his particular form of judicial astrology, at least – Nostradamus attached any particular *esoteric* significance to planetary conjunctions as such. This is not to say that he was unimpressed by them, of course, or that he was incapable of "interpreting' them in traditional fashion. But the fact remains that he makes no reference to the extraordinary lineup of all the then-known planets in Taurus of early May 2000, for example – which, had such things been significant for him, he must surely have mentioned. True, it is possible that he did, but that the verse in question is among the fifty-eight lost quatrains of *Century* VII (see Nostradamus's Writings), and with it, conceivably its twin as well – for Nostradamus, as we shall see, often wrote his verses in "pairs," even though he did not normally place them together (see Dating and Sequencing the Prophecies). But if that is the case, it is something that we shall possibly never know.

More to the point, the seer knew perfectly well that such lineups had occurred before. The same planets had lined themselves up in the self-same house (but this time in Libra) between September 17th and 24th, 1186. They had done the same again (but in Pisces) between February 13th and 25th, 1524, when the young Nostradamus, fresh from college at Avignon, was still roaming the countryside in search of herbs and cures. He therefore knew perfectly well what had happened on both occasions.

Nothing of note, at least in France.

Under the terms of comparative horoscopy, therefore, *nothing of note ought to happen in May of the year 2000, either.* This perhaps rather surprising conclusion points up quite dramatically the difference between traditional astrology and judicial astrology – as Nostradamus practiced it, at least. In the former, the multiple conjunction is of enormous symbolic significance. In the latter, it is more or less ignored.

But then there *are* some differences that could be significant. As the charts for the three occasions reveal (right), Neptune, "inoperative" in 1186, actually formed part of the alignment in 1524 (albeit unknown to Nostradamus), while the moon, similarly "inoperative" on both earlier occasions, will similarly join the general lineup on its final day in 2000. Nostradamus would have had his own ways of interpreting these differences. These would, however, inevitably have been based on traditional astrology, under the terms of which the alignment of the year 2000 will of course differ significantly from both its predecessors. So that, paradoxically, *nothing* is perhaps the one thing that can be relied on *not* to happen in early May, 2000 (compare Selected Sequence of Horographs, Dating and Sequencing the Prophecies, and The Muslim Invasion of Europe). Indeed, the fact that all the planets concerned except the moon and (perhaps significantly) Mars were *also* in Taurus in April/May of 1941, when Hitler's *Reich* was at its most rampant, should possibly give us pause for thought.

3. EONIC ASTROLOGY

Eonic astrology is the astrology of the ages. It is based on the fact that the position of the sun at the spring equinox processes very slowly "backward" through the signs of the zodiac as the centuries go by, completing the full circuit of the heavens in some 25,800 years. Naturally, estimates of the precise length of this cycle have varied since the Greek astronomer Hipparchus first discovered the phenomenon in around 130 B.C.

Thus, the equinoctial point was in the sign of Taurus between 4080 B.C. and 1930 B.C., and in that of Aries between 1930 B.C. and A.D. 221. The current "Age of Pisces" then followed, and is destined to last until A.D. 2371. Barring astronomical catastrophe, the much-anticipated "Age of Aquarius' will then take over – much later than is commonly assumed – eventually giving way to the succeeding "Age of Capricorn" in A.D. 4521. However, traditional

---

[58] Thus, when the ever-devious Nostradamus places Mercury, Mars, and Jupiter "in France" in IX.55, he is in fact referring to their conjunction in Aries.

PLANETARY ALIGNMENT

Horograph for September 17th, 1186 (c. 11a.m.) to September 24th, 1186, (c. 11a.m.)

Houses:	1	2	3	4	5	6	7	8	9	10	11	12
Pluto							★					
Neptune		★										
Uranus				★								
Saturn										★		
Jupiter										★		
Mars										★		
Venus										★		
Mercury										★		
Moon		★									★	★
Sun										★		

Horograph for February 13th, 1524 (c. 11a.m.) to February 25th, 1524 (c. 11a.m.)

Houses:	1	2	3	4	5	6	7	8	9	10	11	12
Pluto								★				
Neptune										★		
Uranus												★
Saturn										★		
Jupiter										★		
Mars										★		
Venus										★		
Mercury										★		
Moon	★	★	★	★	★	★	★					
Sun										★		

Horograph for May 1st, 2000 (c. 11a.m.) to May 3rd, 2000 (c. 11a.m.)

Houses:	1	2	3	4	5	6	7	8	9	10	11	12
Pluto					★							
Neptune							★					
Uranus							★					
Saturn										★		
Jupiter										★		
Mars										★		
Venus										★		
Mercury										★		
Moon									★	★		
Sun										★		

("tropical") astrology staunchly continues to assume that the sun is always at the "first point of Aries" at the time of the spring equinox – which of course means that, strictly in terms of it, no Age of Aquarius can ever actually dawn.

However, no traditional astrologer will actually countenance this conclusion, which means that traditional astrologers, too, are in fact prepared to indulge in eonic (and thus "sidereal") astrology, too – when it suits them, at least. Certainly there are some intriguing links between the latter's potent symbolism and historical developments on earth – ranging from the ancient bull and ram cults, via the repeated fish-symbolism of Christianity, to the "man carrying a pitcher of water" who, in John's gospel, leads the disciples to the Millennium-symbolizing "upper room."

There is no evidence in Nostradamus's writings, however, that he subscribed to this symbolism or used it in his predictions.

As for the length of the cycle as a whole, the seer seems to have taken the figure to be nearer 26,000 years, so making the length of each of its constituent ages some 2,160 years. This period in turn he then apparently divided into six sub-ages (he called them "cycles") of 360 years each – i.e. a symbolic "year of years." Here the prevalence of the number six could suggest an ancient Babylonian origin, possibly during the Jewish captivity in Babylon of roughly 585 to 520 B.C., since the Babylonians' mathematics showed a clear preference for counting in sixes.

Just as each larger age was allotted a *sign*, so each sub-age was now allotted a ruling *planet*. In view of the fact that *seven* "planets" were known at the time – including the sun and moon – this inevitably meant that one of them had to be omitted. The indications are that this was probably Mercury.

In line 1 of *Century* I.48 (first published in 1555) Nostradamus states that twenty years of the age of the moon have already passed. In the light of this and the information in section 14 of the *Préface à César* (q.v.), the system would thus appear to run as follows:

AGE OF THE MOON: 1535–1895
AGE OF THE SUN: 1895–2255
AGE OF SATURN: 2255–2615
AGE OF JUPITER: 2615–2975
AGE OF MARS: 2975–3335
AGE OF VENUS: 3335–3695
AGE OF THE MOON: 3695–4055
AGE OF THE SUN: 4055–4415

. . . and so on.

Quite what developments the prophet expected to occur during each of these ages is not always clear. There are nevertheless a few indications. The Age of Saturn (he suggests in section B.29 of the *Lettre à Henri II*) will be a Golden Age: Rabelais (*Pantagruel*, 31) shares that assumption, which was clearly quite general in his day. In V.53 the seer seems to suggest some kind of dispute as to whether the Messiah will appear during the Age of Venus or that of the sun, but finally plumps for that of the sun. In section 12 of the *Préface à César* he indicates that the "final conflagration" will come sometime after the Age of Mars, which will be characterized by vast world floods, preceded and followed by long rains, as well as by fire and meteorites. The last date actually mentioned by Nostradamus is 3797, which he indeed seems to associate (*Préface à César*, 12) with the moon – and which falls, as indicated, after the Age of Mars (compare *Century* I.48).

4. SCRYING AND THEURGY

Once having established the broad outlines of the future with the aid of judicial astrology and its traditional and eonic adjuncts, Nostradamus now needed to flesh out the picture. This was where ritual magic finally entered the scene.

In his *Préface à César* the seer hints at some of the practices involved. In section 7 (q.v.) he indicates how it is possible for the diviner to open the mind to divine inspiration not merely through the use of judicial astrology, but with the ritual aid of *lymbe* and *exigue flamme* (see explanation below). Almost in the same breath, however, he beseeches his infant son never to dabble in such practices – for, he says, they desiccate the body, disturb the mind, and send the soul to perdition. For that reason he has reduced to ashes the ancient books in which he first discovered the techniques involved. They burned, he says, with an unnatural brilliance.

Fortunately, these slightest of hints are elaborated considerably in the *Centuries* themselves – sufficiently, in fact, for us actually to identify two of the "magic books" in question. Verse I.42, for example, evidently refers to the *De Daemonibus*, a critique of occult practices written by the eleventh-century Byzantine neo-Platonist philosopher, historian, theologian, and statesman Michael Psellus. In damning the practices involved, the latter naturally had first to describe them (a familiar drawback, this, for ancient theologians, to which we owe many a description of long-lost heretical beliefs and practices) – and they include customs ranging from ritual sex and infant cannibalism on Passion Sunday at one end of the spectrum to simple scrying, or future-gazing, with the aid of a basin of water at the other. It is this last that some commentators feel sure was practiced by Nostradamus – though it has to be said that the seer never specifically mentions the practice, and that the verse in question is in fact darkly disapproving of the practices involved.

Indeed, verse I.42 is virtually a paraphrase and precis of Psellus's original, critical words. I therefore present it here in a version that is similarly interpretive – not least because, in the original (see The Major Prophecies), the last line in particular is so heavily disguised (even in the first edition) as to have fooled virtually every commentator since. Below it are the relevant parts of Psellus's own description:

April the tenth – in Gothic style, the first!

The rite's revived by those on evil bent:
Out goes the light, and then that crew accursed
Seek out the filthy demon Psellus meant.

They gather on the evening of the Passion of Our Savior and . . . having put out the lights, copulate promiscuously either with their sisters or with their daughters . . . reckoning that this will . . . facilitate the entry of the demons.

Note that Nostradamus, evidently anticipating the Gregorian calendar that would be introduced only sixteen years after his own death, here identifies the "Gothic" (i.e. medieval or Julian) Passion Sunday, 1554, as the date when (presumably) the verse was composed, but miscalculates slightly its Gregorian equivalent. This is understandable, given that the final conversion formula had not yet even been officially established.

Meanwhile, in the light of his clear note of disapproval, it is rather odd to find so many commentators insisting that Nostradamus actually used Pselline techniques.

If, then, these practices were not among those used by Nostradamus, what was? To answer the question we need do no more than turn to the very first two verses of the *Centuries*, where the seer starts the whole ball rolling by being about as specific as anybody could be. In them he describes a combination of practices that are to be found in another, even more important (indeed, unique) ancient work on ceremonial magic – or rather on the ancient temple mysteries. This is the *De Mysteriis Aegyptiorum* of the respected third/fourth-century neo-Platonist (or rather neo-Pythagorean) philosopher Iamblichus, a Latin translation of which (also incorporating Psellus's work) was published by de Tournes in 1549, even while the newly married seer was still in Italy.

This immensely scholarly work is a response to a letter by Iamblichus's former teacher Porphyry that was critical, even cynical, about the sacred rites generally, and especially about theurgy – the summoning up of gods and spirits in order to gain greater insights into the divine wisdom, and especially into the future. In view of this it is astonishing how carefully, patiently, and even convincingly Iamblichus addresses all of Porphyry's criticisms. There is no hint of rancor, still less of doubt. Indeed, the work comes across as the response of a man who not only believes what he says but knows it to be true from his own and others' long experience. The higher beings, he insists, can indeed be called upon to bestow knowledge – and especially foreknowledge – on those who invoke them in the right way and for the right reasons. But this is the exclusive job of a ritually purified priesthood that has abstained from sex for some time beforehand. Nevertheless, he does hint at the possibility of *two separate* approaches – one for the ritually purified, and one for those still engaged in everyday life.

Iamblichus does not bother to describe in any detail the exact procedures involved. True, he lists the various beings that can be invoked – from gods, through demigods and heroes, to archangels, angels, demons, and archons (both good and evil), and ordinary, everyday spirits. He also explains how they are all mere manifestations (at successively lower levels) of the divine First Cause itself.

This insistence that the approach is, in effect, in no way atheistic or pagan finds repeated echoes both in Nostradamus's *Préface à César* and in his *Lettre à Henri II*.

Then Iamblichus goes on to describe the exact forms in which the various manifestations appear, their sizes, their motions, and the types of light that they emit. He points out that while demigods, angels, and good demons will all give information quite freely, not all of them are reliable. He goes on to list what he calls the "divine tokens of genuine inspiration by the gods" who alone, once successfully invoked in the correct way, "are incapable of untruth."(Hence, conceivably, Nostradamus's insistence in section 12 of the *Préface à César* – which he himself was later to contradict – that his predictions may be regarded as infallible.)

The ancient Syrian philosopher next assesses the various forms of prediction, from dreams and trance, through natural clairvoyance, to that of the ritual Mysteries, which he deems to be the highest and most reliable of all. He explains the place of astrology in all of this – for the stars, he asserts, are mere physical manifestations of those same divinities mentioned earlier, whose own movements they merely reflect. (This, then, clearly, is the underlying principle that links all Nostradamus's own prophetic activities together, too.) And he decries those who would meddle with mere ghosts as being false and unreliable messengers.

He even explains the place of prayer and contemplation in the early stages of the rite, as well as the purposes of the various types of ritual symbols and formulas. He goes on to affirm that there is no other reliable way of salvation and enlightenment, still less of foreknowledge, except "the knowing of the gods" – which he also describes as "the knowing of the Father." "Not all things in the natural world," he insists, "are controlled by Fate."

In the course of all this, as we have seen, Iamblichus says very little about the actual practices involved. In chapter 11 of Book 3, however, he does briefly describe (see facsimile below) three theurgic techniques – namely those employed at ancient Colophon, Delphi, and Branchidai (modern Didym in Turkey). At Colophon, he says, the female oracle

prepares herself by fasting for a day and a night, then pronounces her prophecies while in a trance after drinking from a subterranean spring. At Delphi the prophetess, seated either on a bronze tripod (*super sedem aeneam* – Nostradamus half-quotes the self-same Latin phrase in section A.4 of the *Lettre à Henri II*) or on a four-footed stool above a vent belching forth "fiery vapors," is taken over by them to the point of being "lit up by a ray of divine fire" and totally possessed by the god.

At this point it is clear that Nostradamus based his own work at least in part on a re-creation of the ancient Delphic rite, for his words in verse I.1 are a virtual paraphrase and precis of de Tournes's Latin translation of Iamblichus's text. Once again, therefore, I offer my own verse-translation above the actual words of the former Syrian philosopher:

Seated, at ease, the secret eremite
On brazen tripod studies through the night:
What 'midst the lonely darkness flickers bright
Offers to bring what none should doubt to light.

The prophetess at Delphi . . . being seated in the inner shrine on a brazen tripod . . . surrenders herself to the god . . . and is illuminated with a ray of divine fire.

DE MYSTERIIS AEGYPTIORUM

**Iamblichus describes the Greek rites in
de Tournes's 1549 Latin version
(in all probability the version used by Nostradamus)**

At Branchidai, Iamblichus continues, (de Tournes's Latin text of 1549 – the one almost certainly used by Nostradamus – calls it "Brancis") the prophetess fasts for three days, then – whether by holding a wand in her hand, dipping her feet or the hem of her robe in water or inhaling its vapors – invokes the god while sitting on a wheel, and is infused with divine light. Once again Nostradamus's words in I.2 reflect the ancient words directly, while clearly referring via the word "he" to himself, rather than the ancient priestess:

> *Wand placed in hand as Branchis' rites lay down,*
> *He soaks with water both his hem and feet.*
> *A fearful voice that shakes him in his gown,*
> *Then light divine! The god assumes his seat.*

> *The female oracle at Brancis . . . holding a wand in her hand or dipping her feet or the hem of her robe in the water . . . is filled with a divine light . . . and predicts what is to come . . . The god becomes externally present . . . and the prophetess . . . is inspired.*

As Nostradamus affirms in his *Préface à César* (section 7), *l'entendement crée intellectuellement ne peult voir occultement, sinon par la voix faicte au lymbe moyennant la exigue flamme, en laquelle partie les causes futures se viendront à incliner.*[59] In his *Lettre à Henri II* (section A.4), Nostradamus also explains that it is necessary to still both mind and body, casting aside all everyday worries and concerns, before embarking on this quest. He also protests once again that God alone is the real source of his insights.

There can be little doubt, then, that Nostradamus – already (as he himself repeatedly states) congenitally gifted with "the sight"[60] – used the techniques described to refine and extend that gift. Whether he also used others we cannot be sure. It is not impossible, for example, that he may after all have used some form of scrying involving a vessel of water, as described by Psellus, since Iamblichus also refers to a form of water divination. In this case the first two words of the second line of I.1 could conceivably be taken as a version of *seel* (Old French, "bucket") *repausé* (Latin, "stopped or ceased again," and thus "stilled"). Such "double meanings" are by no means unknown in Nostradamus.

Moreover it would be surprising if he had not also come across the celebrated *Clavicula Salomonis*, or *Key of Solomon*, the magical *grimoire* allegedly written by King Solomon himself. But this would

have involved the seer amassing a huge collection of additional ritual equipment – not merely a wand (if later translations of it are to be believed), but a ritual knife, a sword, a charcoal brazier, a white gown, a hat inscribed with the symbols of power, a supply of mercury and aromatic herbs, a protective circle inscribed on the floor with further symbols of power, and a nearby triangle similarly inscribed for the conjured god or spirit to appear in, to say nothing of a range of sacrificial animals – and it seems unlikely that all this could have gone unnoticed by the authorities, to say nothing of the rite itself. Nevertheless, it is not entirely impossible that the *Clavicula* was the source from which Nostradamus gleaned the *words* of his ritual conjurations – his "magic spells" – since Iamblichus himself notably omits to detail any.

Naturally, as with any activity as subjective as these, his success with the various occult techniques must have varied from day to day and month to month. There were, after all, two young infants in the house (see Table of Events), and many a disturbed night

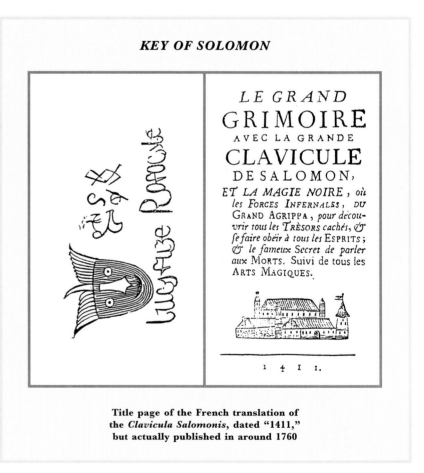

KEY OF SOLOMON

LE GRAND **GRIMOIRE** *AVEC LA GRANDE* **CLAVICULE** *DE SALOMON,* *ET LA MAGIE NOIRE,* où les *FORCES INFERNALES,* DU *GRAND AGRIPPA,* pour découvrir tous les *TRÈSORS* cachés, & se faire obéir à tous les *ESPRITS;* & le fameux *Secret* de parler aux *MORTS.* Suivi de tous les *ARTS MAGIQUES.*

1 ✝ I 1.

Title page of the French translation of the *Clavicula Salomonis*, dated "1411," but actually published in around 1760

59 "Only through the voice produced by the hem, by means of the minute flame, can the intellect perceive occultly in what direction future developments will tend."

60 Or, as he puts it in section A.4 of the *Lettre à Henri II*, with a *naturel instinct qui m'a esté donné par mes aiules.*

must have resulted. In addition, there are veiled hints at IV.24 and IV.25 (q.v.) that at this point operations were seriously interrupted – even desecrated – by some kind of domestic altercation. The admittedly vague signs are that this may have involved either the suspicion of adultery by his wife Anne Ponsarde with his young assistant Chavigny during an absence, or even her connivance in some kind of "sorcerer's apprentice" episode. Reading between the lines, a major row would seem to have followed. As my admittedly fairly free translations of the two verses concerned put it:

> *Our Lady's voice, heard underground, is feigned.*
> *Man's fire shall rise while light Divine shall wane.*
> *Then shall the land with priestly blood be stained*
> *And holy temples wrecked by the profane.*

> *Bodies sublime midst endless vistas bright*
> *Are clouded o'er by reasons such as these.*
> *Bodies grown faceless, headless, lost to sight:*
> *The sacred incantations fade and cease.*

The distracted prophet seems to have reacted (if the next two verses are to be regarded as significant) by abandoning work for a while and taking a trip back to his childhood home at St.-Rémy, encountering a rustic swarm of bees en route and indulging an old passion by visiting the nearby ancient ruins of Roman Glanum. Then follow a couple of 'occult' quatrains whose subtext indicates in arcane, alchemical terms that sexual activities (Venus) have been disguised as divine ones (the sun), but that the seer has been able to use magical techniques (Mercury) involving fire (Vulcan) to discover the truth and restore the divine supremacy. As my further translations of verses IV.28 and IV.29 put it:

Franco – who featured in Nostradamus's predictions – at the head of a military parade in July 1961

> *When Venus with the sun is cloaked about,*
> *Beneath its light shall lurk a form occult.*
> *Then Mercury through fire shall find them out,*
> *Though strife's loud rumors do him sore assault.*

> *The hidden sun, eclipsed by Mercury,*
> *Shall come to rank but second in the sky.*
> *By Vulcan Mercury shall foddered be.*
> *Then shall the white, pure, bright sun rise on high.*

And so, eventually, calm is restored, and the prophet, in the shadow of Salon's citadel, can regain the inspired prophetic state originally described by Iamblichus (IV.30, IV.31):

> *Eleven more times the moon shall shun the sun,*

> *Each raised or lowered in its own degree,*
> *Or so abased that no gold shall be spun –*
> *Then, after dearth and plague, the secret see!*
> *The moon at midnight o'er the lofty mount*
> *The new-found sage's mind alone can claim.*
> *Him for immortal his disciples count,*
> *Eyes southward, hands in lap, body aflame.*

Nevertheless, Nostradamus may well have been knocked sideways by the experience, if experience it was: IV.30 suggests that in its aftermath he felt moved to take an eleventh-month break. Certainly, as the texts make perfectly clear, the first edition was to come to an abrupt halt only twenty-two verses later. However, there may well be other reasons for this (see Nostradamus's Writings).

Distractions apart, however, Nostradamus seems to have managed to receive a whole variety of clairvoyant impressions as a result of reviving the practice of the ancient rites, and on this basis was able to fill in many additional details of the future events that he had already pinpointed with the aid of judicial astrology. Thanks to them, he was sometimes able not only to detect colors, sounds, and smells, *but even to hear actual names* – Franco, Napoleon and de Gaulle among them, though probably not Hitler (see Nostradamus, Napoleon, and "Hister"). Thanks to them, too, he was able to predict future events of staggering complexity – if with a degree of accuracy that admittedly varies.

He himself, after all, admitted that his visions came to him *comme dans un mirouer ardant* [61] (see *Lettre à Henri II*, A.6). True, numerous commentators have seen fit to interpret this expression in terms of some kind of magic device surrounded by flames. In fact, it refers (just as it does in chapter 16 of Rabelais's *Pantagruel*) to a simple burning-mirror – a concave mirror designed to catch and focus the sun's rays. Either one sees nothing except for a hugely magnified foreground or, as one moves away from the mirror, everything becomes distant background – and upside down, at that. On this basis, then, we should expect many of Nostradamus's prophecies to be either extremely detailed but lacking in context, or very generalized and possibly back-to-front.

As, indeed, actual experience tends to confirm.

But that cannot alter the fact that, thanks to a whole variety of Nostradamian techniques, the predictions are now there, and that they foreshadow some very specific dates and events indeed.

---

[61] "as though in a burning mirror."

SEQUENCE OF SELECTED HOROGRAPHS

THE FOLLOWING pairs of horographs show *in order of date* the comparative horoscopy underlying a number of future recapitulations of major past events that seem to be predicted by Nostradamus (see Astrologer and Mage).

While the charts all show the dates of forthcoming astrological "matches," those asterisked also seem to be pinpointed by one or more of the Nostradamian prophecies indicated at the end of the heading, in some cases specifically via at least one of the available dating techniques (see Dating and Sequencing the Prophecies). In each case, the top chart shows the astrology of the original event on which the prediction in the bottom chart is based.

ALCHABITIUS'S
TREATISE ON ASTROLOGY

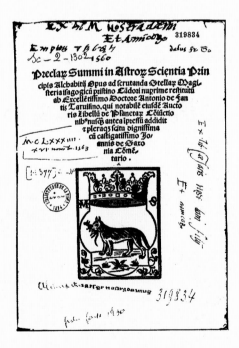

**Title page of Alchabitius's
Treatise on Astrology
bearing the ex-libris signatures of
Nostradamus (top) and his son César (right)**

ORIGINAL EVENT

Horograph for September 16th, 1226, to November 9th, 1226	♈	♌	♊	♋	♍	♃	♎	♏	♐	♑	♒	♓
Pluto						★						
Neptune		★										
Uranus								★				
Saturn										★	★	
Jupiter											★	
Mars									★	★		
Venus							★	★	★			
Mercury							★	★	★			
Moon	★	★	★	★	★	★	★	★	★	★	★	★
Sun								★	★			

Solar noon declination to nearest degree: 3°N to 17°N
Geographical latitude: 48°N 52'N

Location: Paris
Event: Accession of (St.) Louis IX, November 8th

FUTURE EVENT

1997* Accession of crusading king (another St. Louis) in southern France or Switzerland.

Sixain 16

Horograph for September 29th, 1997, to November 4th, 1997	♈	♌	♊	♋	♍	♃	♎	♏	♐	♑	♒	♓
Pluto								★				
Neptune										★	★	
Uranus												
Saturn	★											
Jupiter											★	
Mars								★				
Venus								★	★			
Mercury							★	★	★			
Moon	★	★	★	★	★	★	★	★	★	★	★	★
Sun								★	★			

Solar noon declination to nearest degree: 3°S to 15°S
Relative latitude: 6°S to 2°S   **Geographical latitude:** 43°N to 47°N

Possible location: France from Marseille to Nantes, or elsewhere between same latitudes
Event: Accession of crusading king while in southern France or Switzerland

ORIGINAL EVENT

Horograph for April 8th, 1453, to April 10th, 1453	♈	♉	♊	♋	♌	♍	♎	♏	♐	♑	♒	♓
Pluto				★								
Neptune							★					
Uranus			★									
Saturn							★					
Jupiter												★
Mars		★										
Venus												★
Mercury	★											
Moon	★	★										
Sun	★											

Solar noon declination to nearest degree: 7°N to 8°N
Geographical latitude: 41° 02'N

Location: Constantinople
Event: Turks lay siege to Constantinople

FUTURE EVENT

1998 Istanbul is threatened from the sea by Asiatic forces.

V.86

Horograph for April 6th, 1998, to April 12th, 1998	♈	♉	♊	♋	♌	♍	♎	♏	♐	♑	♒	♓
Pluto									★			
Neptune											★	
Uranus											★	
Saturn	★											
Jupiter												★
Mars	★											
Venus												★
Mercury	★											
Moon				★	★	★						
Sun	★											

Solar noon declination to nearest degree: 6°N to 9°N
Relative latitude: 1°S to 1°N   **Geographical latitude:** 40°N to 42°N

Possible location: Istanbul
Event: Asiatics threaten and/or besiege Istanbul

ORIGINAL EVENT

Horograph for January 8th, 480 B.C. to January 10th, 480 B.C.	♈	♉	♊	♋	♌	♍	♎	♏	♐	♑	♒	♓
Pluto						★						
Neptune								★				
Uranus				★								
Saturn											★	
Jupiter												★
Mars											★	
Venus											★	
Mercury									★			
Moon									★	★		
Sun									★			

Solar noon declination to nearest degree: 22°S
Geographical latitude: 38° 54'N to 41° 02'N

Location: Sardis to Istanbul
Event: Xerxes sets out to invade Greece with massive Persian army

FUTURE EVENT

1999 Huge invasion of western Turkey and Aegean from Ardalan (Iran) by another Xerxes.

Lettre à Henri II (B.3)

Horograph for January 7th, 1999, to January 20th, 1999	♈	♉	♊	♋	♌	♍	♎	♏	♐	♑	♒	♓
Pluto									★			
Neptune											★	
Uranus											★	
Saturn	★											
Jupiter												★
Mars							★					
Venus											★	
Mercury									★			
Moon							★	★	★	★	★	★	★
Sun											★	

Solar noon declination to nearest degree: 22°S to 20°S
Relative latitude: 0°S to 2°S   **Geographical latitude:** 39°N to 38°N

Location: Rhodes to Khios, taking in former province of Ardalan (north Iran)
Event: Huge invasion of western Turkey from east

ORIGINAL EVENT

Horograph for July 17th, 1429, to August 8th, 1429

	♈	♉	♊	♋	♌	♍	♎	♏	♐	♑	♒	♓
Pluto				★								
Neptune					★							
Uranus	★											
Saturn								★				
Jupiter	★											
Mars							★					
Venus					★							
Mercury					★							
Moon	★	★	★	★	★	★	★	★	★		★	★
Sun					★							

Solar noon declination to nearest degree: 21°N to 16°N
Geographical latitude: 48° 27'N

Location: Domrémy-la-Pucelle, France
Event: Joan of Arc leaves to seek the Dauphin at Chinon

FUTURE EVENT

1999 Reemergence of a "Joan of Arc" figure somewhere in England.

VI.74,
VIII.15

Horograph for June 27th, 1999

	♈	♉	♊	♋	♌	♍	♎	♏	♐	♑	♒	♓
Pluto									★			
Neptune											★	
Uranus											★	
Saturn		★										
Jupiter	★											
Mars							★					
Venus						★						
Mercury						★						
Moon										★		
Sun				★								

Solar noon declination to nearest degree: 23°N
Relative latitude: 2°N to 7°N   **Geographical latitude:** 50° 27'N to 55° 27'N

Possible location: English south coast to Scottish border
Event: Return to power of "masculine" woman leader

ORIGINAL EVENT

Horograph for July 24th, 579, to August 2nd, 579

	♈	♉	♊	♋	♌	♍	♎	♏	♐	♑	♒	♓
Pluto												★
Neptune			★									
Uranus											★	
Saturn											★	
Jupiter					★							
Mars									★			
Venus								★				
Mercury							★					
Moon	★	★	★								★	★
Sun						★						

Solar noon declination to nearest degree: 20°N to 18°N
Geographical latitude: 47° 54'N to 41° 02'N

Location: Rome to Constantinople
Event: Future Pope Gregory the Great quits Rome to seek help against Lombard invaders

FUTURE EVENT

1999* The Pope (presumably John-Paul II) flies to Ankara to attempt to buy off the Asiatic invaders, but fails. The Turks side with the invaders, and war resumes (see Interpreting the Prophecies).

X.72

Horograph for July 19th, 1999, to July 28th, 1999

	♈	♉	♊	♋	♌	♍	♎	♏	♐	♑	♒	♓
Pluto									★			
Neptune											★	
Uranus											★	
Saturn		★										
Jupiter		★										
Mars								★				
Venus							★					
Mercury				★								
Moon	★	★	★	★	★							★
Sun						★						

Solar noon declination to nearest degree: 21°N to 19°N
Relative latitude: 1°N   **Geographical latitude:** 43°N to 42°N

Possible location: Rome to Ankara
Event: Pope flies to Turkey to buy off invaders, but merely stirs them up: war resumes

ORIGINAL EVENT

Horograph for November 27th, 1241, to December 13th, 1241

	1	2	3	4	5	6	7	8	9	10	11	12
Pluto						★						
Neptune			★									
Uranus								★				
Saturn				★								
Jupiter		★										
Mars											★	
Venus							★					
Mercury								★				
Moon	★					★	★	★	★	★	★	★
Sun								★				

Solar noon declination to nearest degree: 21°S to 23°S
Geographical latitude: 41°N to 47°N

Location: Hungary and Balkans
Event: Mongol invasion of southeast Europe

FUTURE EVENT

1999 "Mongol" hordes sweep into southeastern Europe and Balkans.

V.48, V.54, Presage 31

Horograph for December 11th, 1999, to December 21st, 1999

	1	2	3	4	5	6	7	8	9	10	11	12
Pluto							★					
Neptune									★			
Uranus									★			
Saturn		★										
Jupiter	★											
Mars										★		
Venus								★				
Mercury									★			
Moon	★	★	★							★	★	★
Sun								★				

Solar noon declination to nearest degree: 32°S
Relative latitude: 2°S to 0°S   **Geographical latitude:** 40°N to 47°N

Possible location: Greece to Hungary
Event: Asiatic invasion of Balkans and southeastern Europe

ORIGINAL EVENT

Horograph for December 17th, A.D. 878

	1	2	3	4	5	6	7	8	9	10	11	12
Pluto		★										
Neptune												★
Uranus						★						
Saturn	★											
Jupiter							★					
Mars										★		
Venus								★				
Mercury									★			
Moon					★							
Sun									★			

Solar noon declination to nearest degree: 23°S
Geographical latitude: 37°N

Location: Sicily
Event: Invasion by Muslim Saracens

FUTURE EVENT

1999 Muslim sea-borne forces invade Sicily.

II.4, VII.6, VIII.84, Presage 31

Horograph for December 31st, 1999, to January 3rd, 2000

	1	2	3	4	5	6	7	8	9	10	11	12
Pluto							★					
Neptune									★			
Uranus									★			
Saturn		★										
Jupiter	★											
Mars										★		
Venus								★				
Mercury									★			
Moon								★	★			
Sun									★			

Solar noon declination to nearest degree: 23°S
Relative latitude: 0°   **Geographical latitude:** 23°N

Possible location: Sicily
Event: Muslim invasion

ORIGINAL EVENT

Horograph for February 2nd, 480 B.C., to February 23rd, 480 B.C.

	1	2	3	4	5	6	7	8	9	10	11	12
Pluto							★					
Neptune								★				
Uranus				★								
Saturn											★	
Jupiter	★											
Mars												★
Venus												★
Mercury											★	
Moon	★	★	★	★	★			★	★	★	★	★
Sun											★	

Solar noon declination to nearest degree: 17°S to 10°S
Geographical latitude: 38°N

Location: Bay of Salamis, just west of Athens
Event: Battle of Salamis; huge Persian fleet defeated by small Athenian fleet (early date)

FUTURE EVENT

2000 European navies defeat a larger Muslim fleet off Libya in a new "Battle of Salamis."

IX.42

Horograph for January 21st, 2000, to February 4th, 2000

	1	2	3	4	5	6	7	8	9	10	11	12
Pluto							★					
Neptune										★		
Uranus										★		
Saturn		★										
Jupiter	★											
Mars												★
Venus								★	★			
Mercury										★		
Moon			★	★	★	★	★	★	★			
Sun										★		

Solar noon declination to nearest degree: 20°S to 16°S
Relative latitude: 3°S to 6°S   **Geographical latitude:** 35°N to 32°N

Possible location: Gulf of Libya
Event: European navies beat off larger Muslim fleet

ORIGINAL EVENT

Horograph for February 22nd, 260 B.C., to March 10th, 260 B.C.

	1	2	3	4	5	6	7	8	9	10	11	12
Pluto					★							
Neptune	★											
Uranus											★	
Saturn					★							
Jupiter							★					
Mars												★
Venus										★		
Mercury												★
Moon	★						★	★	★	★	★	★
Sun												★

Solar noon declination to nearest degree: 10°S to 4°S
Geographical latitude: 38°N

Location: Off Milazzo, northeast Sicily
Event: Battle of Mylae: Roman fleet's first victory over Carthaginians

FUTURE EVENT

2000 European navies beat off a new "Carthaginian" fleet from north Africa off Sicily.

IX.42, I.37(?)

Horograph for February 19th, 2000 to March 12th, 2000

	1	2	3	4	5	6	7	8	9	10	11	12
Pluto							★					
Neptune										★		
Uranus										★		
Saturn		★										
Jupiter		★										
Mars	★											
Venus											★	
Mercury												★
Moon	★	★	★		★	★	★	★	★	★	★	★
Sun												★

Solar noon declination to nearest degree: 11°S to 3°S
Relative latitude: 1°S to 1°N   **Geographical latitude:** 37°N to 39°N

Possible location: Off Sicily and southern Italy
Event: European fleets defeat fleet from North Africa

ORIGINAL EVENT

Horograph for March 24th, 1396, to March 25th, 1396

	Ari	Tau	Gem	Cnc	Leo	Vir	Lib	Sco	Sgr	Cap	Aqr	Psc
Pluto			★									
Neptune		★										
Uranus									★			
Saturn								★				
Jupiter		★										
Mars	★											
Venus	★											
Mercury												★
Moon						★	★					
Sun	★											

Solar noon declination to nearest degree: 2°N
Geographical latitude: 45°N

Location: Lower Danube
Event: Ottomans invade Danube

FUTURE EVENT

2000 Forces from Asia invade the Danube and southeastern Europe.

V.48, Presage 31

Horograph for March 20th, 2000, to March 21st, 2000

	Ari	Tau	Gem	Cnc	Leo	Vir	Lib	Sco	Sgr	Cap	Aqr	Psc
Pluto									★			
Neptune											★	
Uranus											★	
Saturn		★										
Jupiter		★										
Mars	★											
Venus												★
Mercury												★
Moon							★					
Sun	★											

Solar noon declination to nearest degree: 1°N
Relative latitude: 1°S   **Geographical latitude:** 44°N

Possible location: Lower Danube
Event: Asian invasion of southeast Europe and Balkans

ORIGINAL EVENT

Horograph for July 23rd, 1453, to July 24th, 1453

	Ari	Tau	Gem	Cnc	Leo	Vir	Lib	Sco	Sgr	Cap	Aqr	Psc
Pluto					★							
Neptune							★					
Uranus					★							
Saturn							★					
Jupiter	★											
Mars					★							
Venus					★							
Mercury				★								
Moon												★
Sun					★							

Solar noon declination to nearest degree: 20°N
Geographical latitude: 41° 2'N

Location: Constantinople
Event: Aftermath of fall of city to Turks on May 29th at third attempt

FUTURE EVENT

2000 Asiatic forces reach Rhodes and the Mediterranean coast of Turkey.

II.49, V.47, VI.21

Horograph for August 1st, 2000, to August 6th, 2000

	Ari	Tau	Gem	Cnc	Leo	Vir	Lib	Sco	Sgr	Cap	Aqr	Psc
Pluto									★			
Neptune											★	
Uranus											★	
Saturn		★										
Jupiter			★									
Mars					★							
Venus					★							
Mercury				★								
Moon					★	★	★	★				
Sun					★							

Solar noon declination to nearest degree: 18°N to 17°N
Relative latitude: 2°S to 3°S   **Geographical latitude:** 39°N to 38°N

Possible location: Antioch, Rhodes, Izmir
Event: Asiatic invaders in control of Turkish Mediterranean coast

ORIGINAL EVENT

Horograph for July 31st, 585 B.C., to August 12th, 585 BC

	♈	♉	♊	♋	♌	♍	♎	♏	♐	♑	♒	♓
Pluto		★										
Neptune	★											
Uranus	★											
Saturn				★								
Jupiter		★										
Mars				★								
Venus			★									
Mercury				★								
Moon							★	★	★	★	★	★
Sun				★								

Solar noon declination to nearest degree: 18°N to 15°N
Geographical latitude: 31° 47′N

Location: Jerusalem
Event: Sack and desecration of capital by Nebuchadnezzar and deportation of Jews

FUTURE EVENT

2000 "Another Nebuchadnezzar" from Iraq overruns Egypt.

II.86, V.25

Horograph for August 7th, 2000, to August 21st, 2000

	♈	♉	♊	♋	♌	♍	♎	♏	♐	♑	♒	♓
Pluto									★			
Neptune											★	
Uranus											★	
Saturn		★	★									
Jupiter			★									
Mars						★						
Venus							★					
Mercury						★						
Moon	★	★						★	★	★	★	★
Sun						★						

Solar noon declination to nearest degree: 18°N to 12°N
Relative latitude: 2°S to 3°S   **Geographical latitude:** 30°N to 29°N

Possible location: Cairo
Event: Invaders from Iraq overrun Cairo and enslave Egyptians

ORIGINAL EVENT

Horograph for July 19th, A.D., 870 to July 26th, A.D. 870

	♈	♉	♊	♋	♌	♍	♎	♏	♐	♑	♒	♓
Pluto	★											
Neptune												★
Uranus				★								
Saturn								★				
Jupiter									★			
Mars						★						
Venus							★					
Mercury						★						
Moon	★	★										★
Sun						★						

Solar noon declination to nearest degree: 21°N to 19°N
Geographical latitude: 36°N

Location: Malta
Event: Invasion by Moors from North Africa

FUTURE EVENT

2000 North Africans from farther west overrun Egypt.

Compare VI.54, Sixain 19 for 1999.

Horograph for August 7th, 2000, to August 21st, 2000

	♈	♉	♊	♋	♌	♍	♎	♏	♐	♑	♒	♓
Pluto									★			
Neptune											★	
Uranus											★	
Saturn		★	★									
Jupiter			★									
Mars						★						
Venus							★					
Mercury						★						
Moon	★	★						★	★	★	★	★
Sun						★						

Solar noon declination to nearest degree: 16°N to 12°N
Relative latitude: 5°S to 7°S   **Geographical latitude:** 31°N to 29°N

Possible location: Cairo
Event: Forces from northwest Africa invade Egypt (compare chart on left)

SEQUENCE OF SELECTED HOROGRAPHS

ORIGINAL EVENT

Horograph for December 24th, 1479, to January 11th, 1480

	1	2	3	4	5	6	7	8	9	10	11	12
Pluto							★					
Neptune									★			
Uranus									★			
Saturn							★					
Jupiter		★										
Mars								★				
Venus											★	
Mercury										★		
Moon			★	★	★	★	★	★	★	★	★	
Sun										★		

Solar noon declination to nearest degree: 23ºS to 22ºS
Geographical latitude: 40° 10'N

Location: Otranto, southern Italy
Event: Invasion of Italian mainland by Ottomans

FUTURE EVENT

2000 Muslims from Turkey invade southeast Italian mainland.

II.5 (?)

Horograph for December 24th, 2000, to January 2nd, 2001

	1	2	3	4	5	6	7	8	9	10	11	12
Pluto							★					
Neptune											★	
Uranus											★	
Saturn		★										
Jupiter			★									
Mars								★				
Venus											★	
Mercury										★		
Moon	★								★	★	★	★
Sun										★		

Solar noon declination to nearest degree: 23°S
Relative latitude: 0°N to 1°N   **Geographical latitude:** 40°N to 41°N

Possible location: Otranto, Brindisi, Bari, southern Italy
Event: Muslim invasion of mainland Italy

ORIGINAL EVENT

Horograph for December 24th, 1308, to January 9th, 1309

	1	2	3	4	5	6	7	8	9	10	11	12
Pluto												★
Neptune							★					
Uranus							★					
Saturn									★			
Jupiter										★		
Mars									★			
Venus										★		
Mercury										★		
Moon		★	★	★	★	★	★	★	★			
Sun										★		

Solar noon declination to nearest degree: 23°S to 22°S
Geographical latitude: 41° 51'N to 43° 56'N

Location: Rome to Avignon
Event: Pope Clement V forced to flee to France

FUTURE EVENT

2000 Pope forced to flee to the papal palace at Avignon, France.

II.41, VII.22, VIII.99, X.3

Horograph for December 24th, 2000, to January 10th, 2001

	1	2	3	4	5	6	7	8	9	10	11	12
Pluto							★					
Neptune											★	
Uranus											★	
Saturn		★										
Jupiter			★									
Mars									★			
Venus											★	
Mercury										★		
Moon	★	★	★	★					★	★	★	★
Sun										★		

Solar noon declination to nearest degree: 23°S to 22°S
Relative latitude: 0°   **Geographical latitude:** 42°N to 44°N

Possible location: Rome to Avignon
Event: Pope forced to flee to France

ORIGINAL EVENT

Horograph for September 29th, 1517, to October 13th, 1517

	♈	♉	♊	♋	♌	♍	♎	♏	♐	♑	♒	♓
Pluto										★		
Neptune											★	
Uranus		★										
Saturn									★			
Jupiter						★						
Mars							★					
Venus								★				
Mercury							★					
Moon	★	★	★	★	★	★	★					
Sun							★					

Solar noon declination to nearest degree: 2°S to 8°S
Geographical latitude: 30° 03'N

Location: Cairo
Event: Invading Ottomans take Cairo and overrun Egypt

FUTURE EVENT

2002 Asiatic invaders overrun Saudi Arabia and take Riyadh.

[Not predicted by Nostradamus]

Horograph for October 16th, 2002, to October 23rd, 2002

	♈	♉	♊	♋	♌	♍	♎	♏	♐	♑	♒	♓
Pluto							★					
Neptune										★		
Uranus										★		
Saturn			★									
Jupiter					★							
Mars							★					
Venus								★				
Mercury							★					
Moon	★	★										★
Sun							★					

Solar noon declination to nearest degree: 9°S to 11°S
Relative latitude: 7°S to 3°S   **Geographical latitude:** 23°N to 27°N

Possible location: Riyadh, Saudi Arabia
Event: Asiatic invaders overrun Saudi Arabia

ORIGINAL EVENT

Horograph for January 8th, A.D. 711, to January 9th, A.D. 711

	♈	♉	♊	♋	♌	♍	♎	♏	♐	♑	♒	♓
Pluto		★										
Neptune												★
Uranus					★							
Saturn				★								
Jupiter				★								
Mars								★				
Venus										★		
Mercury									★			
Moon			★									
Sun									★			

Solar noon declination to nearest degree: 22°S
Geographical latitude: 36° 07'N

Location: Gibraltar
Event: Moors invade Spain

FUTURE EVENT

2003 Muslims from north Africa invade Sicily and/or Portugal and Spain.

II.30, VI.80, Sixain 41

Horograph for January 18th, 2003, to January 19th, 2003

	♈	♉	♊	♋	♌	♍	♎	♏	♐	♑	♒	♓
Pluto							★					
Neptune										★		
Uranus										★		
Saturn			★									
Jupiter					★							
Mars								★				
Venus							★					
Mercury									★			
Moon			★	★								
Sun									★			

Solar noon declination to nearest degree: 21°S to 20°S
Relative latitude: 1°S to 2°S   **Geographical latitude:** 35°N to 34°N

Possible location: The Algarve to Cartagena, or Sicily
Event: New North African invasion of Sicily and/or Portugal and southwest Spain

ORIGINAL EVENT

Horograph for March 21st, 1423, to March 30th, 1423

	Aries	Taurus	Gemini	Cancer	Leo	Virgo	Libra	Scorpio	Sagittarius	Capricorn	Aquarius	Pisces
Pluto			★									
Neptune				★								
Uranus												★
Saturn							★					
Jupiter						★						
Mars			★									
Venus	★											
Mercury	★											
Moon								★	★	★	★	
Sun	★											

Solar noon declination to nearest degree: 0°N to 4°N
Geographical latitude: 43° 18'N

Location: Marseille
Event: Fleet from Aragon sacks Marseille

FUTURE EVENT

2004 Muslim sea-borne forces from Barcelona invade France and mainland Italy.

I.18, I.28, VI.56, IX.28

Horograph for March 22th, 2004, to April 1st, 2004

	Aries	Taurus	Gemini	Cancer	Leo	Virgo	Libra	Scorpio	Sagittarius	Capricorn	Aquarius	Pisces
Pluto							★					
Neptune											★	
Uranus												★
Saturn			★									
Jupiter						★						
Mars			★									
Venus		★										
Mercury	★											
Moon	★	★	★	★	★							
Sun	★											

Solar noon declination to nearest degree: 1°N to 5°N
Relative latitude: 1°N   **Geographical latitude:** 44°N

Possible location: Marseille and Port-de-Bouc (or Savona, Genoa, and La Spezia)
Event: Sea invasion from Barcelona

ORIGINAL EVENT

Horograph for January 31st, A.D. 472, to February 12th, A.D. 472

	Aries	Taurus	Gemini	Cancer	Leo	Virgo	Libra	Scorpio	Sagittarius	Capricorn	Aquarius	Pisces
Pluto			★									
Neptune						★						
Uranus							★					
Saturn			★									
Jupiter			★									
Mars									★			
Venus											★	
Mercury											★	
Moon	★	★	★	★	★	★						
Sun											★	

Solar noon declination to nearest degree: 18°S to 14°S
Geographical latitude: 40° 48'N to 42° 02'N

Location: Mount Vesuvius to Constantinople
Event: Major eruption of Vesuvius blows ashes all the way to Constantinople

FUTURE EVENT

2005 Volcanic ash or "fire from the sky" descends on much of southern Europe.

II.81, IX.99

Horograph for February 3rd, 2005, to February 6th, 2005

	Aries	Taurus	Gemini	Cancer	Leo	Virgo	Libra	Scorpio	Sagittarius	Capricorn	Aquarius	Pisces
Pluto							★					
Neptune											★	
Uranus												★
Saturn			★									
Jupiter						★						
Mars									★			
Venus											★	
Mercury											★	
Moon									★	★	★	
Sun											★	

Solar noon declination to nearest degree: 17°S to 16°S
Relative latitude: 1°N to 2°S   **Geographical latitude:** 42°N to 39°N

Possible location: Pyrenees and Rome to Lisbon, the Balearics, and Crotona (Italy)
Event: Volcanic ash or "fire from the sky" descends on much of southern Europe

ORIGINAL EVENT

Horograph for January 28th, A.D. 476, to February 14th, A.D. 476	♈	♉	♊	♋	♌	♍	♎	♏	♐	♑	♒	♓
Pluto					★							
Neptune						★						
Uranus								★				
Saturn					★							
Jupiter							★					
Mars									★			
Venus									★			
Mercury									★			
Moon	★				★	★	★	★	★	★	★	★
Sun										★		

Solar noon declination to nearest degree: 18°S to 13°S
Geographical latitude: 41° 54'N

Location: Rome
Event: Last Roman Emperor ("Pontifex") deposed by German chieftain

FUTURE EVENT

2005 Last Pope ejected from office by foreign invaders.

II.93

Horograph for November 6th, 2005, to December 12th, 2005 (minor match only)	♈	♉	♊	♋	♌	♍	♎	♏	♐	♑	♒	♓
Pluto									★			
Neptune											★	
Uranus												★
Saturn				★								
Jupiter							★					
Mars		★										
Venus										★		
Mercury								★	★			
Moon	★	★	★	★	★	★	★	★	★	★	★	★
Sun								★	★			

Solar noon declination to nearest degree: 16°S to 23°S
Relative latitude: 2°N to 10°S **Geographical latitude:** 44°N to 32°N

Possible location: Avignon via Rome, to Tel Aviv
Event: Last Pope ("Pontiff") ejected from office by foreign invaders

ORIGINAL EVENT

Horograph for April 28th, 1537, to May 8th, 1537	♈	♉	♊	♋	♌	♍	♎	♏	♐	♑	♒	♓
Pluto											★	
Neptune	★											
Uranus				★								
Saturn						★						
Jupiter		★										
Mars	★											
Venus				★								
Mercury	★											
Moon	★	★							★	★	★	★
Sun		★										

Solar noon declination to nearest degree: 14°N to 17°N
Geographical latitude: 36° 15'N

Location: Algiers
Event: Ottomans invade and capture Algiers

FUTURE EVENT

2007 Muslim forces invade the Balearics and southeastern Spain.

III.20, VI.88

Horograph for May 16th, 2007, to May 21st, 2007	♈	♉	♊	♋	♌	♍	♎	♏	♐	♑	♒	♓
Pluto									★			
Neptune											★	
Uranus												★
Saturn						★						
Jupiter									★			
Mars	★											
Venus				★								
Mercury			★									
Moon		★	★	★	★							
Sun		★										

Solar noon declination to nearest degree: 19°N to 20°N
Relative latitude: 5°N to 3°N **Geographical latitude:** 42°N to 40°N

Possible location: Balearics and Barcelona to Pyrenees
Event: Muslim invasion of Spain and North Africa

ORIGINAL EVENT

Horograph for March 31st, A.D. 167, to May 9th, A.D. 167

	♈	♉	♊	♋	♌	♍	♎	♏	♐	♑	♒	♓
Pluto		★										
Neptune								★				
Uranus												★
Saturn											★	
Jupiter							★					
Mars						★	★					
Venus			★	★	★							
Mercury	★	★										
Moon	★	★	★	★	★	★	★	★	★	★	★	★
Sun	★	★										

Solar noon declination to nearest degree: 4°N to 16°N

Geographical latitude: 45°N to 38°N

Location: Southeast Europe

Event: German tribes cross Danube, reach northwest Italy, invade Greece, and capture Athens

FUTURE EVENT

2010 Muslim forces advance up the Danube, or up the Rhône into central France.

I.72, V.48, Presage 31

Horograph for April 1st, 2010, to June 10th, 2010

	♈	♉	♊	♋	♌	♍	♎	♏	♐	♑	♒	♓
Pluto									★			
Neptune											★	
Uranus	★											★
Saturn						★	★					
Jupiter	★											★
Mars						★	★					
Venus			★	★	★							
Mercury	★	★										
Moon	★	★	★	★	★	★	★	★	★	★	★	★
Sun	★	★	★									

Solar noon declination to nearest degree: 5°N to 23°N

Relative latitude: 1°N to 7°N **Geographical latitude:** 46°N to 45°N

Possible location: Danube River, or central France

Event: Invaders advance up Danube or up Rhône into central France

ORIGINAL EVENT

Horograph for January 26th, 546 B.C., to February 11th, 546 B.C.

	♈	♉	♊	♋	♌	♍	♎	♏	♐	♑	♒	♓
Pluto		★										
Neptune				★								
Uranus							★					
Saturn							★					
Jupiter						★						
Mars											★	
Venus										★		
Mercury											★	
Moon	★	★	★	★	★	★	★	★				
Sun											★	

Solar noon declination to nearest degree: 19°S to 14°S

Geographical latitude: 39°N

Location: Sardis (modern Turkey)

Event: Cyrus the Great burns Sardis and condemns King Croesus to death (actual fate unknown)

FUTURE EVENT

2011 A "new Cyrus the Great" sets fire to Rome, and the Pope disappears or is murdered.

II.93

Horograph for February 5th, 2011, to February 19th, 2011

	♈	♉	♊	♋	♌	♍	♎	♏	♐	♑	♒	♓
Pluto									★			
Neptune										★		
Uranus												★
Saturn							★					
Jupiter	★											
Mars											★	
Venus										★		
Mercury											★	
Moon	★	★	★	★	★	★						★
Sun											★	

Solar noon declination to nearest degree: 16°S to 11°S

Relative latitude: 3°N **Geographical latitude:** 42°N

Possible location: Rome

Event: Sacking and burning of Rome and disappearance/execution of Pope

ORIGINAL EVENT

Horograph for June 21st, 1348, to July 9th, 1348												
Pluto	★											
Neptune											★	
Uranus		★										
Saturn												★
Jupiter			★									
Mars						★						
Venus				★								
Mercury				★								
Moon		★	★	★	★	★	★	★	★	★		
Sun				★								

Solar noon declination to nearest degree: 23°N to 22°N
Geographical latitude: 38° 10'N northwards

Location: Messina (Sicily) northwards
Event: Black Death invades Europe from south

FUTURE EVENT

2012 A great plague epidemic sweeps Europe from the south.

I.16, II.6, VIII.21, IX.42

Horograph for June 27th, 2012, to July 3rd, 2012												
Pluto									★			
Neptune												★
Uranus	★											
Saturn						★						
Jupiter			★									
Mars						★						
Venus			★									
Mercury				★								
Moon						★	★	★	★			
Sun				★								

Solar noon declination to nearest degree: 23°N
Relative latitude: 0°N to 1°N **Geographical latitude:** 38°N northwards

Possible location: Balearics, Spain, Italy, and France
Event: Severe plague epidemic sweeps Europe from south

ORIGINAL EVENT

Horograph for December 28th, 1901 B.C., to January 19th, 1900 B.C. (traditional date)												
Pluto									★			
Neptune	★											
Uranus				★								
Saturn							★					
Jupiter				★								
Mars										★	★	
Venus								★				
Mercury										★		
Moon	★	★	★	★	★	★	★	★	★	★		★
Sun									★			

Solar noon declination to nearest degree: 23°S to 20°S
Geographical latitude: 31° 25'N

Location: Dead Sea, Palestine
Event: "Fire and brimstone" descend on Sodom and Gomorrah

FUTURE EVENT

2013 "Fire from the sky" descends on southern Europe, including France.

I.87, II.3, II.91, III.7, VI.97, VIII.2, Sixain 27

Horograph for October 8th, 2013, to November 5th, 2013												
Pluto									★			
Neptune												★
Uranus	★											
Saturn							★					
Jupiter			★									
Mars				★	★							
Venus								★				
Mercury							★					
Moon	★	★	★	★	★	★	★	★	★	★	★	★
Sun									★	★		

Solar noon declination to nearest degree: 6°S to 16°S
Relative latitude: 17°N to 4°N   **Geographical latitude:** 48°N to 35°N

Possible location: Sicily and southern Spain via southern France to northern Switzerland
Event: "Fire from the sky" descends on southern Europe

ORIGINAL EVENT

Horograph for September 1st, A.D. 70, to September 2nd, A.D. 70

	♐	♑	♒	♓	♈	♉	♊	♋	♌	♍	♎	♏
Pluto											★	
Neptune	★											
Uranus											★	
Saturn						★						
Jupiter					★							
Mars				★								
Venus					★							
Mercury					★							
Moon									★			
Sun						★						

Solar noon declination to nearest degree: 8°N to 7°N
Geographical latitude: 37° 47'N

Location: Jerusalem
Event: Sack of Jerusalem by Romans and burning of Temple

FUTURE EVENT

2015 Rome is sacked, and the Vatican and St. Peter's burned to the ground.

II.81, II.93, III.84, IV.82

Horograph for August 1st, 2015, to August 7th, 2015

	♐	♑	♒	♓	♈	♉	♊	♋	♌	♍	♎	♏
Pluto										★		
Neptune												★
Uranus	★											
Saturn								★				
Jupiter					★							
Mars				★								
Venus					★							
Mercury					★							
Moon	★	★									★	★
Sun					★							

Solar noon declination to nearest degree: 10°N to 16°N
Relative latitude: 10°N to 9°N **Geographical latitude:** 42°N to 41°N

Possible location: Rome
Event: Sacking of Rome and burning of Vatican and/or St. Peter's

ORIGINAL EVENT

Horograph for December 31st, A.D. 454 to January 6th, A.D. 455

	♐	♑	♒	♓	♈	♉	♊	♋	♌	♍	♎	♏
Pluto			★									
Neptune				★								
Uranus					★							
Saturn						★						
Jupiter									★			
Mars						★						
Venus											★	
Mercury									★			
Moon							★	★	★	★		
Sun									★			

Solar noon declination to nearest degree: 23°S
Geographical latitude: 41° 54'N

Location: Rome
Event: Rome sacked by Vandals

FUTURE EVENT

2019 Rome is reinvaded by forces from North Africa.

I.52 (?)

Horograph for December 30th, 2019, to January 3rd, 2020

	♐	♑	♒	♓	♈	♉	♊	♋	♌	♍	♎	♏
Pluto										★		
Neptune												★
Uranus		★										
Saturn										★		
Jupiter										★		
Mars								★				
Venus											★	
Mercury										★		
Moon	★										★	★
Sun										★		

Solar noon declination to nearest degree: 23°S
Relative latitude: 0° **Geographical latitude:** 42°N

Possible location: Rome
Event: Renewed sacking of Rome by forces from North Africa

ORIGINAL EVENT

Horograph for January 1st, A.D. 543, to January 12th, A.D. 543

	♈	♉	♊	♋	♌	♍	♎	♏	♐	♑	♒	♓
Pluto										★		
Neptune												★
Uranus				★								
Saturn						★						
Jupiter			★									
Mars				★	★							
Venus												★
Mercury									★			
Moon		★	★	★	★	★	★					
Sun										★		

Solar noon declination to nearest degree: 23°S to 22°S
Geographical latitude: 43° 18'N

Location: Marseille
Event: First plague epidemic hits south of France

FUTURE EVENT

2025 A disastrous plague outbreak strikes southern France.

I.16, II.37, VIII.17

Horograph for January 4th, 2025, to January 5th, 2025

	♈	♉	♊	♋	♌	♍	♎	♏	♐	♑	♒	♓
Pluto										★		
Neptune												★
Uranus	★											
Saturn												★
Jupiter			★									
Mars					★							
Venus												★
Mercury									★			
Moon												★
Sun										★		

Solar noon declination to nearest degree: 23°S
Relative latitude: 0°S to 1°S   **Geographical latitude:** 43°N to 42°N

Possible location: French Mediterranean coast
Event: Severe plague outbreak hits south of France from Mediterranean

ORIGINAL EVENT

Horograph for March 26th, 323 B.C. to April 11th, 323 B.C.

	♈	♉	♊	♋	♌	♍	♎	♏	♐	♑	♒	♓
Pluto	★											
Neptune								★				
Uranus		★										
Saturn			★									
Jupiter				★								
Mars				★								
Venus		★										
Mercury												★
Moon						★	★	★	★	★	★	★
Sun	★											

Solar noon declination to nearest degree: 2°N to 8°N
Geographical latitude: 32° 33'N

Location: Babylon, Iraq
Event: Death of Alexander the Great and division of his empire

FUTURE EVENT

2026 Death of alien overlord and division of empire three ways.

II.47, VIII.73

Horograph for March 31st, 2026, to April 15th, 2026

	♈	♉	♊	♋	♌	♍	♎	♏	♐	♑	♒	♓
Pluto										★		
Neptune	★											
Uranus		★										
Saturn	★											
Jupiter				★								
Mars	★											★
Venus		★										
Mercury												★
Moon						★	★	★	★	★	★	★
Sun	★											

Solar noon declination to nearest degree: 4°N to 10°N
Relative latitude: 2°N   **Geographical latitude:** 34°N to 35°N

Possible location: Tripoli, Lebanon/Baghdad
Event: Death of Muslim conqueror and division of empire

ORIGINAL EVENT

Horograph for July 21st, 1017, to August 9th, 1017

	♒	♑	♊	♋	♌	♐	♎	♍	♎	♐	♏	♓
Pluto									★			
Neptune											★	
Uranus		★										
Saturn									★			
Jupiter			★									
Mars							★					
Venus						★						
Mercury						★						
Moon			★	★	★	★	★	★	★	★	★	
Sun						★						

Solar noon declination to nearest degree: 20°N to 16°N
Geographical latitude: c. 45°N

Location: Northern Italy
Event: Normans under Count Roger invade Saracen-occupied Italy

FUTURE EVENT

2027 Western counterinvasion of Muslim-occupied Italy reaches Sicily.

II.16, II.71

Horograph for August 21st, 2027, to August 24th, 2027

	♒	♑	♊	♋	♌	♐	♎	♍	♎	♐	♏	♓
Pluto											★	
Neptune	★											
Uranus			★									
Saturn	★											
Jupiter							★					
Mars								★				
Venus							★					
Mercury							★					
Moon	★	★										
Sun						★						

Solar noon declination to nearest degree: 12°N to 11°N
Relative latitude: 8°S to 5°S   **Geographical latitude:** c. 37°N to 40°N

Possible location: Southern Italy and Sicily
Event: Counterinvasion of Muslim-occupied Italy reaches far south

ORIGINAL EVENT

Horograph for January 29th, 49 B.C. to February 21st, 49 B.C.

	♒	♑	♊	♋	♌	♐	♎	♍	♎	♐	♏	♓
Pluto		★										
Neptune				★								
Uranus						★						
Saturn							★					
Jupiter				★								
Mars	★											
Venus										★		
Mercury										★	★	★
Moon	★	★		★	★	★	★	★	★	★	★	★
Sun										★		

Solar noon declination to nearest degree: 18°S to 11°S
Geographical latitude: 43° 18′N

Location: Marseille
Event: Roman civil war, with Ahenobarbus opposing Julius Caesar from Marseille

FUTURE EVENT

2032 Civil war involving a "new Ahenobarbus" sweeps southern France and Italy.

&II.34, V.23, V.45, VI.7, VI.58, VI.95

Horograph for February 7th, 2032, to February 19th, 2032

	♒	♑	♊	♋	♌	♐	♎	♍	♎	♐	♏	♓
Pluto											★	
Neptune	★											
Uranus			★									
Saturn			★									
Jupiter										★		
Mars	★											
Venus										★	★	
Mercury											★	★
Moon	★	★	★					★	★	★	★	
Sun										★		

Solar noon declination to nearest degree: 16°S to 12°S
Relative latitude: 2°N to 1°S   **Geographical latitude:** 54°N to 42°N

Possible location: Grenoble to Mediterranean coast
Event: European civil war between powers in southern France and Rome

ORIGINAL EVENT

Horograph for January 6th, 190 B.C. to January 22nd, 190 B.C.

	♈	♉	♊	♋	♌	♍	♎	♏	♐	♑	♒	♓
Pluto									★			
Neptune						★						
Uranus									★			
Saturn								★				
Jupiter							★					
Mars	★											
Venus									★			
Mercury										★		
Moon	★	★				★	★	★	★	★	★	★
Sun									★			

Solar noon declination to nearest degree: 22°S to 20°S
Geographical latitude: 33°N to 37°N

Location: Syria
Event: Lucius Scipio Asiaticus defeats Antiochus the Great and destroys Seleucid Syria

FUTURE EVENT

2034 European forces invade Muslim Middle Eastern heartlands in a "new crusade."

II.22, III.64, X.86

Horograph for January 13th, 2034, to January 16th, 2034

	♈	♉	♊	♋	♌	♍	♎	♏	♐	♑	♒	♓
Pluto										★		
Neptune	★											
Uranus				★								
Saturn				★								
Jupiter												★
Mars	★											
Venus									★			
Mercury										★		
Moon								★	★	★		
Sun									★			

Solar noon declination to nearest degree: 22°S to 21°S
Relative latitude: 0°S to 1°S   **Geographical latitude:** 33°N to 36°N

Possible location: Haifa to Antioch (Antakya)
Event: European forces invade Muslim Middle Eastern heartlands

ORIGINAL EVENT

Horograph for May 23rd, 1097, to June 3rd, 1097

	♈	♉	♊	♋	♌	♍	♎	♏	♐	♑	♒	♓
Pluto	★											
Neptune				★								
Uranus		★										
Saturn							★					
Jupiter	★											★
Mars		★										
Venus				★								
Mercury			★									
Moon								★	★	★	★	★
Sun			★									

Solar noon declination to nearest degree: 21°N to 22°N
Geographical latitude: 40°N to 36°N

Location: Turkey
Event: First crusade moves south from Constantinople to Edessa and Antioch

FUTURE EVENT

2034 European forces invade southern Turkey in their "new crusade."

I.74, VI.21, VI.85

Horograph for May 21st, 2034, to June 12th, 2034

	♈	♉	♊	♋	♌	♍	♎	♏	♐	♑	♒	♓
Pluto										★		
Neptune	★											
Uranus				★								
Saturn												
Jupiter	★											
Mars				★	★							
Venus				★								
Mercury			★									
Moon	★			★	★	★	★	★	★	★	★	★
Sun			★									

Solar noon declination to nearest degree: 20°N to 23°N
Relative latitude: 1°S to 1°N   **Geographical latitude:** 39°N to 37°N

Possible location: Lesbos to Tarsus
Event: European forces invade Middle East (Nostradamus gives May 25th at VI.85)

PART TWO

NOSTRADAMUS AS AUTHOR

*Nostradamus's writings and
language; Nostradamus the
joker, poet, historian, and
mythologist; the omens; printing
and publishing details.*

NOSTRADAMUS'S WRITINGS

NO KNOWN writings by Nostradamus survive from before 1547. The subsequent works covered by this section are (with publication dates) as follows:

1. The *Almanachs* (1551 [?] to 1557)
2. The *Traité des fardemens et confitures* (1555)
3. The *Centuries* (1555, 1557, 1558, 1560, 1568)
4. The *Paraphrase de C. Galen* (1557)
5. The *Lettre . . . à la Royne mere du Roy* (1566)
6. The *Orus Apollo* (unpublished)
7. The *Presages* (1605)
8. The *Sixains* (1605)
9. The "extra" quatrains (1605 onward)

1. THE *ALMANACHS*

Michel de Nostredame, identifying himself for the first time as "Nostradamus," wrote an annual *Almanach* virtually every year of his life (as Chavigny confirms) from about 1550 until his death in 1566. There was even a posthumous 1567 *Almanach*. It was presumably to these and their many imitations that his celebrated younger contemporary Pierre de Ronsard was referring when he penned the lines:

> *Tant d'Almanachs qui d'un langage obscur*
> *Comme Démons annoncent le futur . . .* [1]

Variously described as *Pronostications* and *Presages*, these popular publications consisted basically of a combined religious and secular calendar, plus a lunar ephemeris. They also contained a series of long-term weather forecasts (a matter of increasingly vital importance at the time, as Nostradamus in Context and the Table of Events reveal), as well as predictions for a few tersely described political and military events. In addition, they were embellished (from 1555, at least) with a series of four-line verses summarizing both the year as a whole and each individual month in turn. It was these verses that were collected together under the patronage of Vincent Sève in 1605 and incorporated by him into the *Propheties* under the title of *Presages*.

There had been previous works of this kind. The first calendar known to have been printed in France dates from 1457. A *Grand Kalendrier et Compost des Bergiers, avec leur Astrologie et plusieurs autres choses* was published regularly between 1529 and 1541. A similar work, the so-called *Astrologie des Rustiques*, appeared in 1547 and again in 1554. Rabelais parodied such publications in his *Pantagruéline prognostication* and his *Grande et brave pronostication nouvelle pour 1544*.

To judge by the *Presages* extracted from the 1555 *Almanach* (see especially Nos. 11–14 under The Major Prophecies) the budding seer seems to have been seduced by the continuing advances of the Turks along the Mediterranean coasts (see Table of Events) into assuming that an invasion by them of southern France was imminent, and therefore included predictions to that effect. Since a similar invasion, albeit far in the future, was also emerging at the time from his work on comparative horoscopy (see Astrologer and Mage and The Muslim Invasion of Europe), he was evidently persuaded that those future events could somehow be used to inform the more immediate ones, notwithstanding the fact that the comparative horoscopy barely justified the assumption.

1566 ALMANACH

Page from the 1566 *Almanach*:
predictions for July

---

[1] *Prognostiques sur les miseres de nostre temps* (1584), 55:
So many Almanacs whose words arcane
Announce like Demons what must soon obtain . . .

This tendency to bring anticipated future events forward in time is a common failing among would-be psychics, and it is surprising to find Nostradamus succumbing to it. Possibly it was for the first and last time. In the event, the predicted events simply failed to occur. It may be this abject failure that was in part responsible for the fact that there is no known copy of a 1556 *Almanach*, despite the seer's own claims to have written one. The fact that he spent most of the summer and fall of 1555 visiting the Court in Paris, so leaving less time for such work, may also have had more than a little to do with it.

Possibly what Nostradamus learned from the experience was that, in horoscopy as in meteorology, "one swallow doesn't make a summer." In order to be sure of a future prediction, in other words, it is necessary that it should be backed up by others in such a way as to offer a convincing context. Unsurprisingly, therefore, context turns out to be a vital consideration, too, in any attempt to decipher and interpret Nostradamus's *Propheties* (see Dating and Sequencing the Prophecies).

By the following year, however, normal service had been resumed, and while the seer evidently still found it impossible to rid his mind entirely of the suspicion of a coming invasion (see *Presages* 18–20, for example), at least he now expressed himself rather more cautiously on the topic.

The 1566 *Almanach* seems to have been the first one in which Nostradamus offered an actual prediction – or rather, two of them – for every day of the year. It also covered the period three times over – first as a simple calendar, next with detailed daily predictions, and finally in expanded prose form. As a result, the whole publication amounted (in the Volant and Brotot edition at least) to no fewer than 144 pages in 16° (i.e. demi-octavo).

The predictions for July (see left) are particularly interesting. Nostradamus died on the night of the first of the month. The prediction for that day reads *Estrange transmigration*. Could it be that the seer was, knowingly or otherwise, predicting his own death?

2. THE *TRAITÉ DES FARDEMENS ET CONFITURES*

Although it claims to have been completed on April 1st, 1552, this engaging little handbook of cosmetic prescriptions and health recipes was not finally published by Antoine Volant of Lyon until 1555. We may surmise that Nostradamus had had unspecified difficulties with a different publisher – Brotot, possibly, who is known to have been giving him typographical problems at about this time. Alternatively, it may be that his publisher of first choice, anxious not to be accused of poisoning anybody, had simply felt insecure about setting the fairly specialized manuscript from Nostradamus's increasingly illegible handwriting, and that it took the eventual copying skills of Chavigny to render the book ready for publication. It is even possible that the book was indeed published in 1552, but that no copy of it has survived.

At all events, the book, once published, was an astonishing success and went through numerous subsequent editions (see Early Editions). These went under various titles: sometimes the work was called *Singulieres recettes pour entretenir la santé du corps*, sometimes *Excellent & Moult Utile Opuscule . . .* , sometimes *Le Vray et Parfaict Embellissement de la Face et Conservation du Corps . . .* , sometimes *Bastiment de plusieurs receptes . . .* But always it was divided into two parts (sometimes prefaced with an additional *Proeme*) devoted respectively to cosmetics and conserves.

Part one proudly offers recipes (often with alternatives) for preparing cosmetic essences, aromatic pomades, oil of benjamin, natural balsam, and amber; for oil of nutmeg, scented powder and rose pills for repelling the plague (see text quoted under Nostradamus the Physician); for violet powder and perfumed face-paste for the cheeks; for powder to clean and whiten the blackest teeth; for perfumed water to sprinkle on tooth-cleaning wadges and also to whiten the complexion; for other forms of perfumed water;

TRAITÉ DES FARDEMENS

LE VRAY ET
PARFAICT EMBEL
LISSEMENT DE LA FACE,
& conservation du corps en son
entier: contenant plusieurs Receptes secretes & desi-
rées non encores
veûes.
&
LA SECONDE
PARTIE, CONTENANT
LA FAÇON ET MANIERE
de faire toutes confitures liquides,
tant en sucre, miel, qu'en
vin cuit.

Ensemble deux façons pour faire le syrop rosat laxatif, & pour
faire le sucre candi, penites & tourrons d'Helpaigne.

Par M. Michael Nostradamus.

Title page of Plantin's 1557 edition of the *Traité des fardemens*

for muscat soap to whiten the hands; for making clear borax crystals; for distilled water and benzoin skin lotion; for bleaching the hair a golden color, as also the beard; for tonics and restoratives (including the one that the author once prepared for the Bishop-elect of Carcassonne – see Nostradamus's Life Story); for blackening the whitest hair; for black soap to darken the beard; for black, nonwashable oils to darken hair and beard alike; for preparing a cosmetic mother-of-pearl to whiten and rejuvenate the skin; and for permanently removing freckles.

Modern readers, however, might well gulp at the unashamed use of such substances as mercury in several of these preparations.

Part two, similarly, just as proudly offers recipes for preserving the skins or flesh of lemons and gourds; for making candied orange-peel; for preserving oranges and nuts (with or without honey or sugar); for making brandy; for preserving lettuces and heart-cherries; for making heart-cherry jelly; for making green ginger marmalade; for preserving ginger juice in the form of a powder to make a tonic wine; for preserving the root of *hiringus*, which is claimed to be just as good as green ginger for the above; for conserving half-ripe almonds; for making a quince jelly fit for a king (the cheap *and* the expensive methods); for crystallizing the same; for conserving whole limes and oranges while they are still small and green; for preserving quartered quinces with and without brandy, both for medicinal purposes and simply for eating, as well as for making sauces; for making quince sweetmeats; for conserving the rind of alkanet or borage-root to use as a general tonic; for preserving pears; for making sugar candy; for crystallizing pine nuts in sugar; for making marzipan tarts and sugar sticks; and finally two recipes for making laxative rose syrup (both methods originally gleaned from Vigerchio in Savona – see Nostradamus's Life Story).

Throughout, the instructions are practical and very friendly, while wholefood enthusiasts will be impressed by the honest-to-goodness, down-to-earth ingredients. None of the familiar "Take a pound of sugar' here: instead, it is a case of "Take some sugar cane . . . "

3. THE *CENTURIES*
(see full text under The Major Prophecies)

This was the title of Nostradamus's main collection of prophecies. The French word refers not to hundreds of years, but to hundreds of verses, of which there were eventually to be ten, so making one thousand quatrains in all. The seer claims in the preface to his *Propheties* (see *Préface à César*) that they are to cover the entire future history of the world until the year 3797. However, because of the opposition that they are likely to arouse, particularly among the religious, he admits to having deliberately written them *par obstruses et complexes sentences* and under the cover of a *figure nubileuse*.[2] At the same time he confesses in his dedication to the King (see *Lettre à Henri II*) that they are *tellement scabreux, que l'on n'y sçauroit donner voye ny moins aucuns interpreter*.[3]

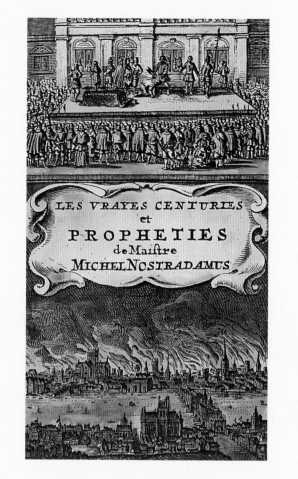

Title page of a 1668 edition of the *Centuries* published in Amsterdam

Certainly the whole work positively bristles with Latin and Greek words (VI.100 being entirely in Latin of a sort), as well as occasionally with words from Provençal (IV.26 and IV.44 are written entirely in the dialect). In addition, the syntax, too, is heavily influenced by Latin – and notably, perhaps, by that of Virgil – with participial phrases (particularly the so-called ablative absolute, see p.99) very much in evidence, and the word-order freely jumbled to fit the demands of rhyme, rhythm, and general obscurity, almost as though the words still retained the word endings that made this reasonable in Latin. None of this is helped, either, by the seer's occasional resort to anagrams (sometimes signaled by capital letters) and his much more frequent resort to abbreviations – especially when he is running out of space in the

2 "cloudy form."

3 "so difficult that there is no way of making sense of them or even of interpreting them."

CENTURIES

> **PROPHETIES**
> DE
> **M. NOSTRADAMVS**
> CENTVRIE PREMIERE.
>
> I
> Estant afsis de nuict fecret eftude,
> Seul repofé fus la felle d'ærain:
> Flambe exigue fortant de folitude,
> Faict profperer qui n'eft à croire vain.
>
> I I
> La verge en main mife au millieu de
> branches,
> De l'onde il moulle & le limbe & le pied:
> Vn peur & voix tremiffent par les mâche
> Splendeur diuine Le diuin pres s'afsied.
>
> I I I
> Quant la lictiere du tourbillon verfée,
> Et feront faces de leurs mâteaux couuers:
> La republique par gens noueaux vexée,
> Lors blancs & roges iugeront à l'enuers.
>
> B 2

**Compare the title page of this 1557 edition
with the much more sophisticated setting
of the original 1555 edition (see p.35)**

last line of a verse. The common sixteenth-century practice of dispensing with subject-pronouns is freely followed, while the future tense is commonly signaled by a plain infinitive – though never, as some commentators would have it, by a past participle (see Nostradamus's Language).

From the structural point of view, the entire work is designedly (though not always entirely successfully) written in decasyllabic quatrains – i.e. the equivalent of English pentameters – having (except in two instances, VI.96 and VII.17) the rhyme-scheme *abab* (see Nostradamus the Poet). The verses are not normally consecutive, but rather in jumbled order – a fact that has led some commentators to propose the existence of some kind of underlying key. The only real sign of one, however, seems to lie in the fact that, unusually, the very first two verses do seem to go together. Conceivably this suggests that other verses, too, come in pairs, if only one can find them. (This might square, too, with Nostradamus's frequent repetition of a word in both halves of a

verse, rather after the semantic model of the Hebrew psalms.) Certainly there is some evidence for such a pairing convention (compare, for example, I.23 and I.38, I.28 and I.71, I.43 and IX.32, I.45 and III.40, I.69 and VIII.16, III:4 and III.5, III:23 and III.24, VI.74 and VIII.15). In this way, some kind of sequence could conceivably be reestablished, especially if shared words, phrases, place names, and time references are also used to help group the various verses. Certain commentators – notably Ruir, Fontbrune, and Lemesurier – have even attempted this (see Dating and Sequencing the Prophecies).

The first of many editions of the *Centuries* was completed on May 4th, 1555, by Macé Bonhomme of Lyon and published as *Les Propheties de M. Michel Nostradamus* (see facsimile of title page under Nostradamus's Life Story). A parallel edition seems to have been produced at the same time by Pierre Roux of Avignon. The former contained only the first three *Centuries*, plus the first fifty-three verses of the fourth. This was seemingly because the full 400 verses would have resulted in a book of 106 pages, ten more than the ideal 96, or 6 x 16 (see Book Printing and Publishing). Four further pages had to be allowed for the temporary paper covers that would have to protect the unbound book until subsequent installments could be published, and so the text had to be printed on 92 pages only.

The second edition, published by Antoine du Rosne of Lyon, appeared in September 1557, this time containing the first six *Centuries* (the last of them minus its last verse), plus the first forty verses of the seventh. Once again the exigencies of printing may have been responsible for the seemingly odd number of verses. From the compositor's point of view it was unfortunately very uneven – indeed, something of a mess, being additionally full of errors, omissions, and eccentric punctuation.

In the dedication to King Henri II (dated June 27th, 1558) that accompanies the final version of the book published by Benoist Rigaud of Lyon in 1568, two years after the seer's death, Nostradamus claims to have completed the full thousand verses – and certainly the last quatrain of the sixth *Century* is now in place, albeit in Dog Latin. Yet all but the first two of the missing quatrains of the seventh *Century* are still missing, and have remained so ever since. This could well argue for some kind of rights dispute between du Rosne and Rigaud, with the former refusing to hand over the text of the missing verses and Nostradamus unable to find his original manuscript. No doubt he was also fearful of asking Queen Catherine de Médicis to return the complete copy that he had undoubtedly already sent her – and which presumably remained in exclusive royal possession for some years afterward (see Early Editions).

Often erroneously described as though they were the sum total of Nostradamus's prophecies, the *Centuries* have never been out of print since his death, though succeeding editions have tended increasingly to corrupt the original text, as well as adding a number of "extra" quatrains (see The Major Prophecies). Clearly they represent a quite astonishing prophetic opus, arguing extraordinary persistence and dedication on the part of their author – which in turn argues that he took his prophetic work very seriously indeed.

4. THE *PARAPHRASE DE C. GALEN, SUS L'EXHORTATION DE MENODOTE, AUX ESTUDES DES BONNES ARTZ, MESMEMENT MEDECINE*

This little book of only sixty-nine pages, first published by Antoine du Rosne of Lyon in 1557, claims to be a French translation of a Latin translation of Galen's original Greek text – though Nostradamus also claims to have referred directly to the Greek itself. Prefaced by a verse eulogy to Galen (quoted under Nostradamus the Physician) and a double dedication to the author's friends the Baron de la Garde (in prose, dated February 17th, 1557) and the Commandeur de Beynes (in verse, castigating bad translators), it takes the form of an extremely free French version of Galen's paraphrase of the Alexandrian Empiricist physician Menodotus's invitation to the human arts, as applied particularly to medicine.

After assuring the reader that he has taken the trouble to confirm his version with a variety of distinguished scholars, Nostradamus presses on with his "translation" (which is actually padded out with his own *ad lib* comments). Basically, the theme is that man is superior to the animals by virtue of his arts and sciences, which in turn derive from his language and thus from his use of reason. It thus becomes a human duty not to be guided by mere brute force and chance, but to cultivate those higher faculties.

Nostradamus at his writing desk

But why should Nostradamus have embarked on "translating" a text that was so obviously obscure and so apparently irrelevant to his purposes as a prophet, especially when Erasmus had already published a Latin version that was much more elegant and faithful to the Greek original? And why, in particular, should he have so obviously skewed its title to try to make it refer to medicine in particular, thanks to nothing more than Menodotus's known medical connections?

Clearly, there has to be some kind of ulterior motive here, presumably connected with Nostradamus's desire to assert that Galen had not been nearly as prescriptive or as limiting as contemporary medical experts were at pains to make him appear (see Nostradamus the Physician). Galen himself, it seems, had gone well beyond the bounds that were currently being set in his name, suggesting that people should not merely accept what was placed in front of them, but should use their own reason to assess it.

Title page of the 1558 edition of the *Paraphrase de C. Galen*

This still does not explain, of course, why Nostradamus should have felt the need to publish the piece as late as 1557, about ten years after he had given up doctoring as a full-time profession – and about ten years, consequently, after he no longer had any need to justify his own medical views in this way. The Belgian anatomy professor Andreas Vesalius, after all, had been publicly demolishing Galen at Padua since as long ago as 1543.

Possibly the seer simply felt that the moment was now ripe in the light of current medical developments. But it is equally possible that this was merely an old manuscript, written during his years as a rebellious young doctor, that he came across one day in his study and decided to publish on the grounds that a little extra cash would not go amiss.

Or perhaps, after all the long years of fighting the medical establishment and its blind dogmas, Nostradamus simply could not resist the temptation to say, "There you are, you see – I was right all along!"

5. THE *LETTRE DE MAISTRE MICHEL NOSTRADAMUS, DE SALON DE CRAUX EN PROVENCE, A LA ROYNE MERE DU ROY*

First published in the year of Nostradamus's death, this letter in fact purports to date from December 21st, 1565. In it the seer ventures to offer his royal patron Queen Catherine de Médicis, newly returned from her two-year progress through the kingdom with the young Charles IX, the official advice for which he has been paid ever since his meeting with them at Arles in November or December the previous year (see Nostradamus's Life Story).

Desirous of discharging his allotted duty of drawing to the Queen's attention any relevant astrological developments, he assures her that, while there are quarrels and disputes ahead, the impending meeting of the Royal Council will result in *une grande paix, & contentement, par tout vostre Royaume.*[4]

The seer concludes by asking the Queen Regent for the young King's latest horoscope and wishing her *vie longue, en santé, et toute constante prosperité, accompagnee de l'entier accomplissement des Royaux desirs de vostre Majesté.*[5]

By and large, both the letter's general attitude and its language seem genuine enough.

6. *ORUS APOLLO, FILS D'OSIRIS, ROI DE AEGIPTE NILIACQUE: DES NOTES HIEROGLYPHIQUES LIVRES DEUX, MIS EN RITHME PAR EPIGRAMMES*

This curious manuscript (No. 2594) in the Bibliothèque Nationale, Paris, was not finally published until the present century. It was seemingly once owned by Jean-Baptiste Colbert, Louis XIV's chief finance minister. Even today, its authorship is disputed. Nevertheless, its language and content are by no means untypical of the prophet.

Evidently based on the Latin-Greek version by Jean Mercier of 1551, the book starts with a verse-dedication to the then Princess of Navarre, Jeanne d'Albret – a fact that would place its composition between that year and 1555, when she became Queen. On the other hand, the fact that the author describes himself as *de Saint-Rémy-en-Provence* would ostensibly require a date prior to 1547. The mismatch is somewhat worrying.

The work comprises two books of verse-epigrams totaling 182 in all and purporting to explain a whole series of Egyptian hieroglyphs. It concludes with ten further verses added by the translator, of which nine are direct versions of Mercier.

Based as they claim to be on a fourth-century Greek version of an Egyptian original, the verse-epigrams seem curiously crude and – like the *Paraphrase* – extremely free in their treatment. Certainly they are less a guide to Egyptian hieroglyphs than to later Greek superstitions and Nostradamian misconceptions about them. Nor is this too surprising, given that the discovery of the interpretationally crucial Rosetta stone still lay more than two centuries in the future.

Nevertheless the work, if genuine, is of considerable relevance to Nostradamus's prophecies, containing as it does a whole range of symbolic creatures and other phenomena, which duly reappear in the *Sixains* particularly (possible references are printed on the next pages in bold type). In the *Orus Apollo*, in short, we may have a key to part of the prophet's symbolism (see Nostradamus's Symbols). In view of this, it seems worthwhile to list overleaf the symbolic attributes attached to each of the main entries.

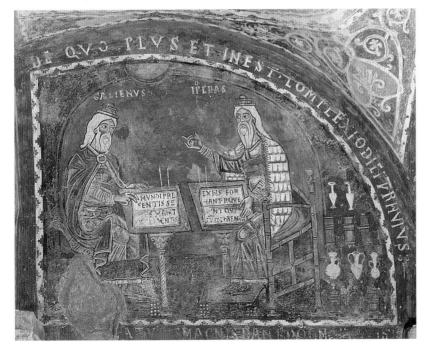

Galen (LEFT), **and Hippocrates** (RIGHT), shown seated in a fresco. Nostradamus respected both eminent physicians and paraphrased one of Galen's works in 1557.

---

4 "great peace and contentment throughout your Kingdom."

5 "long life, in health and ever-continuing prosperity, accompanied by the total fulfillment of Your Majesty's royal desires."

THE *ORUS APOLLO*: SELECTED ALPHABETICAL LIST OF SYMBOLS

ANCIENT BOOKS AND PRAYERS: antiquity

ANIMAL: man concealing his dishonor

ANT: attention/home-lover

ARCHER: upheaval

ASS'S HEAD: man who has never traveled

BAT: steady living / weak man always on the run

BEAR, tethered: congenital deformity

BEAVER: masochist or self-harmer

BEE: law-abiding people

BLIND BREAM: man having regained strength in the sun

BOAR: pernicious man

BULL TETHERED BY RIGHT KNEE: man of dubious temperance

BULL TIED TO WILD FIG TREE: man punished by last adversity

BULL WITH ERECT PENIS: strong, controlled man

BULL'S EAR: hearing

BUNDLE OF PAPERS: ancient lineage

BURNING CENSER: Egypt

BUSTARD: weak man in flight

CAMEL: slow mover

CATFISH: man vomiting meat

CRANE SOARING: celestial knowledge

CRANE WATCHING: man on guard against enemies

CROCODILE: wantonness, lawlessness, fury, madness, looting, enemy attack

CROCODILE EATING PIG: thief and looter

CROCODILE HAVING LEECHES REMOVED FROM MOUTH BY TROCHILLUS BIRD: king opposed to good and friend of flatterers

CROCODILE SWIMMING IN NILE, ATTACKED BY LEECHES: man eating

CROCODILE WITH DOWNCAST EYES: sunset

CROCODILE WITH STORK'S FEATHER ABOVE: rapacious man

CROCODILE'S EYES: sunrise

CROCODILE'S TAIL: shadows

CROW: man of good age

CROW FLYING WHILE CHICKS FLEDGE: restlessness

CROWS, TWO: man consorting with wife

CROWS, TWO: Mars and Venus, marriage

DEWFALL: knowledge

DOG-FACED BABOON: moon, letters, new moon, anger, swimming, Egyptian priesthood, turning world

DOG-FACED BABOON URINATING TWELVE TIMES: equinoxes

DOG-FOX: son

DOG: scribe, prophet, judge, prince, beautiful smell

DOVE: ingratitude / man without own inner fire

DOVE, BLACK: widow

EAGLE: soul, almighty God, depression, loftiness, excellence, blood, victory, man dead from hunger

EAGLE CARRYING PEBBLE: man at home in his city

EAGLE NESTING IN DESERT: lonely, pitiless king

EAGLE, PREGNANT: man so poor as to alienate children

EAGLE RUBBING BEAK ON ROCK: artificial renewal of appetites

EAGLE SOARING EASTWARD: wind

EAGLES, TWO: Mars and Venus

EEL: hostility to everything

ELEPHANT: strong man, initiator of useful things

ELEPHANT WITH SNORTING PIG: king fleeing mockery

EYE AND TONGUE, INJURED: prayer

FEATHER: fair distribution

FIRE SEPARATED FROM WATER: ignorance

FISH: wicked or hateful man

FISH, DRY: man desiring beautiful things

FLIES: worms

FLUTE: man who has lost and found himself

FLY: immodest, shameless man

FROG (= *RANE*): embryo, wanton or sly man, imperfect man

FROG WITH FEET BACK: immobility

GOAT: canny man

GRASSHOPPER: mystic

GUARD: priest

HALF-SUN, HALF-STAR: engaged woman

HALTER: love

HAND OF MAN (*MAIN*, AS IN *POL MANSOL*?): hard work

HARE WITH OPEN EYES: evident fact

HIPPOPOTAMUS CLAWS: unjust judgment

HIPPOPOTAMUS EMERGING FROM NILE: spring

HOOPOE: gratitude

HORN OF FEMALE BEAST: hurt, vengeance

HORN (RIGHT) OF MALE BEAST: work

HORNED SNAKE: eternity / man oppressed by accusations

HORSE: weak man in flight

HORSE, DEAD BODY OF: wasps

HUMAN FINGER: measurement

HYENA AND LEOPARD SKINS TOGETHER: higher vanquished by lower

HYENA ON LEFT: defeat

HYENA ON RIGHT: victory

HYENA SKIN: fearless confrontation of fate

ISIS: year

LADDER: siege

LEECH: [function – to attack and bleed crocodile's mouth without harming it significantly]

LEOPARD: concealed malice

LION: courage, anger, fury

LION EATING MONKEY: self-cure

LION FLICKING TAIL AT CUBS: uncontrollable anger

LION WITH BURNING TORCHES: man punished with fire

LION WITH THREE PITCHERS: inundation of Nile

LION'S FOREPARTS: strength, power

LION'S HEAD: vigilant or redoubtable man

LIONESS: woman who has given birth only once

LOBSTER: leader in control

MAGPIE: man who has cured himself by respecting oracles

MAN, NAKED, WITH DOG AT FEET: magistrate

MAN PRESSING DOWN ERECT PENIS: temperance

MAN STANDING AND EATING HOURS: horoscope

MAN'S EAR IN SHADE: past or future work

MAN'S FEET IN WATER: fuller or washerman

MAN'S FEET IN WATER: impossibility

MAN'S FEET OF EQUAL SIZE AND PARALLEL: winter

MAN'S MOUTH: hanged man

MARE WITH FOOT ON WOLF: woman who has aborted

MEN'S HEADS, TWO: defense, guardianship

MOLE: blindness

MONKEY, SMALL: unwilling bequest

MOON ON BACK: month

MORAY: commerce with strangers and foreigners

MOTHER-OF-PEARL: life-saving

OCTOPUS: indiscriminate and imperfect digestion

OCTOPUS: indiscriminate consumer of others' wealth

OYSTER: lack of care for self

PALM BRANCH: month

PALM TREE: year

PARROT-FISH: greed

PARTRIDGES, TWO, MALE: buggery, sodomy

PELICAN: madman or one lacking understanding

PHOENIX: daily renewal, old man or flood

PHOENIX RETURNING TO EGYPT: late-returning traveler

POPPY, WHITE OR BLACK: illness

QUARTER FIELD: next year

RAT: death, end

RAT FOLLOWING CROCODILE: weak man needing support of others

SALAMANDER: man burned in fire

SCARAB: man having regained strength in the sun

SCARAB: Vulcan, Minerva (androgynes), only child, father & mother, world, generation

SCORPION: enemy attack

SCREECH OWL: death / man vainly seeking help from his lord

SCRIBE: hieroglyphs

SEVEN LETTERS JOINED BY TWO FINGERS: fate

SHEEP AND STAG: king shunning folly and ignorance

SHELLFISH: sexual intercourse

SKULL AND BONES: firmness, security

SMOKE RISING: fire

SNAKE: mouth

SNAKE EATING TAIL WITH NAME IN MIDDLE: wicked king

SNAKE EATING TAIL: world

SNAKE ON GUARD: protective king

SNAKE, WHOLE: king of kings

SNAKE WITHIN HOUSE: victorious king

SNAKE'S FOREPARTS: king dominating part of world

SPARROW: luxury and libidinousness / man vainly seeking help from his lord

SPINE: innards, convolvulus

STAG: fertile human penis

STAG DIGGING: man fearful of grave

STAG RUTTING: long life

STAG WITH FLAUTIST: man fooled by praise

STAG WITH VIPER: timorous man always fleeing

STAR: God, destiny, fortune's wheel, five

STORK: heart, reason, love of parents

SUN AND MOON: month

SWALLOW: inheritance

SWAN: old musician

SWORDSMAN'S TORSO IN FIELD: sin, perversity

THUNDER: distant voices

TONGUE AND TEETH: taste

TONGUE WITH HAND BELOW: prayer

TUFTED LARK: anticipation of good harvest, illness from eating too many grapes

TURTLE-DOVE: executed man / woman giving milk, man delighting in music and dancing

TWO HERONS HUNTING: man burned up with anger

TWO MAGISTRATES: concord

VIPER: woman who hates her husband, children attempting to harm mother

VULTURE: mother, term/end, clairvoyance, year, mercy, Pallas, Juno

WASP ATTACKING CROCODILE: murder, blood

WEASEL: mannish woman

WICKED BEAST "ORUGE" (BIRD WITH BIG FEET AND LONG, BROAD BEAK): sin

WILD MARJORAM: lack of ants

WOLF OR DOG, OR HARE BEING CHASED BY THEM: aversion, repulsion

WOLF HAVING GNAWED OFF PART OF TAIL IN RAGE: resistance to enemy

WOLF WITH STONE: man living in occult fear

Woodcut of Nostradamus in his study, used on the title page of the 1563 *Almanach*; the same design was used on several different works by Nostradamus

7. THE *PRESAGES*

This collection of prophetic quatrains, first published as such in 1605 by Vincent Seve of Beaucaire (possibly a relation of Nostradamus via his daughter Anne – see Nostradamus's Family Tree), claims to have been taken from original manuscripts presented to him by a nephew of the seer by the name of Henry Nostradamus. Since no such name exists in the archives, it has to be assumed either that Henry was a fiction, or that he was the son of one of the seer's various unrecorded brothers (see Nostradamus's Family Tree). Some credence is nevertheless possibly attached to the claim by the fact that the *Presages* themselves are perfectly genuine. In fact, they could have been abstracted from the published *Almanachs* of 1555 to 1567. Perhaps, indeed, they were.

If so, then it was not the first time that they had been so treated. As early as 1594 and 1596, the seer's secretary and amanuensis Jean-Aimé de Chavigny had published some of them in his *La Premiere Face du Janus François* and his *Commentaires du Sr. de Chavigny Beaunois sur les Centuries et Prognostications de feu M. Michel de Nostradamus*, at the same time starting the vogue for interpreting selected lines out of their original context (see opposite).

The verses, after all, had originally been attached to particular years and months within the *Almanachs*, where they had served as summaries of the events predicted in the prose text that followed. These had included such things as weather, disease, and events, both political and military. Usually there had been one summary-*presage* for the year as a whole, followed by one for each month (Chavigny, typically, often suggests that various lines really apply to events *the following year*). By rights, therefore, the collection ought to have contained some (13 + [13x12]), or 169 verses. In fact, various months' quatrains were omitted – possibly as being too specific or too uninteresting – so making a total of only 141.

The verses are for the most part in exactly the same poetic style as the *Centuries* – dense, complex, often telegrammatic, and in the familiar decasyllables, or pentameters, arranged in the customary rhyme-scheme *abab* – except that the usual heavy overlay of classical vocabulary is much lightened. From 1566, however (the year of the seer's death), there is a sudden change. The familiar decasyllables are replaced by twelve-syllable lines, or alexandrines. This has the effect of lightening the style even further, since the prophet now has more space in which to express himself. True, the tendency to telegrammese persists, but at the same time these verses do offer something of a stylistic bridge between the obtuseness of the *Centuries* and the much more limpid and expansive style of the *Sixains* (see The Major Prophecies).

The verses for 1567 show yet other changes. The regular alexandrines for 1566 are now replaced by an irregular mixture of ten- and twelve-syllable lines, plus a change of rhyme-scheme to *aabb* in the last *Presage*. Whether these changes have any bearing on Nostradamus's currently declining health is unknown. Certainly the self-same last verse of the *Presage* – originally for November 1567, but nevertheless written before his death in July 1566 – appears, as Chavigny notes, to predict that very event (see translation in Nostradamus's Life Story).

If, however, it is permissible to apply to July 1566 a verse that ostensibly refers to a date about sixteen months later, then presumably the others can be regarded as similarly "transferable" – and not merely to events long past, but to events in the future, too. So, at least, it seems to have started to be assumed. This deduction could possibly be seen as finding further justification in the fact that the Muslim invasion evidently predicted by the *Presages* for 1555 simply failed to occur – and so must presumably refer to some other occasion entirely, quite possibly lying some centuries in the future. As, indeed, the astrology tends to confirm (see Astrologer and Mage).

It was in response to some such conviction, clearly, that Seve took it upon himself to publish the whole collection of *Presages*. Otherwise he would merely have been resurrecting old history. And if Chavigny likewise shared Seve's "flexible" view, then it is at least possible that he had gleaned it in the first place from his master himself.

In which case, it might be asked, who are we to argue?

Henri II as depicted in the 1558 edition of the *Propheties* in which Nostradamus included a dedicatory letter to the king

8. THE *SIXAINS*

The *Sixains* consist of fifty-eight verses of six lines each, presented in a mixture of octosyllables (tetrameters) and decasyllables (pentameters). They have a variety of rhyme-schemes, of which the favorite is *aabccb*. At least fifteen of them quote actual dates, virtually all in the six(teen) hundreds, and so – having failed to come true at the time – beg to be referred to Nostradamus's "liturgical count," as originally broached in *Centuries* VI.54 and VIII.71 (see Dating and Sequencing the Prophecies).

Like the *Presages*, the *Sixains* were first published in Seve's 1605 edition of the *Propheties*. This time there is not even any claimed genealogical link. Seve simply declares in his dedicatory epistle to the then King Henri IV that he has "verified and checked" them. This lack of claimed independent authentication, plus their evident dissimilarity of format and possibly style, has led numerous commentators to deduce that they are in fact forgeries. Various facts argue against this conclusion, however:

1. A forger will normally do his utmost to emulate the style and format of whatever or whomever he is attempting to counterfeit. *It is precisely the criticism of most commentators, however, that the style and format are nothing like Nostradamus's.* Curiously, therefore, the contention in fact tends to argue for the verses' authenticity. The only "forger" likely to have had sufficient confidence to alter the style and format completely would have been Nostradamus himself.

2. The *Sixains* are fifty-eight in number but do not claim (as other alleged forgeries sometimes do) to be the fifty-eight long-lost verses of the seventh *Century* (see Nostradamus's Life Story and under The Centuries above). Nor, indeed – in view of their obvious incompatibility – could they be. And yet fifty-eight is precisely the number of verses that the seer would have added, had he been endeavoring in his old age to restore the full thousand in a form and style of his own choosing.

3. Even though the *Sixains* introduce a cast of symbolic characters that is for the most part missing from the *Centuries*, their themes mesh in extraordinarily well with those of the earlier work, and their respective dates largely coincide too, insofar as they are quoted at all and are amenable to decoding (see Dating and Sequencing the Prophecies).

CHAVIGNY'S *COMMENTAIRES*

Extract from Chavigny's *Commentaires*, interpreting selected verse-*Presages*

4. Despite the admitted (and very obvious) change of format, the style of the *Sixains* is in fact scarcely any more incompatible with Nostradamus's earlier style than are the *Presages* for 1566 with those for 1565 – and certainly there is no reason why they should not all have been written by the same author at different stages of his life.

5. Finally, the *Sixains*, forged or not, were still written by 1605 at the latest. Whoever their author may have been, consequently, they are indubitably genuine prophecies from about the same period. The execrated Michel Nostradamus le Jeune apart, therefore (see Nostradamus's Family Tree), it is difficult to see who else *could* have written them, in the light of their evident quality and the consistency of their themes with those of the earlier Nostradamian prophecies.

9. THE "EXTRA" QUATRAINS

Seve's 1605 edition of the *Propheties* additionally contained twenty-five supplementary quatrains assigned (apparently at random) to *Centuries* VI and VIII, as well as to two fragmentary "new" *Centuries* numbered XI and XII (two more, VII.43 and VII.44, were added subsequently). In some cases they bear the same numbers as already-existing verses, and so nowadays usually have an *a* appended. They are quoted at the end of the section entitled The Major Prophecies.

The fact that these "extras" appear to be distributed more or less at random, rather than all packed into the semivacant *Century* VII, suggests no attempt at deliberate forgery. Indeed, except for the very much substandard VII.43a, virtually all of them could have been written by the seer himself on stylistic and thematic grounds alone. Certainly Chavigny assumed that those in *Centuries* XI and XII were.

There are, however, some infelicities of rhyme and scansion in the "extra" quatrains. VII.44, for example, uncharacteristically has alternate lines of eight and ten syllables, while XII.69 is incomplete. Most of XII.5, for its part, reads more like an alliterative tongue-twister than a serious verse.

These facts, then, could suggest the intriguing possibility not that they are forgeries, but that most of them at least are early drafts of verses discarded by the seer. In due course, conceivably, they were found scattered among his papers after his death and thereafter incorporated willy-nilly by Seve into the 1605 edition without a thought for their quality or for the prophet's likely wishes on the matter.

Epilogue: questions of authenticity

In view of widely expressed doubts regarding the origins of the *Sixains*, and especially of the "extra" quatrains, it would, of course, be useful to have at our disposal some objective test of authenticity other than mere subjective impressions and arguments after the fact. As it happens, there is such a test.

Computer analysis of Nostradamus's vocabulary (see Nostradamus's Language) throws up certain special characteristics that mark him out from other authors. Like most of us he had his own favorite words and tended to use them more frequently than other people. In this connection it is interesting to compare the relative frequency with which he uses these favorite words in (a) the *Centuries* and *Presages* (which are indubitably genuine), (b) the *Sixains* (regarding which there is more doubt), and (c) the "extra" quatrains (which are almost universally regarded as fakes). A table of the most frequently used words in the *Propheties* (based on the second and subsequent editions, and ignoring small particles such as *et* and *il*) is given opposite. In each case the first figure quoted refers to the total number of uses of each word, while the second (in brackets) is the analytically more useful notional number of uses per hundred verses. Underlined words are common to at least two of the columns. The cutoff point is purely arbitrary.

**Waxwork of
Nostradamus at work
in his study at Salon**

COMPARATIVE WORD COUNTS

Centuries and *Presages*	*Sixains*	'*Extra*' quatrains
grand 446 (41.18)	grand 36 (62.1)	grand 8 (29.6)
mort 172 (15.88)	cens 24 (41.4)	deux 6 (22.2)
deux 131 (12.1)	apres 18 (31.03)	bien 4 (14.8)
viendra 131 (12.1)	peu 17 (29.3)	fort 4 (14.8)
roy 130 (12)	bien 13 (22.41)	fureur 4
terre 122 (11.26)	feu 13 (22.41)	gens 4
sang 117 (10.8)	temps 12 (20.69)	puis 4 (14.8)
feu 100 (9.23)	deux 10 (17.24)	viendront 4
mer 89 (8.2)	Mais 10	entre 3 (11.11)
apres 88 (8.13)	terre 10 (17.24)	farouche 3
Grande 83 (7.66)	verra 10	grands 3 (11.11)
regne 82 (7.57)	dame 9 (15.52)	guerre 3 (11.11)
cité 81 (7.48)	fin 9	mais 3
temps 81 (7.48)	vie 9	mal 3 (11.11)
bien 80 (7.39)	coup 8	paix 3
chef 78 (7.2)	fer 8	plusieurs 3
fort 69 (6.37)	sans 8 (13.79)	roy 3 (11.11)
mis 69 (6.37)	ans 7 (12.07)	sans 3 (11.11)
ciel 65 (6)	cinq 7	vienne 3
dedans 62 (5.72)	encor 7	attente 2 (7.41)
grands 60 (5.54)	France 7 (12.07)	beaucoup 2
peu 59 (5.45)	mort 7 (12.07)	chaud 2
trois 58 (5.36)	sangsue 7	contre 2 (7.41)
puis 56 (5.17)	pays 6 (10.34)	coup 2
Sept 56 (5.17)	plusieurs 6	courir 2
mal 55 (5.08)	Prince 6	dedans 2 (7.41)
Mars 53 (4.89)	eau 5 (8.62)	feu 2 (7.41)
sans 52 (4.8)	franc 5	foy 2
guerre 50 (4.62)	grands 5 (8.62)	France 2 (7.41)
lieu 50 (4.62)	guerre 5 (8.62)	grande 2 (7.41)
peste 48 (4.43)	loup 5	Haine 2
contre 46 (4.25)	luy 5 (8.62)	helas 2
peuple 46 (4.25)	mettra 5	las 2
tiendra 46 (4.25)	neuf 5	mis 2 (7.41)
hors 44 (4.06)	nouvelle 5	mort 2 (7.41)
classe 43 (3.97)	Pourvoyeur 5	nuict 2
luy 43 (3.97)	puissant 5	pied 2
tant 43 (3.97)	avec 4 (6.9)	portant 2
France 41 (3.79)	celuy 4	prince 2

The overall impression, it has to be said, is that all three sets of writings may indeed be by the same author – thanks especially to the extraordinary preponderance of the word *grand* in its various forms in all three columns. On the other hand, the samples are of very unequal size, with the fifty-eight *Sixains* and the paltry twenty-seven "extra" verses no match for the 1,083 *Centuries* and *Presages* – and of course any truly conclusive analysis would also need to conduct similar counts of the vocabulary of likely contenders.

Nevertheless, no author springs to mind who uses the word *grand* with such extraordinary abandon. This characteristic, in fact, seems well-nigh obsessive. This fact alone, therefore, suggests that Nostradamus's authorship of *all three* collections of verses is at least worth adopting as a working hypothesis.

NOSTRADAMUS'S LANGUAGE

NOSTRADAMUS'S language is nowhere near as crude or primitive as is often suggested by frustrated, linguistically ill-qualified commentators (especially non-French ones). Garencières, after all, goes so far as to reveal (1672) that the *Propheties* were actually being used in France *as a standard classroom reader* as late as his own boyhood (roughly 1616).

Clearly this would not have been the case had Nostradamus's verse been either illiterate or indecipherable. What possibly attracted the seventeenth-century pedagogues, indeed, was the fact that it was *highly* literate, and decipherable by anyone who was linguistically in the know. That "know," however, involved a good command not only of classical vocabulary but of classical syntax in particular. Hence the attraction of the texts to the schoolmen. Not only did the former seer's book encourage pupils to broaden their vocabularies with words of classical origin, but it helped to classicize their French grammar, too – as current custom demanded. That fashion, in fact, went back to Nostradamus's own time.

It was in 1549, while Nostradamus was still in Italy (see Nostradamus's Life Story), that Jean Dorat's pupil Joachim du Bellay published the ground-breaking linguistic manifesto entitled *La Deffence et Illustration de la Langue Francoyse.* In this he was encouraged and supported by the poet Ronsard,

> *Qui premier me poussas et me formas la voix*
> *A celebrer l'honneur du langage François.*[6]

Heavily based on earlier Renaissance models, it advocated replacing the conventional use of Latin for many educated literary purposes with a complete reform and reinvigoration of the French language, albeit involving the judicious *borrowing* of Greek and Latin words and constructions, together with the free imitation of great classical writers – to say nothing of the use of allegorical references, dialectal and technical terms, archaisms, and even rank neologisms. In 1556 an influential group of writers known as the *Pléiade* was formed to promulgate these revolutionary principles.

The movement spread far and wide. In England it would be greatly admired by Francis Bacon and would lead to the short-lived movement known as Euphuism, after John Lyly's *Euphues, The Anatomy of Wit* of 1579, which was in due course even to influence Shakespeare. And certainly the bard, in unconscious deference to the *Pléiade's* ideals, would introduce large numbers of classical words into the English language.

In France, too, the movement was to prove enormously influential. Ronsard's whole poetic *œuvre* would itself be redolent of its principles. As he himself would later put it:

> *Adonques pour hausser ma langue maternelle,*
> *Indonté du labeur, je travaillé pour elle,*
> *Je fis des mots nouveaux, je rapellay les vieux*
> *Si bien que son renom je poussay jusqu'aux cieux:*
> *Je fis d'autre façon que n'avoient les antiques,*
> *Vocables composés, et frases poëtiques,*
> *Et mis la poësie en tel ordre qu'apres,*
> *Le François s'egalla aux Romains et aux Grecs.*[7]

But Ronsard's work was not alone in being affected. The *Pléiade* had not only an inner membership but many fringe enthusiasts, too. Given the fact, for example, that Ronsard himself clearly admired Nostradamus (see Criticisms and Reviews), and that Dorat (the group's founding father) was so enthusiastic about him as to send his pupil Chavigny to become his amanuensis and secretary (see Nostradamus's Life Story) – given, too, that Jodelle, another member of the group, seems to have been so publicly critical about him – it is quite certain that Nostradamus and the *Pléiade* were well aware of each other's existence, and perhaps even in close contact.

At which point it starts to appear much less odd that the seer should, like them, have for the most part eschewed Latin and instead written his *Propheties* in French – a French, moreover, that was positively stuffed with terms and constructions drawn straight from the classics. Far from being an isolated, maverick academic, as he is so often portrayed, Nostradamus was in fact merely using the linguistic technology of the moment. The only difference was that in his case he was using it not merely to enrich the French language, but at one and the same time to cloak his meaning from the ignorant and uneducated – a largely accidental side-effect that nevertheless suited his prophetic purposes down to the ground (compare his specific quotation of the highly apposite Matthew 7:6 in section 2 of the *Préface à César*, in The Major Prophecies).

All this is not to say, though, that Nostradamus's verses were "really" in Latin or Greek, as is equally often asserted. That would have been entirely contrary to the founding principles of the *Pléiade.* Despite one verse in Dog Latin (VI.100), two (IV.26 and IV.44) in

---

[6] *Who first did urge me and did school my voice*
To honor French and in it to rejoice.
The words were in fact put into du Bellay's mouth much later by Ronsard himself (*Elegie à Loïs des Masures,* 1560, lines 87-8). Du Bellay had died on January 1st that year at the age of thirty-four.

[7] *So then, my mother-tongue to glorify*
The toil regardless, work for her did I.
I coined new words, recalled to life the old
Till heaven itself her fame could scarcely hold.
In ways that to the ancients never dawned
I cobbled terms, poetic phrases spawned
And poetry so ordered that thenceforth
French would attain to Greek's or Latin's worth.
(Responce aux injures et calomnies, 1563, lines 1019–26)

his native Provençal and his numerous deliberate classical importations, Nostradamus's prophecies were basically written in the French of his day. Yet there was no standard language at the time. Not only did its spoken form vary from north to south, from region to region, even more than it does today (compare Nostradamus in Context) but the written language itself had not yet been standardized. Both authors and printers had their own preferred forms of spelling and punctuation, and even the syntax varied from author to author, depending largely on the degree to which they were trying to imitate the Latin classics.

Nevertheless certain underlying characteristics were widespread, and these duly show up in Nostradamus's writings.

This section covers the following areas:

1. **Grammar and syntax**
2. **Vocabulary**
3. **Spelling**
4. **Punctuation**
5. **Printer's errors**

1. GRAMMAR AND SYNTAX

As simple reference to the writings of Rabelais and especially Ronsard will confirm, sixteenth-century French grammar was not basically very different from seventeenth-century grammar, which even today forms the basis of the written language. Moreover, Nostradamus's verbs in the *Propheties* are mostly confined (for obvious reasons) to the present and future tenses. Consequently we need to concentrate here on only a handful of peculiarities.

Future tense endings

As is well known to students of French, the regular future tense is formed by adding to the infinitive form of the verb the endings of *avoir*. Taking advantage of this fact, Nostradamus often feels free to omit these endings, generally for reasons of space and/or scansion, obviously taking the view that the infinitive form itself is in such cases sufficient to indicate futurity. Indeed, it may be that he is deliberately using the infinitive itself in future mode, much as it can still be used today as a past tense (*Et la bise de souffler*) or as an imperative (*Ne pas marcher sur le gazon*).

As a result, we are faced with a series of apparent infinitives that need to be reinterpreted as futures – *nourir* for *nour(r)ira*, *mourir* for *mourra*, *trembler* for *trembleront*. Needless to say, not *all* infinitives need to be interpreted in this way: sometimes the infinitive is actually what is intended. Moreover, this technique applies *only* to infinitives: *there is absolutely no justification for reading future tenses into other verb forms such as past participles*.

Verbs without pronouns

Under the influence of Latin, sixteenth-century writers such as Rabelais frequently favored an increasingly obsolescent form of French syntax that omitted the subject-pronoun before a verb wherever (as in Latin) the verb ending made the sense obvious anyway. Thus, *fut adverty* ("he was warned or advised"); *partirent* ("they left"). This made for a seemingly crude, but vigorous form of expression that suited the ex-monk's racy narratives admirably. Not surprisingly, then, Nostradamus – one of Rabelais's contemporaries and colleagues – often does the same, though in his case it is often more for reasons of space and/or scansion. Thus, *seras* ("you shall be"); *seront* ("they shall be"). *With each verb, therefore, it is important to establish whether it refers to a previous noun, or instead is intended to stand by itself with its own implied subject.* Apparent mismatches of subject and verb, consequently, may not always be what they seem.

Negatives

In accordance with traditional usage, Nostradamus frequently uses *ne* as a self-contained negative, without the use of the reinforcing *pas* or *point* – just as he also uses *point* without its *ne*.

The so-called ablative absolute

The ablative absolute was a special construction in Latin denoting via a simple participial phrase some already-completed event – as in "Caesar having been advised," or "the prisoners having been freed." By way of imitating Latin, Nostradamus, like his contemporaries, uses such constructions frequently. Among the earliest of his verses to demonstrate this are *Centuries* I.7, I.10, I.25, and I.39.

Relative clauses

Many sixteenth-century writers were obsessed with writing the most complex sentences possible, supposedly after classical models, evidently imagining that the more abstrusely they wrote, the more this would impress their readers. Nostradamus was evidently one such, in his prose writings at least. As a result, a single sentence – as with other writers of the time – can easily go on for two pages

---

GRAMMATICAL ANOMALIES

X

Serpens tranſmis dans la caige de fer,
Ou les enfans ſeptains du roy ſon pris:
Les vieux & pere ſortiront bas de l'enfer
Ains mourir voir de fuict mort & crys.

**Verse I.10 of the 1557 edition
displays various of the
peculiarities listed so far**

**Dr. Theophilus de Garencières,
who translated Nostradamus's
quatrains, and other works**

gender and number sufficiently clearly to indicate which nouns and pronouns they qualified. *It is vital, therefore, for any would-be interpreter to compare all such endings carefully.*

True, the printer occasionally left out the odd letter, while Nostradamus himself sometimes left off a final -*e* or other ending for reasons of scansion or rhyme; but in such cases the fact is generally fairly obvious, especially if the word concerned is a rhyming word and its ending is consequently exposed. *It is never a valid principle of interpretation to assume that Nostradamus was somehow illiterate, and simply mixed singular and plural, masculine and feminine at will.*

A construction particularly dear to Nostradamus is the "inverted possessive," as in "of France the naval victory" (see below). Throughout, it adds a certain stateliness to his verses, especially if read aloud. Good examples of this construction are

du froment le boisseau (II.75),
de la cité le plus grand (III.13),
du Vatican le sang royal (VI.12),
de France la victoire navale (VII.3), and
de Robin la traitreuse entreprinse (Sixain 6).

2. VOCABULARY

Thanks largely to his many classical borrowings (see the introduction to this section), Nostradamus displays a wide vocabulary. At about 8,000 words (including variants), it is equivalent to that of Milton, rather more than that of the Hebrew Old Testament and about half that of Shakespeare (who, as we have noted, would likewise coin large numbers of "new" words of classical origin).

While the bulk of that vocabulary remains familiar to speakers of modern French, a significant proportion of it is peculiar to Old French, and therefore needs to be checked by would-be interpreters in the relevant dictionaries. But the greatest puzzle is set, as ever, by the numerous classical borrowings, which are often Gallicized and so made that much more difficult to look up.

To assist in this process, a comprehensive Nostradamus Dictionary is appended to this volume.

3. SPELLING
Extra letters

Ever since it had developed out of Vulgar Latin, French had been losing the original Latin endings, and a good many of the internal consonants as well. As a result, whole rafts of different words were starting to sound and look the same. This might not be too impor-

and more, its clauses endlessly (if unconvincingly) stitched together with words such as *et, car, qui,* and *que* (compare the two letters reproduced under The Major Prophecies). Such link words appear in his verses as well, if less frequently. *Que*, in particular, needs to be watched out for. It is used as in modern French (sometimes, in accordance with contemporary practice, it stands for *qui*), while on other occasions it means very little at all.

Word order

Sixteenth-century writers such as Rabelais and Nostradamus were much given to inverting their word-order – sometimes, for example, placing the verb (and more especially its participle) at or near the end of its clause, after the classical Latin model. In his verses, Nostradamus took this even further. Taking his cue from the Roman poets, and particularly Virgil, he seems to have felt free to reassemble his words into any order he pleased – whether to make a rhyme, to adjust the number of syllables in a line, or merely to bamboozle the reader. With Virgil, this added to the poetic flavor of the verse and posed few problems. In Latin, after all, all the main words had special endings that showed perfectly clearly which word went with which. In sixteenth-century French, on the other hand, many of the original endings had disappeared. As a result, potential confusion was never far away.

However, verbs did still retain enough of their endings to show which subject they belonged to, while adjectives still showed their tant for ordinary speech, but in areas such as the Law it was of course disastrous, in that it permitted all kinds of confusion. Long before the sixteenth century, consequently, the lawyers' clerks, whose influence on the written language was always considerable, had been trying to set matters right by introducing all kinds of extra letters, mainly borrowed from the presumed original Latin, so as to distinguish one word from another again. Thus, *mes* ("I/you put"), for example, now became *mets*, to relate it to *mettre* (Latin *mittere*) and distinguish it more clearly from *mes* (= "my"). Such useful reforms have largely persisted right down to the present day.

But not all such reforms were quite so useful. Lawyers were paid by the line and, when obliged to reduce costs by writing smaller, countered by using as many words as they could (a tendency that likewise persists, in French as in other languages, right down to the present day). When further curbs were introduced, they simply responded by padding out the spelling as much as possible. And so *animaux* became *animaulx*, for example, while *y* was preferred to *i*, which took up less space. Under the influence of Latin, *savoir* became *sçavoir* or *sçavoir* (supposedly from Latin *scire*), while *diner* became *disner* (modern *dîner*, where the circumflex accent denotes the now "missing" s).

The Latinizing tendency caught on. Extra letters sprouted all over the place, even where not strictly sanctioned by the etymology (compare, for example, the corresponding transformation of English *dout* into *doubt* in order to align it with Latin *dubitare* – a willful scholasticism that has bamboozled schoolchildren ever since). Thus, not merely was *a* ("has" – from Latin *habet*) spelled *ha*, and *uile* respelled *huile* to avoid confusion with the identically printed *vile*, but *un* was often written *ung*, while in his *Orus Apollo* Nostradamus himself (or his copyist) writes *on* as *ont* and *yeux* as *hieulx*.

Eventually it was realized that things were starting to become ridiculous, and during the course of the sixteenth century numerous efforts at resimplification were set in train. At the same time the poet Ronsard and his disciples started a sensible move to distinguish *u* from *v* and *i* from *j* (previously the fashion had been simply to use the one when capital and the other when lower case).

However, none of these reforms was universal. Authors were often quite happy to spell the same word in two or three different ways on the same page. Printers, too, spelled and punctuated largely as they thought fit, often depending on just which letters they had left at the time. And, especially in Nostradamus, many of the various Latin-based additions survived.

There would be little point is trying to catalog them all here: they were not, after all, truly regular features, any more than was any other feature of contemporary spelling. The best that one can do is remain alive to the fact that many words are likely to contain "extra" letters. The word *avenir*, for example, is commonly spelled *advenir*. As ever, the best guide for would-be interpreters is often to say the word aloud, then look up its likely *modern* spelling.

The following typical words from the second edition of the first *Century* all contain such "extra" letters, as well as others that were not "extra" at the time but have since disappeared or been replaced by various accents: *estant* (étant), *faict* (fait), *esleu* (élu), *ieulx* (yeux), *ioinct* (joint), *descouuriront* (découvriront), *sepmaines* (semaines), *repoulsés* (repoussés), *vuidé* (vidé) , *festes* (fêtes), *esloigné* (éloigné), *basty* (bâti), *hault* (haut), *tost* (tôt), *teste* (tête), *infernaulx* (infernaux), *laict* (lait), *prinses* (prises), *neufue* (neuve), and *accompaigné* (accompagné).

Alternative letters

We have already noted the prevalent confusion between *u* and *v*, *i* and *j*. In addition, final *s* was often written *x* or *z*, while *ts* was also rendered as *z* (especially where it corresponded to the Latin ending *-atus* – modern *-é* – at the end of a past participle). The group of letters that we should nowadays write as *ai* was normally written *oi* or *oy* (thus, *estoit* for modern *était*). The letters *f* and *ſ* (initial or medial *s*) are often confused by Nostradamus's later printers, especially du Rosne, with both letters often rendered as *f*, especially when the type for *ſ* ran out. Meanwhile, & is often used to mean not only *et* but almost any other small particle that might be dashed off as a written squiggle, such as *ou* or *de*.

The following spellings are typical of the 1557 edition: *Vn* (un), *couuers* (couverts), *noueaux* (nouveaux), *iugeront* (jugeront), *ſera* (sera), *piedz* (pieds), *loys* (lois), *auoit* (avait), *esclaue* (esclave), *receuz* (reçus), *iours* (jours), *fleues* (fleuves), *viura* (vivra), *deſſoubz* (dessous), *renouuation* (renovation), *ſuaue* (suave), *annichilez* (annihilé), *monnoyes* (monnaies), *eſtainct* (éteint), and *nuictz* (nuits).

Accents

By and large, few of the modern accents had yet come into general use. The apostrophe was only introduced in 1529 (often to replace final *-e*, as in *un'* for *une* etc.) and the acute accent in 1530. In the *Centuries*, written from the 1550s onward, the acute accent is reserved mainly for past participles ending in *-é* (from Latin *-atus*),

---

ADDITIONAL ODDITIES

XCII
Apres le ſiege tenu dixſept ans,
Cinq changeront en tel reuolu terme:
Puis fera l'vn effeu de meſme temps,
Qui des Romains ne fera trop conforme.

Verse V.92 of the 1557 edition displays a variety of further oddities

though Nostradamus sometimes uses the *ez* form instead. Grave accents were used, but only sparingly, in words such as à and *là*. In Nostradamus, the *tilde* (~) is used to indicate a missing *m* or *n* (thus, *ferõt*, *rõger*) – or even some other letter or group of letters – where the printer has left it out in order to cram a particular line onto the page without breaking it. The *cedilla* (,) is used as in modern French. Except for these, his writings are largely accent-free – a fact that makes for a neat text, but can sometimes lead to confusion.

Examples from the second edition of the first *Century* include *chãsons* (chansons), *seigñr* (seigneur), *aurõt* (auront), *nõbre* (nombre), *ſerõt* (seront), *Lõdres* (Londres), *tẽps* (temps), *biẽ* (bien), *blõd* (blond), *chãgemet* (changement), *pl' grand* (plus grand), *quãd* (quand), *grãds* (grands), *vẽtre* (ventre), *hõme* (homme), *tourmẽt* (tourment), *Lyõ* (Lyon), *argẽt* (argent), *lõg* (long), and *pſ̃* (près).

Abbreviations

Abbreviations were by no means uncommon in contemporary printing, but in Nostradamus they are particularly numerous. In his case they are usually just a handy means of cramming more into his brief verses, especially when he is running out of syllables in the last line – as, alas, he all too frequently is. Sometimes, though, it is the printer who has introduced them for reasons of space. For the most part they are applied only to proper names, and particularly to names of places – as, for example, *Gén.* for *Gênes* (Genoa), or *Bru.* for *Bruxelles*. Further examples include *Carcaſ.* (Carcassonne), *Cremo.* (Crémone), *Mãt.* (Mantoue), *Bourd.* (Bordeaux), *Tholo.* (Toulouse), *Bay.* (Bayonne), *Rod.* (Rhodes), *Aſt.* (Asti), *Son.* (Saône), and *Gar.* (Garonne).

4. PUNCTUATION

Our familiar modern punctuation conventions were largely laid down by Aldo Manuzzio, the Venetian printer who in 1497 published Marsilio Ficino's Latin translation of Iamblichus's *De Mysteriis Aegyptiorum* and Psellus's *De Daemonibus*, which Nostradamus may well have studied in Florence's Medici library during his Italian trip of 1548–50 (see Nostradamus's Life Story).

There is some evidence in the surviving manuscript of the *Orus Apollo*, however, that *Nostradamus may simply not have punctuated his original verses at all* (more opportunities for ambiguity!). Certainly such things were very much in the hands of the printers at the time. In the second edition of the *Centuries*, for example, it is fairly evident that a standard format was mechanically applied throughout (except where shortage of space at the end of a line forbade it) – namely, a comma at the end of lines 1 and 3, a colon at the end of line 2, and a full stop or period at the end of line 4. Even as early as verse 2 it is perfectly clear from the sense that this arrangement is linguistically nonsensical. It is all rather reminiscent of the proverbial retired colonel who, when roped in to read the lesson in church, automatically treats every line as though it were a separate sentence: no wonder Nostradamus is so frequently supposed to be illiterate!

In order to recover the original sense, therefore, *Nostradamus's verses may quite often need to be differently divided*. Certainly the punctuation of Bonhomme's first edition is a more sophisticated affair than that of its successors. This apart, it needs only to be pointed out that there are a number of occasions in the 1557 edition where *?* is used instead of *!* Early verses in which the punctuation clearly needs reordering in the second edition (though not in the first) include I.7, I.9, I.28, and I.51.

5. PRINTER'S ERRORS

Misprints are numerous, particularly in the second and subsequent editions. Sometimes they may be due to a simple misreading of the manuscript: certainly there is plenty of evidence of this, with whole groups of letters sometimes being wrongly divided (compare the footnotes appended to The Major Prophecies). On other occasions a letter or spacer seems to have fallen out of its setting-stick: as a result, not only are there occasional blanks, but also many examples of words joined together. Occasionally, too, a word has been omitted completely, as is evident from the scansion (allowing for diphthongs and possible elision of exposed final *e* with a following vowel, each line of the *Centuries* should in theory contain ten syllables). On yet other occasions letters have been transposed, perhaps as a result of having been stored by inexperienced, low-paid apprentices in the wrong compartment, so that the wrong letter entirely was used.

Thus, ∫ is sometimes confused with *l* and *l* with *i* and *t*: *r* is likewise confused with *t*, and both of them with *c*: and ∫ and *f* are, as we have seen, confused throughout the second edition particularly, with *f* preferred when the type for ∫ runs out. As might perhaps be expected in the light of the popular saying about them, *p* is also (understandably) confused with *q*. In addition, doubles are frequently replaced with singles: *nouueaux*, for example, tends to come out as *noueaux*. (The random splitting of a word at the end of a line, or of a verse at the end of a page, is not a misprint, but merely normal sixteenth-century practice.)

In the light of contemporary printers' enormous and rapid turnover, all this is perhaps to some extent excusable: typesetting with movable type had, after all, been invented in Europe only just over a hundred years previously. Nevertheless, it means that modern would-be interpreters need to be constantly on their guard against misprints. This is not, of course, a license for relettering the text at will: but it does mean that where no kind of normal sense emerges from the text it is legitimate to look for possible typographical errors of a kind that is known to occur elsewhere. In the case of most late editions (i.e. those based on the 1605 text or later) this will to a large extent already have been done, and the text amended accordingly. The problem here, though, is that the editor (ancient or modern) may or may not be right. This is, of course, a prime argument for using as early an edition as possible – and the reason why the texts printed in The Major Prophecies do just that.

NOSTRADAMUS THE JOKER

NOSTRADAMUS, it is well known, had a wicked sense of humor (compare, for example, the story of the inscription for the fountain in Salon under Nostradamus's Life Story). Moreover, he lived in an age when word-play was all the rage. Puns and anagrams, especially, were an almost universal obsession. The Elizabethans knew and loved them as "conceits." Even Shakespeare's popular Falstaffian episodes would be positively stuffed with such devices.

But for the French seer it was not merely a question of displaying his sense of humor. As in the case of the classical words and constructions so favored by the *Pléiade*, the contemporary passion for word-play, too, suited his purposes admirably.

He was, after all, presenting himself to the public as a prophet – and prophets had always sought to clothe their predictions in cryptic language in order to veil their true meanings from the ignorant and reveal them only to the wise. So, at least, they claimed. *Cast not your pearls before swine*, Nostradamus might have added – and did (*Préface à César*, section 2) – but then, as it happens, he was by no means the first to do so.

To us today this attitude might seem élitist, but there can be no doubt that Nostradamus shared it. He complained continually about being surrounded in his provincial hometown of Salon by *brutes barbares*, enemies of literature with not a scintilla of true learning between them. As he was to put it in the extraordinary Dog Latin of the incantatory verse printed at VI.100 (not present in the 1557 edition), and punctuated in the by-now familiar way:

Quos legent hosce versus maturè censunto,
Profanum vulgus & inscium ne attrectato:
Omnesq; Astrologi Blenni, Barbari procul sunto,
Qui aliter facit, is ritè, sacer esto.[8]

Certainly the seer was alive to the fact that ignorance was the enemy of his prophetic cause. But then even more so, perhaps, was *semi*-ignorance. The problem was not merely that the uneducated would not be able to understand his verses, but that the *semi*-educated might think that they *could*. Largely ignorant of mythology, history, and even French grammar, they would imagine that, merely because they could read and write, they were entitled to read into his predictions absolutely anything that currently took their fancy, so demonstrating the truth of the old adage that "a little knowledge is a dangerous thing." (One has only to look at the current literature on Nostradamus to appreciate the justness of the prophet's fears.) Well might he, then, make his prophecies as obtuse as possible.

True, this might merely succeed in provoking the Nostradamaniacs even more. Denied predictions of a more obvious kind, they might now be tempted to use his verses simply as one might read tea leaves in a cup. But at least saner commentators would then be able to point out the fact and remind the worried nonreading public that "you can read anything you like into Nostradamus." Indeed, this assertion is all too familiar in our own day.

On the one hand, then, crass credulity on the part of the ignorant, on the other, dismissive rejection on the part of the unknowing. Meanwhile the only people who would stand the slightest chance of finding out what the French seer really did mean would be educated people – scholars, even – who were prepared quietly to analyze his actual words and all their myriad references for what they actually said.

Meanwhile there were other major considerations. A prophet can be wrong. "I am human: I can err, fail, and be deceived," Nostradamus was to write on a later occasion, contradicting what he had earlier claimed in his *Préface à César* (section 12). And so it is all too natural that he should hedge his bets. What better means, then, than to use obscure – indeed, almost impenetrable – language?

He would not be the first. The Delphic oracle, it is said, once assured the almost legendary King Croesus of Lydia ("almost," because nowadays even his proverbial riches are rapidly being cast into the trash can of history, along with much of the rest of classical tradition and mythology) that if he invaded Persia he would destroy a great empire. He did – and promptly destroyed his own. But the oracle, of course, was still seen to be right – just as it would have been had the opposite occurred. And with luck, much the same considerations would apply to Nostradamus, too.

But then there were dangers in being thought right, too. Too much success in this area might hint at Black Magic, which would

Nostradamus, like the Delphic oracle, used obscure language

---

[8] Or, freely translated:
Think on this, reader, sagely as you may,
But shun my verse, you mob profane and shallow.
Star-gazers, snotty Philistines, away!
Let those more reverent my office hallow.

not endear him to the Inquisition. It might even be suggested that, in predicting the events, he had actually helped to cause them – which would not endear him to anybody at all.

By far the best policy, therefore, was to write so obscurely as to make it virtually impossible to prove definitively whether he had been right or wrong in the first place. For this, word-play of every kind would be just as useful as the wholesale importation of classical vocabulary (see Nostradamus's Language). As he himself was to put it in his dedicatory letter to the King (section 2), . . . *la rithme estre autant facile, comme l'intelligence du sens est difficile . . . La plus part des quatrains prophetiques sont tellement scabreux que l'on n'y sçauroit donner voye ny moins aucuns interpreter.*[9]

Perhaps he merely wished to put off his royal patron from any such attempt.

At all events, the result is the verses as we now know them – puns, anagrams, word-plays, and all. These features, therefore, also need to be looked at by anyone hoping to decode and interpret the prophet of Provence.

This section will consider Nostradamus's word-play under the following headings:

1. Anagrams
2. Puns
3. Other forms of word-play

1. ANAGRAMS

The anagram was one of the favorite literary devices of sixteenth-century Europe. It was used for personal concealment, for veiled public criticism, for coded propaganda, and for sheer, unashamed fun. François Rabelais himself published most of his works under the outrageous pseudonym of *ALCOFRIBAS NASIER.* In Nostradamus, puns are used quite freely, especially in the later *Centuries* – though nothing like as often as some of the wilder commentators would like us to believe. (The oft-made suggestion, for example, that *noir* is generally used as an anagram for *roi* seems to have little foundation in fact: the seer, after all, himself uses the undisguised term *roy* constantly.) When he does use them, though, he often draws attention to them in some way.

For a start, most of the words concerned are proper nouns, and therefore already distinguished by a capital letter (the main function of the anagram, in other words, is in such cases to disguise the names of people and places). Second, they generally make no sense at all *as printed and spelt*, and so draw attention to themselves on a semantic level. Third, the word in the text is often so clearly some kind of barbarous neologism as to hit the reader in the eye.

So barbarous are they in some cases, in fact, that Nostradamus himself seems to have feared for the printer's ability to read and reproduce what he had written, and consequently spelled them out for him in capital letters. The printer clearly misunderstood this intention, and promptly *printed* them in capital letters, too. In all

except one case, the capitals were hurriedly removed in the 1557 edition, but stayed put in the 1568 text, which probably went back directly to the original edition (see Nostradamus's Writings). But the result is that, by referring to the 1555 and 1568 editions (see The Major Prophecies) we can have the benefit of this useful pointer.

Not that anagrams are the only thing signaled by Nostradamus's dozen-and-a-half or so capitalized references. They are also used for simple puns and other forms of word-play, as well as occasionally for no apparent reason at all. Nevertheless, they should at least serve to put us on our guard.

Certain characteristics of sixteenth-century anagrams, however, need to be borne in mind. For a start, a repeated letter might be reduced in the final anagram to one, while the odd additional letter might be thrown in as it were for good luck, if it made the resultant word more convincing. Indeed, Nostradamus's anagrams in particular tend to be *sound* anagrams rather than purely literary ones, so that exact transcriptions should not in any case be expected. Finally, *I/Y/J* and *H* seem to have been regarded as interchangeable – just as they were in the contemporary spelling of *yeux/hieulx.* In short, all the features of spelling listed under Nostradamus's Language might reasonably be expected to apply to anagrams, too.

Typical examples from the *Propheties* are *CHYREN* in IV.34 (presumably "Henryc," and thus "Henri"), *NORLARIS* in VIII.60 (probably "Lorraine"), *NERSAF* in VIII.67 (almost certainly "France"), *RAYPOZ* in IX.44 (possibly "pays rose"), and *Angolmois* in X.72 (see Interpreting the Prophecies).

2. PUNS

Even more than visual puzzles, aural ones seem to have fascinated Nostradamus. As noted above, even his anagrams tend to be *sound* anagrams rather than strictly literary ones. What more natural, then, than that he should be particularly drawn to puns and homonyms? Unlike mere anagrams, after all, these generally made sense both in their misleading, "apparent" form and in their true, "cloaked" one.

Contemporary French writers – and lawyers' clerks especially – were already well aware that the loss of their language's former endings and consonants had resulted in an extraordinary capacity for *double entendre*, both in speech and in writing (see Nostradamus's Language). In their case, with the Law's pressing need for clarity, this was something of a curse. But in Nostradamus's, with his equally pressing need for obtuseness, it was of course a positive godsend – especially as the clerks' efforts to put things straight in their documents were to have only the most marginal of influences on the spoken language itself. Even today, as a result, spoken

---

9   Freely: ." . . the rhythm (is) as easy as making out the sense is difficult . . . most of the prophetic quatrains are so demanding that nobody is likely to know how to approach them, let alone interpret any of them."

French remains extraordinarily rich in potentially confusing homonyms, whose true meaning emerges only from the context: compare, for example, *oeufs/eux/euh, deux/d'oeufs/d'eux, on/ont, ou/où/houx, an/ans/en* (= "in")*/en* (= "of it, of them, from it, away".

The field for the punsmith, in short, is as wide open today as it was in Nostradamus's time – so that now, as then, it is often necessary to *say the word aloud* if one is to arrive at the true meaning.

And so it is that the apparently meaningless *cet, main* of II.62 turns out in the end (if one says it often enough) to resolve itself into the much more familiar *sang humain*.

Other puns are to be found at I.2 (*BRANCHES* for *Branchis* – see Astrologer and Mage), VIII.15 (*deux* for *ducs* [from Latin *dux, duces*]), VIII.16 (*Fesulan* – a geographical pun on *Faesulae*, the Roman name for Fiesole, Italy, and its adjectival form *Faesulanum* – for *fessan*), VIII.18 (*Flore* for *Florence*), VIII.46 (*Pol mensolee*, another geographical pun, this time on *(St.-)Paul-de-Mausole* [see Nostradamus's Life Story] as well as for *Paul Main-soleil*, an apparent reference to St. Malachy's famous papal predictions [q.v.]).

3. OTHER FORMS OF WORD-PLAY
Classical homonyms

As well as puns, geographical and otherwise, Nostradamus's sense of linguistic fun and *double entendre* extended to more than just the French language. If he could find "doubles" of French words in Greek and Latin he was more than willing to use them in their Greek or Latin sense, while at the same time he was perfectly prepared to muddy the water by hinting at the possibility that they might equally well be mere versions of some other *French* word.

A classic case in point is the often-used word *pont*. Meaning "bridge" in French, its Greek homonym *pontos* means "sea" (as in "Hellespont," for example) – and Nostradamus in fact uses it far more frequently in this latter sense, as is clear from the contexts in which it is used. Some commentators even suggest – not always very convincingly, it has to be said – that he also uses it as an abbreviation for Latin *Pontifex*, meaning first "bridge-builder," then

---

PREDICTION OF HENRI II'S DEATH

35 Le lyon ieune le vieux furmontera,
En champ bellique par singulier duelle,
Dans caige d'or les yeux luy creuera:
Deux claffes vne, puis mourir, mort cruelle.

Stanza I.35, as printed in the original 1555 edition

"Emperor" and finally "Pope" (whence, of course, the word "Pontiff"). Once again, however, whether or not this is so in any given case can only be determined from the context (see Dating and Sequencing the Prophecies).

Thus, *Negrepont* (II.3 – from Latin *niger* via French *negre*, plus Greek *pontos*) clearly means the same as *marnegro* in V.27 – namely "Black Sea" – while *pont de Laigne* in X.48, which looks as though it ought to mean "wooden (from Latin *legna*) bridge," may in fact go back to Greek *pontos* plus *lagyna* (Latin *lagena*), meaning "narrow-necked bottle." The "bottle-necked sea," then – the reference, seen in context, in fact appears to be to the Strait of Gibraltar.

Classe, similarly, has a Latin homonym – or rather antecedent – in *classis*, meaning a body of men, and more particularly a fleet or army. From the various contexts, it is clear that Nostradamus uses it mostly in the sense of "fleet." However, in the stanza with which Nostradamus first made his name as a national prophet by apparently predicting the death in a tournament of King Henri II of France (I.35, reprinted left), it is clear – as the context once again seems to reveal – that the word *classes* means neither "fleets" nor "armies," let alone "classes." Consequently most commentators hurriedly resort instead to the Greek *klasis*, meaning "breakage" or "fracture" (compare English "icono*clasm*"). This does not mean "wound," as a good many of them would have us believe – *klasis* is word that refers to the breakage of something hard and even brittle, not soft and fleshy – but it still reflects quite faithfully what happened to the fatal lance in question. In fact, though, such abstruseness is quite unnecessary: the familiar Latin word *originally* meant "calling," "call-up" or "summons," so that the verse in fact describes exactly what happened in the event – namely a double challenge, followed by yet another (see translation p.38)

Misleading word-divisions

But Nostradamus was not merely devious – he was positively mischievous at times. Given that his object was to some extent to deceive, this may nevertheless be regarded as legitimate. It gave him a golden opportunity, after all, to indulge his biting sense of humor with a feeling of perfect justification.

This shows up particularly in his apparently deliberate splitting of some words and joining together of others. On one or two occasions, for example, he spells the word *dame* as *d'ame* (IV.24, VIII.70), with the result that the reader is left puzzling over what the phrase "of soul' can possibly have to do with it. On the other hand, the notorious *Roy d'effrayeur* of X.72 originally started out in life as a perfectly innocuous *Roy deffrayeur*, or "defraying leader" (compare original text under Interpreting the Prophecies) – so that in this case it is not Nostradamus who is guilty of all the resulting alarm and despondency.

But Nostradamus reserves what is perhaps his most diabolical pieces of wool-pulling for the simple word *deux*. Not only does the text on one occasion give this instead of *d'eux* (VIII.69) but the reverse can happen, too: *d'eux* appears as *deux* (IV.57). True, the printer may be to blame here. But he is emphatically not to blame for what follows. For the seer's next piece of trickery is to write *deux* for Latin *dux/duces*, meaning "leader." This happens in I.6, IX.56, X.54 and *Presages* 115 and 120, for example, as well as in up to fifteen other verses. As a result, we are left wondering what the formidable *hommasse*, or mannish woman, of VIII.15 (whom some have associated with Margaret Thatcher) could possibly be doing hounding *les deux ecly(p)ses*. Here it is of course the word *les* that gives the game away, since eclipses do not generally come in twos. Make the necessary transpositions, however, and it soon becomes clear that what the seer is really talking about is "failed (from Greek *ekleipsis*, "failure") leaders."

Note, meanwhile, the preconditions for such an approach. Faced with some obvious piece of nonsense, we effectively come up against an interpretational brick wall. *It is this that should then warn us to look out for some typical piece of Nostradamian word-play.*

The same applies at the larger, accretional level, too. Faced with a baffling line such as *Sur le canon du respiral estaige* in II.75, we are left floundering. It is only when we reassemble the line into *Sur le canon dur et spiral estaige* that it starts to make some kind of sense.

Alternative meanings hidden within the sound

True, there are some occasions where even the interpretational brick wall is missing, and we are merely faced – provided that we are clever enough to spot the fact – with two equally possible meanings on the basis of the sound alone. A modern example of this might be the designation that Citroën long ago gave to their classic "space-age" car, the DS. On the face of it, this seems a perfectly innocent abbreviation. Only when French people talk about it aloud does it start to become obvious that the word is really *déesse* ("goddess").

Nostradamus, too, plays tricks of this kind. Sometimes he does so slyly, giving no indication of what he is up to. It is necessary to read the verse aloud in order to realize what he is about. *Consequently this is well worth recommending as a standard interpretational procedure.*

Sometimes, though, he goes even further and reveals quite openly that he is setting us what amounts to a cryptic crossword clue. *Sixain* 42, for example, runs

La grand'Cité où est le premier homme,
Bien amplement la ville je vous nomme,
Tout en alarme, & le soldat és champs
Par fer & eaue, grandement affligee,
Et à la fin, des François soulagee,
Mais re sera des six cens & dix ans.

Here it is clear that Nostradamus is setting us some kind of riddle. In line 2 he maintains that he has just named perfectly clearly the city to which he is referring. The name must therefore

lie concealed somewhere within the first line. Once again, this needs to be read aloud. Moreover, there is a further clue: for Nostradamus, *le premier homme* almost certainly has to mean the Pope. So what is the name of the city? Divide the line into its constituent syllables (in French, a syllable is held to begin with a consonant unless none is available), and the answer (Rome) should become clear.[10]

Code-names

Except for Franco (IX.16) and possibly Pasteur (I.25 – though this may merely be a reference to some unidentified shepherd or bishop) – Nostradamus does not normally name his characters outright. True, he does seem to name Napoleon at VIII.1, but only in anagram form (see section 1 above): *PAU, NAY, LORON* decodes as *Napaulon Roy*. De Gaulle is thought by some to be named, and his three terms of office as France's "standard bearer" predicted, at IX.33. And then there is also the great future ruler of Europe whom the seer names and capitalizes as *CHYREN* (II.79, IV.34), while at the same time revealing at X.27 and at *Sixain* 38 that he is to be the fifth of the name: decoding the anagram and comparing it with French history, it is clear that this has to be *Henryc(us)*, the future Henri V of France so long awaited by French royalists. Though, of course, the accession to power of President Jacques Chirac in May 1995 was a positive gift to the gullible.

As for Hitler, Frau Goebbels's alleged former conviction – avidly taken up by the more credulous of modern commentators – that the recurring word *Hiſter* refers to the notorious Nazi dictator seems more than a little farfetched. The word was in fact the classical name for the Lower Danube, which might explain why Nostradamus is prone to couple it with the Rhine – the two rivers having once formed the northeastern frontier of the Roman Empire. He does so, for example, at IV.68 – a fact that tends to cancel out the unexpected bonus for the "Hitlerian" camp that in the 1557 edition of this verse the word is actually misprinted *hilter*!

Otherwise, most personal references merely take the form of generalized, if often highly suggestive descriptions within even more suggestive contexts. IX.49, for example, has to be seen as a reference to the execution of Charles I of England, since no other monarch has been put to death by Parliament as the verse predicts; the "wretch" described at VIII.76 begs identification with Cromwell; the *moine noir en gris dedans Varennes* of IX.20 who is also *esleu cap.* (i.e. the elected leader) presumably has to be Louis XVI, who had indeed been reelected to the throne; the emperor who *naistra pres d'Italie* of I.60 would seem to be Napoleon; and the *roy*

---

[10] My suggested verse-translation reads:
That mighty Town where roams the first of men
(I've named the place – just read the line again)
Is sore alarmed, with soldiers all afield.
Both war and flood the City shall assail
Till rescuing Frenchmen shall once more prevail.
Six hundred ten: then see these things revealed.

Margaret Thatcher may or may not be predicted by *Centuries* VIII.15 and VI.74

des Isles of X.22 who is forced to flee because of opposition to divorce cannot help but identify himself as the unfortunate Edward VIII.

Whether the northern *hommasse* of VIII.15 who will cause such ructions in Europe, terrify the world, and castigate failed leaders generally – and who also seems to be referred to at VI.74 – really turns out to be Margaret Thatcher, though, only history will reveal.

This is of course an unsatisfactory situation. If the subjects of Nostradamus's verses can be identified only in retrospect, of what use are his predictions, other than to prove him right and demonstrate that prophecy, contrary to all scientific logic, is possible? If they are to have any practical value, some reliable decoding technique needs to be developed that can establish such things in advance, purely from the textual context. It is this particular challenge that will be examined under Dating and Sequencing the Prophecies and Interpreting the Prophecies.

Meanwhile we come to the great symbolic players. In the *Centuries* there are only a few of these – notably "*l'Ogmion*," "*le gryphon*," "*Ahenobarbus*", and "*l'Aemathion.*" In myth, *Ogmion* is Ogmios, the silver-tongued Gallic equivalent of the classical Hercules reported by the second-century Greek rhetor Lucian – presumably, then, some future French "strong man" with the gift of the gab. Indeed, Nostradamus also refers to him repeatedly as *Hercule* (but see Historian and Mythologist). The *Griffon* is a composite mythical beast with a lion's body and an eagle's beak and wings, a solar creature that in ancient Greece symbolized both wisdom and vengeance – but the word is also used to mean a novice, a pony being raced for the first time, and a guardian or watchman: thus, presumably, it stands for some future leader, of comparatively tender years, who will lead an international alliance of nations symbolized by the lion and the eagle in wreaking vengeance on their common enemies. *Ahenobarbus* was the name, not only of the Emperor Nero, but also of Julius Caesar's great military and political rival who was defeated after Caesar's celebrated crossing of the Rubicon, and then raised a further revolt against him from his base in Marseille: thus, he is presumably some future leader operating mainly in the south of France against the authority of a Roman dictator. Finally *l'Aemathion* (or *Haemathien*) means "the Macedonian" – presumably a reference to a future military leader who either comes from that country or whom the prophet sees as another Alexander the Great of Macedon (in the light of Nostradamus's known classicizing tendency, the latter is more likely).

True, Nostradamus also mentions in his *Centuries* such symbolic beasts as the "Camel" – presumably some North African or Middle Eastern power or leader. He repeatedly mentions the invasion of Europe by "locusts" or "grasshoppers," too, as well as by "frogs." But the main playground for Nostradamus's symbolic characters is undoubtedly the *Sixains*. These are peopled by a whole cast of them – notably the Leech, the Wolf, the Phoenix, the Firebrand (also mentioned in the *Centuries*), the Physician, the great Prince, the great Lady, the Crocodile, the Elephant, the Sea Monster, the Griffon (once again), and the great Supplier/Provider/ Steward. Decoding these is not always easy (see Nostradamus the Poet). However, several of them also appear among the hieroglyphic symbols in the *Orus Apollo* (see Nostradamus's Writings), and with various of their characteristics actually spelled out, so that it is possible to assess their likely roles and natures, if not their identities.

The Crocodile, for example, is described as the embodiment of the enemy lawlessness, fury, madness, wantonness, and looting, while the Leech is seen as a bloodsucker that at least attacks and bleeds the Crocodile, even if not to any great effect. It is perhaps going too far to suggest, as some enthusiasts for the *Orus Apollo* do, that the work is a kind of general key to the seer's symbolism. But it at least offers us a few pointers to the sort of ideas that may have been swilling in his mind while he was writing his *Centuries*.

This section has, of course, merely described a few of the linguistic tricks with which Nostradamus seeks to bamboozle us. The rest – most of them boasting complicated and totally unnecessary Greek technical names – barely need describing at all, provided that we stay on our guard. Again and again some classical name is used to summon up a whole raft of associated ideas. In harmony with the underlying principles of *comparative horoscopy* (see Astrologer and Mage), past characters and events are made to stand for future ones. The part is made to stand for the whole, and the whole for the part. And the seer rarely names directly what he can conveniently allude to in more obscure terms.

This, after all, is the man who at III.46 alludes to Lyon as *de Plancus la cité*, so baffling anybody who did not know – or is unable to find out – that Lucius Munatius Plancus was the Roman city's founder in 43 B.C. He it is, too, who at V.81 calls the same city *la cité solaire*, so picking up on the solar symbolism that both tradition and his own *Orus Apollo* associate with the lion (and thus *Lyon*!), but at the same time successfully kidding various commentators into assuming that he is really talking about ancient Heliopolis (Greek for "City of the Sun") in Egypt, and thus about Cairo. Finally, he it is who in his covering letter to the King calls another prominent French city the *port qui prend sa denomination au bœuf marin*[11] – so making its identification impossible for anybody who does not know that the Latin for "seal" was *phoca*, and that *Phocaea* was the Roman name for Marseille.

---

[11] "the port which takes its appellation from the marine bull."

NOSTRADAMUS THE POET

D'esprit divin l'ame presage atteinte
Trouble, famine, peste, guerre courir,
Eauz, siccitez, terre mer de sang teinte,
Paix, tresve, a naistre Prelats, Princes mourir.[12]

Presage 1 (1554 for 1555)

DESPITE his perhaps overmodest disclaimer in the *Proème* of his *Traité des fardemens* to the effect that *ne soions pas trop exercitez en la poësie Francoise,*[13] Nostradamus clearly thought of himself as something of a poet. Otherwise he would never have presumed to publish well over a thousand prophetic verses – starting with the stanza quoted above – that were evidently meant to be read as poetry.

Others shared that view. Ronsard's celebrated critique of the seer in his *Élégie sur les Troubles d'Amboise* of 1560 (see Criticisms and Reviews) casts not the slightest doubt on his qualities as a poet, other than to point out that, in the best prophetic tradition, his words tend to be *douteux*, or "vague." The fact that the *Propheties* were, according to Garencières, still being treated as a standard French classroom reader all of fifty years after Nostradamus's death hardly argues for the common modern assumption that they are little better than doggerel – and clumsy doggerel at that.

True, at least one of the several denunciations of them published in around 1558 (notably the *Monstre d'Abus . . . in Nostradamum*: see Criticisms and Reviews) did suggest that the prophet of Provence was virtually illiterate – but then these were so generally abusive in tone as to devalue their actual criticisms.

Whence, then, the now almost universal view that Nostradamus was a poetic amateur at best?

As ever, the main source has to be the fact that most modern commentators – not excluding French ones – are flummoxed even by perfectly ordinary sixteenth-century French, let alone Nostradamus's deliberately arcane version of it (see Nostradamus's Language).

Add to this the fact that Nostradamus himself admits in his *Lettre à Henri II* (section 2) that his verses are *composees plustost d'un natural instinct, accompagné d'une fureur poëtique, que par reigle de poësie,*[14] and the superficial impression that they are crude and unlettered starts to become understandable. Yet in the very next sentence he also claims that they read perfectly well, even if they are difficult to understand: *respondra quelqu'un qui auroit bien besoin de soy moucher, la rithme estre autant facile, comme l'intelligence du sens est difficile.*[15]

Unfortunately, however, the verses' vigorous rhythm and flow are completely lost in most translations. More to the point, so is their rhyme. As a result, they have come to be seen as about as convincing and as poetic as the average pop lyric or television opera subtitle. No wonder the prophet's reputation as a poet is currently at rock-bottom.

Yet that poor reputation is far from deserved. When read aloud and with due regard for its natural rhythm, his verse is often impressive and stately, to some extent precisely because of its heavy burden of classical words and constructions. Its characteristic "inverted possessive" – as in *de France la victoire navale*[16] (VII.3) – adds particularly to this elevated tone, which is very much consistent with Dylan Thomas's definition of poetry as "prose standing on tiptoe." So do its frequent classical and mythological allusions (see Historian and Mythologist), even if they do tend to baffle most modern readers.

Freed from the constraints of the normal quatrain, or four-line verse, moreover, Nostradamus can become quite graceful and fluent. This is particularly the case in such *Sixains* as 23 and 44:

Quand la grand nef, la proüe & gouvernail,
Du franc pays & son esprit vital,
D'escueils & flots par la mer secoüee,
Six cens & sept, & dix cœur assiegé
Et des reflus de son corps affligé,
Sa vie estant sur[17] *ce mal renoüee.*

La belle roze en la France admiree,
D'un tres-grand Prince à la fin desiree,
Six cens & dix, lors naistront ses amours
Cinq ans apres, sera d'un grand blessee
Du trait d'Amour, elle sera enlassee,
Si à quinze ans du Ciel reçoit secours.[18]

---

[12] *God's sprite prophetic doth my soul o'erflood.*
War, famine, plague, upheaval I espy:
Floods, droughts; stained shall be land and sea with blood,
Ere peace be born prelates and princes die.

---

[13] "(I) may not be all that practised in French poetry."

---

[14] "composed more by natural instinct, accompanied by poetic frenzy, than by the rules of poetry."

---

[15] "The stuffy will retort that the verse is as easy as the making sense of it is difficult."

---

[16] "of France the naval victory."

---

[17] Read as *par*.

---

[18] *When the great ship of state, from stem to stern,*
Of France and all things that its life concern,
With rocks and waves is shattered by the sea,
Its heart assailed, the ebb with corpses strewed –
Yet by this ill its life shall be renewed.
Six hundred seven or ten these things shall be.

The beauteous rose that all in France admire
A mighty Prince shall in the end desire:
Six hundred ten shall see his passion rise.
After five years herself she'll wounded find
By Cupid's dart, and in his arms entwined
If fifteen see him aided from the skies.

In *Sixain* 18, indeed, he becomes positively lyrical:

Considerant la triste Philomelle
Qu'en pleurs & cris sa peine renouvelle,
Racourcissant par tel moyen ses jours,
Six cens & cinq, elle en verra l'issue,
De son tourment, ja la toile tissue,
Par son moyen senestre aura secours.[19]

On top of this, Nostradamus sometimes uses special tricks of his own, which lend a distinctly personal flavor to his verse. Fortunately, alliteration is not normally one of them – since, once he does decide to indulge in it (as in XII.5 in The "Extra" Quatrains), he tends to go completely overboard, to risible effect.

His "echo-technique," however, is much more successful. Here he mirrors a single word or concept in both halves of a quatrain, so creating a technique somewhat reminiscent of the Hebrew psalms – part of whose characteristic poetic technique is simply to say the same thing twice in each verse in different ways. Perhaps, indeed, these were the real source of the idea. Early examples of this technique may be found in II.18 (echoing the word *subite(s)*, though in this case as early as line 2), II.23 (*oiseau*), and II.35 (*deux*). One of its functions is often to emphasize the link between some "omen" in the first half of a verse and its predicted "fulfillment" in the second – and here some significant number frequently plays (as in II.35 above) an important role (see The Nostradamus Omens).

In Nostradamus, however, there is always a tug-of-war between the amount of information that he urgently needs to convey and the space available to express it in. In a greater poet this tension often has a refining tendency – as in the case of the typical sonnet or Japanese *haiku*, for example. But then sonneteers and composers of *haiku* are rarely burdened with the need to convey much in the way of factual information. In Nostradamus, on the other hand, this consideration is paramount – and consequently the demands of the poetry tend to come off very much the worse in the resulting conflict.

As a result, not only does breadth of imagery tend to get relegated very much to the sidelines, but the seer often finds himself running out of room in the last line of a verse. Faced with the inevitable, he then resorts to crude abbreviations and rank telegrammese. In the later *Centuries* (perhaps because he is starting to run out of poetic ideas) he is even prepared to perpetrate entirely bodged rhymes. It is not just that occasional ones (as in V.92 and VII.10) are left false. Even worse are the cases where, in an effort to make the rhyme, perfectly ordinary words are suddenly given seminonsense endings, with what appears to be a total lack of literary shame on the seer's part. It is almost as if an English versifier were to start a limerick with the lines:

A pilot who came from Northampton
Used to fly by the seat of his pampton . . .

Portrait miniature of
Nostradamus the poet

Needless to say, such undignified antics do little to maintain the high solemnity of the verse.

Examples of the seer's use of abbreviations and telegrammese are too numerous to catalog here (see, however, section 3(d) under Nostradamus's Language), but readers will find bodged rhymes involving nonsense-words at VIII.51 (*pamplation*), VIII.88 (*marrit scome*), VIII.89 (*Peloncle*), and perhaps IX.22 (*halbe*).

Possibly, then, such cases may be regarded as Nostradamus's poetic Achilles' heel (to apply a standard piece of mythological imagery that is, as it happens, unused by the seer). Nevertheless, in most other respects he deserves to be counted as a poet of at least some distinction – even though a much less graceful one that his contemporary Clement Marot, or even than the often delightful, but sometimes tedious, Ronsard.

The remainder of this section will be devoted to detailing the various technical aspects of the *Propheties* under the following headings:

1. Verse-form
2. Vocabulary
3. Imagery and symbolism
4. Arrangement of verses

---

[19] *Considering the sad, Greek Nightingale*
Who shall her woes with cries and tears bewail
And in such wise consume her earthly days,
Six hundred five she shall deliverance see
From all her pains: so does Fate's web decree.
By means sinister she shall succour raise.

1. VERSE-FORM

Nostradamus's standard verse-form is the quatrain, or four-line stanza. This is used for

(a) the *Centuries*,
(b) the *Presages*,
(c) the "extra" quatrains

Six-line stanzas are reserved, as their name suggests, for the *Sixains*.

The standard line is of ten syllables (the equivalent of the standard English pentameter), though the *Presages* for 1566 (Nos. 118–29) are in alexandrines (lines of twelve syllables, or hexameters, then only recently resurrected after classical models), while the last twelve *Presages* display a mixture of the two. Some of the *Sixains* are in decasyllables, the rest in shorter lines of eight syllables (i.e. tetrameters), as is the first of the "extra" quatrains (the second of which is in a mixture of the two).

Throughout, the standard rhyme-scheme for the quatrains is *abab*, though *Century* VII.17 and *Presage* 141 have *aabb*, while IV.96 has *abba*. The usual rhyme-scheme for the *Sixains* is *aabccb*, but Nostradamus clearly feels free to vary this at will.

Nostradamus's Symbolic Beasts and other Characters (See Concordance for actual verses involved)

Aemathien (or *[H]aemathion*): "Macedonian": read as "another Alexander the Great"

Aenobarbe: "Ahenobarbus": read as "guerilla leader from Marseille"

Boutefeu: "firebrand": read as "Arab invaders with thermal weapons"

Chameau: "camel": read as "invading leader from North Africa"

Chyren: anagram for "Henri": read as "the future Henri V of France"

Fenix: see *Phoenix*

Crocodil[l]e: "crocodile": read as "resurgent North African Arabs"

Dame: "lady": read as "France" or "Church"

Elephant: "elephant": read as "mighty African invader"

Gryphon: fabulous beast, part-lion, part-eagle, but also hunting dog, novice, pony and guardian or watchman: read as "young allied Western leader"

Lion: "lion": possibly read as "Pope"

Locustes: "locusts": read as "hordes of invaders"[20]

Loup: "wolf": read as "eastern invader"

Mastin: "mastiff": name for Cerberus, Hound of Hell: read as "loud-mouthed invading general"

Medecin: "doctor": read as "healer of the world's ills"

Monstre marin: "sea-monster": read as "Britain"

Neptune: "Neptune or Poseidon": read as "Britain"

Ogmion: eloquent Gallic version of Hercules: read as "powerful defender of Provence against power from northern Italy" (see Historian and Mythologist)

Phoenix: "Phoenix": read as "revived Middle Eastern military power"

Pol mansol/mensolee: "(St.-)Paul-de-Mausole": sometimes used as geographical pun on "Paul Manus Solis" or (possibly) "John Paul II"

Pourvoyeur: "supplier, provider, steward": possibly read as "American leader"

Prince: "prince": possibly read (with *grand*) as "American leader"

Sangsue: "leech": read as "despised, parasitical Northern or Western European power" (possibly Britain)

Sauterelles: "grasshoppers": see *Locustes*.

2. VOCABULARY

At about 8,000 words (including variants), the vocabulary of the verses is roughly equivalent to Milton's, or about half that of Shakespeare. It consists of a mixture of French (including Old French), Latin, Greek, and Provençal, with occasional words from Italian, Spanish, and, in one case (*north* in II.17), English. Only one verse, however, (VI.100) is entirely in Latin (Dog Latin, to be precise), and only two (IV.26 and IV.44) in Provençal.

In the *Orus Apollo* the lion stands for courage, anger, fury; in the quatrains it may be read as "Pope"

---

[20] Compare Ronsard, *Continuation de discours des miseres de ce temps* (1572), 71–2, with reference to the Protestant armies of the time, who were supported by the dread *Reiter*, or German cavalry:
Tandis vous exercez vos malices cruelles,
Et de l'Apocalypse estes les sauterelles . . .
or, freely rendered:
Meanwhile, as cruel of deed as cruel of lips,
You are the locusts of Apocalypse . . .

For the sake of scansion, names of places in particular are often abbreviated, while those of people and places are occasionally anagrammatized (see Nostradamus's Language).

By and large, Nostradamus's vocabulary is varied, selective, and always precise. For specialized analyses consult the Nostradamus Dictionary and the Concordance at the end of this volume.

3. IMAGERY AND SYMBOLISM

Despite occasional flashes of poetic originality – and with the exception of a range of racy everyday idioms – Nostradamus's imagery and symbolism are generally drawn straight from the classics, and notably from the poet Virgil. He does, however, introduce a whole cast of symbolic beasts and other characters (see left), as well as a range of symbolic colors (see below).

Nostradamus's Color Symbolism
(characteristic meanings: see Concordance for examples)

blanc (white): no obvious general meaning

bleu (blue): "Persian or Iranian"

jaune (yellow): possibly "oriental"

noir (black): "African": some commentators suggest "king" (anagram for *roi*)

rose (pink): "Persian or Iranian" (from the flower, a major emblem of Iranian Shi'ite martyrs)

rouge (red): "of Roman Catholic cardinals" or possibly "bearing a red flag"

vert (green): "new, young"

> NOTE: *Some commentators additionally ascribe various of the above colors to particular groups during (a) the French Revolution, (b) the Russian Revolution, and/ or (c) the Spanish Civil War of 1936.*

4. ARRANGEMENT OF VERSES

Except in the case of the *Presages*, the verses are not consecutive, but in random order – in all probability set down simply in the sequence suggested by Nostradamus's application of the principles of comparative horoscopy to ancient events, which themselves were not necessarily even considered by him in chronological order (see Astrologer and Mage). To this extent, they form the scattered, individual pieces of a jigsaw puzzle, which can be reassembled only by applying a range of dating and sequencing techniques (see Dating and Sequencing the Prophecies).

Vital to these is the fact that many of the verses clearly form "pairs," albeit widely separated in most cases. It is verses I.1 and I.2 that supply the initial clue that this may be the case. Further inspection then reveals a whole series of such pairs – including,

possibly, I.23 and I.38, I.28 and I.71, I.43 and IX.32, I.45 and III.40, I.53 and X.72, I.69 and VIII.16, III.4 and III.5, III.23 and III.24, VI.74 and VIII.15. Indeed, subsequent investigation may eventually reveal that *all* verses have pairs.

Further clues to the correct sequence of the verses may be gleaned from the fact that certain of them are quite obviously designed as summary-verses covering whole periods of the future, just as the *Presages* for each year generally come under the umbrella of a similar summary-verse for the year as a whole. A series of summary-verses covering the predicted future Muslim invasion of Europe, for example, appears to be provided by *Centuries* XII.36, VI.80, V.68, VII.34. IX.55, and V.13 (see Dating and Sequencing the Prophecies).

Clearly, without some such effort at sequencing, any given individual verse will lack context, and so be incapable of reliable interpretation (see Interpreting the Prophecies). This is unfortunately all too evident from the many published interpretations that simply fail to address this task.

There remains, then, the question of just *why* Nostradamus chose to write his prophecies in verse, rather than in straightforward prose. The likely reasons can be summarized fairly briefly:

1. The precedent of similarly "inspired' biblical prophets such as Isaiah, and classical ones such as Virgil and the celebrated Sybilline oracle of Cumae, the last of whom may well have been particularly prominent in Nostradamus's mind (see Nostradamus's Life Story);
2. The opportunities that verse offered for veiling the predictions' meaning through the use of obscure, terse, elliptical expressions, highly literary vocabulary, and unusual turns of phrase;
3. The contemporary fashion for expressing even quite prosaic ideas in verse (compare, for example, the *Orus Apollo* and various of the subsequent literary attacks on Nostradamus cited under Criticisms and Reviews);
4. The fact that rhyming verse in particular is easy to remember and extremely difficult to tamper with (not that this latter fact would put off subsequent meddlers in practice).

To our own age, admittedly – much less familiar as it is with verse as a medium for serious communication – Nostradamus's poetic approach can very easily pose a major obstacle to communication. There are some, indeed (often the very same people, paradoxically enough, who can live quite happily with rap or modern song lyrics), who simply cannot make head or tail of it at all. For such people some kind of translation or paraphrase is therefore *de rigueur*, and so it is vital that such versions be as reliable as the material allows. The paraphrases and summaries of interpretations offered under The Major Prophecies are designed to fulfill this need.

HISTORIAN AND MYTHOLOGIST

NOSTRADAMUS'S entire opus is steeped in classical history and myth, which he clearly knew inside out. In this he was not merely typical of his day, bathed as it still was in the lingering glow of the High Renaissance. In his case classical historical references provided the very basis of his prognostic technique, giving as they did the very dates on which his comparative horoscopy for the future was based (see Astrologer and Mage, and Sequence of Selected Horographs).

And so the major players of classical history – Alexander and Nero, Ahenobarbus and Hannibal among them – bestride Nostradamus's pages anew, every bit as large as life as they were in

Hercules, the classical hero, was also a local hero for Nostradamus, having defeated his foe on the "Stony Plain" west of Salon

ancient Greece or Rome. And where history fades into myth at the edges – as in the cases of Jason or Romulus – even the mere denizens of the human imagination start in his writings to take on human flesh and blood.

Like most of his contemporaries, however, Nostradamus turned far more readily to the Roman world than to the Greek. Like them, he knew Greek – he even quoted and translated it in the *Proème* to his *Traité des fardemens* – but he thought and worked much more easily in Latin. Like the Romans themselves, scholars of his day may have looked back with awe at ancient Greece and the lofty heights of its culture, but it was the massive achievements of the Roman Empire that still loomed supreme in their minds, visible as its titanic monuments were still all around them, and notably in Rome itself.

The Romans, it seemed, had been a veritable race of giants.

And so even such Greek figures as do appear in the seer's pages typically take on Roman garb. Ancient Greek gods such as Hermes and Artemis, Aphrodite and Ares, Zeus and Kronos are resurrected in his texts as Mercury and lunar Diana, Venus and Mars, Jupiter and Saturn, bringing their planets with them. Poseidon with his trident resurges as fishy Neptune. And Herakles in particular re-performs his labors as Hercules, and even as the Gallic *Ogmion*.

This last point is of special interest and importance for the *Propheties*. Just as the historical Lucius Domitius Ahenobarbus, mortal foe of Julius Caesar, had resisted the overweening Roman dictator to the death from his local base in Marseille, so the mythical Hercules had had a local aspect, too, and one that lay even closer to Nostradamus and his particular concerns.

The Temple of Hercules at Agrigento in Sicily, built in the late part of the 6th century

True, it was very much the fashion at the time to appropriate such figures as Hercules for ceremonial purposes. In 1549 and 1550 the new King Henri II himself had been welcomed to Paris and Rouen amid extravagant municipal junketings as the "French Hercules," and Nostradamus, now safely installed in Salon, had been well aware of the fact. Yet Hercules had not been a king. He had, though, been a notable warrior.

It was during his tenth labor (ran the legend), while on his way back to Greece with the rustled cattle of Geryon, King of Tartessus in Spain, that Herakles/Hercules had been attacked by the Ligurians (who then occupied both southern France and northern Italy) while crossing an arid wasteland, ever since known as the "Stony Plain," where only briny springs were to be found.

That "stony plain" was in fact the *Crau*, immediately to the west of Nostrodamus's hometown of Salon.

Wounded, exhausted and despairing (the story continued), the mighty hero had knelt down and prayed to Zeus, who in pity had summoned up a storm cloud and rained down stones upon the muddy earth for him to hurl at his enemies. This he did, and duly put the murderous foe to flight. And the stones remain to this day.

Hercules, then, was not merely a hero. He was a *local* hero.

And so when the seer writes (as he often does – see the Concordance at the back of this book) of a future Hercules – or even of his eloquent Gallic equivalent, Ogmius or *Ogmion* – he is likely to be referring to one aspect of the ancient champion in particular. His future role, it seems, will be not merely to perform great acts generally, *but specifically to defend Provence by taking on and defeating powerful occupiers of southern France and northern Italy*.

At once, then, the role of the mythical Hercules starts to merge into that of the historical Ahenobarbus – a fact that then enables us to see the relevant predictions in their true mutual relationship. At some future time of overwhelming invasion from northern Italy, it seems, Provence will be sorely oppressed by a foreign dictatorship, but a doughty local leader, somehow finding weapons and strength literally from heaven knows where, will eventually succeed in driving the aliens back, even if he himself possibly has to die in the process (see The Muslim Invasion of Europe).

The case is an instructive one, warning us to think carefully about Nostradamus's historical and mythological references. Far from being mere scholastic throwaways, they are likely to carry within them all sorts of characteristic clues as to what Nostradamus expects to happen. Those clues need to be prised out, examined, and coordinated with the rest of his prophetic blueprint.

NOSTRADAMUS,
THE BIBLE, AND THE CHURCH

LIKE MOST of the world's major prophets, Nostradamus was deeply religious. There is absolutely no warrant for the suggestion, supported by various modern commentators, that this may have been mere religiosity, or some kind of blind to cover up the more nefarious of his magical practices. His revelations, he constantly claimed, were of Divine, not human, origin – let alone the product of mere magic. Indeed, *only* such Divine revelations, he repeatedly pointed out in his dedicatory letters (see sections 4 and 6 of the *Préface à César* and section A.6 of the *Lettre à Henri II* under The Major Prophecies), could possibly hope to foretell the future.

To cite once again the very first of his verse-*Presages*, published in the *Almanach* for 1555:

D'esprit divin l'ame presage atteinte
Trouble, famine, peste, guerre courir,
Eauz, siccitez, terre mer de sang teinte,
Paix, tresve, a naistre Prelats, Princes mourir.[21]

The evidence is overwhelming. Not only did he quote constantly from the scriptures in the dedicatory prefaces to his *Propheties* (compare the footnotes to the *Préface à César* and *Lettre à Henri II*). He supported the Church, argued in favor of Catholic doctrines, defended them fiercely against the new Protestant ideas, observed fasts, prayed, made charitable donations, quoted the Bible to those to whom he gave them, was apparently on good terms with his near neighbor the Archbishop of Arles, stayed in Paris with the powerful Archbishop of Sens, treated both the Bishop of Béziers and the Bishop-elect of Carcassonne, left money to at least two Franciscan convents, and asked to be buried in Salon's now-defunct Franciscan chapel (see Portrait of the Prophet and Nostradamus's Lifestory). Moreover, not only was this request granted, along with full civic honors, but Nostradamus's son André subsequently joined a branch of the Order himself, albeit under some duress.

Evidently, then, the seer was drawn more to the austere and charitable Franciscans that to the much more acquisitive and cult-obsessed mainstream Church, as represented by the Église St.-Michel just behind his own house in Salon. Reform, both Catholic and Protestant, was very much in the air at the time, but Nostradamus, already under suspicion as a Jew, naturally preferred the safer, Catholic version. The impression, reinforced by Chavigny's listing of *jeusnes, oraisons, ausmones et . . . patience*[22] as his main religious activities, suggests the self-same leaning toward reformed or primitive Catholicism as is reflected in *Century* II.8:

THE SEER'S RELIGIOUS LEANINGS

8 Temples ſacrés prime façon Romaine
   Reieteront les goffes fondements,
   Prenant leurs loys premieres & humaines,
   Chaſſant, non tout, des ſaints les cultements.

Century **II.8 in the original,**
1555 edition[23]

True, Nostradamus's biblical quotations are often inaccurate, giving the distinct impression of having been summoned up purely from memory. This may have been because, as a good Catholic, he simply did not read the scriptures or have a copy of his own. The Church, after all, asserted (with some reason) that it had chosen the Bible, and not the reverse. Reading the scriptures (especially in the vernacular) was until quite modern times actually forbidden to lay Catholics as potentially dangerous to their spiritual salvation. Such things were for the experts only.

Alternatively, it may be that Nostradamus simply treated the scriptures with much the same airy abandon as he did the ancient texts that he was wont to translate (see Nostradamus's Writings), evidently taking the view that a measure of intuitive interpretation was permissible in both cases. Once again, the view (if such it was) was more redolent of Catholic doctrinal scholarship than of its Protestant equivalent, with its much sterner regard for literal truth. Moreover, typical mid-sixteenth-century scholarship was in any

---

21 *God's sprite prophetic doth my soul o'erflood.*
War, famine, plague, upheaval I espy:
Floods, droughts; stained shall be land and sea with blood,
Ere peace be born prelates and princes die.

22 "fasts, prayers, alms and . . . austerities": see Portrait of the Prophet.

23 *Of churches hallowed in old Roman manner*
They shall reject the very fundaments,
Making base-principles their human banner
At many a former saintly cult's expense.

case (rather like much that passes for Nostradamus scholarship today) much vaguer and worse-informed than we usually expect modern scholarship to be, and tended, on the whole, to be essentially an amateur rather than a professional job.

Nevertheless, the fact remains that not only Nostradamus's prefaces, but his prophecies, too, are suffused with biblical ideas – and not merely the Old Testament ideas which, as an ancestral Jew, he might reasonably be expected to have inherited, but New Testament ideas too. Above all, the Revelation of John and the First Letter of John clearly inform many of his more apocalyptic visions of the future. The Great Whore of Babylon, the dreaded "Kings (originally angels) from the East" released from beyond the Euphrates, the rains of blood and fire, the Great Comet and premonitory eagle, the invading hordes of "locusts," the darkening of sun and moon, the expected Antichrist – all these duly re-people the *Propheties* (in the case of the Antichrist on several different occasions, much as comparative horoscopy demands) no less vividly than do the characters from ancient history and myth considered under Historian and Mythologist.

In a sense, all three provide the very stuff of Nostradamus's visions, leaving him as an astrologer with the sole function of determining (once again with the aid of comparative horoscopy – see Astrologer and Mage) just where and when the inevitable blow must fall, even if not specifically the biblical Armageddon.

It is entirely erroneous, however, to suggest that this astrological function somehow excluded him from the Church's fold. The Church, as Nostradamus himself was at constant pains to point out in his prefaces, was not opposed at the time to judicial astrology – i.e. the astrology of foretelling the future. Nor, indeed, would it have had a leg to stand on if it had been, given that the infant Jesus himself had allegedly been discovered by three "Magi," or astrologers, who were supposedly engaged at the time in *following a star*.

Indeed, when the reverend canons of Orange had their church treasures looted during a Protestant riot in early 1562, it was to Nostradamus that they turned for the *preparation of a horoscope* that would reveal the culprit (see Nostradamus's Life Story).

Nostradamus, after all (see Astrologer and Mage), had based

The ancient Eglise St.-Michel, just behind Nostradamus's house in Salon

many of his allegedly magical practices on the *De Mysteriis Aegyptiorum*, the seminal work by the classical Iamblichus, who had asserted specifically that not only the planets, whose movements informed astrology, but also the ancient gods themselves were merely aspects or manifestations of the Divine First Cause – i.e. God Himself – and that their revelations were therefore infallible.

How, then, could the Church possibly presume to gainsay the insights that they afforded – especially as the Church at the time was only just coming to grips with its characteristic post-Renaissance *Angst* over how to reconcile the decidedly permissive glories of classical paganism with the much sterner and more prescriptive demands of traditional Christianity, as typified by the celebrated argument over Michelangelo's Sistine Chapel ceiling?

True, Nostradamus would subsequently be reviled by Protestant intellectuals for his apparent castigation of them in his *Propheties* (see Criticisms and Reviews), just as he would paradoxically be reviled by the ignorant local Catholic peasantry (the so-called *Cabans*) as some kind of crypto-Protestant (see Nostradamus's Lifestory). He had already had one brush with the Inquisition of Toulouse, too – though more, it would seem, for his free thinking and his oddball sense of humor than for any perceived act of deliberate irreligion.

All this was no more than might be expected of a prominent thinker and intellectual with unusual and somewhat worrying views. The message, after all, was not necessarily welcome. What could be more natural or more usual, then, than to blame the messenger himself?

However, the suggestion that his prophecies were disapproved of by the official Church of his day, let alone condemned by it, is entirely a modern misconception. When the Vatican's official *Index Librorum Prohibitorum*, or Index of Forbidden books, appeared in 1556–9, a variety of names such as Martin Luther's figured prominently in it. But of Nostradamus there was conspicuously no mention, even though at least one of his *Almanachs* had by then been published in Italy. Nor, indeed, would there ever be. Only in the even more orthodox and suspicious Spanish equivalent would various selective bans be imposed (see illustration on page 55).

THE NOSTRADAMUS OMENS

LIKE MOST PEOPLE of his day, and many of ours, Nostradamus was deeply sensitive to signs and portents of every description. Unusually, he was also extremely skilled in interpreting them.

Apocryphal tales excepted (see Forgeries and Fairy Tales), the first two Nostradamian omens of which we have any record both occurred in 1554, the year before his *Propheties* were first published. According to César, a two-headed child was born that year in nearby Sénas, a short distance south of the town of Orgon, and brought to his father for examination. A month and a half later, a black–and–white kid with the self-same deformity was brought in from the little village of Aurons, in the hills just to the east of Salon and north of Pélissanne.

Nostradamus, it seems, promptly showed the beast to Palamede Marc, the then First Consul of Salon and a long-time friend, who was currently entertaining the Duc de Tende, Governor of Provence, the Baron de la Garde, Admiral of the Eastern Fleet, and the Commandeur de Beynes – all of them being on their way to an important society baptism at St.-Rémy.

Il ne fut parlé durant presque tout le souper, César would later write,[24] *que de ces monstres hideux et des malheurs et divisions qu'ils semblent pronostiquer tousjours infailliblement, voir du schisme sanglant et des guerres de Religion que suyvirent peu apres, estans tousjours produits contre l'ordre et l'art de nature, non certainment comme causes, mais vrais signes et nonces extraordinaires et certains de choses tristes et funestes.*[25]

The first experience particularly made its mark. Nostradamus duly used it in verse 90 of his first *Century* (see right), so indicating not only the point in his work that he had probably reached at the time (compare Nostradamus's Lifestory), but also the precise manner in which he proposed to use such omens in his predictions.

Ever and anon he would announce some such *monstre* (from Latin *monstrum,* "omen") in one half of a verse, using it as a "sign" (much as César indicates) of some other, much greater event described in the other. Once again, in other words, he would have the satisfaction of saying the same thing in two different ways in the two halves of a verse.

---

24 *Histoire et Chronique de Provence,* Simon Rigaud, Lyon, 1614: evidently he did so from hearsay only, since he was barely born at the time.

25 "Nothing was spoken of during almost the whole of supper apart from these hideous monsters and the disasters and divisions that they always seem infallibly to presage, namely the bloody schism and the Wars of Religion that would follow shortly afterwards, always manifesting themselves contrary to the laws and customs of nature – not, indeed, as causes, but as true signs and extraordinary yet certain portents of unhappy and baleful events."

26 *When sounds the tocsin, Poitiers and Bordeaux*
Shall send a mighty army to Langon.
Against the French their great north wind shall blow
When hideous monster's born hard by Orgon.

USE OF THE *MONSTRE*

90 Bourdeaux, Poitiers, au son de la campane'
A grande classe ira iusques à l'Angon,
Contre Gauloys sera leur tramontane,
Quād mōstres hideux naistra près de Orgon.

**Verse 90 of the first *Century*
in the 1555 edition[26]**

The quatrain on the left duly shows this technique in action. Typically these tales of *monstres* (I.80, I.90, II.32, II.70, III.34, III.41, V.20, V.88, VI.19, X.5, X.98, Pr.82, Pr.84) refer to two-headed births (I.58), babies born with teeth already in place (II.7, III.42), animal hybrids (VI.44), and possibly even human-animal hybrids (I.64, III.69). And almost always they contain the word *quand*, clearly indicating that their prime function is to serve not as mere grisly newscopy, but rather as omens and portents, or "signs of the times."

It was, of course, perfectly normal at the time to interpret events in this way. Let the poet Ronsard, for example, act as spokesman for his age:

> *Et quand on voit tant de monstres difformes,*
> *Qui en naissant prennent diverses formes,*
> *Les pieds à haut, la teste contre-bas,*
> *Enfants morts-nez, chiens, veaux, aigneaux et chats*
> *A double corps, trois yeux et cinq oreilles:*
> *Bref, quand on voit tant d'estranges merveilles*
> *Qui tout d'un coup paroissent en maints lieux,*
> *Monstres non veus de nos premiers ayeux,*
> *C'est signe seur qu'incontinent la terre*
> *Doit soustenir la famine et la guerre,*
> *Les fleaux de Dieu qui marchent les premiers,*
> *Du changement certains avant-courriers.*[27]

Moreover, such warnings needed to be taken seriously. Recent history showed all too clearly the folly of failing to do so. Thus it was the prime task of prophets such as Nostradamus to draw people's attention to them:

> *Dés long temps les escrits des antiques prophetes,*
> *Les songes menaçans, les hideuses comettes,*
> *Nous avoient bien predit que l'an soixante et deux*
> *Rendroit de tous costés les François malheureux,*
> *Tués, assassinés: mais pour n'estre pas sages,*
> *Nous n'avons jamais creu à si divins presages,*
> *Obstinés, aveuglés: ainsi le peuple Hebrieu*
> *N'adjoutoit point de foy aux prophetes de Dieu:*
> *Lequel ayant pitié du François qui forvoye,*
> *Comme pere benin du haut Ciel luy envoye*
> *Songes, et visions, et prophetes, à fin*
> *Qu'il pleure, et se repente, et s'amande à la fin.*[28]

We "scientific modern people" may imagine that we are immune to such superstitions. Yet still we are prone to see in the sinking of great passenger liners signs that the existing world order is about to go under.

In major pollution disasters we see portents of what we are likely to do to ourselves if we do not cleanse our own hearts and minds and stop passing on our messy internal problems to less

Nostradamus frequently announced a *monstre* – a misshapen human or animal – in his verse as a portent of some great event

[27] *Prognostiques sur les miseres de nostre temps* (1584), 57–68:
> *And when we see so many monsters gross*
> *Born all around in various forms, with toes*
> *In place of heads, or heads where feet should be,*
> *Infants stillborn, dogs, calves, lambs, cats with three*
> *Eyes or five ears or double body found;*
> *In short, so many portents all around*
> *Appearing suddenly, now here, now there,*
> *Of which no forefather was e'er aware;*
> *It is a certain sign that soon the earth*
> *Will bring both famine and dread war to birth –*
> *God's punishments, the first of many more,*
> *Sure harbingers of mighty change in store.*

[28] *Discours des miseres de ce temps* (1562), 95-106:
> *Long time the writings of the seers of old,*
> *Menacing dreams and comets have foretold*
> *In all their hideousness how 62*
> *Would bring disasters for us Frenchmen, who*
> *Would suffer death and murder: but, deceived,*
> *Such heavenly presages we ne'er believed,*
> *Blind as we were and obstinate. The Jews*
> *Likewise God's prophets did their faith refuse.*
> *Yet, pitying the errant French in love*
> *Like some kind father, He from heaven above*
> *Sent prophets, visions, dreams, that in the end*
> *They might repent, and weep and so amend.*

**The wreckage of the Lockerbie air disaster
– was it a portent of a greater tragedy?**

fortunate parts of the world to solve for us. We are acutely aware of how, if one airliner crashes, so do half a dozen others, or how, when one epidemic or environmental disaster strikes, so do a whole rash of them. Surely, we find ourselves thinking, all this has to *mean* something?

And if our society were as willing as Nostradamus's to allow deformed fetuses to come to term, instead of averting our eyes and expecting the professionals to incinerate them or flush them down the waste-disposal system at the first sign of trouble, possibly we,

too, would be more aware of them, and more inclined to read them as "signs of the times."

Indeed, our very unwillingness to do any such thing may be a sign in itself, indicating our fundamental unwillingness to look either at the state of our own minds or at the future consequences of our own acts. This last, at least, is not an accusation that can reasonably be leveled at Nostradamus.

CRITICISMS AND REVIEWS

THE UNCONVENTIONAL Nostradamus was always the object of a certain amount of natural suspicion on the part of his contemporaries. When he actually went into print, however, he brought down upon his head a whole rash of public literary and religious criticism as well. This peaked in around 1558, apparently following Jean de Tournes's publication of the last three *Centuries* in that year. It seems to have been none other than the poet Jodelle, a member of Dorat's *Pléiade*, who started on its way a poisonous little Latin distich that ran:

*Nostra damus cum falsa damus, nam fallere nostrum est
Et cum falsa damus, nil nisi nostra damus.*[29]

A riposte duly appeared, possibly composed by Chavigny:

*Vera damus cum verba damus quae Nostradamus dat;
Sed cum nostra damus, nil nisi falsa damus.*[30]

A further variant also appeared (could it have been suggested by the seer himself?):

*Nostra damus cum verba damus quae Nostradamus dat:
Nam quaecumque dedit nil nisi vera dat.*[31]

Soon, however, much more serious criticisms started to appear in print. One of them was *La premiere invective du Seigneur Hercules le François contre Monstradamus (sic!)*. Allegedly translated from the Latin – and written in terms that suggest that the author had already read an early draft of Ronsard's later pseudo-sonnet about the prophet (see below) – this accused him of infecting the people with a plague of execrable heresies, of usurping the place of God, and of playing on people's credulity. He was, it alleged, a "twenty-four-carat liar" spouting a babble of double-edged words, who in his *Almanachs* made bold to tell the whole world when to travel, when to get married, when to do business, even when to change its shirt. Replacing God with a form of fatalism that insulted the good name of astrology, the slippery prophet (it continued) nevertheless kept changing his alleged predictions to fit events, a bit like a snake changing its skin.

Like all other sorcerers, charmers, diviners, enchanters, mountebanks, and magicians, he should therefore be exterminated, for all his pretensions to education and medical knowledge. He was a purveyor of darkness against whom all lovers of truth should rise as one, a son of iniquity fashioned out of lies who fed the people with fables and falsehoods. Unless he returned to the paths of truth and salvation (the tract threatened), he would be exposed and held up to ridicule for all to see as the hideous monster he was – tortuous, enigmatic riddles and all – or hauled down out of the firmament into which he had presumed to soar with his borrowed artistic feathers (the expression is curiously redolent of later criticisms of the young Shakespeare). He should be content to be a simple mathematician, philosopher, or astrologer, without attempting to play the soothsayer as well – let alone aping some oracle out of Greek or Roman mythology – and in future he should confine his *Almanachs* to mere descriptions of the movements of the planets, the seasons, and changes in the weather.

Just to rub the point in, the estimable "French Hercules" (an obvious reference, this, to the future leader whom the seer had called *Ogmion* in his prophecies) concluded with a short verse:

A DAMNING CRITIQUE

*Deſcrie ma muſe à ſon de trompe
(Comme argent de mauuais alloy)
Ce ſorcier qui le monde trompe,
Soubs pretexte de bonne foy.
De remonſtrer ſouuienne toy,
Que ſi ſon caquet auoit lieu,
Il fauldroit tous changer de loy,
Puis qu'il nous forge vn aultre Dieu.*

In translation this might read:

*Denounce, my Muse, with clarion call,
(Like silver mixed with metals base)
This sorc'rer who'd deceive us all,
False candor writ across his face.
Be sure to argue and to say
That if his prattle came to be
The world would work a different way,
Ruled by a different Deity.*

---

[29] Or, freely translated:
*We give our own when lies we give, for it is ours to err:
And when we lie our own we give, and none but ours we share.*

[30] Or, freely rendered – as was the way with Nostradamus himself (see Nostradamus's Writings):
*'Tis truth we wreak when words we speak that Nostradamus gave us:
For words we choose are of no use and, lying, cannot save us.*

[31] Free rendering:
*Our own we wreak when words we speak as Nostradamus spake them,
For, line by line, they're true and fine as truth itself can make them.*

The poet Pierre de Ronsard was criticized for eulogizing Nostradamus and for warning his fellow-countrymen to heed the seer's prophecies

Next, there was the *Monstre d'Abus . . . in Nostradamum*, allegedly translated from the Latin by a fictitious university rector, one "Jan de la Daguenière," who was clearly a Calvinist. He may even have been Calvin's leading disciple and successor in Geneva, Théodore de Bèze. Written in even more insulting vein, it bore on its title page a piece of Latin invective accusing the seer of not yet having mastered even the basic rudiments of the French language, yet daring to attribute heavenly virtue to his magic wand. Curiously, the tract was issued in Paris by Barbe Regnault, a former publisher of Nostradamus himself.

A further defamatory tract was the *Déclaration des abus, ignorances et séditions de Michel Nostradamus, de Salon de Craux en Provence*, once again allegedly translated from the Latin, but this time by one Laurens Vedel, a well-known secretary to the aristocracy who had

at least had the courage to use his own name. According to him, the seer was a scabby, mangy blockhead, a great ass and a poor brute, and needed his brain fumigated. Just as curiously, this tract, too, was printed by a former publisher of Nostradamus – one Pierre Roux of Avignon.

At some point, too, Joseph Justus, illustrious son of Jules César Scaliger, seems to have joined in, referring to Nostradamus's *malefice juif*,[32] castigating him as a *charlatan malfaiteur*,[33] and describing his work quite simply as *des sottises*.[34]

---

[32] "Jewish malevolence."

[33] "criminal charlatan."

[34] "idiocies."

Fortunately, however, there were more serious, carefully balanced criticisms, too. The most noteworthy was a pseudo-sonnet incorporated into his *Élégie sur les Troubles d'Amboise* of 1560 by the poet Pierre de Ronsard, the most outstanding member of the *Pléiade* and an enthusiast – if a somewhat guarded one – of Nostradamus. After upbraiding his fellow countrymen for mocking the warnings of their own homeborn seers in the wake of the Protestant attempt to kidnap the young King François II at Amboise and the subsequent bloody reprisals by the Catholic Guises, he continued:

> *Ou soit que du grand Dieu l'immense eternité*
> *Ait de Nostradamus l'entousiasme excité,*
> *Ou soit que le daimon bon ou mauvais l'agite,*
> *Ou soit que de nature il ayt l'ame subite,*
> *Et outre le mortel s'eslance jusqu'aux cieulx,*
> *Et de lâ nous redit des faicts prodigieux:*
> *Ou soit que son esprit sombre et melancolique,*
> *D'humeurs grasses repeu, le rende fantastique;*
> *Bref, il est ce qu'il est, si est ce toutesfois*
> *Que par les mots douteux de sa profette voix,*
> *Comme un oracle anticque, il a des mainte année*
> *Predit la plus grand part de nostre destinée.*
> *Je ne l'eusse pas cru, si le ciel, qui depart*
> *Bien et mal aux humains, n'eust esté de sa part . . .*[35]

Even Ronsard, however, was not immune to the critics, and especially not to the Protestant ones. Indeed, his passing eulogy merely served, in their eyes at least, to align him with the execrated Nostradamus himself. In the anonymous *Palinodies de Pierre de Ronsard* of early 1563 and the *Remonstrance à la Royne* of later the same year, Ronsard was heavily castigated for being so superstitious as to believe this "impostor," this "mad magician," this "devilish dreamer," this "stinking liar." Naturally, the poet protested at the various criticisms, but this merely produced a further counterblast. In the *Defence aux injures et calomnies contenues en la Response de M. Pierre Ronsard, contre les Ministres (qu'il appelle Predicans) de l'Eglise de Geneve*[36] he was further damned for allegedly sharing the prophet's fatalistic view of events.

Clearly, then, Nostradamus could do nothing right, for some people at least, and anybody who associated with him risked being tarred with the self-same brush. Curiously enough, however, this merely confirmed his own prophecies on the subject. In section 2 of the *Préface à César*, after all, (see The Major Prophecies) he had stated in so many words that *si je venois à referer ce que a l'advenir sera, ceulx de regne, secte, religion, & foy trouveroient si mal accordant à leur fantasie auriculaire, qu'ilz viendroient à damner, ce que par les siecles advenir on congnoistra estre vue & appercue.*[37] In section A.4 of his *Lettre à Henri II*, similarly, he had prayed to be spared from *la calomnie des meschans,*[38] and had expressed his conviction that his writings would be better understood after his death than before it.

In this, too, he was possibly right – so, in a sense, condemning his critics out of their own mouths.

And so it was that in 1584, long after the prophet's death, Ronsard could once again take up his former theme, if this time in more generalized form:

> *Ou soit que Dieu, comme en lettres de chiffre*
> *Douteusement son vouloir nous dechiffre*
> *D'un caractere obscur et mal-aisé,*
> *Soit qu'un Démon de soy-mesme avisé,*
> *Qui vit long temps, et a veu mainte chose,*
> *Voyant le Ciel qui ses Astres dispose*
> *A bien ou mal, comme il veut les virer,*
> *Se mesle en l'homme, et luy vient inspirer,*
> *En le troublant, une parolle obscure,*
> *Soit que cela se face d'aventure,*
> *Je n'en sçay rien: l'homme qui est humain,*
> *Ne tient de Dieu le secret en la main.*
> *Mais je sçay bien que Dieu qui tout ordonne,*
> *Par signes tels tesmoignage nous donne*
> *De son courroux, et qu'il est irrité*
> *Contre le Prince, ou contre la Cité . . .*[39]

---

[37] "if I were to set down (in clear language) what will happen in the future, people in power and members of various sects, religions, and faiths would find it so out of harmony with what they had heard and imagined that they would condemn what by future centuries will be seen and perceived (as true)."

---

[38] "the calumny of the wicked."

---

[39] *Prognostiques sur les miseres de nostre temps* (1584), 69–84:
Be it that God in letters that we know
To us but vaguely does his bidding show
In form obscure and difficult of sense;
Be it some Daemon whose experience
O'er many years has seen of things its fill –
Seen how high Heaven wields for good or ill
Its stars, and how it turns them on a whim –
Instils itself in man and stirs in him
Words all too dark and many a troubled trance;
Be it that all of it occurs by chance –
I know not: while man lives in human mould
God's secret is not his to have or hold.
But yet I know that God the All-Disposing
To us his signs in witness is exposing
Of His displeasure and His anger great
Against the Prince, or else against the State . . .

---

[35] Suggested translation:
Be it Great God beyond all space and time
Roused Nostradamus' rapture into rhyme;
Be he by daemon good or evil stirred,
Or gifted with a soul that like some bird
Soars up to heavens no mortal man may know
To bring back auguries for us below;
Be his a mind so gloomy, dark and dim,
Crammed with gross humours, as to cozen him –
Whate'er he is, he is: yet none the less
Through the vague portents that his words express
Like some old oracle he has foretold
For many a year what fate for us shall hold.
I'd doubt him, did not heaven, that disburses
Both good and ill to men, inform his verses.

---

[36] "Defense against the Insults and Calumnies in the reply of M. Pierre Ronsard against the Ministers (whom he calls Preachers) of the Church of Geneva."

BOOK PRINTING AND PUBLISHING

THE TECHNIQUE of printing using movable type was still only about a hundred years old in Europe when Nostradamus first appeared on the publishing scene. Individual letters (themselves handcrafted) were still set manually from the cases in which they had been stored after printing the previous book, often by unskilled apprentices – upper cases for capitals, lower cases for small letters (whence the continued use of the terms today). Opportunities were thus legion for *u* to become mixed up with *v* and *n*, *d* with *b*, *l* with *t*, and *p* with *q* (whence, once again, the still-current saying about minding one's *p* s and *q* s). Even more to the point, ∫ (initial and medial *s*) was liable to be confused with *f*. Moreover, letters could quite easily fall out of their setting-sticks, so leaving blanks in the resulting text.

The results were predictable – though it did not, of course, take a seer of Nostradamus's stature to predict them. All of the above confusions and omissions duly occurred. In the case of Antoine du Rosne of Lyon, printer and publisher of Nostradamus's second edition of 1557, that between ∫ and *f* was particularly frequent. Or perhaps it was simply that, as the printers ran out of ∫, they simply felt free to substitute *f* instead. At all events, the result is that, in this edition particularly, these two letters are in a state of permanent confusion, with *f* vastly predominating. Consequently the reader is left to decide which is which in any given case, purely on the basis of sense and context.

Meanwhile the amount of type available was itself limited – both as to its total amount and as to the numbers of each letter available. As a result, printers – unlike lawyers (see Nostradamus's

USE OF THE TILDE

x x
Freres & ſeurs en diuers lieux captifz,
Se trouueront paſſer pres du monarque:
Les contempler les rameaux ententifz,
Deſplaiſant voir mētō, frōt, nez, les marqs.

Century **II.20 from the
1557 edition**

Language) – were keen to cut down on the number of letters wherever they could. Nostradamus's verses gave them a golden opportunity to do so. Wherever a line threatened to spill over onto the next line, du Rosne's compositors particularly grabbed the chance with both hands, freely superimposing the tilde (~) over a vowel in place of a following *m* or *n* – and sometimes using it to indicate whole groups of other missing letters as well (compare *Century* II.20 below left, for example, and see Nostradamus's Language).

But the limited amount of type available had other consequences, too. It was important not to keep any given book set up in print for a moment longer than was necessary. As a result there was generally no question of returning proofs to the author for checking. In the case of Nostradamus, for example, the return journey time between Lyon and Salon alone might well have been anything up to one month, depending on the time of year. Instead, proofreading was normally done in-house, with proofreaders often more concerned to see that the printed text was consistent with itself than to ensure that it remained true to the original manuscript. No doubt partly as a result, books were produced at astonishing speed, despite the limitations of the technology available.

Meanwhile there was also the question of legality to consider. All books at the time had to receive official approval before publication, primarily in order to ensure that they were not offensive to the Catholic faith. This imprimatur, often printed within the book itself, was issued not by the Church, but by the King's local representative. In the case of Nostradamus this was generally the Seneschal, or Lord Lieutenant of Lyon, and it therefore applied only to the domains within his jurisdiction. Publication in Paris was a separate matter arranged with different publishers and sanctioned by the authorities there.

But the official imprimatur carried certain positive benefits, too. It was, to use the French term, a *privilège*, explicitly forbidding any other publisher in the region to reprint or sell the book, often for a fixed period, on pain of confiscation and/or other summary punishment. It was, in effect, an early form of licensed copyright.

At the same time, under an edict of King François I issued in 1522, a copy of every book had to be lodged with the royal library in Paris at the time of publication. It was no doubt in this way that the first edition of Nostradamus's *Propheties* managed to reach Queen Catherine de Médicis within just a few weeks of its publication in May 1555.

The book once printed, distribution was the next task. Since no roads to speak of existed at the time outside the major cities (see Nostradamus in Context), all transportation had to be by packhorse. This placed a considerable premium both on volume and on weight. This could have been one of the reasons why so many contemporary editions (Nostradamus's included) were produced not in octavo (roughly six by nine inches) but in 16°, or demi-octavo – which of course also made for an excellent pocketbook. But there were other results, too. Books were normally distributed to the French provinces *unbound*, so saving the weight and space of two covers per book; binding was then the responsibility of retailers or purchasers, the more aristocratic of whom might well take advantage of the fact to have the family arms or other decorations printed on the cover.

A further upshot was that publishers were particularly eager to keep the length of any given book strictly within bounds. Since books were normally produced (as they still are today) in multiples of sixteen pages – the purely mathematical result of the printer's repeated folding of a large sheet of paper – there seems to have been considerable pressure on publishers to shorten texts to the next sixteen pages below, rather than above, the initial printed length. Not only does this help to explain why the earliest editions of Nostradamus cheerfully split verses between pages, rather than starting the next verse on a new page; it may well also explain the distinctly odd numbers of verses that were actually printed in the various early editions of the *Centuries*.

As in England, the initial cost of the venture was generally funded by some generous and probably noble patron to whom the author had addressed a suitably deferential dedication. Thereafter royalties of one kind or another might be paid by the publisher to the author as funds appeared. Out of this relationship there then arose a mutual dependence that amounted to a business partnership with all sorts of ramifications. In particular, the publisher's premises might (as in the case of Sebastien Gryphe of Lyon and the

much-respected Jean de Tournes) become a kind of meeting house for his authors. (No doubt it is significant that Nostradamus at one stage routed all his foreign mail via one of his other Lyon publishers, Jean Brotot.) It was at least partly due to the intellectual ferment generated by the Lyon publishers, in fact, that the city managed for so long to remain a major center of original thought and speculation relatively free from the constraints imposed on their Paris counterparts by the religiously and academically conservative Sorbonne.

All the difficulties notwithstanding, the printed results, decorated with woodcuts and other ornaments, were often a delight to the eye. The original 1555 edition of the *Centuries* is a case in point. In addition, Jean de Tournes, a former employee of Sebastien Gryphe (better known as "Gryphius") who set up as a printer and publisher on his own account in 1542, was particularly renowned for his exquisite work – and he it was who published the last three of Nostradamus's *Centuries* in 1558.

The seer's relations with his publishers may not always have been as fortunate, however. The mere fact that he changed publisher so often suggests some nagging dissatisfaction on his part – unless, of course, he was merely a "difficult author." The very fact that the last fifty-eight verses of the seventh *Century* remain missing to this day may itself go back to some kind of triangular dispute between Nostradamus, Antoine du Rosne, and his fellow Lyon publisher Benoist Rigaud (see Nostradamus's Writings).

**William Caxton's early
printing press, as depicted
by Daniel Marclise**

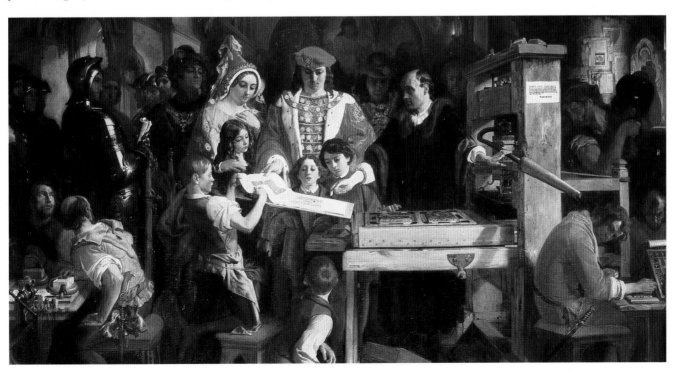

EARLY EDITIONS

THE FOLLOWING is a complete list of the currently known early editions of Nostradamus's works up to 1605. Principal source: CHOMARAT AND LAROCHE.

1. ORIGINAL EDITIONS

Almanachs

1552 for 1553 (Chaussard, Lyon); 1553 for 1554 ("Bertot," Lyon); 1554 for 1555 (Brotot, Lyon); 1555 for 1556 (by report only); 1556 for 1557 (Kerver, Paris); 1557 for 1557 (Kerver, Paris); 1557 for 1558 (Brotot & Volant, Lyon); transl., 1557 for 1557 (Cicognera, Milan); 1558 for 1558 (Antwerp); 1558 for 1558 (Brotot & Volant, Lyon); 1558 for 1559 (Brotot, Lyon); 1558 for 1558 (Antwerp); pirated English transl., 1558 for 1559 ("Antwerp," but possibly London); 1559 for 1560 (le Noir, Paris); transl., 1559 for 1559 (Sutton, London); transl., 1559 (Copland, London); 1559 for 1560 (Brotot & Volant, Lyon); 1560 for 1560 (?); 1560 for 1561 (Regnault, Paris); transl., 1560 for 1561 (Hackett, London); 1560 for 1561 (?); transl., 1560 for 1560 (Germany?); 1561 for 1562 (le Noir & Bonfons, Paris); 1561 for 1562 (Volant & Brotot, Lyon); 1561 for 1562 (Regnault, Paris); 1562 for 1563 (Roux, Avignon); 1562 for 1563 (Regnault, Paris); transl., 1562 for 1562 (Powell, London); transl., 1562 for 1563 (Benaccio, Bologna); transl., 1563 for 1564 (London); transl., 1564 for 1565 (Genoa); 1564 for 1565 (Benoist Rigaud, Lyon); 1565 for 1565 (Odo, Lyon); 1565 for 1566 (Volant & Brotot, Lyon); transl., 1565, summary predictions for 1565 to 1570 (Genoa); 1566 for 1566/7 (Gerard, Lyon); transl., 1566 for 1566 (Florence); 1566 for 1567 (Volant & Brotot, Lyon); 1566 for 1567 (Odo, Lyon); transl., 1566 for 1566 (Denham, London); 1566 for 1567 (Nyverd, Paris); transl., 1566 for 1567 (Bynnyman, London); 1566 for 1567/8 (Nyverd, Paris); transl., 1566 for 1566 (Benatio, Bologna); transl., 1566 for 1566 (Giolito?, Venice?); transl., 1566 for 1567 (Italy); transl.?, 1566 for 1568? (London); 1566 for 1567/8 (Jove, Lyon)

Propheties

❖ First edition (*Préface à César* and *Centuries* I.1 to IV.53): 1555 (Roux, Avignon); 1555 (Bonhomme, Lyon); 1556 (Roux, Avignon); 1556 (Denyse, Lyon); 1588 (du Petit Val, Rouen); 1589 (ditto)

❖ Second edition (*Préface à César* and *Centuries* I.1 to VII.40): 1557 (du Rosne, Lyon)

❖ Third edition (*Centuries* VIII.1 to X.100): 1558 (reported only); 1558 (de Tournes, Lyon)

❖ Fourth edition (*Préface à César* and *Centuries* I.1 to VII.42, followed by *Lettre à Henri II* and *Centuries* VIII.1 to X.100): 1561 (Regnault, Paris); 1568 (Benoist Rigaud, Lyon); 1588 (Roffet, Paris); 1588 (Ménier, Paris); 1589 (ditto); 1589 (Roger, Paris); 1590 (Roux, Avignon); 1590 (Rousseau, Cahors); 1594–6 (Benoist Rigaud, Lyon); 1597 (heirs of Benoist Rigaud, Lyon); 1600 (Poyet, Lyon); 1604 (Pierre Rigaud, Lyon)

❖ Fifth edition (*Préface à César* and *Centuries* I.1 to IV.53, followed by *Lettre à Henri II* and *Centuries* VIII.1 to X.100, plus 141 *Presages*, 58 *Sixains* and 25 "extra" quatrains for *Centuries* VII, VIII, "XI" and "XII": 1605 (Seve / Benoist Rigaud)

Traité des fardemens / Excellent & Moult Utile Opuscule / Le Vray et Parfaict Embellissement de la Face etc.

1555 (Volant, Lyon); 1556 (Volant, Lyon); 1556 (de Harsy, Paris); 1557 (Plantin, Antwerp); 1560 (Volant, Lyon); 1567 (de Marnefz & Bouchetz, Poitiers); ed. César, 1568 (Nyverd, Paris); 1572 (Bonfons, Paris); 1572 (Benoist Rigaud, Lyon); transl. Mertz, 1572 (Manger, Augsburg); transl., 1573 (ditto); transl., 1589 (ditto)

Paraphrase de C Galen (transl. Nostradamus)

1557 (du Rosne, Lyon); 1558 (du Rosne, Lyon); 1559 (du Rosne, Lyon);

Les Significations de l'Eclipse, qui sera le 16. Septembre 1559 . . .

1559 for 1559/60 (le Noir, Paris); transl., 1559 for 1560 (Daye, London)

Prophetie Merveilleuse for 1560–8

1560 (de Nyverd, Paris)

Le Remede tres utile contre la peste . . .

1561 (Nyverd, Paris)

Traité d'Astrologie

1563 (Paris)

Lettre . . . A la Royne mere du Roy

1566 (Benoist Rigaud, Lyon)

2. ANTEDATED EDITIONS

Propheties

"1566" (Pierre Rigaud, Lyon); "1568" (Sève/Pierre Rigaud, Lyon, probably 1610)

CENTURIES

Extraict des regiſtres de la
Seneſchaucée de Lion.

S.VR CE que Macé Bonhomme Imprimeur
demeurant à Lyon, ha dict auoir recouuert certain
liure, intitulé, LES PROPHETIES DE MICHEL
NOSTRADAMVS, qu'il feroit volentiers imprimer
s'il nous plaiſoit, luy permettre ce requerāt: & outre
ce defenſes eſtre faictes à tous Imprimeurs & autres de ne l'imprimer, ou faire imprimer de deux
ans. Et apres que le dict liure ha eſté par nous veu en
auctis poincts d'iceluy & que le dict Macé Bōhōme
ha affermé en tout icelui liure n'auoir aucune choſe
concernant la foy prohibée. Auons, ouy ſur ce le procureur du Roy permis, & permetons au dict Macé
Bonhomme de pouoir imprimer, & faire imprimer
le dict liure. Et ſi auons faict defences de par le Roy
à tous imprimeurs d'icellui n'imprimer dès deux ans
à conter du iour & date de la preſente à peine de
confiſcation deſdicts liures: et d'amende arbitraire.
Faict à Lyon par nous Hugues du Puis, ſeigneur
de la Mothe, Conſeillier du Roy, & Lieutenant par-
ticulier en la Senechaucée de Lyon: le dernier iour
d'Apuril, l'an mil cinq cents cinquante cinq.
Collation faicte.
Signé,   Du Puys.   I. Croppet.

PREFACE

DE M. MICHEL
NOSTRADAMVS
à ſes Propheties.

Ad Cæſarem Noſtradamum filium
VIE ET FELICITE.

 ON TARD aduenement
CESAR NOSTRADAME
mon filz, m'a faict mettre mon
long temps par continuelles
vigilations nocturnes referer
par eſcript, toy delaiſſer me-
moire, apres la corporelle extinction de ton
progeniteur, au commun profit des humains
de ce que la Diuine eſſence par Aſtronomi-
ques reuolutions m'ont donné congnoiſſan-
ce. Et depuis qu'il a pleu au Dieu immortel
A ij

Privilège and first page of Bonhomme's 1555 edition of the *Centuries*

SURVIVING COPIES OF EARLY EDITIONS

THE FOLLOWING institutions hold original copies of the early editions listed. The Almanacs are variously described and cataloged as *Almanachs*, *Prognostications* or *Presages*. Principal source: Chomarat and Laroche

Aarau Cantonal Library: *Propheties* (SEVE, RIGAUD, 1605)

Aix-en-Provence, Arbaud Library: *Almanachs* (KERVER, PARIS, 1557 FOR 1557; ROUX, 1562 FOR 1563); *Lettre . . . A la Royne mere du Roy* (RIGAUD, 1566); *Propheties* (RIGAUD, 1568, THREE VERSIONS; SEVE/RIGAUD, 1605); *Traité des fardemens* (DE HARSY, PARIS, 1556; RIGAUD, 1572[40])

Albi Municipal Library: *Propheties* (BONHOMME, 1555)

Amiens Municipal Library: *Propheties* (SEVE, 1611)

Angers Municipal Library: *Propheties* (MÉNIER, 1589)

Ann Arbor University Library: *Almanachs* (TRANSL. INTO ENGLISH, SUTTON, LONDON, 1559 FOR 1559)

Antwerp, Plantin-Moretus Library: *Traité des fardemens*[41] (PLANTIN, ANTWERP, C. 1557)

Arles Municipal Library: *Propheties* (HEIRS OF BENOIST RIGAUD, 1597; PIERRE RIGAUD, 1604)

Besançon Municipal Library: *Paraphrase de C. Galen* (DU ROSNE, 1558)

Bethesda, N. Library of Medicine: *Traité des fardemens* (TRANSL. INTO GERMAN BY MERTZ, AUGSBURG, 1572; DITTO 1573)

Brussels, AG: *Almanachs* (LE NOIR & BONFONS, 1561 FOR 1562)

Brussels, Royal Library: *Propheties* (SEVE, 1611; DITTO, ANTEDATED "1568")

Budapest National Library: *Propheties* (DU ROSNE, 1557)

Caen Municipal Library: *Propheties* (SEVE, 1611, ANTEDATED "1568")

Caen University Library: *Propheties* (SEVE, 1611, ANTEDATED "1568")

Cambridge, University Library: *Propheties* (SEVE, 1611, ANTEDATED "1568"); *Traité des fardemens* (VOLANT, 1555; PLANTIN, ANTWERP, C. 1557)

Carpentras Municipal Library: *Traité des fardemens* (DE HARSY, PARIS, 1556)

Châlons-sur-Marne Municipal Library: Propheties (SEVE, 1611, TWO VERSIONS)

Châteauroux Municipal Library: *Propheties* (RIGAUD, 1568)

Cherbourg Municipal Library: *Propheties* (SEVE, 1611, ANTEDATED "1568")

Chicago, John Crerar Library: *Traité des fardemens* (DE HARSY, PARIS, 1556)

Nostradamus at work in his study

Chicago, Newberry Library: *Propheties* (SEVE, 1605, ANTEDATED "1568")

Copenhagen, Royal Library: *Propheties* (SEVE/RIGAUD, 1605; SEVE, 1611, ANTEDATED "1568"; SEVE 1611)

Dijon Municipal Library: *Propheties* (SEVE, 1611, ANTEDATED "1568")

Dôle Municipal Library: *Propheties* (RIGAUD, 1568)

Dresden, Landsbibliothek: *Propheties* (RIGAUD, 1568; SEVE, 1611, ANTEDATED "1568")

Edinburgh, National Library: *Propheties* (SEVE, 1605, ANTEDATED "1568")

Florence, National Library: *Propheties* (RIGAUD, 1568)

Grenoble Municipal Library: *Propheties* (RIGAUD, 1568; SEVE/RIGAUD, 1605; SEVE, 1611, ANTEDATED "1568")

Harvard City Library: *Propheties* (SEVE, 1611)

Harvard University Library: *Propheties* (PIERRE RIGAUD, 1610; SEVE, 1611); *Traité des fardemens* (TRANSL. INTO GERMAN BY MERTZ, AUGSBURG, 1572)

Heidelberg University Library: *Propheties* (RIGAUD, 1568)

Ithaca University Library: *Propheties* (SEVE, 1611)

Krakow Library: *Almanachs* (TRANSL. INTO ITALIAN, 1567 FOR 1567)

Le Mans Municipal Library: *Propheties* (SEVE, 1611); *Traité des fardemens* (DE HARSY, PARIS, 1556)

Libourne Municipal Library: *Propheties* (SEVE/RIGAUD, 1605)

Lille Municipal Library: *Almanachs* (REGNAULT, 1562 FOR 1563)

London, British Library: *Almanachs* (TRANSL. INTO ENGLISH, "ANTWERP," 1558 FOR 1559; DITTO, LONDON [?],

---

40 *As Excellent & Moult Utile Opuscule . . .*

41 *As Le Vray et Parfaict Embellissement de la Face . . .*

1567 FOR 1568 [!], INCOMPLETE); *Propheties* (MÉNIER, 1588; ROFFET, 1588; MÉNIER, 1589; SEVE/RIGAUD, 1605; SEVE, 1611); *Traité des fardemens* (VOLANT 1556;[42] PLANTIN, ANTWERP, CA 1557;[43] NYVERD, 1567, INCOMPLETE; TRANSL. INTO GERMAN BY MERTZ, AUGSBURG, 1589)

London, Harry Price Library: *Propheties* (RIGAUD, 1594-6)

London, Lambeth Palace: *Almanachs* (TRANSL. INTO ENGLISH, COPLAND, 1559 FOR 1559)

London, Wellcome Library: *Propheties* (RIGAUD, 1568; SEVE/RIGAUD, 1605); *Traité des fardemens* (TRANSL. INTO GERMAN BY MERTZ, AUGSBURG, 1572; DITTO 1589)

Lyon Municipal Library: *Paraphrase de C. Galen* (DU ROSNE, 1557); *Propheties* (RIGAUD, 1568, INCOMPLETE; PIERRE RIGAUD, 1610; SEVE, 1611; SEVE, 1611, ANTEDATED "1568")

Marseille Municipal Library: *Propheties* (RIGAUD, 1568, TWO COPIES)

Milan, Ambrosiana Library: *Almanachs* (TRANSL. INTO ITALIAN, CICOGNERA, 1557; TRANSL. INTO ENGLISH, DENHAM, LONDON, 1566 FOR 1566)

Montreal, Osler Medical Library: *Almanachs* (VOLANT & BROTOT, C. 1565 FOR 1566)

Montpellier University Library; *Propheties* (SEVE, 1611, ANTEDATED "1568")

Moscow, Lenin Library: *Propheties* (DU ROSNE, 1557)

Munich, State Library: *Almanachs* (KERVER, PARIS, 1556 FOR 1557; KERVER, PARIS, 1557 FOR 1557; ANTWERP, 1558 FOR 1558; BROTOT & VOLANT, 1558 FOR 1558; ANTWERP, 1558 FOR 1558; TRANSL. INTO ENGLISH, "ANTWERP," 1558 FOR 1559; PARIS, 1560 FOR 1560; TRANSL. INTO GERMAN, 1560 FOR 1560; REGNAULT, PARIS, 1561 FOR 1562; TRANSL. INTO ITALIAN, 1565 FOR 1566); *Traité des fardemens* (TRANSL. INTO GERMAN BY MERTZ, AUGSBURG, 1572)

Nantes Municipal Library: *Propheties* (RIGAUD, 1568)

Naples, National Library: *Almanachs* (VOLANT & BROTOT, C. 1565 FOR 1566)

New Brunswick University Library: *Propheties* (SEVE, 1611)

New York, Columbia University Library: *Propheties* (SEVE, 1611)

Oxford, Bodleian Library: *Propheties* (Seve/Rigaud, 1605)

Oxford, Taylorian: *Propheties* (Rigaud, 1568)

Paris, Arsenal Library: *Propheties* (SAINCT JAURE, 1590; MOREAU, 1603; SEVE/RIGAUD, 1605; SEVE, 1605, ANTEDATED "1568"); *Traité des fardemens* (VOLANT, 1555;[44] DE HARSY, PARIS, 1556; PLANTIN, ANTWERP, 1557; MARNEFZ & BOUCHETZ, 1567[45])

Paris, Mazarine Library: *Paraphrase de C. Galen* (DU ROSNE, 1557); *Propheties* (MÉNIER, 1588, MOREAU, 1603); *Traité des fardemens* (BONFONS, 1572;[46] TRANSL. INTO GERMAN BY MERTZ, AUGSBURG, 1589); RIGAUD, 1572)

Paris, National Library: *Almanachs* (NYVERD, PARIS, C. 1560 FOR 1560; TRANSL. INTO ITALIAN, 1564 FOR 1564; RIGAUD, 1564 FOR 1564; TRANSL. INTO ITALIAN, C. 1565 FOR 1565; TRANSL. INTO ITALIAN, 1566 FOR 1566); *Propheties* (MÉNIER, 1589; POYET, 1600; PIERRE RIGAUD, 1610; CHEVILLOT, 1611; SEVE, 1611, TWO VERSIONS; SEVE, 1605, ANTEDATED "1568"); *Traité des fardemens* (VOLANT, 1555)

Paris, Ste-Geneviève: *Propheties* (SEVE/RIGAUD, 1605; SEVE, 1605, ANTEDATED "1568"); *Traité des fardemens* (NYVERD, 1567,[47] INCOMPLETE; RIGAUD, 1572[48])

Philadelphia, Krauth Memorial Library: *Traité des fardemens* (TRANSL. INTO GERMAN BY MERTZ, AUGSBURG, 1572)

Rome, Vatican Library: *Traité des fardemens* (TRANSL. INTO GERMAN BY MERTZ, AUGSBURG, 1573)

Salon, Maison de Nostradamus: *Propheties* (LYON, "1558")

San Marino, Huntington Library: *Almanachs* (TRANSL. INTO ENGLISH, POWELL, LONDON, 1562 FOR 1563)

Schaffhausen Municipal Library: *Propheties*

(RIGAUD, 1568)

Strasbourg Municipal Library: *Propheties* (SEVE, 1611, ANTEDATED "1568")

Toulouse Municipal Library: *Propheties* (PIERRE RIGAUD, 1610)

Troyes Municipal Library: *Propheties* (CHEVILLOT, 1611; SEVE, 1611, TWO VERSIONS)

Urbana University Library, Illinois: *Almanachs* (TRANSL. INTO ENGLISH, 1562 FOR 1563; DITTO 1563 FOR 1564)

Utrecht University Library: *Propheties* (DU ROSNE, 1557)

Venice, National Library: *Almanachs* (TRANSL. INTO ITALIAN, 1566 FOR 1566)

Venice, St. Mark's Library: *Propheties* (PIERRE RIGAUD, 1604)

Vienna, National Library: *Propheties* (BONHOMME, 1555; SEVE/RIGAUD, 1605)

Washington, Folger Shakespeare Library: *Almanachs* (TRANSL. INTO ENGLISH, POWELL, LONDON, 1562 FOR 1563, INCOMPLETE; TRANSL. INTO ENGLISH, BYNNYMAN, LONDON, 1566 FOR 1567)

Washington City Library: *Propheties* (SEVE, 1611)

Wolfenbüttel HA Library: *Almanachs* (TRANSL. INTO GERMAN, C. 1560 FOR 1560; NYVERD, 1566 FOR 1567); *Traité des fardemens* (TRANSL. INTO GERMAN BY MERTZ, AUGSBURG, 1589)

Wrozlaw University Library: *Propheties* (RIGAUD, 1568)

Yale Medical School: *Traité des fardemens* (TRANSL. INTO GERMAN BY MERTZ, AUGSBURG, 1572)

---

[42] As *Excellent & Moult Utile Opuscule* . . .

[43] As *Le Vray et Parfaict Embellissement de la Face* . . .

[44] As *Excellent & Moult Utile Opuscule* . . .

[45] As *Excellent & Utile Opuscule* . . .

[46] As *L'embellissement de la face* . . .

[47] As *Bastiment de plusieurs receptes* . . .

[48] As *Excellent Et Tres Util Opuscule* . . .

BOOKS, FILMS, VIDEOS, DISKS, AND INTERNET

European/American publishers are indicated by obliques.

BOOKS

Amadou, R.: *L'Astrologie de Nostradamus* (DOSSIER, 1992/)
French translations of fifty-one pieces of Nostradamus's Latin correspondence.

Benazra, R.: *Répertoire Chronologique Nostradamique* (*1545–1989*) (1990)
A bibliographical survey of the Nostradamus literature to 1990.

Boeser, K. (ed.): *The Elixirs of Nostradamus* (BLOOMSBURY/HARPERCOLLINS, 1995)
1995 English translation of a 1994 German version of a 1572 German translation of the 1555 French original of the *Traité des fardemens*. Not surprisingly, more like Chinese whispers. *Un personnaige à jeun* (which means a person fasting) comes out, with depressing predictability, as "a young man"; *roses rouges incarnées* (infolded red roses) repeatedly as "black orchids"; *urines* (urine) as "drinking wells"; *seignées* (blood-lettings) as "permitted remedies." If *you* permit them, you will have only yourself to blame.

Boeser, K.: *Nostradamus* (BLOOMSBURY, 1994/)
The book of the film (see below).

Brennan, J.H.: *Nostradamus; Visions of the Future* (AQUARIAN, 1992/)
An informed book that nevertheless argues the case for a range of common assumptions about Nostradamus.

Cannon, D.: *Conversations with Nostradamus: His Prophecies Explained*, Vols 1, 2 and 3 (/OZARK MOUNTAIN, 1989 ONWARD)
Original and creative, this proposes (among other things) the view that Nostradamus saw the future world through our eyes:

evidently, too, it invites us to see his world through the author's.

Capel, S.: *Nostradamus: His Life and Predictions* (STUDIO EDITIONS, 1995/)
A relatively slim "coffeetable book," padded out with creative artwork.

Cheetham, E.: *The Final Prophecies of Nostradamus* (FUTURA/PERIGREE, 1989)
Basically a fatter and almost equally reliable version of its original predecessor, this in fact contains (despite its title) the same old prophecies (i.e. the *Centuries* only), but this time in the 1568 edition's original typography: highly recommended for this reason alone.

Cheetham, E.: *The Further Prophecies of Nostradamus* (CORGI/PERIGREE, 1985–91)
A selection of the same prophecies again, but this time amplified and mulled over at greater length.

Cheetham, E.: *The Prophecies of Nostradamus* (CORGI/PERIGREE, 1973; /BERKELEY, 1981)
This volume is a good deal more valuable for its complete French transliteration of the 1568 edition of the *Centuries* (see Early Editions) than for the reliability of its word-

for-word translations, its biographical details, or its etymological research.

Chomarat, M. & Laroche, Dr. J.-P.: *Bibliographie Nostradamus* (KOERNER, 1989/)
The definitive guide to early editions of Nostradamus, written by the two foremost authorities on the subject.

Dupèbe, J.: *Nostradamus, Lettres Inédites* (1993)
Fifty-one previously unpublished Latin letters to and from Nostradamus, mainly on the subject of personal horoscopes (see **Amadou** above).

Erickstad, H.G.B.: *The Prophecies of Nostradamus in Historical Order* (JANUS, 1996/VANTAGE, 1982)
Literalistic renderings of some 350 of the *Centuries*, displaying an antipodean slant on Cheetham's view of history and Nostradamus's of the coming Muslim invasion. Improbably, if predictably, identifies Jacques Chirac as *CHYREN*.

Fontbrune, J.-C. de: *Nostradamus 1: Countdown to Apocalypse* (PAN/HOLT, 1983; CRESSET, 1993, PT. 1)
An English translation of *Nostradamus, historien et prophète*, this is an inventive, if dense, interpretation of the first of 600 or so of the *Centuries*, *Presages*, and *Sixains* in the 1605 edition (see Early Editions), arranged in proposed sequence.

Fontbrune, J.-C. de: *Nostradamus 2: Into the Twenty-First Century* (/HOLT, 1984; CRESSET 1993, PT. 2)
Seemingly designed to mop up the residue of the verses unclaimed by Book 1, this volume alone contains the all-important index for both volumes.

Hewitt, V.J.: *Nostradamus: The Key to the Centuries* (HUTCHINSON, 1994/)
Demonstrates the remarkable technique whereby the writer, apparently despairing of making sense of the prophecies as they

stand, treats them instead as anagrammatical oracles, so offering remarkable insights into the author's mind.

Hewitt, V.J. & Lorie, P.: *Nostradamus: the End of the Millennium* (BLOOMSBURY / SIMON & SCHUSTER, 1991)

This distinctly original book once again treats the prophecies as anagrammatical oracles to be dismembered and intuitively re-assembled into what claims to be French.

Hogue, J.: *Nostradamus and the Millennium* (BLOOMSBURY, 1987/)

Hogue's original "coffeetable book" on Nostradamus, full of dire warnings and colorful illustrations.

Hogue, J.: *The Nostradamus Date Book* (BLOOMSBURY, 1989/)

Evidently a spinoff of the above.

Hogue, J.: *Nostradamus: The New Revelations* (ELEMENT / ELEMENT, 1994)

Another "coffeetable book," this lavish production at least attempts honest interpretations of some 600 of the *Centuries* and *Presages*, even if only in isolation.

Ionescu, V.: *Les dernières victoires de Nostradamus* (Filipacchi, 1993/)

Interpretations and commentaries by a much-respected scholar who actually got it right.

Kidogo, Bardo (BARRY POPKESS): *The Keys to the Predictions of Nostradamus* (FOULSHAM, 1994/)

A sober, if complex, guide for decoding Nostradamus that possibly credits the seer with an even more devious mind than he actually possessed: incorporates a useful, if select, Nostradamus glossary.

King, Francis X.: *Nostradamus: Prophecies Fulfilled and Predictions for the Millennium and Beyond* (BCA, 1993/)

Perhaps the most genuinely informative of all the "coffeetable books" to date.

Laver, J.: *Nostradamus or the Future Foretold* (MANN, 1942–81/)

Almost the first English book on Nostradamus to be even halfway rational for some hundreds of years – and arguably the last for another fifty or more. By way of a bonus, offers translations of the prophecies of Olivarius and Orval.

Lemesurier, P.: *Nostradamus: The Final Reckoning* (PIATKUS, 1995 / BERKELEY, 1997)

Mixes predictions by Nostradamus and others in an effort to map out the next 2,500 years, quoting over 150 specific dates, as well as verse-translations of many of the *Sixains*: the "final reckoning" may refer either to the author's dates or to the prospects for his interpretation.

Nineteenth-century impression of Nostradamus (the telescope was not officially invented until 1608)

Lemesurier, P.: *Nostradamus – The Next 50 Years* (PIATKUS, 1993 / BERKELEY, 1994)

Despite a derivative potted biography uncorrected by later research, this offers the first sequenced English verse translation of some 430 of the *Centuries*, *Presages*, and *Sixains* with commentaries.

Leoni, E.: *Nostradamus and his Prophecies* (WINGS, 1961–82)

Widely read American account, with trans-

lations and commentaries.

Leroy, Dr. E.: *Nostradamus: ses origines, sa vie, son œuvre* (LAFITTE, 1993/)

The authoritative guide to the seer's life and work, based on years of research into local archives and original sources.

Lorie, P. (with Greene, L): *Nostradamus: The Millennium and Beyond* (BLOOMSBURY / SIMON & SCHUSTER, 1993)

A creative "coffeetable" treatment of (a) astrology and (b) Nostradamus.

Lorie, P. (with Mascetti): *Nostradamus's Prophecies for Women* (BLOOMSBURY, 1995/)

A further "coffeetable book" about (a) women and (b) Nostradamus.

Mareuil, J. de: *Les ultimes prophéties de Nostradamus* (GRANCHER, 1994/)

If the author is right in suggesting that the sixty-five anonymous verses quoted and analyzed are by Nostradamus, no wonder the seer left them at Orval.

Mézo, E.: *Ainsi parlait Nostradamus* (DU ROCHER, 1995–6/)

A French perspective.

Nostradamus, M.: *Lettre à Catherine de Médicis* (CHOMARAT, 1996/)

A beautifully produced facsimile of the seer's last known letter in his capacity as Royal Councilor.

Nostradamus, M.: *Orus Apollo*, ed. Rollet, P., as *Interprétation des hiéroglyphes de Horapollo* (MARCEL PETIT, 1993/)

First publication (with extremely enthusiastic commentary) of manuscript 2594 from the Bibliothèque Nationale, which possibly sheds some light on Nostradamus's (a) symbolism and (b) view of translation.

Nostradamus, M.: *Les Prophéties*, Lyon, 1557 (CHOMARAT, 1993/)

Facsimile of du Rhône's second edition, published by the man who rediscovered the long-lost first edition in 1984 and has done more than anybody else to rescue the real Nostradamus from centuries of falsification and misrepresentation.

Nostradamus, M.: *Traité des fardemens et confitures*, published as *Le Vray et Parfaict Embellissement de la Face*, in Plantin's Antwerp edition of 1557
(GUTENBERG REPRINTS, 1979/)
Facsimile of complete text (compare Boeser (ed.), above).

Ovason, D.: *The Secrets of Nostradamus* (CENTURY, 1997/)
Undoubtedly the best-informed general book in English on Nostradamus to date, based on recent French research. Some readers may find it a bit heavy on esoteric language and astrology; others will feel that this is just what the doctor ordered.

Pitt Francis, D.: *Nostradamus: Prophecies of Present Times?*
(AQUARIAN, 1984/)
A sober biblical scholar seeks to demonstrate with tables, statistics, and careful arguments that Nostradamus was merely amplifying and blurring biblical prophecies to predict events up to the end of the world at the end of the twentieth century; then wonders if he himself is not the final interpreter predicted by the prophet.

Roberts, H.C.: *The Complete Prophecies of Nostradamus*
(GRAFTON/NOSTRADAMUS CO., 1985)
The complete French text of the *Centuries* (including "extras" – see Nostradamus's Writings) in a version based on the corrupt 1672 edition by Garencières and accompanied by mercifully brief interpretive comments.

Thing Enterprises, N.E.: *Nostradamus Magic Eye*
(JOSEPH, 1995/)
Not everybody will see Anything in this genre puzzle-book, which is full of illusions.

Ward, C.A.: *Oracles of Nostradamus* (SOCIETY OF METAOPHYSICICIANS [FACSIMILE OF 1890 ED.], 1990, 1995/MODERN LIBRARY [SCRIBNER], 1940)
A highly literary early survey of Nostradamus and his work, all the better for having never heard of later speculations.

Engraving from Torné-Chavigny's *Influence de Nostradamus*

Woldben, A. (trans. from Italian): *After Nostradamus*
(MAYFLOWER, 1975/)
This book summarizes a wide range of prophecies in addition to some of Nostradamus's and claims to have been translated from the Italian.

FILMS

Nostradamus (NOSTRADAMUS ENTERPRISES LTD.)
Tells an inventive story with flair: allegedly caused much laughter at its British première.

VIDEOS

Nostradamus (VA 30610: FIRST INDEPENDENT)
The video of the film (see above).

The Man Who Saw Tomorrow
(WARNER HOME VIDEOS: PES 61246: 1981)
Superbly narrated by Orson Welles and featuring the American prophetess Jeane Dixon, this production, based on selective extracts from Cheetham's interpretations, illustrates allegedly predicted past events with excerpts from period drama and newsreel footage that put in the shade its somewhat meager predictions for the future.

Nostradamus: A Voice from the Past (POWER SPORTS INTERNATIONAL: DCL 1062: 1994)
With the aid of a laryngitic Nostradamus and wholesale borrowings from the earlier video, this technically mediocre production somehow manages to combine half-sensible speculations about past fullfilments with some of V.J. Hewitt's interpretations for the future (see above).

Nostradamus, Prophète de l'an 2000? (SOCIÉTÉ YN PRODUCTIONS, LYON)
An authoritative survey by Michel Chomarat, produced by Lionel Chomarat, in which local and foreign experts rehabilitate the real Nostradamus and put off the end of the world.

Nostradamus: Prophet of Doom (IMC 082: GREYSTONE)
Commentators who should know better trot out all the usual misconceptions, and add a host of others besides.

DISKS

Salon-de-Provence: Maison de Nostradamus (INTERSIGNE MÉDITERRANÉE / STUDIOS CAAV-ARTHEA, 1992)
The official *guide sonore* to the Maison de Nostradamus at Salon (available on site in various languages), delivered in best French literary style.

Stewart, A.l.: *Live*
(RCA LP 9001/PL 25391)
Album including the track entitled Nostradamus, which contains the memorable refrain:

> *Man, man, your time is sand, your ways are leaves upon the sea.*
> *I am the eyes of Nostradamus. All your ways are known to me.*

THE INTERNET

NOTE: *There are numerous Nostradamus Websites on the Internet, including the complete Propheties (both in French and in translation). There is also a lively Nostradamus Newsgroup at alt.prophecies.nostradamus.*

PART THREE

PROPHECIES

Dating, sequencing, and interpreting the prophecies; a selection of the prophecies themselves.

DATING AND SEQUENCING
THE PROPHECIES

NOSTRADAMUS'S prophecies are self-evidently in scrambled order. Sequencing them is thus one of the most urgent – yet at the same time one of the most challenging – of the would-be interpreter's tasks. Fulfilling it, however, is dependent upon the discovery of certain guiding clues, and above all

    1. dated predictions,
    2. summary-verses,
    3. linked verses,
    4. paired verses.

This article will consider each of these in turn.

1. DATED PREDICTIONS

In his *Lettre à Henri II*, Nostradamus claims to be able to put a date on each of his prophecies: *si je voulois à un chacun quatrain mettre le denombrement du temps*, he writes, *se pourroit faire: mais à tous ne seroit aggreable, ne moins les interpreter, iusques à ce, Sire, que vostre Majesté m'aye octroyé ample puissance pour ce faire, pour ne donner cause aux calomniateurs de me mordre.*[1]

Clearly, he felt vulnerable, and having left his quatrains in random order so as to avoid accusations of witchcraft and worse, he was not now about to blow his cover by putting dates on them all. On the other hand, if he left *no dates at all* he might just as easily be accused of merely fishing in the dark – of writing prophecies so general and unspecific that they were bound to be fulfilled somewhere or other, sooner or later.

On the one hand, then, he might be seen as too good a prophet for his own good; on the other, as too poor a one to be taken seriously.

The obvious answer was some kind of compromise – the inclusion of just sufficient dated predictions to permit those with the necessary intelligence to erect some kind of basic temporal framework around which to assemble the rest of the prophecies in some sort of rational sequence. Yet even these dates must not be too obvious. For the most part they must require more than a little knowledge and experience on the part of the would-be decoder – and a good deal of patience to boot.

The upshot is a multiple system. A few of Nostradamus's dates are *en clair* – that is, normal calendar dates. Some are purely astrological. Others are based on his little-known "liturgical" count, first introduced in quatrains VI.54 and VIII.71 and wielded generously in his *Sixains*. Yet others can be deduced by applying the principles of comparative horoscopy to the details presented.

Calendar datings

These are based on the ordinary, familiar system of year numbering – though, except in his *Presages*, the dates are spelled out in words rather than set down in figures. This means, of course, that researchers are faced with the former French words for seventy, eighty, and ninety – *septante*, *octante*, and *nonante* – which are still used in Belgium and Switzerland (and, though old-fashioned, are in fact much less clumsy than their current French equivalents, which correspond to old English "three score and ten" and so on).

Incidentally, it was fairly normal at the time to omit the *mil* from the beginning of a date, just as today we are happy to talk of the '14 to '18 war, or of the prospects of Hong Kong after '97. César, indeed, follows the modern practice in his *Histoire et Chronique de Provence* when dating the affair of the two-headed kid to '54 (see Nostradamus's Omens). The former practice shows up in both "calendrical" and "liturgical" counts.

Thus, while I.49 specifies *mil sept cens* (1700), III.77 *mil sept cens vingt & sept* (1727), and the famous X.72 *mil neuf cens nonante neuf* (1999), VI.2 merely offers *cinq cens octante* ('580).

Astrological datings

Only five planets were known in Nostradamus's time – Mercury, Venus, Mars, Jupiter, and Saturn. So all astrological datings had to be in terms of these, plus the sun and moon. In the *Propheties*, such datings are often defined by the presence of one or more of them in a particular sign. Sometimes actual *conjunctions* are specified.

Heavenly bodies are normally said to be "in conjunction" when they are within a couple of degrees or so of each other (even this, after all, amounts to four lunar or solar diameters), though many authorities accept up to four degrees, while others seem happy to extend this to a dozen degrees or more. Precisely which definition Nostradamus used is not known, though it seems possible that he regarded planets as "in conjunction" even if they were merely within the same sign or house. Nevertheless it would seem wise to apply one of the smaller figures when decoding his astrological fixes, since this tends to narrow down the "window of possibilities" somewhat.

"Window," however, is the operative word. With Saturn – the "slowest" of the then known planets – orbiting the sun once every $29\frac{1}{2}$ years or so, and the others more often, it follows that each of Nostradamus's astrological "datings" is a kind of "movable feast,"

---

1   "If I wished to set down in figures the timing of each quatrain, this could be done, but it would not be to the liking of everybody – still less interpreting them – until such time, Sire, as Your Majesty has granted me ample authority to do so, lest the slanderers be given occasion to attack me."

potentially liable to repeat itself at least once every thirty years.

In order to "tie down" a particular astrological dating, consequently, it is necessary to relate it to some other verse containing a particular *calendrical, liturgical,* or *horoscopic* date (see below), or at very least to establish whether or not the verse in question has already been fulfilled. If it has not, then the date in question presumably has to be related either to the *next* time that the particular alignment occurs, or to some subsequent occasion.

It should always be borne in mind, then, that Nostradamus's astrological datings can seldom, if ever, be regarded as absolute.

As far as practicalities are concerned, the best technique for consulting a planetary Ephemeris in this connection – and certainly the one that is least time-consuming – is probably to work from the outermost planetary body inward. In other words, pinpoint the likely limiting dates for Saturn first, then, within these, the dates for Jupiter, Mars, Venus, Mercury, the sun, and the moon, in that order. *Less specific Nostradamian definitions such as "under Cancer" normally refer to the sun's zodiacal position, and thus primarily to the time of year.*

The next likely datings for some of the main astrologically dated quatrains are (in chronological order) as follows:

V.25: August 21st–22nd, 1998
I.51: February 13th–28th, 1999
I.83: May 1st–8th, 2002
VI.24: June 29th–July 8th, 2002
III.3: August 17th, 2004
*II.65 (*if *fenera* implies retrograde*):* December 2004
III.96: February 13th, 2006
IX.73: February 15th–18th, 2009
IX.55: April 2nd–May 11th, 2011
I.52 (deux malins = Saturn, Mars*):* August 23rd–29th, 2014
VIII.2: August 9th–23rd, 2015
II.48:28(?) January 2017
X.50 (& trois = "3 others"*):* February 2nd–18th, 2021
IV.86 (eau = Aquarius*):* January 21st–26th, 2021
Sixain 46: April 16th, 2026
V.23: June 1st–15th, 2032
VIII.48: February 2034

Liturgical dates

Nostradamus is quite specific about this particular system of dating. At VI.54 he offers the following quatrain:

> Au point du iour au second chant du coq,
> Ceulx de Tunes, de Fez, & de Bugie:
> Par les Arabes captif le roy Maroq,
> L'an mil six cens & sept de Liturgie.

The pan-Arabic rising in question, clearly, is due to occur during the "year 1607 of the Liturgy." Totally ignoring what the seer actually says, most commentators – those who have bothered to think about it at all, that is – have tried to relate this to the Council of Nicaea of A.D. 325. But this council, well known though it is, had little if anything to do with the Church's liturgy. Its main concern was with matters of belief – whence, of course, the now celebrated Nicene Creed.

The simple question therefore has to be asked: when was the Roman Church's liturgy actually founded? There is no mystery about this. The Roman Church first became truly catholic – i.e. both mandatory and universal throughout the Roman Empire – on November 8th, A.D. 392, when the Emperor Theodosius I issued an edict to that effect. But precisely what was it that was thereby made mandatory and universal? Inevitably, the Church's beliefs and practices. The former had of course been largely settled by the Council of Nicaea – but the latter had only just been formalized by St. Ambrose into what is nowadays known as the Canon of the Mass, which constitutes the liturgical core of the office of Holy Communion. It is the year 392, consequently, that may be said to mark the effective foundation of the Church's liturgy.

The "year 1607 of the Liturgy," therefore, has to be the calendrical year (392 + 1607), *which works out at 1999.*

Just to rub the point home, Nostradamus refers to this count once again at VIII.71. This time he predicts a persecution of astrologers and/or astronomers that will occur in *l'an mil six cens & sept par sacre glomes.* The word *glomes* (on the evidence of the word *sacre,* apparently a singular noun) is a puzzle. It appears to be a form of Latin *glomus,* originally meaning a ball of twine (hence the English words "conglomerate" and "agglomeration"). Some commentators therefore assume that it refers to a Church gathering or council – and thus, once again, to the long-suffering Council of Nicaea – but this is no more likely to be right here than it was before. It could, of course, refer to the "congregation" of the Church here on earth, or to a "collection" of liturgical practices, which was what St. Ambrose's new rubric actually was. More likely, perhaps, it could be a reference to the "thread" of church history. Or possibly the word is simply a misprint for *gnomes* (from Paracelsus's Latin *gnomus,* based on the Greek *gnome*), meaning "intelligence, understanding, opinion." In this form, indeed, the word could even represent Greek *gnomon,* "pointer" or "sundial." The expression, on this basis, would simply mean "by the Church's time." One way or the other, then, the reference has once again to be to the foundation of the Catholic Church and its liturgy, and thus *to the year 1999.*

Quite why Nostradamus should have resorted to this particular dating system is not known. It is not impossible that he had foreseen the demise of the traditional calendar at the time of what he called *le commun advenement* (*Préface à César,* 2) – i.e. the French Revolution – as indeed actually happened. On top of this, such an arcane dating system would allow him to give actual dates while at the same time concealing them – a paradox that would certainly have appealed to his distinctly devious mind.

At all events, having broached the system in the *Centuries*, Nostradamus now proceeded to use it extensively, not in the *Centuries* themselves, but in the *Sixains* – a late collection of prophecies which, he could be fairly sure, would never be published during his lifetime and so would leave him quite safe in the event that somebody managed to break the dating code.

True, he does not explicitly state that their dates are liturgical ones. On the other hand, if they are calendar dates, they are flatly wrong – for almost all of them fall within the sixteen hundreds, yet remained unfulfilled during the historical seventeenth century. Moreover, once they are taken as *liturgical* dates they turn out to fit the other calendrical and astrological datings of the *Centuries* more or less like a glove (see below). The simple principle, therefore, needs to be stated: the *datings of the Sixains are evidently liturgical ones*. On this basis we are thus presented with a whole new series of dated prophecies – virtually all of them, as it happens, apparently referring to our own future.

In chronological order these are as follows:

Sixain 11:1996
Sixain 12:1997
Sixain 14:1997
Sixain 18:1997
Sixain 16:1997/8
Sixain 19:1997/8 to 2009
Sixain 25:1998/2001
Sixain 13:1998/2001
Sixain 28:1998 to 2001/6
Sixain 21:1999
Sixain 23:1999/2002
Sixain 24:2000/2012
Sixain 44:2002/7
Sixain 42:2002
Sixain 38:2007/2011
Sixain 54:2007/2012
Sixain 53:2062/2007/13/31

Dates fixed by comparative horoscopy

As with astrological datings, comparative horoscopy (see Astrologer and Mage and Sequence of Selected Horographs) is not of itself capable of fixing *absolute* dates. It can, however, suggest a range of *possible* dates that can then be compared with the datings already established by means of the other three methods above. The resulting "integrated list" *combining all four dating methods* can then serve as a basic framework for sequencing the rest of the prophecies.

The following is tentatively offered as a possible "integrated list" of dated predictions for the next half-century or so:

Date	Verse	Event	Dating method
1997	**Sixain 12**	*Feud between leaders*	*Liturgical*
1997	**Sixain 14**	*"Great siege" resumes in spring*	*Liturgical*
1997	**Sixain 18**	*"Greek nightingale" saved*	*Liturgical*
1997/8	**Sixain 16**	*British coronation or American inauguration (?)*	*Liturgical*
1997/8/ 2009	**Sixain 19**	*"Firebrand" arises and "Crocodile" reawakens*	*Liturgical*
1998	**V.25**	*"Arab Prince" from Iran (?) invades Turkey and Egypt with forces some million strong*	*Astrological*
1998	**V.86**	*Istanbul threatened from sea by Asiatic forces*	*Comparative horoscopy*
1998/ 2001	**Sixain 25**	*Chancellor "as big as an ox" visits Paris on retiring*	*Liturgical*
1998/ 2001	**Sixain 13**	*"Adventurer" dismissed by "supreme Emperor"*	*Liturgical*
1998/ 2001/6	**Sixain 28**	*"Old Charon" rewrites calendar, to the surprise of "Doctor"*	*Liturgical*
1999	**Lettre à Henri II (B.2)**	*Huge invasion of Turkey and Aegean by "another Xerxes" from Iran*	*Comparative horoscopy*
1999	**I.51**	*Vast disasters threaten France and Italy*	*Astrological*
1999	**Sixain 21**	*"Author of all ills" drives out "Leech," who flees home via France*	*Liturgical*
1999	**X.72**	*Pope flies to Ankara to try to buy off Asiatic invaders, but merely stirs the pot (see below)*	*Calendrical / Comparative horoscopy*
1999	**V.48, V.54, Presage 31**	*"Mongol" hordes invade southeast Europe and Balkans*	*Comparative horoscopy*
1999	**VIII.15**	*Reemergence of English "Joan of Arc" figure*	*Comparative horoscopy*
1999	**VI.54**	*Pan-Arabic rising in North Africa: King of Morocco imprisoned*	*Liturgical*
1999	**VIII.71**	*Growth in numbers of astrologers brings about ban on their books and persecution*	*Liturgical*
1999	**II.4, VII.6, VIII.84, Presage 31**	*Muslim sea-borne forces invade Sicily*	*Comparative horoscopy*
1999/ 2002	**Sixain 23**	*Violent attack on France from the sea*	*Liturgical*
2000/ 2012	**Sixain 24**	*"Mercurial" leader threatened, betrayed, and killed*	*Liturgical*

Date	Verse	Event	Dating method	Date	Verse	Event	Dating method
2000	IX.42	European navies beat off a larger Muslim fleet in new "Battle of Salamis"	Comparative horoscopy	2010	I.72, V.48, Presage 31	Further Muslim forces advance up Rhône into France	Astrological/ comparative horoscopy
2000	IX.42, I.37	European navies defeat new "Carthaginian" fleet off Sicily	Comparative horoscopy	2011	II.93	New "Cyrus the Great" sets fire to Rome and executes Pope	Comparative horoscopy
2000	II.49, V.47, VI.21	Asiatic forces reach Rhodes and Mediterranean coast of Turkey	Comparative horoscopy	2011+	IX.55	Huge epidemic wipes out man and beast in France	Astrological
2000	II.86, V.25	Another "Nebuchadnezzar" from Iraq invades Egypt	Comparative horoscopy	2012	I.16, II.6, VIII.21, IX.42	Plague epidemic sweeps Europe from south	Comparative horoscopy
2000		Arab forces from farther west overrun Egypt	Comparative horoscopy	2013	I.87, II.3, II.91, III.7, V.10, VI.97 VIII.2, Sixain 27	"Fire from the sky" falls on southern Europe, especially SW France	Comparative horoscopy
2000	II.5	Muslims from Turkey invade southeast Italian mainland	Comparative horoscopy				
2000	V.48, Presage	Asiatic forces invade Danube and southeast Europe	Comparative horoscopy	2014	I.52	Last Pope (?) murdered; "plague" devastates Church in France	Astrological
2000	II.41, VII.22, VIII.99, X.3,	Pope forced to flee to Avignon France	Comparative horoscopy	2015	II.81, II.93, III.84, IV.82	Rome sacked: Vatican burned	Comparative horoscopy
2002	I.83	Aliens plunder Italy	Astrological	2015 (or 2017/ 19/21)	VIII.2	"Fire from the sky" descends on SW France: Garonne defense-line falls	Astrological
2002	Sixain 42	Rome surrounded by armies	Liturgical				
2002	VI.24	Calamitous war	Astrological	2017	II.48	Great army crosses mountains wielding chemical weapons	Astrological
2002		Asiatic invaders overrun Saudi Arabia and take Riyadh	Comparative horoscopy	2019	I.52	Rome reinvaded by forces from North Africa	Comparative horoscopy
2002/7	Sixain 44	France succumbs to arrows of powerful "lover"	Liturgical	2021	X.50	Floods and treason in Lorraine and Luxembourg	Astrological
2003	II.30, VI.80, Sixain 41	Muslims from North Africa invade Portugal and/or Spain	Comparative horoscopy	2021	IV.86	New overlord crowned at Reims and Aachen	Astrological
2004	III.3	Drought in south: earthquakes in Middle East	Astrological	2025	I.16, II.37, VIII.17	Plague hits southern France	Comparative horoscopy
2004	II.65	Western economies collapse, Church in flames, plague, and captivity	Astrological	2026	II.47, VIII.73,	Alien overlord dies: empire divided	Comparative horoscopy
2004	I.18, I.28, VI,56, IX.28	Muslim sea-borne forces from Barcelona invade France and mainland Italy	Comparative horoscopy	2026	Sixain 46	"Great Provider" routs both "Wolf" and "Leech": disaster befalls France	Astrological
2005	II.81, IX.99	Volcanic ash or "fire from the sky" falls on much of southern Europe	Comparative horoscopy	2027	II.16, II.71	Western counterinvasion of Muslim-occupied Italy reaches Sicily	Comparative horoscopy
2005	II.93	Last Pope ejected from office by foreign invaders	Comparative horoscopy	2032	V.23	Allies strike fear into African leader, until "Duumvirate" is split	Astrological
2006	III.96	Local Italian leader murdered on orders from Rome	Astrological	2032	II.34, V.23, V.45, VI.7, VI.58, VI.95	Civil war involving "Ahenobarbus" sweeps southern France and Italy	Comparative horoscopy
2007	III.20, VI.88	Muslim forces invade Balearics and southeastern Spain	Comparative horoscopy				
2007/11	Sixain 38	"Great Provider" shows his mettle, and future Henri V is baptised	Liturgical	2034	VIII.48	War of words changes to deeds, as southern Spain is liberated	Astrological
2007/12	Sixain 54	"Great Lady" of France dies, then England and Flanders are besieged and attacked	Liturgical	2034	II.22, III.64, X.86	European forces attack Muslim Middle Eastern heartlands in "new crusade"	Comparative horoscopy
2009	IX.73	"Blue-turbaned" leader invades southwest France	Astrological	2034	I.74, VI.21, VI.85	European forces invade southern Turkey	Comparative horoscopy
				2062	Sixain 53	Death of "Phoenix"	Liturgical

2. SUMMARY VERSES

Once having established a basic dating framework, the next task has to be to relate the remaining verses to it. Basic to this task – as to any interpretation of Nostradamus whatever – has to be the notion of *context*. The dating framework already suggests one of its own, of course, but fortunately this can be checked and confirmed against the seer's summary verses.

The concept of the summary verse first surfaces in the *Almanach* of 1555. As represented by *Presage* 1 (translated under Nostradamus the Poet), this offers a general context for the subsequent predictions for each individual month of the year. The *Presages* for 1559, 1561, and every subsequent year (q.v.) are similarly preceded by a such a verse.

Unsurprisingly, therefore, similar summary verses are to be found in the *Centuries*, too. Unlike the *Presages*, though, the predictions in the *Centuries* are in no particular order, and so the relevant verses need to be actively looked for.

This is not too difficult. Such verses are typically marked by their vast generalizations, their long-term historical coverage and/or their broad geographical sweep. Consequently they do not need to be listed here. A collection of such verses relative to the predicted Muslim invasion of Europe, for example, is listed and quoted in translation in the relevant section below.

Once the summary verses have been allocated their likely places within the overall dating framework, they in turn can then be linked in a variety of ways with other, less general verses.

3. LINKED VERSES

Nostradamus's predictions are linked both with the summary verses and with each other by various distinguishing features. Of these the main ones are the following:

Verbal links

Self-evidently, numbers of the verses share common phrases. The phrase *feu du ciel*, for example, appears in I.46, II.81, III.7, V.98, V.100, VIII.2, and *Presages* 9, 17, and 28. It is not unreasonable to assume that at least some of these may refer to one and the same occasion, and the possibility is thus worth exploring, especially where one or more of these can be related to the overall dating framework (as is the case with VIII.2). Other characteristic phrases, and even individual words – such as *selin(e)*, *rouge*, and *rose* – may be worth exploring in a similar way.

Personal names

Other common features may then start to become apparent. Self-evidently again, certain personal names recur in a number of different verses. Among these are *Aenobarbe*, *l'Aemathien*, *Ogmion*, *Hercule*, *Chyren*, and *Pol mansol/mensolee*, and, in the *Sixains* particularly, the Wolf, Leech, Crocodile, Provider, Lady, and Phoenix (see Concordance). Once again, then, it is not unreasonable to assume

that these verses belong together and that they can thus be related to the overall dating framework as in (a) above.

Place names

Similar considerations apply to the seer's numerous geographical place names. If a large number of verses mention the city of Lyon, for example (as I.31, I.33, I.35, I.72, I.93, II.83, II.85, II.94, III.52, III.56, III.93, V.25, V.99, VIII.02-3, VIII.6, VIII.34, IX.19, IX.69-70, X.99, *Presages* 56, 62, and 69, and *Sixain* 52 all do), then the probability is considerable that some of them belong together. Here, then, reference to the Concordance (see the end of this book) can prove invaluable.

Moreover, if the predictions describe an invading army's advance from town A to town C, then it is reasonable to assume that it will pass through town B in the process. Reference to a good map, then, can help to "place" any verse that refers to that town (and here a large-scale tourist road-map can prove invaluable).

Time references

There are some verses that are not themselves dated but seem to refer to others that are, via such expressions as "six months after" or "the year before." All that is necessary, therefore, is to identify the event in question and match it up, and such verses can effectively be dated, too.

Thematic links

Here the adoption of a slightly broader view is involved. Identifying thematically linked verses must of course be based in the first place on the features already outlined. But, behind these, a number of more general, underlying themes now start to emerge, and these in turn can act as umbrella-contexts for other verses that it has not proved possible to identify via the more specific means already referred to.

Typical cases in point are, for example, the papal flight from Rome or the Muslim Invasion of Europe.

4. PAIRED VERSES

Finally, we come to the various paired verses. These are, in effect, a special case of the "linked verses" covered above.

As the very first two verses of the *Centuries* seem to hint, Nostradamus may actually have written – whether deliberately or otherwise – *two* verses on each event, even if in the final text they were to finish up widely separated. To date, this has not been definitely confirmed as a general principle. But certainly a remarkable number of verses do seem to have pairs. Some of those in the first edition, indeed, actually end with a comma or colon, so suggesting that they are to be continued (see, for example, I.21, I.65, II.85, III.42, III.63, and III.86), while others refer to their protagonists only via pronouns, so suggesting a previous reference. The possible cases have already been mentioned of I.23 and I.38, I.28 and I.71, I.43 and IX.32, I.45 and III.40, I.53 and X.72, I.69 and VIII.16, III:4 and 5, III:23 and 24, VIII.15, and VI.74. The two apparent pairs from *Century* III are particularly interesting, falling as they atypically do *together*.

Clearly, then, where it is possible to date either one of a pair, or at least to place it in some sort of context, it follows that the other verse, too, is *ipso facto* "placed" as well.

In this way it is possible via a process of patient reconstruction gradually to assemble an even more extensive framework for interpreting Nostradamus's predictions than is afforded by the dated verses alone. It is probably not too optimistic to suggest that well over half the predictions can be sequenced in this way – in which case there can no longer be any excuse for the grand, "intuitive," pick'n'mix approach affected by most of the popular would-be interpreters.

Nostradamus, it is clear, has his own agenda, and there can thus be no justification anymore for commentators to superimpose on his prophecies credulous, doom-laden, end-of-the-world agendas of their own, let alone for bamboozling the public into believing that they were ever Nostradamus's.

The phenomenon of selective *biblical* quotation is well enough known. Anybody determined to see in Exodus 34:4 a recipe for the treatment of constipation is welcome to do so: *and Moses arose early in the morning*, it reads, *went up into the mountain . . . and took two tablets.* But this would be willfully to select merely the words one wants to see, and equally willfully to take them totally out of context.

Yet precisely the same kind of approach is widely offered as if it were a serious treatment of Nostradamus by interpreters who, for the most part, cannot even cope reliably with Nostradamus's language (see Interpreting the Prophecies). And a public that is naturally ill-qualified to judge has little option but to believe them.

The time for such nonsense, surely, is over.

Defeat of Saladin and the Turks by the Christians, 1189–92, from *Chronicle* by David Aubert

INTERPRETING THE PROPHECIES

FOR REASONS that seem to be directly connected with the technique of comparative horoscopy (see Astrologer and Mage), Nostradamus's predictions in the *Centuries* and *Sixains* come in no particular order – and in view of the circumstances of the day (see Nostradamus in Context, Table of Events, and Nostradamus's Life Story) it is clear that he had no great incentive to clarify their sequence, either.

The result is that, with the exception of the *Presages*, the collected *Propheties* present us with what is, in effect, a massive verbal jigsaw puzzle.

Moreover, their language is often obtuse and sometimes positively arcane. This may well have at least as much to do with the fashionable classicizing tendency of the seer's day as with any intent to bamboozle (see Nostradamus's Language). Nevertheless, the result is that a further layer of impenetrability is added to an already chaotic text.

The upshot is a familiar one where such texts are concerned. As with the Bible, the whole thing becomes a kind of Rorschach test, reflecting back to the would-be interpreter not what is actually there, but what he or she assumes is there – at which point enormous and totally unwarranted significance starts to be attached to individual pieces of the jigsaw puzzle *in isolation*, in much the same way as biblical proof-texts are often waved around out of context by zealots more concerned to justify their own oddball preconceptions than with establishing the truth.

Yet even a moment's thought makes it perfectly clear that this approach is quite untenable, as anybody who has ever actually done a jigsaw puzzle will readily confirm. The time to make confident statements about the picture on the box is when you have finally succeeded in reconstructing it – and not until you have done so will you have much idea of the true significance of any given individual piece.

As with the Bible, then, the only person qualified to interpret any individual verse of the Nostradamian *Propheties* is a linguistic and cultural scholar who has already studied and analyzed the whole opus from a totally dispassionate viewpoint. Needless to say, there are not many such. Respected academics, fearful of their reputations, usually refuse to touch Nostradamus with a bargepole, while most of those who would rush in to fill the vacuum not only have all-too-obvious philosophical, eschatological, or commercial axes to grind, but often lack the basic linguistic qualifications to carry out the task in the first place.

No wonder that the seer, echoing Virgil's resounding *Procul este, profani*,[2] inveighs so heavily at VI.100 against the "profane and ignorant mob," warns off astrologers and the great unwashed, and apparently urges serious students to involve themselves directly and at first hand in his prophetic process (see The Major Prophecies):

Think on this, reader, sagely as you may,
But shun my verse, you mob profane and shallow.
Star-gazers, snotty Philistines, away!
Let those more reverent my office hallow.[3]

What, then, is involved in interpreting Nostradamus's predictions? Clearly, there are a number of distinct steps. For any given case, they may be summarized as follows:

1. ESTABLISH THE TRUE TEXT

This means
(a) tracing the *original text*, prior to any subsequent editorial or typographical corruptions,
(b) examining it for any typographical errors of its own in the light of what is already known about
(i) Nostradamus's spelling, vocabulary, and grammar (see Nostradamus's Language) and
(ii) contemporary typographical practices (see Book Printing and Publishing), and then
(c) establishing the definitive version.

On this basis alone, many existing commentaries and interpretations disqualify themselves at the outset (see, for example, Books, Films, Videos, Disks, and Internet).

2. CARRY OUT ANY NECESSARY DECODING

This means
(a) analyzing the text from the viewpoint of
(i) sixteenth-century vocabulary and grammar (see Nostradamus's Language),
(ii) provincial variants (fairly common),
(iii) obsolescent Old French forms,
(iv) Latin antecedents (always very much in the seer's mind), and
(v) Greek antecedents (also constantly present in his consciousness);
(b) spotting and solving (see Nostradamus the Joker, Nostradamus the Poet, and Historian and Mythologist) any obvious
(i) anagrams,
(ii) other word-plays (extremely frequent),
(iii) historical references (also extremely frequent),
(iv) mythological references (see Nostradamus and Mythology),
(v) deliberate classicisms (extremely frequent),
(vi) specialized technical terms,
(vii) foreign loan-words, or

---

[2] "Stay away, you uninitiated!" (*Aeneid* VI.258).

[3] Revised version of translation from Lemesurier: *Nostradamus: The Final Reckoning* (Piatkus, 1995).

(viii) neologisms and invented words;

(c) using such features as the verse's own scansion and rhyme-scheme to unscramble and reconstitute any

   (i) scrambled grammar (see Nostradamus's Language),

   (ii) compressed grammar, and

   (iii) "understood" grammar.

3. PROVISIONALLY ESTABLISH THE VERSE'S LIKELY PLACE IN THE OVERALL SEQUENCE

It may well have been the sequential nature of the predictions emerging from the comparative horoscopy (see Sequence of Selected Horographs) that originally convinced Nostradamus that he had stumbled not on a mere series of astrological coincidences, but on real chains of future events. Nevertheless, the published order of the verses still does not reflect that sequence, and so unearthing any particular verse's sequential context demands that the interpreter

(a) find the verse's "pair," if any (see Dating and Sequencing the Predictions), and

(b) relate the verse(s) to others in terms of

   (i) theme,

   (ii) vocabulary,

   (iii) shared phrases,

   (iv) shared names of places or people,

   (v) time references ("after *x*" . . . "before *y*"),

   (vi) relevant summary verses, and

   (vii) any overt datings (see below).

Here again, few existing interpretations and commentaries even attempt this.

4. ESTABLISH A LIKELY DATING FOR THE PREDICTION

This involves

(a) decoding any direct datings indicated by the text (see Dating and Sequencing the Predictions), whether in terms of

   (i) overt calendar dates,

   (ii) astrological datings, and/or

   (iii) "liturgical" datings;

(b) working toward an approximate dating by establishing the verse's likely place in the overall sequence (see 3 above); or

(c) establishing a dating by identifying the predicted event's historical precursor and applying comparative horoscopy (see Astrologer and Mage and Sequence of Selected Horographs)

Once again, hardly any existing commentaries manage anything beyond (a)(i) above.

5. FINALLY, ON THE BASIS OF THE ABOVE, ATTEMPT AN INTERPRETATION

If it is to reflect the original, this will need to

(a) be linguistically accurate (most published interpretations and translations immediately fall down on this criterion alone, being for the most part full of the most elementary schoolboy howlers),[4]

(b) be placed in some kind of temporal and spacial context (a prophecy that does not indicate when and where in some way is manifestly not really a prophecy at all),

(c) be comprehensible, and not some kind of impenetrable, literalized gobbledygook (a literal, word-for-word version is clearly *not a translation* and usually indicates that the would-be translator has not understood the text in the first place),

(d) be in some kind of verse commensurate with the original (verse translated into prose usually reads like bad opera subtitles, and certainly misses the "feel" of the original), and

(e) follow the same rhyme-scheme as the original wherever possible.

Self-evidently, most existing versions of Nostradamus (see Books, Films, Videos, Disks, and Internet) fail nearly all of the above criteria, and consequently scarcely one of them can be regarded as either reliable or representative.

In order to demonstrate the technique in action, perhaps the best plan is to take a sample verse and treat it accordingly. Since the most quoted and least understood of all Nostradamus's predictions is undoubtedly the notorious X.72 – commonly assumed to presage the advent of the Antichrist and the onset of Armageddon and the Apocalypse – it is this verse that I now propose to subject to model analysis along the lines just laid down.

---

4 One prominent series of modern English commentaries alone yields the following prime examples: "inhabitable" instead of "uninhabitable" for *inhabitable*; "horse" instead of "kid" for *chevrau*; "fog" instead of "drizzle" for *bruine*; "unwanted" instead of "unwonted" for *insolit*; "left" instead of "wounded" for *lesé*; "America" instead of "Armenia" for *Armenie*; "less" instead of "more" for *plus*; "towards" instead of "will see" for *verra*; "escapes" instead of "caught" for *attrapé*; "consort" instead of "conqueror" for *vitrix*; "shroud" instead of "coffin" for *cercueil*; "queen" instead of "green" for *vert*; "troubling" instead of "trembling" for *tremblement*; "severe" instead of "serene" for *serein* – to say nothing of feminines taken as masculines, plurals taken as singulars, past participles taken as futures, and a whole series of simple factual errors both biographical and etymological.

1. ESTABLISH THE TRUE TEXT

This first stage necessarily has to involve tracing the original words. The earliest extant version of X.72 is that of 1568, and I therefore reproduce it here in Benoist Rigaud's edition of that year:

> L'an mil neuf cens nonante neuf sept mois
> Du ciel viendra vn grand Roy deffraieur
> Refusciter le grand Roy d'Angolmois,
> Auant apres Mars regner par bon heur.

The usual "literal" version of this reads something like:

In the year nineteen hundred and ninety-nine, seven months,
From the sky will come a great King of Terror
To resuscitate the great King of Angoumois.
Before and after Mars reigns happily.

It has to be said, though, that even most literalist interpreters immediately substitute "of the Mongols" for "of Angoumois," thus severely denting at the outset their claimed literalist credentials – and revealing just how strong the tendency is, even at this stage, to let one's prior assumptions color one's eventual interpretation.

Since there is no evidence of misspellings or misprints in this version, we can move straight onto the next stage in interpreting the prediction.

2. CARRY OUT ANY NECESSARY DECODING

Here it has to be said at the outset that Nostradamus, having stated the dating of the prophecy with unusual clarity, seems to have felt that this justified his having a great deal of linguistic fun with the rest of the verse and setting all manner of traps for the unwary. Virtually all the commentators have then obligingly fallen into them, so contriving to bamboozle not only themselves but everybody else as well.

To take the various features in the order set out above:

(a)(i) *nonante* This old form for "ninety" is still used in Belgium and Switzerland, as well as in parts of southern France.

sept mois While the New Year was celebrated in Nostradamus's time at the spring equinox, the calendar itself was nevertheless reckoned in the normal way from January (as his own *Almanachs* reveal): the seventh month is therefore July.

viendra . . . refusciter This construction, which is intertwined in best Virgilian style with the rest of the syntax, has little or nothing to do with the idea of "coming"; instead, it is used extremely frequently (over a hundred times in the *Propheties* alone) as an emphatic form of future tense, just as it often is in English ("You will come to regret it."). The second word is, of course, merely the normal sixteenth-century spelling of modern *ressusciter* (but see (a)(iv) below).

Roy The term admittedly means "king": but since other types of rulers were virtually unknown in Nostradamus's day, it may be assumed to apply to any kind of sovereign ruler.

regner This is either governed by *viendra* (above) or is a "future infinitive" – a form frequently used by Nostradamus, mainly because it uses one syllable less than the conventional future tense. It is perhaps worth bearing in mind that this latter is itself regularly formed simply by adding the endings of *avoir* ("to have") *to the infinitive.* Even seen as a straight infinitive, the form is not necessarily "ungrammatical": even today the infinitive can still be used both as a past tense (*Et mon père de partir*) and as an imperative (*Ne pas se pencher au dehors*).

par bon heur [*Schoolboy howler number one*] This expression does not mean the same as the modern *par bonheur*, despite the common assumption to the contrary. In fact, its "split" format makes its meaning here quite clear – "by good fortune," or "by luck." It is thus far better rendered by the word "haply" than by "happily."

(a)(iii) *deffraieur* [*Schoolboy howler number two*] Except in corrupt later editions, this word contains no apostrophe. It therefore does not mean "of terror" (even though it is not impossible that Nostradamus, who loved playing with omitted and inserted apostrophes, may deliberately have sought to lay a trap to that effect for would-be interpreters). Instead, the term (from Old French *defrayer*, modern *défrayer*) simply means "defrayer" or "paymaster": indeed, it may even have the sense of "appeaser," as in near-contemporary Spenserian English.

(a)(iv) *refusciter* Although this word normally means "to resuscitate or revive," we need to bear in mind that Nostradamus was always extremely conscious of the Latin roots of the words he used (he was used to working in Latin, after all). In this case the original Latin word was made up of three elements (*re+sub+citare*), which meant something like "to bring into rapid movement again from below": in other words, "to stir up again." This, then, is probably the gloss that the seer intended.

(b)(i) *Angolmois* Even though this is a standard term (modern *Angoumois*) referring to the region around Angoulême in western France, most commentators assume that it is actually an anagram – presumably because they cannot conceive of the area in question having a great king or ruler capable of doubling as the expected Antichrist (even though, as we shall see, the verse in fact raises no such expectation). True, at least one commentator does manage to associate the region with a marauding leader from the East by asserting that Attila the Hun once conquered it. Most commentators, however, prefer to assume that the word is a straightforward anagram of *Mongolois*. Clearly, however, it is not – or at least not exactly. Nevertheless, near-anagrams seem to have been almost as widely enjoyed as exact ones in Nostradamus's day, so that the possibility still deserves to be borne in mind for comparison with the true context of the prediction, once it has finally been established (see 3 and 4 below).

(b)(iv) *Mars* This word could refer to the Roman god, to the planet named after him, or to war, the main activity for which he was held responsible. Since, for lack of any other detail, the reference does not appear to be astrological, the best plan seems to be to assume a combination of the other two possibilities.

(c)(i) *Du ciel . . . un grand Roy deffraieur* This is a splendidly typical example of the classically inspired "inverted possessive" ("Of heaven a great defraying King"), which peppers the *Propheties* from end to end and lends a certain stately air to so many of the verses. Consequently it needs to be reemphasized at this point that (once again in best Virgilian style) *Du ciel* here belongs with *un grand Roy deffraieur*, rather than with *viendra*, which in fact goes with *refuſciter* (see (a)(i) and 4 below).

(ii) *regner* Either this is elliptically governed, like *refuſciter*, by *viendra* in line 5, or it is a standard Nostradamian compression of *regnera* (as already explained under (a)(i) above). Under the terms of this, it represents a future, not a present tense.

3. PROVISIONALLY ESTABLISH THE VERSE'S LIKELY PLACE IN THE OVERALL SEQUENCE

Normally this would involve (a) finding the verse's "pair" (if any) and (b) relating it to other verses with known dates (see section 4 below). Indeed, a possible "pair" does suggest itself in I.53, albeit somewhat remotely, while a whole complex of other verses seem to provide a possible context (see The Muslim Invasion of Europe).

However, in the present case there is no immediate need for such research, since the verse (unusually) comes with a perfectly clear dating of its own. It is thus possible, by relating it to other dated verses (see Dating and Sequencing the Prophecies and the commentaries attached to The Major Prophecies), to place it directly in context without more ado.

Nevertheless, since that context will in turn contribute to the final interpretation of the verse (as is inevitably the case with any version or translation), it is still important to spell it out. And in the present case it is a context that apparently involves a massive Asiatic and Muslim invasion of Europe starting shortly before the turn of the twentieth century and extending some decades into the twenty-first, with dire results for the papacy and for southern and western Europe generally.

4. ESTABLISH A LIKELY DATING FOR THE PREDICTION

As we have seen, Nostradamus has already done this for us, presumably with the aid of comparative horoscopy (see Astrologer and Mage). But if so, then a curious problem presents itself. If the event described is to be seen (as the system requires) as a recapitulation of some earlier event, possibly from classical times, when did a historical "defraying ruler" (other than Moses, perhaps) ever descend from the sky to do his business? The answer, of course, is

"Never." Such antics are for modern rulers with the benefit of airplanes, not antique ones who had to rely on horses, carriages, or their own flat feet. This brings us back, then, to our earlier point – namely that the words *Du ciel* belong with *un grand Roy deffraieur*, and not with *refuſciter*. The personage concerned, in other words, is "a great defraying heavenly ruler," or even a "great holy appeaser," and not (as countless modern commentaries assure us) a "great King of Terror" who descends upon us from the skies. Though, in the modern context, such a descent is of course for the first time by no means impossible.

But what, in this case, *was* that earlier event? Here we ourselves can apply comparative horoscopy to find the answer, taking advantage of the fact that, with the dating of the future event already known, the planetary positions at the time can be determined, and known history then searched for a suitable "match."

That "match" turns out to be a surprising one – in terms of the conventional interpretation. For the original date turns out (as the horographs overleaf reveal) to be A.D. 579, and the historical figure in question none other than the future Pope Gregory the Great.

The "coincidences" are little short of amazing. Born in around A.D. 540, Gregory rose to early prominence, becoming Prefect of Rome in 573. The following year, however, he threw up a promising career to become a monk. On doing so, he gave up his Sicilian estates for the foundation of monasteries and surrendered his mansion in Rome for conversion into a religious house. That mansion stood on one of the seven hills of Rome known as the Caelian Hill (*Mons Caelius*), named after the Caelius ("heavenly") family. Already, then, he had distinguished himself not only as *Du ciel* ("of Caelius"), but also as a *deffraieur* (a funder or payer-out).

In 578 Gregory, now one of the seven Deacons of Rome, was sent on a mission to Constantinople to beg for help from the Emperor against the Lombards (*Langobardi*) who had just defeated the related *Gepidae* on the Danube with the aid of the Avars – an oriental tribe of possibly Mongol origin – and were now invading Italy. Indeed, they had already overrun the plain of the Po and were in the process of setting up their capital at Pavia. Despite six years of effort, the Emperor not only refused but made peace with the invaders, so Gregory was forced to return to a Rome that was threatened by invaders who, in effect, had merely been encouraged by the exercise.

In 590 he was nevertheless made Pope and soon distinguished himself by organizing a massive relief program for the refugees currently flooding into the city (*deffraieur* again). For the invading Lombards were still on the march and were eventually to reach Rome itself. Indeed, he managed to save the city only by buying them off at the last moment (*deffraieur* yet again, but this time definitely in the sense of "appeaser").

In every respect, then, Gregory fits the picture painted by the prophecy. He had come from the Caelian hill (*du ciel*). He was a great ruler, and (as Pope) a "heavenly" one at that (*du ciel* again).

He was a notable philanthropist, and an appeaser into the bargain (*deffraieur* in both senses). And he saw the very war that he had attempted to damp down resume again in earnest.

But what of *Angolmois*? And what of the *Langobardi* on the one hand and the allegedly anagrammatical Mongols on the other (line 3)? We have already seen, of course, that there was a possible Mongol involvement in the Lombards" invasion. Moreover, where anagrams are concerned, it is worth noting that the first two syllables of *Angolmois* are a direct (and this time not a mere pseudo-) anagram of the first two syllables of *Langobardi*. What, though, of the rest of Nostradamus's intriguing term? Here what seems to have happened is that, faced with a "difficult" rhyme, he simply adds a nonsense ending to the last word of the line (see Nostradamus the Poet). *Angolmois*, in other words, is simply a portmanteau-word designed to fulfill three functions at once – namely to refer to the *Langobardi*, to hint at the Mongols, and to rhyme.

5. FINALLY, ON THE BASIS OF THE ABOVE, ATTEMPT AN INTERPRETATION

Here, requirement (b) is already partially satisfied by the verse itself, and so the stated date of July 1999 needs only to be amplified with reference to the context supplied by a host of other verses (see The Muslim Invasion of Europe). Otherwise we need to concentrate mainly on requirements (a), (c), (d), and (e). Our interpretation, in other words, has to be linguistically accurate, in comprehensible English, in verse, and in rhyme. Not that these last four requirements are always entirely compatible. A measure of poetic license is virtually inevitable, yet this still does not need to falsify the verse's overall meaning. Nor, indeed, should it.

Our interpretation, then, needs to relate how, in July of 1999, the then Pope (in all probability the current one) flies to Ankara (the latitude is marked out by the bottom horograph) in an attempt to buy off the Muslim invaders who are threatening the shores of Europe. In the event, he merely succeeds in stirring the pot, and the massing hordes from the east are able to use the respite to build up their strength even further. The Turks having finally thrown in their lot with them, the invasion then resumes.

A possible verse-translation of X.72 consistent with all the above might thus read:

> *When 1999 is seven months o'er*
> *Shall heaven's great Vicar, anxious to appease,*
> *Stir up the Mongol-Lombard King once more,*
> *And war reign haply where it once did cease.*

Arriving at a version such as the above, however, demands a great deal of study and analysis. With over a thousand verses to tackle, perhaps it is not too surprising that most would-be interpreters prefer simply to dive straight in and make of each verse what they will. Unfortunately this does little to reflect what Nostradamus actually wrote or meant.

ORIGINAL EVENT

These horoscopic charts compare planetary positions and show astrological "matches" between events from classical times and major events predicted by Nostradamus.

Horograph for July 24th, 579, to August 2nd, 579

	1	2	3	4	5	6	7	8	9	10	11	12
Pluto												★
Neptune			★									
Uranus											★	
Saturn											★	
Jupiter				★								
Mars								★				
Venus							★					
Mercury				★								
Moon	★	★	★								★	★
Sun					★							

Solar noon declination to nearest degree: 20°N to 18°N

Geographical latitude: 41° 54'N to 41° 02'N

Location: Rome to Constantinople

Event: Future Pope Gregory the Great quits Rome to seek help against Lombard invaders

FUTURE EVENT

Horograph for July 19th, 1999, to July 28th, 1999

	1	2	3	4	5	6	7	8	9	10	11	12
Pluto								★				
Neptune											★	
Uranus											★	
Saturn		★										
Jupiter		★										
Mars								★				
Venus							★					
Mercury				★								
Moon	★	★	★	★	★							★
Sun						★						

Solar noon declination to nearest degree: 21°N to 10°N

Relative latitude: 1°N   **Geographical latitude:** 43°N to 42°N

Possible location: Rome to Ankara

Event: Pope flees to Turkey to buy off invaders, but merely stirs them up: war resumes

NOSTRADAMUS AND THE FRENCH REVOLUTION

EVEN LONG BEFORE the time of Nostradamus, astrologers had been predicting a period of major social upheaval for the late 1780s. The Nostradamus scholar James Laver, for example, reports the following:

❖ A manuscript dated "1414" in the Douai municipal library entitled *Imago Mundi* in which the author, one Pierre d'Ailly, foreshadows great changes – especially political and religious ones – specifically for 1789.

❖ A work entitled *La Période, c'est-à-dire la fin du monde; contenant la disposition des chouses terrestres par la vertu et influence des corps celestes* by the eminent mathematician and astrologer Pierre Turrel of Autun (d.1531), which once again predicts that great changes, especially political and religious ones, will begin with the "eighth major and marvelous conjunction" of the year 1789 and last for some twenty-five years.

❖ The *Liber Mirabilis* of 1524, based on a set of Latin distichs allegedly written by Jean Muller in 1476, forecasting the overthrow of the world's empires for 1788.

❖ The *Livre de l'estat et mutations des temps* by Richard Roussat, a canon at Langres, published in 1550, which not only quotes Turrel's prediction (thus verifying its prior existence) but foreshadows on its own account a "renovation of the world" to take place 243 years after the book's completion in 1549 – which once again gives the year 1789.

What, then, was so "major and marvelous" about the planetary conjunction expected for 1789? The astronomical data are quite specific. Between March 11th and 19th of that year all the then-known planets except the moon and (curiously)[5] Jupiter would be grouped together in Pisces, with the sun, Mercury, and Saturn all initially within six degrees of each other. Indeed, Venus and Mars would come into exact conjunction at the end of the period, just as the sun and Saturn would equally do on the 3rd of the month.

The horograph for the period of the general conjunction, shown above, thus offers fairly convincing evidence (if evidence were still needed) that astronomical observations at the time were quite accurate enough to permit the calculation of planetary positions for some centuries to come.

Whatever their reasons for deducing that this particular astrological situation would be so literally epoch-making, their expectation was certainly quite specific. Granted, the suggestion by Turrel's title that the period might mark in some way the end of the world was overdramatic: but that it marked the end of *a* world can, in the light of history, scarcely be doubted.

Characteristically, however (see Astrologer and Mage), Nostradamus himself seems to ignore the "marvelous conjunction" completely. Or at least he studiously omits to mention it. Instead, he is apparently attracted (as usual) more to the major horoscopic linkages to the period in question. The planetary situation for April 1789, for example, closely matches that for April 16th, 72 B.C., during the celebrated Roman slave revolt under Spartacus:

ASTRONOMICAL DATA FOR MARCH 1789

Horograph for March 11th, 1789, to March 19th 1789												
	♈	♉	♊	♋	♌	♍	♎	♏	♐	♑	♒	♓
Pluto											★	
Neptune						★						
Uranus				★								
Saturn												★
Jupiter			★									
Mars												★
Venus												★
Mercury												★
Moon							★	★	★	★	★	
Sun												★

***The Taking of the Louvre* by Jean Louis Bezard**

---

[5] In Nostradamus's view, Jupiter was the planet preeminently concerned with the matters of rulership and state (see Astrologer and Mage).

SPARTACUS SLAVE REVOLT

Horograph for April 16th, 72 B.C.

	Aries	Taurus	Gemini	Cancer	Leo	Virgo	Libra	Scorpio	Sagittarius	Capricorn	Aquarius	Pisces
Pluto		★										
Neptune			★									
Uranus		★										
Saturn										★		
Jupiter						★						
Mars	★											
Venus	★											
Mercury	★											
Moon								★				
Sun	★											

Solar noon declination to nearest degree: 10°N

Geographical latitude: 46°N to 38°N

Location: Italy

Event: Roman slave revolt under Spartacus

FRENCH REVOLUTION

Horograph for April 15th, 1789, to April 19th, 1789

	Aries	Taurus	Gemini	Cancer	Leo	Virgo	Libra	Scorpio	Sagittarius	Capricorn	Aquarius	Pisces
Pluto											★	
Neptune							★					
Uranus				★								
Saturn												★
Jupiter					★							
Mars	★											
Venus	★											
Mercury	★											
Moon									★	★		
Sun	★											

Solar noon declination to nearest degree: 10°N to 11°N

Relative latitude: 0°N to 1°N   **Geographical latitude:** 46°N to 39°N

Possible location: Southern France to southern Italy

Event: French Revolution (and possible Italian analogue)

Moreover, even though the chart for 1789 (below left) could apply both to France and to Italy, the fact that all the "operative" planets are *in Aries* would inevitably have suggested to Nostradamus that the events involved were earmarked *specifically for France* (see Astrologer and Mage).

However, he signally fails to mention the year 1789 either in his *Prophecies* or in his letters. Instead, he seems to go for another match with the Spartacus slave revolt – *namely that for 1792*. At all events, that is the date that he specifically mentions in his *Lettre à Henri II* (section B.17). Compare the relevant horographs shown on the right.

However, he immediately precedes this reference in the *Lettre* with an extraordinarily detailed astrological rundown of a "peaceful year" during which the following conditions (among others) will apply: "Saturn in Capricorn; Jupiter in Aquarius; Mars in Scorpio; Venus in Pisces; Mercury in Capricorn, Aquarius, and Pisces all within the space of a month; the moon in Aquarius; a conjunction of Jupiter and Mercury; and a conjunction of the sun and Jupiter."

All of these conditions were in fact satisfied *at various times during the year 1783* – in which case what follows is highly relevant. "Starting in that year [Nostradamus warns] there will be a greater persecution of the Christian Church than ever occurred in North Africa, and it will last until the year 1792, which will be thought of as the beginning of a new order."

1792 – the year marking the eventual proclamation of the French Republic.

Not that this is by any means Nostradamus's only apparent reference to the French Revolution. Among them, the various modern commentators cited under The Major Prophecies (q.v.) have managed to identify about forty or so different references to the great upheaval (see The Major Prophecies) – and many of these, it has to be said, are remarkably convincing. They range from the suggestive I.3 to the even more celebrated and remarkable IX.20.

The former reads (in my own translation):

When litter by the whirlwind is o'erthrown
And face is covered by concealing cloak,
Then the republic 'neath new powers shall groan
And whites and reds false judgments shall invoke.

It is claimed to refer to the "great tornado" of 1788.

The latter runs:

Through woods of Reims by night shall make her way
Herne the white butterfly, by byways sent.
Th' elected head, Varennes' black monk in gray
Sows storm, fire, blood, and foul dismemberment.

This astonishingly detailed prediction evidently foreshadows the famous flight to Varennes on June 21st, 1791, by the newly elected

END OF THE
SPARTACUS SLAVE REVOLT

Horograph for May 25th, 71 B.C., to May 27th, 71 B.C.												
	♐	♈	♊	♋	♌	♒	♎	♏	♐	♑	♒	♓
Pluto		★										
Neptune			★									
Uranus		★										
Saturn										★		
Jupiter							★					
Mars						★						
Venus			★									
Mercury		★										
Moon						★	★					
Sun			★									

Solar noon declination to nearest degree: 21°N

Geographical latitude: 46°N to 38°N

Location: Italy

Event: Roman slave revolt under Spartacus (final stages)

PROCLAMATION OF
THE FRENCH REPUBLIC

Horograph for May 20th, 1792, to June 6th, 1792												
	♐	♈	♊	♋	♌	♒	♎	♏	♐	♑	♒	♓
Pluto											★	
Neptune						★						
Uranus					★							
Saturn	★											
Jupiter							★					
Mars					★							
Venus		★										
Mercury		★										
Moon		★	★	★	★	★	★	★	★	★		
Sun			★									

Solar noon declination to nearest degree: 20°N to 23°N

Relative latitude: 1°N to 2°N   **Geographical latitude:** 47°N to 40°N

Possible location: Central France southward to Corsica, Sardinia, and southern Italy

Event: Closing stages of French Revolution and possible spread to Italy

King Louis XVI and his queen,[6] Marie Antoinette, which helped finally to discredit the French monarchy and led to its eventual abolition the following year.

Among the further revolutionary references suggested by Laver are I.51, I.53, VII.14, II.2, I.14, VI.23, IX.34, IX.22, IX.23, VIII.87, VII.44 (one of the "extra" Quatrains, with its arch reference to a *bour . . . bon*), X.43, I.57, VI.92, VIII.19, IX.17, III.59, VIII.80, V.33, IX.77, X.17, *Sixain* 55, I.58, IX.11, IX.51, and 1.31. But then, even the academically respectable Laver is sometimes tempted to take verses (and even parts of verses) out of their likely context and to read into them meanings that may never have been intended by Nostradamus.

Lest it be alleged, however, that this is all a matter of retrospective interpretation only, it should be pointed out that the revolutionaries themselves clearly recognized at the time that the seer's prophecies foreshadowed *themselves*. In the closing stages of the Revolution itself, a copy of the *Propheties* was reportedly put on public display in Paris for the people themselves to consult, open at the famous "1792" reference already mentioned.

Nor was this to be Nostradamus's only brush with the Revolution. In the same year (1792) an unruly gang of national guardsmen from Marseille (some say from Vaucluse) broke open his tomb out of a mixture of devilry and curiosity, scattering his moldering bones. Local tradition has it that one of the hooligans even made bold to drink from his skull.

Certainly drink is likely to have had more than a chance connection with the incident. The superstitious tend to be more impressed, however, by the fact that the first man to open the tomb was apparently shot dead a few days later for stealing money from his own lodgings.

As for the bones, along with César's portraits of his father and himself, these were soon circulating among the citizenry as souvenirs. The shocked local mayor, one David by name, did his best to gather them up again and reminded his fellow citizens that "citizen Nostradamus predicted the coming of liberty."

All the more reason, one would have thought, to hang on to the souvenirs.

Nevertheless, some of the remains at least were successfully recovered – along, no doubt, with a variety of dogs' bones and other unconnected detritus – and reverentially re-entombed, this time in the wall of the chapel of St.-Roch (appropriately, the patron saint of plague sufferers) in the town's Collégiale St.-Laurent. Now converted, even more appropriately, into the chapel of *Notre Dame*, this quiet bay against the north wall continues to house Nostradamus's remains to this day, marked by a stone plaque that was finally installed in 1813. Precisely, as it happens, as a subsequent deleted clause in the seer's will had laid down that it should . . .

---

6 *reine*, here anagrammatized as *Herne* (see Nostradamus the Joker).

NOSTRADAMUS, NAPOLEON, AND "HISTER"

JUST AS HE evidently prophesied the French Revolution, Nostradamus also famously seems to have predicted the advent of the great Napoleon Bonaparte. Two quatrains especially are often quoted in this regard. The first is I.60, which in my earlier translation reads:

Near Italy an emperor is born
Who'll cost the Empire dear; and ever since
Those even who his hand decline to scorn
Shall say he is more butcher than a prince.

This could, of course, refer to almost any future ruler born in or near Italy, but it does fit Napoleon's birth in Corsica quite satisfactorily. In this case one imagines that Nostradamus would have arrived at his prediction by horoscopic analogy with one of the ancient Roman emperors (see Astrologer and Mage).

The second oft-quoted major Napoleonic quatrain is VIII.1, which refers to *PAU, NAY, LORON*. Here the capitals would tend to signal some kind of word-play such as an anagram (see Nostradamus the Joker), to which the solution could well be NAPAULON ROY – a perfectly acceptable spelling (for the time) of the Corsican's name.

But this is by no means the full extent of the suggested Napoleonic links. Among them, the various commentators cited below under The Major Prophecies have managed to identify no fewer than 110 references to the great man in the *Propheties*. James Laver, for his part, cites III.35, I.76 (which refers etymologically to his "foreign" or "barbaric" name), IV.54 (which again refers to his regally unprecedented name, and so may be seen as the earlier verse's "pair" – see Dating and Sequencing the Prophecies), VII.13, III.37, I.24, II.94, I.98, IV.26, II.29, VIII.57, V.60, VIII.53, I.4, V.15, II.99, I.88, IV.82, IX.76, X.87, X.23, I.23, and I.32, to say nothing of a whole variety of other verses referring to the Napoleonic wars rather than to the Emperor himself. It has to be said, however, that many of these are applied by other commentators to different characters and circumstances – a fact which, under the terms of comparative horoscopy, does not necessarily rule out the possibility of a Napoleonic reference as well.

Napoleon himself, it seems, was acutely aware that his advent had been predicted in the *Propheties*. Current Bonapartist propa-

Hitler at Munich, September 1937 – the name "Hister" was interpreted as referring to him

ganda – such as the *Nouvelles Considérations puisées dans la Clairvoyance* of 1806 by Théodore Bouys – pointed explicitly to the fact. On the other hand, the Emperor himself seems to have been drawn more to a Nostradamian fake first published in 1792, the so-called *Prophecies of Orval* (see Forgeries and Fairy Tales), than to the genuine article. The book, it is reported, was one that he constantly carried around with him.

But then the romantically inclined Emperor seems to have been something of a sucker for literary forgeries. Not only did his favorite bedside reading include Goethe's hugely successful series of fictional love letters of 1774 entitled *Die Leiden des jungen Werthers*; it also included the claimed poems of the third-or fourth-century Ossian (first published from 1760 onward). Dr Johnson and others had already exposed this opus (as early as 1797) as having been largely fostered onto the ancient Irish bard by one James Macpherson. Yet this blast of cold reality seems in no way to have upset most contemporary Europeans' continuing faith in the bogus texts.

The phenomenon of self-identification with the *Propheties* was, as we have seen, not a new one. Already it had been used by the revolutionaries of 1792 as a form of recommendation and self-justification. To an extent it could be seen as a case of prophetic self-fulfillment.

But this was as nothing compared with what was to follow during the twentieth century.

It was Magda Goebbels, wife of Nazi Germany's infamous but canny minister of propaganda, who in late 1939 seems first to have drawn her husband's attention to *Century* III.57, as interpreted by one Dr. H. H. Kritzinger in a 1922 publication entitled *Mysterien von Sonne and Seele*. According to earlier interpretations still, this suggested that a war would break out in 1939 involving Poland, France, Germany, and Britain – as, indeed, had just happened.

More followed. As Frau Goebbels looked further into the prophecies, a familiar name kept jumping out at her. This was the name *Hifter* – which, in the ancient Gothic German script that, under Hitler's influence, prevailed at the time, still preserved its long *s*. There it was in II.24, in IV.68, in V.29. Indeed, had she had access to the 1557 edition, she would have seen something even more spine-tingling: in IV.68 the printer had actually misspelled the word *hilter*.

Could all this, then, have been a direct reference – albeit an anagrammatical one – to her beloved *Führer*, Adolf Hitler himself?

In fact, we do not know whether Frau Goebbels herself ever made this particular connection. But later commentators certainly would do. The fact that *Hister* was actually the ancient classical name for the lower Danube, and clearly used by Nostradamus as such – in both the first two cases in conjunction with the word *Rin*,[7] the Rhine and Danube having together formed the northeastern frontier of the former Roman Empire – would be brushed aside as irrelevant. The fact, equally, that the subject of II.24 is specifically the *crossing of river*s would be blithely disregarded. And the fact that the seer uses the name again in *Presages* 15 and 31 – this time without its *H*, but indubitably with reference not only to the Danube but to the years 1557 and 1558, long before anybody of note called Hitler was ever heard of – would simply be ignored.

Dr. Josef Goebbels, however, was no fool. Certainly he knew which side his bread was buttered. As hostilities switched from the eastern to the western front, German aircraft were soon dropping leaflets over France bearing selected and edited Nostradamian quotations designed to show that Nazi victory was inevitable.

It was Frau Goebbels who drew her husband's attention to *Century* III.57's prediction of war

But Winston Churchill was no fool either, and it was not long before British propaganda started to retaliate in kind. *Century* III.63 in particular was a positive gift, apparently indicating as it did that both Fascist Italy and Nazi Germany were run by idiots and would sooner or later come a catastrophic cropper:

> *The Roman power is cast down in the mire,*
> *Of its great neighbor following in the wake,*
> *While hidden hate and civil feuds conspire*
> *The stupid fools somewhat aback to take.*

But it was the Americans' propaganda machine that, once they had finally been persuaded to enter the war, really came up trumps. Committing itself to what it did best, no less a company than MGM launched a series of short films designed to boost home morale, once again appropriating the Nostradamian predictions. In the first of the series, entitled *Nostradamus Says So*, the seer's support was claimed for America and all things American, quoting (among others) *Sixain* 15, which in my translation reads:

> *The new-elected Captain of the Barque*
> *Long time shall see the torch's brilliant spark*
> *That serves to light the whole of this domain;*
> *What time the armies 'neath his flag shall fight*
> *Alongside those of Bourbon leader bright.*
> *From east to west his memory shall remain.*

The MGM version, for its part, carefully avoided the embarrassing fact that line 5 dragged in the French by simply leaving it out, along with lines 4 and 6. It then substituted an original line of its own to complete what seemed to be a highly satisfactory reference to New York's own Statue of Liberty. It ran:

> *The chosen protector of the great country*
> *For endless years will hold the famed torch.*
> *It will serve to guide this great people*
> *And in its name they will struggle and triumph.*

Such, it seems, is the price of freedom and truth.

Unsurprisingly, then, translators and commentators with varying degrees of loyalty to the original text have continued to find in the Nostradamian prophecies numerous other references to Hitler, specifically as a kind of "second Antichrist" (the first one having allegedly been Napoleon). The interpreters cited below under The Major Prophecies between them claim about forty-one such references – and there is no reason to suppose that by any means all of them are in error. IX.90, after all, even refers specifically to *Un capitaine de la grand Germanie* – as direct (if unnamed) an apparent reference to the *Führer* and his beloved *Grossdeutschland* as one could wish to find.

---

[7]   In II.24 of the second edition this loses its capital, so paving the way for its transformation in the 1568 edition into *rien*, which is the word that most modern commentators then assume.

NOSTRADAMUS AND THE MUSLIM INVASION OF EUROPE

A HUGE MUSLIM INVASION of Europe was already in progress during Nostradamus's own lifetime. For the last century or so the Ottoman Turks had been steadily advancing westward from Constantinople, which they had first conquered in 1453. Indeed, they had by then already overrun most of the rest of the southeast Balkans as well. By the time Nostradamus was born they had extended their conquests to include most of Greece, Albania, Bosnia, Herzegovina, Hungary,

and Transylvania, as well as briefly occupying Otranto on the Italian mainland. In 1529, when the budding doctor went up to Montpellier, their armies were before the very gates of Vienna. And by the time he was writing his *Propheties* they had conquered most of North Africa, too, and were threatening the Mediterranean shores of Europe all the way from Gibraltar to Venice.

But then those shores had already been subject to Muslim attack and invasion for long centuries past. As early as the year 711

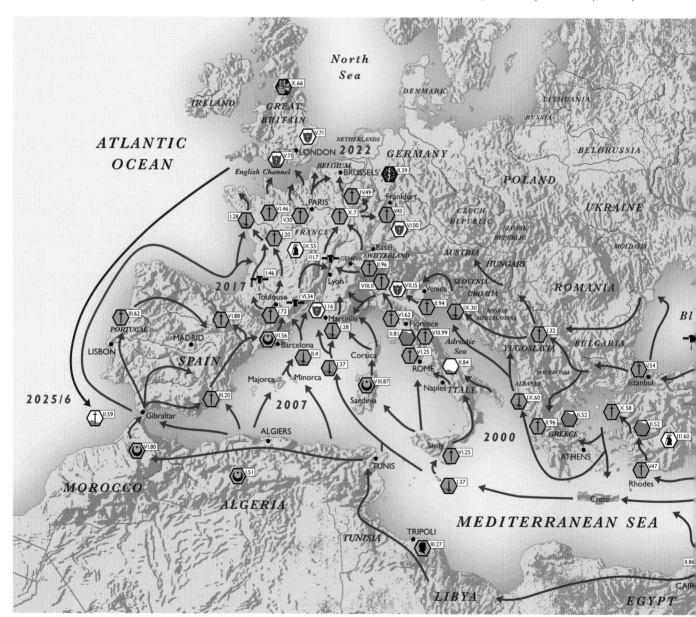

the Moors had entered Spain from North Africa (originally by invitation), eventually overrunning the whole country and even parts of western France. Indeed, they had not finally been expelled again until 1492, shortly before Nostradamus's birth. Their architectural and racial legacy in southern Spain remains to this day, as does their considerable influence on the language.

From the late ninth to the late eleventh centuries Sicily, too, had been in the hands of the Muslim Saracens, a fact that both its religious architecture and its racial characteristics, like those of Spain, continue even now to reflect. Mainland Italy had likewise suffered dreadfully at the invaders' hands. Even in France, the results were – and are – still there for everyone to see. At Stes-Maries-de-la-Mer and at Agde the ancient coastal churches remain strongly battlemented and fortified, as though expecting that any day now the former invaders will sweep in once more from the sea.

If the *Presages* for 1555 especially are to be believed (see Nos. 2, 9, 11, 12), Nostradamus himself shared that expectation. Unsurprisingly, therefore, under the terms of comparative horoscopy (see Astrologer and Mage), he predicted that the former events would repeat themselves almost blow for blow in the future. So overwhelmingly threatening were those coming events seen to be at the time, indeed, that they figure in the resulting predictions with a vivid remorselessness that is almost frightening.

The *Propheties* duly set out the resulting scenario, and a combination of dating methods serves to time it. While the dates resulting from comparative horoscopy and simple astrology (see Astrologer and Mage and Sequence of Selected Horographs) offer only a range of possibilities, the *Sixains*' "liturgical count" pinpoints fairly specific timings.

The general drift of events, meanwhile, is summed up by a remarkably explicit series of summary verses (see Dating and Sequencing the Prophecies). In apparent chronological order these are XII.36, VI.80, IX.55, V.68, VII.34, and V.13. In my own translations (published by Piatkus Books) these read:

> *In Cyprus they the fierce assault prepare*
> *(Weep now your coming ruin at the altar!)*
> *Arabs and Turks the evil deed shall share*
> *'Twixt separate fleets: huge ruin via Gibraltar.*

> *From Fez shall rulership to Europe spread,*
> *Firing its cities, slashing with the sword.*
> *O'er land and sea by Asia's Great One led,*
> *Christians, blues, greens fall prey to his vast horde.*

> *To drink he comes by Rhine's and Danube's shore:*
> *The Mighty Camel no remorse shall show.*
> *Quake, you of Rhône; of Loire quake even more.*
> *Yet near the Alps the Cock shall lay him low.*

> *After dread war that westward is prepared*
> *Pestilence comes with but a year's demur.*
> *In France nor old nor young nor beast is spared:*
> *In Aries,[8] Mercury, Mars, Jupiter.*

> *In grief the land of France shall mope and pine,*
> *Light-heartedness be foolishness decreed.*
> *No bread, salt, water, beer, medicine nor wine:*
> *Their leaders captive: hunger, cold and need.*

> *The lord from Rome in furious anger black*
> *Shall send his Arab horde Belgium to rape:*
> *But just as furious they shall chase them back*
> *From Hungary to stern Gibraltar's cape.*

Map of the Muslim invasion apparently predicted by Nostradamus for the near future (after original by Christopher DeJager)

---

8   i.e. also France: see Astrologer and Mage.

The selection of verses may admittedly seem arbitrary, yet all of them do seem to share a common subject, and the sheer facts of geography make it difficult to avoid the conclusion that the sequence suggested is the right one.

The general context, then is firmly established. The dates, too, are established by a variety of means. And the resulting scenario, which no fewer than 240 separate verses can be seen as supporting, appears to run more or less as follows (compare summary chart under Dating and Sequencing the Prophecies):

After severe disturbances in North Africa starting in 1997, a massive Muslim invasion starts in the Middle East in the summer of 1998, when Turkey and Egypt are attacked by Central Asian, Iranian and/ or Iraqi forces around a million strong. Western leaders immediately hold talks to discuss the situation. After a pause in hostilities the following summer while an emissary – probably the Pope – flies to Ankara to attempt to "buy off" the invaders, the Asiatic advance resumes again, led by a "new Xerxes." Southeastern Europe is quickly overrun by the "Mongol" invaders, and soon, following a militant Arab uprising in North Africa, Sicily, too, is invaded, with raids even mounted on the Mediterranean coast of France.

During the year 2000, violent sea-battles between Western and Muslim fleets take place in the Mediterranean, while in the Middle East the invading forces finally reach Rhodes and overrun Egypt. Later the same year the incoming hordes not only move up the Danube, but also attack mainland Italy itself. The Pope (seemingly the present one) is forced to flee to France, where he takes up residence in the former papal palace at Avignon until, chased out of it again, he finally meets his death near Lyon.

Within two years, the marauders have started to invade Provence in strength, mainly via Marseille, while by 2003 Muslim forces from North Africa are starting to mount separate seaborne attacks on southern Spain and Portugal. In 2004 – a year of drought, earthquakes, plague, persecution, and general financial collapse – they also start to make raids all along the Mediterranean coast of France. With ghastly aerial thermal weapons already being brought into play, the last Pope is ejected from office by the invaders in 2005. The year 2007 sees a major Muslim invasion of southeastern Spain, soon destined to threaten France itself. By 2009 the invaders are starting to cross the Pyrenees, and the following year sees further advances into France. In 2011 Rome is put to the torch and the last Pope murdered, while southern Europe is swept by an epidemic that eventually wipes out not only most of the French population but their livestock too. In 2015, with Rome finally razed to the ground and the Vatican destroyed by fire, a massive northward advance starts from southwestern France, accompanied by more "fire from the sky." Within two years chemical weapons, too, are being deployed.

Rome is now overrun yet again, this time by forces from North Africa, and 2021 sees the final triumph of the Muslim overlord, as his invading forces reach their farthest point on the borders of Belgium and the English Channel coast. Brutal atrocities and deprivation are by now affecting the whole of France, and the Church in particular is suffering bloody persecution.

With the death in 2026 of the enemy overlord – or the Antichrist, as many will see him – dissension suddenly splits the Muslim camp, and the Western allies are able to mount a huge counterinvasion that quickly liberates France, reaching Sicily by 2027.

Patient efforts to reestablish civilization throughout France and Italy are threatened in 2032, however, when a major civil war breaks out, resulting in

the death of the corrupt French leader. By 2034, however, the young Henri V of France [CHYREN in the original] has acceded to power and set matters to rights. After successfully liberating Spain, he turns his attention to the Middle East, which is duly invaded and liberated in turn by massed allied forces.

Such, then, is the gruesome scenario that jumps out again and again from the seer's pages, as (in general terms, at least) French commentators in particular have long recognized. No doubt thanks largely to the typically pick'n'mix approach more usually employed by British commentators, on the other hand, most of the latter have been so transfixed by possible Armageddons and Third World Wars between NATO and the former Warsaw Pact (none of which are in actual fact mentioned by Nostradamus) that they have failed to make much of the possible Muslim dimension at all. Perhaps the inherent geography of the case makes this difference relatively understandable.

Nevertheless, it must be quite clear by now that the coming Muslim invasion is perhaps, of all themes, the prophet's overriding concern, particularly as – thanks to its obvious religious dimension – it spells the end of the Roman Catholic Church as he knows it. In agreement with the ancient papal prophecies of St. Malachy, to which on one occasion at least he seems to refer via his pseudonym of *Pol mansol* for the present Pope (Malachy's *De Labore Solis* – "something to do with the labor of the sun"), he foresees only two more Popes after the present one. Then will follow the destruction of Rome, including St. Peter's and the Vatican, and the end of the old religious order.

The new Christianity that will arise after the great conflict will, he hints, be marked by a new return to basics, a resurgence of primitive Christianity, and an abandonment of its accumulated ritual extravagances.

But then, as an apparent crypto-Franciscan (see Nostradamus, the Bible, and the Church), we should hardly expect him to be saying anything else.

Armageddon or not, then, the coming conflict, if such it proves to be, will be more devastating than anything that Western Europe has ever known in all its long history. It will make the First and Second World Wars look positively gentlemanly by comparison, resulting as it will in the deaths of millions and the eventual destruction of the present World Order. Yet it may also result in the birth of a new order entirely, and one that offers far better prospects for humanity's ultimate survival than the present scenario of ever-growing decay, disintegration, and despair.

Whether or not this proves to be the long-promised millennial World Order expected by many of the religious remains to be seen. It remains to be seen, too, whether Nostradamus's predictions for it were ever in fact accurate in the first place. But at very least the latter should serve as a warning to us of what may be to come and a reassurance of what, if we play our cards right, may ultimately follow.

FROM SUBMARINES TO EXTRATERRESTRIALS

THE REAL TEST of Nostradamus's visionary powers has, of course, to be his ability to foresee future developments never before known in the history of the world. No amount of comparative horoscopy could, after all, ever predict such things on its own (see Astrologer and Mage). And yet he repeatedly comes up with such science-fiction visions.

Whether or not his reference to chariots at IX.93 has any possible reference to modern tanks, there can be little doubt that at III.21, for example, he is referring to the submarine:

> *Where Conca's waters to the ocean race*
> *There shall appear a fish of fearful look*
> *With fishy tail and yet a human face*
> *That lands itself with neither net nor hook.*

Especially when this is referred to the verse's evident "twin," II.5, which in my earlier translation reads:

> *From out a fish where papers, arms are stowed*
> *One shall emerge who then shall go to war.*
> *Across the sea he shall his fleet have rowed*
> *At length to appear off the Italian shore.*

Moreover, III.13 times its own fulfillment specifically to an occasion when *submergée la classe nagera* ("the fleet will sail underwater").

As for submarines, so for air travel. True though it may be that the infamous X.72 does not, after all, predict specifically that a "King of Terror" will descend *from the skies* in 1999 (see Interpreting the Prophecies), the fact remains that the seer refers at I.64, as well as apparently at II.45, to battles in the sky, and at I.63 makes a confident prediction of safe travel "by sky, land and sea."

When it comes to space travel, however, we are on shakier ground. British commentators in particular are prone to take IX.65's mention of someone surrendering in *le coin de luna* as a reference to NASA's famous moon missions: presumably they are unaware that the expression simply means a patch of moonlight. I.81, similarly, has no explicit connection with space travel, despite the commentators' proneness to link it (with dubious mathematical aptness) to the *Challenger* disaster of 1986.

What, then, of extraterrestrials? Here two verses in particular might conceivably be relevant. The first is the already mentioned II.45, which in my previous translation reads:

> *Too much high heaven the Androgyne bewails*
> *New-born aloft the sky where blood is sprayed.*
> *Too late that death a mighty race avails.*
> *Sooner or later comes the hoped-for aid.*

– which may or may not have deep space connections. The second is the remarkable VI.5:

> *A wave of plague shall bring so great a dearth*
> *While ceaseless rains the Arctic Pole shall sweep:*
> *Samarobryn, a hundred leagues from Earth,*
> *Law-free themselves from politics shall keep.*

Here the main puzzle is the *Samarobryn*. This word, evidently based on the Celtic *Samarobriva* (Amiens),[9] and treated by Nostradamus as a plural, may also have more than a chance connection with the word *Samaritain* (compare the evident relief-work referred to by III.5 and II.45 above). It may thus just conceivably suggest some kind of race of extraterrestrial saviours.

The main point, however, is the quoted distance of one hundred leagues "from the hemisphere" (as the original has it). If, after all, this is intended to be measured vertically, then the *Samarobryn* are literally in orbit, at roughly the altitude (some 276.4 miles/445km) of the former American *Skylab* . . .

Evidently, in this case, *someone* has made it into space. But there is absolutely no indication anywhere in Nostradamus's work as to whether that someone will be human or extraterrestrial. Nor is there any suggestion of future manned visits (*pace* IX.65) to either the moon or the planets. Perhaps, then, the seer was more closely tied to his comparative horoscopy than enthusiasts for his clairvoyance would like to admit. He had visions of the future, certainly – but possibly he was prepared to accept them only all the while they fitted in with his astrology (see Astrologer and Mage).

H.M.S. *Upholder* under way – Nostradamus clearly foresaw the existence of submarines

---

9 Some commentators even claim to see in the term references to the Russian words for "self" and "operating."

NOSTRADAMUS AND THE END OF THE WORLD

SINCE NOSTRADAMUS in fact nowhere predicts the end of the world, this section can be mercifully brief. True, the strong popular conviction that he does is ably fostered by a host of modern would-be interpreters. Typically, it centers on *Century* X.72's alleged prediction of the advent of a "King of Terror" in 1999 – even though the verse turns out not to be on a "King of Terror" at all, let alone about the end of the world (see Interpreting the Prophecies).

The seer admittedly expects (apparently on the basis of the ancient *Book of Enoch*) some kind of apocalypse to occur at the beginning of the seventh millennium after the biblical creation of the world – which works out, on the basis of the figures supplied in the *Lettre à Henri II* (section B.16, below), to be the year A.D. 2828 or thereabouts. But this turns out to be merely the beginning of a new age – nothing less than the long-promised kingdom of heaven on earth (an ancient Jewish concept long since abandoned by most latter-day Christians in favor of a purely heavenly paradise) during which, as the Bible suggests, all things will be made new.

The details, it is true, seem somewhat scary. After a long period of extraordinary prosperity for a much reduced world population – a time of safe travel by air, sea, and land (I.63) – everything is shattered by what appears to be a cometary or asteroidal impact (V.32). The result is forty years of apparent "nuclear winter" during which both sun and moon are obscured by dust clouds (III.5, III.4, III.34). The earth is stricken first by a long period of drought (I.17) and then by ceaseless rain and flooding (III.4, VI.5). Famine (I.67, II.75), cannibalism (II.75), and war (I.63, IV.67) ensue. Then come the celestial *Samarobryn* (see From Submarines to Extraterrestrials), whose extraordinary name may bear more than a chance resemblance to the biblical term "Samaritan," given that their role seems to be essentially a rescuing and redeeming one (III.5, VI.5) . . .

True, none of these events is dated, and so almost any of them could as easily apply to a much more imminent future. The first of them particularly (I.67) might well apply to our own age, as could the second (V.32). Indeed, the seer predicts that the Pope's flight from Rome in the year 2000 (see Dating and Sequencing the Prophecies) will be accompanied by the appearance of just such a comet as this verse seems to describe (see II.41, II.15, V.VI).

Yet the world continues to survive. And so it is that eventually, one May, huge earthquakes strike and the dead are, as already predicted by the Bible, seen rising from the grave (IX.83, X.74). This stunning event apparently occurs in the very midst of the Olympic games of the year in question, which on the basis of Nostradamus's chronology in the *Lettre à Henri II* (section B.16), seems to be marked out as A.D. 2828.

Nostradamus predicted the dawn of a new age, in which we see God face to face

But the result is still not so much the end of the world as the beginning of a new age – an era during which humanity at last sees God face to face and gains access to almost unlimited future possibilities (II.13, III.2).

Even so, yet another mighty conflagration then occurs, after "hidden fires," which some commentators associate with the residue of former nuclear activities, have broken out and devastated the face of the planet (IV.67). Yet, despite further wars, the world will still be here as late as 3797 (*Préface à César*, 12), and humanity presumably with it.

Granted, Nostradamus does give this as the final date for his prophecies, which might imply that it is the final date for world history as well. Yet he does not implicitly say so – and if he does not, then it ill becomes modern commentators with infinitesimal prophetic credentials of their own to say so in his name.

It would seem, then, that as far as the end of the world is concerned, we at the end of the twentieth century and the beginning of the twenty-first can collectively breathe a sigh of relief and sleep safely in our beds again, even if as individuals and nations we may yet have many trials and tribulations to endure and survive in the meantime.

FORGERIES AND FAIRY TALES

AS IS VIRTUALLY inevitable with a figure as mysterious and unusual as Nostradamus, an enormous number of bogus texts and apocryphal stories have sprung up around his name since his death. Leaving aside the various modern commentaries – many of which are themselves almost misleading enough to be classed in this same general category – these will be listed and addressed here.

BOGUS TEXTS

1. The prophecies of "Michel Nostradamus le Jeune"

This shadowy figure's real name is unknown. He first climbed on to the Nostradamus literary bandwagon in 1568, when his *Predictions pour vint ans* were published in Rouen by Pierre Brenouzer. He followed this in 1571 with his *Prediction Des Choses Plus Memorables Qui sont a advenir, Depuis Cette presente Année, jusques à l'an mil cinq cens quatre vingt & cinq*, published in Troyes by Claude Garnier. Republished by Nostradamus's own publisher Benoist Rigaud of Lyon in 1574, this was followed by a collection of prophecies from various sources in 1575 and by a Dutch Almanac in 1577.

Seemingly famed in his lifetime for the sheer *in*accuracy of his predictions, he is reported as having finally met his nemesis when, having forecast that the then-besieged town of Le Pouzin, in Ardèche, would be burned to the ground, he was caught actually setting fire to it. According to one account, he then failed to predict the ironic sequel – namely that he would be kicked to death by his own horse.

2. The prophecies of Antoine Crespin
dict Nostradamus (alias Archidamus)

Antoine Crespin (or Crispin), allegedly of Marseille, first went into print in 1570 with an Almanac for 1571 that was published in Paris by Robert Colembel. A whole series of books and pamphlets followed – further almanacs, commentaries on royal births, eclipses and comets, letters to royalty on a variety of phenomena. He seems even to have managed to get himself appointed astrologer to the King on the strength of them. His last prophecies (for the years up to 1598) appeared in 1590.

3. "Extra" quatrains VII.43 and VII.44
(see The Major Prophecies)

These two verses, first published in 1643, differ sufficiently from Nostradamus's usual style and format to suggest that they are the work of different hands entirely. Most French commentators regard them as politically inspired forgeries relating to Mazarin and the insurrectionary *Fronde* of the 1640s.

Woodcut of Nostradamus from the title page of the 1698 edition of the *Propheties*

4. The prophecies of Olivarius

These mysterious predictions, ostensibly written by a doctor and astrologer by the name of Philippe Dieudonné Noël Olivarius, are reported by Laver as bearing the date "1542" – a fact that, in conjunction with their author's claimed profession, has caused a number of commentators to surmise that they might really be the work of the then still-wandering Nostradamus. According to Bareste, indeed (reporting in 1839 a story handed down by the Empress Josephine's favorite fortuneteller), the great Napoleon himself was convinced of this and reportedly took a copy of the slim volume with him wherever he went (for further details of his literary tastes, see Nostradamus, Napoleon, and "Hister").

In studiedly antique language, these lofty effusions anticipate the coming of a "supernatural being . . . from the sea" who will raise great armies, overrun Europe, be defeated and exiled, return to power, and then be dethroned once again in favor of the old royal line. Eventually, however, a new, young savior will appear to raise France to new heights of glory.

Their chief subject, then, is clearly Napoleon – which would of course explain his evident interest in them. However, their reported language, style, and general content supply ample evidence that they are in fact of *eighteenth- or nineteenth-century* origin – which might explain why Bareste's own copy of them was dated "1793." Indeed,

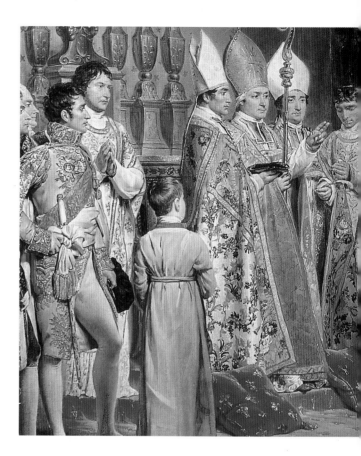

the fact that they refer quite clearly to the Emperor's second exile, yet are only very vague about anything thereafter (evidently drawing heavily on Nostradamus's predictions for the future Henri V), would actually tend to date them to the very end of Napoleon's reign, or even just after it. Which is bad news, unfortunately, for Bareste's story.

5. The prophecy of Orval

This short prophetic screed is clearly (on the evidence of its language and content) a product of the same prophetic stable as the prophecies of Olivarius (above) – as the anagrammatical similarity between the two names tends to confirm.

Allegedly discovered in 1793 at the Cistercian abbey of Orval in the Ardennes, shortly before the house's destruction, it claims to have been originally produced in 1544. The similarity of dates with the claimed prophecies of Olivarius is striking. Moreover, it carries on more or less from where the previous prophecies left off.

In even more obtuse language than before, it refers once again to somebody who is obviously Napoleon, then seemingly adumbrates (among other things) the return of the monarchy, a huge oriental invasion, the eventual expulsion of the invaders, and a Western liberation of the Holy Land. The ideas could have been taken straight from Nostradamus (compare Nostradamus and the Muslim Invasion of Europe). Once again, therefore, his authorship of them has been widely proposed. However, the likelihood that the future seer was even in the region at the time of their alleged composition is remote, given that the entire area was currently wracked by war between France and the Empire. Besides, he had in any case not yet had a chance to lay down the essential astronomical groundwork on which his prophetic work would largely be based (see Nostradamus's Life Story).

Style, language, and general content once again make it plain, in fact, that the prophecy of Orval is a nineteenth-century forgery. Laver, for his part, sees good reason for tying it down to some point between 1830 and 1840.

6. Subsequent "Orval" prophecies

A number of modern writers – seemingly inspired by the "Olivarius" syndrome – have claimed to discover further Nostradamian manuscripts from the abbey of Orval (ruined in 1793) and have duly published their texts. Some of the resulting collections of verses (see Books, Films, Videos, Disks and Internet) are quite good, if slightly atypical. At least one collection (one of several suggestively entitled *Les ultimes prophéties de Nostradamus*) even numbers fifty-eight quatrains – precisely the number required to restore the incomplete seventh *Century* to its original length.

On the other hand, none of the authors has succeeded in explaining what the seer was doing rewriting verses before 1544 that would not actually go missing until after 1558: in section 2 of his *Lettre à Henri II* of that year, after all, he specifically states that the collection of a thousand verses is *complete*.

Perhaps, then, Nostradamus was even more of prophet than anybody realizes.

FAIRY TALES

A number of legends about Nostradamus are recounted with great gusto by each succeeding generation of commentators as though they were actual facts. Often these tales seem to take precedence over actual biographical truth. Moreover, their details tend to proliferate as time goes on. This phenomenon is a well-known characteristic of the so-called urban myth, and thus tends to expose their true nature.

Every great man, from Alexander the Great to Winston Churchill, attracts such stories – and Nostradamus was no exception.

1. Nostradamus and the Wrong Pig

The story is told of how the future seer, while visiting a Monsieur and Madame de Florinville at the Château de Fains, near Bar-le-Duc in northeastern France (an area that, as we have seen, seems to spawn Nostradamian forgeries), spotted two piglets in the farm-

place to partake of the flesh of an animal whose consumption was so famously forbidden by his ancestral religion.

2. Nostradamus and the Surprised Monk

Another story relates how, while traveling near Ancona in Italy, Nostredame encountered a young swineherd (those pigs again!), or alternatively a traveling Franciscan friar (some versions of the story, evidently anxious to stack up the odds, even mention a whole group of them). At once Nostradamus fell down at his feet, explaining that he must kneel before "his Holiness." Sure enough, the young Felice Peretti duly became Pope Sixtus V in 1585.

Except for the fact that there is no other record of a visit by the future seer to the region of Ancona, the details almost fit. Born in 1521 the son of a gardener from Montalto in the March of Ancona, Peretti had indeed been a Franciscan ever since the age of twelve. Before that he may even have been employed as a swineherd. If so, though, he must have been a very young one.

But the main chronological weakness in the story is another one. Peretti was ordained priest in 1547, at least a year before he is likely to have encountered Nostradamus – during his known visit to Italy, that is (see Nostradamus's Life Story). This makes it marginally less likely that he would have been traveling the roads around Ancona at the time, least of all as one of group of friars . . .

3. Nostradamus and the Secret Tryst

One day, goes another story, Nostradamus was sitting outside his house in Salon when the pretty young daughter of a neighbor passed by on her way to gather firewood in the forest (the actual details vary from account to account). "Good day, young maid," he said (the actual words, similarly, vary). A little while later she returned with her bundle – no doubt looking just a little flushed. "Good day, young woman," ventured the ever-impish seer.

The story does not seem at all improbable – but for the fact that it is also told of no less a figure than Hippocrates . . .

4. Nostradamus and the Lost Dog

A story recounted by Chavigny himself in his *Vie et testament de Nostradamus* has, by virtue of its authorship alone, a somewhat better pedigree (the word, as we shall see, is an apt one) – even though this former pupil of Dorat was, like most scholars of the day, never overcritical of his sources at the best of times.

While visiting the court in Paris during 1555, it seems, the newly famous seer was called on at his lodgings near St.-Germain-l'Auxerrois by the young page of the de Beauveau family, who had lost a magnificent hound of which he had been placed in charge. Before he could even answer the door or ask what he wanted, Nostradamus, hearing him call out that he had come from the King (a lie if ever there was one), shouted from inside that he would find his stray dog on a leash on the Orléans road.

And there, indeed, it was.

yard and predicted to his host that the white one would be eaten by a wolf, while the black one would finish up on the dinner table. Florinville, however, wishing to put the would-be seer to the test, expressly ordered his cook to kill and prepare the *white* one.

The cook did as he was told right up to the point where the piglet was ready for roasting, then had to leave the kitchen for a moment – presumably for a call of nature. At this point, a wolf cub that was being kept for taming seized its chance and, entering the kitchen, laid into the piglet's rump.

At dinner that night Florinville mockingly informed his guest that they were in fact eating the white piglet, not the black. When Nostredame ventured to disagree and stuck to his original prediction, the cook was summoned to support his master. In the event, however, he had to confess that the guest was right. Another dish was therefore served so as not to upset either party.

The story, certainly, is an engaging one. There are various worrying features about it, however. First of all it was not reported in print until the latter end of the seventeenth century, and then only on the authority of an anonymous *Testament de Nostradamus*. Second, it is highly unlikely (see Nostradamus's Life Story) that the then Nostredame would have risked going anywhere near war-torn northeastern France in the early 1540s, which is when the visit would presumably have had to occur. Finally, one wonders quite how keen the "wandering Jew" would really have been in the first

Unfortunately, there is no independent confirmation of this story. Indeed, the specific mention of St.-Germain-l'Auxerrois does seem to suggest that its author may have either muddled or invented his facts. St.-Germain-l'Auxerrois is the name, not of a district, but of a church in Paris on the place du Louvre from which the signal was given for the St. Bartholomew's Day Massacre of 1572. St.-Germain-*en-Laye* was where Nostradamus visited the King and Queen – though not where he was lodged. Much, therefore, hinges on whether the town residence of the powerful Archbishop of Sens, his host at the time, was near the Louvre or not, and if so why it should be described instead as "near St.-Germain." Moreover, since Chavigny was not in any case there at the time – and only wrote up the story about forty years after the event – there is also the question of where he got his information from. To judge by the details, it was probably some source subsequent to 1572.

And what, in any case, was Nostradamus doing taking over the job of the regular doorman?

5. Nostradamus and the Upright Burial

In view of the very slightest of hints in Nostradamus's grave epitaph (see Nostradamus's Life Story) that he might have been concerned lest posterity ever dig up his remains, it is perhaps not surprising that later legend should have attributed to him a curse on anybody who did. (Compare *Century* IX.7, as also the inscription on Shakespeare's grave at Stratford.)

In the aftermath of the so-called *presse des Cabans*, similarly, it was said that the seer had cursed the rioting peasantry of the time with the unprepossessing words: *Allez, méchants pieds poudreux, vous ne me les mettrez pas sur la gorge, ni pendant ma vie, ni après ma mort.*[10] Logically, perhaps, it was therefore supposed that he had been buried upright, rather than lying down. A report of 1668, however, merely indicates that his tomb was in the wall of the local Franciscan chapel – a by no means unknown arrangement that would have served much the same purpose, as well as more or less squaring with the provisions of his will and corresponding to the situation of his *current* tomb in the Collégiale St.-Laurent. But then, by the end of the eighteenth century, the legend had developed further: the prophet was now supposed to be still alive in his tomb, and still writing his prophecies.

Unsurprisingly, neither when the tomb was opened in 1792, nor when the church was finally sacked by the revolutionaries in 1793,[11] was any evidence found to support this theory . . .

6. Nostradamus and the Message in the Tomb

A favorite hair-raising story of fairly recent provenance none the less purports to describe what *was* found. When grave robbers (or was it the local council?) first opened the tomb in 1700 (or was it the drunken revolutionary solders of 1792, or 1793?), what they discovered around the seer's bony neck was a medallion bearing a date in Roman numerals (a deft touch, this!). That date was none

other than "1700" – or "1792," or even "1793," depending on the particular version of the story. Sometimes the month is even added for good measure.

This interesting ability of the date to change with the account is truly magical – and clearly has nothing to do with actual fact. Neither, consequently, is the story itself likely to have. Indeed, it is difficult to see how the dying seer, who knew perfectly well that his body would be stripped and washed before burial, could have ensured that the medallion would be hung around his neck thereafter. Certainly, nothing of the kind was specified in his will (compare Nostradamus's Last Will and Testament). Nor is any desecration of the tomb in 1700 known to local history.

But then the dry-witted seer would no doubt still have enjoyed the joke. He might even have wished that he had been the one to think of it . . .

7. Other stories

A whole variety of other rumors – ranging from tales of successful horoscopic predictions to an actual raising from the dead – have surfaced over the centuries and duly been embellished (as is the way of things) with names, places, dates, and/or other would-be verificatory details. Most of them are reported in the form of mere passing references of dubious pedigree by very late commentators. None of them, consequently, is cogent enough to detain us here.

A crude portrait of the seer from the title page of the 1664 edition of the *Propheties*

---

10 "Clear off, you evil clod-hoppers: living or dead, you shan't tread on my throat!"

11 Possibly the two events are in reality one: the church may already have been sacked and ruined when the curious soldiery came across the famous prophet's tomb among the rubble and decided to tempt Providence . . .

PART FOUR

MILIEU

*Nostradamus's
hometown;
gazetteer
and who's who.*

NOSTRADAMUS'S HOMETOWN

SALON-DE-PROVENCE is a busy market town on the eastern edge of the vast, stony plain known as the *Crau*. The town's lofty central rock, crowned with its ancient castle, is, in effect, the last outlier of the limestone hills that run southwestward toward Salon all the way from the Durance River. Once surrounded by a salt marsh, the Rocher du Puech was formerly the site of the Roman fort of *Castrum Salonense*. This not only marked the start of the *Via Aurelia* where the latter launched itself westward, straight as an arrow, across the *Crau* to Arles; it also guarded the Roman road's junction with the important route between Avignon to the north and Marseille to the south.

Even today, the modern highway and the railway between the two cities both pass directly through the town, and so provide easy access from either direction. Arriving by car (certainly by far the best way to visit both the town and its surrounding area), the best plan is to seek out the place Morgan (see map on the right), directly to the west of the castle on its rock, which offers free parking every day except market day (normally Wednesday morning). Underground parking lots are also available, but metered street parking is much more problematical.

GETTING INTO TOWN

From the place Morgan it is only a short walk into the center of the town. Skirting the castle to your right, follow the arc of shops and business premises that form the boulevard Jean-Jaurès, the cours Pelletan, and the cours Carnot as they follow the line of what was formerly one of the town walls. This brings you around to the north of the castle until you reach the place Crousillat (known locally as the place de la Fontaine Moussue), with its extraordinary, moss-covered fountain – one of several in the region. On your right now stands the magnificent porte de l'Horloge – so called because of the seventeenth-century clock-tower with which, after the fashion of the region, this ancient north gate is crowned.

From here you have two main choices:

Route 1 – The Way of the Living Seer

Passing through the porte de l'Horloge, head directly into the heart of the old town. After only a few yards you come to the place de l'Ancienne Halle (the former fish-market). Ignoring for a moment the enormous portrait of Nostradamus on the wall of the shop directly ahead of you, turn immediately to your left into the inevitable rue Nostradamus.

This brings you almost at once to the impressively restored Maison de Nostradamus on your right. Open every day from 9 a.m. until 6 p.m., this offers a kind of *son-et-lumière* self-guided tour of Nostradamus's former house in a variety of languages, as well as a range of museum exhibits: numerous books and publica-

The recently rebuilt *Maison de Nostradamus* at Salon bears only a passing resemblance to the original (see p.31)

tions on the seer and his milieu may also be purchased. Unfortunately the commentary has little to say about the house itself, since both it and the *quartier* around it are for the most part modern reconstructions, having been devastated by the disastrous Vernègues earthquake of 1909. The cellar has been filled in and the walls – even the exterior ones – largely rebuilt. The circular stone staircase leading up into the building from the little courtyard, however, may go back to the seer's time, while the medieval stone window-casement let into its wall almost certainly does. The engaging waxworks of Nostradamus and others help to lend a little atmosphere to the experience. The wall of the metal staircase leading back down into the entrance lobby bears the reprinted text of a very early edition of the *Propheties*. Students of the seer can obtain from the desk details of the nearby Centre Nostradamus

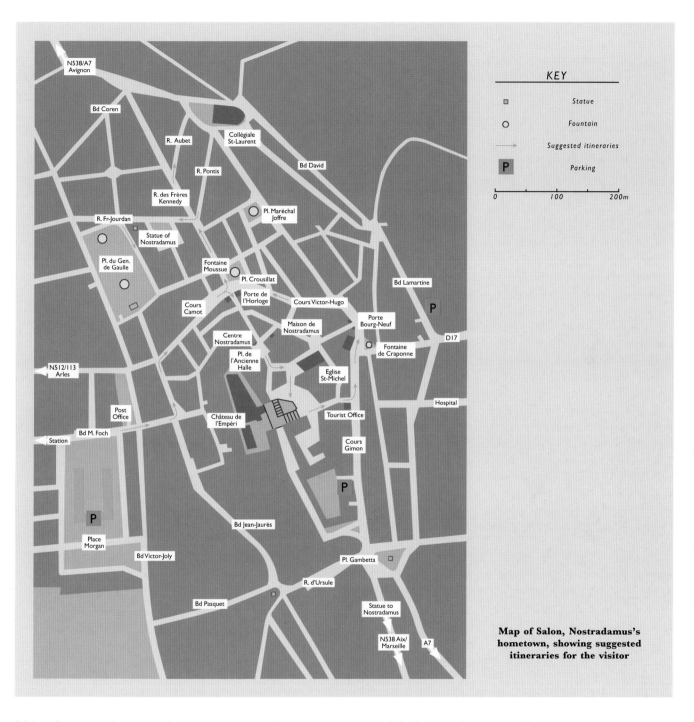

KEY

▫	Statue
○	Fountain
→	Suggested itineraries
P	Parking

0   100   200m

Map of Salon, Nostradamus's hometown, showing suggested itineraries for the visitor

(Maison Benoît, on the corner of the rue Moulin-Isnard).

Emerging from the Maison de Nostradamus, turn left and return to the place de l'Ancienne Halle. The Centre Nostradamus is now on the right-hand corner facing you. Should you, as a scholar, wish to explore its many documents, this is perhaps the moment to announce yourself – though any long-term study of them may need to await a later occasion.

On reemerging into the sunlight, resume your original itinerary toward the far end of the square. You now come (on your left) to the appropriately-named Église St.-Michel, with its twelfth-century tympanum over the doorway and its separate thirteenth- and fifteenth-century belfries. Descending into its relative darkness, you are in the very midst of the thirteenth century. The seer himself would probably not have joined you, however: he seems to have preferred to worship elsewhere (see below, and compare Nostradamus, the Bible, and the Church).

Emerging once more into the light, bear left and continue on your way, heading for the castle via the place des Centuries, and passing beneath the huge modern mural of Nostradamus and Catherine de Médicis (the purely imaginative original drawing on which this is based can be seen in the Musée des Alpilles Pierre de Brun at St.-Rémy). You now have the option of mounting a frontal assault on the castle via the steps.

Unfortunately, thanks to the 1909 earthquake, much of the castle as you see it today is a modern reconstruction, and is consequently far more impressive from the outside than from the inside. Here the only genuine architectural features of note are the *cour d'honneur* with its Renaissance gallery (which you can see just inside the entrance without having to pay any entrance-fee), plus the twelfth-century chapel and the great, sculpted fireplace in the *salle d'honneur*, where Nostradamus is said to have been consulted by King Charles IX and his mother Catherine de Médicis in October 1564, less than two years before his own death (see Nostradamus's Life Story). Otherwise, the interior of the castle is of interest mainly to enthusiasts for ancient weapons and military uniforms, of which the castle offers a vast display.

On leaving the castle and taking your final view of Salon from above, you can now proceed via the street directly opposite the steps into the town's main shopping-center in the cours Victor-Hugo. On the right-hand corner as you enter it is the Office de Tourisme, where you can pick up leaflets and information on a variety of topics from accommodation to parking facilities and forthcoming events.

Turn left now and wander gently down to the place de l'Hôtel de Ville where, opposite the Town Hall, a delightful statue and fountain celebrates Adam de Craponne, the local architect and hydraulic engineer who, with Nostradamus's financial support, helped to transform the *Crau* from a stony desert into the green and flowering plain that it is today by digging the ambitious canal that still bears his name.

Continuing on down the hill, you pass on your left the thirteenth-century town gate known as the porte Bourg-Neuf, which serves to remind you that the whole frontage of which it forms part was once the inner town wall. This passed close by Nostradamus's house, which now lies a short distance inside the gate and one street to the right. Provided, however, that you can resist the temptation to take another peek at it, and instead continue to follow the line of shops down the main street, you now come back again to the place Crousillat with its mossy fountain, so completing this particular itinerary.

An early twentieth-century statue of Nostradamus in period costume marks the site of his original burial

Route 2 – The Way of the Dead Seer

From the place Crousillat, follow the street directly opposite the porte de l'Horloge (latterly renamed the rue des Frères Kennedy) for a hundred yards or so until you can see on the high ground slightly to your right the ancient church known as the Collégiale St.-Laurent, with its heavy stone buttresses and ornate fifteenth-century steeple. This is Nostradamus's second and (hopefully) final resting-place. Entering by the south door that faces you, you are immediately struck by the deep gloom that the meager light from the narrow windows scarcely manages to penetrate. Despite this, you still manage to catch sight of the Craponne family tomb on your left.

However, the main point of interest is the Lady Chapel (i.e. the chapel of *Notre Dame*!) opposite the door, for it is here that Nostradamus's mortal remains now repose, having been reburied here in around 1792 after his original tomb had been desecrated (see Nostradamus's Lifestory and Nostradamus and the French Revolution). You will find the replacement tomb slab in the left-hand wall of the chapel as you enter it, its situation in the wall possibly reflecting that of the original burial. Beneath is a modern French translation of the Latin inscription of 1813. Because of its dark coloration, photographing the slab is not easy. Fortunately, flash photography is not explicitly forbidden, provided that a service is not in progress at the time: it is best done either from one side or from below, though, in order to avoid reflection-dazzle.

Having discovered the site of the seer's last resting place, it is now time to discover that of his original burial. Leaving by the same door as you entered by, follow the rue Pontis back down towards the town, leaving the greenery of the little square Jean XXIII (formerly the square Saint-Laurent) well to your left, until you rejoin the same rue des Frères Kennedy up which you came earlier. At this point take the street immediately opposite (formerly the rue des Cordeliers, now the rue Fr.-Jourdan). After passing the place des Martyres on your left, you will come to the northeast corner of the large place du Général de Gaulle. Here, immediately on your left, you will find a stone statue of Nostradamus.

Despite its antique appearance, this dates only from the beginning of the present century. Nevertheless, its "Shakespearean" garb at least serves as a useful reminder of just when Nostradamus lived. Even more interestingly, it marks the approximate site of the former Franciscan convent in whose chapel the seer was originally buried, and which he quite possibly attended in his lifetime (see

Nostradamus, the Bible, and the Church). Certainly he felt attached enough to it to leave money to it in his will (see Nostradamus's Last Will and Testament), and his son André was actually to enter the order in due course.

By walking the length of the place du Général de Gaulle, you can now regain the place Crousillat and the porte de l'Horloge by taking any one of the streets to your left.

Other attractions

1. The extraordinary, bat-winged monument to the spirit of Nostradamus (*Évocation de l'idée de Nostradamus*) is situated in the far southern part of the town on its roundabout beyond the end of the allées de Craponne. It was erected in 1979 after its predecessor had been demolished by a careering truck in the middle of a thunderstorm. *Be warned: the monument is an abstract, and in no way intended to look like Nostradamus!*

2. The Musée de Salon et de la Crau lies in the eastern part of the town, and contains numerous exhibits covering local arts, crafts, industries and geology, including a light-operated audio-visual display (not always well coordinated) of the region's geological and geographical formation. To find it, head for the hospital, leave it on your right, then follow the signs that lead you up the hill and to the left at the roundabout.

3. Events and festivals: enquire at the Office de Tourisme in the main shopping street (the cours Gimon) for details of the summer jazz festivals, the barrel organ festival (*orgues de Barbarie*), the various fairs, concerts, plays, art and craft exhibitions etc.

Shopping and eating

The place Crousillat with its mossy fountain offers easy access to the shops and restaurants. Most of the main shops are in the street that runs along the curving line of the former town wall on either side of the porte de l'Horloge. To its right, the cours Carnot will also lead you back towards the place Morgan.

Most of the restaurants lie either hereabouts or through the gate in the ancient town-centre. All of them, from the most expensive "private restaurants" to the cheapest pizzeria, can be relied upon to provide good French meals. Often, indeed, the cheapest will offer the best value and the most efficient service. For special tastes, Chinese and Vietnamese restaurants are also available and as cheap as any.

Leaving the town centre

(a) From the place Crousillat and its mossy fountain, simply follow the cours Carnot back the way you originally came, turning left into the cours Pelletan and then right. Alternatively, keep following the cours Carnot until you reach the boulevard Victor Joly, then turn left and follow it all the way to the place Morgan.

(b) From the place de l'Ancienne Halle in the heart of the town, take the first narrow street that leads around the right-hand flank

Salon: the rue de l'Horloge leads to the town's sixteenth-century north gate, surmounted by its seventeenth-century clock-tower

of the castle, leaving its lofty eminence hard to your left. Turn left at the end, and then right until you reach the boulevard Victor Joly. Cross it, and the place Morgan will lie to your left.

When to go

Spring and early fall are the best times to avoid the crowds and the heat. Of the two, spring is greener, but subject to the occasional *Mistral*; fall is dry and brown until the heavy rains arrive in mid-September. The main fairs and festivals start at the end of April and finish in August, with the big musical events (including the international jazz festival at the castle) grouped mainly around June, July and August. Several markets are held weekly. Contact the Office de Tourisme (see below) for the current year's brochure containing full details. Above all, go soon, while it is still there: Nostradamus (compare Dating and Sequencing the Predictions) seems to foresee a huge Muslim invasion overrunning the whole area from around the year 2002.

Tourist information

For details of travel routes to Salon-de-Provence, and of accommodation and parking facilites within the town, contact the Office de Tourisme at 56, cours Gimon, Salon-de-Provence, 13300 (Tel. 4.90.56.27.60: Fax 4.90.56.77.09).

GAZETTEER AND WHO'S WHO

Roman figures refer to numbers of *Centuries*

A

Adrian VI
Pope from Jan. 9th, 1522, to Sept. 14th, 1523, during Nostradamus's years of student wandering. Appointed tutor to the future Emperor Charles V in 1507, he was for six years responsible for overseeing the Spanish Inquisition. Of high character, he espoused Church reform, but opposed Martin Luther.

Aemathien
See *Haemathien*

Aenobarbe
Name used by Nostradamus to refer at V.45, V.59, and apparently IX.6 to a future military leader and governor from the south of France. Evident reference not to the Emperor Nero, whose name it also was, but to Lucius Domitius Ahenobarbus (d.48 B.C.), a Roman politician and general who was appointed to replace Julius Caesar as commander in Gaul and passionately opposed his assumption of power on his return home. He later led a revolt against him from his base in Marseille. Thus, the name *Aenobarbe* appears to denote a doughty future fighter for freedom against some overwhelming foreign tyranny (see Nostradamus and the Muslim Invasion of Europe).

Agde (Pop. 18,000)
Fishing port and vacation resort with a medieval cathedral in southwest France, mentioned at III.99 as the site of a massive future (and probably North African Muslim) invasion involving a million troops.

Agen (Pop. 34,500)
Ancient city in southwestern France (formerly the Roman Aginnum) on Garonne River, mentioned at IV.72, VII.12, IX.38, and IX.85. The home of Julius Caesar Scaliger, it became Nostradamus's, too, when he first settled down there to join the circle of the doctor and philosopher in around 1533.

Aigues Mortes ("Dead Waters") (Pop. 4,500)
Ancient fortified town on the coastlands of the Camargue. It was built by Louis IX (Saint Louis) as a base-port for mounting the Seventh Crusade in 1248, complete with medieval lighthouse (mentioned at XII.52 – see The Major Prophecies: The "Extra" Quatrains).

Aix-en-Provence (Pop. 124,500)
Chief city of Provence and former capital of Good King René, its last king, Aix is mentioned

at I.71, II.88, IV.86, and V.76. On the last day of May 1546, the city was struck by plague, and Nostradamus was hurriedly summoned from Marseille. Nostradamus describes the outbreak vividly in his *Traité*, as well as giving his recipe for rose pills to combat it.

Albret, Jeanne d' (1528–72)
Niece of François I, Viscountess of Béarn, and Queen of Navarre, she married Antoine de Bourbon and was the mother of Henri IV. She was a leading protagonist in France's Wars of Religion.

Alençon, Hercule-François, Duc d' (1554–84)
Youngest son of Henri II and Catherine de Médicis, he was one of the royal children examined by Nostradamus at Blois in 1555. Notoriously ugly, he subsequently proposed himself as suitor to Queen Elizabeth of England, possibly at the seer's suggestion.

Alleins
Village just north of Salon, mentioned by Nostradamus at III.99 as being on the site of the final battle to expel the future Muslim invaders from France (see Nostradamus and the Muslim Invasion of Europe).

Allemand, Jacqueline
Founding Director from 1992 of the Maison de Nostradamus in Salon.

Alpilles
Low mountain range to the south of St.-Rémy and to the west of Salon. The ancient Roman city of Glanum lies concealed in a valley below its northern escarpment.

Antiques, les
Local name for the complex of Roman ruins at St.-Paul-de-Mausole, just to the south of St.-Rémy-de-Provence. They include the Mausoleum of Sextus, the municipal gateway and the extensive remnants of the ancient city of Glanum.

Arles (Pop. 51,000)
The former Roman Arelate, the ancient city of Arles (mentioned at I.71, VII.2, VIII.68, and X.93–4) stands on the left bank of the Rhône, on a low hill commanding the delta. It marks the southernmost crossing of the river by the Roman *Via Domitia* as well as the western terminus of the canal de Craponne.

It was in the bishop's palace that the now-elderly Nostradamus, summoned from Salon for

consultation, met King Charles IX and his mother, Catherine de Médicis, for the last time in November 1564. He was formally appointed to the office of Councilor and Physician-in-Ordinary to the King, "with all the rights, privileges and honors pertaining thereto."

Aubespine, Claude de l' (d.1567)
Secretary of State to François I, as well as to Henri II at the time of Nostradamus's visit to the Court at St.-Germain-en-Laye in 1555.

Aurons
Small hill-village northeast of Salon from where, in 1554, a black-and-white kid with two heads was brought to Palamède Marc, First Consul of Salon, who on the advice of Nostradamus then showed it to the Governor of Provence (see Tende, Claude, Duc de), the Baron de la Garde, and the Commandeur de Beynes. The seer seems to have interpreted the omen as signifying imminent wars and divisions in the land – as indeed occurred in the form of the bloody Wars of Religion that were to devastate France for much of the rest of the century.

Avicenna (980-1037)
Classicized form of Ibn Sina, doctor to the Persian Court, and known as "Prince of Physicians." He introduced the medical teachings of Aristotle to the Middle East and in his *Canon of Medicine* strove to reconcile them with those of Galen. Burnt by Paracelsus, this was still in use at Nostradamus's old medical faculty at Montpellier as late as 1650.

Avignon (Pop. 91,500)
Capital city of Vaucluse, mentioned at I.71, III.56, III.93, VIII.38, VIII.52, and IX.41. In the fourteenth century it became the headquarters of the French Popes. The enormous Palais des Papes still stands, as does the famous ruined bridge leading from it across the Rhône. Nostradamus attended college in the city until late 1520.

The beautiful cloister of the cathedral of St.-Trophime, Arles

B

The citadel of Les Baux-de-Provence, now in ruins

Barbares
Contemptuous term frequently used by Nostradamus of the future invaders of Europe, as well as of anybody else he disapproves of (see VI.100, for example). The ancient Greek word *barbaros* simply meant "foreign", since "bar-bar" (i.e. babble) was all that the somewhat chauvinistic Greeks imagined that foreign languages amounted to. By extension, however, it also carried connotations of Philistinism, uncouthness, and lack of civilization. But the word *barbares* also relates to *la Barbarie* – i.e. the country of the North African Berbers. In Nostradamus's writing, consequently, the term tends to refer not only to foreigners in general but to North African foreigners in particular – and thus, by false extension, first to Arabs and then to Muslims generally.

Barben, Château de la
Spectacular medieval fortress in the secluded valley of the Touloubre River, east of Salon. At one time it served as a country residence of Good King René.

Bareste, Eugène
Prominent nineteenth-century Nostradamian biographer, bibliographer, and commentator. His book *Nostradamus* (1840) contains numerous absorbing anecdotes concerning the seer, many of them otherwise unsubstantiated.

Baume, La Sainte
Celebrated cave in the forest of the same name, east of Marseille. The remote pilgrimage site of a prehistoric fertility cult, it became sacred to St. Mary Magdalene in early Christian times, after which it continued to be a major pilgrimage-center for royalty and commoners alike, including Good King René of Provence. King Charles IX of France, and his mother, Queen Catherine de Médicis, likewise made the pilgrimage directly after visiting Nostradamus at Salon in 1564. Local Provençal legend has it that Mary Magdalene, driven out of Palestine, was shipwrecked on the south coast of France at what is now Les Stes-Maries-de-la-Mer. She then set out across Provence on a preaching-tour, finishing up at the already-celebrated cave of La Sainte Baume (Prov. *baoumo*, 'cave, grotto') where she spent the final 33 years of her life in prayer and contemplation.

Baux-de-Provence, Les
Ancient rock fortress and village perched spectacularly on a rock promontory jutting out from the southern slopes of the Alpilles. At the time of Nostradamus it was part of the fiefdom of the High Constable of France, Anne de Montmorency, who renovated it considerably. It was here that, in 1822, the mineralogist Pierre Berthier discovered aluminum ore, since known as bauxite in commemoration of the fact.

Beaucaire (Pop. 13,000)
Town on the right bank of the Rhône (the Roman Ugernum), opposite Tarascon. Nostradamus mentions Beaucaire not only at X.93, but at *Sixain* 43. It was one Vincent Seve of Beaucaire who undertook in 1605 the publication of the first edition of the *Propheties* to contain the so-called *Presages* and *Sixains*.

Beaulme, Jean
Rich Salon lawyer and deceased first husband of Anne Ponsarde, Nostradamus's second wife.

Bellay, Cardinal Jean du
Cousin of Joachim du Bellay, Bishop of Paris and French Ambassador to Rome, for whom François Rabelais worked as secretary between 1532 and 1547.

Bellay, Joachim du (c.1525–60)
Distinguished French sonneteer and lyric poet, who in 1549 published *La Deffense et Illustration de la langue Françoyse*, the manifesto of the pioneering literary group *la Pléiade*, whose ideas seem greatly to have influenced Nostradamus's language, and especially his use of Greek and Latin words and syntax.

Berre, Étang de
Vast inland lagoon lying south of Salon. Apparently referred to by Nostradamus at I.16 as a major future invasion site for Muslim forces attacking Marseille (see Nostradamus and the Muslim Invasion of Europe), it was also the site in the first decades of the twentieth century of the first recorded French seaplane flight.

Beynes, Commandeur de
Long-time crony of Nostradamus at Salon and prominent local dignitary. With the Baron de la Garde, he was a dedicatee of the *Paraphase de C. Galen* of 1557.

Béza (or de Bèze), Théodore (1519–1605)
Burgundian former Professor of Greek at Lausanne who subsequently became head of the Genevan reformed Church on Calvin's death in 1564. He may have been the author of the *Monstre d'Abus . . . in Nostradamum*, a violent criticism of Nostradamus published in 1558.

Béziers (Pop. 71,000)
Former Roman town of *Julia Baeterrae*, southwest of Montpellier, Béziers is referred to at III.56, IV.94, VIII.3, VIII.36, and IX.25. It was for the bishop of his day, the thirty-six-year-old Cardinal Lorenzo Strozzi, that Nostradamus, while on a trip to Narbonne in October 1559, prescribed a particularly painful treatment for gout, involving a specially designed cauterizing instrument. It is not known how successful the treatment was – though it may safely be assumed that the seer was never summoned back to Béziers to repeat it.

Bibliographie Nostradamus
Prime source of information cataloging the dates, details and current whereabouts of the various sixteenth- to eighteenth-century editions of Nostradamus, as well as of other contemporary publications relating to them. Compiled by Michel Chomarat (below) and Dr. Jean-Paul Laroche, it was published in 1989 in Germany by Éditions Valentin Koerner under the collection "Bibliotheca Bibliographica Aureliana."

Blois (Pop. 45,000)
Capital city of Loir-et-Cher, on the north bank of the Loire River, mentioned at I.20, III.51, III.55, V.34, VIII.38, VIII.52, IX.21, and X.44. It has a magnificent renaissance castle, famous chiefly for the murder of Henri Duc de Guise on December 25th, 1588.

It was here that (according to his son César) Nostradamus was sent from Paris by Queen Catherine de Médicis in the summer of 1555 to examine all seven royal children and cast their horoscopes. As the seer had already anticipated (albeit obtusely) in his *Centuries*, their prospects turned out to be uniformly catastrophic. One of them, indeed (the future Henri III), was himself to become responsible for the grisly murder mentioned above. Nostradamus is said, however, to have contented himself with informing her blandly that "all her sons would become kings."

Bonhomme, Macé (= Matthieu)
Lyon printer and publisher, active from around 1535 or 1540, who published the first edition of the *Propheties* on May 4th, 1555. This was a beautifully printed edition of the first 353 quatrains of the *Centuries* only, accompanied by the *Préface à César* and the royal *"privilège"* or imprimatur (see Book Printing and Publishing). Remarkable for some dozen-and-a-half words in capital letters, this was extended in Du Rosne's second edition of 1557.

The Calès caves were inhabited from Neolithic times until the Middle Ages

Bordeaux (Pop. 271,000)

Major city and seaport of southwestern France, mentioned at I.72, I.79, I.90, III.9, and IV.44, and by inference at IV.79 and IX.6. Nostradamus is said to have stayed in the city in around 1539, following his flight from Agen – certainly in his *Traité* he claims to have practiced there.

Bouc, Port-de- (Pop. 20,000)

Fortified port at the entrance to the Canal de Caronte and étang de Berre. The twelfth-century tower incorporated into the seventeenth-century fort is mentioned by Nostradamus at I.28 as being attacked first by North African, then by Western forces at some time in the future, with devastating consequences (see Nostradamus and the Muslim Invasion of Europe).

Bourbon, Antoine de (1518–62)

Son of Charles de Bourbon (see below) and rightful successor to the Valois princes, he married Jeanne d'Albret, Queen of Navarre. He died at the siege of Rouen of 1562 before he could claim the succession.

Bourbon, Charles de (1490–1527)

Constable of France from 1515. He deserted to the Holy Roman Empire in 1521 on the death of his wife and commanded the Emperor's forces in Italy until his death in 1527.

Bourbon, Cardinal Louis de

Leading churchman and powerful politician who, as Archbishop of Sens, acted as Nostradamus's host during his visit to Paris of 1555. It was in his town residence that the seer was taken ill with gout after visiting Queen Catherine de Médicis. He also received many visitors and would-be patients there, reportedly becoming very rich in the process. *Century* VI.86 evidently refers either to the Cardinal or to one of his successors.

Brennan, J.H.

Author of *Nostradamus: Visions of the Future*, which briefly recounts the seer's life and offers a speculative, thematic account and literal translation of some of his prophecies.

Brotot, Jean

Lyon publisher responsible for many of Nostradamus's *Almanachs*, including those for 1554 (despite the seer's complaints of incompetent typesetting); 1557 (with Jacques Kerver of Paris); 1558 (with Antoine Volant of Lyon); 1559 (also translated into English and published by Henry Sutton of London); and 1560, 1562, 1566, and 1567 (once again published with Antoine Volant).

C

Cabans

Catholic peasants of the Salon area – so-called after their gray winter cloaks – who were possibly among the *bestes brutes et gens barbares* to whom Nostradamus refers in the *proeme* of his *Traité des fardemens*. In May 1560 they started to arrest and persecute local Protestants, one of whom the eccentric seer was (however illogically) locally suspected of being, and in April 1561 the growing threat forced him to rent a house in Avignon, though he seems never to have taken up residence there, possibly because the violence subsided.

Calès, Grottes de

Ancient cave-city excavated into the upper slopes of the Montagne du Défens just behind the village of Lamanon.

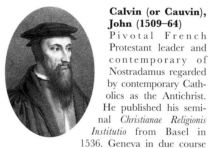

Calvin (or Cauvin), John (1509–64)

Pivotal French Protestant leader and contemporary of Nostradamus regarded by contemporary Catholics as the Antichrist. He published his seminal *Christianae Religionis Institutio* from Basel in 1536. Geneva in due course became his base for the training of Protestant ministers from France and elsewhere, who were then sent back to reevangelize their own countries, with turbulent results that were to lead directly to the French Wars of Religion.

Camargue

Vast area of bleak, coastal marshland occupying the western part of the Rhône delta to the south and west of Arles. Characterized by its famous white horses, bulls, flamingoes, paddy-fields, and vast lagoons sheltering behind long, shifting coastal sandbars.

Canal de Craponne

Network of irrigation canals, partly financed by Nostradamus, and designed and constructed by Adam de Craponne and his successors, the brothers Ravel, during and shortly after the seer's lifetime (1554 onward). Its purpose was to water and bring to life the long-arid Désert de la Crau to the west of Salon.

Fed by the Durance River, it leads the river's waters southwards through the Lamanon gap, where it divides. One branch leads westwards across the Crau below the southern slopes of the Alpilles to empty into the Rhône at Arles, passing just south of the Roman theater. The other passes through the western suburbs of Salon, then south to empty into the Mediterranean via the Étang de Berre.

Cannon, Dolores

Author of *Conversations with Nostradamus*, a three-volume work purporting to explain Nostradamus's prophecies with reference to Erika Cheetham's translations (see below), and with the "channeled" authority of the seer himself. It is interesting mainly for the suggestion that the seer arrived at many of his prophetic insights telepathically via our own eyes.

Carcassonne (Pop. 43,500)

Ancient city and former stronghold of the Albigenses on the river Aude in southwestern France. The young Nostradamus is rumored to have visited the city in around 1525 while acting as a peripatetic physician in pursuit of the plague. Certainly he claims in his *Traité des fardemens* of 1552/1555 to have worked there at some stage. A later alleged visit to treat its bishop, one Amamien de Foix, probably never actually took place.

Carcassonne figures no fewer than seven times in the *Centuries* (I.5, III.62, V.100, VIII.67, IX.10, IX.71, and X.5), notably in connection with a future invasion of Europe by Muslim forces from Africa and Spain (see Nostradamus and the Muslim Invasion of Europe).

Carpentras (Pop. 26,000)

Town lying northeast of Avignon, much patronized by the fourteenth-century French Popes and their entourages, and mentioned at V.76 and IX.41. Formerly fortified, it also had a large Jewish ghetto. Its cathedral had a door specifically for Jewish converts.

The celebrated porte des Juifs at the former cathedral of St.-Siffrein, Carpentras

Cateau-Cambrésis, Treaty of

Crucial treaty of April 1559 between Spain and France which, following the disastrous French defeat at St.-Quentin two years earlier, provided for the marriage of Philip II to Henri II's daughter Élisabeth de Valois, the betrothal of Henri's sister Marguerite de Valois to Emmanuel Philibert Duc de Savoie, the ceding by France of Savoy, Piedmont, Bresse, Brugey, Corsica, and Lombardy, and her retention or regaining of a variety of towns.

Leading directly to the royal marriage celebrations during which Henri II was killed in a tournament, and having the effect of demobilizing thousands of soldiers, the Treaty can be said to have provided the final spark igniting the Wars of Religion and leading to the catastrophic disintegration of the kingdom that characterized most of the rest of the sixteenth century.

Catherine de Médicis, Queen (1519–89)

Powerful Queen and Regent of France, deeply involved with the occult. The daughter of Lorenzo de' Medici, she married the future Henri II in 1533, and became queen on his accession in 1544. On his death in 1559 she acted as Queen Regent for their son François II, and later for their next son Charles IX.

A patron of arts and letters, and a capable architect in her own right, her main concerns were always the unity of France and the survival of her own family. Ever torn between promoting religious toleration and siding with one side or the other, she is notorious for either urging or actually ordering the St. Bartholomew's Day massacre of Protestants in August 1572.

On the appearance in print of Nostradamus's first edition in May 1555, she promptly sent for the prophet to attend her in Paris (see Nostradamus's Life-Story). He next met the Queen in Salon on October 17th, 1564, during a royal progress that she was making with her son Charles. At Arles a few weeks later, he was appointed Physician in Ordinary to the King and Royal Councillor and given a pension to match. It is said that he also proposed a marriage between the young King and Elizabeth I of England (now thirty-one).

On December 21st, 1565 Nostradamus sent the Queen a letter predicting further difficulties and quarrels for the kingdom at large, but an eventual happy outcome of the meeting of the Royal Council then in prospect.

Cavaillon (Pop. 21,000)

Marshland town (the ancient *Cabellio*) north of Salon, mentioned in *Century* V.76.

Centre Nostradamus

Documentation centre founded in Salon-de-Provence (Maison Benoît, rue Moulin-Isnard) in 1996 to provide local research facilities for Nostradamus-scholars. President: Michel Chomarat.

Centuries

Title of Nostradamus's main collection of prophecies. See Nostradamus's Writings and The Major Prophecies.

César Nostradamus

See **Nostredame, César de**

Charles V (1500–58)

King of Spain (1518) and Germany (1519), and Holy Roman Emperor (1520). A brilliant strategist, yet tortured politician, he was the long-term enemy and rival of King François I, whom he captured and imprisoned in Italy in 1525, prior to sacking Rome two years later. Confronted by the Turks in the east, by the French under François's son Henri II in the west, and by Luther and his Protestants at home, he started to lose his ascendancy when the last two groups joined forces against him. He abdicated in 1556 in favor of his brother Ferdinand as Emperor and of his son Philip II as King of Spain.

Charles IX (1550–74)

King of France 1560–74. He was among the royal children examined by Nostradamus at Blois in 1555. Unstable, moody, and withdrawn, and with an inborn streak of cruelty, he acceded to the throne at the age of ten on his brother François's death in 1560, with his mother Catherine de Médicis and Antoine, King of Navarre, acting as regents. Declared of age in 1563, he nevertheless continued to be ruled by his mother. In Salon in October 1564, the teenage king is said to have remarked that he had "only come to see Nostradamus." Pressured by his mother to order the St. Bartholomew's Day massacre, he increasingly became prey to depression and died childless in 1574.

Chavigny, Jean-Aymes (Aimé) de

Long-time secretary, amanuensis, editor, and disciple of Nostradamus, and the first interpreter of his prophecies. Described in later publications as *Sieur* de Chavigny, he was a lawyer and former magistrate of Beaune in Burgundy. He was sent by Jean Dorat to Salon to assist with the *Propheties* at some point in or after 1554, and remained until Nostradamus's death. He then seems to have assisted Anne Ponsarde in administering the will and arranging subsequent publication of the complete *Propheties*.

His publications include *Jani Gallici Facies Prior / La Premiere Face du Janus François* (Roussin, 1594) – a history of the Wars of Religion to 1589, expressed in terms of 347 of Nostradamus's prophecies, with a biography of the prophet, including a poem on him by Ronsard; *Prognostication de l'advenement à la Couronne de France . . . (du) Prince Henry de Bourbon roy de Navarre* (1595); *Commentaires Du Sr de Chavigny Beaunois sur les Centuries et Prognostications*

du feu M. Michel de Nostradamus . . . (du Breuil, 1596); and *Les Pleiades du Sr. de Chavigny, Beaunois . . .* (Rigaud, 1600).

Cheetham, Erika

Pioneering twentieth-century editor of Nostradamus's prophecies. Her books include *The Prophecies of Nostradamus*, *The Further Prophecies of Nostradamus*, and *The Final Prophecies of Nostradamus*.

Her books have been criticized as being littered with factual and linguistic errors that have served to encourage many public misconceptions about Nostradamus and his prophecies. Some of her influential interpretations, likewise, have been described as unduly credulous. But Ms Cheetham was breaking much new ground at the time, and such criticisms must be set against her immensely valuable service in making the 1568 text of the *Centuries* readily available for the first time to the English-speaking world at large.

Chomarat, Michel

Lyon publisher, archivist, prize-winning author, and passionate promoter of the real Nostradamus. As founder and director of the Association des Amis de Michel Nostradamus, he was chiefly responsible for tracking down a large number of early Nostradamus editions and commentaries, and for publishing extracts from them in the organization's journal, the *Cahiers Michel Nostradamus*, between 1983 and 1988. Closely associated with the Maison de Nostradamus in Salon, he also published in 1984 a facsimile of the newly rediscovered 1555 edition of the *Propheties*, and in 1993 a similar facsimile of du Rosne's 1557 edition. A further facsimile of Rigaud's edition of *Nostradamus's Lettre . . . à la Royne mere du Roy* followed in 1996 under the title *Lettre à Catherine de Médicis*. In collaboration with Dr. Jean-Paul Laroche, he also compiled the definitive and seminal work entitled the *Bibliographie Nostradamus*.

Personally responsible for a vast collection (the Fonds Michel Chomarat) of over 2,000 pieces of Nostradamian documentation in the Bibliothèque Municipale de Lyon, he became founder-president in 1995 of the new Centre Nostradamus at Salon-de-Provence, dedicated to facilitating public research into the seer. His active cooperation has been vital to the present encyclopedia.

The young Charles IX of France, best remembered for ordering the St. Bartholomew's Day massacre in 1572

Chyren

Code name for predicted ruler and savior of France, of royal blood, referred to at II.79, IV.34, VI.27, VI.70, VIII.54, and X.41. The name is usually assumed to be an anagram of "Henryc(us)", which would make him the future Henry V so long expected by French royalists. Certainly the idea of his being the fifth of the name is supported by X.27 and *Sixain* 38, and would seem to rule out the inevitable recent claims on behalf of Jacques Chirac.

Clavicula Salomonis or Key of Solomon

Grimoire or magical book often claimed to have been owned by Nostradamus and used by him as the basis for his supposed nocturnal ceremonies (see Astrologer and Mage). Said to have been composed by King Solomon himself in a variety of tongues (compare the seer's own practice in this regard). Purported versions of it still survive, while a bowdlerized English translation was made by the Order of the Golden Dawn's S. L. Mathers as recently as the last century.

Clement VII

Pope from 1523 to 1534, during Nostradamus's later years of student wandering and his time at the medical faculty of Montpellier. The illegitimate son of Giuliano de' Medici, he was morally upright, but a born procrastinator and vacillator, causing him constantly to switch sides in the long quarrel between Henri II and the Emperor Charles V.

Coligny, Admiral Gaspard de (1519–72)

Huguenot leader of Condé's Protestant party from around 1557, he reluctantly took up arms against the crown in 1562. He was one of the Protestant leaders murdered apparently at Catherine de Médicis's behest during the St. Bartholomew's Day massacre in 1572.

Collégiale St.-Laurent

Fourteenth-/fifteenth-century church situated on high ground in the northern part of Salon. In the left-hand wall of the chapel of the Blessed Virgin (*Nostre Dame!*) is the current tomb of Nostradamus, placed there following his exhumation at the time of the French

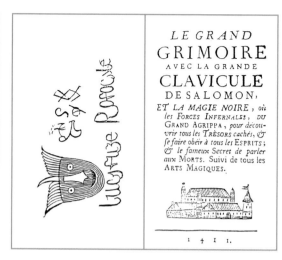

Title page of a French translation of the *Clavicula Salomonis* or *Key of Solomon*

Revolution. The church also contains the Craponne family tomb.

Condé, Henri, Prince de (1552–88)

Strongly Calvinist son of Louis (see below), he became coleader of the Huguenot cause on the latter's death in 1569. Imprisoned at Court, he escaped in 1573 to help raise the Fifth War of Religion. He was poisoned in 1588.

Condé, Louis, Prince de (1530–69)

Founder of the House of Bourbon-Condé, he distinguished himself at the battles of Metz (1552) and St. Quentin (1557). A member of the Huguenot conspiracy to overthrow the ruling Guises, he was spared execution only by the death of François II in 1560. Governor of Picardy under Catherine de Médicis, he went on to lead a new Huguenot revolt until shot at the Battle of Jarnac in 1569.

Coudoulet, Pierre Tronc de

Consul of Salon in 1560 and 1565, and relation by marriage (from 1565) of Nostradamus through the latter's niece Jeanne, daughter of his brother Bertrand. It was in his house that that the future Henri IV was lodged at the time of Queen Catherine's visit to Salon in October

1564, when Nostradamus is said to have "spotted" the boy as a great future monarch (see Nostradamus's Life Story).

Craponne, Adam de (1525–76)

Architect and hydraulic engineer, in whose grandiose project to divert the waters of the Durance River southward to water the Désert de la Crau Nostradamus and his wife eventually acquired at least a thirteenth share – some 688 crowns in four installments between 1556 and 1567.

    Craponne was educated at the local Franciscan Collège des Cordeliers, then distinguished himself as a military architect. It was on returning from the army at the age of only twenty-eight that he embarked on his ambitious project to water the *Crau*, selling much of his inheritance to pay for it.

    Work on the project started in 1554, with the "pilot" canal to Salon completed in 1557. The full-sized canal followed in April 1559, and was soon making large profits from irrigation and water-mill revenues. However, extending the system further proved expensive and, with the project running into increasing financial difficulties, Craponne eventually returned to his first love, military architecture. He was allegedly poisoned in 1575 and died the following year. His project was taken over by his brother Frédéric and the brothers Ravel, who finally extended the canal to Arles.

Craponne, Frédéric de (b. 1523)

Merchant and older brother of Adam (above), who took over the engineer's various projects after his death.

Crau, la

Pebble-strewn area of former desert stretching westward from Salon toward Arles, and crossed by the former Roman *Via Aurelia*. It was part of the delta of the Durance River until it changed course in prehistoric times to join the Rhône River south of Avignon. Marshy in winter and arid in summer, it was formerly inhabited exclusively by lizards and snakes, scorpions and birds of prey, along with occasional goatherds and their flocks. In its northern part especially, the desert has now been transformed by the canal de Craponne and its successors into fertile, if stony, farmland.

Crocodil(les)

Symbolic term frequently applied in the *Sixains* to future (presumably Muslim) invaders of Europe from North Africa (see Nostradamus and the Muslim Invasion of Europe). In his *Orus Apollo* (see Nostradamus's Writings) Nostradamus associates the creature chiefly with wantonness, lawlessness, looting, uncontrolled fury, and madness.

The Collégiale St.-Laurent, Salon, final resting place of Nostradamus

D

Daurat, Jean
See **Dorat, Jean**

Dee, Dr. John (1527–1608)
English mathematician and magician, and younger contemporary of Nostradamus. He was imprisoned under Queen Mary, but became court astrologer to Queen Elizabeth I from 1558, being responsible for selecting the date of her coronation, as well as claiming visionary support for various unsuccessful searches for the fabled Northwest Passage.

Like Nostradamus, he studied theurgy intensively, possibly from the same books (see Astrologer and Mage), but there is no evidence that the two ever met, although they may have corresponded.

Nostradamus may have corresponded with Dr. John Dee, court astrologer to Elizabeth I, although they never met

Dorat, Jean (1508–88)
Brilliant Greek scholar, humanist, inveterate enthuser of young students, and father of the *Pléiade*. He became tutor to Pierre da Ronsard and later Professor of Greek at the Collège Royal from 1556. A great admirer of Nostradamus, he encouraged his pupil Jean-Aymes de Chavigny to travel to Salon and become the seer's secretary and amanuensis.

Durance River
Major tributary of the Rhône River, which it joins at Avignon. Rising in the Alps, it skirts the Lubéron to the east and south and runs just north of Salon and the Alpilles. On adopting its current, westerly course, it left behind to the south the cargo of large pebbles that still characterizes its modern bed, so forming the Désert de la Crau. Nostradamus mentions the river at III.99 and VIII.1.

E

Edward VI (1537–53)
Youthful King of England, 1547–53. The sickly son of Henry VIII and Jane Seymour, Edward was initially governed by the Protestant Duke of Somerset as Protector, then by the Earl of Warwick, who was chiefly responsible for the iconoclastic "Great Pillage" of the English Church.

Eglise St.-Michel
Ancient church just behind Nostradamus's house in Salon. The seer probably never attended it, however. His sympathies seem to have lain with the Franciscans, in whose chapel he was eventually buried before being transferred to the Collégiale St.-Laurent.

Elephant
Typical Nostradamian term used (in the *Sixains*) to refer to future invading forces from North Africa (see Nostradamus the Poet).

Elisabeth de Valois (b. 1545)
Oldest daughter of Henri II and Catherine de Médicis, she was one of the royal children examined by Nostradamus at Blois in 1555. It was at the proxy marriage-celebrations for her union with Phillip II of Spain in 1559 that the King was mortally wounded in a tournament, as apparently predicted by Nostradamus, so precipitating sudden success for the seer.

Elizabeth I acceded to the English throne in 1558

Elizabeth I (1533–1603)
Queen of England from 1558 on the death of her half-sister Mary, Elizabeth used her much-proclaimed virginity as a political weapon, tantalizing a whole succession of proposed suitors, including Philip II of Spain, the young Charles IX of France, and both of his brothers – Henri, Duc d'Anjou and Hercule-François, Duke of Alençon.

Emmanuel-Philibert, Duc de Savoie
See **Savoie, Emmanuel-Philibert, Duc de**

Empéri, Château de l'
Crowning fortress of Salon, built on the site of an ancient Roman encampment. It was here that Nostradamus met not only Emmanuel-Philibert, Duc de Savoie, and his bride, Marguerite de Valois in late 1559, but also Charles IX and Catherine de Médicis herself in August 1564.

Erasmus, Desiderius (1466–1536)
Outstanding Dutch humanist, scholar, and translator. An Augustinian monk, he became a priest in 1492. While living at Basel and Freiburg from 1521 until his death, he edited numerous classical authors and in 1516 produced an epoch-making new Latin translation of the Greek New Testament. Erasmus was constantly attacked by Nostradamus's mentor Scaliger, and also corresponded with Rabelais, who himself complained to him of Scaliger's attacks.

Erickstad, Herbert G. B.
New Zealand ferry-operator and lifelong student of Nostradamus, who in 1986 published *The Prophecies of Nostradamus in Historical Order*. Engagingly unpretentious, his text is derivative and original by turns – in the former case benefiting from his readings of Cheetham and others, and in the latter from his own travels and military experiences in the Middle East.

Eyguières
Village northwest of Salon, nestling among the foothills of the Alpilles. It incorporates a twelfth-century church.

F

Fontbrune, Jean-Charles de
French author of the influential modern presentation of a selection of 600 or so of Nostradamus's prophecies entitled *Nostradamus, historien et prophète*, based on the earlier work of his father Dr. Max de Fontbrune (see below). The book is unusual in that it attempts to place the prophecies (quoted in the somewhat corrupt 1605 version) in sequence, while justifying its interpretations with lengthy, verbatim quotes from a variety of academic textbooks. Critics often accuse the work of twisting the seer's language unnecessarily to fit certain preconceived conclusions.

Fontbrune, Max de
Respected scholar and author of a number of books on Nostradamus published between 1937 and 1950, and notably the much-reprinted *Les prophéties de Maistre Michel Nostradamus expliquées et commentées* of 1938. In it he used the seer's verses to predict many of the events of World War II, including the defeat and partition of Germany – with the result that he was persecuted by the Gestapo from 1940 and his book banned.

Fontvieille
Village northeast of Arles, close to the ruins of two Roman aqueducts.

François I (1494–1547)
King of France from 1515 who, having failed to attain the Imperial crown in 1519, spent most of his life fighting the successful contender, Charles V. Captured at Pavia in 1525, he was freed in 1526 on surrendering Burgundy and giving up his two sons as hostages against what, in the event, proved to be a huge ransom. The most powerful monarch of his day, much involved in forging alliances with Henry VIII of England and the Ottoman Suleiman the Magnificent, he did much to reinforce and centralize government power.

François II (1544–60)
Sickly oldest son of Henri II and Catherine de Médicis, and briefly King from 1559 under the regency of the Guises. He was among the royal children examined by Nostradamus at Blois in 1555. In April 1558 he married Mary Queen of Scots, who survived him and subsequently returned to Scotland.

François, Duc d'Alençon
See **Alençon, Hercule-François, Duc d'**

Fulke, William
English author of a 1560 tirade against Nostradamus and others entitled *Anti-prognosticon contra inutiles Astrologorum Praedictiones Nostradami, Cunninghami, Lovi, Hilli, Vaghani et reliquorum omnium* – one of a number of such works circulating at about this time, especially in France (see Criticisms and Reviews).

G

Galen (*c.* 130–200)
More familiar name of Claudius Galenus of Pergamum, Greek pioneering anatomist and physician to the son of the Roman Emperor Marcus Aurelius. Generally regarded as the founder of modern medicine, he took an allopathic view of treatment and reinforced the traditional doctrine of the Humors with that of the *pneuma*, or all-pervading "breath" (see Nostradamus the Physician). The seer published a free translation of his paraphrase of Menodotus's exhortation to medicine (the so-called *Paraphrase de C. Galen*) in 1557, apparently in an attempt to show that Galen did not regard his own teachings in the same blinkered way as most of his sixteenth-century would-be disciples did.

Gard, or Gardon
River rising in the Cévennes, which runs into the Rhône just north of Beaucaire. Chiefly known for the famous Pont du Gard aqueduct, the river is mentioned by Nostradamus at *Centuries* V.58, VIII.6, and X.6, as well as at *Sixain* 11.

Garde, Baron de la, chevalier des Ordres du Roy, admiral des mers du Levant
Long-time friend and associate of Nostradamus at Salon, local notable, and one of the dedicatees of the *Paraphrase de C. Galen*. He was one of those present at the presentation of the two-headed kid from Aurons in 1554.

Garencières, Théophile de
Seventeenth-century French academic who edited, translated, and interpreted Nostradamus in his influential *The True Prophecies; or, Prognostications of Michael Nostradamus . . . ,* of 1672. In this last major English version for some 274 years he reveals that the *Propheties* were being used as a basic French reader in French schools during his own childhood (i.e. around 1618). In the course of his critique he points to the numerous errors that have crept into the texts over the years, but nevertheless helps to promulgate a good many of them himself.

Gaurico, Luca (b. 1476)
Celebrated Italian astrologer and magician and older contemporary of Nostradamus. Better known in France as Luc Gauric, he is also said at some time to have tutored the latter's mentor, Scaliger. Among his many correct prophesies, he warned Henri II of France to "avoid all single combat in an enclosed place, especially around his forty-first year", adding that at this time a wound in the head threatened to blind or even kill him. The prediction duly came to pass in 1559.

The municipal arch and Mausoleum of Sextus at the ancient city of Glanum

Glanum
Ancient Graeco-Roman city whose remains lie just to the south of Nostradamus's birthplace of St-Rémy. The various relics that were above ground at the time (notably the Mausoleum of Sextus, the municipal arch and the so-called *Pyranide*) evidently excited the young man's interest considerably, and they are duly mentioned in a number of quatrains, as well as referred to in the *Proème* of his *Traité des fardemens*.

Goebbels, Magda
Wife of Dr. Josef Goebbels, propaganda minister to Adolf Hitler, who in the 1930s first drew her husband's attention to the apparent rele-

vance of Nostradamus's prophecies to current developments in Germany, so leading to a concentrated effort to use them for Nazi propaganda purposes and even to determine early German military strategy.

Grans
Small town on Touloubre River southwest of Salon, served by Craponne's canal.

Gryphe, Sébastien (1493–1556)
French name of Sebastian Greyff, better known as Gryphius. A Swabian, he became the pre-eminent Lyon publisher from 1520, especially of classical works. His editions of Hippocrates and Galen were edited by Rabelais, and his premises served as a meeting-house for pioneering writers, thinkers, and academics. His outstanding compositor was Jean de Tournes.

Gryphon
Name of fabulous beast, part-lion, part-eagle, said to symbolize strength and vigilance; also used of hunting dogs and ponies. Used by Nostradamus at X.86 and *Sixains* 29 and 56 apparently to represent a future northern European leader of a massive counterinvasion against occupying Muslim forces.

Guise, Claude, Duc de (1496–1550)
A distinguished soldier, peer and Court official, he headed the Catholic Guise faction against the more centrist Montmorency on the one hand and the mainly Protestant Bourbons on the other.

Guise, François, Duc de (1519–63)
Son of Claude, duc de Guise, he was a renowned soldier and commander against Spain and the Empire both in the East and in Italy, and acquired the nickname "Scarface." His brilliant defense of Metz against the Emperor in 1552 was greatly assisted by the engineering efforts of the young Adam de Craponne. In 1558 he succeeded in recovering Calais from the English. On becoming virtual co-ruler of France through his niece, the new Queen Mary Stuart, on Henri II's death in 1559, he ruthlessly suppressed all rival factions and formed a

Catholic triumvirate with Montmorency and the Maréchal Saint André to thwart Catherine de Médicis's frantic efforts to reconcile Catholic and Protestants. He was mortally wounded at the siege of Orléans in 1563.

H

Haemathien, Haemathion or Aemathien
Term (from Latin *Aemathius*, "Macedonian") used by Nostradamus at IX.38, IX.64, IX.93, X.7, and X.58 to indicate either a future Greek military commander or a leader comparable to Alexander the Great, in either case apparently fighting on the side of the invading Muslims (see Nostradamus and the Muslim Invasion of Europe).

Harsy, Olivier de
Paris publisher of the 1556 edition of the *Traité des fardemens*.

Henri II (1519–59)
Younger son of François I who was held hostage in Spain from 1526–30. In 1533 he married Catherine de Médicis, and in 1536 succeeded his deceased older brother François as Dauphin. King of France from 1547, he continued both his father's administrative reforms and his war with the Holy Roman Empire until around 1559, when growing religious quarrels forced him to disband much of the army and concentrate on problems at home.

In 1555 he received Nostradamus and paid him 100 crowns for his trouble. At the celebrations in late June 1559 to mark both the wedding of his sister Marguerite de Valois and the engagement of his daughter Élisabeth de Valois, Henri was mortally wounded by a splintered lance in a tournament with the captain of his Scottish guard, as apparently predicted by the seer at I.35. As seemingly predicted, too, he died in agony eleven days later.

Henri III (1551–89)
Third son of Henri II and Catherine de Médicis, and among the royal children examined by Nostradamus at Blois in 1555. He was unwillingly elected King of Poland in 1573, and succeeded his brother Charles IX as King of France in 1574. Opposed by the Guises, he was nearly overthrown in 1588, but reacted by arranging for the assassination of Henri, Duc de Guise at Blois. He himself was assassinated at St.-Cloud in 1589.

Henri IV (1553–1610)
Prince of Navarre and son of Antoine de Bourbon and Jeanne d'Albret, he was brought up a Protestant but nevertheless attended Court in Paris. In the summer of 1564 he accompanied Charles IX and Catherine de Médicis on their visit to Salon, where the seer intuitively "spotted" the unlikely eleven-year-old as a future King of Navarre and of France.

In 1572, the year of the St. Bartholomew's Day massacre, the youngster duly became King of Navarre, and in 1589 mounted the throne as

Rabelais's edition of Hippocrates and Galen, published by Sébastien Gryphe in 1532

Henri IV of France. His assassination in May 1610 led directly to the relative "golden age" initiated under his son Louis XIII and finally presided over by his grandson Louis XIV.

Henri V
Future leader and savior of France foreshadowed by Nostradamus under the name *Chyren* (q.v.), as well as anonymously at *Sixain* 38.

Henry VIII (1491–1547)
King of England from 1509 and contemporary of François I. After spending much of his life attempting to maintain the balance between France and the Holy Roman Empire, he eventually sided with the latter, while maintaining the quarrel with the Pope that eventually led to the English Reformation and the suppression of the monasteries.

Hercule-François, Duc d'Alençon
See **Alençon, Hercule-François, Duc d'**

Hercules
Name of classical Greek hero used by Nostradamus, to refer at V.13, V.51, IX.33, IX.93, X.27, and X.79 to a future French military leader and ruler destined to expel Muslim invaders from France (see Historian and Mythologist). Also referred to as Ogmion or Ogmyon (q.v.), his ancient Gallic equivalent.

Hewitt, V. J.
Author of a number of books on Nostradamus, in which she proposes an anagrammatical method for interrogating given verses on predetermined subjects as though they were designed to be used as oracles, rather than accepting them for what they actually say.

Rabelais's edition of Hippocrates and Galen, published by Sébastien Gryphe in 1532

Hippocrates (c. 460–377 B.C.)
Asclepian "Father of Medicine" from the Greek island of Cos, much respected by Nostradamus, and on whom the work of Galen and virtually all subsequent ancient physicians was based. He saw the doctor's task as to aid nature rather than oppose it, and stressed good diet, rest, clean water, and fresh air. Author of a treatise on *Epidemics*, his basic principles seem to have been adopted by Louis Serres, under whom Nostradamus studied the treatment of the plague at Marseille from 1544 (see Nostradamus the Physician).

Hister
Classical name for the lower Danube, used by Nostradamus at II.24, IV.68 and V.29, as well as (without its initial "H") in *Presages* 15 and 31. Sometimes supposed by commentators such as Erika Cheetham to refer to Adolf Hitler (see **Goebbels, Magda**).

Hogue, John
Author of *Nostradamus and the Millennium* and *Nostradamus: The New Revelations*, both lavishly illustrated coffee-table books that do their best to divine the future by selective application of verses from the *Propheties* in sometimes dubious literal translations.

Hôpital, Michel de l' (d. 1573)
President of the Council and Chancellor to Henri II's sister Marguerite de Valois, and Chancellor of France from 1560 to 1568. He endeavored with Catherine de Médicis to encourage religious tolerance and reconciliation, permitting Protestant freedom of conscience and (to some degree) of worship through the celebrated "Edict of January" of 1562.

Michel de l'Hôpital was a supporter of Ronsard against Protestant critics of his work, and was an associate of the *Pléiade*

Hozier, Maître Etienne
Lawyer and first cousin of Nostradamus's second wife Anne Ponsarde, he married them at Salon on November 11th, 1547. On November 11th, 1553, he issued a procuration authorizing one Antoine de Royer to withdraw from Nostradamus's publisher Jean Brotot the manuscript of the 1554 *Almanach*, as well as of the seer's *Ephemerides*, on grounds of having corrupted and mutilated the text.

I

Iamblichus of Chalcis (d. c. A.D. 330)
Syrian neo-Platonist philosopher, much given to Pythagorean numerology, and author of the *De Mysteriis Aegyptiorum: Chaldaeorum: assyriorum*. A Latin translation of this celebrated account of the theurgic practices of the ancient world was available in Florence's Medici library at the time of Nostradamus's visit to Italy in 1548. Extracts from it are paraphrased in French translation in verses I.1 and I.2 of the *Propheties*. This suggests that it was among the most basic of the seer's "magic books" (see Nostradamus's Lifestory, and Astrologer and Mage).

Index Librorum Prohibitorum
The Catholic Church's list of "forbidden books", first published between 1556 and 1559 and regularly updated until 1925. Contrary to tradition, the Vatican versions *never* named Nostradamus among their banned authors – a fact that reflects his evident piety and often-expressed Catholic affiliations (see Nostradamus, the Bible, and the Church). The lists issued by the Spanish authorities between 1570 and 1790, on the other hand, *all* ban various of the seer's writings.

J

Jodelle, Etienne (1532–73)
High-born French poet and dramatist, and prominent member of the *Pléiade*. His *Cléopâtre captive*, first performed in 1553, is generally regarded as the original French tragedy, and his equally weak *Didon se sacrifiant* followed soon afterward. He is generally credited with having written in around 1558 the satirical Latin distich about Nostradamus that ran:

Nostra damus cum falsa damus, nam fallere nostrum est
Et cum falsa damus, nil nisi nostra damus.

Some commentators, however, attribute this to the Calvinist Théodore Béza (or de Bèze) (see Criticisms and Reviews).

Julius II, Pope (1443–1513)
Nephew of Pope Sixtus V, he was made cardinal in 1471 and bribed his way to the papacy in 1503, the year of Nostradamus's birth. He then quickly reestablished the Papal States, as well as acting as patron to both Raphael and Michelangelo. A soldier and diplomat, he succeeded in driving the French out of Italy in 1512.

Julius III, Pope (1487–1555)
Archbishop of Siponto from 1512, he was made cardinal in 1536 and presided over the opening of the Council of Trent in 1545. Pope from 1550, he allied himself with the Emperor Charles V against Henri II of France, but was forced to make peace with the latter in 1552.

K

Kerver, Jacques
Paris publisher of Nostradamus's *Almanachs* for 1556 and 1557.

Kidogo, Bardo
Pseudonym of Barry Popkess, author of *The Keys to the Predictions of Nostradamus*, a relatively sober, academic exposition of suggested principles for Nostradamian interpretation, incorporating a useful glossary.

King, Francis X
Author of the informative and relatively well-researched *Nostradamus: Prophecies Fulfilled and Predictions for the Millennium and Beyond*.

L

Adam de Craponne's bust at Lamanon

Lamanon
Village north of Salon commanding the Lamanon gap, through which the main Avignon road, the railway and Craponne's canal pass. Craponne's bust still stands amid the waters of his distribution-pool.

Lançon
Village southeast of Salon, served by Craponne's canal.

Laroche, Dr. Jean-Paul
Psychiatrist, researcher, and author, who collaborated with Michel Chomarat to compile and produce the truly seminal *Bibliographie Nostradamus* of 1989.

Laver, James
Author of the influential *Nostradamus or the Future Foretold*. This thoroughly respectable study of the seer is the result of a great deal of careful research, putting most subsequent books to shame in this regard, though it naturally does not benefit from more recent documentary discoveries.

Le Noir, Guillaume
Paris publisher of Nostradamus's *Almanachs* for 1560 and 1562, as well as of the *Significations de l'Eclipse* of 1559.

Lemesurier, Peter (b. 1936)
British author of the present volume, as of numerous other books on esoteric or occult matters, including *Nostradamus – The Next 50 Years* and *Nostradamus: The Final Reckoning*. These offer the first known sequenced, verse-translations of the seer into English.

Pope Leo X subsidized Raphael and other artists of the day, presiding over the culmination of the Roman Renaissance

Leo X, Pope (1475–1521)
Second son of Lorenzo de' Medici ("The Magnificent"), he was made cardinal at thirteen and became Pope on the death of Julius II in 1513, as predicted by Luca Gaurico. A lavish patron of the arts, politically he supported France and the Empire alternately. The financial greed of his Court and his unwillingness to undertake any kind of religious reform helped to fuel Luther's revolt and the subsequent Protestant Reformation.

Leroy, Dr. Edgar (1883–1965)
French physician, soldier, distinguished epidemiologist, sometime psychiatrist at St.-Paul-de-Mausole, and author of the seminal *Nostradamus: ses origines, sa vie, son oeuvre*. The result of many years of documentary and local archival research, this represents by far the most reliable and complete account of Nostradamus thus far.

Lettre à Henri Roy de France Second

Dedicatory letter to Henri II prefaced by Nostradamus to the third edition of his *Propheties* – i.e. the text of *Centuries* VIII, IX, and X of 1558 – and therefore generally included at this point in later, complete editions (see Early Editions). For full text, see The Major Prophecies.

Locustes

Term used at V.85 and *Presage 36* – replaced at III.82 and IV.48 by *sauterelles* ("grasshoppers") and at IX.69 by *Langoust* – apparently to signify swarms of future invaders (possibly airborne) from the Mediterranean, in reflection of the "locusts" of the biblical Revelation of John.

Lorie, Peter

Co-author of attractive, lavishly presented books placing great emphasis on post-Nostradamian speculation, and somewhat less on the seer's actual words.

Lorraine, Charles, Cardinal de (d. 1574)

Ecclesiastical brother of François, Duc de Guise, who sat with him on the King's Council and shared power with him during the brief reign of François II.

Lubéron

Mountain range and natural park to the north of the Durance River.

Luther, Martin (1483–1546)

German Augustinian monk and lecturer at Wittenberg, whose posting in 1517 of his ninety-five theses against Papal indulgences is generally reckoned to mark the start of the Protestant Reformation. After publicly burning the Pope's condemnation of his views in 1520, he refused to recant at the Diet of Worms of 1521 and married a former nun in 1525. Unfortunately Luther's admirable work has to be set against the resulting centuries of religious turmoil and bloody conflict, especially in contemporary France.

Lyon (Pop. 1,305,000)

Major city, bishop's see, university town, and industrial center of southern France at the confluence of Rhône and Saône Rivers. Founded by the Greeks in the sixth century B.C., it became (as *Lugdunum*) capital of Roman Gaul. Rebuilt by Nero after the fire of A.D. 59, it was the birthplace of the emperors Claudius, Marcus Aurelius, and Caracalla.

It was to Lyon that Nostradamus was summoned in 1547 to put down an epidemic of the plague. The city was also the southern center of the then-vital printing industry, as well as of Calvinism and industrial unrest, too. Unsurprisingly, it was in Lyon that virtually all of Nostradamus's works were first published.

The city is mentioned at I.31, I.33, I.35, I.72, I.93, II.83, II.85, II.94, III.52, III.56, III.93, V.25, V.99, VIII.2-3, VIII.6, VIII.34, IX.19, IX.69-70, X.99, *Presages* 56, 62, and 69, and *Sixain* 52, as well as via a variety of pseudonyms in other verses too.

M

Maison de Nostradamus

The former house of Nostradamus at Salon (rue Nostradamus), now converted into a pilgrimage site, museum, and documentation center, open daily. The visitor is offered a *guide sonore* including a variety of waxworks and tableaux and a speculative reconstruction of the seer's study. See Nostradamus's Hometown.

Malachy, St. (*c.* 1094–1148)

Prophetically gifted Archbishop of Armagh, who left behind a list of Latin tags purporting to identify all the 111 Popes from his day until the end of the papacy. First published in 1595, it has often proved startlingly accurate, and the Vatican has long since matched the list to the actual papal succession.

De Labore Solis ("Something to do with the Labor of the Sun") is the present John Paul II, who as a young man under the occupying Nazis worked with his bare hands in the Polish stone quarries. This same title may possibly be referred to by Nostradamus at V.57 via the geographical pun *Mansol* (i.e. *Manus Solis* or, once again, "Handiwork-of-the-Sun"), based on the name of St.-Paul-de-Mausole. The case of VIII.46 is even more compelling.

Mallemort

Rock-perched village northeast of Salon, whose ruined castle overlooks the Durance River from opposite the Lubéron.

Marc, Palamède

Sieur de Chasteauneuf, close friend of Nostradamus and sometime First Consul of Salon, under whom the seer composed a Latin inscription for a municipal fountain in 1553. On the seer's advice he displayed the famous two-headed kid from Aurons to his supper guests in 1554, and in 1566 he was one of the signatories of the prophet's will.

Lyon *c.* 1550, showing the house (center) where Nostradamus stayed

Marcellus II, Pope (d. 1555)

Short-lived Pope, of promising character and ideals, who died after less than a month in office in May 1555.

Marguerite de Valois

Sister of King Henri II. It was at the celebrations for her engagement to Emmanuel-Philibert, duc de Savoie that the King was killed in a tournament in July 1559. As the new duchess, she then visited Nostradamus with her husband on her way back to Nice in October. In 1561, now pregnant, she is said to have asked for a further consultation regarding the imminent birth: the seer (whether in person or by letter) correctly predicted a son.

Also the name of the youngest daughter (1552–1610) of Henri II and Catherine de Médicis, who was among the royal children examined by Nostradamus at Blois in 1555.

Marot, Clément (1496–1544)

Court poet, much favored by François I, who was taken prisoner with him at Pavia in 1525. Arrested in 1526 for his "heretical" translation of the Psalms, he took refuge in Italy, but returned soon after 1535.

Marseille (Pop. 1,015,000)

Major French city and seaport on the Mediterranean. Founded by Greek colonists from Phocaea, Asia Minor, in around 600 B.C. (whence the common Nostradamian terms *Phoce* and *Phocen*), it was then known as *Massilia* (whence the term *Port Massiliolique* at IX.28). After supporting Pompey, it was subjugated by Julius Caesar in 49 B.C., and its rebel leader Lucius Domitius Ahenobarbus (alluded to as Aenobarbe by the seer) killed the following year. In 543 it was racked by the first of many devastating plague epidemics (see Sequence of Selected Horographs, under "2025"), and it was here that Nostradamus studied the treatment of the Plague from 1544 under the physician Louis Serres (see Nostradamus the Physician).

Martha, Saint

Sister of the biblical Lazarus and companion of Mary Magdalene, who was allegedly washed ashore at Stes-Maries-de-la-Mer following the crucifixion, then evangelized Tarascon, where her later church still stands.

Mary Magdalene, Saint

Reformed prostitute and disciple of Jesus who was allegedly washed ashore at Stes-Maries-de-la-Mer following the crucifixion, then passed the rest of her life as a penitent at La Ste Baume. She is said by some "underground" traditions to have married Jesus and given birth to a son from whom the French Merovingian line subsequently descended: this is destined eventually to produce the future Henri V of France.

Mary Tudor (1516–58)
Daughter of Henry VIII and Catherine of Aragon, a fervent Catholic, she became Queen of England in July 1553. After strenuous efforts to restore Catholicism and repair her father's breach with Rome, she married Philip II of Spain in 1554, then embarked on a campaign of Protestant persecutions in the name of the old laws of heresy.

Mary Stuart, Queen of Scots (1542–87)
Daughter of James V of Scotland, and Queen of that country from birth. Brought up in France by the Guises, she married the Dauphin François in 1558 and became Queen of France when he ascended the throne as François II the following year. Her marriage is apparently referred to by Nostradamus in the virtually contemporary X.55. Following the King's death a year later, she returned to Scotland in 1561 and married her cousin Henry Stuart, Lord Darnley, in 1565. After various intrigues, she was imprisoned by Queen Elizabeth for eighteen years and eventually executed in 1587.

Mastin
Term for "mastiff" used by Nostradamus at II.41, V.4, X.59, and X.99, sometimes prefaced by *le gros*. Also used in this form by Ronsard in his *Responce . . . aux Injures et Calomnies* of 1563 (lines 161–72) to signify Cerberus, three-headed watchdog of the Underworld, who is similarly referred to by Homer as "The dog." He thus represents the "Hound of Hell" – in Nostradamus's case probably a future invading Muslim military leader, who is issuing loud threats and serving a dread oriental overlord (see Nostradamus and the Muslim Invasion of Europe).

Medici
Prominent family of Florentine traders and bankers many of whose members rose to become either Popes or rulers of Florence. It was Caterina de Medici who in 1533 married the future Henri II of France and changed her name to Catherine de Médicis (q.v.).

Menodotus of Nicomedia
Alexandrian empirical physician of the early Christian era, whose exhortation to medicine, as paraphrased by the great Galen, Nostradamus

freely translated and published in 1557 (see Nostradamus's Writings).

Miramas-le-Vieux
Picturesque rock-perched village southwest of Salon, overlooking the Étang de Berre.

Montgomery, Gabriel, Comte de (c. 1530–74)
Soldier and captain of Henri II's Scottish guard who on June 30th, 1559, accidentally inflicted a mortal wound on the King during a tournament in Paris to celebrate the engagement of the latter's sister Marguerite de Valois and the proxy marriage of his daughter Élisabeth de Valois to Philip II of Spain. Fleeing to Scotland, Montgomery converted to Protestantism, then returned to join the French Huguenot armies in 1562. Eventually captured at Domfront in 1573, he was executed in Paris in 1574. Verse III.30 seems to predict the event.

Montmajour, Abbaye de
Former Benedictine monastery overlooking the plain of Arles. Founded in the tenth century, it became a noted pilgrimage site in the eleventh century. It was finally suppressed by Louis XVI in 1786, but is now owned by the state and has been partially restored.

Montmorency, Anne de (1492–1567)
Distinguished French soldier, named after his godmother Anne de Bretagne. In 1522, after distinguished service at the battles of Marignano (1515) and Mézières (1521), he was made a Marshal. He defeated Charles V at Susa in 1536 and became High Constable (i.e. royal commander-in-chief) in 1538. In August 1555 he was seemingly sent to welcome Nostradamus on his command visit to the Court at the behest of the Queen.

The medical faculty at Montpellier, whose predecessor Nostradamus attended, with the Cathedral of St. Peter

In 1557 Montmorency was largely responsible for the national disaster of St.-Quentin, when his particularly incompetent generalship resulted in huge French losses. He later played an important role in trying to reconcile the extreme Catholic and Protestant factions under the Guises and Bourbon-Condés respectively. Mortally wounded while fighting the Huguenots in 1567, he died in Paris in November.

Nostradamus mentions the name Montmorency at IX.18, but it is unclear whether the reference is to the Constable, one of his three sons or a descendant.

Montpellier (Pop. 208,000)
Capital of Bas Languedoc, with a cathedral of St. Peter and adjoining medical faculty. The city is mentioned by Nostradamus at III.56, VIII.64, and *Sixain* 52.

Montpellier first arose in the tenth century, came under the control of Spain between 1204 and 1349, then was sold to France. It became a major trading center with the Orient, specializing in herbs and spices. Out of this activity arose the first medical schools, then the university – subsequently attended by both Nostradamus (1529 onwards) and Rabelais.

With the absorption of Provence into France in 1481, much of the foreign trade was lost to Marseille, but in the next century the city acquired a new preeminence as a major center of Calvinism.

Moral, Jean
Paris moneylender who advanced Nostradamus two rose nobles and two crowns in August 1555 when the seer arrived too low in funds to pay his hotel bill at the Auberge St.-Michel.

Muller, Jean
Author of a set of Latin distichs written in 1476, and cited in the *Liber Mirabilis* of 1524, which allegedly predicted revolutionary times starting in 1788 (see Nostradamus and the French Revolution).

N

Nîmes (Pop. 130,000)
Ancient Roman city seemingly founded by the Emperor Augustus for veterans of the Egyptian campaign in around 31 B.C. It stands on the site of the former native center of *Nemausus*, with its sacred spring. The ancient spring still survives (mentioned by Nostradamus at IX.12), as do the Roman amphitheater or Arènes (described as the *colosse*, or Colosseum, at X.6), the gate of Augustus, the temple of Jupiter (the remarkable Maison Carrée) and parts of the celebrated Pont du Gard aqueduct (V.66). So do the Temple of Diana (V.66 and IX.12) and the pre-Roman Tour Magne, which an amateur sixteenth-century archeologist nearly destroyed in his search for the buried treasure apparently located by the seer in the vicinity (V.66, IX.12). The city is mentioned at III.56, X.94, and *Sixain* 52.

NOSTRADAMUS, MICHEL (1503–66)
Scholar, physician, astrologer, mage, seer, poet, Royal Counselor, crypto-Franciscan, patron of public works, and the subject of this encyclopedia. See Nostradamus's Life Story and The Nostradamus Family Tree.

Nostradamus le Jeune, Michel (d. 1629?)
Well-known impostor, unrelated to Nostradamus, who published collections of prophecies in 1568, 1571, and 1575, as well as an Almanac in 1577. He met his nemesis when, having predicted the burning of Le Pouzin in Ardèche, he was caught actually setting fire to it (see Forgeries and Fairy Tales).

Nostredame, André de (1557–1601)
Third son of Nostradamus, born November 3rd, 1557, he in due course entered the service of the then Governor of Provence, Henri d'Angoulême, as a "gentleman." After inadvertently killing one Cornillon of Salon in a duel, he vowed to become a monk if released from jail. He duly entered the Capuchin (Franciscan) Order in 1587 at the age of thirty, taking the name Séraphin. He is said to have died at Brignoles on December 2nd, 1601.

Nostredame, Anne de (1558[?]–c.1596)
Second daughter of Nostradamus, she married Pierre de Seva, co-seigneur of Pierrefeu (Toulon) and bore one son, Melchior de Seva (possibly a relation of Vincent Seve, q.v.).

Nostredame, Antoine de (1523–97)
Younger brother of Nostradamus. Lawyer, deputy judge, tax-collector and sometime Consul of St.-Rémy, he married Louise Berle of Cavaillon and had at least ten children.

Nostredame, "Capitaine" Bertrand de (1518–1602)
Younger brother of Nostradamus, prosperous citizen and merchant of St.-Rémy and, from 1568, armed retainer in the service of Claude de Savoie, Comte de Tende and governor of Provence. Subsequently appointed captain in charge of one of the town's four defense companies during the Wars of Religion, he married Tomyne Rousse of Lamanon and had four chil-

Nostradamus, physician, seer, astrologer, and poet, at work in his study

dren. A noted country landowner, clerk of the court and First Consul of St.-Rémy for 1573–4, he was much engaged in agricultural commerce, and devoted large sums of money to rebuilding and developing the Mas (now Château) de Roussan, his beloved country house.

Nostredame, César de (c.1554–1630)
The seer's oldest son and infant dedicatee of the *Préface* to the first edition of his *Propheties*, also known as César Nostradamus. He allegedly managed to compose the Latin epitaph for his father's tomb in 1566.

By 1572 he was studying mathematics in Paris, where he witnessed the St. Bartholomew's Day massacre. Describing himself as a *gentilhomme provençal*, he subsequently devoted himself to arts and letters. By 1592 César had become a prominent citizen of Salon, accompanying the First Consul during a visit by Charles-Emmanuel de Savoie, the son of Emmanuel-Philibert whose birth had been predicted by Nostradamus. In 1598 he was made First Consul, and in that capacity welcomed Marie de Médicis to the town in 1600.

In 1604 he caused something of a stir by belatedly marrying one Claire de Grignan, and in 1614 published his important *Histoire et chronique de Provence*, which was heavily subsidized by the regional authorities. By now he had taken to

The Maison Carrée, or temple of Jupiter, at Nîmes

painting miniatures and portraits, of which one of his father and another of himself both survive. By 1629, however, the old man was in decline, begging his cousin Pierre d'Hozier to arrange a modest royal pension. Childless, he was seemingly carried off by the plague at St.-Rémy in 1630.

Self-portrait by César

Nostredame, Charles de (1556–1629)
Second son of Nostradamus. He married one Louise Becq and settled down at Alleins, where a daughter Anne was baptized on February 1st, 1590. In 1594 Hozier described him as *Capitaine de la ville de Salon*. Reckoned in his day as one of the three leading poets of Provence, he was described by César as "recently deceased" at the end of 1629.

Nostredame, Dauphine or Delphine de (dates unknown)
Unmarried sister of Nostradamus, mentioned in legal documents of 1545, 1558, and 1559. Apparently somewhat contrary, she refused all offers of lodging with her brother Antoine on the grounds that she would have continually to talk to his wife and children.

Nostredame, Diane de (1561–1630+)
Youngest daughter of Nostradamus. Cooed over as an infant by Queen Catherine de Médicis herself during the royal visit to Salon of 1564, she nevertheless turned out to be a cantankerous old spinster, for whom even her brother César could find few kind words in his will, despite leaving her his house, most of his furniture, and 200 crowns in cash.

Nostredame, Hector de (dates unknown)
Younger brother of Nostradamus, he married Antoinette (or Thonète) Mourguète. Their daughter Florimonde was baptized in 1558.

Nostredame, Henry de
Alleged nephew of Nostradamus, mentioned by Vincent Seve in the preface to his 1605 edition of the *Propheties* as the source of the manuscript of the *Presages*. May have been the son of one of the seer's unrecorded brothers.

Nostredame, Jaume de (c.1470–c.1547)
Son of Pierre (or Peyrot) de Nostredame and prosperous merchant of St.-Rémy, and also

known as Jacques de Sainte-Marie. In 1495 he married Reynière (or Renée) de St.-Rémy, thereby acquiring considerable land and property. From 1503 he additionally described himself as a notary, signing himself *Jacobus de nostra domina* and acting as scribe, bailiff, and clerk of the court. Naturalized, along with his brother Pierre, in letters patent signed by François I in 1540, he seems to have died in 1546 or 1547, since his sons are named as his "co-heirs" in a document of February 6th, 1547.

Nostredame, Jehan de (1522–c.1577)
Distinguished younger brother of Nostradamus, and lawyer at St.-Rémy from around 1545 to around 1555. From 1557 he was attached to the Parlement at Aix, becoming Attorney General for the province. It was in this capacity that Nostradamus dedicated to him his *Traité des fardemens et confitures* of 1555.

He was the author of *Les Vies des plus celebres et anciens poetes provensaulx* (Lyon, 1575), covering seventy-five poets from the twelfth to the fifteenth centuries, as of other literary and historical pieces, all of which were freely used by César in his *Histoire et chronique de Provence*, despite being subsequently much criticized for their (for the time) typical inaccuracies and exaggerations.

Nostredame, Louis de
Younger brother of Nostradamus. No other details are known.

Nostredame, Madeleine de (1551[?]–1623)
Oldest child of Nostradamus and Anne Ponsarde, she married Claude de Perussis, baron of Lauris and Oppède (according to César an accomplished lutenist), and had one son, Claude, who became municipal attorney for Vitrolles. She was buried at Lauris (in the Lubéron) on April 7th, 1623.

Nostredame, Michel de
See **Nostradamus, Michel**

Nostredame, Pierre de (dates unknown)
Uncle of Nostradamus. Naturalized in 1540 by François I, along with his brother Jaume, he was a merchant at Arles.

Also the name of a younger brother of Nostradamus about whom no further details are known.

Nostredame, Pierre or Peyrot de (dates unknown)
Paternal grandfather of Nostradamus. Of Jewish descent, and born Guy Gassonet (see Nostradamus's Family Tree), the son of Arnaud de Vélorgues, he was a merchant and money-lender of Avignon. He converted to Christianity, taking the name Peyrot de Nostredame or de Sainte-Marie, but his second wife Benastrugue refused to join him, so he legally repudiated her at Orange in 1463, marrying one Blanche (recorded as "de Sainte-Marie") instead. They had six known children, among them Nostradamus's father, Jaume, and uncle, Pierre.

O

Ogmion or Ogmyon
Reference to Ogmios, a Gallic god reported by the Greek rhetor Lucian as a wrinkled, balding old man who, like Hercules, was dressed in a lion-skin and wielded a club (see Hercules). His strength, however, lay more in his gift of the gab than in his physical strength. He is referred to in his Herculean role – generally as a liberating hero and leader – at V.80, VI.42, VIII.4, VIII.44, IX.89, and *Presage 39*.

Olivarius, Philippe Dieudonné Noel
Alleged physician, astrologer, and author of a *Livre des Prophéties* dated "1542", often erroneously thought to be by Nostradamus and reportedly discovered by the state librarian and censor François de Metz among the manuscripts of the Bibliothèque Ste-Geneviève in Paris at the time of the French Revolution. Chiefly referring to Napoleon, Metz's copy of them, dated 1793, was posthumously discovered by Bareste among his papers, and a translation of them is reproduced by Laver in his *Nostradamus, or the Future Foretold*. The language and style of the so-called *Prophecies of Master Olivarius*, however, betray them as early nineteenth-century forgeries (see Forgeries and Fairy Tales).

Orange (Pop. 27,000)
City north of Avignon, formerly the Roman *Arausio*. It has a Roman triumphal arch and a huge second-century theater. The city is mentioned at *Sixain 5*.

In December 1560 the treasures of its cathedral of Notre Dame were ransacked in the course of a Protestant riot, and early in 1561 the canons wrote to Nostradamus asking him to identify the culprits. He replied with a horoscope – curiously dated for February 11th and with a letter revealing that the treasures had been stolen by two of their own number, recommending that the missive be read out in the presence of all concerned so that the guilty parties might betray themselves by their reactions, and threatening all concerned with the plague and worse should the advice be disregarded.

An eighteenth-century copy of both horoscope and letter are preserved in the Bibliothèque d'Arles (mss. 96–7).

Orgon (Pop. 2,000)
Town on the south bank of the Durance, mentioned at I.90 and V.62. It has a fourteenth-century church and the Chapelle Notre-Dame-de-Beauregard, superbly situated on a lofty rock.

Orus Apollo
Manuscript apparently by Nostradamus in the Bibliothèque Nationale, Paris.

Paracelsus, founder of modern pharmaceutics, whom Nostradamus may have regarded as a model

Allegedly based on a fourth-century Greek version of an Egyptian original, it comprises an extremely free verse-translation of a series of notes on the meaning of selected Egyptian hieroglyphs, and may have some bearing on the symbolism of the *Propheties* (see Nostradamus's Writings).

Orval, Prophecy of
Collection of prophecies dated 1544, often erroneously supposed to have been composed by Nostradamus while staying at the abbey of Orval, near the Belgian border. A copy was allegedly made of them in 1793, and Bareste speaks of a further, 1823 copy. They are reproduced in translation by Laver, but refer mainly to Napoleon and seem to date from the early nineteenth century (see Forgeries and Fairy Tales).

P

Palais des Tournelles
Palace near the Bastille in Paris, used as royal residence during the rebuilding of the Palais du Louvre from 1546 onward. It was here that the celebrations were held in June/July 1559 during which Henri II was mortally wounded in a tournament, as apparently predicted both by Gaurico and by Nostradamus at I.35.

Paracelsus (c.1492–1541)
"Beyond Celsus": typically boastful pseudonym of Theophrastus Aureolus Bombastus von Hohenheim, Swiss natural philosopher, pioneering chemist, medical revolutionary, unconventional physician, and vastly popular lecturer. He empirically devised a whole pharmacopeia of mineral medicines, thus laying many of the foundations of modern pharmaceutics.

After his controversial appointment as lecturer in medicine at Basel university, he scan-

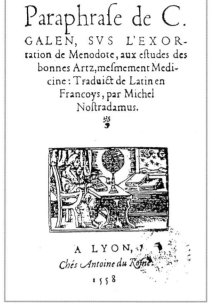

Paraphrafe de C.
GALEN, SVS L'EXOR-
ration de Menodote, aux eftudes des
bonnes Artz, mefmement Medicine : Traduiſt de Latin en
Francoys, par Michel
Noſtradamus.

A LYON,
Chés Antoine du Rofne
1558

**Title page of the 1558 edition of
Nostradamus's *Paraphase de C. Galen***

The curious
rock-pinnacle
known as *la
Piramide* at
Glanum is
specifically
mentioned in
Nostradamus's
writings

dalized the authorities by inviting all and sundry
to his German lectures and publicly burning the
works of Galen and Avicenna. Forced by his
very fame as a rebel to flee, he staged a notable
comeback with his celebrated *Die grosse
Wundartzney* ("The Great Surgery Manual") of
1536, only to be apparently murdered in 1541
at Salzburg.

While there is no record of Paracelsus ever
having met Nostradamus, there are sufficient
echoes of his ideas in the latter's medical
approach to suggest that the slightly younger
(and similarly rebellious) French doctor may
have regarded Paracelsus as something of a
model and kindred spirit.

Paraphrase de C. Galen

Extremely free French version by Nostradamus
of a Latin translation of the Greek text of Galen's
paraphrase of the Alexandrian empirical physician Menodotus's exhortation to "the good
arts", and notably medicine. Apparently
designed to show that Galen himself had not
been nearly so blinkered in his approach as
his latter-day medical disciples, the translation
was first published by Antoine du Rosne of
Lyon in 1557.

Paris (Pop. 2,580,000)

Ancient capital city of France and favored royal
residence from the time of François I. It was visited by Nostradamus in the summer of 1555 at
the request of Queen Catherine de Médicis.
The seer duly attended the Court at St.-
Germain-en-Laye before returning to stay at the
town residence of the Cardinal de Bourbon,
Archbishop of Sens. He apparently left again
in a hurry on hearing that the justices of the
city, which harbored thousands of astrologers

and magicians, were about to investigate his
occult practices.

The city is mentioned at III.51, III.56,
III.93, V.30, XI.23, VIII.67, IX.45, and IX.86.
At least eight of Nostradamus's *Almanachs*, several versions of the fourth edition of the
Propheties, a number of editions of the *Traité des
fardemens*, the 1559 treatise on the eclipse of that
year, the astrological treatise of 1563, and various other works were published in Paris (see
Early Editions).

Paul III, Pope (1468–1549)

An early associate of the Medici in Florence
who became cardinal in 1493 and Pope in
1534. As such he presided over the fiercely anti-
Protestant Counter-Reformation and set up the
defining Council of Trent in 1545. The day of
his death (November 20th, 1549) was correctly
predicted by Luca Gaurico.

Paul IV, Pope (1476–1559)

Elected Pope in 1555 at the age of seventy-nine,
he allied with France against Philip II's Spain,
bestowed riches on his own nephews at the
expense of the prominent Colonna family of
Rome and sharpened the Inquisition's teeth.

Pelissanne

Small town east of Salon on the Touloubre
River. Its ancient street-plan survives, as does its
church.

Pelletier, Anatole le

Prominent Nostradamian commentator who
published two volumes entitled *Les Oracles de
Michel de Nostredame* in 1876.

Pézenas (Pop. 7,500)

This extraordinarily well-preserved
sixteenth/seventeenth-century town (formerly
the Gallic *Piscenae*) northeast of Béziers still pre-
serves its ancient Jewish ghetto.

Philip II (1527–98)

Son of the Emperor Charles V and from 1556
King of Spain, the Two Sicilies, and the entire
Spanish Empire. In 1543 he married Mary of
Portugal, in 1554 Queen Mary of England, and
on her death Elisabeth de Valois, oldest daugh

ter of Henri II and Catherine de Médicis, as
agreed by the Treaty of Cateau-Cambrésis of
the same year.

Ruthlessly determined, hard-working, and
intensely religious, he saw himself as the Pope's
senior in the deadly struggle against
Protestantism, sending the celebrated and ill-
fated Spanish Armada against England in 1588.

The name "Philip" occurs several times in
the *Propheties*, but it is unclear whether any of the
references are specifically to the Spanish King.

Pilierverd, René le

Apothecary of Lyon who concocted medical
preparations for Nostradamus with great skill
during the plague epidemic of 1547. The seer
commends him heartily in his *Traité des fardemens*
of 1555.

Piramide or *Pyramide, la*

Extraordinary, isolated rock-pinnacle in the
middle of the ancient Roman stone quarry at
Glanum, apparently intended to mark the various
rock levels from which the ancient city's stones
were taken, but possibly also serving some ritual purpose. The curious name may derive from
la pierre en mi (i.e. "the stone in the middle"). It
is mentioned at IV.27.

**The death in 1549 of Pope Paul III was
accurately predicted by Luca Gaurico**

Pitt Francis, David

Author of a scholarly assessment of Nostradamus entitled *Nostradamus: Prophecies of Present Time?* which is somewhat undermined by substandard translations. Replete with tables and graphs, this seeks to show that most of Nostradamus's more apocalyptic predictions are merely biblical glosses based on the concept of history repeating itself (compare Astrologer and Mage), while such successes as the seer has had to date have relied heavily on reasonable expectation, interpretational "fudge" and near-deliberate self-fulfillment.

Pius IV, Pope (1599–1565)

Medici Pope, elected in 1559, who summoned the third session of the Council of Trent.

Pius V, Pope (St.) (1504–72)

Dominican bishop of Sutri from 1556 and Inquisitor General and cardinal from 1557, who became Pope in 1566, the year of Nostradamus's death. He strengthened the Inquisition, opposed the Turks, excommunicated Queen Elizabeth I, and supported Mary Queen of Scots.

Pléiade, la

Influential group of seven pioneering poets (including de Baïf, Belleau, and Jodelle), named after the ancient school of Alexandrian poets that was formed under Ptolemy II. Spearheaded by Joachim du Bellay and Pierre de Ronsard, it was founded in 1553 under the tutelage of the classicist Jean Dorat in order to reform and rehabilitate the French language along classical lines. Its principles were outlined in du Bellay's *Deffence et Illustration de la langue Francoyse* of 1549: they included imitation of the ancients, judicious importation of classical words and syntax, the use of regional, foreign, specialized, and obsolete terms, and even the creation of new words as occasion demanded. The fact that Nostradamus, too, did all these things – possibly to excess – suggests that he had close links with the group, and especially with Ronsard, who admired his work.

Poissonnerie, place de la

Small square close to Nostradamus's house in Salon, now the place de l'Ancienne Halle (see Nostradamus's Hometown).

Ponsarde or Ponsart, Anne (d. 1582)

Rich widow of the Salon lawyer Jean Beaulme, young second wife of Nostradamus, and mother of his six surviving children. They were married by her first cousin Etienne Hozier on November 11th, 1547. After arranging, as the seer's legal heir and executor, for the engraving of his tombstone in July 1566, she lived for a further sixteen years. She was buried beside her husband in the local Franciscan chapel.

Pont du Gard

Magnificent surviving section (where it crosses the Gard or Gardon River) of the Roman aqueduct that originally brought water into the city of Nîmes from the Cévennes to the north. It is referred to at V.58, while the aqueduct of which it forms part is also mentioned at V.66.

Préface à Cesar

Dedicatory letter to his infant son César prefaced by Nostradamus to the first edition of his *Propheties*. For full text, see The Major Prophecies.

Presages

Title of a collection of 141 four-line verse-predictions drawn from Nostradamus's *Almanachs* for 1555–67 and first published as such by Vincent Seve in 1605. They were originally designed as verse summaries for given months or years. However, the seer's amanuensis Chavigny had by then already extracted and freely interpreted selected verses, in the process sowing the seeds of a tradition of prophetic interpretation that would apply such verses to later events entirely, and that has lasted until the present day (see Nostradamus's Writings and Interpreting the Prophecies).

Pro(g)nostications

Alternative name for Nostradamus's *Almanachs*, as of other general publications of the type.

Propheties

Overall title of Nostradamus's planned ten books of *Centuries*, both as originally published and as subsequently supplemented with 141 *Presages* and 58 *Sixains* (1605) (see Nostradamus's Writings).

Provençal

Regional language of Provence, presumed native tongue of Nostradamus and most important variant of the ancient *langue d'oc* – a form of Vulgar Latin formerly spoken across much of southern Europe and known as *occitan*. Besides using a number of individual words from Provençal in his *Propheties*, Nostradamus wrote two verses (IV.26 and IV.44) in the language.

Provence

Former province of the Roman Empire (Latin *Provincia*), previously colonized by the Greeks, and lying between the Rhône, the Alps, and the Mediterranean. Overrun first by the Visigoths and then by the Franks, it repeatedly changed hands until Good King René, Duke of Anjou, finally bequeathed it to France in 1474, with the final transfer taking place in 1482. It is mentioned at II.59, V.43, and IX.75, *Présages* 2 and 128, and *Sixain* 33, with possible further references at IV.21 and *Sixains* 4 and 40.

Psellus, Michael (c.1019–c.1078)

Byzantine theologian, historian, statesman, first professor of philosophy at the university of Constantinople, and secretary of state to the Emperor Constantine IX. Among his many treatises, speeches, letters, and poems is the celebrated attack on alleged Messalian practices entitled *Peri energeias daimonon*. A version of this was published in Latin translation as the *De Daemonibus* by Jean de Tournes of Lyon in 1549, conceivably at Nostradamus's own suggestion (see Astrologer and Mage). Certainly it seems to been one of the major magical source-books that he later (a) owned and (b) subsequently probably destroyed (compare *Préface à César*, 9 under The Major Prophecies).

Puys or Puis, Hugues du

Seigneur de la Mothe, Royal Councilor, and Seneschal of Lyon who signed the royal *privilège* for the printing and publication of the first edition of the *Propheties* on April 30th, 1555.

The spectacular Roman Pont du Gard aqueduct was referred to by Nostradamus in the *Centuries*

R

Rabelais, François (c.1494–1553)

Larger-than-life monk, scholar, humanist, editor, doctor, and world-famous pioneering novelist. He became successively a Franciscan friar and Benedictine monk before quitting religious orders for university studies in law and medicine, joining Nostradamus at Montpellier in 1530 (see Nostradamus's Life Story). Controversially appointed chief hospital physician at Lyon in 1532, he edited Hippocrates and Galen (see Nostradamus the Physician) for Sebastien Gryphe while corresponding with Erasmus, then published his astonishing first novel *Pantagruel*.

Next came the *Pantagrueline Prognostication* of 1533, in which he unmercifully sent up the various astrological almanacs that were by then all the rage (see Nostradamus's Writings); *Gargantua* (1534); then the rather deeper *Tiers Livre* of 1546, and *Quart Livre* of 1552. Both were subsequently condemned by the Sorbonne as heretical and the latter banned completely. The Rabelaisian opus subsequently found its way into the Church's *Index Librorum Prohibitorum*.

A study of Rabelais's language offers an ideal introduction to that of the contemporary Nostradamus (see Nostradamus's Language).

Ravel brothers

Canal-building successors of Adam de Craponne, who took over his project to water the *Crau* in about 1581 from his brother

The title page of Rabelais's *Gargantua*, published in 1534

Frédéric. Their major achievement was finally to complete the planned canal to Arles.

Regnault, Barbe

Paris publisher of the 1561, 1562, and 1563 *Almanachs*, as also of a reported 1561 version of the fourth edition of the *Propheties*.

René, "Good King", Duc d'Anjou (1409–80)

The son of Louis II of Anjou, "Good King René" inherited Anjou and Provence in 1434 and proved a popular patron of arts, letters, trade, and agriculture, as well as a gifted poet and author in his own right. After the death of his son John of Calabria in 1470 he was persuaded by Louis XII of France to bequeath his possessions to Charles, Duc de Maine and thus eventually to France. His daughter Margaret married Henry VI of England in 1445.

Reynaud-Plense, Charles

Editor of the comprehensive *Les vraies centuries et prophéties de Michel Nostradamus* (Salon, 1940), based on the texts of 1558, 1568, 1605, 1611, and 1650, and including the complete *Presages* and *Sixains*.

Reynière or Renée de St.-Rémy (dates unknown)

Daughter of René de St.-Rémy and Béatrice Tourrel, wife of the merchant and notary Jaume de Nostredame – and mother of Nostradamus.

Rhône, river

Major water-artery of Provence that rises in Switzerland, passes through Lake Geneva, is joined by the Saône at Lyon, the Durance at Avignon, and the Gard or Gardon near Beaucaire, and divides at Arles into the Petit Rhône and Grand Rhône to enclose the Camargue delta before finally discharging into the Mediterranean. It is mentioned by Nostradamus at II.25, II.60, II.74, II.96, IV.3, IV.76, IV.94, V.17, V.68, V.71, VII.22, VIII.38, VIII.46, VIII.62, IX.68, IX.85, and *Presage* 14.

Rigaud, Benoist (d. 1597)

Lyon publisher of the *Almanach* for 1565, the *Lettre . . . A la Royne mere du Roy* of 1566, and the *Traité des fardemens* of 1572, as well as of the complete editions of the *Propheties* published in 1568 and 1594–6.

Rigaud, Pierre

Son of Benoist Rigaud. He took over his father's business in 1597 and published a series of editions of the *Propheties* dated "1566" (actually a reprint of his father's 1568 edition) and "1568", as well as an edition of his own in 1604.

Roberts, Henry C.

American author of the pioneering 1947 translation and commentary somewhat optimistically entitled *The Complete Prophecies of Nostradamus*. Even though the interpretations are sometimes geographically and historically rather wild, it offers a useful basis for comparison with other interpretations.

Roche, Maître Joseph

Salon lawyer who drew up Nostradamus's will in June 1566.

Ronsard, Pierre de (1524–85)

Pioneering French poet and younger contemporary of Nostradamus. A former royal page and soldier, he entered the Church's minor orders, then studied the classics under Jean Dorat at the Collège de Coqueret. At the same time he devoted himself to writing poetry. In 1549 he and a number of other poets formed the pro-classical group known as the *Pléiade*.

He published a number of major poetic works, notably the *Odes* (1550–3), modeled mainly on Horace and Pindar, the often moving sonnets (1552–78), and the delightful if sentimental *Amours* (1552 and 1555). With the advent of the Wars of Religion, however, he embarked on a series of long and tedious religio-political tracts judiciously supporting the monarchy and the Catholic cause in verse. In one of these he incorporated an admiring pseudo-sonnet on Nostradamus. This roused the ire of Protestant critics. Various blasts and counterblasts followed (see Criticisms and Reviews).

In 1572 the unfinished epic poem *La Franciade* was published, in which Ronsard floated the idea, already familiar from Nostradamus's *Propheties*, that the French royal family was descended from one Francus, son of Hector of Troy (see I.19, III.51, V.74, V.87, and VI.52).

Pierre de Ronsard, a pioneering and original writer of graceful odes and sonnets

Rosne, Antoine du

Lyon publisher of the 1557 *Paraphrase de C. Galen*, as well as of the second edition of Nostradamus's *Propheties* of November 3rd the same year and subsequently. This latter publication, which stops short at VII.40 (see Nostradamus's Writings, and Book Printing and Publishing), removes all but one of the superfluous capitalizations of Macé Bonhomme's first edition of 1555, but is otherwise of poor quality. Verses VII.41–2 were added in subsequent editions, a possible rights dispute between Du Rosne, Nostradamus, and Benoist Rigaud seems to have resulted in the complete loss of the remaining verses of the seventh *Century*.

The present-day Mas de Roussan, on the country estate of Nostradamus's brother, Bertrand

Roussan, Mas de
Country home of Bertrand de Nostredame, just west of St.-Rémy-de-Provence, it was much rebuilt and landscaped during his lifetime. Now replaced by the later Château de Roussan.

Rousse, Thomine
Wife of Nostradamus's younger brother Bertrand de Nostredame from around 1540, and mother of their six children. She seems to have given her name to the Mas de Roussan (see above).

Ruggieri, Cosmo
Celebrated sixteenth-century Italian astrologer and chief familiar of Catherine de Médicis at the time of Nostradamus's 1555 visit to Paris, for whom she built an observatory at Chaumont.

Ruir, Émile
Author of the obviously prophetic *Le grand carnage d'après les prophéties de Nostradamus de 1938 à 1947* (Paris, 1938) and *L'Écroulement de l'Europe, d'après les prophéties de Nostradamus* (Sarlat, 1939), as well as of *Nostradamus, ses prophéties* (Paris, 1947) and *Nostradamus, les proches et derniers événements* (Médicis, Paris, 1953). One of the first twentieth-century Nostradamian commentators (along with Fontbrune) to succeed in interpreting the *Prophéties* in some kind of rational sequence and in drawing from them the picture both of a future World War II and of a Muslim invasion of Europe.

S

St.-Chamas (Pop. 5,000)
Small town beside the Étang de Berre marking one terminus of Craponne's canal and notable for its aqueduct. Just to the southeast, the magnificent Roman Pont Flavien stands forlornly.

St.-Germain-en-Laye
Town west of Paris, whose magnificent castle, largely rebuilt by François I, formerly served as the royal summer residence. It was here that Nostradamus visited King Henri II and Queen Catherine de Médicis in August 1555.

St.-Martin-de-Crau
Village in the middle of the Plaine de la Crau, at the western end of the arrow-straight section of the former Roman *Via Aurelia* leading to Salon-de-Provence.

St.-Paul-de-Mausole
Twelfth-century Augustinian priory, then Franciscan convent, then Van Gogh's asylum just south of St.-Rémy and hard by the ruins of ancient Roman *Glanum*. Nostradamus clearly knew the site well, referring to it on a number of occasions, now as Mausol (VIII.34), now as Mauseole (IX.85), now as Mansol (IV.27, V.57, X.29). See also **Malachy, St.**.

St. Rémy-de-Provence (Pop. 8,500)
Ancient market-town just north of the Alpilles and close by the ruins of Roman *Glanum*. It was here that Michel Nostradamus was born and grew up. The frontage of his alleged birthplace still stands in the rue Hoche, though the attribution is dubious. A room devoted to Nostradamian memorabilia is to be found in the sixteenth-century Musée des Alpilles Pierre de Brun, in the elegant place Favier. In the same square the Hôtel de Sade houses numerous relics recovered from ancient *Glanum*.

St.-Rémy, Jean de
Respected doctor and treasurer (1481–1504) of St.-Rémy, and maternal great-grandfather of Nostradamus. It seems to have been he who

St.-Paul-de-Mausole; the former priory, now *Clinique Van Gogh*

gave the future seer his early education, presumably in Latin, Greek, and possibly Hebrew, to say nothing of mathematics, astrology, and possibly herbalism and chemistry. There is no evidence to prove that he was ever official Court-physician to Good King René of Provence, but every reason to suppose that he may have been called upon to attend the King during the latter's periodic visits to St.-Rémy.

St.-Rémy, René de (d.1479?)
Maternal grandfather of Nostradamus. No other details are known.

St.-Rémy, Reynière or Renée de
See **Reynière or Renée de St.-Rémy**.

Sainte-Marie, Blanche de
Third wife and first Christian spouse of Nostradamus's paternal grandfather Pierre or Peyrot de Nostredame of Avignon, who outlived her husband and was still alive in 1503, the year of the future seer's birth.

Stes-Maries-de-la-Mer, Les (Pop. 2,000)
Coastal town and major pilgrimage center of the Camargue, clustered around the fortified medieval church alleged to contain the relics of Sts Mary Jacobi, Mary Salome, and their servant Sara, who were reputedly washed ashore there with Lazarus, Mary Magdalene, and others after the Crucifixion.

Salon-de-Provence (Pop. 36,000)
Nostradamus's hometown (the former *Castrum Salonense*) located on the eastern edge of the Plaine de la Crau. A busy market town, and long a center of the olive-oil and soap industries, today it also deals in mineral oils, boasts an important military air-training school, and hosts major jazz and arts festivals (see Nostradamus's Hometown).

Samarobryn
Plural name given by Nostradamus at VI.5 to what appear to some commentators to be a fleet of future extraterrestrial spaceships. The term derives from *Samarobriva*, the Celtic name for Amiens, but also bears interesting (if possibly accidental) resemblances to the Russian words for "self" and "operating."

Sangsüe
"Leech": term applied by Nostradamus at *Sixains* 7, 21, 30, 40, 45–6, 49, and 58 to a future parasitic world power (possibly Britain) that will help to defeat the future Muslim invaders of Europe, but will then need to be put firmly in its place.

Saône River
Major tributary of the Rhône, which it joins at Lyon. It rises in the Vosges mountains and is mentioned by Nostradamus at II.25, VI.79, and IX.68.

Sarrazin, Philibert
Prominent Lyon physician, referred to by Nostradamus in his *Traité des fardemens* as *Phil.*

Sarracenus, and described by him as *un notable personnaige de incomparable sçavoir* ("a notable personage of incomparable knowledge"). He may have made an enemy of the future seer as early as the latter's time at Agen, and certainly opposed his methods of treating the plague at Lyon in 1547, insisting on a public confrontation before the city authorities. Defeated, he retired to live at Villefranche, to the north of the city. *Antoine Sarrazin*, a prominent physician with whom he is often confused, but who did not enter the Montpellier medical faculty until 1565, may have been his grandson (see Nostradamus's Life Story).

Savoie, Emmanuel-Philibert, Duc de (d. 1569)
Duke of Savoy, and brilliant imperial general serving Charles V, who fought Montmorency for control of Brussels in 1554 and was placed by Philip II in command of the the most powerful army of the century to defeat the French at St.-Quentin in northern France in August 1557. Under the ensuing peace of Cateau-Cambrésis of 1559, Emmanuel-Philibert was to marry Marguerite de Valois, Henri's sister. It was at the engagement celebrations that the King was, as previously predicted, mortally wounded in a joust.

In October 1559 Emmanuel-Philibert and his new wife called on Nostradamus at Salon and two years later the seer was commanded by Catherine de Médicis to attend them in Turin for a consultation regarding the imminent birth of their child. He is said to have correctly predicted the birth of a son (Charles-Emmanuel), an imminent leg injury to the Duke and his eventual death "when a nine precedes a seventh" – the Duke died in 1569.

Savoie, Marguerite de
See **Marguerite de Valois**

Scaliger, Joseph Justus (1540–1609)
Tenth of fifteen children of Julius Caesar Scaliger. Educated by his father, he became a brilliant polymath, learned thirteen languages, and became acknowledged as the foremost scholar of his age. It seems to have been he, rather than his father, who violently attacked Nostradamus's "Jewish malevolence", described him in print as a "criminal charlatan" and dismissed his work as so many "idiocies" (see Criticisms and Reviews).

Scaliger, Julius Caesar (1484–1558)
Brilliant Italian polymath – soldier, scholar, poet, grammarian, physician, scientist, and astrologer – and violent polemicist. Born Giulio Cesare della Scala (Gallicized as Jules César de l'Escalle), he settled in Agen in 1525 and became the center of a lively group of scholars and philosophers. In 1533 Nostradamus, who had long corresponded with him, went to live in the great man's shadow, setting up in medicine there on his own account. The association did not last, however. Scaliger, already the scourge of other scholars, soon fell out with his protégé as well, causing Nostradamus to leave the town

(see Nostradamus's Life Story). Nevertheless, the seer remained devoted to Scaliger and eulogized him almost ecstatically in his *Traité des fardemens* as possessing a soul that might have been "father to the eloquence of Cicero", and as "in his perfect and supreme poetry another Virgil, and to whom I remain more indebted than to anybody else in this world."

Sénas
Small town located north of Salon from which a two-headed child was brought to Nostradamus in 1544. It boasts a thirteenth-century church and a Roman bridge (see The Nostradamus Omens).

Serres, Louis
Eminent French physician under whom Nostradamus studied and fought the plague in Marseille during 1544–6, and whom the seer later praised in his *Traité des fardemens* for his "Hippocratic perspicacity and knowledge."

Seva, Melchior
Grandson of Nostradamus by his daughter Anne and her husband Pierre de Seva.

Seva, Pierre de
Son-in-law of Nostradamus and husband of his daughter Anne.

Seve, Vincent
Beaucaire publisher of the comprehensive 1605 edition of the *Propheties*, apparently printed at Troyes and incorporating for the first time both the 141 *Presages* collected from the *Almanachs* of 1555-67 and the fifty-eight *Sixains*, which he flags as *pour les ans courans en ce siecle* (i.e. for the seventeenth century). The former he claims to have acquired from an otherwise unknown nephew of the seer named Henry Nostradamus. The claim is not necessarily false, for Seve himself may have been related to Nostradamus via the seer's son-in-law Pierre de Seve (see above).

Silvacane, Abbaye de
Latin: "forest of reeds." Former Cistercian monastery by the Durance, just west of the entrance to Craponne's canal. It was sacked during the Wars of Religion, and at the time of the French Revolution was turned into a farm.

Simeoni, Gabriel
Eminent Jewish-Italian astrologer and magician to the Court of Catherine de Médicis at the time of Nostradamus's 1555 visit.

Sixains
Collection of fifty-eight six-line verses apparently designed to replace the fifty-eight missing verses of *Century* VII, and allegedly discovered by Chavigny among the seer's papers after his death. First incorporated into the *Propheties* in Vincent Seve's 1605 edition, they are more poetic and expansive than the *Centuries*, and thus their authorship has sometimes been questioned. See Nostradamus's Writings, and the full text under The Major Prophecies.

Suleiman the Magnificent (1495–1566)
Celebrated Ottoman Emperor. The son of Selim I, he ascended the Peacock Throne in 1520 as an already successful general. An enlightened ruler at home, he nevertheless waged almost continual war abroad against the West, overrunning Belgrade in 1521, Rhodes in 1522, and then Buda. He was only prevented from overrunning Vienna in 1532 by the timely intervention of the Holy Roman Emperor Charles V. Meanwhile Suleiman was also pushing across North Africa, while his navies continually ravaged the Mediterranean coasts of Europe as far as Nice and Tripoli.

A great deal of all this duly surfaces in Nostradamus's *Propheties*, and seems to have led, via comparative horoscopy (see Astrologer and Mage, and Sequence of Selected Horographs), to his many predictions of a future Muslim invasion of southern Europe, and of France in particular. Suleiman (whom the seer more correctly spells "Sol(i)man") is even mentioned by name at III.31. In his *Almanach* for 1555 Nostradamus seems to have felt that the great invasion was imminent, only subsequently revising this view (see The Muslim Invasion of Europe).

Sutton, Henry
London printer who was the first officially to publish Nostradamus's *Almanachs* (specifically, that for 1559) in English translation: there had been a pirated translation the previous year.

The Abbaye de Silvacane was sacked during the Wars of Religion but has now been restored by the state

The almost perfectly preserved fifteenth-century castle of Tarascon, a favorite residence of Good King René

T

Tarascon (Pop. 11,000)
Former frontier-town of Provence on the Rhône opposite Beaucaire. Nostradamus mentions the town at IV.27, as well as referring at VIII.46 to the monster known as the *Tarasque* (a personification of the frequent Rhône floods) said to emerge regularly from the waters to claim many victims until finally subdued by St. Martha.

Tende, Claude de Savoie, Duc de
Governor of Provence, personal friend of Nostradamus, and member of the ruling house of Savoy. He was present in Salon in 1544 when a two-headed kid was brought for Nostradamus's consideration, and it was he who was allegedly asked by Queen Catherine de Médicis to persuade the seer to come to Paris in 1555 following the publication of the first edition of the *Propheties*. He seems to be mentioned at X.11, and in *Présage* 2.

Torné, Chavigny, Abbé H
Late nineteenth-century Nostradamian commentator, parish priest, and claimed descendant of the seer's secretary Jean-Aymes de Chavigny, who devoted his life to Nostradamus and published many volumes on the seer. These included three volumes of translations and interpretations designed to relate Pierre Rigaud's antedated "1566" edition of the *Propheties* to subsequent history, a *Concordance des Prophéties de Nostradamus avec l'Apocalypse*, an interpretation of the prophecies of Olivarius and Orval (attributed by the author to Nostradamus), the *Lettres et nouvelles lettres du Grand Prophète*, and the *Almanachs du grand Prophète* for 1872, 1873, 1877, and 1878 (!).

Torné-Chavigny possibly did more than anybody else to establish the modern tradition of twisting the prophecies via ingenious, self-deluding linguistic sleight-of-hand to fit both the known facts of history and the interpreter's prior expectations.

Touloubre
Small river that rises near Aix-en-Provence, runs westward past the Château de la Barben, passes through Pélissanne and is joined by Craponne's canal before entering the Étang de Berre at St.-Chamas.

Toulouse (Pop. 359,000)
Major city of southwestern France (formerly the Visigoths' capital *Tolosa*) on the upper Garonne and the Canal du Midi. Its famous mill known as the Basacle is referred to by both Rabelais (*Pantagruel*, 22) and Nostradamus (VIII.30, *Sixain* 31). At the time of Nostradamus (who in his *Traité des fardemens* claims to have practised medicine there in his younger days) it was governed by a powerful Parlement, and was the seat of a branch of the Inquisition, whose summons to attend it is alleged to have been one of the reasons for his hurried departure from Agen in around 1534. The city is referred to at I.72, I.79, III.45, VIII.30, VIII.39, VIII.86, IX.9-10, IX.37, IX.46, IX.72, and X.5.

Tourrel, Beatrice
Maternal grandmother of Nostradamus and wife of René de St.-Rémy.

Tournes, Jean de (d.1564)
Outstanding compositor of the renowned Lyon publisher Sebastien Gryphe. In 1542 he set up in business on his own account, publishing Erasmus, Aesop, the Bible, Simeoni, Petrarch, and others in illustrated editions notable for their beautiful printing and ornaments. An erudite scholar in his own right, in 1558 he published the third (partial) edition of Nostradamus's *Propheties* containing only the last three *Centuries*, and in 1559 was appointed official royal publisher at Lyon. His son Jean II took over the business with similar distinction (see Book Printing and Publishing).

Traité des fardemens et confitures
Nostradamus's variously entitled book of cosmetics and conserves, apparently completed in 1552, but of which only the 1555 and subsequent editions survive (see Early Editions). A major money-spinner for the seer, it went through around a dozen editions in its first thirty-five years and covered a vast range of preparations. See Nostradamus's Writings.

V

Vernègues
Small hill-village northeast of Salon destroyed by earthquake in 1909. It is referred to at III.99 as the site of a final battle to expel future Muslim invaders.

Via Aurelia
Arrow-straight section of the former Roman *Via Domitia* joining Salon to Arles, and named after the Emperor Marcus Aurelius.

Via Domitia
Former Roman trunk road, named after the Emperor Domitius, linking Italy with Spain, of which the *Via Aurelia* forms part.

Vigerchio, Antonio
Renowned Italian apothecary resident at Genoa whom Nostradamus (according to his *Traité des fardemens*) visited during his Italian journeys. One of his prescriptions (for constipation) is reported at the end of the same book.

Visier, Éric
Modern French student, translator, interpreter, and publisher of Nostradamus. In 1995 he published a collection of facsimiles of ten Nostradamian documents entitled *Nostradamus au XVIe siècle*.

Volant, Antoine
Lyon publisher (with Brotot) of the 1558, 1560, 1562, 1566, and 1567 *Almanachs* and (on his own account) of the 1555, 1556, and 1560 editions of the *Traité des fardemens*.

W

Ward, Charles A.
Author of the influential and scholarly *Oracles of Nostradamus* of 1891. Replete with classical quotations and liberal footnotes, it reflects the partial but nevertheless fascinated interest of the time and offers an excellent, if dated, introduction to Nostradamus.

Portrait of Nostradamus from the title page of a German printing of *Les Vraye Centuries*, 1691

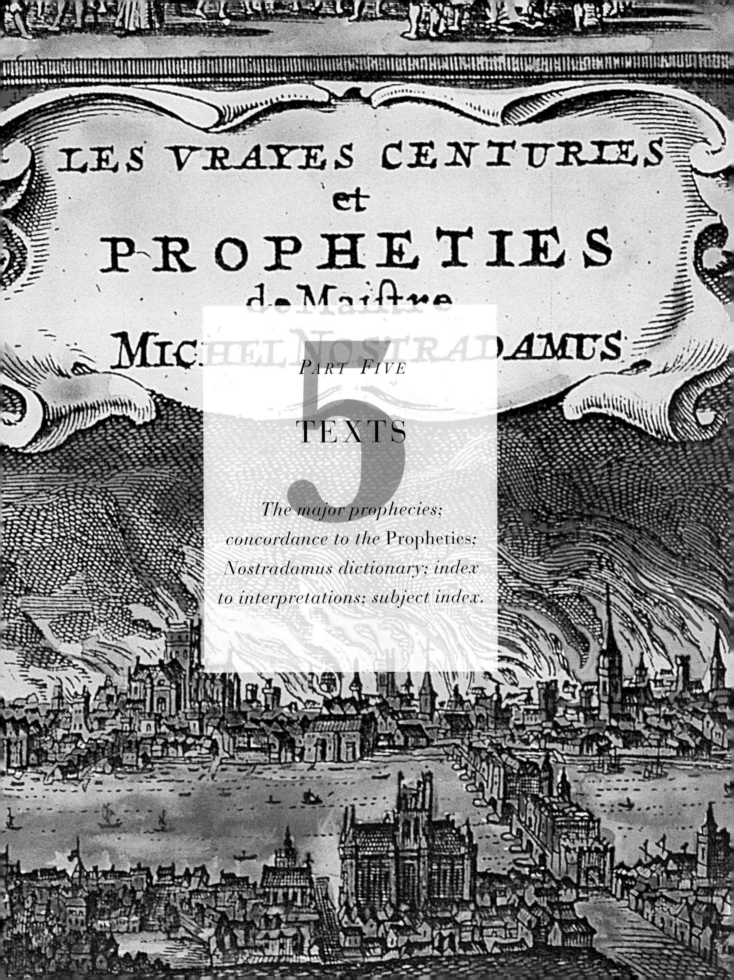

PART FIVE

5

TEXTS

The major prophecies;
concordance to the Propheties;
Nostradamus dictionary; index
to interpretations; subject index.

THE MAJOR PROPHECIES

This section contains the following texts:

The *Préface à César* (1555 edition)

The *Centuries* (1555, 1557 and 1568 editions)

The *Lettre à Henri II* (1568 edition)

The *Presages* (1605 edition)

The *Sixains* (1605 edition)

The "extra" quatrains (various subsequent editions)

THE *PRÉFACE À CÉSAR*

(Transliterated from **Bonhomme**'s 1555 edition and divided into sections with commentary.)

PREFACE DE M. MICHEL NOSTRADAMUS à ses Propheties.

Ad Caesarem Nostradamum Filium VIE ET FELICITE.

1

Convinced that his prophetic gift will die with him, Nostradamus explains to his now one-year-old son how he has decided to preserve for him in writing (as for the world at large) the fruits of his nocturnal scrying and astrological labors.

TON tard advenement Cesar Nostradame mon filz, m'a faict mettre mon long temps par continuelles vigilations nocturnes reserer par escript, toy delaisser[1] memoire apres la corporelle extinction de ton progeniteur, au commun profit des humains de ce que la Divine essence par Astronomiques revolutions m'ont[2] donne congnoissance. Et depuis qu'il a pleu au Dieu immortel que tu ne soys venu en naturelle lumiere dans ceste terrene plaige, & ne veulx dire tes ans qui ne sont encores acompaignés, mais tes moys Martiaulx incapables à recepvoir dans ton debile entendement ce que je seray contrainct apres mes jours definer: veu qu'il n'est possible te laisser par escript ce que seroit par l'injure du temps obliteré: car la parolle hereditaire de l'occulte prediction sera dans mon estomach intercluse: consyderant aussi les adventures de l'humain definement estre incertaines, & que le tout est regi & guberné par la puissance de Dieu inextimable, nous inspirant non par baccante fureur, ne par lymphatique monument, mais par astronomiques assertions Soli numine

divino afflati praesagiunt & spiritu prophetico particularia.[3]

2

Claiming many past prophetic successes, the seer admits to having avoided revealing what future generations would see as true prophecies, for fear of religious persecution in the interim: he has disguised his predictions in abstruse language, so that his gist may be hidden from the powers-that-be but revealed to the humble and meek.

Combien que de long temps par plusieurs foys j'aye predict long temps au-paravant ce que despuis est advenu, & en particulieres regions, attribuant le tout estre faict par la vertu & inspiration divine & aultres felices & sinistres adventures de accelerée promptitude prenoncées, que despuis sont advenues par les climats du monde ayant volu taire & delaissé par cause de l'injure, & non tant seulement du temps present, mais aussi de la plus grande part du futur, de mettre par escrit pource que les regnes sectes & religions feront changes si opposites, voyre au respect du present diametralement, que si je venoys à reserer ce que à l'advenir sera, ceux de regne, secte, religion, & foy trouveroient si mal accordant à leur fantasie auriculaire, qu'il viendroent à damner ce que par les siecles advenir on congnoistra estre veu & apperceu: Consyderant aussi la sentence du vray Sauveur: Nolite sanctum dare canibus nec mittatis margaritas ante porcos ne conculcent pedibus & conversi dirumpant vos.[4] Qui a[5] esté la cause de faire retirer ma langue au populaire, & la plume au papier: puis me suis volu extendre declarant pour le commun advenement, par obstruses & perplexes sentences les causes futures, mesmes les plus urgentes, & celles que j'ay apperceu, quelque humaine mutation que adviene ne scandalizer l'auriculaire fragilité, & le tout escrit sous figure nubileuse, plus que du tout prophetique, combien que, Absconditi haec àsapientibus, & prudentibus, id est. potentibus & regibus, & enucleasti ea exiguis & tenuibus,[6] & aux Prophetes: . . .

3

The true prophet, he asserts, is illumined directly by the spirit of God, as by the rays of the sun itself.

. . . par le moyen de Dieu immortel & des bons anges ont receu l'esprit de vaticination, par lequel ilz voyent les causes loingtaines, & viennent à prevoir les futurs advenementz, car rien ne se peult parachever sans luy, ausquelz si grande est la puissance & la bonté aux subjectz, que pendant qu'ilz demeurent en eulx, toutefois aux autres effects subjectz, pour la similitude de la cause du bon genius, celle challeur & puissance vaticinatrice s'approche de nous: comme il nous advient des rayons du Soleil, qui se viennent getans leur influence aux corps elementeres, & non elementeres.

4

Humans cannot of themselves have such knowledge: aided by astrology, however, divine knowledge of the future can appear to the prophet as in a flame of fire.

Quant à nous qui sommes humains ne pouvons rien de nos-

tre naturelle cognoissance, & inclination d'engin congnoistre des secretz obstruses de Dieu le createur, Quia non est nostrum noscere tempora, nec momenta etc.[7] Combien que aussi de present peuvent advenir & estre personnaiges que Dieu le createur aye voulu reveler par imaginatives impressions, quelques secretz de l'advenir accordés à l'astrologie judicielle, comme du passé, que certaine puissance & voluntaire faculté venoit par eulx, comme flambe de feu apparoit, que luy inspirant on venoit à juger les divines & humaines inspirations. Car les œuvres divines, que totalement sont absoluës, Dieu les vient parachever: la moyenne qui est au millieu, les Anges: la troisiesme, les mauvais.

5

The prophecies, he repeats, are no mere vain spoutings, but of divine origin, received via the medium of fire and the stars.

Mais mon filz, je te parle icy un peu trop obstrusement: mais quant aux occultes vaticinations que lon vient à recevoyr par le subtil esperit du feu qui quelque foys par l'entendement agité contemplant le plus hault des astres comme estant vigilant, mesmes que aux prononciations estant surprins escritz, prononceant sans crainte moins attainct[8] d'inverecunde loquacité: mais quoy? tout procedoit de la puissance divine du grand Dieu eternel, du qui toute bonté procede.

6

The seer himself, however, declines the title of prophet in his own right: his insights derive from a combination of effort and free will on the one hand and divine revelation via astrology on the other.

Encores mon filz que j'aye inseré le nom de prophete je ne me veux attribuer tiltre de si haulte sublimité, pour le temps present: car qui propheta dicitur, hodie, olim vocabatur videns:[9] car prophete proprement mon filz est celuy qui voit choses loingtaines de la cognoissance naturelle de toute creature. Et cas advenant que le prophete moyennant la parfaicte lumiere de la pphetie, luy appaire manifestement des choses divines, comme humaines: que ce ne peult fayre, veu les effectz de la future prediction s'estendant loing. Car les secretz de Dieu sont incomprehensibles, & la vertu effectrice contingent de longue estendue de la cognoissance naturelle, prenent son plus prochain origine du liberal arbitre, faict apparoir les causes que d'elles mesmes ne peuvent aquerir celle notice pour estre cognuës, ne par les humains augures, ne par aultre cognoissance ou vertu occulte, comprise soubz la concavité du ciel, mesmes du faict present de la totale eternité que vient en soy embrasser tout le temps. Mais moiennant quelque indivisible eternité par comitiale agitation Hiraclienne, les causes par le celeste mouvement sont congnuës.

7

Not that such things are unamenable to reason, aided by luck and science, but without divine inspiration they cannot be fully revealed: and to perceive them, the ritual use of fire and the hearing of

---

3 de laisser.

2 m'a (!).

---

3 "Only those inspired by the divine godhead and the spirit of prophecy can predict detailed events."

4 "Do not give what is holy to the dogs or cast pearls before swine, lest they trample them under their feet, turn upon you and tear you in pieces" (Matth.7:6).

5 *a.*

---

6 "Thou hast hidden these things from the wise and prudent, i.e. the mighty and kings, and hast revealed them to the small and weak" (expanded version of Matth.11.25).

7 "For it is not ours to know the dates or times . . ." (version of Acts 7:1).

8 *teint.*

9 "He who was formerly called a seer is nowadays described as a prophet."

voices consequent upon ritually moistening the hem of one's garment are essential.

Je ne dis pas mon filz, affin que bien l'entendes, que la cognoissance de ceste matiere ne se peult encores imprimer dans ton debile cerveau, que les causes futures bien loingtaines ne soient à la cognoissance de la creature raisonable: si sont nonobstant bonement la creature de l'ame intellectuelle des causes presentes loingtaines, ne luy sont du tout ne trop occultes, ne trop reserées: mais la parfaicte des causes notice[10] ne se peult aquerir sans celle divine inspiration: veu que toute inspiration prophetique reçoit prenant son principal principe movant de Dieu le createur, puis de l'heur, et de nature. Parquoy estans les causes indifferantes, indifferentement produictes, & non produictes, le presaige partie advient, ou àesté predit. Car l'entendement crée intellectuellement ne peult voir occultement, sinon par la voix faicte au lymbe moyennant la exigue flamme, en laquelle partie les causes futures se viendront à incliner.

8

Nevertheless, the seer warns his son César against such dangerous and disturbing practices, let alone full-blown magic itself. Only judicial astrology, as sanctioned by the Church (and as used to prepare the current prophecies), is to be encouraged.

Et aussi mon filz je te supplie que jamais tu ne vueilles emploier ton entendement à telles resveries & vanités, qui seichent le corps & mettent à perdition l'ame, donnant trouble au foyble sens: mesmes la vanité de la plus que execrable magie reprouvée jadis par les sacrées escriptures, & par les divins canons: au chef du-quel est excepté le jugement de l'astrologie judicielle: par laquelle & moyennant inspiration & revelation divine par continuelles veilles et supputations, avons noz propheties redigé par escript.

9

True, the seer has studied many ancient occult scripts, but in order to preserve his son from their dangers, he has now committed them to the flames and reduced them to ashes. They burned, he says, with an unnatural brightness.

Et combien que celle occulte Philosophie ne fusse reprouvée. m'ay onques volu presenter leurs effrenées persuations: combien que plusieurs volumes qui ont esté cachés par long siecles me sont estés manifestés. Mais doutant ce qui adviendroit en ay faict apres la lecture, present à Vulcan, que, pendant quil les venoit àdevorer, la flamme leschant l'air rendoit une clarté insolite, plus claire que naturelle flamme, comme lumiere de feu de clistre fulgurant illuminant subit la maison, comme si elle fust esté en subite conflagration. Parquoy affin que à l'avenir ni feusses abusé perscrutant la parfaicte transformation tant seline solaire, & soubz terre metaulx incorruptibles, & aux undes occultes, les ay en cendres convertis.

10

In his book he will nevertheless give details of what the stars have revealed to him, avoiding mere imaginative speculation and limiting himself to stating (thanks to inspired interpretaton of astrological patterns) what is to happen where, and in some cases when.

Mais quant au jugement qu se vient parachever moyennant le jugement celeste cela te veulz je manifester: parquoy avoir congnoissance des causes futures rejectant loing les fantastiques imaginations qui adviendront, limitant la particularité des lieux par divine inspirations supernaturelle accordant aux celestes figures, les lieux, & une partie du temps de propri-

---

10 *la parfaicte notice des causes.*

eté occulte par vertu, puissance & faculté divine: en presence de laquelle les troys temps sont comprins par eternité, revolution tenant à la cause passée, presente & future: *quia omnia sunt nuda & aperta &c.[11]*

11

The prophecies, he repeats, are the result of astrological study combined with divine inspiration.

Parquoy mon filz, tu peulx facilement nonobstant ton tendre cerveau, comprendre que les choses qui doivent avenir se peuvent prophetizer par les nocturnes & celestes lumieres, que sont naturelles, & par l'esprit de prophetie: non que je me vueille attribuer nomination ny effect prophetique, mais par revelée insipiration, comme homme mortel esloigné non moins de sens au ciel, que des piedz en terre.

12

The prophecies are infallible, and (surprising though it may seem) extend all the way to the year 3797: hopefully César himself will see them start to come true during his own lifetime.

Possum non errare falli decipi:[12] suis pecheur plus grand qu nul de ce monde, subject à toutes humaines afflictions. Mais estant surprins par foys la sepmaine lymphatiquant, par longue calculation rendant les estudes nocturnes de souefue odeur jay composé livres de propheties contenant chascun cent quatrains astronomiques de propheties, lesquelles j'ay un peu voulu raboter obscurement: & sont perpetuelles vaticinations, pour d'yci à l'année 3797. Que possible fera retirer le front à quelque uns en voyant si longue extension, & par souz toute la concavité de la Lune aura lieu & intelligence: & ce entendant universellement par toute la terre, les causes mon filz. Que si tu vis l'aage naturel & humani, tu verras devers ton climat au propre ciel de ta nativité les futures avantures prevoyr.

13

The process of prophecy is a combination of natural gift and astrological study aided by divine revelation, thanks to the ritual use of fire, which also inspired many ancient philosophers.

Combien que le seul Dieu eternel, soit celuy seul qui congnoit l'eternité de sa lumiere, procedant de luy mesmes: & je dis franchement que à ceulx à qui sa magnitude immense, qui est sans mesure et incomprehensible, ha voulu par longue inspiration melancolique reveler, que moyennant icelle cause occulte manifestée divinement, principallement de deux causes principales qui sont comprinses à l'entendement de celuy inspiré qui prophetise l'une est que vient à infuser, esclarcissant la lumiere supernaturelle au personaige qui predit par la doctrine des astres, & prophetise par inspiré revelation: laquelle est une certe participation de la divine eternité: moyennant le prophete vient à juger de cela que son divin esperit luy ha donné par le moyen de Dieu le createur, & par une naturelle instigation: c'est assavoir que ce que predit, est vray, & a prins son origine ethereement: & telle lumiere & flambe exigue est de toute efficace, & de telle altitude: non moins que la naturelle clarté, & naturelle lumiere

---

11 "For all things are naked and open . . ." (half-remembered version of Matth. 10.26).

---

12 "It is possible for me not to err, fail or be deceived": Nostradamus was later to have second thoughts about this. In his letter of February 4th, 1562 to the canons of Orange, he omits the word *non* and prefaces the statement with the words *Humanus sum*, thus admitting that, as a mere human being, he is bound to be susceptible to error.

rend les philosophes si asseurés que moyennant les principes de la premiere cause ont attainct à plus profondes abysmes de plus haultes doctrines.

14

Anxious not to confuse his son by theorizing further (and fearing a future catastrophic decline in general literacy),[13] the seer now begins to summarize some of the main prophecies themselves. Before the final conflagration, he says, there will be vast world floods during the "Age of Mars," preceded and followed both by long rains and by fire and stones from the sky. Long before this, however, the current "Age of the Moon"[14] has to give way to that of the Sun,[15] and then to that of Saturn.[16] Within 177 years, 3 months, and 11 days[17] pestilence, famine, war, and flood will then wipe out most of humanity, leaving the fields largely untended. Nevertheless, the Last Judgment will not come until the end of the seventh millennium.[18]

Mais à celle fin, mon filz, que je ne vague trop profondement pour la capacité future de ton sens, & aussi que je trouve que les lettres feront si grande & incomparable jacture, que je trouve le monde avant l'universelle conflagration advenir tant de deluges & si hautes inundations, qu'il ne sera gueres terroir qui ne soit couvert d'eau: & sera par si long temps que hors mis enographies[19] & topographies, que le tout ne soit pery: aussi avant telles & apres inundations, en plusieurs contrées les pluies seront si exigues, & tombera du ciel si grande abondance de feu, & de pierres candentes, que ni demoura rien qu'il ne soit consummé: & cecy avenir, & en brief, & avant la derniere conflagration. Car encores que la planette de Mars paracheve son siecle, & à la fin de son dernier periode, si le reprendra il: mais assemblés les uns en Aquarius par plusieurs années, les autres en Cancer par plus longues & continues. Et maintenant que sommes conduicts par la lune, moyennant la totale puissance de Dieu eternel, que avant qu'elle aye parachevé son total circuit, le soleil viendra, & puis Saturne. Car selon les signes celestes le regne de Saturne sera de retour, que le tout calculé le monde s'approche, d'une anaragonique revolution: & que de present que ceci j'escriptz avant cent & septante sept ans troys moys unze jours, par pestilence, longue famine, & guerres, & plus par les inundations le monde entre cy & ce terme prefix, avant & apres par plusieurs foys, sera si diminué, & si peu de monde sera, que l'on ne trouvera qui vueille prendre les champs, qui deviendront liberes aussi longuement qu'ilz sont

---

13 A fear apparently shared by **Rabelais** (*Pantagruel*, Prologue).

---

14 1535 to 1889, according to Erika **Cheetham**, but more likely 1535 to 1895 – i.e. a 360-year "year of years" – or possibly 1535 to 1900, if a "year" of 365 years is involved.

---

15 On the same basis, presumably 1895 to 2255 (or possibly 1900 to 2265).

---

16 Presumably 2255 to 2615 (or possibly 2265 to 2630): **Hogue** suggests 4000–6000.

---

17 i.e. presumably by 2793 or 2808: the "Age of Mars" (mentioned earlier), seems destined for 2975 to 3335.

---

18 2828, by Nostradamus's calculations in the **Lettre à Henri II**.

---

19 *ethnographies.*

estés en servitude: & ce quant au visible jugemeut[20] celeste, que encores que nous soyons au septiesme nombre de mille qui paracheve le tout, nous approchant du huictiesme, ou est le firmament de la huictiesme sphere, qui est en dimension latitudinaire ou le grand Dieu eternel viendra parachever la revolution: ou les images celestes retourneront à se mouvoir, & le mouvement superieur qui nous rend la terre stable & ferme, non inclinabitur in saeculum saeculi:[21] hors mis que quand son vouloir sera accomply, ce sera, mais non point aultrement: . . .

15

Meanwhile, via heavenly visions God reveals to those of his prophets who choose to open themselves to them what the direct knowledge of the senses cannot reveal.

. . . combien que par ambigues opinions excedantes toutes raisons naturelles par songes Machometiques, aussi aucune fois Dieu le createur par les ministres de ses messagiers de feu en flamme missive vient à proposer aux sens exterieurs, mesmement à nos yeulx, les causes de future predictions significatrices du cas futur, qui se doibt à celuì qui presaige manifester. Car le presaige qui se faict de la lumiere exterieure vient infailliblement à juger partie avecques & moyennant le lume exterieur: combien vrayement que la partie qui semble avoir par l'œil de l'entendement, ce que n'est par la lesion du sens imaginatif: la raison est par trop evidente, le tout estre predict par afflation de divinité, & par le moyen de l'esprit angelique inspiré à l'homme prophetisant, rendant oinctes de vaticinations, le venant à illuminer, luy esmouvant le devant de la phantasie par diverses nocturnes aparitions, que par diurne certitude spphetise[22] par administration astronomique, conjoincte de la sanctissime future prediction, ne consistant ailleurs que au courage libre.

16

In the immediate future, César should expect a more deadly war than for three generations past, but the Final Judgment itself will not come until most of the prophecies have been fulfilled.

Vient asture[23] entendre mon filz que je trouve par mes revolutions que sont accordantes àrevellée inspiration, que le mortel glaive s'aproche de nous pour asture, par peste, guerre plus horrible que à vie de trois hommes n'à esté, & famine lequel tombera en terre, & y retournera souvent, car les astres s'accordent à la revolution: & aussi a dit, Visitabo in virga ferrea iniquitates eorum, & in verberibus percutiam eos:[24] car la misericorde du Seigneur ne sera point dispergée un temps mon filz, que la pluspart de mes propheties seront acomplies, & viendront estre par acomplissement revoluës.

17

Dreadful storms, floods and rains will also come, as predicted more specifically in the seer's collection of plain prose prophecies.[25] Even the meanings of the more obscure predictions will become clear

---

[20] Misprint for *jugement*.

---

[21] "It shall not vary from age to age."

---

[22] *prophetise.*

---

[23] Possible misprint for *Viendras-tu à*, influenced by line 4.

---

[24] "I will visit their iniquities with a rod of iron and will strike them with blows" (corrupt version of Ps.2.9 or Rev.2.27).

---

when the time comes for ignorance to be banished.

Alors par plusieurs foys durant les sinistres tempestes, Centeram ergo, dira le Seigneur, & confringam, & non miserebor:[26] & mille autres aventures qui aviendront par eaux & continuelles pluies comme plus à plain j'ay redigé par escript aux miennes autres propheties qui sont composées tout au long, in soluta oratione,[27] limitant les lieux, temps, & le terme prefix que les humains apres venus, verront cognoissants les aventures avenues infailliblement, comme avons noté par les autres, parlants plus clairement: nonobstant que sous nuée seront comprinses les intelligences: sid quando submovenda erit ignorantia,[28] le cas sera plus esclarci.

18

Finally Nostradamus signs off, wishing his son long life, prosperity and happiness.

Faisant fin mon filz, prends donc ce don de ton pere M. Nostradamus, esperant toy declarer une chascune prophetie des quatrains ici mis. Priant au Dieu immortel qu'il te veuille prester vie longue, en bonne & prospere felicité. De Salon ce i de Mars 1555.

THE *CENTURIES*

Roman numerals denote *Centuries*. Summaries are tentative, pending establishment of sequence and thus context. Possible subject-references are as suggested by **Cheetham**(C), **Fontbrune**(F), **Hogue**(H), **Lemesurier**(L), and **Roberts**(R). For translations see all except **Fontbrune**. Words given in **bold** indicate cross-references via the Indexes or in the Gazetteer and Who's Who.

CENTURY I

Transliterated from **Bonhomme**'s original 1555 edition.

I.1

With the aid of a brazen tripod, **Nostradamus** sees the future flicker before him out of the darkness. C,F,H,L,R.

Estant assis de nuict secret estude,
Seul repousé[1] sus la selle d'aerain,
Flambe exigue sortant de solitude,
Faict proferer qui n'est à croire vain.

I.2

Sprinkling his hem and feet after the Apollonian rite of Branchidai, C,F,L the trembling seer hears voices and sees a divine apparition. C,F,H,L,R.

---

[25] Presumably the **Almanachs** (q.v.).

---

[26] "I will trample and break them, and will have no pity" (vague reference to Isa.63.3).

---

[27] "In plain prose": if these are *not* the **Almanachs**, they were never published and have long since disappeared.

---

[28] "But when the time comes for ignorance to be removed."

---

[1] Either "resting alone" or possibly from O.Fr. *seel* (mod. Fr. *seau*, "bucket") and Lat. *repausare*, "to cease, stop again": thus, "the stilled bucket" (see **Astrologer and Mage**) – the first of a long line of possible Nostradamian riddles in the *Centuries*, doubling as a word play on *selle* later in the same line.

La verge en main mise au milieu de branches
De l'onde il moulle & le limbe & le pied.
Un[2] peur & voix fremissent par les manches,
Splendeur divine. Le Divin prés s'assied.

I.3

With nobles' litters overturned by a whirlwind and faces cloaked, new powers take over the republic, while reds and whites are at loggerheads: **French Revolution** C,H / future Muslims and Russia F / **Russian Revolution**, 1917 R.

Quant la lictiere du tourbillon versée,
Et seront faces de leurs manteaux couvers,
La republique par gens nouveaux vexée,
Lors blancs & rouges jugeront à l'envers.

I.4

During the brief reign of a world ruler, the Church is deeply damaged and its power lost: **Napoleon** and papacy C / future **Henri V** of France F / future secular world empire R.

Par l'univers sera faict ung monarque,
Qu'en paix & vie ne sera longuement:
Lors se perdra la piscature barque,
Sera regie en plus grand detriment.

I.5

Persecution across the southwest of France is resisted in the main towns: C16 Huguenots C,R / World War II F / **Muslim invasion** of France, 2011–13 L.

Chassés seront sans faire long combat,
Par le pays seront plus fort grevés:
Bourg & cité auront plus grand debat,
Carcas.[3] Narbonne auront cueurs esprouvés.

I.6

Northern Italy is overwhelmed by French troops: France and papal states, C16 C / ditto, C19 F / final rout of Muslim invaders of Europe, 2027 L.

L'œil de Ravenne sera destitué,
Quand à ses pieds les aelles failliront,
Les deux de Bresse auront constitué,
Turin, Verseil que Gauloys fouleront.

I.7

An execution is carried out at the behest of one Rousseau (or "red-head") before contrary evidence can arrive: Dreyfus case, 1899 C,H / future fall of French Republic F / execution of Tsar, 1918 R.

Tard arrivé l'execution faicte,
Le vent contraire, letres au chemin prinses
Les conjures xiiij. d'une secte
Par le Rosseau senez les entreprinses.

I.8

The "City of the Sun" is overrun by barbarians from the Adriatic: siege of **Paris**, 1590 C,H / **Napoleon** in Cairo, 1798 F / Muslims attack Lyon, 2005 L.

Combien de foys prinse cité solaire
Seras, changeant les loys barbares & vaines:
Ton mal s'aproche: Plus seras tributaire
La grand Hadrie reovrira tes veines.

---

[2] For *un'*.

---

[3] Abbreviation for *Carcassonne*.

I.9

An African fleet attacks the Adriatic and Italy from the east, storming the Mediterranean islands: Malta, 1565 and **Henri IV**, 1590 [C] / Third World War [F] / **Muslim invasion of Europe**, 1999–2000 [H,L] / Haile Selassie [R].

De l'Orient viendra le cuer Punique,
Facher Hadrie & les hoirs Romulides,
Acompaigne de la classe Libycque,
Trembler Mellites: et proches isles vuides.

I.10

"Snakes" in an iron cage kill seven imprisoned royal children while their parents look on: House of Valois, 1610 [C,H] / Mussolini, 1945 [F] / **French Revolution** ("Reign of Terror") [R].

Serpens transmis dens⁴ la caige de fer
Ou les enfans septains du roy son pris:
Les vieux & peres sortiront bas de l'enfer,
Ains mourir voir de son fruict mort & crys.

I.11

War overtakes Spain and Italy thanks to addled thinking: failed prediction for Spanish Empire [C] / Garibaldi and Francis II of Sicily [F] / **Muslim invasion of Europe**, 1999–2000 [L] / Mussolini and Spanish Falangists [R].

Le mouvement de sens, cueur, pieds, & mains
Seront d'acord. Naples, Leon, Secille,
Glaifves, feus, eaux: puis aux nobles Romains
Plongés, tués, mors par cerveau debile.

I.12

An untrustworthy brute betrays the trust of those who have rushed him to power in Verona: Jacobo Sansabastiani, 1539–62 [C] / Verona, 1805, and **Napoleon** [F] / Mussolini [R].

Dans peu dira faulce brute, fragile,
De bas en hault eslevé promptement:
Puys en instant desloyale & labile
Qui de Veronne aura gouvernement.

I.13

Exiles conspire against a ruler and send in insurgents: conspiracy of Amboise, 1560 [C] / **Napoleon** on Elba, 1815 [F] / Victor Emmanuel III of Italy [R].

Les exiles par ire, haine intestine,
Feront au roy grand conjuration:
Secret mettront ennemis par la mine,
Et ses vieux siens contre eux sedition.

I.14

An enslaved (or Slavic) people clamors for freedom from its overlords, only to be comforted by religious halfwits: **French Revolution** [C,H] / Russia in 1930s [F] / **Russian Revolution** [H,R].

De gent esclave chansons, chantz & requestes,
Captifs par princes & seigneur aux prisons:
A l'avenir par idiots sans testes
Seront receus par divins oraisons.

I.15

War threatens the French with seventy blood-lettings, while the Church first flourishes, then is ruined: **Napoleon** or modern Iran [C] / Franco-Prussian War, 1870 [F] / wars threatening Europe, 1999 onward [L,R].

I.16

A new astrological cycle brings war to France: late twentieth-century war [C,H] / **Muslim invasion** of southeast France via Étang de **Berre**, 1999–2002 [L] / War of Wars, 1999 [R].

Faulx a l'estang joinct vers le Sagitaire
En son hault AUGE de l'exaltation,
Peste, famine, mort de main militaire:
Le siecle approche de renovation.

I.17

No rainbow appears during forty years of drought, then it is seen daily during another forty years of deluge: war, 1830–70; peace, 1871–1914 [F] / future severe climatic disturbance (see **I.91**) [L] / aftermath of **Armageddon** [R].

Par quarante ans l'Iris n'aparoistra,
Par quarante ans tous les jours sera veu:
La terre aride en siccité croistra,
Et grans deluges quand sera aperceu.

I.18

With the Gulf of Genoa awash with blood, internal French dissension allows a Muslim invasion-fleet to enter **Marseille**: chaos in French colonies, 1940 [C] / future **Muslim invasion of Europe** [H,R] / Ditto, 2005 [L].

Par la discorde negligence Gauloyse,
Sera passaige à Mahommet ouvert:
De sang trempé la terre & mer Senoyse,⁵
Le port Phocen de voiles & nefs couvert.

I.19

The leader of the Franco-Spanish monarchy, decimated by the Spanish, is forced to flee into the marshes: Wars of Spanish Succession (?) [C] / Spanish anarchism, exile of Alfonso XIII, 1931, and Spanish Civil War [F].

Lors que serpens viendront circuir l'are,
Le sang Troien⁶ vexé par les Hespaignes
Par eux grand nombre en sera faicte tare,
Chief, fuyct caché aux mares dans les saignes.

I.20

Northern French cities, mainly along the Loire, are besieged by foreigners, with earth-shaking effect: **Muslim invasion of Europe**, 2020 [L] / World War II [R].

Tours, Orleans, Bloys, Angiers, Reims, & nantes
Cités vexées par subit changement:
Par langues estranges seront tendues tentes
Fluves,⁷ dars Renes, terre & mer tremblement.

I.21

White clay, oozing from beneath a rock, serves as an unknown protection: discovery of new natural resources [R].

I.22

Some kind of robot harms its creator amid freezing weather: technology of far future [L] / ballistic missiles [R].

Ce qui vivra & n'aiant aucun sens,
Viendra leser à mort son artifice:⁸
Autun Chalon, Langres & les deux Sens,
La gresle & glace fera grand malefice.

I.23

After three months, boar and leopard fight at sunrise, until the worn-out leopard sees an eagle flying against the sun: Battle of Waterloo, 1815, three months after **Napoleon**'s return from Elba [C,F] / World War I or II (?) [R].

Au mois troisiesme se levant le soleil,
Sanglier, liepard, au champ mars pour combatre.
Liepard laisse, au ciel extend son œil,
Un aigle autour du soleil voyt s'esbatre.

I.24

The eaglelike attacker of a "New City" is at first uncertain, then magnanimous in victory, despite damage to Cremona and Mantua: **Napoleon** at Villanova during Italian campaigns of 1795–7 [C,F] / Nuremberg trials [R].

A cité neufve pensif pour condemner,
Loysel⁹ de proye au ciel se vient offrir:
Apres victoire a captifs pardonner,
Cremone & Mantoue grands maulx aura souffert

I.25

A shepherd or priest is half-deified for discovering some long-lost secret, but debunked at the end of a lunar cycle: foundation of Institut Pasteur, 1889 [C,L,R].

Perdu, trouvé, caché de long siecle
Sera pasteur demy dieu honore,
Ains que la Lune acheve son grand cycle
Par autres veux sera deshonoré.

I.26

One great man is killed by a daytime thunderbolt, another at night, while Reims, London, and Tuscany undergo pestilential attack: Kennedy assassinations, 1963 and 1968 [C,H] / **Muslim invasion of Europe**, 2019–20 [L] / Hitler's invasion of Czechoslovakia, 1939 [R].

Le grand du fouldre tumbe d'heure diurne,
Mal & predict par porteur postulaire
Suivant presaige tumbe d'heure nocturne,
Conflit Reins, Londres, Etrusque pestifere.

I.27

Ancient treasure is discovered near a blasted, mistled oak, but the discoverer is found dead: Nazis execute airborne attack-troops seeking their treasure hoard [R].

Dessoubz de chaine Guien du ciel frappe,
Non loing de la est caché le tresor,
Qui pour longs siecles avoit este grappé,
Trouve mourra, l'œil crevé de ressort.

---

4 Syllable missing: read as *dedans*.

5 Presumed misprint for *Genoise*, "of Genoa."

6 Reference to the French kings' alleged descent from Francus, son of Hector of Troy, as later celebrated by **Ronsard** in his abortive *Franciade* (1572).

7 Read as either *fleuves* or *fléaux*.

8 Probable abbreviation of *artificier*.

9 *l'oiseau*.

I.28

The fort at **Port-de-Bouc** is attacked by Muslim craft, then, later, by ships from the west, causing devastation (see **I.71**): siege of Tobruk, 1941 [C] / future **Muslim invasion of Europe** [F] / ditto, 2005 and 2019 or 2025–6 [L] / gas-attack by Spaniards [R].

La tour de Bouq gaindra[10] fuste Barbare,
Un temps, long temps apres barque hesperique,
Bestail, gens, meubles tous deux feront granttare
Taurus & Libra quelle mortelle picque!

I.29

Strange amphibious craft come ashore, permitting sea-borne enemies to attack (see **II.5**): submarine missile [C] / Normandy invasion, 1944 [F,L] or future equivalent, 2000 [L].

Quand le poisson terrestre & aquatique
Par forte vague au gravier sera mis,
Sa forme estrange suave & horrifique,
Par mer aux murs bien tost les ennemis.

I.30

When a storm-bound foreign vessel puts in under peaceful colors at an unknown port, death and pillage result from tardy intelligence: pre-World-War-II France [R].

La nef estrange par le tourment marin
Abourdera pres de port incongneu,
Nonobstant signes de rameau palmerin
Apres mort, pille: bon avis tard venu.

I.31

Multinational war afflicts France for many years: World War II [C,R] / World War III [F] / **Muslim invasion** of France, 2002–2026 [L].

Tant d'ans' les guerres en Gaule dureront,
Oultre la course du Castulon monarque,
Victoire incerte trois grands couronneront
Aigle, coq, lune, lyon, soleil en marque.

I.32

A great ruler bases himself in a tiny spot which subsequently grows: **Napoleon** on Elba and St. Helena [C,H] / future **Henri V** [F] / **Ogmion** or "French **Hercules**," 2025 [L].

Le grand empire sera tost translaté
En lieu petit qui bien tost viendra croistre:
Lieu bien infime d'exigue comté
Ou au milieu viendra poser son sceptre.[11]

I.33

A "great lion" uses imperial forces to besiege an austere city: hoped-for fall of Geneva to Holy Roman Empire [C] / restoration and final defeat of Winston Churchill [R].

Près d'un grant pont de plaine spatieuse,
Le grand lyon par force Cesarées
Fera abbatre hors cité rigoreuse,
Par effroy portes luy seront reserées.

I.34

A bird of prey, variously interpreted, appears shortly before France is attacked: Blitzkrieg 1940 [C] / Peace declarations 1938 [F].

L'oyseau de proye volant a la fenestre
Avant conflit faict aux Francoys pareure
L'un bon prendra, l'un ambigue sinistre,
La partie foyble tiendra par bon augure.

I.35

A young lion overcomes an old one in a triple duel, putting out his eyes in a golden cage and dealing him a cruel death: death of **Henri II**, 1559 [C,F,H,L,R] – the quatrain that made **Nostradamus's** name as a prophet.

Le lyon jeune le vieux surmontera.
En champ bellique par singulier duelle,
Dans caige d'or les yeux luy crevera:
Deux classes une, puis mourir, mort cruelle.

I.36

A king rues not having liquidated his adversary, but consents to far worse, to the mortal detriment of his family: **Guise** brothers, 1588 or Louis XVI [C] / **Napoleon** and Toussaint L'Ouverture, black governor of Haiti [R].

Tard le monarque se viendra repentir
De n'avoir mis à mort son adversaire:
Mais viendra bien à plus hault consentir
Que tout son sang par mort fera defaire.

I.37

Battle commences just before sunset and a fleet, abandoned by those ashore, is sunk: sea-battle and Pope **Pius V**,[12] 1799 [C] / **Muslim invasion of Europe**, 2005 [L] / Armageddon [R].

Ung peu devant que le soleil s'esconce
Conflit donné, grand peuple dubieux:
Proffligés, port marin ne faict responce,
Pont & sepulchre en deux estranges lieux.

I.38

Sun and eagle appear to the victor while the death of the losers helps assure peace: Battle of Waterloo, 1815 (see **I.23**) [C,H] / future Peace Movement [R].

Le Sol & l'aigle au victeur paroistront:
Responce vaine au vaincu l'on asseure,
Par cor ne crys harnoys n'arresteront
Vindicte, paix par mort si acheve à l'heure.

I.39

A leader is strangled in his bed, his defense unread, for his links with a blond heir-elect, while a triumvirate takes over the Empire: the last of the **Condés** [C,F], the comte de Chambord and the successors of Charles X [C] / **Philip II** of Spain [R].

De nuict dans lict le supresme estrangle
Pour trop avoir subjourné, blond eslue:
Par troys l'empire subroge exancle,
A mort mettra carte, pacquet ne leu.

I.40

False spoutings bring new rulers to power in Istanbul, while currency reforms take place in Egypt: **Ottomans** or French Directoire [C] / prelude to **Muslim invasion of Europe**, 1998–9 [L] / new Middle Eastern trade convention [R].

La trombe faulse dissimulant folie
Fera Bisance un changement de loys:
Hystra d'Egypte qui veult que l'on deslie
Edict changeant monnoyes & aloys.

I.41

A maritime city is besieged by night, while family reunions and poisonings take place: **Paris** in World War III [F] / **Marseille** and **Muslim invasion of Europe**, 2005 (?) [L] / siege of Leningrad, 1941 [R].

Siege en cité, & de nuict assaillie,
Peu eschapés: non loing de mer conflict.
Femme de joye, retours filz defaillie
Poison & lettres cachées dans le plic.

I.42

Malign devil-worshipers revive an ancient occult ceremony on April 1st by the Julian calendar (April 10th proto-Gregorian): revival by **Nostradamus** [C] of the conjuration rites described in **Psellus's** *De Daemonibus* [R].

Le dix Kalendes d'Apvril de faict Gotique
Resuscité encor par gens malins:
Le feu estainct, assemblée diabolique
Cherchant les or du d'Amant & Pselyn.[13]

I.43

Just before a new empire takes over, an ancient porphyry pillar is unearthed: **French Revolution**, 1789 [C] / **Muslim invasion of Europe** and/or flight of Pope to France, 2000 [L] / new direction for British Empire [R].

Avant qu'avienne le changement d'empire,
Il aviendra un cas bien merveilleux,
Le champ mué, le pilier de porphyre,
Mis, translaté sus le rochier noilleux.

I.44

A new era of inflation and persecution wipes out the Church: **French Revolution**, 1790–4 [C] / Last Times [F] / far future [L] / Protestant repression of Roman Catholics [R].

En brief seront de retour sacrifices,
Contrevenans seront mis à martyre:
Plus ne seront moines abbés ne novices:
Le miel sera beaucoup plus cher que cire.

I.45

Amid religious conflicts, ancient forms of public entertainment are revived (see **III.40**): C16 religious schisms [C,R].

Secteur de sectes grand preme[14] au delateur:
Beste en theatre, dressé le jeu scenique:
Du faict antique ennobly l'inventeur,
Par sectes monde confus & scismatique.

I.46

Earth-shaking "fire from the sky" falls on southwestern France (see **VIII.2, VI.97, I,87**): World War III [F] / **Muslim invasion** of France, 2013–17 [L] / extraterrestrial close encounters [R].

---

[10] Later editions have *craindra*: *geindra* ("will whimper") is also possible: but *gagnera* (compare It. *guadagnare*) is perhaps more likely.

[11] Dubious rhyme could suggest a misprint at the end of lines 2 or 4.

[12] Presumably Pius VI.

[13] Probable disguise for *Cherchant les ordures du démon Psellin* (see **Astrologer and Mage**).

[14] Later editions have *peine*.

Tout aupres d'Aux, de Lectore & Mirande
Grand feu du ciel en troys nuicts tumbera:
Cause aviendra bien stupende & mirande:
Bien peu apres la terre tremblera.

I.47

After dragging on for some time, the pronouncements issuing from Geneva fail and attract censure: League of Nations, 1920–47 [C,H,R] / Geneva Conventions [F].

Du lac Leman les sermons facheront:
Des jours seront reduicts par les sepmaines,
Puis moys, puis an, puis tous deffailliront,
Les magistrats damneront leurs loys vaines.

I.48

Fulfillment of **Nostradamus**'s prophecies by the year 7000 [C,R] / ditto, by the year 1999 [F] / ditto, by 2828 [L].

Vingt ans du regne de la lune passés
Sept mil ans autre tiendra sa monarchie:
Quand le soleil prendra ses jours lassés
Lors accomplir & mine ma prophetie.

I.49

Expected eastern, "lunar" **invasion of Europe** in "1700" [C] / Chinese invasion 2025 [R] / ditto, preceded by **Russian Revolution** [F].

Beaucoup beaucoup avant telles menées
Ceux d'Orient par la vertu lunaire
L'an mil sept cens feront grand emmenées
Subjugant presque le coing Aquilonaire.

I.50

One born of a watery triad, with Thursday as his feast day, triumphs in the east: third **Antichrist** [C] / World War III and future King of France [F] / General Douglas MacArthur or future equivalent [L] / birth of USA [R].

De l'aquatique triplicité naistra
D'un qui fera le jeudy pour sa feste:
Son bruit, loz, regne, sa puissance croistra,
Par terre & mer aux oriens tempeste.

I.51

With Jupiter and Saturn at the point of Aries, bad times are due to return for France and Italy [R]: **Napoleon** in Italy, 1802 [C,H], and World War III(?) [C] / **Muslim invasion of Europe**, 1999 [F,L].

Chef d'Aries, Juppiter & Saturne,
Dieu eternel quelles mutations!
Puis par long siecle son maling temps retourne,
Gaule & Italie quelles esmotions!

I.52

With Mars and Saturn in Scorpio, a great leader is murdered and the Church persecuted throughout Europe [R]: **Napoleon** and Sultan of Turkey, 1807 [C] / murder of last Pope, 2014 [L].

Les deux malins de Scorpion conjoints,
Le grand seigneur meurtry dedans sa salle:
Peste à l'eglise par le nouveau roy joint,
L'Europe basse & Septentrionale.

I.53

Thanks to new funding, the Church is laid waste: discovery of oil in Near East [C] / **Muslim invasion of Europe** after refinancing, 1999 (see X.72) [L] / Industrial Revolution [R].

Las qu'on verra grand peuple tormenté
Et la loy saincte en totale ruine:
Par autres loyx toute Chrestienté,
Quand d'or d'argent trouve nouvelle mine.

I.54

Two revolutions of Saturn changes kingdoms and dispensations: **French and Russian Revolutions**, 1789 and 1917 [C] / French Revolutions, 1830 and 1848 [F] / Disintegration of USSR, 1990 [H] / New World Order within fifty-nine years of 1999 [L] / Swastika [R].

Deux revolts faits du malin falcigere,
De regne & siecles faict permutation:
Le mobil signe à son endroict si[15] ingere,
Aux deux egaux & d'inclination.

I.55

Great bloodshed, hunger, and atmospheric pollution afflict the region adjoining Iraq: air warfare [C] / future catastrophe [H] / Gulf War, 1991 [L] / cataclysmic destruction in Antipodes [R].

Sous l'opposite climat Babylonique
Grande sera de sang effusion,
Que terre & mer, air, ciel sera inique:
Sectes, faim, regnes, pestes, confusion.

I.56

Changes in the heavens bring future changes of leadership and horrific acts of vengeance [C]: Muslim **Armageddon**, 1999 [F,H] / future world religion [H] / summary of far future [L,R].

Vous verrés tost & tard faire grand change
Horreurs extremes, & vindications:
Que si la lune conduicte par son ange
Le ciel s'approche des inclinations.

I.57

In the course of a great upheaval, a bloody royal head rolls: **French Revolution** and execution of Louis XVI, 1793 [C,F,H] / Japanese betrayal of USA, 1941 [R].

Par grand discord la trombe tremblera.
Accord rompu dressent la teste au ciel:
Bouche sanglante dans le sang nagera:
Au sol la face ointe de laict & miel.

I.58

When a human monster is born, an Italian leader flees on a local feast day: **Napoleon** and death of Louis XVI [C] / return of Bourbons [F].

Tranché le ventre, naistra avec deux testes,
Et quatre bras: quelques ans entier vivra:
Jour qui Alquilloye celebrera ses festes
Foussan, Turin, chief Ferrare fuyvra.

I.59

Exiles, deported to the islands (see II.7), are murdered, the more talkative of them burned to death: Coup d'État of 1857 (?) [C] / Jewish holocaust of World War II [R].

Les exilés deportés dans les isles
Au changement d'ung plus cruel monarque,
Seront meurtrys: & mis deux des[16] scintilles
Qui de parler ne seront estés parques.

---

[15] *s'y.*

[16] Possible misprint for *dans les.*

I.60

A butcherlike Emperor, born near Italy, will cost the Empire dear: birth of **Napoleon**, 1769 [C,F,H,L,R].

Un Empereur naistra pres d'Italie,
Qui a l'Empire sera vendu bien cher:
Diront avecques quels gens il se ralie
Qu'on trouvera moins prince que boucher.

I.61

A new overlord ruins the republic, while the Swabians break their agreement: Franco-Prussian war, 1870–1 (?) [C] / accession of **Napoleon** as First Consul, 1799 [F] / repudiation of France by Sweden, 1804 [R].

La republique miserable infelice
Sera vastée du nouveau magistrat:
Leur grand amas de l'exil malefice
Fera Sueve ravir leur grand contract.

I.62

The very knowledge of letters is lost before the cycle of sun and moon is at an end and the final deluge comes: scholarship lost or vulgarized before 1889 [C] / decline of civilization in far future [L] / literature paves the way for the **French Revolution** [F].

La grande perte las que feront les letres:
Avant le cicle de Latona parfaict:
Feu, grand deluge plus par ignares sceptres
Que de long siecle ne se verra refaict.

I.63

After great disasters, population declines; peace ensues, with safe land, sea, and air travel, before war resumes: Europe, 1945 onward (?) [C,H] / ditto, 1871–1914 [F] / population decrease, peace and prosperity, either 2034 to 2100 (?) or much later [L] / interwar period, 1918–39 [R].

Les fleaux passés diminue le monde
Long temps la paix terres inhabitées
Seur marchera par ciel, terre, mer, & onde:
Puis de nouveau les guerres suscitées.

I.64

The sun is seen at night, half-human pigs and talking animals appear and aerial battles occur: Battle of Britain, 1940 [C,H,L] or similar [R].

De nuit soleil penseront avoir veu
Quand le pourceau demy-homme on verra,
Bruict, chant, bataille, au ciel battre aperceu
Et bestes brutes a parler lon orra.

I.65

A child is born without hands, a huge bolt of lightning strikes, a royal prince is injured at tennis and three are enchained: **French Revolution**, 1789 [F,R].

Enfant sans mains jamais veu si grand foudre:
L'enfant royal au jeu d'oesteuf blessé.
Au puy brises: fulgures alant mouldre:
Trois sous les chaines par le milieu troussés:

I.66

A breathless messenger announces the bombardment of various French towns: spread of **French Revolution** [R].

Celui qui lors portera les nouvelles,
Apres un peu il viendra respirer.
Viviers, Tournon, Montserrant & Pradelles,
Gresle & tempestes les fera souspirer.

I.67

Severe famine, at first intermittent, spreads world-wide: warning of future [C] / ecological **Armageddon** [H] / far-future world wasteland [L] / late C20 [R].

La grand famine que je sens approcher,
Souvent tourner, puis estre universele:
Si grande & longue qu'on viendra arracher
Du bois racine, & l'enfant de mammelle.

I.68

Three ill-guarded innocents are poisoned by drunken executioners [R]: **French Revolution** (?) [C].

O quel horrible & malheureux torment
Troys innocens qu'on viendra à livrer:
Poyson suspecte, mal garde tradiment
Mis en horreur par bourreaux enyvrés.

I.69

After peace and war, a great mountain will be beset by floods that will devastate many countries (see **VIII.16**): future asteroid impact [H] / ruin of Rome by **Muslim invasion**, 1999–2000 [F] / Mount Olympus beset by floods following Middle Eastern earthquakes, 2004 [L].

La grand montaigne ronde de sept estades,
Apres paix, guerre, faim, inundation:
Roulera loing abysmant grands contrades,
Mesmes antiques, & grand fondation.

I.70

On top of other disasters in Persia, the monarchy is undone by excessive religious zeal emanating from France: Ayatollah Khomeini's revolution and deposition of Shah, 1979 [C,F,H,L] / fatal vacillation of Louis XVI [R].

Pluie, faim, guerre en Perse non cessée
La foy trop grande trahira le monarque,
Par la finie en Gaule commencée:
Secret augure pour à ung estre parque.

I.71

A marine fort is fought over by Muslims and Europeans, and **Provence** overrun from Italy (see **I.28** [C,F,L,R]): World War III [F] / **Muslim invasion of Europe**, 2005 and 2019 [L] / World War II [R].

La tour marine troys foys prise & reprise
Par Hespagnolz, barbares, Ligurins:
Marseille & Aix, Arles par ceux de Pise
Vast, feu, fer, pillé Avignon des Thurins.

I.72

The people of **Marseille** are pursued to Lyon, while huge massacres occur in the southwest: World War II [C,H,R] / Muslim Third World War [F] / **Muslim invasion of Europe**, 2005–6 [L].

Du tout Marseille des habitans changée,
Course & poursuitte jusques au pres de Lyon:
Narbon. Tholoze par Bourdeaux outragée:
Tués captifz presque d'un milion.

I.73

After the fall of Spain, France undergoes avoidable fivefold attack from North Africa: France and Libyan revolution, 1969 [C] / **Muslim invasion of Europe** [F], 2013 [L] / expected Muslim *jihad*, 1988 [H].

France à cinq pars par neglect assaillie
Tunys, Argiels esmeus par Persiens,
Leon, Seville, Barcelone faillie
N'aura la classe par les Venitiens.

I.74

Forces led by a "black curly-beard" set out to liberate Greece and attack Turkey, incinerating the enemy: C16 Algerian pirates [C] / **Napoleon**'s Egyptian campaign, 1799 [F] / cremation of Hitler, 1945 [H] / European counterinvasion against Muslims, 2036+ [L] / Mussolini's Italian empire [R].

Apres sejourné vogueront en Epire:
Le grand secours viendra vers Antioche,
Le noir poil crespe tendra fort à l'Empire:
Barbe d'aerain se roustira en broche.

I.75

Two invading armies land at the Marches of Ancona and spread across northern Italy, to the consternation of the defending commander: annexation of Papal States, 1807 / **Muslim invasion of Europe**, 2000 [L] / World War II [R].

Le tyran Siene occupera Savone:
Le fort gaigné tiendra classe marine:
Les deux armées par la marque d'Ancone.
Par effraieur le chef s'en examine.

I.76

A leader with a ferocious name achieves great renown: **Napoleon** [C,F] / future Messiah [R].

D'un nom farouche tel proferé sera,
Que les troys seurs auront fato le nom:
Puis grand peuple par langue & faict duira
Plus que nul autre aura bruit & renom.

I.77

Between Gibraltar and Cape Roche (?) a man is killed by a horse bite and the English raise a black sail: Battle of Trafalgar, 1805 [C,H] / **Napoleon** on St. Helena [F] / Greek myth of Theseus [R].

Entre deux mers dressera promontoire
Que puis mourra par le mords du cheval:
Le sien Neptune pliera voyle noire,
Par Calpre & classe aupres de Rocheval.

I.78

An idiot heir is born to an old leader, while France's chief terrorizes his sister and the military take over: Marshal Pétain, 1940 (?) [C,F] / Louis XV, 1715–74 [R].

D'un chef viellard naistra sens hebete,
Degenerant par savoir & par armes
Le chef de Françe par sa sœur redouté:
Champs divisés, concedés aux gendarmes.

I.79

Murderous quarrels and disputes rack southwestern France: World War III(?) [F] / civil war in southwest after liberation of France from Muslims, 2026 [L].

Bazaz, Lectore, Condon, Ausch, & Agine
Esmeus par loys, querele & monopole.
Car Bourd. Thoulouze Bay.[17] metra en ruine
Renouveler voulant leur tauropole.

I.80

Saturn brings thunder in Burgundy, an animal monster and four months' bloodshed: World War III [F].

De la sixiesme claire splendeur celeste
Viendra tonner si fort en la Bourgoigne:
Puis naistra monstre de treshideuse beste.
Mars, apvril, May, Juing grand charpin & rongne.

I.81

Nine humans are set apart and on their own, their fate sealed, and "K," "Th," and "L" banished: pioneer astronauts harmed [C] / *Challenger* disaster, 1986 [H] / ditto, or future space disaster [L] / US Supreme Court and Soviet Politburo [R].

D'humain troupeau neuf seront mis à part
De jugement & conseil separés:
Leur sort sera divisé en depart
ΚΥπ, θhita and λambda [18] mors, bannis esgarés.

I.82

When tree trunks, smeared with red, tremble in the south wind, Austria trembles before a mighty host: Austrian revolution, 1918 [C] / World War III [F] / Austrian uprising, 1934 [R].

Quand les colomnes de bois grande tremblée
D'Auster conducte couverte de rubriche
Tant vuidera dehors grand assemblée,
Trembler Vienne & le païs d'Austriche.

I.83

With Saturn in Aries or badly aspected with Mars, occupying powers share out the spoils amid horrors in Italy and Greece: Mussolini's forces [C] / **Muslim invasion of Europe**, 2002 [L] / extraterrestrial landings [R].

La gent estrange divisera butins,
Saturne en Mars son regard furieux:
Horrible strage[19] aux Tosquans & Latins,
Grecs, qui seront à frapper curieux.

I.84

With the moon obscured, a lord stabs his brother in the darkness: Comte d'Artois and Duc de Berry, 1820 [C,H].

Lune obscurcie aux profondes tenebres,
Son frere passe de couleur ferrugine:
Le grand caché long temps sous les latebres,
Tiedera[20] fer dans la plaie sanguine.

I.85

A king is angered by a lady's response, while a lord fatally double-crosses his brothers: **Henri III** and **Catherine de Médicis** [C,H] / abdication of Edward VIII, and Kennedy brothers [R].

Par la response de dame, roy troublé:
Ambassadeurs mespriseront leur vie:
Le grand ses freres contrefera doublé
Par deus mourront ire, haine, envie.

---

17 *Carcassonne, Bordeaux, Toulouse, Bayonne.*

18 i.e. the Greek letters *kappa* (k), *theta* (th) and *lambda* (l), as spelled out in later editions.

19 Should probably read *estrange*, as in line 1: such echoes within verses are typical of Nostradamus: otherwise possibly *oultrage*.

20 Read as *tiendera*.

I.86

A great queen shows manly courage in defeat, riding across a river naked, though outraging her religion: escape of Mary Queen of Scots, 1568 [C,H] / Marie-Antoinette, 1793 [F] / women's movement [R].

La grande royne quant se verta[21] vaincu,
Fera exces de masculin couraige:
Sus cheval, fluve passera toute nue,
Suite par fer: à foy fera oultrage.

I.87

Earth-shaking fire from the world's center burns around a "new city," and two "rocks" make war on each other, staining a river red: Eruption of Mount St. Helens, Oregon, 1980 [C] / destruction of New York, 1994–6 [H] / Muslim assault on Villeneuve-sur-Lot, 2017 [L] / World War III, and nuclear holocaust [R].

Ennosigée feu du centre de terre
Fera trembler au tour de cité neufve:
Deux grands rochiers long temps feront la guerre
Puis Arethusa rougira nouveau fleuve.

I.88

Epilepsy strikes a prince before his marriage, sapping his support and leading to his death at the hands of shaven-heads: troubles and death of Charles I [C,H] / collapse of **Napoleon**ic Empire [F] / **Napoleon** [R].

Le divin mal surprendra le grand prince
Un peu devant aura femme espousée,
Son puy[22] & credit à un coup viendra mince,
Conseil mourra pour la teste rasée.

I.89

Spanish invaders inflict bloodshed on northern France, while a rescuing armada approaches: Peninsular War, 1808–14 [C] / **Muslim invasion of Europe**, 2020–1 [L].

Tous ceux de Ilerde seront dedans Mosselle,
Metants à mort tous ceux de Loyre & Seine:
Secour marin viendra pres d'haulte velle
Quand Hespagnols ouvrira toute vaine.

I.90

Southwestern France rises in revolt when a monster is born near Orgon: **Muslim invasion of Europe** [F] / civil war in southwest France, 2026 [L].

Bourdeaux, Poitiers, au son de la campane'
A grande classe ira jusques à l'Angon,
Contre Gauloys sera leur tramontane,
Quand monstres hydeux naistra pres de Orgon.

I.91

Before the sky clears and war starts, the gods warn humanity that it alone is to blame for it: future war from China [C] / pacifist myths [F] / war of far future (compare **III,5, III,4, III.34, I.17**) [L].

Les dieux feront aux humains apparence
Ce quils seront auteurs de grand conflit:
Avant ciel veu serain espée & lance,
Que vers main gauche sera plus grand afflit.[23]

I.92

Peace does not last, and pillage and rebellion produce some 300,000 dead: Franco-Prussian War, 1870 [C,H] / World War III [F] / revolt of southwest France, 2032 [L] / Pearl Harbor, 1941 [R].

Sous un la paix par tout sera clamée,
Main non long temps pille & rebellion,
Par refus ville, terre & mer entamée,
Morts & captifz le tiers d'un milion.

I.93

With England and France at loggerheads, and Castile and Galicia (?) disinclined to interfere, northern Italy trembles: **Napoleon**'s Italian campaign, 1795 [C] / World War III [F] / **Muslim invasion of Europe**, 2000 [L] / World War II [R].

Terre Italique pres des monts tremblera,
Lyon & coq non trop confederés,
En lieu de peur l'un l'autre saidera[24]
Seul Castulon & Celtes moderés.

I.94

Although the Muslim tyrant is killed at sea, liberty remains elusive: death of Admiral Ali Pasha at Lepanto, 1571 [C] / future Muslim war [F] / Margaret Thatcher honored after Falklands War, 1982 [R].

Au port Selin le tyran mis à mort
La liberté non pourtant recouvrée:
Le nouveau Mars par vindicte & remort,
Dame par force de frayeur honorée.

I.95

The twin son of a monk and a nun achieves great fame.

Devant monstier trouvé enfant besson
D'heroic sang de moine & vestutisque:
Son bruit par secte langue & puissance son
Qu'on dira fort elevé le vopisque.[25]

I.96

An official destroyer of churches is persuaded to attack buildings rather than people: religious revival [C] / rejection of future oriental religious leader [H] / **Muslim invasion of Europe**, 2017–21 [L].

Celuy qu'aura la charge de destruire
Temples, & sectes, changés par fantasie,
Plus aux rochiers qu'aux vivans viendra nuire
Par langue ornée d'oreilles ressasies.

I.97

A king, dreaming of bloodshed, achieves more by soft speech: death of **Henri III** [C,H] / United Nations [R].

Ce que fer flamme n'a sceu parachever,
La doulce langue au conseil viendra faire.
Par repos, songe, le roy fera resver.
Plus l'ennemi en feu, sang militaire.

I.98

Having lost 5,000 of his huge foreign army in Crete and Greece, a general eludes capture in a "marine barn": **Napoleon**'s flight from Egypt, 1798–9 [C] / **Napoleon** on St. Helena [F] / Sino-Soviet war [R].

Le chef qu'aura conduit peuple infini
Loing de son ciel, de meurs & langue estrange:
Cinq mil en Crete & Thessale fini,
Le chef fuiant sauvé en marine grange.

I.99

The alliance of a king with two others brings dire consequences for the children of Narbonne: **Henri V** of France [F,L] / **Napoleon** [R].

Le grand monarque que fera compaignie
Avecq deux roys unis par amitié:
O quel souspir fera la grand mesnie,
Enfans Narbon, à l'entour quel pitié!

I.100

Over Dole and Tuscany a gray bird of peace is seen, presaging the death of a leader and the end of a war: Comte de Chambord, 1846 [C] / US President Franklin D. Roosevelt [R].

Long temps au ciel sera veu gris oiseau
Aupres de Dole & de Tousquane terre,
Tenant au bec un verdoiant rameau,
Mourra tost grand, & finira la guerre.

CENTURY II

Transliterated from **Bonhomme**'s original 1555 edition.

II.1

A huge British invasion-force descends on southwest France and a "lunar" or Muslim port amid freezing weather: World War I Dardanelles campaign, 1915 [C,H] / future **Muslim invasion of Europe** [F] / European counterinvasion against Muslims and attack on Genoa, 2025 [L] / World War II D-Day, 1944 [R].

Vers Aquitaine par insults Britanniques,
De par eux mesmes grandes incursions
Pluies, gelées feront terroirs iniques,
Port Selyn fortes fera invasions.

II.2

A "blue-head" attacks and hangs a "white-head" when news of prisoner numbers arrives (see **IX.73**): Persian Ayatollah's future dealings with France [C] / **French Revolution** and end of *Ancien Régime*, 1792 [F] / future Iranian Shiite quarrels with Sunnis [H] / **Muslim invasion of Europe**, 2017 [L] / death of Mussolini, 1945 [R].

La teste blue fera la teste blanche
Autant de mal que France a fait leur bien.
Mort à l'anthenne grand pendu sus la branche,
Quand prins des siens le roy dira combien.

II.3

While Rhodes and Genoa are starving, solar heat enables people to collect the Black Sea's fish ready-cooked (see **V.98**): Aegean atomic explosion [C] / World War III [F] / future asteroid impact [H] / **Muslim invasion of Europe**, 2013 [L] / Mediterranean volcanic eruptions, 1944–51 [R].

Pour la chaleur solaire sus la mer
De Negrepont les poissons demis cuits:
Les habitans les viendront entamer
Quand Rod.[1] & Gennes leur faudra le biscuit.

---

[21] Misprint for *verra*.

[22] *appui*.

[23] Abbreviation of *affliction*.

[24] *s'aidera* in later editions.

[25] "*Dominus vobiscum.*"

[1] *Rhodes.*

II.4

The Mediterranean coast from Monaco to Sicily is plundered and laid waste by Muslim raiders: unidentified barbarian attackers [C,R] / **Muslim invasion of Europe**, 2000–7 [L].

Depuis Monech jusques au pres de Secile
Toute la plage demourra desolée,
Il ny aura fauxbourg, cité, ne vile
Que par Barbares pillée soit & vollée.

II.5

Submarine-borne invaders descend on Italy (see **I.29**): Third **Antichrist**, 1996 (?) [C] / **Muslim invasion of Europe**, 1996 [H] / ditto, 2000 [L] / World War II, North African campaign [R].

Qu'en dans poisson, fer & letre enfermée
Hors sortira qui puys fera la guerre,
Aura par mer sa classe bien ramée
Apparoissant pres de Latine terre.

II.6

Two cities suffer unheard-of calamities of famine, plague, war and eviction: Hiroshima and Nagasaki, 1945 [C,H] / **Muslim invasion of Europe** [F] / ditto at Narbonne and **Carcassonne**, 2017 [L] / former Berlin Wall [R].

Aupres des portes & dedans deux cités
Seront deux fleaux onques n'aperceu un tel,
Faim dedans peste, de fer hors gens boutés,
Crier secours au grand Dieu immortel.

II.7

Among the starving island exiles (see **I.59**) a child with two teeth is born and a new dispensation looms: French penal colonies [C] / birth of **Antichrist** [F] / British maltreatment of Australian aborigines [R].

Entre plusieurs aux isles deportés
L'un estre nay à deux dens en la gorge
Mourront de faim les arbres esbrotés
Pour eux neuf roy novel edict leur forge.

II.8

Former Roman Catholic traditions are abandoned as a return is made to religious first principles: C16 Huguenots [C,R] / new world order, 2037 [L].

Temples sacrés prime façon Romaine
Rejeteront les goffes fondements,
Prenant leur loys premieres & humaines,
Chassant, non tout, des saints les cultements.

II.9

A thin man rules for nine years before falling ill, while his subjects fall prey to a more gracious figure: AIDS [C] / Louis XVI [R].

Neuf ans le regne le maigre en paix tiendra,
Puis il cherra en soif si sanguinaire:
Pour luy grand peuple sans foy & loy mourra,
Tué par un beaucop plus de bonnaire.

II.10

During a worrying new era that finally settles everything, aristocracy and Church are both transformed and social classes mingled (see *Sixain* 1): **French Revolution**, 1790, [R] or USSR [C] / C20 social regimentation [H].

Avant long temps le tout sera range
Nous esperons un siecle bien senestre:
L'estat des masques & des seulz bien changé
Peu trouveront qu'a son rang veuille estre.

II.11

The second-in-line succeeds, achieving a bitter glory by exiling his own children: **Napoleon** [C,H] / Lord of L'Aisnier [R].

Le prochain fils de l'asnier parviendra
Tant eslevé jusques au regne des fors,
Son aspre gloire un chascun la craindra,
Mais ses enfans du regne getés hors.

II.12

New spiritual cults that despise traditional religion are abolished by a great king: **French Revolution** and suppression of clergy, 1790 [C] / **Henri V** [F] and new world order, 2037 [L].

Yeux clos, ouverts d'antique fantasie
L'habit des seulz seront mis à neant,
Le grand monarque chastiera leur frenesie:[2]
Ravir des temples le tresor par devant.

II.13

The faithful are reborn and God is finally revealed: Nostradamus's belief in transmigration (see **Almanach** for 1966, July 1st)[C] / Last Judgment, 2828 [L].

Le corps sans ame plus n'estre en sacrifice:
Jour de la mort mis en nativité.
L'esprit divin fera l'ame felice
Voiant le verbe en son eternité.

II.14

Those on the Loire watch the approach of Her Serene Greatness: regency of **Catherine de Médicis**, 1559–89 [C] / Falklands War, 1982 [R].

A. Tours, Jean,[3] garde seront yeux penetrants
Descouvriront de loing la grand sereyne,
Elle & sa suitte au port seront entrants
Combat, poulsés, puissance souveraine.

II.15

Shortly before a monarch is killed, with a comet aloft in Argo during May/June, the economy collapses and northern Italy is cut off (see **VI.6**): death of Pope **John Paul II** [H,F,L] / Middle Eastern unrest [R].

Un peu devant monarque trucidé?[4]
Castor Pollux en nef, astre crinite.
L'erain publiq par terre & mer vuidé
Pise, Ast, Ferrare, Turin, terre interdicte.

II.16

Amid aerial bombardments and great bloodshed, new powers from the north take over in Italy: World War II defeat of Mussolini [C,R] / recapture of Italy from Muslims, 2028 [L].

Naples, Palerme, Secille, Syracuses
Nouveaux tyrans, fulgures feuz celestes:
Force de Londres, Gand, Brucelles, & Suses
Grand hecatombe, triumphe, faire festes.

II.17

Amid severe winter weather, with the army in southwest. France, a leader arrives incognito: preparations for European reinvasion of Spain, 2033–4 [L] / flood at Tivoli [R].

Le camp du temple de la vierge vestale,
Non esloigné d'Ethne & monts Pyrenées:
Le grand conduict est caché dens la male
North. getés[5] fluves & vignes mastinées.

II.18

Two armies are held up by rain and falls of pumice (?): death of the last Valois children of **Catherine de Médicis** [C] / collapse of Warsaw Pact [F] / World War II D-Day, 1944 [R].

Nouvelle & pluie subite impetueuse
Empeschera subit deux exercites.
Pierre, ciel, feuz, faire la mer pierreuse,
La mort de sept terre & marin subites.

II.19

Incomers take over a virtually empty country and recommence farming: foundation of Israel, 1948 [F,H] / reoccupation of France after **Muslim invasion**, 2026 [L] / Normandy landings, 1944 [R].

Nouveaux venus, lieu basti sans defense
Occuper place par lors inhabitable.
Prez, maisons, champs, villes prendre a plaisance,
Faim, peste, guerre, arpen long labourable.

II.20

Marked or mutilated captives are paraded before a monarch and his family: **Henri II** and captured Huguenots, 1557 [C] / **French Revolution** [F] / Nazi enslavement during World War II [R].

Freres & seurs en divers lieux captifs
Se trouveront passer pres du monarque,
Les contempler ses rameaux ententifs,
Desplaisant voir menton, front, nez, les marques.

II.21

On the Black Sea an ambassador is repulsed and his ships impounded: incident in Greek waters [C] / British rejection of Rudolf Hess's World War II mission, 1941 [R].

L'embassadeur envoyé par biremes
A mi chemin d'incogneuz repoulses:
De sel renfort viendront quatre triremes,
Cordes & chaines en Negrepont troussés.

II.22

A northern military force sets out for the Middle East: US takeover of Persian Gulf [C] / Warsaw Pact invasion, World War III [F] / reinvasion of Middle East, 2037 [L] / Atlantis [R].

Le camp Asop d'Eurotte[6] partira,
S'adjoignant proche de l[']isle submergée:
D'Arton classe phalange pliera,
Nombril du monde plus grand voix subrogée.

II.23

Birds are chased away by birds, the enemy pushed back beyond the river and a bird seen carrying an arrow (see **II.44**): government hangers-on [R].

---

[2] Two syllables too many: should presumably read *Le grand monarq. chastier leur frenesie.*

[3] Later editions have *Gien: Joue-les-Tours* is conceivably more likely.

[4] Misprint for comma.

---

[5] Probable misprint for *gelés.*

[6] Later editions have *Europe.*

Palais, oyseaux, par oyseau dechassé,
Bien tost apres le prince prevenu,
Combien qu'hors fleuve enemis repoulsé
Dehors saisi trait d'oyseau soustenu.

II.24

Armies frantically cross the lower Danube, and a leader is captured as the Germans approach the Rhine: Hitler (see **Nostradamus Dictionary**, under **Hister**) and World War II C / east–west link-up on Danube, 1945, and fall of Hitler F / defeat of Hitler H / **Muslim invasion** of Hungary, 2000 L / death of Hitler R.

Bestes farouches de faim fluves tranner:
Plus part du camp encontre Hister sera,
En caige de fer le grand fera treisner,
Quand Rin enfant Germain observera.

II.25

Betrayed by its foreign garrison in hope of political advantage, a fortress is taken and all France outraged: surrender of Metz to Germans, 1870 C,F / arrival of **extraterrestrials** R.

La garde estrange trahira forteresse:
Espoir & umbre de plus hault mariage.
Garde deceu, fort prinse dans la presse,
Loyre, Son. Rosne, Gar.7 à mort oultrage.

II.26

Because of a city's misplaced favor, northern Italy is overrun and put to the sword: **Muslim invasion of Europe** F / reinvasion of Muslim-occupied Italy, 2026–8 L.

Pour la faveur que la cité fera
Au gran qui tost perdra champ de bataille,
Fuis le rang Po, [ ]8 Thesin versera
De sang, feuz, morts, noyes de coup de taille.

II.27

Heavenly forces are baulked in their efforts while a secret remains concealed from passers-by: Nostradamus's original tomb C / **Fontbrune's** own book (!) F.

Le divin verbe sera du ciel frapé,
Qui ne pourra proceder plus avant.
Du reserant le secret estoupé
Qu'on marchera par dessus & devant.

II.28

The last-but-one to bear the prophet's name uses Monday as a rest day from his incessant travels to free a great people from tribute: Mahomet (?) C / papal successor of **John Paul II** F / future world religious leader, 1979–2000 H / Pope **John Paul II** himself L / demented future leader and new long weekend R.

Le penultime du surnom du prophete
Prendra Diane pour son jour & 9 repos:
Loing vaguera par frenetique teste,
Et delivrant un grand peuple d'impos.

II.29

An eastern leader flies across Italy to France, striking all with his rod: Third **Antichrist** C / ditto and **Muslim invasion of Europe** F,L and/or Ayatollah Khomeini L / future world religious leader H / nuclear bombardment of France from beyond Urals R.

L'oriental sortira de son siege,
Passer les monts Apennins, voir la Gaule:
Transpercera du ciel les eaux & neige:
Et un chascun frapera de sa gaule.

II.30

A North African invader of the stamp of Hannibal inflicts almost unprecedented terror on Europe: North African leader destroys Catholic religion C / **Muslim invasion of Europe** F, 2006+ L / **Antichrist** H / oil-rich kingdoms terrorize Italy with nuclear weapons R.

Un qui les dieux d'Annibal infernaulx
Fera renaistre, effrayeur des humains
Onq' plus d'horreurs ne plus pire journaux
Qu'avint viendra par Babel aux Romains.

II.31

Long rains and floods afflict Italy: Capua C / Spanish rape of Italy R.

En Campanie Cassilin. sera tant
Qu'on ne verra que d'eaux les champs couverts
Devant apres la pluye de long temps
Hors mis les arbres rien l'on verra de vert.

II.32

The former Yugoslavia is knee-deep in blood and "milky rain," while pestilence breaks out in Italy and a monster is born in Ravenna: future rain of frogs C / Russian invasion of World War III F / **Muslim invasion of Europe**, 2000 L/ Dalmatia, Basel and Czechoslovakia R.

Laict, sang, grenoilles10 escoudre en Dalmatie
Conflit donné, peste pres de Balenne:
Cry sera grand par toute Esclavonie
Lors naistra monstre pres & dedans Ravenne.

II.33

A huge human disaster occurs on the Adige River, as well as on the Garonne when forces invade from Italy: **Muslim invasion of Europe**, 2000 L.

Par le torrent qui descent de Verone,
Par lors qu'au Po guindera11 son entrée:
Un grand naufraige, & non moins en Garonne
Quant ceux de Gênes marcheront leur contrée.

II.34

Pride causes a feud between two brothers that harms France: Duc de Mayenne's attempted coup d'état, 1594 (?) / disastrous future Arab-Jewish conference F / beginning of European civil war, 2032 L.

L'ire insensée du combat furieux
Fera à table par freres le feu luire
Les12 despartir mort, blessé, curieux:
Le fier duelle viendra en France nuire.

II.35.

Two fatal fires break out at night near two rivers at the behest of a priest on December 22nd: great fire of **Lyon**, 1582 (?) C / death of Pope **John Paul II** F.

Dans deux logis de nuit le feu prendra,
Plusieurs dedans estoufês & rostis.
Pres de deux fleuves pour seur il aviendra
Sol, l'Arq, & Caper tous seront amortis.

II.36

A prophet's warnings of deception are delivered to a tyrant whose crimes later trouble him: Nostradamus in **Paris** (?) C / **Napoleon's** annexation of Church F / Ernst Krafft and Hitler H.

Du grand Prophete les letres seront prinses
Entre les mains du tyrant deviendront:
Frauder son roy seront ses entreprinses,
Mais ses rapines bien tost le troubleront.

II.37

Murder, disease and famine afflict the would-be rescuers of a besieged fortress: battles over **Port-de-Bouc**, 2005, 2019 or 2025–6 L / biological warfare R.

De ce grand nombre que lon envoyera
Pour secourir dans le fort assiegés,
Peste & famine tous les devorera
Hors mis septante qui seront profligés.

II.38

A barely successful reconciliation of leaders condemns many: Hitler-Stalin pact, 1939–41 C,H,R / Nuremberg trials, 1945, and Cold War F / end of European civil war, 2032–3 L.

Des condemnés sera fait un grand nombre
Quand les monarques seront conciliés:
Mais a l'un d'eux viendra si malencombre
Que guerres ensemble ne seront raliés.

II.39

A "schoolhouse republic," founded the previous year by European powers, collapses on the outbreak of war in Italy: outbreak of World War II, 1939 C / war between France, Germany, and Spain, 1795 F / collapse of European Union, 2000 L / nuclear attack on **Paris** just before World War III R.

Un an devant le conflit Italique,
Germain,13 Gaulois, Hespaignols pour le fort:
Cherra l'escolle maison de republique,
Òu, hors mis peu, seront suffoqués morrs.14

II.40

Renewed naval warfare breaks out after a year, with fires and "strange creatures" involved: World War II submarine warfare C,H / World Wars II and III F / Afro-European sea-battles, 2005–6 L / nuclear missiles and World War III R.

Un peu apres non point longue intervalle.
Par mer & terre sera fait grand tumulte,
Beaucoup plus grande sera pugne navale,
Feus, animaux, qui plus feront d'insulte.

---

7 Abbreviation for *Saône, Rhône, Garonne.*

8 Syllable missing: possibly &.

9 Probably stands here for *de.*

10 Second edition has *genoilles,* "knees."

11 Read as *guidera* or (more likely) *gagnera* (compare **I.28**).

12 Possibly *lesé.*

13 Read as *Germains.*

14 Misprint for *morts.*

II.41

A comet bright as the sun, and the baying of the "Great Mastiff," mark a Pope's change of abode: papal flight from World War III [F], 1993 [C] / flight of **John Paul II** in face of **Muslim invasion of Europe**, 2000 [L] / installation of **John Paul II** [R].

La grand' estoile par sept jours bruslera,
Nuée[15] fera deux soleils apparoir:
Le gros mastin toute nuit hurlera
Quand grand pontife changera de terroir.

II.42

Animals lick the blood of a fearless tyrant found dead in another's bed: death of Robespierre, 1794 [C,R].

Coq, chiens & chats de sang seront repeus,
Et de la plaie du tyrant trouvé mort,
Au lict d'un autre jambes & bras rompus,
Qui n'avoit peur mourir de cruel mort.

II.43

A comet marks the outbreak of war between three great leaders and the landing of "serpents" in Italy: Triple Alliance, 1881, or early C20 Triple Entente [C] / World War III [F] / future Arab terrorist attack on Italy [H] / **Muslim invasion of Europe**, 2000 [L] / Halley's comet, 1985 [R].

Durant l'estoyle chevelue apparente,
Les trois grands princes seront fait ennemis,
Frappes du ciel, paix terre tremulente.
Po, Timbre undants, serpant sus le bort mis.

II.44

An eagle above a noisy battlefield is chased off by other birds as a lady faints (see II.23): **Napoleon**'s retreat from Moscow, 1912 [C] / Napoleon III's defeat at Sedan, 1870 [F] / Arabs chase off US aircraft [R].

L'aigle pousée en tour des pavillons
Par autres oyseaux d'entour sera chassée,
Quand bruit des cymbres, tubes & sonaillons
Rendront le sens de la dame insensée.

II.45

With celestial bloodshed, Heaven bewails the death of an androgyne, even though vital aid results: far future contact with extraterrestrials [L] / events following death of Ayatollah Khomeini in 1980s [R].

Trop le ciel pleure l'Androgyn procrée,
Pres de ce ciel sang humain respandu,
Par mort trop tarde grand peuple recrée
Tard & tost vient le secours attendu.

II.46

A new and greater cycle is heralded by disasters and a major comet: World War III [F,H] in 1990s [C] / new era starting in 2828 [L] / future technology and warfare [R].

Apres grand trouble[16] humain, plus grands'aprest(e)
Le grand mouteur les siecles renouvele.
Pluie, sang, laict, famine, fer, & peste
Au ciel veu, feu courant longue estincele.

---

15 Second edition has *Nuict* – possibly an author's correction.

16 Later editions have *troche* – possibly a correction by the seer (see **Nostradamus Dictionary**).

II.47

Having overrun much of the world with his hordes, a great enemy leader is poisoned, blaming his impending death on a variety of unlikely agents: events during World War III [F] / assassination of Muslim overlord, 2026 [L] / future abolition of war and poverty [R].

L'ennemy grant viel dueil meurt de poison:
Les souverains par infinis subjuguez:
Pierres plouvoir, cachés sous la toison:
Par mort articles en vain sont allegués.

II.48

A great army crosses the mountains, armed with **chemical** weapons, while a leader is hanged: 2193 (?) [C] / **Muslim invasion** of France via the Pyrenees, 2017 [L].

La grand copie que passera les monts.
Saturne en l'Arq tournant du poisson Mars
Venins cachés sous testes de saulmons:
Leur chief pendu à fil de polemars.

II.49

A primary confederacy, already in control of Rhodes and Istanbul and in quest of further territory, has its eyes set on Malta: Ottoman Empire [C] / Balkan wars, 1908–19 / **Muslim invasion of Europe**, 1999–2000 [L].

Les conseilliers du premier monopole,
Les conquerants seduits pour la Melite:
Rodes, Bisance pour leurs exposant pole:
Terre faudra les poursuivants de fuite.[17]

II.50

Fighting based on ancient feuds breaks out in Belgium once Langres is under siege: Netherlands uprising, 1568 [C] / aftermath of **Muslim invasion of Europe**, 2025 (?) [L].

Quant ceux d'Ainault, de Gand et de Brucelles
Verront à Langres le siege devant mis
Derrier leurs flancz seront guerres crueles,
La plaie antique fera pis qu'ennemis.

II.51

"Lightnings" in London strike six out of twenty-three of a Just One's family (see **II.53** below), while an ancient lady falls and the faithful are killed: Great Fire of London, 1666 [C,H,L,R].

Le sang du juste à Londres fera faute
Bruslés par fouldres de vingt trois les six.
La dame antique cherra de place haute:
De mesme secte plusieurs seront occis.

II.52

Two spring earthquakes hit Greece and western Turkey with tidal waves (see **III.3**) while war continues: events during World War III [F] / England and Holland hit by future floods [H] / seismic events during **Muslim invasion of Europe**, 2004 [L].

Dans plusieurs nuits la terre tremblera:
Sur le prinstemps deux effors [feront[18]] suite:
Corynthe, Ephese aux deux mers nagera:
Guerre s'esmeut par deux vaillans de luite.

---

17 Possible misprint for *suite*

18 Two syllables missing: possible omitted word.

II.53

A maritime city's Great **Plague** ceases only when a Just One's family, their fate studiedly ignored by a great lady, is avenged (see **II.51** above): Great **Plague** of London, 1665 [C,H,L] as retribution for execution of Charles I, 1649 [R] / **Plague** of **Marseille**, 1720 [F].

La grande peste de cité maritime
Ne cessera que mort ne soit vengée
Du juste sang, par pris damne sans crime
De la grand dame par feincte n'outraigée.

II.54

Alien invaders trouble a depopulated Rome by sea, while a local girl is insecurely imprisoned: **Muslim invasion of Europe**, 2000 or 2014 (?) [L] / Japan attacks Pearl Harbor, 1941 [R].

Par gent estrange, & Romains loingtaine
Leur grand cité apres eaue fort troublee,
Fille sans main, trop different domaine,
Prins chief, sarreure n'avoir esté riblée.

II.55

An undervalued leader eventually excels himself in the face of attackers from the Adriatic by stabbing a "proud one" at a banquet: Duc de Mayenne's attempted coup d'état, 1594 [C,H] / **Muslim invasion of Europe**, 2000 (?) [L].

Dans le conflit le grand qui peu valloyt,
A son dernier fera cas merveilleux:
Pendant qu'Hadrie verra ce qu'il falloyt,
Dans le banquet pongnale l'orguilleux.

II.56

One who has survived plague and war is struck by lightning and dies in a well, while a priest dies in a shipwreck: last hours of Hitler [R].

Que peste & glaive n'a peu seu definer
Mort dans le puys, sommet du ciel frappé.
L'abbé mourra quand verra ruiner
Ceux du naufraige l'escueil voulant grapper.

II.57

The fall of a great wall presages a war, while a deformed leader dies suddenly and a river bank is red with blood (see **VIII.2**): John F. Kennedy and Cuba crisis [C] / storming of Bastille, 1789 [F,H] / **Muslim invasion** of southwest France, 2019 (?) [L] / Sino-Soviet war and destruction of Great Wall of China [R].

Avant conflit le grand mur tumbera:
Le grand à mort, mort trop subite & plainte:
Nay imparfaict: la plus part nagera:
Aupres du fleuve de sang la terre tainte.

II.58

A traitor who can speak aggressively, but actually do nothing, is rushed to a fortified port with his first-born by moonlight: **Napoleon** (?) [C] / Louis XVII's escape from Temple prison, 1793 [F] / kidnapping of Lindbergh baby, 1932 [R]

Sans pied ne main par dend ayguë & forte
Par globe au fort deporc[19] & laisné nay:
Pres du portail desloyal se transporte
Silene luit, petit grand emmené.

---

19 Probable misprint for *de port*, as in later editions.

II.59

With the French fleet supported by the British, **Provence** is laid waste by marauding troops, while Narbonne is attacked with missiles: failed prediction re Turks [C] / World War III [F] / **Muslim invasion** of France, 2005–6 or 2017 [L] / French and British invade France [R].

Classe Gauloyse par apuy de grand garde
Du grand Neptune, & ses tridents souldars
Rousgée[20] Provence pour sostenir grand bande:
Plus Mars Narbon. par javelotz & dards.

II.60

After a greedy, duplicitous eastern regime breaks its promises, fleets are scattered and disaster reigns from Portugal to Palestine: troubles in Africa [C] / Muslim duplicity and World War III [F] / **Muslim invasion of Europe**, 1999–2034 [L] / aftermath of war [R].

La foy Punicque en Orient rompue
Gang. Jud.[21] & Rosne, Loyre & Tag.[22] changeront,
Quand du mulet la faim sera repue,
Classe espargie, sang & corps nageront.

II.61

Invading British liberators led by a member of France's royal house are welcomed on the west coast of France, as a waterside fortress is stormed: reinvasion of Muslim-occupied France, 2025 (?) [L] / French civil wars [R].

Euge Tamins, Gironde & la Rochele:
O sang Troien! Mars au port de la flesche
Derrier le fleuve au fort mise l'eschele,
Pointes a feu grand meurtre sus la bresche.

II.62

The death of one "Mabus" precipitates a wholesale slaughter, followed by bloody vengeance and famine marked by a comet: Third Antichrist [C] 1985–2000 [H] / **Muslim invasion of Europe**, 1999+ (see **X.72**) [L].

Mabus[23] puis tost alors mourra, viendra
De gens & bestes une horrible defaite:
Puis tout à coup la vengence on verra
Cent, main,[24] soif, faim, quand courra la comete.

II.63

As Ivry becomes another Parma, neither French nor Italians are so much defeated as forced to accept that resistance would be fatal: Duke of Parma, 1590 [C] / **Muslim invasion of Europe**, 2000–22 [L] / World War II sinking of French fleet in Bordeaux [R].

---

[20] Possible misprint: later editions have *ronsgé* or *rongée*.

[21] Abbreviation for *Gange judaïque* – i.e. the Jordan, the Jews' holy river.

[22] Abbreviation for *Tagus*.

[23] Until November 1995 Raymond E. Mabus was the US ambassador to Riyadh, Saudi Arabia – a political appointee since returned to Mississippi, and thus a potential future "roving ambassador" to the Arab world.

[24] Typical Nostradamian blind for *sang humain*.

Gaulois, Ausone bien peu subjugera:
Po, Marne, & Seine fera Perme l'vrie[25]
Qui le grand mur contre eux dressera
Du moindre au mur le grand perdra la vie.

II.64

Switzerland loses hope of resupply as the south of France is cut off by sea: Cévennes revolt after Edict of Nantes, 1685 [C] / destruction of Geneva and defeat of Muslim invaders [F] / **Muslim invasion of Europe**, 2005+ [L].

Seicher de faim, de soif gent Genevoise
Espoir prochain viendra au deffaillir,
Sur point tremblant sera loy Gebenoise.
Classe au grand port ne se peult acuilir.

II.65

Financial disaster strikes northern Italy and western Europe as the Vatican is sacked: 2044 [C] / World War III [F] / events surrounding **Muslim invasion of Europe**, 2000 [L] / Spain and the House of Savoy [R].

Le parc enclin grande calamité
Par l'Hesperie & Insubre fera:
Le feu en nef, peste & captivité:
Mercure en l'Arq Saturne fenera.

II.66

An important prisoner escapes and his fortunes change, while the people are trapped in the palace and the city is besieged: **Napoleon's** escape from Elba, battle of Waterloo [C,R] and restoration of Louis XVIII, 1815 [C] / Last Pope (?) [H].

Par grans dangiers le captif echapé:
Peu de temps grand la fortune changée.
Dans le palais le peuple est atrapé
Par bon augure la cité est assiegée.

II.67

A blond (see **IV.89**) routs an aquiline opponent and some exiles are repatriated, while the strongest are sent to sea: William of Orange and James II, 1688 [C] / second restoration of Louis XVIII, 1815 [F] / French expulsion of intruders [R].

Le blonde au nez forche viendra commetre
Par le duelle & chassera dehors:
Les exiles dedans fera remetre,
Aux lieux marins commetans les plus forts.

II.68

The northern powers exert themselves by sea as England pulls itself together, especially when it becomes aware of an invasion fleet: William III's invasion of England, 1688 [C] / World War III invasion of Britain by Russians [F] / **Muslim invasion of Europe**, 2022 [L] / restoration of Charles II, 1660 [R].

De l'Aquilon les effors seront grands:
Sus l'Ocean sera la porte ouverte,
Le regne en l'isle sera reintegrand:
Tremblera Londres par voile descouverte.

II.69

A French king from the right reunites tripartite Gaul against a great ruling power: expulsion of

---

[25] Possible misprint for *Ivry* (probably either Ivry-le-François, on the Marne, or Ivry-la-Bataille, on the Eure).

James II by William III, 1688 [C] / fall of Bourbons, 1830 [F] / **Henri V** of France, 2034+ [L] / **Henri II** of France's aid in restoring Charles II (?!) [R].

Le roy Gauloys par la Celtique dextre
Voiant discorde de la grand Monarchie,
Sus les trois pars[26] fera fleurir son sceptre,
Contre la cappe de la grand Hirarchie.

II.70

A deadly missile causes devastation and brings about the surrender of a great power amid rumors of omens: Battle of Waterloo, 1815 (?) [C] / closing stages of European counterinvasion against Muslims, 2037 [L] / London Blitz, 1940 [R].

Le dard du ciel fera son estendue
Mors en parlant: grande execution.
La pierre en l'arbre, la fiere gent rendue,
Bruit, humain monstre, purge expiation.

II.71

Exiles arrive in Sicily to feed starving aliens, though the French decline to support the leader: **French Revolution** and Age of Reason [C] / European counterinvasion against Muslims, 2028 [L] / re-establishment of Israel, 1948 [R].

Les exilés en Secile viendront
Pour deliver de faim la gent estrange:
Au point du jour les Celtes luy faudront:
La vie demeure à raison: roy se range.

II.72

French armies are routed and chased virtually out of Italy: Battle of Pavia, 1525 [C] / World War III [F] / **Muslim invasion** of Italy, 2000–4 [L].

Armée Celtique en Italie vexée
De toutes pars conflit & grande perte:
Romains fuis, ò Gaule repoulsée!
Pres du Thesin, Rubicon pugne incerte.

II.73

All over southern Europe, omens predict attacks by three powers on a sleepy and apathetic continent, ripe for a "lunar" takeover: USA-Vatican alliance (? [C] / imminent **invasion of Europe** by triple Muslim confederacy, 1999–2000 [L] / birth of Italian fascism [R].

Au lac Fucin de Benac[27] le rivaige
Prins de Leman au port de l'Orguion:
Nay de troys bras predict belliq image,
Par troys couronnes au grand Endymion.[28]

II.74

Forces from the Marches of Ancona chase armies or populations westward across France: invasion of Italy [C] / World War III [F] / **Muslim invasion of Europe**, 2005 [L] / World War II Maquis [R].

De Sens, d'Autun viendront jusques au Rosne
Pour passer outre vers les monts Pyrenées:
La gent sortir de la Marque d'Anconne:
Par terre & mer le suivra à grans trainées.

---

[26] Probable reference to the tripartite Gaul of Julius Caesar's *Gallic War*.

[27] Lake Garda, Italy.

[28] Mythical Greek shepherd made to sleep forever by a possessive Selene, the moon-goddess.

II.75

An "unwonted bird" presages massive shortages and inflation leading to cannibalism: unwanted (!) owl [C] announces world famine [C,H] / apocalyptic famines of the far future [L] / space-warfare and natural catastrophes [R].

La voix ouye de l'insolit oyseau,
Sur le canon du respiral estaige:[29]
Si hault viendra du froment le boisseau,
Que l'homme d'homme sera Anthropophage.

II.76

Thunderbolts in Burgundy presage trickery and betrayal of the local senate by a lamed priest: Talleyrand, 1791–1814 [C] / Marshal Ney and **Napoleon**, 1815.

Foudre en Bourgoigne fera cas portenteux,
Que par engin [oncques[30]] ne pourroit faire
De leur senat sacriste fait boiteux
Fera savoir aux ennemis l'affaire.

II.77

A midnight barrage admits attackers into a city, while betrayers flee via underground tunnels: Paris Commune and civil war, 1871 [F] / Spanish Civil War and Madrid fifth column [R].

Par arcs feuz poix & par feuz repoussés:
Cris, hurlemens sur la minuit ouys.
Dedans sont mis par les ramparts cassés
Par cunicules les traditeurs fuis.

II.78

British submarines arrive late, to find the sea and its islands red with African and French blood, thanks partly to poor security: Barbary pirates and AIDS [C] / **Muslim invasion of Europe** [F], 2005 [L] / threatened Nazi invasion of Britain, 1942–3 [R].

Le grand Neptune du profond de la mer
De gent Punique & sang Gauloys meslé,
Les Isles à sang, pour le tardif ramer:
Plus luy nuira que l'occult mal celé.

II.79

Black curly-bearded **Chyren** subdues a cruel, proud race, and rescues all prisoners from Muslim captivity: battle of Lepanto, 1571 (?) [C] / final defeat of **Muslim invasion** and **Henri V** [F,L].

La barbe crespe & noire par engin
Subjugera la gent cruelle & fiere.
Un grand CHYREN ostera du longin
Tous les captifs par Seline baniere.

II.80

Clever words cobble together a truce that fails to free the leaders until the proper time: death of F. D. Roosevelt and Nuremberg trials, 1945 [R].

Apres conflit du lesé l'eloquence
Par peu de temps se tramme faint repos:
Point l'on n'admet les grands à delivrance:
Les ennemis sont remis à propos.

II.81

While "fire from the sky" devastates a city and December floods threaten, a North African fleet attacks Sardinia: C20 war [C] / future asteroid impact [H] / **Muslim invasion of Europe** [F], 2005 [L].

Par feu du ciel la cité presque aduste:
L'Urne menasse encor Deucalion:[31]
Vexée Sardaigne par la Punique fuste
Apres que Libra lairra son Phaëton.

II.82

An attacking "wolf" is trapped by shortage of food and a leader is hemmed in: World War II and Mussolini [R].

Par faim la proye fera loup prisonnier,
L'assaillant lors en extreme detresse.
Le nay ayant au devant le dernier,
Le grand n'eschappe au milieu de la presse.

II.83

The city of **Lyon** is sacked, while "drizzle" falls on Swabia/Switzerland and the Jura mountains: revolutionary troops at **Lyon**, 1795 [C] / **Muslim invasion of Europe**, 2005–6 [L] / British lion [R].

Le[32] gros trafficq du grand Lyon changé
La plus part tourne en pristine ruine,
Proye aux souldars par pille vendange
Par Jura mont & [par[33]] Sueve bruine.

II.84

Six months of drought in Italy presage an alien invasion and the devastation of western Yugoslavia: failed quatrain [C] / World War III [F] / **Muslim invasion of Europe**, 2000 [L] / Albanian expansion [R].

Entre Campaigne, Sienne, Flora, Tuscie
Six moys neufz jours ne plouvra une goute.
L'estrange langue en terre Dalmatie
Courira sus, vastant la terre toute.

II.85

The French authorities in **Lyon** overextend themselves, while air-battles ensue and the Ligurian Sea is red with blood: **Napoleon** [C] / **Muslim invasion** of France, 2005 [L] / World War II Luftwaffe [R].

Le vieux plain barbe sous l'estatut severe,
A Lyon fait dessus l'Aigle Celtique:
Le petit grand trop outre persevere:
Bruit d'arme au ciel: mer rouge Lygustique:

II.86

Adriatic tidal waves wreck a fleet, while Egypt surrenders to growing Muslim power: **Napoleon** and siege of Acre, 1799 [C] / World War III [F] / **Muslim invasion**, 1999+ [L] / increasing Muslim power [R].

Naufraige a classe pres d'onde Hadriatique:
La terre esmeuë sus l'air en terre mis:
Egypte tremble augment Mahommetique
L'Herault soy rendre à crier est commis.

II.87

A German prince from abroad is enthroned, while a subject lady's time runs out: accession of George I, 1714 [C,R].

Apres viendra des extremes contrées
Prince Germain dessus le throsne doré:
La servitude & [par] eaux rencontrées
La dame serve, son temps plus n'adoré.

II.88

When a fifth lord is called the seventh, a foreign attacker endangers the France of a third: **Henri IV** and ruin of Valois dynasty [C] / World War III [F] / league against **Henri III** and **Henri IV** [R].

Le circuit du grand faict ruineux
Le nom septiesme du cinquiesme sera:
D'un tiers plus grand l'estrange belliqueux,
Monton,[34] Lutece, Aix ne guarantira.

II.89

Two great "masters" eventually become powerful allies, as the New World's star rises and a "bloody one" takes account of it: US-Russian alliance [C,H,L] and removal of Gorbachev [C] / US-Chinese alliance against Russia [R].

Du jou seront demis[35] les deux grandz maistres
Leur grand pouvoir se verra augmenté:
La terre neufve sera en ses haults estres,[36]
Au sanguinaire le nombre racompté.

II.90

Hungary is subjected to a harsh regime (see **VIII.15**), its twin cities the heart of murderous conflict: Hungarian revolution, 1957 [C] / Ditto, 1956 [P] / **Muslim invasion of Europe**, 1999–2000 [L] / Russian subjection of Hungary [R].

Par vie & mort changé regne d'Ongrie:
La loy sera plus aspre que service,
Leur grand cité d'urlemens plaincts & crie,
Castor & Pollux ennemis dans la lyce.

II.91

At sunrise a huge blaze extends northward, with dreadful slaughter and screams within it: future nuclear attack on Russia or USA [C,H] / World War III nuclear attack on Russia [F] / **Muslim invasion of Europe**, 2013–17 [L].

Soleil levant un grand feu lon verra,
Bruit & clarté vers Aquilon tendant:
Dedans le rond mort & cris lont orra
Par glaive, feu, faim, mort les attendants.

---

[31] Greek version of the biblical Noah.

[32] A multitude of shared printing errors at around this point in the two subsequent editions suggests that both were based on a single spoilt copy, rendered semi-illegible near the spine of the right-hand page.

[33] One syllable missing, unless diphthongs differentiated – as is in fact often the case in Nostradamus.

[34] *Menton.*

[35] Late editions have *Un jour seront amis*, but the original is perfectly clear. *Du jou(g) seront demis* simply means "will be subjected to the (same) yoke."

[36] Possibly *astres*.

---

[29] Read as *Sur le canon dur et spiral estaige.*

[30] Two syllables missing: *oncques* added from 1568.

II.92

As gold is discovered underground, a leader's grandson is murdered, but a "proud one" escapes during a show: attempted assassination of Napoleon III, 1870 [C] / nuclear fission or fusion [R].

Feu couleur d'or du ciel en terre veu:
Frappé de hault, nay, fait cas merveilleuz:
Grand meurtre humain: prins du grand le nepveu,
Morts d'expectacles eschappé l'orguilleux.

II.93

Death, followed by flood, overtakes Rome, as a leader is consigned to a dungeon, and castle and palace go up in flames: future Pope [C,R] / last Pope [H,L] and asteroid impact [H].

Bien pres du Tymbre presse la Libytine,
Ung peu devant grand inundation:
Le chef du nef prins, mis a la sentine:
Chasteau, palais en conflagration.

II.94

Italy suffers much for France's sake as alien hordes invade and a quarter of a million are captured, while the British navy is scared off: **Napoleon** [C] / **Muslim invasion of Europe**, 2000 [L] / Italian attacks on French [R].

GRAN. Po, grand mal pour Gauloys recevra,
Vaine terreur an maritin Lyon:
Peuple infini par la mer passera,
Sans eschapper un quart d'un milion.

II.95

The field-boundaries of a deserted land are re-defined, while kingdoms are allocated to wise incompetents and fratricidal disputes rage: Kennedy brothers [C,H] / Third World War in Palestine [F] / collapse of US-Soviet alliance, 1994–9 [H] / aftermath of **Muslim invasion** of France, 2032 [L] and civil war [L,R].

Les lieux peuples seront inhabitables:
Pour champs avoir grande division:
Regnes livrés a prudents incapables:
Lors les grands freres mort & dissension.

II.96

While a glare is seen in the sky over a starving, war-racked Switzerland, Iranian forces attack Greece: Persian attack on Turkey [C] / World War III [F] / future nuclear terrorist attack or jihad against southern Europe [H] / **Muslim invasion of Europe**, 2000 [L].

Flambeau ardant au ciel soir sera veu
Pres de la fin & principe du Rosne:
Famine, glaive: tard le secours pourveu,
La Perse tourne envahir Macedoine.

II.97

The Pope is warned that any approach to a "city that waters two rivers" will prove fatal to him and his followers: death of Pius VI at Valence, 1799 [C] / death of **John Paul II** at **Lyon**, 2000 [L] / attempted assassination of **John Paul II**, 1981 [R].

Romain Pontife garde de l'approcher
De la cité qui deux fleuves arrouse,
Ton sang viendras au pres de la cracher,
Toy & les tiens quand fleurira la rose.

II.98

Following ominous thunder, the face of a victim is bloodied for the sake of a fiancée: death of Philippe of Orléans, 1793 [F].

Celuy du sang resperse le visaige
De la victime proche sacrifiée:
Tonant en Leo augure par presaige:
Mis estre à mort lors pour la fiancée.

II.99

Rome's domains are harried by the French, despite fears that their fleet (or army) has gone too far to the north: French takeover of Papal States, 1810, and **Napoleon**'s retreat from Moscow, 1812 [C] / Franco-Italian conflict [R].

Terroir Romain qu'interpretoit augure,
Par gent Gauloyse seras par trop vexée:
Mais nation Celtique craindra l'heure,
Boreas, classe trop loing l'avoir poussée.

II.100

War sweeps the islands, despite the forging of alliances against the marauders: anti-Ottoman alliance, 1565 [C] / **Muslim invasion of Europe**, 2000–5 / London Blitz, 1940 [R].

Dedans les isles si horrible tumulte,
Rien on n'orra qu'une bellique brigue,
Tant grand sera des predateurs l'insulte,
Qu'on se viendra ranger à la grand ligue.

CENTURY III

Transliterated from **Bonhomme**'s original 1555 edition.

III.1

Following a great sea battle (see **II.78**), Britain rides high, terrorizing the "red enemy": failed quatrain [C] / World War III [F] / aftermath of Mediterranean sea-battle, 2005 [L] / Japanese attack on Pearl Harbor, 1941 [R].

Apres combat & bataille navale,
Le grand Neptune à son plus haut beffroy,
Rouge aversaire de fraieur viendra pasle,
Metant le grand ocean en effroy.

III.2

God grants to humanity mystic sovereignty over all creation: Nostradamus scrying [C,H] / media's propagation of **Fontbrune**, 1981 (!) [F] / Last Judgment and Kingdom of Heaven on earth, 2828+ [L] / hermetic secret of Philosopher's Stone [R].

Le divin verbe donrra à la sustance,
Comprins ciel terre, or occult au fait mystique.
Corps, ame, esprit aiant toute puissance,
Tant sous ses pieds, comme au siege celique.

III.3

Southern drought and an astrological conjunction accompany earthquakes in Greece and western Turkey (see **II.52**): events during World War III [F] / future superquakes, 1987+, and/or Apocalypse 1994–2000 [H] / seismic events during **Muslim invasion of Europe**, 2004 [L] / C21 quakes [R].

Mars & Mercure & l'argent[1] joint ensemble
Vers le midi extreme siccité:
Au fond d'Asie on dira terre tremble,
Corinthe, Ephese lors en perplexité.

III.4

Shortly before sun and moon are dimmed (see next verse), cold, drought, and danger are abroad: Islamic collapse and Third Antichrist [C] / fall of Asiatic Empire and danger at **Salon** [F] / Last Times, C29 [L], and danger at Salon [R].

Quand seront proches le defaut des lunaires,[2]
De l'un a l'autre ne distant grandement,
Ftoid,[3] siccité, danger vers les frontieres,
Mesmes ou l'oracle a prins commencement.

III.5

With the far future dimming of sun and moon, two mighty rescuers appear: cessation of hostilities between Iran and Iraq, 1989 (?) [C] / World War II inflation and precious-metal shortage [F] / Last Times and appearance of extraterrestrials, C29 [L] / as previous verse [R].

Pres, loin defaut de deux grands luminaires
Qui surviendra entre l'Avril & Mars.
O quel cherté! mais deux grands debonaires
Par terre & mer secourront toutes pars.

III.6

Lightning strikes within the churches and strong-holds where people are sheltering, as floods, famine, and thirst spread and all take up arms: failed quatrain [C] / **Napoleon**'s papal coup, 1809 [F] / **Muslim invasion** of Italy, 2000+ [L].

Dans temples clos le foudre y entrera,
Les citadins dedans leurs forts grevés:
Chevaux, beufs, hommes, l'onde leur touchera,
Par faim, soif sous les plus foibles arnés.[4]

III.7

As fighting reaches the walls, refugees are attacked from the air, where "crows" are fighting: World War II fall of France, 1940 [C] / fall of **Lyon** to Muslims amid air-battles, 2005–6 [L] / battles around Berlin Wall, late C20 [R].

Les fuitifs,[5] feu du ciel sus les piques:
Conflit prochain des courbeaux s'esbatans,
De terre on crie aide secours celiques,
Quand pres des murs seront les combatans

III.8

German and French forces depopulate Spain: Spanish Civil War, 1936–9 [C], and French World War II resistance [F] / C18 Anglo-French colonial rivalry [R].

Les Cimbres joints avecques leurs voisins,
Depopuler viendront presque l'Hespaigne:
Gens amassés Guienne & Limosins
Seront en ligue, & leur feront compaignie.[6]

---

[1] In traditional alchemy, silver stands for the moon.

[2] Probable compression of *luminaires* (see next verse).

[3] Misprint for *froid*.

[4] Later editions have *armés: sous* may be a misprint for *tous*.

[5] Later editions have *fugitifs*.

[6] Rhyme (and later editions) demand *compaigne*.

III.9

The English, Bretons, and Dutch pursue forces from **Bordeaux**, Rouen, and La Rochelle into eastern France: World War II liberation of France, 1944 [F] / counterinvasion of Muslim-occupied Europe, 2022–6 [L].

Bourdeaux, Rouen, & la Rochele joints
Tiendront autour la grand mer oceane:
Anglois, Bretons, & les Flamans conjoints
Les chasseront jusques au-pres de Roane

III.10

Coastal France is devastated seven times, Monaco starved and taken and its head imprisoned: death of Princess Grace of Monaco (?) [C] / liberation of **Provence**, 1943–4 [F] / future asteroid impact [H] / Muslim raids on Riviera, 2000–5 [L].

De sang & faim plus grande calamité
Sept fois s'apreste à la marine plage,
Monech de faim, lieu prins, captivité,
Le grand mené croc en ferrée caige.

III.11

After long air-battles and privations, the city's central tree falls and the leader of Venice (?) succumbs: assassination of **Henri IV**, 1610 [C,H] / **Muslim invasion** of Italy, 2000 [L] / air-warfare [R].

Les armes batre au ciel longue saison,
L'arbre au milieu de la cité tumbé:
Vermine, rongne, glaive en face tyson,
Lors le Monarque d'Hadrie succombé.

III.12

All over Europe, leaders are either killed or taken prisoner: millennial flooding from greenhouse effect [C] / **Muslim invasion of Europe** [F], 2000 [H] to 2022 [L].

Par la tumeur de Heb. Po, Tag. Timbre & Rosne,
Et par l'estang Leman & Aretin,
Les deux grans chefs &[7] cités de Garonne
Prins, morts, noies. Partir humain butin.

III.13

As lightnings melt soft metals and captives attack each other, a submarine fleet sets out: submarine missile [C,H] / abdication of **Napoleon**, 1815 [F] / Muslim attacks on Riviera, 2000–5 [L].

Par foudre en l'arche or & argent fondu:
Des deux captifs l'un l'autre mangera,
De la cité le plus grand estendu,
Quand submergée la classe nagera.

III.14

The son of a valiant but unlucky father makes good in his old age on accepting advice from an amateur: Louis XV [C] / Louis Philippe, 1830 [R].

Par le rameau du vaillant personage
De France infme: par le pere infelice
Honneurs, richesses travail en son viel aage
Pour avoir creu le conseil d'homme nice.

III.15

Beset on all sides, the kingdom shows its true mettle, as a death brings a more aggressive, youthful leader: Louis XV [C] / the French Regency, 1715 [F] / accession of **Henri V**, 2033–4 [L] / **Napoleon** [R].

Cueur, vigueur, gloire le regne changera,
De tous points contre aiant son adversaire.
Lors France enfance par mort subjuguera.
Le grand regent sera lors plus contraire.

III.16

An English prince with Mars/Aries as his birth-planet/sign, determined to seek his own fortune, takes part in a duel that pierces the gallbladder of one whom he hates but his mother likes: unfulfilled [C] / Edward VIII [R].

Le prince Anglois Mars à son cuer de ciel
Vouldra poursuivre sa fortune prospere:
Des deux duelles l'un percera le fiel:
Hay de luy, bien aymé de sa mere.

III.17

Rome burns and Flanders is in darkness, while a king pursues his nephew and churchmen are involved in scandals: **Napoleon** (?) [C] / future burning of Rome [F], 2002 [L] / future war [R].

Mont Aventine brusler nuict sera veu:
Le ciel obscur tout à un coup en Flandres,
Quand le Monarque chassera son nepveu:
Leurs gens d'eglise commetront les esclandres.

III.18

Reims suffers chemical attack while war rages all around: World War I [F] / **Muslim invasion of Europe**, 2021–2 [L].

Apres la pluie laict assés longuete,
En plusieurs lieux de Reins le ciel touché
Helas quel meurtre de seng pres d'eux s'apreste.
Peres & filz rois n'oseront aprocher.

III.19

A rain of blood and milk presages war and general disaster for Lucca, while its leader dies far away: future AIDS (?) [C] / future catastrophe [H] / **Muslim invasion** of Italy, 2000 [L].

En Luques sang & laict viendra plouvoir:
Un peu devant changement de preteur,
Grand peste & guerre, faim & soif fera voyr
Loing, ou mourra leur prince [et leur[8]] recteur.

III.20

Muslim forces overrun southern Spain, thanks to betrayal by a Cordoban: expulsion of Moors and Jews from Spain, 1492 and 1610 [C] / Moorish revolt in Granada, 1567, and expulsion, 1610 [F] / **Muslim invasion of Europe**, 2007+ [L,R(?)].

Par les contrées du grand fleuve Bethique
Loing d'Ibere, au regne de Granade:
Croix repoussées par gens Mahumetiques
Un de Cordube trahira la contrade.

III.21

A horrible sea-creature lands itself on the east coast of Italy: "mermaid," 1523 or 1531 (?) [C] / **Muslim invasion** of Italy using amphibious craft, 2000 [L] / manatee [R].

Au crustamin par mer Hadriatique
Apparoistra un horride poisson,
De face humaine, & la fin aquatique,
Qui se prendra dehors de l'ameçon.

III.22

As a city falls after six days of fighting, the three who betrayed it are spared, but the rest slaughtered: battle for Jerusalem, 1967, or 1994–9 [H] / Arab-Israeli Six-Day War, 1967, [R].

Six jours l'assaut devant cité donné:
Livrée sera forte & aspre bataille:
Trois la rendront & à eux pardonné:
Le reste à feu & sang [l'on[9]] tranche [&[10]]traille.

III.23

France is warned not to intervene in Italy against Muslims invading from the Adriatic, who will trap its forces among the islands and reduce them to starvation: C16 France and the Ottomans [C] / **Muslim invasion** of Italy [F], 2000 [L].

Si France passes outre mer lygustique,
Tu te verras en isles & mers enclos:
Mahommet contraire: plus mer Hadriatique:
Chevaulx & d'asnes tu rougeras[11] les os.

III.24

France is again warned of enormous losses if it intervenes (see **III.23**): Ottomans [C] / **Muslim invasion** of Italy, 2000 [L].

De l'entreprinse grande confusion,
Perte de gens, thresor innumerable:
Tu ny dois faire encor extension
France a mon dire fais que sois recordable.

III.25

The heir to Navarre acquires dominions from an ally of Spain: **Henri IV** [C,H] / **Napoleon**ic Wars, 1806–8 [F].

Qui au royaume Navarrois parviendra
Quand de Secile & naples seront joints:
Bigorre & Landes par Foyx Loron[12] tiendra,
D'un qui d'Hespaigne sera par trop conjoint

III.26

A wave of strange, esoteric spiritual beliefs and practices arises: inflation, violence and the fulfillment of Nostradamus's prophecies [F] / new spiritual free-for-all following European liberation, 2034+ [L] / victimization of oil sheikhs [R].

Des roys & princes dresseront simulacres,
Augures, creuz eslevez aruspices:
Corne, victime d'orée,[13] & d'azur, d'acre,[14]
Interpretés seront les extispices.

III.27

A Libyan leader angers the French by appointing himself spokesman for the Arabs: President Gaddafi [C,L] / Franco-Libyan nuclear alliance [R].

---

[7] Possibly stands here for *des*.

[8] Two syllables missing.

[9] Presumed omission.

[10] Presumed omission.

[11] Misprint: later editions have *rongeras*.

[12] Possibly *Oloran*.

[13] *dorée*.

[14] Presumably *d'nacre*.

Prince Libyque puissant en Occident
Francois d'Arabe viendra tant enflammer:
Scavans aux lettres fera condescendent,
La langue Arabe en Francois translater.

III.28

A young woman of poor background gains power and long wields it to terrible effect: Anne Boleyn (?) C / **Napoleon** III F / Margaret Thatcher (?) L / Indira Gandhi R.

De terre foible & pauvre parentele,
Par bout & paix parviendra dans l'empire:
Long temps regner une jeune femele,
Qu'oncq en regne n'en survint un si pire.

III.29

Two nephews avenge the deaths of their fathers in war: nephews of Anne de **Montmorency**, or failed quatrain C / Anglo-American struggle against Nazi Germany R.

Les deux nepveus en divers lieux nourris:
Navale pugne, terre, peres tumbés
Viendront si haut eslevés enguerris
Venger l'injure: ennemis succombés.

III.30

One who has defeated his superior (see **I.35**) is arrested by six men at night: comte de **Montgomery**, 1574 C,H,L,R / assassination of Admiral **Coligny**, 1572 F.

Celuy qu'en luite & fer au fait bellique,
Aura porté plus grand que lui le pris,
De nuit au lit six luy feront la pique,
Nud sans harnois subit sera surpris.

III.31

Two armies thrice face each other in Iran, Arabia and Armenia, and "Soliman" is defeated on the River Araks: Battle of Lepanto, 1571 C / future defeat of Muslims on Iranian-Armenian border F, 1998–9 L / war, with dire results for Israel R.

Aux champs de Mede, d'Arabe & d'Armenie,
Deux grands copies trois foys s'assembleront:
Pres du rivage d'Araxes la mesnie,
Du grand Solman en terre tomberont.

III.32

With war in Italy and eastern Europe, a great massacre of troops from western France takes place in Tuscany: World War II C / **Muslim invasion of Europe**, 2000 L.

Le grand sepulcre du peuple Aquitanique
S'aprochera aupres de la Tousquane,
Quand Mars sera pres du coing Germanique,
Et au terroir de la gent Mantuane.

III.33

A city beset by wolves has its heartlands laid waste, while allies look on from the Alps: Paris and World War II F / **Muslim invasion** of Switzerland or northern Italy, 2000 L.

En la cité ou le loup entrera,
Bien pres de là les ennemis seront:
Copie estrange grand païs gastera.
Aux murs & Alpes les amis passeront.

III.34

While the sun is dimmed (see **III,4**, **III.5**) a mysterious monster unexpectedly appears: death of Louis XVI, 1793, and Robespierre F / far future events, C29 L.

Quand le defaut du Soleil lors sera,
Sus le plain jour le monstre sera veu:
Tout autrement on l'interpretera.
Cherté n'a garde: nul ny aura pourveu.

III.35

A child of poor parentage from the heart of western Europe grows up to seduce a great people and become famous even in the East: Adolf Hitler C,F,H,L,R.

Du plus profond de l'Occident d'Europe,
De pauvres gens un jeune enfant naistra,
Qui par sa langue seduira grande troupe:
Son bruit au regne d'Orient plus croistra.

III.36

A subversive heretic, who is buried alive, is rediscovered with mutilated hands: downfall of President Nixon, 1974 R.

Enseveli non mort apopletique
Sera trowe avoir les mains mangées:
Quand la cité damnera l'heretique,
Qu'avoit leur loys si leur sembloit changées.[15]

III.37

Despite exhortations, Milan is captured and sacked by the "eagle," its walls blasted apart: **Napoleon**'s capture of Milan, 1796 and 1800 C / **Napoleon** III at Milan, 1870 F.

Avant l'assaut oraison prononcée:
Milan prins d'aigle par embusches deceuz:
Muraille antique par canons enfoncée,
Par feu & sang à mercy peu receuz.

III.38

After casualties beyond the mountains (see **III.32**, **III.43**), a peace accord in reached in the autumn: Spanish peace with Pope, 1557, or World War II C / European counterinvasion of Italy, 2028 L / Franco-British ultimatum to Hitler, 1939 R.

La gent Gauloise & nation estrange
Outre les monts, mors prins & profligés:
Au mois contraire & proche de vendange
Par les seigneurs en accord rediges.

III.39

Seven powers combine to subdue the Apennines, but bad weather and Italian cowardice destroy their enterprise (see **III.38**): Italian Holy League, 1576 C / **Napoleon** in Italy and Sardinia, 1796–7 F / setbacks to European counterinvasion of Muslim-occupied Italy, 2028 L.

Les sept [païs[16]*] en trois mis en concorde*
Pour subjuguer des[17] *alpes Apennines:*
Mais le tempeste & Ligure couarde,
Les profligent en subites ruines.

III.40

Ancient theatrical and sporting traditions are revived, but prove overdemanding: reestablishment of European civilization by "**Hercules**," 2028+ L / post World War II reconstruction R.

Le grand theatre se viendra redresser:
Le dez getés & les rets ja tendus.
Trop le premier en glaz viendra lasser,
Par arcz prostraits de log[18] *temps ja fendus.*

III.41

A hideous hunchback is elected, and the assassin of a bishop approved by the King: Prince Louis de **Condé**, 1569 C.

Bosseu sera esleu par le conseil,
Plus hideux monstre en terre n'aperceu.
Le coup volant prelat crevera l'œil,
Le traistre au roy pour fidele receu.

III.42

The birth of a child with two teeth (see **II.7**) and a rain of stones in Tuscany presage great famine: Louis XIV (?) C / birth of **Antichrist** F / world famine R.

L'enfant naistra à deux dents à la gorge
Pierres en Tuscie par pluie tomberont:
Peu d'ans apres ne sera bled, ne orge,
Pour saouler ceux qui de faim failliront:

III.43

The French are warned not to pass the Apennines, lest a future black curly-beard (see **I.74**, **II.79**) raise cenotaphs to their dead (see **III.32, 38, 39, 43**): future war C / **Napoleonic** monuments F / setbacks to counterinvasion of Italy, 2028 L.

Gents d'alentour de Tarn, Loth, & Garonne,
Gardés les monts Apennines passer,
Vostre tombeau pres de Rome & d'Anconne
Le noir poil crespe fera trophée dresser.

III.44

A domestic animal learns to speak, but has to be suspended in mid-air: invention of wireless C,H,L / **Napoleon**'s return from Elba, 1815 F.

Quand l'animal à l'homme domestique
Apres grans peines & saults[19] *viendra parler:*
Le fouldre à vierge[20] *sera si malefique,*
De terre prinse, & suspendue en l'air.

III.45

Toulouse learns what to expect from new overlords when five foreigners are murdered in church: battle of Toulouse, 1814 C / World War III F / revolt in southwest France, 2032 L.

Les cinq estranges entrés dedans le temple,
Leur sang viendra la terre prophaner:
Aux Thoulosains sera bien dur exemple
D'un qui viendra ses loys exterminer.

---

[15] Read as *Qui avoit leur loys (si leur sembloit) changées.*

[16] Two syllables missing: possible word.

[17] Much later editions give *les*.

[18] *long*: compare this verse to **I.45**.

[19] i.e. *assaults.*

[20] Possibly *verge.*

III.46

The stars foretell either good times or disaster for Lyon: World War III [F] / **Muslim invasion of Europe**, 2005–6 [L].

Le ciel (de Plancus la cité) nous presaige
Par clairs insignes & par estoiles fixes,
Que de son change subit s'aproche l'aage,
Ne pour son bien, ne pour ses malefices.

III.47

An old ruler is deposed by Christian forces and seeks help from Lesbos: fall of Marshal Pétain, 1944–5 [F] / European counterinvasion of Mediterranean, 2036+ [L] / Greek monarchy, 1941 and 1967 [R].

Le vieux monarque deschassé de son regne
Aux Orients son secours ira querre:
Pour peur des croix pliera son enseigne:
En Mitilene ira pour port & terre.

III.48

700 prisoners are staked out, and not rescued until fifteen have died: World War II Nazi brutalities [R].

Sept cens captifs estaches rudement
Pour la moitie meurtrir, donné le sort,
Le proche espoir viendra si promptement,
Mais non si tost qu'une quinzieme mort.

III.49

French sovereignty is transferred abroad and its traditions overthrown by powers based in Rouen and Chartres: Code **Napoléon** [C] / Vichy government, 1940–4 [F] / Muslim occupation of France, 2005–26 [L] / **French Revolution** [R].

Regne Gauloys tu seras bien changé:
En lieu estrange est translaté l'Empire
En autres mœurs, & loys seras rangé:
Rouan & Chartres te feront bien du pire.

III.50

A democratic city-state is stormed and forced to submit to a king: journée des barricades, 1588 [C] / siege of **Paris**, 1870 [F] / **French Revolution** and storming of Bastille, 1789 [R].

La republique de la grande cité
A grand rigueur ne voudra consentir:
Roy sortir hors par trompete cité
L'eschele au mur, la cité repentir.

III.51

Paris and **Blois** plot grand murder, while Orléans tries to restore its leader and other cities make mischief: **Guise** murders, 1588 [C,F,L] / Reign of Terror and Louis Philippe [R].

PARIS conjure un grand meurtre commetre,
Bloys le fera sortir en plain effet:
Ceulx d'Orleans vouldront leur chef remetre,
Angiers, Troye, langres leur feront grand forfait.

III.52

With Italy either inundated or parched, France sees the immature "eagle's wing" threatened by the "lion": **Napoleonic** Wars [C].

En la Campaigne sera si longue pluie,
Et en la Pouille si grande siccité.
Coq verra l'aigle, l'aesle mal accomplie:
Par Lyon mise sera en extremité.

III.53

With southwest Germany and Switzerland overcome, German forces capture Frankfurt and advance via Flanders into France: Nuremberg rallies [C] and fall of France, 1940 [C,F,H].

Quand le plus grand emportera le pris
De Nuremberg d'Auspurg,[21] & ceux de Basle
Par Aggripine chef Francfort repris
Transverseront par Flamans jusques en Gale.

III.54

A great leader flees to Spain with his forces, and after years of devastation rules in peace: Franco and Spanish Civil War [C] / World War III [F] / Juan Peron and Argentina [R].

L'un des plus grands fuira aux Hespaignes,
Qu'en longue plaie apres viendra saigner:
Passant copies par les hautes montaignes
Devastant tout & puis en paix regner.

III.55

When "one-eye" rules in France, the court is disturbed and the lord of **Blois** murders his friend (see **I.35**, **III.51**): death of **Henri II**, 1559 [C], and **Guise** murders, 1588 [C,F,H].

En l'an qu'un œil en France regnera,
La court sera à[22] un bien fascheux trouble:
Le grand de Bloys son ami tuera:
Le regne mis en mal & doute double.

III.56

With plague and storms in southern France in March, twenty-three divisions afflict the major cities from '607: failed quatrain (?) [C] / raids in south cause major disturbances, 1999 [L].

Montauban, Nismes, Avignon, & Besier,[23]
Peste, tonnerre & gresle à fin de Mars:
De Paris pont, Lyon mur, Montpellier,
Depuis six cent & sept. xxiii. pars.

III.57

Britain, unlike German-supported France, undergoes seven bloodstained "changes" in 290 years, while war-threats lessen from the east: dynastic and political events, 1603–1939 [C] / rise and fall of British Empire [H] / British alliances 1628–1918 [F] / events 1555–1845 [R].

Sept foys changer verrés gent Britannique
Taintz en sang en deux cent nonante an:
Franche non point par apui Germanique.
Aries doute son pole Bastarnan.

III.58

A leader is born in south Germany who wards off the eastern Europeans, then disappears without trace: Lech Walesa [C] / Adolf Hitler [F,H,R].

Aupres du Rin des montaignes Noriques
Naistra un grand de gents trop tart venu,
Qui defendra SAUROME & Pannoniques,
Qu'on ne saura qu'il sera devenu.

III.59

A fratricidal usurper takes over a "barbarian" empire, while another condemns opponents to life-imprisonment: **French Revolution** and **Napoleon** [C] / Third and Fourth Republics, 1881–1911 and 1958 [F] / **Muslim invasion**, 1998–9 [L] / Iranian revolution and Ayatollah Khomeini [R].

Barbare empire par le tiers usurpé
La plus grand part de son sang metra à mort:
Par mort senile par luy le quart frapé,
Pour peur que sang par le sang ne soit mort.

III.60

Persecution sweeps Asia Minor, with much blame heaped on one young black: Chinese mobilization and prophet of **Antichrist** [C] / Abu Abbas [H] /Asiatic invasion of Turkey, 1998–9 [L] / Middle East and World War III [F].

Par toute Asie grande proscription,
Mesmes en Mysie, Lysie & Pamphylie:
Sang versera par absolution
D'un jeune noir rempli de felonnie.

III.61

A violently anti-Christian army moves in from Iraq against weaker opponents: Iran-Iraq war [C] / World War III [F] / **Muslim invasion**, 1998 [L].

La grande bande & secte crucigere
Se dressera en Mesopotamie:
Du proche fleuve compaignie legiere,
Que telle loy tiendra pour ennemie.

III.62

Forces cross the Pyrenees in order to attack **Carcassonne**: World War III [F] / **Muslim invasion** of France, 2013 [L].

Proche del duero par mer Tyrene close
Viendra percer les grans monts Pyrenées.
La main plus courte & sa percée gloze,
A Carcassonne conduira ses menées

III.63

An imitative Italian regime collapses, while arguments behind the scenes hold up stupid decisions: Mussolini and Hitler [C,H,R] / end of Pope's temporal power, 1870 [F] / dissensions in newly liberated Italy, 2028 [L].

Romain pouvoir sera du tout abas,[24]
Son grand voysin imiter ses vestiges:
Occultes haines civiles, & debats
Retarderont aux bouffons leurs folligges,

III.64

Warships and cargo vessels captured from Iran attack Iranian Muslims and sack the Greek islands before retiring to an Ionian port: Battle of Lepanto, 1571 [F] / European counterinvasion of Middle East, 2034+ [L].

Le chef de Perse remplira grande OLXAÚES[25]
Classe trireme contre gent Mahumetique
De Parthe, & Mede: & piller les Cyclades:
Repos long temps au grand port Ionique.

---

[21] Normal sixteenth-century spelling of *Augsburg*.

[22] *en* in much later editions.

[23] *Béziers*.

---

[24] Some late editions give *a bas*.

[25] Later editions have *Olchades*.

III.65

A Pope is elected the day after a prominent Roman tomb is unearthed, but is promptly poisoned: John Paul I, 1978 [C,H] / attempt to restore papacy after European liberation, 2028+ [L].

Quand le sepulcre du grand Romain trouvé,
Le jour apres sera esleu pontife,
Du senat gueres il ne sera prouvé
Empoisonné son sang au sacré scyphe.

III.66

The Bailiff of Orléans, at first insecurely detained, is undeservedly killed for reasons of revenge: death of Jerôme Greslot, 1569 [C] / execution of Philippe-Égalité, 1793 [F].

Le grand baillif d'Orleans mis à mort
Sera par un de sang vindicatif:
De mort merite ne mourra, ne par sort:
Des pieds & mains mal le faisoit captif.

III.67

A new, idealistic philosophical sect achieves popularity beyond Germany (see **III.76**): C16 Anabaptists [C] / Nazism in early C20 Austria [F,R(?)] / "New Age" sects after the liberation of Europe, 2034 [L].

Une nouvele secte de Philosophes
Meprisant mort, or, honneurs & richesses
Des monts Germains ne seront limitrophes:
A les ensuivre auront apui & presses.

III.68

Leaderless people throughout Italy and Spain are betrayed and slaughtered: Mussolini (?) [C] / weak government, 1855, and Sebastopol [F] / **Muslim invasion of Europe**, 2000–12 [L] / World War II Russian front [R].

Peuple sans chef d'Espagne & d'Italie
Morts, profligés dedans le Cherronnesse:
Leur duyct trahy par legiere folie,
Le sang nager par tout à la traverse.

III.69

A young leader surrenders his army, but the old son of a "half-pig" (see **I.64**) forges alliances in Burgundy: C20 flier in oxygen mask [C].

Grand exercite conduit par jouvenceau,
Se viendra rendre aux mains des ennemis:
Mais le viellard nay au demi pourceau,
Fera Chalon & Mascon estre amis.

III.70

A flooded Britain secures allies against a new, aggressive regime in Italy: renewal of Holy League, 1606 [C] / revolutions in Britain and Italy [F] / **Muslim invasion of Europe**, 2004 [L].

La grand Bretagne comprinse l'Angleterre
Viendra par eaux si hault à inunder
La ligue neufve d'Ausonne fera guerre,
Que contre eux mesmes il se viendront bander

III.71

While famine rages abroad, those besieged in the islands build up their strength against the foe: World War II [C,H] / World War III [F] / **Muslim invasion of Europe**, 2022+ [L] / Dutch wartime breaching of dykes [R].

III.72

A good old man is unjustifiably buried alive (see **III.36**), while his successor pockets the ransom: failed quatrain [C] / ousting of Churchill, 1945 [R].

Le bon viellard tout vif enseveli,
Pres du grand fleuve par fauce souspeçon
Le nouveau vieux de richesse ennobli
Prins au chemin tout l'or de la rançon.

III.73

A new, lame ruler takes a long time to repair the damage caused by a bastard competitor: Duke of Bordeaux and Franco-Prussian War, 1870 [C] / obscure C16 event [R].

Quand dans le regne parviendra le boiteux
Competiteur aura proche bastard:
Luy & le regne viendront si fort rogneux,
Qu'ains qu'il guerisse son fait sera bien tard.

III.74

Several Italian cities agree unsatisfactory terms so as to go along with the "wretches of Nola": failed quatrain [C] / Italian factional disputes [R].

Naples, Florence, Favence[26] & Imole,
Seront en termes de telle facherie,
Que pour complaire aux malheureux de Nolle,
Plainct d'avoir fait à son chef moquerie.

III.75

Bloody war and shell-borne plague from distant lands overtake Italy and Spain, while counter-measures remain "so near and yet so far": chemical warfare and/or AIDS from China [C] / Siege of Saragossa, 1809 [F] / **Muslim invasion of Europe**, 2000–12 [L].

PAU. Veronne, Vicence, Sarragousse
De glaifves loings terroirs de sang humides:
Peste si grande viendra à la grand gousse,
Proche secours, & bien loing les remedes.

III.76

New, semipagan cults in Germany or eastern Europe (see **II.67**) eventually return to the Christian fold: Hitler's abolition of religion [C] / Nazism in Germany [F,R] / "New Age" sects after liberation of Europe, 2034 [L].

En Germanie naistront diverses sectes,
S'approchans fort de l'heureux paganisme,
Le cueur captif & petites receptes,
Feront retour à payer le vray disme.

III.77

In October 1727 the King of Persia is captured by the Egyptians and Christianity is disgraced: Turco-Persian peace, 1727 [C] / events in 2025 [R].

Le tiers climat soubz Aries comprins
L'an mil sept cents vingt & sept en Octobre,
Le roy de Perse par ceux d'Egypte prins:
Conflit, mort, pte[27]: à la croix grand opprobre.

III.78

A Scottish chief and six Germans, captured by oriental sailors, are brought before Iran's new ruler: failed quatrain [C] / Antichrist (?) [H] / **Muslim invasion of Europe** [F,L].

Le chef d'Escosse avec six d'Alemagne
Par gens de mer Orientaux captifs:[28]
Transverseront le Calpre & Hespagne
Present en Perse au nouveau roy craintif.

III.79

As the ancient former order is overthrown, Marseille is attacked and invaded from the sea: liberation at end of World War II [F] / Lebanon, 1979 [H] / **Muslim invasion of Europe**, 2005 [L].

L'ordre fatal sempiternel par chaisne
Viendra tourner par ordre consequent:
Du port Phocen sera rompue la chaisne:
La cité prinse, l'ennemy quand & quand.

III.80

After a wretch is expelled from England and his adviser burned, his followers install a bastard: Charles I and Cromwell [C].

Du regne Anglois l'indigne deschassé,
Le conseillier par ire mis à feu:
Ses adherans iront si bas tracer,
Que le bastard sera demi receu.

III.81

A daring loud-mouth, elected to lead the army, leads a breakout and terrifies a city: Charles I, Cromwell, and Siege of Pontefract [C] / **Muslim invasion of Europe**, 2017–18 [L].

Le grand criard sans honte audacieux.
Sera esleu gouverneur de l'armée:
La hardiesse de son contentieux,
Le pont rompu, cité de peur pasmée:

III.82

"Grasshoppers" devastate the French Riviera, while prisoners are ill-treated: aerial invasion of southern France [C] / **Muslim invasion** of France [F], 2005 [L] / air-fleets [R].

Freins,[29] Antibol,[30] villes au tour de Nice,
Seront vastées fer, par mer & par terre:
Les sauterelles terre & mer vent propice,
Prins, mors, troussés, pilles sans loy de guerre.

III.83

Long-haired French warriors, allied with foreigners, capture and subdue the Aquitainians: Louis XVIII [C] / allied counterinvasion of western France, 2024–5 [L] / northern French intellectuals imprison their opponents [R].

Les lons cheveux de la Gaule Celtique
Accompagnés d'estranges nations,
Metront captif la gent Aquitanique,
Pour succomber à interniions.[31]

---

26 *Faenza.*

27 Later editions have *perte.*

28 Grammar, rhyme, and later editions all suggest *captif.*

29 Misprint for *Freius (Fréjus).*

30 *Antibes.*

31 Late editions give *leurs intentions.*

III.84

A great city is emptied and sacked, its people killed by war and disease: sack of Rome, 1775–9 [C] / World War III destruction of Paris [F] / Muslim destruction of Rome, 2000–2 [L] / destructive effects of removal of Berlin Wall [R].

La grand cité sera bien desolée
Des habitans un seul ny demeurra:
Mur, sexe, temple, & vierge violée,
Par fer, feu, peste, canon peuple mourra.

III.85

A southwestern French city is betrayed and captured: **Paris** and Narbonne in World War III [F] / **Muslim invasion** of France and capture of Narbonne, 2017 [L] / Fifth Column during Spanish Civil War, 1936–9 [R].

La cité prinse par tromperie & fraude,
Par le moyen d'un beau jeune atrapé:
Lassaut donné Roubine pres de l'AUDE
Luy & touts morts pour avoir bien trompé.

III.86

An Italian leader, traveling to Spain via **Marseille**, suffers a long death but leaves a remarkable legacy: Mafia (?) [C] / events in **Bordeaux** [R].

Le chef d'Ausonne aux Hespagnes ira
Par mer fera arrest dedans Marseille:
Avant sa mort un long temps languira:
Apres sa mort on verra grand merveille:

III.87

The French fleet is warned that any approach to Corsica or Sardinia will result in bloodshed, capture and death (see **III.23–4**): wreck of French fleet, 1655 [C] / ditto, 1646 [F] / reference to **Napoleon** [R].

Classe Gauloyse n'aproches de Corseigne[32]
Moins de sardaigne, tu t'en repentiras
Trestous mourres frustrés de laide Grogne:[33]
Sang nagera: captifs ne me croyras.

III.88

A seaborne force from Barcelona attacks **Marseille** and the islands (see **I.28, I.71**), while a betrayer is bloodily killed ashore (see **VII.37**): Spanish attack on **Marseille**, 1596 [C] / World War III [F] / **Muslim invasion** of France, 2005, 2009, or 2025–6 [L].

De Barcelonne par mer si grand armée,
Toute Marseille de frayeur tremblera:
Isles saisies de mer aide fermée,
Ton traditeur en terre nagera.

III.89

Cyprus is cut off from aid, while old people are killed and leaders are seduced and outraged: Cyprus troubles, 1950s [C,R] / Greek War of Independence, 1810 [F].

En ce temps la sera frustré Cypres
De son secours, de ceux de mer Egée:
Vieux trucidés: mais par masles & lyphres
Seduìct leur roy, royne plus outragée.

---

[32] Presumed misprint for *Corsegue* (Corsica), as per later editions: compare **III.99** below.

[33] Should read *l'aide gregue* (= *grecque*), to rhyme with corrected line 1.

III.90

A wild and lecherous Iranian leader allows an eastern European admiral based in southern Italy to take the area around **Marseille**: failed quatrain [C] / World War III [F] / **Muslim invasion** of France, 2005 [L].

Le grand Satyre & Tigre de Hyrcanie,
Don presenté à ceux de l'Ocean:
Un chef de classe istra de Carmanie
Qui prendra terre au Tyrren Phocean.

III.91

A long-dead tree bursts into leaf overnight, as leaders are incapacitated and ships set sail: birth, 1820, and exile, 1830, of duc de Bordeaux [C] / future rebirth of understanding [R].

L'arbre qu'avoit par long temps mort seché,
Dans une nuit viendra a reverdir:
Cron.[34] roy malade, prince pied estaché
Craint d'ennemis fera voile bondir.

III.92

Toward the end of the age, sovereignty is transferred to an eastern, dark-skinned nation as Narbonne is blinded by a "hawk": future decadence and growing power of Africa [C] / World War III [F] / **Muslim invasion** of France, 2017 [L] / rise of black Africa and Third World [R].

Le monde proche du dernier periode,
Saturne encor tard sera de retour:
Translat empire devers nation Brodde:
L'œil arraché à Narbon par Autour.

III.93

As North African forces are held off to the east, **Avignon** replaces a ruined **Paris** as capital, to the chagrin of **Lyon**: indeterminate future events [C] / reestablishment of France after liberation [F], 2025–6 [L,R].

Dans Avignon tout le chef de l'Empire
Fera arrest pour Paris desole:
Tricast tiendra l'Annibalique ire:
Lyon par change sera mal consolé.

III.94

In 500 years the "jewel of his age" is finally understood, to everybody's gratification: final decoding of the ***Prophecies*** by 2055 [C,H,L,R].

De cinq cents ans plus compte lon tiendra
Celuy qu'estoit l'ornement de son temps:
Puis à un coup grande clarté donrra
Que par ce siecle les rendra trescontens.

III.95

A more seductive dispensation follows the collapse of North African power, after Russian power has yielded to a more attractive regime: collapse of US-Soviet detente [C] / collapse of Russo-Muslim bloc [F] / decline of Islam and rise of Communism [R].

La loy Moricque on verra defaillir,
Apres une autre beaucoup plus seductive,
Boristhenes premier viendra faillir:
Pardons[35] & langue une plus attractive.

---

[34] Late editions give *son*.

[35] Later editions have *par dons*.

III.96

A leader from Fossano is murdered by his dog-handler at Rome's behest on February 13th [36]: stabbing of duc de Berry, 1820 [C] / atrocities in Muslim-occupied Italy, 2006 [L].

Chef de FOUSSAN aura gorge couper[37]
Par le ducteur du limier & levrier:
Le faict patré par ceux du mont TARPEE
Saturne en Leo. xiii de Fevrier.

III.97

A new dispensation takes over in the Levant, and the "barbarian empire" collapses before the end of the solar cycle: foundation of Israel, 1948 [C,L,R] or **Muslim invasion**, 1999 [L] / Six-Day War, 1967 [F] / Armageddon, 1997 [H].

Nouvelle loy terre neufve occuper
Vers la Syrie, Judee, & Palestine:
Le grand empire barbare corruer,
Avant que Phebés son siecle determine.

III.98

Two royal brothers fight for power and start a civil war: **Henri III** and duc d'**Alençon**, 1574–84, and/or Louis XIII and duc d'Orléans, 1662 [C] / Fifth War of Religion, 1574–6 [F] / future of World Organizations [R].

Deux royals freres si fort guerroyeront
Qu'entre eulx sera la guerre si mortelle,
Qu'un chacun places fortes occuperont:
De regne & vie sera leur grand querele.

III.99

A bitter final battle just to the northeast of **Salon** leads to the collapse of Iraqi power in France: World War III [F] / final liberation of France from Muslims, 2026 [L].

Aux champs herbeux d'Alein & du Varneigne,[38]
Du mont Lebron[39] proche de la Durance,
Camp de deux pars conflict sera sy aigre:
Mesopotamie deffallira en la France.

III.100

An undervalued leader defeats the foe by taking advantage of an envious one's death: Charles de Gaulle and Admiral Darlan [C,R].

Entre Gaulois le dernier honoré.
D'homme ennemi sera victorieux:
Force & terroir en moment exploré,
D'un coup de trait quand mourra l'envieux.

CENTURY IV

Transliterated from **Bonhomme**'s original 1555 edition.

IV.1

Venice seeks long-awaited help, but surrenders at the first bugle-call: Turkish attack on Cyprus, 1560–73 [C] / Ottomans in Crete (1545–64) and Cyprus [H] / Siege of Candia (Crete), 1667–9 [R].

---

[36] On Julian calendar.

[37] *coupee*.

[38] Read as *de Vernègues*: compare *Corseigne* for *Corsegue* in **III.87** above.

[39] Read as *Lubéron*.

Cela du reste de sang non espandu:
Venise quiert secours estre donné:
Apres avoir bien long temps attendu.
Cité livrée au premier corn sonné.

IV.2

France attacks Spain by sea and land, abducting many great ladies: War of Spanish Succession, 1701–13 [C] / Peninsular War, 1808–13 [F] / **French Revolution**, 1789, and the Spanish Civil War, 1936–9 [R].

Par mort la France prendra voyage à faire
Classe par mer, marcher monts Pyrenées,
Hespaigne en trouble, marcher gent militaire:
Des plus grand dames en France emmenées.

IV.3

Dark-skinned troops are expelled from eastern France, while forces from the **Rhône** valley attack southern Spain: French invasion of Spain, 1701, and/or C20 [C] / final expulsion of Muslim occupiers from France and Spain, 2032–4 [L].

D'Arras & Bourges, de Brodes grans enseignes
Un plus grand nombre de Gascons batre à pied,
Ceulx long du Rosne saigneront les Espaignes:
Proche du mont ou Sagonte s'assied.

IV.4

A criticized leader can do nothing as French and North Africans attack each other and huge invasion fleets expel the French from Italy: unsuccessful contemporary quatrain [C] / **Muslim invasion of Europe**, 2000–2 [L] / French and Italian colonization [R].

L'impotent prince faché, plainctz & quereles.
De rapts & pilles par coqz & par libyques:
Grand est par terre, par mer infinies voiles,
Seure Italie sera chassant Celtiques.

IV.5

As France and Spain are united under one religion, a disastrous conflict looms: War of Spanish Succession, 1710–13 [C] / conclusion of World War III [F] / final liberation of western Europe from Muslim occupation, 2034 [L] / Spanish membership of NATO and European Common Market [R].

Croix, paix, sous un accompli divin verbe,
L'Hespaigne & Gaule seront unis ensemble.
Grand clade proche, & combat tresacerbe,
Cueur si hardi ne sera qui ne tremble.

IV.6

After a truce, deadly cloak-and-dagger activities go on in Venice: **Muslim invasion** of Italy, 2000 [L].

D'habits nouveaux apres faicte la treuve,
Malice tramme & machination:
Premier mourra qui en fera la preuve
Couleur[1] venise insidiation.

IV.7

After the younger son of a hated ruler contracts leprosy, both he and his mother die: cancer (?) [C] / death of **Napoleon** II, 1832.

Le mineur filz du grand & hay prince,
De lepre aura à vingt ans grande tache:
De dueil sa mere mourra bien triste & mince.
Et il mourra la ou toumbe chef[2] lasche.

IV.8

St-Quentin is overcome by surprise nighttime attack: battle of St-Quentin, 1557 [C,F] / battle of St-Quentin in World War I, 1918 [R].

La grand cité d'assaut prompt repentin
Surprins de nuict, gardes interrompus
Les excubies & veilles sainct Quintin,
Trucidés, gardes & les pourtails rompus.

IV.9

A general is wounded in battle, while Geneva is betrayed by the rest of Switzerland: anti-Calvinist tirade [C] / World War III [F] / Treaty of Lausanne's sabotage of League of Nations [R].

Le chef du camp au milieu de la presse
Dun coup de fleche sera blessé aux cuisses,
Lors que Geneve en larmes & detresse
Sera trahie par Lozan & Souysses.

IV.10

False accusations against a prince cause military ructions and the leader's murder, followed by a royal accession: accession of future **Henri V** [F] / Edward VIII [R].

Le jeune prince accusé faulsement
Metra en trouble le camp & en querelles:
Meurtri le chef pour le soustenement:
Sceptre apaiser: puis guerir escroueles.

IV.11

A Pope commits an indiscretion and twelve "reds" are involved in murder: death of John Paul I, 1978 [C,H] / Committee of Twelve, 1793 [F] / Roman Catholic Church [R].

Celuy qu'aura gouvert de la grand cappe
Sera induict a quelque cas patrer:
Les XII rouges viendront souiller la nappe
Sous meurtre, meutre se viendra perpetrer

IV.12

A larger army is routed, reduced, and finally expelled from France: German invasions of World Wars I [C,F,R] and II [C,R] / final expulsion of Muslim occupiers, 2036 [L].

Le camp plus grand de route mis en fuite,
Gueres plus outre ne sera pourchassé:
Ost recampé, & legion reduicte
Puis hors des Gaules du tout sera chassé.

IV.13

News of a defeat causes dissension and desertions among the army: recapture of Antwerp from Duke of Parma, 1580s [C] / revolt of Spanish army and chief Falangist, Primo de Rivera, against Franco [R].

De plus grand perte nouvelles raportées,
Le raport fait le camp s'estonnera:
Bandes unies encontre revoltées:
Double phalange grand abandonnera.

IV.14

A young, new, redoubtable ruler succeeds on the sudden death of his predecessor: John F. Kennedy (?) [C,H] / future **Henri V** of France [F], 2034 [L] / assassination attempt on Ronald Reagan, 1981 [R].

La mort subite du premier personnaige
Aura changé & mis un autre au regne:
Tost, tard venu à si haut & bas aage,
Que terre & mer faudra que lon le craigne.

IV.15

Amid famine, supplies of oil and flour arrive under the eyes of a greedy, watching "sea-dog": World War II Atlantic convoys [C,H,L] / submarine oil exploration [R].

D'ou pensera faire venir famine,
De la viendra le rassasiement:
L'eil de la mer par avare canine
Pour de l'un autre donrra huyle, froment.

IV.16

A "free city" offers asylum to more and more refugees despite a new, more critical government: Orange [C] / Garibaldi's Thousand at Genoa, 1859 [F] / Danzig under Nazis [R].

La cité franche de liberté fait serve:
Des profligés & resveurs faict asyle.
Le roy changé à eux non si proterve:
De cent seront devenus plus de mille.

IV.17

A leader, walking by the **Saône** River, tries in vain to change the Carmelites in eastern France: submarine [R].

Changer à Beaune, Nuy,[3] Chalons & Digeon
Le duc voulant amander la Barrée
Marchant pres fleuve, poisson, bec de plongeon
Verra la queue: porte sera serrée.

IV.18

Astronomers and/or astrologers are persecuted by ignorant leaders (see **VIII.71**): Copernicus and Galileo [F,L] / or ban on astrological books, 1999 [L] / contempt for science [R].

Des plus letrés dessus les faits celestes
Seront par princes ignorants reprouvés:
Punis d'Edit, chassés, commes sceleftes,
Et mis à mort la ou seront trouvés.

IV.19

Forces from Italy besiege Rouen and go on to ravage the Belgian border: unfulfilled quatrain [C] / **Muslim invasion of Europe**, 2020–1 [L].

Devant ROUAN d'Insubres mis le siege,
Par terre & mer enfermés les passages:
D'Haynault, & Flandres, de Gand[4] & ceux de Liege,
Par dons laenees[5] raviront les rivages.

IV.20

Peace descends on a deserted France, to which the bodies of the fallen are now returned: end of Muslim occupation, 2026 [L] / famine and flood in France [R].

Paix uberté long temps lieu louera
Par tout son regne desert la fleur de lis:
Corps morts d'eau, terre la lon apportera,
Sperants vain heur d'estre la ensevelis.

---

[1] Possibly *Coule en.*

[2] Misprint for *chef.*

[3] *Nuits-St-Georges.*

[4] i.e. Ghent.

[5] Possibly *par dons & langue* (see **III.95**).

IV.21

Great changes to the social order prove profitable, but immensely difficult: France in World War II [C] / transfer of government to **Avignon** (see **III.93**, **VIII.38**) [F], 2036 [L], under future **Henri V** [F] / revolution [R].

Le changement sera fort difficile:
Cité, province au change gain fera:
Cueur haut, prudent mis, chassé lui habile.
Mer, terre, peuple son estat changera.

IV.22

Just when a king needs an absent army, it fails to arrive as promised: defeat of **Napoleon**'s Grand Army, 1812–13 [F] / Iranian Revolution, 1979 [R].

La grand copie qui sera deschassée,
Dans un moment fera besoing au roy:
La foy promise de loing sera fauscée
Nud se verra en piteux desarroy.

IV.23

Having embarked his army, "**Hercules**" attacks a "lunar" port with "Greek fire": Louis XIV's attack on Genoa, 1684 [C] / **Henri V** burns Istanbul [F] / counterattack on Muslim-occupied Genoa, 2026 [L] / repulsion of chemical attack on New York [R].

La legion dans la marine classe
Calcine, Magnes soulphre, & poix bruslera:
Le long repos de l'asseurée place:
Port Selyn, Hercle feu les consumera.

IV.24

A female voice underground presages an era of human, rather than divine, inspiration, plus persecution of the Church: **French Revolution** [C] / future coming of Maitreya (Buddhist "Messiah") [H] / temporary disruption of Nostradamus's nocturnal activities by family noise below [L].

Ouy sous terre saincte d'ame,[6] voix fainte,
Humaine flamme pour divine voyr luire,
Fera des seuls de leur sang terre tainte
Et les saints temples pour les impurs destruire.

IV.25

The seer's visions fade and are disrupted by exterior influences: disembodied experiences during trance [C,H] / disruption of visions, possibly by infant crying [L] / future occult knowledge and prophecies [R].

Corps sublimes sans fin à l'œil visibles
Obnubiler viendront par ses raisons:
Corps, front comprins, sens, chief,[7] & invisibles,
Diminuant les sacrées oraisons.

IV.26

[**Provençal quatrain**] A swarm of bees arises from nowhere, there is a nighttime ambush, and a city is betrayed by five speaking in code: **Napoleon**'s coup d'état of 1799 [C,H] and the Directory [R].

Lou grand eyssame se levera d'abelhos,
Que non sauran don te siegen venguddos
De nuech l'embousq;, lou gach dessous las treilhos,
Cieutad trahido p[8] cinq lengos non nudos.

IV.27

Salon, **Tarascon**, and **St-Paul-de-Mausole** unworthily ransom a Danish prince: John Paul II at Tarascon [F].

Salon, Mansol,[9] Tarascon de SEX l'arc,
Ou est debout encor la piramide,
Viendront livrer le prince Dannemarc
Rachat honni au temple d'Artemide.

IV.28

The sun's eclipsing of Venus reveals an occult form discovered by alchemical means and threatened by sounds of conflict: hermetic quatrain [C,R] / C18 philosophers [F] / the seer's conjurations disrupted by domestic strife [L].

Lors que Venus du sol sera couvert,
Souz l'esplendeur sera forme occulte:
Mercure au feu les aura descouvert
Par bruit bellique sera mis à l'insulte.

IV.29

The sun takes second place to Mercury, while Hermes is sacrificed to the fire, creating a "bright sun" in its own right: Hermetic quatrain [C] / the seer commits his Hermetic books to the flames [L] / alchemical practices [R].

Le Sol caché eclipse par Mercure
Ne sera mis que pour le ciel second:
De Vulcan Hermes sera faite pasture:
Sol sera veu pur rutilant & blond.

IV.30

Eleven months of prophetic dearth are sufficient to discover the secret: hermetic quatrain [C] / prophetic "lean period" [L] / alchemical practices [R].

Plus xi. fois Luna Sol[10] ne voudra,
Tous augmentés & baissés de degré:
Et si bas mis que peu si lon coudra:
Qu'apres faim peste descouvert le secret.

IV.31

Full moon sees the seer resume his practice, fully respected by his disciples: Nostradamus in meditation [C,R] / future world religious leader [H] / resumption of the seer's nightly sessions with order and authority restored [L] / success and secrecy [R].

La Lune au plain de nuit sus le haut mont,
Le nouveau sophe d'un seul cerveau la veu:[11]
Par ses disciples estre immortel semond
Yeux au mydi. En seins mains, corps au feu.

IV.32

As meat gives way to fish, the old dispensation is destroyed from within and common ownership abolished: collapse of Communism [C,H] / retreat of Communism, 1942 [F].

Es lieux & temps chair au poiss. donra lieu.
La loy commune sera faicte au contraire:
Vieux tiendra fort, puis oste du milieu
Le πάτα χοîναφιλῶμ[12] mis fort arriere.

IV.33

With Jupiter nearer Venus than the moon, Britain abandons veiled sex to fall under the spell of war: occult quatrain [C] / British debauchery [F] / sex gives way to war [R].

Juppiter joint plus Venus qu'à la Lune
Apparoissant de plenitude blanche:
Venus cachée soubs la blancheur Neptune,
De Mars frappé par la granée[13] branche.

IV.34

A great foreign leader, defeated in Italy, is brought before "**Chyren**" in chains: failed quatrain [C] / World War III and future Henri V [F] / European victory over Muslims, 2034 [L].

Le grand mené captif d'estrange terre,
D'or enchainé au roy CHYREN offert,
Qui dans Ausonne, Millan perdra la guerre,
Et tout son ost mis à feu & à fer.

IV.35

A flame is put out as virgins betray a new force, while monks or priests guard a king and throats are slit in Tuscany and Corsica: betrayal of **Napoleon** by women, then imprisonment and death, 1821 [F].

Le feu estaint, les vierges trahiront
La plus grand part de la bande nouvelle:
Fouldre à fer, lance les seulz roy garderont:
Etrusque & Corse, de nuit gorge allumelle.[14]

IV.36

After victory in Italy the games are restored in France, while the Pyrenees are subdued and Spain and the Holy Roman Empire tremble: **Napoleon**ic campaigns [C,F] / European counter-invasion of Europe, 2032 [L].

Les jeux nouveaux en Gaule redressés,
Apres victoire de l'Insubre champaigne:
Monts d'Esperie, les grands liés, troussés:
De peur trembler la Romaigne & l'Espaigne.

IV.37

French forces cross the Alps and occupy northern Italy, while Genoa and Monaco fight off a "red" fleet: **Napoleon**ic campaigns, 1800 [C] / World War III [F] / **Muslim invasion of Europe**, 2000, or subsequent liberation, 2027 [L] / **Henri IV** [R].

Gaulois par saults, monts viendra penetrer:
Occupera le grand lieu de l'Insubre:
Au plus profond son ost fera entrer:
Gennes, Monech pousseront classe rubre.

IV.38

War follows long hostility and the imprisonment of a Turkish leader on the Greek island of Samothrace: war between Greece and Turkey [F].

---

[6] Typical Nostradamian version of *dame*.

[7] Should probably read *sans chief*, as per later editions.

[8] *per*.

---

[9] Possible reference both to the Latin *Manus Solis* and to **St-Paul-De-Mausole** near **St-Rémy**.

[10] The words *Luna Sol* are from the second edition: the first substitutes astrological symbols.

[11] *l'a veu*.

---

[12] *pánta choìna philòm*: Greek for "all things held in common."

[13] Misprint for *gravée?*

[14] *à lamelle*.

[15] Apparently superfluous word, possibly misprint for *un*.

Pendant que duc, roy, royne occupera
Chef Bizant. dn[15] captif en Samothrace:
Avant l'assauit[16] l'un l'autre mangera:
Rebours ferré[17] suyvra du sang la trasse.

IV.39

As an Arab empire retreats, Western powers supply the aid implored by a neglected Rhodes: Iran-Iraq War [C] / European victory over Muslims [F], 2037 [L] / Syrian-Iraqi alliance [H] / economic decline of Saudi Arabia [R].

Les Rodiens demanderont secours
Par le neglet de ses hoyrs delaissée.
L'empire Arabe revalera son cours
Par Hesperies la cause redressée.

IV.40

Besieged fortresses are reduced to rubble, while priestly traitors are locked up: the last days of Hitler [C,H] / World War III [F] / warning to C16 heretics [R].

Les forteresses des assieges sarrés
Par pouldre à feu profondés en abysme:
Les prodeiters seront tous vifs serrés
Onc aux sacristes n'avint si piteux scisme.

IV.41

A general abandons escaped female prisoners to his army after being hoodwinked by them: tribulations of American Patti Hearst, 1974–5 [R].

Gymnique sexe captive par hostaige
Viendra de nuit custodes deceuvr:
Le chef du camp deceu par son langaige
Lairra à la gente, fera[18] piteux à voyr.

IV.42

Swiss prisoners in France, plus French sympathizers, are sold out by their own countrymen: World War III [F] / French civil disturbances [R].

Geneve & Langres par ceux de Chartres & Dolle,
Et par Grenoble captif au Montlimard:
Seysset, Losanne par fraudulente dole,
Les trahiront par or soyxante marc.

IV.43

Battles between "divine enemies" are heard in heaven, as enemies of holy laws put believers to death: C20 air battles [C,H] / invention of rockets, 1806, and **Napoleon**, 1809 [F] / C16 Wars of Religion, or Muslim assault on European Christianity, 2017+ [L] / religious war, and air-warfare [R].

Seront oys au ciel les armes batre:
Celuy an mesme les divins ennemis
Voudront loix sainctes injustement debatre
Par foudre & guerre bien croyans à mort mis.

IV.44

[**Provençal quatrain**] Civil war overtakes the southwest of France: civil war, 2026 [L] / rising against tax collectors [R].

Lous gros de Mende, de Roudés & Milhau
Cahors, Limoges, Castres malo sepmano
De nuech l'intrado, de Bourdeaux un cailhau
Par Perigort au toc de la campano.

IV.45

A ruler abandons his country to almost universal massacre: **Napoleon**, Napoleon III, or Kaiser Wilhelm II [C] / **Nostradamus** and Battle of Waterloo, 1815 [R].

Par conflit roy, regne abandonera:
Le plus grand chef faillira au besoing:
Mors profligés peu en rechapera,
Tous destranchés, un en sera tesmoing.

IV.46

The strong city of Tours is warned of coming ruin and noxious drizzle, despite protection by Britain: warning of ruin and fog (!) [C,R] / **Muslim invasion** of France, 2021–2 [L].

Bien defendu le faict par excelence,
Garde toy Tours de ta proche ruine.
Londres & Nantes par Reims fera defense
Ne passés outre au temps de la bruine.

IV.47

Using a whole arsenal of weapons, a ferocious "black" terrifies the people and strings up its leaders: Third World War (?) [C] / Charles IX and St. Bartholomew's Day Massacre, 1572 [H] / death of Mussolini, 1945 [R].

Le noir farouche quand aura essayé
Sa main sanguine par feu, fer, arcs tendus:
Trestout le peuple sera tant effraie,
Voyr les plus grads[19] par col & pieds pendus.

IV.48

Swarms of ravenous flies and grasshoppers veil the Italian sun while spreading disease: future spread of locusts to Europe (?) [C] / World War II aerial bombings [F] / **Muslim invasion of Europe**, 2000 [L] / World War II D-Day landings, 1944 [R].

Plannure Ausonne fertile, spacieuse
Produira taons si trestant sauterelles:
Clarté solaire deviendra nubileuse,
Ronger le tout, grand peste venir d'elles.

IV.49

Only after blood is shed aloft the sky is heaven's voice heard, thanks to a solitary spiritual witness (see **II.45**): execution of Louis XVI, 1792 [F] / assassination of President John F. Kennedy, 1963 [H,R] and his brother Robert R./ far-future extraterrestrial encounters, 2500+ [L].

Devant le peuple sang sera respandu
Que du haut ciel ne viendra esloigner:
Mais d'un long temps ne sera entendu
L'esprit d'un seul le viendra tesmoigner.

IV.50

Despite Western land- and air-victory, Asia's power is destroyed only after seven administrations: Third **Antichrist** [C] / Future Buddha Maitreya and new age of Light [H] / end of World War III [F] / victory of West over Muslim invaders, 2037 [L] / defeat of Asian forces after seven Spanish Popes [R].

Libra verra regner les Hesperies,
De ciel, & terre tenir la monarchie:
D'Asie forces nul ne verra peries
Que sept ne tiennent par rang la hierarchie.

IV.51

Near **Montpellier** a pursuing leader gets ahead of his army: Lord Louis Mountbatten [R].

Le duc cupide son ennemi ensuivre
Dans entrera empeschant la phalange:
Astes[20] à pied si pres viendront poursuivre,
Que la journee conflite pres de Gange.

IV.52

The besiegers of a city are seen off by a rain of fire just when its leader is about to surrender: urban America [R].

La cité obsese aux murs hommes & femmes
Ennemis hors le chef prestz à soy rendres
Vent sera fort encontre les gens-darmes:
Chassés seront par chaux, poussiere & cendre.

IV.53

Among returning exiles, a father, son, and family are killed while improving fortifications: failed quatrain (?) [C].

Les fuitifs & bannis revoqués:
Peres & filz grand garnisent les hauts puids:
Le cruel pere & les siens suffoqués:
Son filz plus pire submergé dans le puis.

Bonhomme's original edition ends at this point: the remaining prophecies are transliterated from du **Rosne's** edition of 1557, whose punctuation particularly should be taken with a pinch of salt.

IV.54

A fearsome ruler with an unheard-of name, and much attracted to foreign women, strikes fear into Italy, Spain, and England: **Napoleon** [C,F,H,R].

Du nom qui onques ne fut au Roy gaulois,
Jamais ne fut un foudre si craintif,
Tremblant l'Italie, l'Espagne, & les Anglois
De femme[21] estrangiers grandement attentif.

IV.55

When a crow calls for seven hours on a brick tower and a statue is stained with blood, a tyrant is set to be murdered.

Quant la corneille sur tour de brique joincte,
Durant sept heures ne fera que crier:
Mort presagee de sang statue taincte,
Tyran murtry, aux Dieux peuple prier.

IV.56

The incendiary spoutings of a bloody conqueror (see **III.81**) are more than flesh and blood can bear: **Muslim invasion of Europe**, 2017 [L] / Adolf Hitler and Jewish holocaust [R].

Apres victoire de rabieuse langue,
L'esprit tempté en tranquil & repos:
Victeur sanguin par conflict faict harangue,
Roustir la langue & la chair & les oz.

---

[16] Misprint for *l'assault.*

[17] Possible misprint for *serré.*

[18] Presumably *sera.*

[19] Misprint for *grands.*

[20] Later editions have *hastez.*

[21] Should presumably read *femmes.*

IV.57

Prompted by envy, a ruler proposes to ban certain writings, while his unmarried partner has an affair: cool reception of *Propheties* by **Henri II** [C], and his mistress Diane de Poitiers [C,H].

Ignare envie du grand Roy supportee,
Tiendra propos deffendre les escriptz:
Sa femme non femme par un autre tentee,
Plus double deux ne sort[22] ne crys.

IV.58

Under a burning sun, the leader of a bloodstained Tuscany, his wife abducted to Turkey, leads away his infant son: World War III [F] / **Muslim invasion of Europe**, 2000 [L].

Soleil ardant dans le gosier coller,
De sang humain arrouser terre Etrusque:
Chef seille d'eaue mener son fiz filet,
Captive dame conduicte en terre turque.

IV.59

Besieged leaders die of thirst, while an old dreamer shows the Genevans what Iran has done, now that the "strong man has been bound": World War II Teheran Conference, 1943 [F] / aftermath of **Muslim invasion of Europe**, 2024–6 (?) [L].

Deux assiegés en ardante ferveur,
De soif [sont][23] estainctz pour deux plainnes tasses
Le fort limé, & un vieillart resveur,
Aux Genevois de Nira monstra trasse.

IV.60

Of seven children left hostage, the third kills his child, while his son stabs two leaders and Genoa and Florence are demolished: assassination of **Henri III**, 1589, and Guises, 1588 [F].

Les sept enfans en hostaige laissés,
Le tiers viendra son enfant trucider:
Deux par son filz seront d'estoc percés,
Gennes, Florence lors viendra encunder.

IV.61

An old man is replaced and mocked by a foreigner, while his son's hands are mutilated (or his armies decimated) and his brother betrays Chartres, Orléans, and Rouen: Marshal Pétain [C,F,H] 1944 [F] / the Watergate affair and Richard Nixon, 1974 [R].

Le vieulz mocqué, & privé de sa place,
Par l'estrangier qui le subornera:
Main de son filz mangees devant sa face
Le frere à chatres, Orl.[24] Rouan trahira.

IV.62

An ambitious colonel stages a coup, but is discovered hiding: Cromwell [C], or Colonel Muammar Gaddafi of Libya [C,H,R] / the Conspiracy of Amboise, 1560 [F].

Un coronel machine ambition,
Se saisira de la plus grande armee:
Contre son prince feincte invention,
Et descouvert sera soubz la ramee.

IV.63

The French army traps and routs mountain-forces with the aid of local peasants: Marshal Villards' campaign against camisard rebels of Cévennes, 1702–4 [C] / White Terror, 1794 [F] / Andreas Hofer's Austrian peasant rebellion, 1797 [R].

L'armee Celtique contre les montaignars,
Qui seront sceuz & prins à la lipee
Paysans fresz poulseront tost faugnars,
Precipitez tous au fil de l'espee.

IV.64

A citizen-defaulter tries a king, and fifteen tenants deprive him of life and estates: fall of Louis-Philippe, 1848 [F] / fall of Shah of Persia, 1979 [R].

Le deffaillant en habit de bourgois,
Viendra le Roy tempter de son offence:
Quinze souldarts la pluspart Ustagois,
Vie derniere & chef de sa chevance.

IV.65

Because a fortress is abandoned, an enemy is able to put an emperor to death: **Napoleon** III [C,H] and loss of Metz, 1870 [F].

Au deserteur de la grand forteresse,
Apres qu'aura son lieu abandonné:
Son adversaire fera si grand prouesse,
L'Empereur tost mort sera condemné.

IV.66

Seven undercover "shaven-heads" poison wells, and cannibalism breaks out in Genoa: false prediction [C] / **Muslim invasion** of Italy [L].

Soubz couleur faincte de sept testes rasees
Serons[25] semés divers explorateurs:
Puys & fontaines de poyson arrousees,
Au fort de Gennes humains devorateurs.

IV.67

A conjunction of Saturn and Mars brings drought, spontaneous fires, hot winds, wars, and raids: future major famine [C] / far future [L].

L'an que Saturne & Mars esgaulx combust,
L'air fort seiché, longue trajection:
Par feux secretz, d'ardeur grand lieu adust,
Peu pluie, vent, chault, guerres, incursions.

IV.68

While screams are heard in the Mediterranean, leaders from North Africa and Asia Minor meet near Venice, representing the Rhine and Danube respectively: meeting of Hitler and Mussolini [C,H] / World War III [F] / **Muslim invasion of Europe**, 2003 [L].

En l'an bien proche [non][26] esloigné de Venus,
Les deux plus grands le l'Asie & d'Affrique:
Du Ryn & hilter,[27] qu'on dira sont venus,
Crys, pleurs à Malte & coste ligustique.

IV.69

Aquileans reveal to forces from Parma a secret way into a city full of casualties and refugees: liberation of Rome, 2028 [L] / intercity warfare [R].

La cité grande les exilés tiendront,
Les citadins mors, murtris, & chassés:
Ceulx d'Aquillee à Parme promettront,
Monstrer l'entree par les lieux non trassés.

IV.70

Near the Pyrenees a great army attacks the "eagle," but is wiped out and its leader pursued as far as Pau: Wellington and Peninsular War [C,F].

Bien contigue des grans monts Pyrenees,
Un contre l'aigle grand copie adresser:
Ouvertes vaines, forces extermines,
Que jusque à Pau, le chef viendra chasser.

IV.71

Vestal virgins are drowned or poisoned before marriage.

En lieu d'espouse les filles trucidees,
Murtre à grand faulte ne sera superstie:[28]
Dedans le puys vestules inondees,
L'espouse estaincte par hausse d'Aconile.[29]

IV.72

Northerners hold talks in southwestern France, but are too late to seize Condom and Mont-de-Marsan: World War II invasion of southwest France [F] / French civil war, 2026 [L].

Les Artoniques par Agen & l'Estore,
A sainct Felix feront le parlement:
Ceulx de Basas viendront à la mal'heure,
Saisir Condon & Marsan promptement.

IV.73

A nephew or grandson brutally exposes a half-hearted pact at an evening performance at Ferrara and Asti: assassination of Duc de Berry, 1820 [C,H,M] / attempted assassination of **Napoleon** III, 1858 [F].

Le nepveu grand par forces prouvera,
La pache faict du cœur pusillanime:
Ferrare & Ast le Duc esprovera,
Par lors qu'au soir sera le pantamime.

IV.74

Germans, Swiss, and French ally against forces from Aquitaine, but are defeated: World War III invasion of France [F] / **Muslim invasion** of France, 2020–1 [L] / World War II Italian campaign [R].

Du lac lyman & ceulx de Brannonices,
Tous assemblez contre ceulx d'Aquitaine:
Germains beaucoup [&][30] encor plus Souisses,
Seront deffaictz avec[31] ceulx d'Humaine.[32]

---

[22] Possibly *fort, font,* or even (to satisfy scansion) *feront bruyt.*

[23] Demanded by scansion.

[24] *Chartres, Orleans.*

[25] *seront.*

[26] Word inserted in later editions.

[27] Suggestive misprint for *Hifter (Hister).*

[28] Misprint for *supersite.*

[29] Misprint for *Aconite.*

[30] Syllable missing.

[31] Should read *avecque* for scansion.

[32] Typical Nostradamian blind for *de Maine.*

IV.75

Because of defectors an enemy is victorious, though the rearguard holds them up and the defectors die: Marshal Grouchy and Battle of Waterloo, 1815 C and **Napoleon**'s retreat from Moscow, 1812 C,F,H / World War II Pacific campaigns R.

Prest a combatre fera defection,
Chef adversaire obtiendra la victoire:
Larriere[33] garde fera defention,
Les deffaillans mort[34] au blanc territoire.

IV.76

Forces around **Agen** are harried all the way to the **Rhône**, while collaborators betray the Church: C16 **Wars of Religion** C / **Muslim invasion** of France, 2017 L.

Les Nictobriges par ceulx de Perigort,
Seront vexez tenant jusques au Rosne:
Lassotie de Gascons & Begorn,[35]
Trahir le temple, le prestre estant au prosne.

IV.77

With Araby and Italy pacified, a Christian world-ruler wishes to be buried at Blois: **Henri II** H and Diane de Poitiers C / **Henri V** of France F, 2037 L.

Selin monarque l'Italie pacifique,
Regnes unis Roy chrestien du monde:
Mourant vouldra coucher en terre blesique,
Apres [pyrates[36]] avoir chassé de l'onde.

IV.78

An army in a civil war successfully defends Parma against foreign insurgents.

La grand armee de la pugne civille,
Pour de nuict Parme à l'estrange trouvee:
Septante neuf murtris dedans la ville,
Les estrangiers passez tous à l'espee.

IV.79

The blood royal is warned to flee southwest France as the Bordelais rampage and famine spreads: civil war in southwest France, 2026 L.

Sang roy fuis Monthurt, Mas, Eguillon,
Remplis seront de Bourdelois les landes:
Navarre, Bigorre, pointes & eguillons,
Profondz de faim vorer de liege glandes.

IV.80

A great ditch divides a river into fifteen parts, while citizens of a captured town seek refuge in their amphitheater (see **X.6**): World War II Maginot Line (built in response to this prophecy!) C,H and occupation of **Paris**, 1940 F / disorder in Rome R.

Pres du grand fluve grand fosse terre egeste,
En quinze pars sera l'eaue divisee:
La cité prinse, feu, sang, crys, conflit mettre,[37]
Et la plus part concerne au collisee.

---

33 *l'arriere.*

34 Should read *mors.*

35 Should read *Begor* (Bigorre).

36 As per later editions.

37 Should presumably read *mestre*, as in late editions.

IV.81

A pontoon-bridge is built for a Belgian army, though some are cut down: Philip II's attack on France across Scheldt, 1560s C / Siege of Antwerp, 1585 R.

Pont on fera promptement de nacelles,
Passer l'armee du grand prince Belgique:
Dans profondrés & non loing de Brucelles,
Oultre passés detrenchés sept à picque.

IV.82

A horde advances from Slavonia, irreparably devastating Romania or the Holy Roman Empire: **Napoleon**'s retreat from Moscow, 1812 C,H or future Muslim jihad H / World War III F / **Muslim invasion of Europe**, 2000–6 L / decline of USSR R.

Amas s'approche venant d'Esclavonie,
L'Olestant vieulx cité ruynera:
Fort desolee verra la Romanie,
Puis la grand flamme estaindre ne scaura.

IV.83

A brave commander flees at night with his forces largely intact, despite sedition and attack by his own son.

Combat nocturne le vaillant capitaine,
Vaincu fuira, peu de gens profligez:
Son peuple esmu sedition non vaine,
Son propre filz le tiendra assiegé.

IV.84

A leader from Auxerre is persecuted and killed by his subordinates: distant past R.

Un grand d'Auserre mourra bien miserable,
Chassé de ceulx qui soubz luy ont esté:
Serré de chaisnes, apres d'un rude cable,
En l'an que Mars, Venus, Sol mis en esté.

IV.85

As one kind of plague follows another, a prisoner dies and the Moorish Camel is left on its feet: Louis XVI and VIII C / **Muslim invasion of Europe** (?) L.

Le charbon blanc du noir sera chassé,
Prisonnier faict mené au tombereau:
More Chameau sur piedz entrelassez,
Lors le puisnay sillera[38] l'auberau.

IV.86

With Saturn in Aquarius, a victorious, persecuting king is anointed at Reims and Aix: failed quatrain C / coronation of future **Henri V** F / installation of Muslim overlord, 2022 L.

L'an que Saturne en eaue sera conjoinct,
Avecques Sol, le Roy fort & puissant:
A Reims & Aix sera receu & oingt,
Apres conquestes murtrira innocent.

IV.87

A prince skilled in languages has his chief supporter killed by his father-in-law.

Un filz du Roy tant de langues aprins,
A son aisné au regne different:
Son pere beau au plus beau filz comprins,
Fera perir principe adeerant.[39]

---

38 Possibly *filera.*

39 Read as *principal adherant.*

IV.88

A base person called Antoine is attacked by lice, while a lead-thief is drowned in a harbor: death of Antoine, King of Navarre, at the Siege of Rouen, 1562 F.

Le grand Antoine du moindre fait sordide,
De Phintriase à son dernier rongé:
Un qui de plomb vouldra estre cupide,
Passant le port d'esleu sera plonge.

IV.89

Thirty Londoners conspire against their King, who is disinclined to die, and so a blond Frisian is elected King: James II and William III, 1688 C,F,L / Guy Fawkes plot, 1605 R.

Trente de Londres secret conjureront,
Contre leur roy sur le pont l'entreprise:
Luy, fatalistes la mort degousteront,
Un roy esleu blonde, natif de Frize.

IV.90

Because two armies fail to join up, Milan and Pavia are shaken and starved: failed quatrain C / World War III F / **Muslim invasion** of Italy, 2000–1 L / World War II R.

Les deux copies aux murs ne porront joindre,
Dans cest instant tremble Milan, Ticin:
Faim, soif, doutance, si fort les viendra poindre,
Chair, pain, ne vivres n'auront un seul bocin.

IV.91

A French leader, forced to fight a duel, is unjustly imprisoned for life as his son takes over and his ship fails to land in Malta or Monaco: "Man in Iron Mask," Count Mattioli, 1678 R.

Au duc gaulois contraint battre au duelle,
La nef Meselle[40] monech n?aprochera:
Tort accusé, prison perpetuelle,
Son filz regner avant mort taschera.

IV.92

A brave leader is beheaded and his body hanged from the yardarm as his discomfited fleet rows off against the wind: radio (?) R.

Teste tranchee du vaillant capitaine,
Sera getté devant son adversaire:
Son corps pendu de sa classe à l'antenne,
Confus fuira par rames à vent contraire.

IV.93

When a serpent is seen near the royal bed, a French prince is born whom all leaders see as heaven-sent: birth of comte de Chambord, 1820 C / birth of future **Henri V**, 2007–12 (?) L / future prince compared with Alexander the Great R.

Un serpent veu proche du lict royal,
Sera par dame, nuict chiens n'abayeront:
Lors naistra en France un prince tant royal,
Du ciel venu tous les princes verront.

---

40 Spelt *Meselle*: probable error for *Mélitte* – later editions have *Melelle.*

IV.94

One of two allies chased from Spain is defeated in the Pyrenees, forces from Germany stain the Rhône and Lake Geneva with blood, and Narbonne and **Béziers** are infected via **Agde** (see VIII.21): World War III [F] / **Muslim invasion** of France, 2017 [L].

Deux grands freres seront chassés d'Espaigne,
L'aisné vaincu soubz les monts Pyrenees:
Rougir mer, rosne, sang leman d'alemaigne,
Narbon, Bliterre, D'Atheniens[41] contaminees.

IV.95

When twin rulers attack each other and two "vestals" rebel, the younger, Breton "brother" is the winner: US-Soviet attack on Muslims [C] / World War III [F] / collapse of US-Soviet alliance, and nuclear winter [H] / French civil war, 2032 [L].

Le regne à deux laissé bien peu tiendront,
Trois ans sept mois passés feront la guerre:
Les deux vestales[42] contre rebelleront,
Victor puis nay en Armonique[43] terre.

IV.96

An older sister is born in Britain fifteen years before her brother, succeeding to the "kingdom of the balance": Mary, Queen of William III [C] / Britain's entry into European Common Market, 1970 [F] / American and **French Revolution**s, 1776 and 1791 [H,R].

La saeur[44] aisnee de l'isle Britannique,
Quinze ans devant le frere aura naissance:
Par son promis moyennant verrifique,
Succedera au regne de balance.

IV.97

When three planets go retrograde, the Portuguese royal line is prolonged by election: Portuguese succession, 1640 (?) [C,R].

L'an que Mercure, Mars. Ven' retrograde,
Du grand Monarque la ligne ne faillir:
Esleu du peuple l'usitant[45] pres de Gandole,[46]
Qu'en paix & regne viendra fort envieillir.

IV.98

As a result of public reactions to events at Langres, merciless "Albanian" forces inflict fire, bloodshed, disease, and famine on Rome: liberation of Muslim-occupied Europe, 2022–6 [L].

Les Albanois passeront dedans Rome,
Moyennant Langres de miples[47] affublés:
Marquis & Duc ne pardonner à homme,
Feu, sang morbile,[48] point d'eau, faillir les blés.

IV.99

A leader's grandson pushes back the French far into the west with massed "thunderbolts": World War II ballistic missile attack (?) [C] / William III and War of League of Augsburg, 1672–1702 [F] / **Muslim invasion of Europe**, 2005 [L].

L'aisné vaillant de la fille du Roy,
Repoulsera si profond les Celtiques:
Qu'il mettra fouldres, combien en tel arroy,
Peu & loing puis profond es Hesperiques.

IV.100

Fire from the sky descends on a royal palace, and seven months' war and slaughter ensue, while Rouen and Evreux remain loyal: Franco-Prussian War, 1870–1, and bombardment of Tuileries [C] / War of **Antichrist** and fall of **Henri V** [F].

De feu celeste au royal edifice.
Quant la lumiere de Mars deffaillira:
Sept mois grand guer,[49] mort gent de malefice,
Rouan, Evreux au Roy ne faillira.

CENTURY V

Transliterated from **du Rosne**'s 1557 edition.

V.1

Talks between leaders precede the ruin of France, as one of them is stabbed and secretly buried: death of Louis XVII, 1792 [C] / Northern Ireland conflict [R].

Avant venue de ruyne Celtique,
Dedans le temple deux parlamenteront
Poignard cœur d'un monté au coursier & picque,
Sans faire bruit le grand enterreront.

V.2

Seven draw swords against three at a banquet, and a shooting causes fleets or armies to change their allegiance.

Sept conjurés au banquet feront lu ye,[1]
Contre les trois le fer hors de navire:
L'un les deux classes au grand fera conduire,
Quant par le mail Denier[2] au front luy tire.

V.3

A new duke sails to Tuscany to offer peace and a naval agreement to Florence: duc de Lorraine, 1737 [C] / Victor Emmanuel II, Cavour, and unification of Italy, 1859–61 [F] / Mussolini's downfall [R].

Le successeur de la duché viendra.
Beaucop plus oultre que la mer de Toscane,
Gauloise branche la Florence tiendra,
Dans son giron d'accord nautique Rane.[3]

V.4

A "Great Mastiff," expelled from a city (see **II.41**), is angered at a foreign alliance, while Wolf and Bear defy each other: World War II [C,F].

Le gros mastin de cité descassé,[4]
Sera fasché de l'estrange alliance:
Apres aux camps avoir le chef[5] chassé,
Le Loup & l'Ours se donront defiance.

V.5

A claimed savior becomes a tyrant by using all the wiles and disinformation of a whore: **French Revolution**, 1789–92 [C] / Adolf Hitler, 1933, and Mein Kampf, 1925 [F] / last days of Hitler [R].

Soubz umbre faincte d'oster de servitude,
Peuple & cité, l'usurpera luy mesme:
Pire fera par fraulx de jeune pute,
Livré au champ lisant le faulx proësme.

V.6

A king blessed by a prophet changes into an emperor of peace: Napoleon III, 1848–51 [C] / **Henri V** crowned [L] by Pope [F], 2037 [L] / **Napoleon** [R].

Au roy l'Agur[6] sus le chef la main mettre,
Viendra prier pour la paix Italique:
A la main gauche viendra changer le septre,
De Roy viendra Empereur pacifique.

V.7

The bones of an ancient Triumvir are discovered by treasure seekers, much to the disquiet of locals: return of **Napoleon**'s ashes from St. Helena [C] / Rome after liberation from Muslims, 2028 [L] / Roman history [R].

Du triumvir seront trouvez les oz,
Cherchant profond tresor aenigmatique,
Ceulx d'alentour ne seront en repoz,
De concaver marbre & plomb metalique.

V.8

Bombs reduce a city to powder, while the resulting fires help the enemy: World War II [C] and/or nuclear holocaust [R], 1987–99 [H] / World War III destruction of **Paris** [F].

Sera laissé le feu vif mort caché,
Dedans les globes horribles espouventables,
De nuict à classe cité en pouldre lasché,
La cité à feu l'ennemy favorable.

V.9

As a great arch falls, a prisoner awaits a friend, and an omen foretells the death of a leader: attempted assassination of Napoleon III, 1858 [C].

Jusques aux fondz la grand arq demolue,
Par chef captif l'amy anticipé:
Naistra de dame front face chevelue,
Lors par astuce duc à mort attrape.[7]

V.10

A wounded French leader has to watch his followers killed until four unknown rescuers arrive: attempted assassination of Napoleon III, 1858 [C,F].

---

[41] Later editions all not unreasonably substitute *Agath* (Agde).

[42] Possible misprint for *vassales*, "subject regions."

[43] Possible misprint for *Armorique*, as in some late editions.

[44] Misprint for *sœur*.

[45] Nostradamian code for *Lusitan*.

[46] Error for *Gades* or *Gaddes*, as rhyme confirms.

[47] Later editions have *demipler* or *demiples*.

---

[48] *morbilles.*

[49] *guerre.*

[1] One letter has disappeared: should read *luyre*.

[2] Possibly *dernier*.

[3] *Rame*, altered so as to rhyme with line 2.

---

[4] Later editions have *deschassée*.

[5] Some editions have *cerf*.

[6] *l'augur.*

[7] Should read *attrapé*.

Un chef Celtique dans le conflit blessé
Aupres de cave voyant siens mort abatre:
De sang & playes & d'ennemis pressé,
Et secouruz par incogneuz de quatre.

V.11
The "solar" powers can no longer safely sail the seas once Venice controls North Africa and disaster has overwhelmed Asia Minor: Japan in World War II [C,H] / Chinese invasion [F] / **Muslim invasion** of Mediterranean [L] / British colonialism [R].

Mer par solaires seure ne passera,
Ceulx de Venus tiendront toute l'Affrique:
Leur regne plus Sol, Saturne n'occupera,
Et changera la part Asiatique.

V.12
A young woman betrays Geneva, and a great flight from Augsburg ensues as forces from the Rhine invade it: Battle of Augsburg, 1636 [C] / World War III [F] / birth of Fascism [R].

Aupres du lac Leman sera conduite,
Par garse estrange cité voulant trahir:
Avant son murtre à Auspurg la grand fuitte,[8]
Et ceulx du Ryn la viendront invahir.

V.13
From Rome a commander sends his Muslim forces to attack Belgium, but a ferocious counterattack chases the North Africans back from Hungary to Gibraltar: Thirty Years War, 1618–48, and Treaty of Pyrenees, 1659 [C] / European counterinvasion, 2025 [L] / collapse of balance between NATO and Warsaw Pact [R].

Par grand fureur le roy Romain belgique,
Vexer vouldra par phalange barbare:
Fureur grinsant chassera gent libique,
Despuis Panons jusques Hercules la hare.

V.14
With Spain under the heel of North Africa, an heir is captured near Malta, while France attacks Italy: Peninsular War, 1807–8, and **Napoleon**'s Egyptian campaign, 1798 [C] / **Muslim invasion of Europe** [F] / European counterinvasion, 2027 [L].

Saturne & Mars en Leo Espaigne captive,
Par chef libique au conflit attrapé:
Proche de Malthe, Heredde prinse vive,
Et Romain sceptre sera par coq frappé.

V.15
After a traveling Pope is taken prisoner (to the impotent horror of his priests) his successor wastes resources and sees his favorite killed: Pius VII's capture by **Napoleon**, 1808 [C] / capture of John Paul II [F], 2000 [L] / Catholic controversy [R].

En navigant captif prins grand pontife,
Grans apretz faillir les clercz tumultuez:
Second esleu absent son bien debife,
Son favory bastard à mort tué.

V.16
As deaths mount, the price of frankincense (from southern Arabia) reaches a peak, while Paros and Rhodes are threatened by Christian forces: World War II [C] / World War III [F] / European counter-invasion of Middle East, 2036–7 [L].

A son hault pris plus la lerme sabee,
D'humaine chair p'mort en cendre mettre:
A l'isle Pharos[9] par croisars perturbee,
Alors qu'a Rodes paroistra dur espectre.

V.17
After his army flees along the **Rhône**, a Cypriot leader is pursued at night by murderous plotters: death of World War III red leader [F] during liberation of Muslim-occupied Europe, 2026 [L].

De nuict passant le roy pres d'une Andronne,
Celuy de Cipres & principal guetto:[10]
Le roy failly la main fuict long du Rosne
Les conjurés l'iront à mort mettre.

V.18
After seven days a city falls and a princely victor celebrates, while a victim dies and true law is reestablished: liberation of Muslim-occupied Europe (?) [L].

De dueil mourra l'infelix profligé,
Celebrera son vitrix l'heccatombe:
Pristine loy franc edict redigé,
Le mur & Prince au septiesme jour tombe.

V.19
Once refinanced, the young, royal successor of a flawed leader breaks a truce and resumes murderous hostilities against the Muslims: resumption of European counterinvasion by future **Henri V**, 2035–6 [L].

Le grand Royal d'or, d'aerain augmenté,
Rompu la pache, par jeune ouverte guerre:
Peuple affligé par un chef lamenté,
De sang barbare sera couverte terre.

V.20
Encouraged by an omen, an army crosses the Alps and the leader of Tuscany suddenly retreats: Napoleon III and Duke Leopold II of Tuscany, 1854–9 [C] / **Napoleon** [R] and Duke Ferdinand III of Tuscany, 1801 [F] / European liberation of Italy, 2027+ [L].

Dela les Alpes grand armee passera,
Un peu devant naistra monstre vapin:
Prodigieux & subit tournera,
Le grand Toscan à son lieu plus propin.

V.21
On the death of a leader in Italy, his cronies and protégés loot everything and persecute the honest: Mussolini (?) [C] / death of "**Hercules**," 2033–4 [L].

Par le trespas du monarque latin,
Ceulx qu'il aura par regne secouruz:
Le feu luyra, divisé le butin,
La mort publique aux hardis incoruz.

V.22
Before a Roman leader dies, alarm spreads as a foreign army reaches Parma and joins another: Sino-Russian alliance after breakdown of US-Soviet one [C] / **Muslim invasion** of Italy, 2000 [L] / Communist leaders celebrate Pope's death [R].

Avant qu'a Rome grand ave rendu l'ame,
Effrayeur grande à l'armee estrangiere:
Par Esquadrons, l'embusche pres de Parme,
Puis les deux roges ensemble feront chere.

V.23
A wartime alliance between two leaders strikes fear into a North African leader, who tries to disrupt it by sea: disruption of US-Soviet alliance [C] / World War III [F] / USA joins campaign against Muslims, 2022+ [L] / Israeli-Egyptian alliance [R].

Les deux contens[11] seront unis ensemble,
Quant la pluspart à Mars seront conjoinct:
Le grand d'Affrique en effraieur & tremble,
Duumvirat par la classe desjoinct.

V.24
While Venus reigns, Saturn rules Jupiter, but the sun's reign bodes ill for Saturnians: World War III [F] / astrology predicts bad times for kingdoms, 3335 to 3696, but better times from 4055 onward[12] [L] / Louis XV [R].

Le regne & loy soubz Venus eslevé,
Saturne aura sur Jupiter empire:
La loy & regne par le Soleil levé,
Par Saturnins endurera le pire.

V.25
With Mars, Venus, and sun in Leo, Christendom is attacked by sea and a "coiled serpent" from the area of Iran invades Turkey and Egypt with forces a million strong: Iran-Iraq War, 1987 [C] / **Muslim invasion** [F], August 1998 [L] / **Antichrist**, 1987 [H] / oriental ideology overcomes Christian ideals [R].

Le prince Arabe, Mars, Sol, Venus, Lyon,
Regne d'Eglise par mer succombera:
Devers la Perse bien pres d'un million,
Bisance, Egipte ver. serp invadera.

V.26
A Slav (or enslaved) race rises up against its prince and mountain forces cross the sea under a leader from the provinces: exile of King Constantine of Greece, 1917 and 1922 [C] / USSR and Stalin [F,L,R].

La gent esclave par un heur martial,
Vien[13] en hault degré tant esleuee:
Changeront prince, naistre un provincial,
Passer la mer copie aux montz leuee.

---

[8] Or *suitte.*

[9] Probably *Paros.*

[10] Should presumably read *guette*, though some late editions have *guerre.*

[11] Possible contraction of *continens:* or "pleased leaders" (from Lat. *duces*).

[12] Reference to cycle of six 360-year ages apparently referred to in **Préface à César** (section **14**).

[13] *viendra.*

V.27

After forces from Persia occupy Trabzon (see V.25), Paros and Lesbos quake and the Adriatic flows with Arab blood: Middle Eastern war [C] / World War III [F] / **Muslim invasion of Europe**, 1998–9 [L] / Russian invasion [R].

Par feu & armes non loing de la marnegro
Viendra de Perse occuper trebisonde:
Trembler Pharos Methelin, Sol alegro,
De sang Arabe d'Adrie couvert unde.

V.28

A Genoan leader is strung up and slaughtered by three rabble-rousers: assassination of King Umberto of Italy, 1900 (?) [C] / attempted assassination of Hitler, 1944 [R].

Le bras pendu & la jambe liee,
Visaige, passe[14] au seing poingard caché:
Trois qui seront jurés de la meslee,
Au grand de Gennes sera le fert[15] lasché.

V.29

Liberty is denied while a proud black villain is in control, and maritime activities disrupt Venice and the lower Danube: Mussolini-Hitler meetings in Venice, 1934–8 [C] / **Napoleon** in Venice, 1797, and subsequent Austrian history to 1849 [F] / **Muslim invasion of Europe**, 2000 [L] / Mussolini [R].

La liberté ne sera recouvree,
L'occupera noir fier vilain inique:
Quant la matiere du pont sera ouvree,
D'Hister, Venise fachee la republique.

V.30

With **Paris** besieged by troops from Rome, massacres occur on its bridges (or pillage at sea): the French sack of Rome, 1797 and 1808 [C,R] / World War III [F] / **Muslim invasion** of France, 2021–2 [L].

Tout à l'entour de la grande cité,
Seront soldartz logés par champs & ville:
Donner l'assault Paris, Rome incité,
Sur le pont lors sera faicte grand pille.

V.31

Glorious Greece is ruined by the sea: tidal waves following Middle Eastern earthquakes, 2004 [L].

Par terre Attique chef de la sapience,
Qui de present est la rose du monde:
Pont ruyné & sa grand preeminence,
Sera subdite & naufragé des undes:

V.32

Disaster from the skies, like the seventh stone (of St. John's Revelation?), strikes when least expected: Franco-Prussian War, 1870–1 [C] / future global warming and economic collapse [H] / "Last Times" and cometary or asteroidal impact, 2020+ [L] / religious civil war [R].

Ou tout bon est, tout bien Soleil & Lune,
Est abondant sa ruyne s'approche:
Du ciel s'advance varier ta fortune,
En mesme estat que la septiesme roche.

V.33

Rebels stage a murderous rising at Nantes: revolutionary atrocities at Nantes, 1793 [C,F,H,R].

Des principaulx de [la][16] cité rebelle,
Qui tiendront fort pour liberté ravoir:
Detrencher masses infelice meslee,
Crys, hurlemens à Nantes piteux voir.

V.34

An invasion fleet from the west of Britain unexpectedly invades the Gironde estuary on behalf of the French monarchy: European counterinvasion of Muslim-occupied Europe, 2024+ [L].

Du plus profond de l'occident Anglois,
Ou est le chef de l'isle britannique:
Entrera classe dans Gyrande[17] par Blois,
Par vin & sel, feuz caché aux barriques.

V.35

At the start of a new campaign, a British fleet attacks Genoa beneath a "drizzle": European counterinvasion of Muslim-occupied Italy, 2026–7 [L].

Par cité franche de la grand mer Seline,
Qui porte encores à l'estomach la pierre:
Angloise classe viendra soubz la bruine,
Un rameau prendre du grand overte guerre.

V.36

A brother poisons his sister and her old female taster.

De sœur le frere par simulte faintise,
Viendra mesler rosee en myneral:
Sur la plancente[18] donne à vieille tardifue,
Meurt. le goustant sera simple & rural.

V.37

After twenty months, 300 conspirators succeed in betraying their King: Louis XVI committed for trial [R].

Trois cens seront d'un vouloir & accord,
Que pour venir au bout de leur attainte:
Vingtz moys apres tous & recordz,
Leur roy trahir simulant haine faincte.

V.38

A new king leads a debauched life that leads to the end of the Salic Law: Louis XV and **French Revolution** [C] / male degeneracy leading to female succession [R].

Ce grand monarque qu'au mort succedera,
Donnera vie illicite & lubrique:
Par nonchalence à tous concedera,
Qu'à la parfin fauldra la loy Salique.

V.39

A true-blooded French king inherits Tuscany and Florence: comte de Chambord [C] / Victor Emmanuel II, 1860, with Florence as capital [F] / **Henri II** and **Catherine de Médicis** [R].

Du vray rameau de fleur de lys issu,
Mis & logé heritier d'Hetrurie:
Son sang antique de longue main issue,
Fera Florence florir en l'armoirie.

V.40

An impure blood-line causes Western pressure on France until it dies out: Charles de Gaulle [C] / Franco-Spanish alliance [R].

Le sang royal sera si tresmeslé,
Constraint seron[t] Gaulois de l'Hesperie:
On attendra que terme soit coulé,
Et que memoire de la voix soit perie.

V.41

A great and good king born in obscurity of an ancient blood-line ushers in a Golden Age: C20 [C] / birth of **Henri V** of France, 2007–12 [L].

Nay soubs les umbres & journee nocturne,
Sera en regne & bonté souveraine:
Fera renaistre son sang de l'antique urne,
Renouvelant siecle d'or pour l'aerain.

V.42

Violent war drives Easterners out of France (see **III.99**), while the occupiers of northern Italy terrorize the West's Italian sympathizers: return of Savoy to France by Cavour, 1860 [C,F] / European counterinvasion of Italy, 2026 [L].

Mars eslevé en son plus hault beffroy,
Fera retraire les Allobrox de France:
La gent lombarde fera si grand effroy,
A ceux de l'Aigle comprins soubs la balance.

V.43

All over southern Europe the Church is devastated, while the Rhineland is ravaged by forces from Mainz: Protestant revolution [C] / **Muslim invasion of Europe**, 2021–2 [L] / World War II bombing of Cologne [R].

La grand ruyne des sacrés ne s'esloigne,
Provence, Naples, Secile, seez & Ponce:
En Germanie, au Ryn & à Colonge,
Vexés à mort par tous ceulx de Magonce.

V.44

Sea pirates capture "the Red," endangering peace, and the papal army is doubled: World War III [F] / Cardinal Mindszenty and the Hungarian uprising, 1956 [R].

Par mer le rouge sera prins des pyrates,
La paix sera par son moyen troublee:
L'ire & l'avare commettra par fainct[19] acte,
Au grand Pontife sera l'armee double[e].

V.45

The empire is desolated and transferred to the Ardennes as two bastards are killed and "hook-nosed **Aenobarbe** (Ahenobarbus)" takes over: World War II [C,H], or future Africa [C] / **Napoleon** III [F] / European civil war, 2032 [L].

Le grand Empire sera roi[20] desolé,
Et translaté pres d'arduer ne[21] silve:
Les deux bastardz par l'aisné decollé,
Et regnera Aenobarbe nay[22] de milve.

---

[19] Possibly *sainct*.

[20] Possible misprint for *droit*, though later editions have *tost*.

[21] Misprint for *arduenne*, as in later editions.

[22] Typical Nostradamian substitution for *nez*.

---

[14] *paſſe*, misprint for *paſle* (*pâle*).

[15] Later editions have *fer*.

---

[16] Syllable missing.

[17] Misprint for *Gyronde*.

[18] *placente*.

V.46

Cardinals feud over the election of a Sabine candidate, while Rome is damaged by Albanians (or people from Albano): events during World War III [F] / beginning of **Muslim invasion** of Italy, 2000 [L]. (Lines 1 and 2 are as printed.)

Par chapeaux rouges qrelles nouveaux,
Quant on aura esleu le Sabinois: (scismes
On produira contre luy grans sophismes,
Et sera Rome lesee par Albanois.

V.47

An advancing Arab leader is betrayed by Turks, Rhodians, and southern Hungarians: future events [C] / World War III [F] / **Muslim invasion of Europe**, 1999–2000 [L] / NATO versus Arab League [R].

Le grand Arabe marchera bien avant,
Trahy sera par les Bisantinois:
L'antique Rodes luy viendra au devant,
Et plus grand mal par austre[23] Pannonois.

V.48

After a major attack on the kingdom is repulsed, forces from North Africa launch murderous attacks on Hungary: future events [C] / **Muslim invasion of Europe**, 2000 [L].

Apres le grande affliction de sceptre,
Deux ennemis par eulx seront deffaictz:
Classe d'Affrique aux Pannons viendra naistre,
Par mer & terre seront horribles faictz.

V.49

A new Pope, of ancient French origin, makes a pact with a pestiferous foe: John Paul II [C,H] and AIDS [C] / War of Spanish Succession, 1701–14 [F] / next Pope at time of **Muslim invasion** of Italy, 2000 [L].

Nul de l'Espagne mais de l'antique France,
Ne sera esleu pour le tremblant nacelle:
A l'ennemy sera faicte fiance,
Qui dans son regne sera peste cruelle.

V.50

By the time two brothers are of age, one of them has conquered Rome and is about to take on the "strong man from Armenia": defeat of **Muslim invasion of Europe** [F], 2027–8 [L].

L'an que les freres du lys seront en aage,
L'un d'eulx tiendra la grande Romanie:
Trembler les monts ouvert latin passaige,
Pache marcher contre fort d'Armenie.

V.51

Czechs, British, Poles, and Romanians ally to attack North African tyrants in Spain and Italy: World War II [C] / counterinvasion of Muslim-occupied Europe, 2026 [L].

La gent de Dace, d'Angleterre & Palonne[24]
Et de Bohesme feront nouvelle ligue:
Pour passer oultre d'Hercules la colonne,
Barcins, Tyrrens dresser cruelle brigue.

V.52

A king turns everything upsidedown, promoting exiles and either supporting or persecuting the pure and chaste: future tyrant [C] / future **Henri V** [L] / Greek government turmoil [R].

Un Roy sera qui dourra[25] l'opposite,
Les exilés eslevés sur le regne:
De sang nager la gent caste hyppolite,
Et florira long temps soubz telle enseigne.[26]

V.53

People will not listen to competing "solar" or "Venusian" prophecies, even though the former are truly Messianic: Jewish ideas on Second Coming [C] / Messianic fulfillment of prophecies [L] / coming Savior resolves war between darkness and light [R].

La loy du Sol, & Venus contendens,
Appropriant l'esprit de prophetie.
Ne lun ne lautre ne seront entendens,
Par Sol tiendra la loy du grand Messie.

V.54

[**Summary verse**] From the area of the Black Sea and Turkestan (Central Asia) a leader penetrates the Caucasus, leaves a bloody rod in Turkey and continues as far as France (see II.29): Third Antichrist from Asia [C] / War of Antichrist [F] / **Muslim invasion of Europe**, 1998–2022 [L].

Du pont Euxine, & la grand Tartarie,
Un roy sera qui viendra voir la Gaule:
Transpercera Alane & l'Armenie,
Et dans Bisance lairra sanglante Gaule.

V.55

[**Summary verse**] A Muslim from a fortunate Arab land conquers Spain and invades Italy from the sea (see **V.54**): failed or retroactive prediction [C] / **Muslim invasion of Europe** [F], 2000–7 [L] / Ayatollah Khomeini and Iranian Revolution, 1979 [R].

De la felice Arabie contrade,
Naistra puissant de loy Mahometique:
Vexer l'Espaigne conquester la Grenade,
Et plus par mer à la gent lygustique.

V.56

A middle-aged Pope succeeds a very old one and reigns long and effectively, though accused of weakening the papacy: John XXIII and Paul VI [C,H] / Pius XI and XII [F] / C16 schisms [R].

Par le trespas de tresvieillart pontife,
Sera esleu [un] Romain de bon aage:
Qu'il sera dict que le siege debiffe,
Et long tiendra & de picquant ouvraige.

V.57

From Rome and northern Italy, a leader diverts his army through a tunnel, and "*Sext. mansol*" is captured between two rocks: Montgolfier brothers and Pius VI, 1775–99 [C,H,R] / flight of John Paul II [F], 2000 [L].

Istra du mont Gaulsier & Aventin,
Qui par le trou advertira l'armee:
Entre deux rocz sera prins le butin,
De Sext. mansol[27] faillir la renommee.

V.58

A leader from **Nîmes** chases his enemy across country and brutally ties him to the **Pont du Gard**: duc de Rohan reinforcing Calvinists, 1627 [C] / future war [R].

De l'archeduc[28] d'Uticense, Gardoing,
Par la forest & mont inaccessible:
Emmy[29] du pont sera tasché[30] au poing,
Le chef Nemans qui tant sera terrible.

V.59

A British leader, hurrying to help "Ahenobarbus" in Spain, delays too long at Nîmes, and several are killed by the war that then starts, as a meteor falls in Artois: future Antichrist [C] / counterinvasion of Muslim-occupied Europe, 2032–4 [L].

Au chef Anglois à Nymes trop sejour,
Devers l'Espaigne au secours Aenobarbe:
Plusieurs morront par Mars ouvert ce jour,
Quant en Artoys faillir estoille en barbe.

V.60

A "shaven-head" mistakenly appoints an incompetent who goes on to commit massacres: Oliver Cromwell [C] / **Napoleon**'s megalomania [F] / St. Bartholomew's Day massacre, 1572 [R].

Par teste rase viendra bien mal eslire,
Plus que sa charge ne porte passera:
Si grand fureur & raige fera dire,
Qu'a feu & sang tout sexe trenchera.

V.61

One whose father deserted him at birth conquers the Apennines and advances to the French border, terrifying "those of the balance": Eugène de Beauharnais, son of **Napoleon** [C] / World War III [F] / **Muslim invasion** of Italy, 2000–1 [L].

L'enfant du grand n'estant à sa naissance,
Subjuguera les haultz mont Apennis:
Fera trembler tous ceulx de la balance,
Et des monts feux jusques à mont Senis.

V.62

Blood spatters rocks at dawn, as ships are sunk, war reaches Orgon, disasters occur in Rome and the area around Trento is taken: future war of Antichrist [C] / World War III and occupation of Britain [F] / **Muslim invasion of Europe**, 2002–5 [L] / East–West war [R].

Sur les rochers sang on verra plouvoir,
Sol Orient, Saturne Occidental:
Pres Orgon guerre, à Rome grand mal voir,
Nefz parfondrees & prins le Tridental.

---

23 *auſtre*: possible misprint for *aultre*, or read as Latin *auster*, "south."

24 *Polonne.*

---

25 Either *douera* or *donrra.*

26 Possibly line 3 describes their former, and the contradictory line 4 their latter state.

---

27 Misprint for *mausol(e).* Most of the names in this verse are either direct references to, or geographical puns on, the area around the ancient Roman city of **Glanum** (**St-Rémy**).

28 Later editions not unreasonably substitute *aqueduct.*

29 *en my.*

30 Elision: read as *sera attaché.*

V.63

French forces vainly roam a devastated, flooded Italy, as blood flows near the Tiber and disease spreads: future war of Antichrist [C] / liberation of Italy, 1944 [F] / **Muslim invasion** of Italy [H], 2004 [L] / future events [C].

De vaine emprise l'honneur indue plaincte
Gallotz errans par latins froit, faim, vagues:
Non loing du tymbre de sang terre taincte,
Et sur humains seront diverses plagues.

V.64

Thanks to democratic apathy, authority is subverted and opposed along the Mediterranean coast: failed quatrain [C] / European civil war, 2032 (?) [L].

Les assemblés par repos du grand nombre,
Par terre & mer conseil contremandé:
Pres d l'Automne[31] Gennes, Nice de l'ombre,
Par champs & villes le chef contrebandé.

V.65

An undercover development causes great shock, as leaders object to the fact that witches are no longer burned: democratic agitation [R].

Subit venu l'effrayeur sera grande,
Des principaulx de l'affaire cachés:
Et dame en braise plus ne sera en veue,
De peu à peu seront les grans faschés.

V.66

Beneath a former Vestal temple, by a ruined aqueduct, gold and silver and an eternal lamp are discovered: future discoveries under former convent of St-Sauveur-de-la-Fontaine, **Nîmes** [C,L].

Soubz les antiques edifices vestaulx,
Non esloignez d'aqueduct ruyné:
De Sol & Luna sont les luisans metaulx.
Ardante lampe Traian d'or buriné.

V.67

When a leader from Pérouges (or Perugia) dares not wear his tunic, seven lords are captured and two of them are killed: Pope Sixtus V and the Valois [C].

Quant chef Perouse n'osera sa tunique,
Sens au couvert tout nud s'expolier:[32]
Seront prins sept faict Aristocratique,
Le pere & filz mors par poincte au colier.

V.68

[**Summary verse**] The "Great Camel" (see **IV.85**) comes to drink from Danube and Rhine, terrorizing the **Rhône** and even more the Loire, until defeated by the French near the Alps: failed quatrain [C] / Russo [F]-**Muslim invasion of Europe**, 2000–26 [L] / Turkish invasion [R].

Dans le Dannube & du Rin viendra boire,
Le grand Chameau ne s'en repentira:
Trembler du rosne & pl' fort ceux de loire:
Et pres des Alpes coq le ruynera.

V.69

A great leader rouses himself, overcomes any doubts and crushes North Africa with red, blue and gold battalions: French conquest of North Africa, 1830 [C] / tripartite Asiatic invasion of North Africa, 1999+ (?) [L] / US invasion, 1942 [R].

Plus ne sera le grand en faulx sommeil,
L'inquietude viendra prendre repoz:
Dresser phalange d'or, azur, & vermeil,
Subjuguer Affrique la ronger jusques aux oz.

V.70

Certain "Regions of the Balance" invade the mountains, taking prisoner a much-lamented Muslim army: Austrian troubles in Balkans, early C20 [C] / World War III [F] / counterinvasion of Muslim-occupied Europe, 2025–6 [L].

Des regions subjectes à la Balance,
Feront troubler les monts par grande guerre:
Captif tout sexe deu, & toute bisance,
Qu'on criera à l'aube terre à terre.

V.71

An army excitedly awaits the tide of events with seventeen boat-loads of nobles (or money), but a messenger arrives late: **Napoleon** or Hitler (?) [C] / World War III [F] / would-be **Muslim** [L] **invasion** of England [R], 2022–3 [L].

Par la fureur d'un qui attendra l'eaue,
Par sa grand raige tout l'exercite esmeu:
Chargé des nobles a dix sept basteulx,[33]
Au long du rosne tard messagier venu.

V.72

Drugs are mixed for use as aphrodisiacs but instinctive sex has its way: **Henri III**'s sexual deviancy [C] / pornography and moral laxity [R].

Pour le plaisir d'Edict voluptueux,
On meslera la poyson dans l'aloy:[34]
Venus sera en cours si vertueux,
Qu'obfusquera du Soleil tout aloy.[35]

V.73

As Arabs ally with Poles (or followers of Paul), the Church is persecuted and ransacked and children neglected: future events [C] / religion persecuted in Poland [F] / **Muslim invasion** of Italy, 2000–2 [L] / anti-Semitism and persecution of Catholics [R].

Persecutee sera de Dieu l'eglise,
Et les sainctz temples seront expoliez:
L'enfant la mere mettra nud en chemise,
Seront Arabes aux Polons raliez.

V.74

A Franco-German king frees Europe of Arabs and restores the Church: failed quatrain [C] / future **Henri V**, 2034–7 [L].

De sang Troyen naistra cœur Germanique,
Qu'il deviendra en si haulte puissance:
Hors chassera gent estrange Arabique,
Tournant l'eglise en pristine preeminence.

V.75

At noon a Pope(?) sits in the window high above St. Peter's Square and to the right, crook in hand, saying nothing: Pope(?) [C] / departure and flight of John Paul II, 2000 [L] / **French Revolution** and National Assembly [R].

Montera hault sur le bien plus à dextre,
Demoura assis sur la pierre quarree:
Vers le midy posé à la fenestre,
Baston tortu en main, bouche serree.

V.76

A general takes care to fight in open country, leaving no mark on the towns of **Provence** (see **III.99**): future **Henri V** makes **Avignon** his capital [F] / counterinvasion of Muslim-occupied France, 2026 [L].

En lieu libere[36] tendra son pavillon,
Et ne voldra en cités prendre place:
Aix, Carpen[37] l'isle volce, mont Cavaillon,
Par tous les lieux abolira la[38] trasse.

V.77

Classical paganism takes over in the Church until a king expunges it: C20 decline of religion, or militant Islam [C] / **Henri V** reimposes Christianity, 2034+ [L] / C16 clerical affairs [R].

Tous les degrés d'honneur ecclesiastique,
Seront changez en dial quirinal:
En Martial quirinal flaminique,
Un roy de France le rendre vulcanal.

V.78

After a thirteen-year inter-Muslim feud, Islam is wiped out and Christianity restored: breakdown of US-Soviet alliance [C,H] / collapse of Muslim occupation of Europe, 2023+ [L] / Hindenburg and Hitler, 1920–33 [R].

Les deux unys ne tiendront longuement,
Et dans treze ans au Barbare satrappe:
Aux deux costés seront tel perdement,
Qu'on benira la barque & sa cappe.

V.79

A peerless "Great Lawgiver" abolishes religious pomp, raises the lowly, and prosecutes rebels: **Napoleon** [C,F] / **Henri V**, 2034+ [L] / Abraham Lincoln [R].

La sacree pompe viendra baisser les aesles
Par la venue du grand legislateur:
Humble haulsera vexera les rebelles,
Naistra sur terre aucun aemulateur.

V.80

A "Gallic **Hercules**" chases the Muslim overlords out of Istanbul and paganism is rooted out, though the Muslim-Christian feud continues: European counterinvasion against Muslims [F], 2037 [L].

Logmion[39] grand bisance approuchera,
Chassé sera la barbarique ligne:[40]
Des deux loix l'une l'estinique lechera,[41]
Barbare & franche en perpetuelle brigue.

---

[31] Possibly misprint for *Ausonne*: later editions have *autonne*.

[32] Presumed misprint for *expofier* (*exposier*).

[33] Misprint for *basteaux*.

[34] Some late editions have *la loy*.

[35] Later editions have *à loy*.

[36] Presumably either *libéré* or *libre*.

[37] Abbreviation for *Carpentras*.

[38] Later editions suggest a misprint for *ʃa* (*sa*).

[39] *L'Ogmion*.

[40] *ligue*, to rhyme with line 4, as in late editions.

[41] *lachera*.

V.81

For seven months a premonitory eagle flies above a "solar city" at night, then within a week the eastern wall falls amid thunderbolts; Paris, Rome, and fall of Berlin Wall [C] / propaganda aircraft [L] and phoney war, 1939 [H] / **Muslim invasion** of France at **Lyon**, 2005–6 [L].

L'oiseau royal sur la cité solaire,
Sept moys devant fera nocturne augure:
Mur d'Orient cherra tonnaire, esclaire,
Sept jours aux portes les ennem.[42] à l'heure.

V.82

After a truce, despairing defenders of la Bresse fail to leave their fortress: Franco-German War, 1871 [F].

Au conclud pache hors de la forteresse
Ne sortira celuy en desespoir mys:
Quant ceux d'Albois de Lang,[43] contre Bresse,
Auront monts Dolle bouscade d'ennemis.

V.83

A ruler is warned of three plotters against a "kingdom without compare" while he is reading the Bible: Protestant Huguenots (?) [C] / plot against **Henri V**, 2033–4 (?) [L].

Ceulx qui auront entreprins subvertir,
Nompariel regne puissant & invincible:
Feront par fraude, nuictz trois advertir,
Quand le plus grand à table lira Bible.

V.84

[**Summary verse**] An obscurely born leader "from the Gulf and city measureless" is determined to destroy papal power all the way to northern France: Antichrist [F,L].

Naistra du gouffre & cité immesuree,
Nay de parens obscurs & tenebreux:
Qui la puissance du grand roy reveree,
Vouldra destruire par Rouan & Evreux.

V.85

The Swiss are assailed and their weaknesses exposed by swarms of military "locusts" from the coast: collapse of League of Nations and World War II [C,R] / World War III [F] / **Muslim invasion of Europe**, 2000–2 [L].

Par les Sueves & lieux circonvoisins,
Seront en guerre pour cause des nuees:
Camp marins locustes & confins,[44]
Du Leman faultes seront bien desnuees.

V.86

A city divided by two heads and three arms[45] is attacked from the sea, while Turkish leaders are forced to flee by Iranian invaders: **Paris** flooding, C17–18 [C] / **Muslim invasion of Europe** via Istanbul, 1998–9 [L] / surrender of **Paris**, 1940 [R].

Par les deux testes &[46] trois bras separés,
La cité grande par eaues sera vexee:
Des grans d'entre eulx par exil esgarés,
Par teste perse Bisance fort pressee.

V.87

With Saturn better aspected, France is flooded, while the "blood royal" marries in Spain: flooding in Midi, 1554 and marriage of **Philip II** to **Elisabeth de Valois**, 1559 [C] / marriage of **Henri V** as better times return, 2032 [L].

L'an que Saturne sera hors de servage
Au franc terroir sera d'eaue inondé:
De sang Troyen fera son mariage.
Et sera seur d'Espaignolz circonder.[47]

V.88

An exotic monster washed up after a storm presages the enslavement of Savona by Turin: ceding of Savona to Savoy, 1815 (?) [C] / Italian political infighting [R].

Sur le sablon par un hideux deluge,
Des autres mers trouvé monstre marins:[48]
Proche du lieu sera faict un refuge,
Tenant Savone esclave de Turin.

V.89

Foreign-instigated sedition arises in Hungary, while a Bourbon attacks Orléans: Bohemian Revolt, Thirty Years' War, 1618–48, and Gaston of Orleans, 1630 [F] / C16 religious troubles and Prince of **Condé** [R].

Dedans Hongrie par Boëme,[49] Navarre,
Et par banniere fainctes seditions:
Par fleurs de lys pays pourtant la barre,
Contre Orleans fera esmoutions.

V.90

Famine and plague caused by Muslims afflict Greece for nine months: disaster from "false dust" in Greece and Balkans [C] / Middle East and Balkans, 1821–56 [F] / pollution [H] / **Muslim invasion** of Europe, 2000–1 [L].

Dans les cyclades, en perinthe & larisse,
Dedans Sparte tout le Pelloponnesse:
Si grand famine, peste, par faulx connisse,[50]
Neuf moys tiendra & tout le cherrouesse.[51]

V.91

After Greece joins the "Market of Liars" (1993 or 2021), it is surprised by light cavalry from Albania: spread of Balkan War [H] / Greek membership of European Common Market and **Muslim invasion of Europe**, 2000–2 (?) [L] / invasion of Greece by Nordics [R].

Au grand marché qu'on dit des mensongers
Du bout[52] Torrent & champ Athenien:
Seront surprins par les chevaulx legiers,
Par Albanois Mars, Leo, Sat.[53] un versie.[54]

V.92

After a Pope has reigned for seventeen years, his term is changed to five years, and a less acceptable Pope is then elected: five Popes in seventeen years after Pius XII [C,H] / Pius XI and XII, 1939 [F] / John Paul II, 1995–2000 [L] / Louis Philippe and **Napoleon** III [R].

Apres le siege tenu dixsept ans,
Cinq changeront en tel revolue terme:[55]
Puis sera l'un esseu[56] de mesme temps,
Qui des Romains ne sera trop conforme.

V.93

Under the moon and Mercury, Scotland proves a source of disturbance to England: Bonnie Prince Charlie [C] / Scotland, then England, attacked by Muslims [F] / Scottish-instigated revolution in England [R].

Soubz le terroir du rond globe lunaire,
Lors que sera dominateur Mercure:
L'isle d'Escosse sera un luminaire,
Qui les Anglois mettra à desconfiture.

V.94

Northeastern France is incorporated into Greater Germany, while an Armenian leader breaks a pact and attacks Vienna and Cologne: World War II, Hitler and Stalin [C,H] / World War III [F].

Translatera en la grand Germanie,
Brabant & Flandres, Gand, Bruges, Bologne,
La tresve faincte le grand duc d'Armenie
Assaillira Vienne & la Cologne.

V.95

A great empire's fleet sails off into oblivion, leaving wrecked ships behind off Greece and Italy: Battle of Navarino, 1827 [F].

Nautique rame invitera les umbres,
Du grand Empire lors viendra conciter:
La mer Egee des lignes les encombres,
Empeschant l'onde Tyrrene desflotez.[57]

V.96

The "Rose" rules over the world's center, spilling public blood and compelling silence until rescue eventually comes: reaction against future oriental religion [H] / Mitterrand regime in France, 1981 [F] / **Muslim invasion** of Israel, 1999 [L] / Franklin D. Roosevelt [R].

Sur le millieu du grand monde la rose,
Pour nouveaux faictz sang public espandu:
A dire vray on aura bouche close,
Lors au besoing viendra tard l'attendu.

---

[42] Printer's abbreviation for *ennemis*.

[43] Later editions have *d'Arbois, de Langres*.

[44] Later editions not unreasonably have *cousins*.

[45] Presumably Istanbul, divided into three parts on two continents.

[46] Here possibly stands for *en*.

[47] Read as *circundé*.

[48] Should read *marin*.

[49] Read as *Boheme*.

[50] See **Nostradamus Dictionary**.

[51] Misprint for *cherronesse*.

[52] Later editions have *du tout* or *de tout*.

[53] *Saturne*.

[54] Misprint for *versie (versien)*.

[55] Read as *Tel terme révolu, (ils le) changeront en cinq (ans)*. The mutilated rhyme-scheme suggests that the too "dangerous" original may have read: *Changeront en cinq (ans) du terme la forme*.

[56] *esseu*, misprint for *esleu*.

[57] *de floter*.

V.97

When a deformed child is horribly suffocated in the capital, prisoners' rights are revoked and hail and thunderbolts afflict Condom: Edict of Nantes, 1598 (?) [C] / **Muslim invasion** of France, 2017 (?) [L].

Le nay difforme par horreur suffoqué,
Dans la cité du grand Roy habitable:
L'edict seure des captifz revoqué,
Gresle & tonnerre Condom inestimable.

V.98

On Latitude 48 drought strikes and fish are boiled alive as they swim (see **II.3**), while "fire from the sky" descends on southwest France: future events [C] / greenhouse effect, 1998–2000 [H] / World War III [F] / **Muslim invasion** of France, 2013–17 [L].

A quarante huict degré climaterique,
A fin de Cancer si grande seicheresse:
Poisson en mer fleuve, lac cuit hectique,
Bearn, Bigorre par feu ciel en detresse.

V.99

Franco-British forces attack northern and south-eastern Italy at a time when an old British general is in command of Rome: Cardinal York and **Napoleon**ic campaigns [C] / allied liberation of Italy under General Bernard Montgomery, 1944 [F].

Milan, Ferrare, Turin, & Aquilloye,
Capne, Brundis[58] vexés par gent Celtique,
Par le Lyon & phalange aquilee,
Quant Rome aura le chef vieux Britanique.

V.100

A firebrand is burned by his own fire in southwest France, while an old leader is rescued by Germans: future events [C] / nuclear war [H] / **Muslim invasion** of France, 2017 [L] / trials of former Nazi war-criminals [R].

Le boutefeu par son feu attrapé,
De feu du ciel à Carcas & Cominge:
Foix, Aux, Mazeres haut viellart eschapé,
Par ceulx de Hasse, des Saxons & Turinge.

CENTURY VI

Transliterated from **du Rosne**'s 1557 edition.

VI.1

Masses of foreigners rescue a new king in the Pyrenees, while a leader from Rome cowers in the water at Mas d'Agenais: future **Henri V** liberates southwest France [F], 2033–4 [L].

Autour des monts Pirenees grand amas,
De gent estrange, secourir roy noveau:
Pres de Garonne du grand temple du Mas,
Un Romain chef le caindra[1] dedans l'eau.

VI.2

In around the year '580 a strange new era begins, while in '703 up to five kingdoms change: Seventh **War of Religion** and War of Spanish Succession [C] / or 1972 and 2095 by **liturgical count** [L] / or 1914 and 2028 from Council of Nicaea [R].

En l'an cinq cens octante plus & [2] moins,
On attend[3] le siecle bien estrange:
En l'an sept cens & trois cieulx en tesmoins,
Que plusieurs regnes un à cinq feront change.

VI.3

A young French prince goes to war against an Empire over a river for religious reasons: conflict over Rhine [C,R] (?) and **Napoleon** [C] / or counter-invasion of Muslim-occupied Europe, 2022–6 [L].

Fleuve qu'esprove le noveau nay Celtique,
Sera en grande de l'Empire discorde:
Le jeune prince par gent ecclesiastique,
Ostera le sceptre coronal de concorde.

VI.4

Cologne and the lands bordering on the Rhine change hands, though the language remains as it was: Franco-Prussian War and Alsace and Lorraine, 1870–1 [C,H] / World War III destruction of **Paris** [F].

Le Celtique fleuve changera de rivaige
Plus ne tiendra la cité d'Aripine:[4]
Tout transmué ormis le viel langaige,
Saturne Leo, Mars, Cancer en rapine.

VI.5

As the northern hemisphere is swept by plague, famine and long rains, **Samarobryn** (plural) orbit at an altitude of 276.4 miles/445 kms, well clear of laws and politics: space-research on AIDS (?) [C,H] / **Russian Revolution** [F] / far future extra terrestrials [L].

Si grand famine par unde pestifere,
Par pluye longue le long du polle artique:
Samarobryn cent lieux de l'hemispere,[5]
Vivront sans loy, exemp[6] de pollitique.

VI.6

After a comet appears in the northern sky over Greece, a Pope dies the night it disappears: death of Pius IX, 1878, and election of Leo XIII [C] / death of John Paul II [F], 2000 [L].

Apparoistra vers le Septentrion,
Non loing de Cancer l'estoille chevelue:
Suze, Sienne, Boece Eretrion,
Mourra de Rome grand, la nuict disperue.

VI.7

Norway, Romania and Britain are disturbed by "two brothers," while the forces of a French-born ruler of Rome are driven into the forests (see **V.45**): French Maquis during World War II [C] / World War III [F] / European civil war, 2032 [L] / French Pope and conflict between NATO and Warsaw Pact [R].

Norneigre[7] & Dace, & l'isle Britanique,
Par les unis freres seront vexees:
Le chef Romain issue de sang Gallique,
Et les copies aux forestz repoulsees.

VI.8

Students and exiles are impoverished under a new regime, and scholars and learning despised: general quatrain [C] / far future [L].

Ceulx qui estoient en regne pour scavoir,
Au Royal change deviendront apouvrie:
Uns exilés sans appuy, or n'avoir,
Jettés[8] & lettres ne seront à grans pris.

VI.9

Honors are awarded for atrocities against the churches, but the one who issues the resulting medals meets a bad end: assassination attempt on John Paul II, 1981 [H] / **Muslim invasion of Europe**, 2017–22 [L] / St. Bartholomew's Day massacre, 1572, and **Henri IV** [R].

Aux sacres temples seront faicts escandales
Comptés seront par honneurs & louanges:
D'un que on grave d'argent dor[9] les medalles,
La fin sera en tourmens bien estranges.

VI.10

During a time of disasters, "reds" and "yellows" rob the churches of mixed "blacks" and "whites": Sino-Soviet invasion and Last Times [C] / intermingling of faiths, and Apocalypse [H] / **Muslim invasion of Europe**, 2000–2 [L] / world unity [R].

Un peu de temps les temples des couleurs
De blanc & noir des deux entre meslee:
Roges & jaunes leur embleront les leurs,
Sang, terre, peste, faim, feu, d'eaue affollee.

VI.11

Seven heirs are reduced to three as two kill two others and then are themselves murdered in their sleep: Valois princes, 1588, and Guise murders, 1588 [C,F,H].

Des sept rameaulx à trois seront reductz
Les plus aînés seront surprins par mort:
Fratricider les deux seront seduictz,
Les conjurés en dormant seront mort.

VI.12

Authorized by the Vatican, a king allies with Holland and England to attack Italy and France with Spanish moral support: **Napoleon**ic Wars [C,F] / counterinvasion of Muslim-occupied Europe, 2022+ [L] / conflict over papal election [R].

Dresser copie [pour][10] monter à l'Empire,
Du Vatican le sang Royal tiendra:
Flamans, Anglois, Espaigne avec Aspire,
Contre l'Italie & France contendra.

---

[58] Misprint for *Capue, Brindis.*

[1] *craindra.*

[2] Here stands for *ou.*

[3] Scansion demands *attendra*, as in some later editions.

[4] Should read *Agripine* (from Latin *Colonia Agrippina*, Cologne).

[5] Misprint for *hemisphere.*

[6] Misprint for *exempt.*

[7] *Norveige.*

[8] Later editions have *Lettrez.*

[9] *d'or.*

[10] Missing word inserted in later editions.

VI.13

People and government argue over the claims of a doubtful ruler who in any case proves unequal to the task: Pius IX, 1846–70 [F] / **Napoleon** [R].

Un dubieux ne viendra loing du regne,
La plus gtand[11] part le vouldra soustenir:
Un capitole ne vouldra point qu'il regne,
Sa grande charge ne pourra maintenir.

VI.14

A king loses a foreign battle, then escapes and is recaptured after concealing his golden armor under a disguise: crusade of Sebastian of Portugal, 1578 [C] / **Napoleon** before Moscow [R].

Loing de sa terre Roy perdra la bataille,
Prompt eschappé poursuivy suivant prins
Ignare prins soubz la doree maille
Soubz fainct[12] habit & l'ennemy surprins.

VI.15

A Spanish conqueror of Nuremberg is found under a tomb after being betrayed by a leader from Wittenberg: Nuremberg trials [R].

Dessoubz la tombe sera trouvé le prince,
Qu'aura le pris par dessus Nuremberg:
L'Espaingnol Roy en Capricorne mince,
Fainct & trahy par le grand Vitemberg.[13]

VI.16

Black Forest Benedictines turn a prize taken by northern French forces from a "young hawk" in Lombardy into a hostel: counterinvasion of Muslim-occupied Europe, 2026–7 [L].

Ce que ravy sera du jeune Milve,
Par les Normans de France & Picardie:
Les noirs du temple du lieu Negresilve,
Feront aulberge & feu de Lombardie.

VI.17

After books are burned and "Saturnine" ass-drivers are forced to change clothes, those who do so are burned: Nazi book-burning [R].

Apres les limes[14] bruslez les asiniers,
Constrainctz seront changer habitz divers:
Les Saturnins bruslez par les musniers,[15]
Hors la pluspart qui ne sera couvers.

VI.18

After a ruler is cured by luck rather than medicine, a Jewish physician attains great eminence for himself and his Christ-denying race: Nostradamus, and rehabilitation of Jews [C,R].

Par les physiques le grand Roy delaissé,
Par sort non art ne l'Ebrieu est en vie:
Luy & son genre au regne hault poulsé,
Grace donnee à gent qui Christ envie.

VI.19

A female firebrand is burned with her own fire (see **V.100**), and an army prepares to attack when an oxlike monster is seen in Seville: Spanish Civil War, 1936–9 [F].

La vraye flamme engloutira la dame,
Que vouldra mettre les Innocens à feu:
Pres de l'assault l'exercite s'enflamme,
Quant dans Seville monstre en bœuf sera veu.

VI.20

An alliance fails to last, a battle-hardened army comes ashore and a new "Lion" takes over in Rome: failed quatrain [C], or Pope John XXIII [C,H] / **Muslim invasion** of Italy and new Pope, 2001 [L] / collapse of union between Egypt and Israel [R].

L'union faincte sera peu de duree,
Des uns changés reformés la pluspart:
Dans les vaisseaux sera gent enduree,
Lors aura Rome un nouveau liepart.

VI.21

The East trembles as the North unites under a new, Church-supported leader and Rhodes and Istanbul are stained with blood: AIDS research, John Paul II [C], and Middle Eastern wars [C,H] / World War III and John Paul II [F] / future **Henri V**'s Middle-Eastern campaign, 2034–5 [L].

Quant ceulx de polle artiq unis ensemble,
En Orient grand effraieur & crainte:
Esleu nouveau sustenu le grand temple,
Rode Bisance de sang Barbare taincte.

VI.22

When a grandson is murdered in London, the Church is split and sacred liberty proclaimed: Archbishop Lefèvre [C,F] / murdered corpse found in St. Paul's cathedral [R].

Dedans la terre du grand temple celique,
Nepveu à londres par paix faincte meurtry
La barque alors deviendta scimatique,[16]
Liberté faincte[17] sera au corn & cry.

VI.23

The coinage depreciates as the people rebel, new laws are passed and **Paris** is in turmoil: **French Revolution** [C,H,L,R] / World War III financial crisis [F].

D'esprit de regne munismes[18] descriees,
Et seront peuples esmeuz contre leur Roy:
Paix, faict nouveau sainctes loix empirees,
Rapis onc fut en si tresdur arroy.

VI.24

War under Mars and Jupiter is followed by the anointing of a king who brings long-term peace: war, 2002, followed by peace [C] / World Redeemer, 2002, and Age of Aquarius [H] / **Muslim invasion of Europe** and **Henri V**, 2002+ [L].

Mars & le sceptre se trouvera conjoinct,
Dessoubz Cancer calamiteuse guerre:
Un peu apres sera nouveau Roy oingt,
Qui par long temps pacifiera la terre.

VI.25

War ruins the Papacy on a day of drizzle, as a new, "red black" ruler takes over: **Napoleon** and papacy [C,H], and King Victor Emmanuel [C] / **French Revolution** [F] / **Muslim invasion** of Italy, 2000 [L] / **Napoleon**'s overthrow of Directory, 1798 [R].

Par Mars contraire sera la monarchie.
Du grand pescheur en trouble ruyneux:
Jeune noir rouge prendra la hierarchie,
Les proditeurs iront jour bruyneux.

VI.26

After an uncertain four-year reign, a new, lecherous Pope is nevertheless supported by three Italian cities: John XXIII and Paul VI [C,H] / Pius VI, 1795–9 [F].

Quatre an[s][19] le siege que[20] peu bien tiendra,
Un surviendra libidineux de vie:
Ravenne & Pyse, Veronne soustiendront,
Pour eslever la croix de Pape envie.

VI.27

"**Chyren**" attacks the "lunar crescent" among islands at the head of a five-fold alliance and, as drizzle falls, only six escape: from Britain future **Henri V** counterattacks Muslims [F] / ditto in the Cyclades [L].

Dedans les isles de cinq fleuves[21] à un,
Par le croissant du grand Chyren Selin:
Par les bruynes de l'aër fureur en l'un,
Six eschapés cachés fardeaux de lyn.

VI.28

When a Frenchman enters Rome at the head of an army of exiles, the Pope kills (or shelters) those who fought for France in the Alps: **Napoleon** [R] and Pius VII [C] / future **Henri V** enters Rome [F] on liberation of Muslim-occupied Italy [L].

Le grand Celtique entrera dedans Rome,
Menant amas d'exilés & bannis:
La grand pasteur mettra à mort[22] tout homme
Qui pour le coq estoient aux Alpes unys.

VI.29

A holy widow is disturbed by news of her children, but they are triumphantly ransomed from the "shaven-heads": **Catherine de Médicis** [C] / papal interregnum [R].

La vefue saincte entendant les nouvelles,
De ses rameaux mis en perplex & trouble:
Qui sera duict appaiser les quererelles,[23]
Par son pourchas des razes fera comble.

---

[11] Misprint for *grand*.

[12] Or *sainct*.

[13] i.e. Wittenberg.

[14] Some late editions have *livres*.

[15] Later editions have *meusniers*.

[16] Should read *deviendra scismatique*.

[17] Or *saincte*.

[18] Probable misprint for *numismes*, as in some later editions.

[19] Missing letter.

[20] Later editions have *quelque*.

[21] Possible misprint for *peuples*.

[22] One edition [F] suggests *port*.

[23] *querelles*.

VI.30

"Faked sanctity" betrays the Vatican to the foe in a night-attack, while Belgium is on the march: World War II invasion of Low Countries, 1940 F / **Muslim invasion of Europe**, 2000 or 2002 L.

Par l'apparence de faincte saincteté,
Sera trahy aux ennemis le siege:
Nuict qu'on cuidoit dormir en seureté,
Pres de Braban marcheront ceulx du liege.

VI.31

A king is pleased at the wrongful recapture of a bishop, but angered by a general's killings in Milan: King Umberto of Italy and Mussolini C / Mussolini and Cardinal Schuster, 1945 F.

Roy trouvera ce qu'il desiroit tant,
Quant le Prelat sera reprins à tort:
Responce au[24] duc le rendra mal content,
Qui dans Milan mettre plusieurs à mort.

VI.32

A leader, overcome by disorders resulting from wrongful killings, is furious at being deceived about an attack by Turkey (or Berry): assassination of duc de Berry, 1820 F.

Par trahysons de vers[25] gens à mort battu,
Prins surmonté sera par son desordre:
Conseil frivole au grand captif sentu,
Nez p'fureur quant Begich[26] viendra mordre.

VI.33

Because "Alus" cannot assure his safety overseas, an Iraqi leader cowers before an army and a "Furious Black" subdues him: Antichrist C / future defeat of Saddam Hussein H / Gulf War, 1981 L / Black Power riots in USA R.

Sa main derniere par Alus sanguinaire,
Ne se pourra par la mer guarantir:
Entre deux fluves[27] caindre[28] main militaire,
Le noir l'ireux le fera repentir.

VI.34

A "flying-fire" device troubles a besieged leader, while sedition leads to despair: C20 rocket attack C on Paris F, or flame-throwing tanks R / **Muslim invasion** of France, 2013–17 L.

De feu volant la machination.
Viendra troubler au grand chef assigés:[29]
Dedans sera telle sedition,
Qu'en desespoir seront les proffigés.[30]

VI.35

From March until September widespread fires or droughts occur, while undercover intelligence goes on.

---

[24] Possible misprint: *du* would make more sense here.

[25] *devers.*

[26] *Berich* in later editions.

[27] Usual spelling for *fleuves.*

[28] *craindre.*

[29] *assiegés.*

[30] Misprint for *profligés.*

Pres de Rion,[31] & proche à blanche laine,[32]
Aries, Taurus, Cancer, Leo la Vierge:
Mars Jupiter le Sol ardra grant plaine,
Boys & cités, lettres cachés au cierge.

VI.36

While an indecisive battle is fought near Perugia, Pisa rebels, Florence does badly and a leader flees wretchedly at night: **Muslim invasion** of Italy, 2000 L.

Ne bien ne mal par bataille terrestre,
Ne parviendra aux confins de Perouse:
Rebeller Pise, Florence voir mal estre,
Roy nuict blessé sus mulet à noire house.

VI.37

An innocent is accused of murdering a leader from a rooftop, while the culprit hides amid misty woods: assassination of John F. Kennedy, 1963 H / Louis XVI R.

L'œuvre ancienne se parachevera,
Du toict cherra sur le grand mal ruyne:
Innocent faict mort on accusera:
Nocent caiché, taillis à la bruyne.

VI.38

Once Italy is subdued, a "bloody Black" embarks on an orgy of arson and bloodshed: Abu Abbas H / **French Revolution**, 1799, and **Napoleon** in Italy, 1797 F / **Muslim invasion** of Italy, 2000 L / Mussolini's Fascist rape of Italy R.

Aux profligés de paix les ennemis,
Apres avoir l'Italie supperee:
Noir sanguinaire, rouge sera commis,
Feu, sang verser, eaue de sang couloree.

VI.39

Hostages celebrate when a prince is exchanged for his captured father.

L'enfant du regne par paternelle prinse,
Expolié sera pour delivrer:
Aupres du lac Trasimen l'azur prinse,
La trope hostaige pour trop fort s'enyvrer.

VI.40

When a leader from Mainz is demoted for his greed, Cologne insists that he be thrown into the Rhine: sacking of Archbishops of Mainz and Cologne as Electors, 1803 and 1806 C / death of Hitler R.

Grand de magonce pour grande soif estaindre,
Sera privé de sa grand dignité:
Ceux de cologne si fort le viendront plaindre
Que le grand groppe[33] au Ryn sera getté.

VI.41

At Holland's and Britain's behest, Denmark's second-in-command spends a fortune on a trip to Italy: counterinvasion of Europe, 2026–7 (?) L / future invasion of Italy R.

Le second chef du regne Dannemarc.
Par ceulx de Frise & l'isle Britannique,
Fera despendre plus de cent mille marc,
Vain exploicter voyage en Italique.

---

[31] Typical Nostradamian version of *d'Orion.*

[32] Ignore printer's standard comma.

[33] *groupe.*

VI.42

"Ogmion" takes over from the defeated "lunar leader" and extends his crafty rule throughout Italy: **Muslim invasion** of France F / liberation of Muslim-occupied Italy, 2027–8 L / King of France's influence over Vatican R.

A logmyon[34] sera laissé le regne,
Du grand Selin qui plus sera de faict:[35]
Par les Italies estendra son enseigne,
Regifera par prudent contrefaict.

VI.43

From the long-uninhabited **Paris** region armies are tempted to invade England, whose defenders will know no rest: World War III F / **Muslim invasion of Europe**, 2022 L.

Long temps sera sans estre habitee,
Ou Seine & Marne autour vient arrouser
De la Tamise & martiaulx temptee,
Deceuz les gardes en cuidant reposer.

VI.44

A nocturnal rainbow and artificial "rain" occur near Nantes, while a fleet is sunk in the Arabian Gulf and a monster appears in Saxony: C20 C / World War III liberation of France F / **Muslim invasion of Europe**, 2021–2, or liberation 2022–5 L / World War II R.

De nuict par Nantes Lyris apparoistra,
Des artz marins susciteront la pluye:
Arabiq gouffre grand classe parfondra,
Un monstre en Saxe naistra d'ours & truye.

VI.45

When an educated ruler resists a royal advent, a fleet sailing upwind from Morocco confirms his disloyalty: Spanish Civil War (?) C / scuttling of French fleet, 1942 R.

Le gouverneur du regne bien scavant,
Ne consentir voulant au faict Royal:
Mellile[36] classe par le contraire vent,
Le remettra a son plus desloyal,

VI.46

An innocent flees to Corsica while plague rages, misleading a "red one" as he retreats before "Frog" and "Eagle": Louis XVIII (?) C / Franco-Russian alliance R.

Un juste sera en exil renvoyé,
Par pestilence aux confins de Nonseggle:
Responce au rouge le fera desvoyé,
Roy retirant à la Rane & à l'aigle.

VI.47

Two great armies launch attacks between two mountains when forces from France attack the Low Countries: Israeli-Egyptian accord between Begin and Sadat, 1978 R.

Entre deux monts les deux grands assemblés,
Delaisseront leur simulte secrete
Brucelles & Dolle par Langres accablés,
Pour à Malignes executer leur peste.

---

[34] *l'Ogmyon.*

[35] Letter missing: read as *deffaict.*

[36] Possible misprint for *Mellite.*

VI.48

Feigned sanctity, eloquence, and too hasty a peace merely succeed in laying waste Florence and Siena.

La saincteté trop faincte & seductive,
Accompaigné d'une langue diserte:
La cité vieille & Palme trop hastive,
Florence & Sienne rendront plus desertes.

VI.49

A great Muslim potentate subjugates the Danube basin and pursues its Christians, claiming vast booty: Nazis [R] and Pius XII [C,H] / John Paul II's campaign against Communism [F] / **Muslim invasion** of Hungary, 2000–2 [L].

De la partie de Mammer[37] grand Pontife,
Subjuguera les confins du Dannube:
Chasser les croix par fer raffe ne riffe,
Captifz, or, bagues plus de cent mille rubes.

VI.50

When bones in a well witness a stepmother's incest, a reformed state, in search of glory, is marked out for war: new regime of "**Hercules**" in liberated Italy, 2027–8 [L].

Dedans le puys seront trouvés les oz,
Sera lincest[38] commis par la maratre:
L'estant changé on querra bruit & loz,
Et aura Mars ascendant pour son astre.

VI.51

At an assembly of princes and people, a building collapses, but the King and thirty others are saved: assassination attempt on Hitler, 1944 [C,H] / demolition of Bastille and survival of Bourbons [F] / Congress of Vienna, 1814–15 [R].

Peuple assemblé voir nouveau expectacle,
Princes & Roys par plusieurs[39] assistans:
Pilliers faillir, murs, mis comme miracle
Le Roy sauvé & trente des instans.

VI.52

A friend stands in for an imprisoned leader who is captured six months later in winter: death of Louis XVII (?) [C] / fall of Napoleon III, 1870 [F] / Richard Nixon and Spiro Agnew [R].

En lieu du grand qui sera condemné,
De prison hors son amy en sa place:
L'espoir Troyen en six moys joinct mort nay,
Le Sol à l'urne seront prins fluves en glace.

VI.53

A suspect bishop flees the kingdom for Britain's or Brittany's sake, unknown to the Muslim powers: event during World War III [F] or **Muslim invasion of Europe** [L].

Le grand Prelat Celtique à Roy suspect,
De nuict par cours sortira hors du regne:
Par duc fertile à son grand roy Bretaigne,
Bisance à Cipres & Tunes insuspect.

VI.54

An Arab revolution takes place all across North Africa at dawn: in 1999 [L] / failed quatrain [C] / Spanish Civil War, and events in 1932 [R].

Au point du jour au second chant du coq,
Ceulx de Tunes, de Fez, & de Bugie:
Par les Arabes captif le roy Maroq,
L'an mil six cens & sept de Liturgie.

VI.55

A leader diving for sponges at midday sees an "Arab" fleet sail by, and Greek or Black Sea cities are invaded: Greek War of Independence, 1821–8 [F] / start of **Muslim invasion**, 1998–9 [L] / Turkish conflict [R].

Au chalmé Duc en arrachant l'esponce,
Voille arabesque voir, subit descouverte:
Tripolis, Chio, & ceulx de Trapesonce,
Duc prins, Marnegro, & sa cité deserte.

VI.56

When a hostile army blinds Narbonne (see **III.92**) and strikes fear into the West, Perpignan is evacuated as a fleet from Barcelona attacks by sea: 1597 (?) [C] / World War III [F] / **Muslim invasion** of France, 2013–17 [L].

La crainte armee de l'ennemy Narbon,
Effrayera si fort les Hesperiques:
Parpignan vuide par l'aveuglé darbon,
Lors Barcelon par mer donra les piques.

VI.57

A prominent cardinal assumes the papacy under the looming threat of a "red" leader: failed quatrain [C] / **Muslim invasion** of Italy [L] / Robespierre and fall of monarchy, 1792 [F].

Celuy qu'estoit bien avant dans le regne,
Ayant chef rouge proche à la hierarchie:
Aspre & cruel, & se fera tant craindre,
Succedera à sacree monarchie.

VI.58

Even with part of Italy liberated, hostility still reigns between a "solar" leader and his "lunar" defeated opponent: **Henri II** and **Philip II** of Spain [C] / liberation of Muslim-occupied Europe [F], 2028+ [L].

Entre les deux monarques esloignés,
Lors que le Sol par Selin clair perdue:
Simulte grande entre deux indignés,
Qu'aux isles & Sienne la liberté rendue.

VI.59

A lady, incensed by a crime, tries to dissuade her prince, and seventeen are martyred.

Dame en fureur par raige d'adultere,
Viendra son prince conjurer non de dire:
Mais bref cogneu sera le vitupere
Que seront mis [les] dixsept à martire.

VI.60

A French prince is betrayed by an interpreter abroad, while Breton priests deceive those of Rouen and La Rochelle at Blaye: failed quatrain [C] / Siege of La Rochelle, 1625–8 [F] / counterinvasion of Muslim-occupied Europe, 2022–6 [L] / political uproar in France [R].

Le prince hors de son terroir Celtique,
Sera trahy deceu par interprete:
Rouan, Rochelle par ceulx de l'Armorique,
Au port de Blaue[40] deceux par moine & prestre.

VI.61

The seer's prophetic tapestry [L] reveals only half of the story and, banned from France, appears harsh until wars force general acceptance of it: future of Nostradamus's prophecies [L] / concealment of truth regarding exiled leader [R].

Le grand tappis plié ne monstrera,
Fors qu'à demy la pluspart de l'histoire:
Chassé du regne loing aspre apparoistra,
Qu'au fait bellique chascun le viendra croire.

VI.62

"Two flowers" are lost too late and a "serpent" confronted by the French hesitates to attack, but murderous raids afflict the Riviera: failed quatrain [C] / **Henri III** and **IV**, 1590–6 [F] / **Muslim invasion** of Italy, 2000 [L] / persecution of heretics [R].

Trop tard to[41] deux, les fleurs seront pdues,[42]
Contre la loy serpent ne vouldra faire:
Des ligueurs forces par gallotz confondues,
Savone, Albinge par monech grand martire.

VI.63

Her first husband dead, a lady rules alone, and after seven years of mourning reigns long and fortunately: **Catherine de Médicis** [C,H,L,R] / First Republic, 1792–9 [F].

La dame seulle au regne demouree,
L'unic estaint premier au lict d'honneur:
Sept ans sera de douleur exploree,
Puis longue vie au regne par grand heur.

VI.64

As pacts are ignored, Barcelona seizes a fleet by ruse: World War III [F] / **Muslim invasion of Europe** [L].

On ne tiendra pache aucune arresté,
Tous recevans iront par tromperie:
De paix & tresve terre & mer proteste,[43]
Par Barcelone classe prins d'industrie.

VI.65

As war half-starts, "gray" and "russet" are attacked and robbed, the latter escaping to reveal two walled up in their church: monastic feud [C] / class warfare [R].

Gris & bureau, demie ouverte guerre,
De nuict seront assaillis & pillés:
Le bureau prins passera par serre,
Son temple overt deux au plastre grillés.

VI.66

When a new sect is founded, a prominent Roman's tomb is revealed by an earthquake: discovery of St. Peter's tomb [C] / new religion and transformation of consciousness [H] / attempted reestablishment of the Vatican, 2027–8 [L] / future San Francisco earthquake [R].

Au fondement de la nouvelle secte,
Seront les oz du grand Romain trouvés:
Sepulcre en marbre apparoistra couverte,
Terre trembler en Avril, mal enfouetz.

---

[37] Possible misprint for *Mahomet*.

[38] *l'incest*.

[39] *plusieurs*.

---

[40] *Blaye*.

---

[41] *toutes*.

[42] *perdues*.

[43] *protesté*.

VI.67

One wicked, wretched empire ruled by a criminal replaces another: **Napoleon** [C,H] / Hitler [F] / rise of Communism [R].

Au grand empire parviendra tout un autre,
Bonté distant plus de felicité:
Regi par un issu non loing du peaultre,
Corruer regnes grande infelicité.

VI.68

At the time of a nocturnal mutiny, an enemy threatens Rome from the direction of Alba and seduces its leaders: Duke of Alba [R] and Netherlands Revolt [C] / **Muslim invasion** of Italy, 2000 (?) [L].

Lors que souldartz fureur seditieuse,
Contre leur chef feront de nuict fer luire
Ennemy d'Albe soir par main furieuse,
Lors vexer Rome & principaulx seduire.

VI.69

Severe deprivation forces formerly generous people to protest and cross the mountains: French disbandment of Catholic clergy, 1792 [C].

La pitié grande sera sans loing tarder,
Ceulx qui donnoient, [seront][44] constraints de prendre:
Nudz affamez de froit, soif, foy bender,
Les monts passer faisant grand esclandre.

VI.70

The victorious "**Chyren**" becomes a widely praised world ruler: future King Henri [C] / **Henri V** [F], 2037 [L] / **Henri II** [H] / future worldpresident [R].

Au chef du monde le grand Chyren sera,
Plus oultre apres aymé, craint, redoubté:
Son bruit & loz les cieulx surpassera,
Et du seul tiltre victeur fort contenté.

VI.71

Unsympathetic associates try to bury a king and sell off his symbols of power even before he is dead: death of "**Hercules**," 2034 [L] / death of future world-president [R].

Quand on viendra le grand roy parenter,
Avant qu'il ait du tout l'ame rendue:
Celuy qui moins le viendra lamenter,
Par lyons, d'aigles croix, coronne vendue.

VI.72

When a woman is raped under the guise of spirituality, the rapist is handed over to the mob: Rasputin [C] / execution of Marie Antoinette [R].

Par fureur faincte d'esmotion divine,
Sera la femme du grand fort violee:
Juges voulans damner telle doctrine,
Victime au peuple ignorant imolee.

VI.73

A monk and artisan spying on Modena under cover of a wedding are betrayed: Reverend Daniel Berrigan [R].

En cité grande un moyne & artisan,
Pres de la porte logés & aux murailles:
Contre Modene secret, cave[45] disant,
Trahis faisant soubz couleur d'esposailles.

VI.74

A woman hounded from power by conspirators returns triumphantly to rule from age seventy-three until her death: Elizabeth I (?) [C] / Empress Eugénie [H] / Margaret Thatcher (?) [L] / **Napoleon** I and III [R].

La deschassee au regne tournera,
Ses ennemis trouvés des conjurés:
Plus que jamais son temps triomphera,
Trois & septante à mort trop asseurés.

VI.75

A king permits his forces to pillage, but seven years later Venice cowers before a Muslim army: Admiral Gaspard de **Coligny**, 1552 and 1559, and Ottomans, 1570 [C] / Don John of Austria at Lepanto, 1571, and Netherlands Rebellion, 1578 [F].

Le grand pillot par Roy sera mandé,
Laisser la classe à plus halt lieu attaindre
Sept ans apres sera contrebandé,
Barbare armee viendra Venise caindre.[46]

VI.76

A tyrannized Padua murders its priests.

La cité antique d'antenoree forge,
Plus ne pouvant le tyran supporter:
Le manchet sainct, au temple couper gorge
Les siens le peuple à mort viendra bouter.

VI.77

A dishonest victory causes two armies to unite (but compare **I.35**) in a German revolt, while a leader is murdered and Florence and Imola are persecuted: Holy Roman Empire (?) [C] / death of **Henri II** (?) [L] / Germans and Italians in World War II [R].

Par la victoire du deceu fraudulente,
Deux classes une, la revolte Germaine:
Un chef murtry [&] son filz dans la tente,
Florence, Imole pourchassés dans romaine.

VI.78

Romans proclaim the victory of the "crescent moon," but the northern Italian cities at first object, then make their own proclamation: Ottoman and Holy Roman Empires [C] / final Muslim defeat in Italy [F], 2028 [L] / or creeping **Muslim invasion** of Italy, 2000 [L].

Crier victoire du grand Selin croissant,
Par les Romains sera l'Aigle clamé:
Turin, Milan, & Gennes n'y consent,
Puis par eulx mesmes Basil grand reclamé.

VI.79

French forces invade northern Italy, crossing the Alps, the Ticino and the Po: **Napoleon** at Battle of Lodi, 1796 [C] / World War III [F] / counterinvasion of Muslim-occupied Italy, 2026-7 [L] / wouldbe Italian imperial expansion [R].

Pres de Thesin les habitans de loire,
Garonne & Saone, Seine, Tain, & Gironde
Oultre les monts dresseront promontoire,
Conflict donné Pau granci, submergé onde.

VI.80

[**Summary verse**] Moroccan forces savagely invade Europe, Asian hordes pour in and Iranians kill Christians: War of Antichrist [C,F] / Mongol War, 1990s [H] / **Muslim invasion of Europe**, 2007 [L] / Spanish Civil War, 1936-9 [R].

De Fez le regne pviendra[47] à ceulx d'Europe,
Feu leur cité, & l'ame[48] trenchera:
Le grand d'Asie terre & mer à grand trope,
Que bleux, pers, croix, à mort deschassera.

VI.81

Corsica and Sardinia suffer murderous invasion and famine at the hands of a "cruel black": War of Antichrist [C] / World War III [F] / **Muslim invasion of Europe**, 2000-5 [L] / future World War and Dodecanese Islands [R].

Pleurs, crys, & plaintz, hurlement[s,] effraieur,
Cœur inhumain cruel noir transy:
Leman les isles de Gennes les maieurs,
Sang espancher frofaim[49] à nul mercy.

VI.82

A Pope's nephew or grandson, wandering in the wilds, is murdered by seven who then take over the papacy.

Par les desers de lieu libre & farouche,
Viendra errer nepveu du grand Pontife:
Assomé à sept avecques lourde souche,
Par ceulx qu'apres occuperont le cyphe.

VI.83

A much-welcomed immigrant to Belgium later commits barbarisms and war against the "flower": **Philip II** of Spain, 1558, and **Henri IV** [C] / duc d'**Alençon** at Antwerp [R].

Celuy qu'aura tant d'honneurs & caresses,
A son entree de la gaule Belgique:
Un temps apres fera tant de rudesses,
Et sera contre à la fleur tant bellique.

VI.84

One unable to rule Sparta because of lameness achieves much by seduction, but is eventually accused of treason: Talleyrand or Lord Byron [C] / Hitler [F].

Celuy qo'en[50] Sparte claude ne peut regner,
Il fera tant par voye seductive:
Que du court, long, le fera araigner,
Que contre Roy fera sa perspective.

VI.85

The French sack Tarsus and take Muslims prisoner, aided by Portuguese ships: failed quatrain [C] / World War III [F] / European counterinvasion of Middle East, 2036-7 [L] / persecution of non-Christians under early Popes [R].

La grand cité de Tharse par Gaulois,
Sera destruicte, captifz tous à Turban:
Secours par mer du grand Portugalois,
Premier d'esté le jour du sacré Urban.

---

[44] Missing word inserted in later editions.

[45] Possibly *cause*.

[46] Later editions have *craindre*.

[47] *parviendra*.

[48] Familiar Nostradamian treatment of *lame*.

[49] *froit, faim*.

[50] *qu'en*.

VI.86

By interpreting a bishop's dream in reverse, a Gascon monk causes the election of a new Bishop of Sens.

Au grand Prelat un jour apres son songe,
Interpreté au rebours de son sens:
De la Gascogne luy surviendra un monge,
Que fera eslire le grand Prelat de sens.[51]

VI.87

An election in Frankfurt is opposed by Milan, and a powerful figure is chased over the Rhine and into the marshes: **Philip II** and Emperor Ferdinand, 1558 [C] / Peace of Frankfurt, 1871, and annexation of Alsace and Lorraine [F].

L'eslection faicte dans[52] *Frankfort,*
N'aura nul lieu Milan s'opposera:
Le sien proche semblera si grand fort
Que oultre le Ryn es marestz chassera.

VI.88

His kingdom desolate, a leader gathers his forces near the Ebro to recuperate at the time of a May earthquake: US west-coast earthquake in 1990s [C] / migration following World War III or earthshift, 2000 [H] / **Muslim invasion of Europe**, 2007 [L].

Un regne grand demoura desolé,
Aupres de l'Hebro se feront[53] *assemblees:*
Monts Pyrenees le rendront consolé,
Lors que dans May seront terres tremblees.

VI.89

Fatherly indignation causes a prisoner to be stretched between two poles and smeared with honey and milk to attract stinging insects: execution of Louis XVI [C].

Entre deux cimbes[54] *piez & mains estachés,*
De miel face oingt & de laict substanté:
Guespes & mouches, fitine amour faschés
Poccilateur faulcer,[55] *Cyphe temptee.*

VI.90

A British war-leader is actually congratulated for his disgraceful lack of support, so as to discourage Britain from making peace: aftermath of Mediterranean sea-battle with Muslims, 2005 [L] / Munich Pact and Neville Chamberlain, 1939 [R].

L'honnissement puant abhominable,
Apres le faict sera felicité:
Grand excusé pour n'estre favorable,
Qu'a paix Neptune ne sera incité.

VI.91

An "irate red" is brutally attacked by a new Agrippa in a new Battle of Actium,[56] and a captive escapes in a packing-case when "Agrippa" has a son: Cornelius Agrippa, 1486–1535 [R].

Du conducteur de la guerre navalle,
Rouge effrené severe horrible grippe,
Captif eschappé de l'aisné dans la basle:[57]
Quant il naistra du grand un filz Agrippe.

VI.92

One handsome prince is brought before a leader who has another betrayed and then offends his King by his atrocities: Louis XVI [C,R] / World War III [F].

Prince [sera][58] *de beauté tant venuste,*
Au chef menee le second faict trahy:
La cité au glaifue de pouldre, face aduste,
Par trop grand meurtre le chef du roy hay.

VI.93

An ambitious bishop acts cautiously by allowing messengers to see his other side: counterreligious movement against TV evangelists [R].

Prelat avare d'ambition trompé,
Rien ne fera que trop viendra cuider:[59]
Ses messagiers & luy bien attrapé,
Tout au rebours voir, qui le bois fendroit.[60]

VI.94

A king, angry at opponents of the Vatican during a time of imposed peace, is poisoned: Protestant sects [C].

Un roy iré sera aux sedifragues,
Quant interdictz seront harnois de guerre:
La poison taincte au sucre par les fragues,
Par eaux[61] *meurtris mors, disat terre, terre.*[62]

VI.95

Because a younger brother is slandered at a time of war, doubts grow about his older brother, and religious schism spreads: Orleanists versus Legitimists, 1871 [F] / Edward Kennedy as US President [R].

Par detracteur calumnié à puis nay,
Quant istront faictz enormes & martiaulx:
La moindre part dubieuse à l'aisnay,
Et tost au regne seront faictz partiaulx.

VI.96

When a great city is abandoned to the soldiery, almost total catastrophe results: cometary impact and/or nuclear winter [C] / World War III destruction of **Paris** [F].

Grande cité a souldartz habandonnee,
Onques ny eust mortel tumult si proche,
O quel hideuse calamité s'approche,
Fors une offence ny sera pardonnee.[63]

VI.97

A "New City" on latitude 45° is attacked with fire from the sky as the "North" is put to the test: nuclear [H] attack on New York [C], 1997, [H] and other major cities [R] / **Muslim invasion** of France and aerial attack (possibly nuclear) on Villeneuve-sur-Lot, 2017 [L].

Cinq & quarante degrés ciel bruslera,
Feu approucher de la grand cité neufve,
Instant grand flamme esparse saultera,
Quant on voudra des normans faire preuve.

VI.98

A city in Languedoc is ruined and infected with pestilence, its churches pillaged and its two rivers red with blood: **Toulouse** [C] / **Muslim invasion** of France and destruction of **Toulouse**, 2017 [L] / Hiroshima, 1945 [R].

Ruyné aux volsques de peur si fort terribles,
Leur grand cité taincte, faict pestilent:
Pillier,[64] *Sol, Lune & violer leurs temples,*
Et les deux fleuves rougir de sang coulant.

VI.99

As antique urns are discovered, a learned enemy retires in confusion, his army sick and ambushed and denied refuge in the mountains.

L'ennemy docte se tournera confus,
Grand camp malade, & defaict p[65] *embusches,*
Montz pyrenees & pœn[66] *luy seront fait refus,*
Proche du fluve descourant antiques oruches.[67]

VI.100

[1568 edition] The seer curses his critics, warning off the profane, the ignorant, astrologers, fools, and barbarians.

LEGIS CANTIO CONTRA INEPTOS CRITICOS
Quos legent hosce versus mature censunto,
Profanum vulgus & inscium ne attrectato:
Omnesq; Astrologi Blenni, Barbari procul sunto,
Qui aliter facit, is ritè, sacer esto.

---

[51] *Sens.*

[52] Scansion demands *dedans.*

[53] Or *seront.*

[54] Presumably *cimes.*

[55] *faulcé.*

[56] Sea-battle of 31 B.C., in which the fleet of Antony and Cleopatra was defeated by Octavian's commander Agrippa. See **Sequence of Selected Horographs** for a whole range of historical events apparently foreseen by Nostradamus as repeating themselves as contemporary planetary configurations recur.

[57] *balle* (?).

[58] Missing word inserted in some late editions.

[59] Should possibly read *cuider viendra*, to rhyme with line 4, as in late editions.

[60] Conceivably *fendra*, to rhyme with revised line 1, as in late editions.

[61] Presumably *eux.*

[62] More likely *serre, serre*, as in later editions.

[63] Note unique rhyme-scheme *abba.*

[64] *piller.*

[65] Abbreviation for *par.*

[66] *Pœnus.*

[67] Read as *descouvrant antiques cruches.*

CENTURY VII

Transliterated from **du Rosne**'s 1557 edition.

VII.1

The Treasury is tricked by "Achilles," but details are known to the government, and a public hanging ensues: magical conjuration (?) [C] / exposure and execution of Marshal d'Ancre by Achilles de Harlay for misuse of public funds, 1617 [R].

L'ac[1] du tresor par Achiles deceu,
Aux procrees sceu la quadrangulaire:
Au faict Royal le comment sera sceu,
Corps veu pendu au veu du populaire.

VII.2

While **Arles** refuses to fight, spies are exposed by troops: **Muslim invasion** of France, 2005–6 [L] / lasers [R].

Par Mars ouvert Arles ne donra guerre,
De nuict seront les souldarts estonnés:
Noir, blanc, à l'inde dissimulés en terre,
Soubs la faicte umbre trai[2] verez & sonnés.

VII.3

After a French naval victory, a bullion robbery is connived at by Toulon (see **III.13**).

Apres, de France la victoire navale,
Les Barchinons, Saillinons, les Phocens:
Lierre d'or l'enclume serré dedans la basle[3]
Ceulx de Ptolon[4] au frand[5] seront consens.

VII.4

While a leader from Langres is besieged in Dôle, allied troops cross the Alps to attack forces from Ancona: duc de **Guise**, Spain and papal states [C] / World War III [F] / counterinvasion of Muslim-occupied Italy, 2026–7 [L].

Le duc de Langres assiegé dedans Dolle,
Accompaigné d'Ostun & Lyonnais:
Gene,[6] Auspurg, joinct ceulx de Mirandole,
Passer les monts contre les Anconnois.

VII.5

Wine is spilled and a third participant is denied his portion, but Perugia treats Pisa as anticipated.

Vin sur la table en sera espandu,
Le tiers n'aura celle qu'il pretendoit:
Deux fois du noir de Parme descendu,
Perouse à Pize fera ce qu'il cuidoit.

VII.6

Muslim-occupied Italy and the Mediterranean islands treat famine, plague, and war as omens of better times: earlier Barbary pirates [C] / ecological catastrophe, 1999 (?) [H] / **Muslim invasion of Europe** [F], 2000 [L] / World War II [R].

Naples, Palerme, & toute la Secile,
Par main Barbare sera inhabitee,
Corsicque, Salerne & de Sardaigne l'isle,
Faim peste, guerre fin de maulx intepree.[7]

VII.7

A light cavalry engagement apparently defeats the "crescent," but covert operations go on at night in the mountains: local defeat of Ottomans [C] / **Muslim invasion of Europe**, 2000–2 [L] / defeat of USSR [R].

Sur le combat des chevaulx legiers,
On criera le grand croissant confond:
De nuict ruer monts, habitz de bergiers,
Abismes rouges dans le fossé profond.

VII.8

Florence is warned to flee advancing troops from Rome that are about to attack Fiesole: failed quatrain [C] / **Muslim invasion** of Italy, 2000 [L] / retreat of Nazis from Florence, 1944 [R].

Flora fuis fuis le plus proche Romain,
Au Fesulan sera conflict donné:
Sang espandu les plus grans prins à main,
Temple ne sexe ne sera pardonné.

VII.9

A viceroy seduces a military leader's wife when the King controls Bar-le-Duc: Diane de Poitiers (?) [C] / Gaston d'Orléans and Marguerite de Lorraine [F] / **Henri IV**, his sister Catherine and her marriage to the duc de Lorraine [R].

Dame à l'absence de son grand capitaine,
Sera priee d'amours du Viceroy:
Faincte promesse & malheureuse estraine
Entre les mains du grand prince Barroys.

VII.10

A commander from le Mans leads a daring French expeditionary force to attack the Balearics via the Straits of Gibraltar: failed quatrain [C] / World War III [F] / counterinvasion of Muslim-occupied Europe, 2022–5 [L] / Charles de Gaulle [R].

Par le grand prince l'imitrophe[8] du Mans,
Preux & vaillant chef de grand exercite:
Par mer & terre de Gallotz & Normans,
Caspre passer Barcelone pillé isle.[9]

VII.11

A wounded, disobedient prince despises his mother, who learns that over 500 of her followers have been killed: struggle between Louis XIII and Marie de Médicis, 1615 [C,R].

L'enfant Royal contennera la mere,
Oeil, piedz blesses, rude, inhobeissant:
Nouvelle à dame estrange & bien amere,
Seront tués des siens plus de cinq cens.

VII.12

A younger brother brings a war to a close, pardoning some, but Protestants at Lectoure and **Agen** decline the offer (or Lectoure declines and **Agen** is destroyed): Edward Kennedy as President [R].

VII.13

A "shaven-head" takes over a subject maritime city, removes a degenerate who proceeds to oppose him, and enjoys absolute power for fourteen years: Toulon [C,R] and **Napoleon**, 1799–1814 [C,F,H,R].

De la cité marine & tributaire,
La teste raze prendra la satrapie:
Chasser sordide qui puis sera contraire,
Par quatorze ans tiendra la tyrannie.

VII.14

Monuments revealed by harvesting are opened, and a new, "black" spiritual philosophy arises: **French Revolution** and desecration of royal tombs [C] / religious conflicts [R].

Faulx exposer viendra topographie,
Seront les cruches des monuments ouvertes
Pulluler secte saincte philosophie,
Pour blancs, noires, & pour antiques verts.

VII.15

Milan, besieged for seven years, is liberated by a great king: failed quatrain [C] / **Napoleon**ic campaigns, 1792–1800 [F] / **Muslim invasion**, 2000+ and 2027 [L] / Netherlands Revolt [R].

Devant cité de l'insubre contree,
Sept ans sera le siege devant mis:
Le tresgrand Roy y fera son eutree,[12]
Cité puis libre hors de ses ennemis.

VII.16

A great queen fortifies a stronghold and an army of "three lions" is defeated, with atrocities committed within: **Mary** Tudor, and Calais until 1558 [C].

Entree profonde par la grand royne faicte,
Rendra le lieu puissant inaccessible:
L'armee des trois lyons sera deffaicte,
Faisant dedans cas hideux & terrible.

VII.17

A merciful prince is honored after his death for trouncing an overlord and bringing peace: future **Henri V** (?) [L] / **Henri IV** [R].

Le prince rare de pitié & clemence,
Viedra[13] changer par mort grand cognoissace[14]
Par grand repos le regne travaillé,
Lors que le grand toit sera estrillé.[15]

VII.18

Besieged defenders break a truce and attack, then are repulsed, with seven executed and a female negotiator imprisoned: Peace of Cambrai, 1529 [C] / "Chicago Seven" [R].

---

[1] Later editions have *l'arc.*

[2] Printer's abbreviation of *traitres,* as in later editions.

[3] *balle.*

[4] Pseudo-Greek disguise-word for Toulon.

[5] Misprint for *fraud,* as in later editions.

[6] *Geneve* in later editions.

[7] Later editions have *intentee.*

[8] Typical Nostradamian version of *limitrophe.*

[9] False rhyme.

[10] Scansion demands *assemblera.*

[11] Presumably *loing.*

[12] Misprint for *entree.*

[13] Misprint for *viedra (viendra).*

[14] Misprint for *cognoissance (cognoissance).*

[15] Note unique rhyme-scheme *aabb.*

Le grand puisné fera fin de la guerre,
Aux Dieux assemble[10] les excusés:
Cahors Moissac iront long[11] de la serre,
Reffus Lestore, les Agennois razés.

Les assiegés couloureront leurs paches,
Sept jours apres feront cruelle issue:
Dans repousés,[16] feu sang, sept mis à l'ache,[17]
Dame captive qu'avoit la paix tissue.

VII.19

To the citizens' horror, the fort at Nice (or a strong man from Nice) is overcome not by combat but by "red-hot metal": Garibaldi [F] / **Muslim invasion** of France, 2002–5 [L] / Monaco's riches [R].

Le fort Nicene ne sera combatu,
Vaincu sera par rutilant metal:
Son faict sera un long temps debatu,
Aux citadins estrange espouvental.

VII.20

Envoys from Italy cross the Alps in the spring, and a "man of the calf" expounds an argument that is not anti-French: Cavour, 1854 [C] / Mussolini in Berlin, 1938 [R].

Ambassadeurs de la Tosquane langue,
Avril & May Alpes & mer passer:
Celuy de veau exposusera l'harangue,
Vie Gauloise ne venant effacer.

VII.21

Hidden Languedocian hatred pursues and kills a tyrant and his henchman at Sorgues: **Muslim invasion of Europe**, 2005–6 [L] / World War II expulsion and execution of Premier Pierre Laval [R].

Par pestilente inimitié Volsicque,
Dissimulee chassera le tyran:
Au pont de Sorgues se fera la traffique,
De mettre à mort luy & son adherant.

VII.22

As a result of Iraqi hatred of Spain's allies, a sleepy, festive Italy is overrun while the Pope is by the **Rhône**: Pius VI, 1799 [C] / World War III [F] / **Muslim invasion** of Italy and flight of John Paul II, 2000 [L] / quarrel involving **Bordeaux** [R].

Les citoyens de Mesopotamie,
Yrés encontre amis de Tarraconne:
Geux, ritz, banquetz, toute gent endormie,
Vicaire au rosne, prins cité, ceux d'Ausone.

VII.23

An underling is forced to assume power, but little is heard from him when the palace is sacked: successor of John Paul II and sacking of Vatican, 2001 [L] / abdication of Shah of Persia, 1979 [R].

Le Royal sceptre sera constrainct de prendre
Ce que ses predecesseurs avoient engaigé,
Puis par l'aneau on fera mal entendre,
Lors qu'on viendra le palays saccager.

VII.24

A "corpse" leaves his tomb and enchains an overlord, while the Marquis du Pont poisons the Duc de Lorraine: failed quatrain [C] / **Henri V** [F].

L'ensevely sortira du tombeau,
Fera de chaines lier le fort du pont:
Empoysoné avec œuf de barbeau,
Grand de lorraine par le Marquis du Pont.

VII.25

As French bronze faces the "lunar crescent," long war depletes both army and exchequer until "leather" money has to be introduced: World War I [C,F] and introduction of paper money [L] / currency before discovery of West Indies [R].

Par guerre longue tout l'exercite expuise,
Que pour souldartz ne trouveront pecune:
Lieu d'or, d'argent, car[18] on viendra cuser,
Gaulois aerain, signe croissant de lune.

VII.26

Out of seven ships that attack a Spanish leader, five of them are captured and two escape: privateers' attack on Spanish fleet, November 1555 [C] / Battle of Trafalgar, 1805 [F] / flying boats and Trident missiles [R].

Fustes & Galees autour de sept navires,
Sera livree une mortelle guerre:
Chef de Madric[19] recevra coup de vires:
Deux eschapees & cinq menees à terre.

VII.27

Cavalry, held up near Ferrara by a baggage train, sack Turin and take hostages.

Au cainct de Vast le grand cavalerie,
Proche à Ferrare empeschee au bagaige,
Prompt à Turin feront tel volerie,
Que dans le fort raviront leur hostaige.

VII.28

A general leads a booty caravan too near the enemy in the mountains and is surrounded, but all except thirty escape.

Le capitaine conduira grande proye,
Sur la montaigne des ennemis plus proche:
Environné, par feu fera tel voye,
Tous eschapez or[20] trente mis en broche.

VII.29

When a Duke of Alba betrays his ancestors by rebelling, a **Guise** captures him and erects a monument: wishful thinking [C] / Duke of Alba's revolt against **Paul IV**, 1557 [F].

Le grand duc d'Albe se viendra rebeller,
A ses grans peres fera le tradiment:
Le grand de Guise le viendra debeller:
Captif mené & dressé monument.

VII.30

Pillaging herdsmen sack the Po valley and later take Genoa, Nice, Fossano, Turin, and Savigliano: **Muslim invasion** of Italy, 2000–1 (?) [L] / Italian conflicts, 1555–9 [R].

Le sac s'aproche, feu grand sang espandu,
Po grand fluwes, aux bouviers l'entreprinse
De Gennes, Nice, apres long attendu,
Foussan, Turin, à Savillan la prinse.

VII.31

More than 10,000 from Savoy and southwest France attempt to recross the Alps and march on Brindisi, but forces from Aquino and Breschia (?) chase them back into eastern France: unrevised quatrain (?) [C] / Garibaldi's Thousand, 1860 [F] / setback [R] to counterinvasion of Muslim-occupied Italy, 2027–8 [L].

De languedoc, & Guienne plus de dix,
Mille voudront les Alpes repasser:
Grans Allobroges marcher contre Brundis,
Aquin & Bresse les viendront rechasser.

VII.32

A humbly born tyrant from Montereale, Florence [C] drains Faenza and Florence of money and men to raise an army around Milan: failed quatrain [C] / Pierre Trudeau and Canadian separatists [R].

Du mont Royal naistra d'une casane,
Qui cave[21] & comte viendra tyranniser,
Dresser copie de la marche Millane,
Favene Florence d'or & gents expuiser.

VII.33

As subversion grips the kingdom and an army is besieged, two pretended friends join in reawakening old hatreds: fall of France, 1940 [C] / European civil war, 2032 [L] / alliance between Hitler and Mussolini [R].

Par fraulde regne, forces expolier,
La classe obsese, passaiges à l'espie:
Deux faincts amys se viendront rallier,
Esveiller hayne de long temps assopie.

VII.34

With the French downcast and desperate, deprivation and oppression are total: World War II occupation of France [C,R] / Muslim occupation of France, 2017–26 [L].

En grand regret sera la gent Gauloise,
Cœur vain, legier, croit à temerité:
Pain, sel, ne vin, eaue venim ne cervoise,
Plus grand captif, faim, froit, necessité.

VII.35

After the "big catch" complains about his election, he disappoints his electors by leaving at the false behest of his own countrymen: **Henri III** as King of Poland [C] / future economic crisis [F] / World War II sabotaging of Vichy regime [R].

La grande pesche viendra plaindre, plorer,
D'avoir esleu, trompés seront en l'aage:
Guiere avec eulx ne vouldra demourer,
Deceu sera par ceulx de son langaige.

VII.36

When the Divine Word is brought to Istanbul by seven "red shaven-heads," 300 at Trabzon are at first horrified, then believe: failed quatrain [C] / future peace in Middle East [H] / end of European campaign against Muslims, 2037 [L].

Dieu le ciel tout le divin verbe à l'unde,
Pourté[22] par rouges sept razes à Bisance.
Contre les oingz trois cens de Trebisonde,
Deux loix mettront, horreur, [&] puis credence.

---

[16] Later editions have *repoulsés.*

[17] *l'hache.*

[18] Later editions have *cuir.*

[19] *Madrid,* as in some late editions.

[20] Should read *hors.*

[21] Possible misprint for *eaue.*

[22] *porté.*

VII.37

During a Mediterranean naval mutiny, a captain's life is threatened, but he is warned and stays ashore at La Nerthe: failed quatrain [C] / assassination of Pope [F] / event during **Muslim invasion of Europe**, 2025 [L] / German naval mutiny [R].

Dix envoyés chef de nef mettre à mort,
D'un adverty, en classe guerre ouverte:
Confusion de chef, l'un se picque & mord,
Leryn, stecades nefz, cap dedans la nerte.

VII.38

An older royal prince dies horribly by being dragged by his horse with his foot caught in the stirrup: death of Crown Prince Ferdinand, oldest son of Louis-Philippe, 1842 [C,F].

L'aisné Royal sur coursier voltigeant,
Picquer viendra si durement à courir:
Gueule, lypee, pied dans l'estrein pleigant,[23]
Trainé, tiré, horriblement mourir.

VII.39

A French commander, unsure about food or shelter for his troops, collapses before aliens from Genoa: defeat of **Napoleon**'s army at Genoa, 1800 [F] / **Muslim invasion of Europe**, 2000–1 [L].

Le conducteur de l'armee Francoise,
Cuidant perdre le principal phalange:
Par sus pavé de livaigne[24] & d'ardoise,
Soy profondra par Gennes gent estrange.

VII.40

Twenty-one commandos are landed at a port in barrels, then they overwhelm the watch and reach the gates, only to be killed: failed quatrain [C] / European counterinvasion of Europe (?), 2022–6 [L].

Dedans tonneaux hors oingz d'huril?[25] & gresse
Seront vingtun devant le port fermés:
Au second guet par mort feront prouesse,
Gaigner les portes & du guet assommés.

Du Rosne's 1557 edition ends abruptly at this point.

Transliterated from **Benoist Rigaud**'s 1568 edition.

VII.41

Because of noises and disturbed sleep caused by an immured prisoner, a house stays unlived-in until it becomes quiet: exorcism of ghost [C,R] / First Resurrection [F].

Les oz des piedz & des mains enserrés,
Par bruit maison long temps inhabitee:
Seront par songes concavant deterrés,
Maison salubre & sans bruyt habitee.

VII.42

Two would-be poisoners of a prince are apprehended by a scullion and one of them is killed.

Deux de poison saisiz nouveau venuz,
Dans la cuisine du grand Prince verser:
Par le souillard tous deux au faict congneux,
Prins qui cuidoit de mort l'aisné vexer.

Apart from a rag-bag of quatrains added in various late versions (see the "Extra" Quatrains), the seventh *Century* ends here.

CENTURY VIII

Transliterated from **Benoist Rigaud**'s 1568 edition.

VIII.1

While a leader flees, the much-praised "Napaulon Roy" [C,H], more fiery than bloody, confines the "magpies" to Pamplona and the Durance: **Napoleon** [C,H,R].

PAU, NAY, LORON plus feu qu'à sang sera,
Laude nager, fuir grand aux surrez:
Les agassas entree refusera,
Pampon,[1] Durance les tiendra enserrez.

VIII.2

Fire and hail from the sky descend on towns in the southwest, and a wall falls in Garonne: World War III [F] / **Muslim invasion** of France, 2017 [L] / extraterrestrials and war [R].

Condon & Aux & autour de Mirande
Je voy du ciel feu qui les environne.
Sol Mars conjoint au Lyon puis marmande
Fouldre, grand gresle, mur tombe dans Garonne.

VIII.3

The older prince of Nancy is imprisoned, while burnings take place in Turin and Lyon mourns: failed quatrain [C] / C16 political events [R].

Au fort chasteau de Viglanne & Resviers[2]
Sera serré le puisnay de Nancy:
Dedans Turin seront ards les premiers,
Lors que de dueil Lyon sera transy.

VIII.4

When a French cardinal is received in Monaco, **Ogmion** [L] tricks Rome, Italy weakens, and France grows stronger: erroneous quatrain [C] / World War III [F] / counterinvasion of Muslim-occupied Europe, 2025–6 [L] / Cardinal Richelieu [R].

Dedans Monech le coq sera receu,
Le Cardinal de France apparoistra
Par Logarion[3] Romain sera deceu
Foiblesse à l'aigle, & force au coq naistra.

VIII.5

A great French leader's corpse draws crowds in northeast France and Switzerland: failed quatrain [C] / death of the future **Henri V** / death of "**Hercules**" [L].

Apparoistra temple luisant orné,
La lampe & cierge à Borne & [à] Breteuil.
Pour la lucerne le canton destorné,
Quand on verra le grand coq au cercueil.

VIII.6

A brilliant flash appears over Lyon, Malta is overrun, **Nîmes** [L] is tricked by the Moors and Switzerland plots with Britain: C16 events [C] / World War III [F] / **Muslim invasion of Europe**, 2002–5 [L].

Clarté fulgure à Lyon apparante
Luysant, print Malte subit sera estainte,
Sardon,[4] Mauris[5] traitera decepvante,
Geneve à Londes à coq trahyson fainte.

VIII.7

As news arrives of attacks around Pavia, Siena, and Florence, a festive Italy falls (see **VII.22**): World War III [F] / **Muslim invasion** of Italy, 2000–1 [L].

Verceil, Milan donra intelligence,
Dedans Tycin, sera faite la paye.[6]
Courir par Siene eau, sang, feu par Florence.
Unique choir d'hault en bas faisant maye.

VIII.8

Chivasso attacks Focia for the "eagle," imprisons its leader and his followers, and carries off his wife to Turin.

Pres de linterne dans de tonnes fermez,
Chivaz fera pour l'aigle la menee,
L'esleu cassé[7] luy ses gens enfermez,
Dedans Turin rapt espouse emmenee.

VIII.9

[**Summary verse**] With "eagle" and "cock" fighting at Savona, at sea, in the Middle East and Hungary, and troops coming ashore at Naples, Palermo and Ancona, the Muezzin [L] already calls over Rome and Venice: failed quatrain [C] / liberation of Italy, 1945 [H] / **Muslim invasion of Europe**, 2000–1 [L].

Pendant que l'aigle & le coq à Savone
Seront unis Mer Levant & Ongrie,
L'armee à Naples, Palerne,[8] Marque d'Ancone
Rome, Venise par Barb' horrible crie.

VIII.10

A stench emanates from Lausanne as aliens are defeated and expelled under fiery skies: Calvinists or Marxists [C] / World War III [F] / liberation of Muslim-occupied Europe, 2022–5 [L] / Conference of Lausanne, 1923 [R].

Puanteur grande sortira de Lausanne,
Qu'on ne scaura l'origine du fait,
Lon mettra hors toute la gent loingtaine
Feu veu au ciel, peuple estranger deffait.

---

[23] Should presumably read *dans l'etrier piegeant*.

[24] Later editions have *l'avaigne* (l'avoine).

[25] *d'huile* in later editions.

---

[1] Possibly Pamplona.

[2] Could just possibly stand for *vigilance à Besiers*.

[3] Some editions give *legation*, but more likely a misprint for *Logmion* (l'Ogmion).

---

[4] Probable misprint for *Gardon*, as in **X.6**: otherwise *Sardeigne* (Sardinia).

[5] *Maures.*

[6] Some later editions have *playe.*

[7] *chassé.*

[8] *Palerme.*

VIII.11

Hordes enter Vicenza peacefully as its basilica burns, while a leader from Valenza is defeated near Lugano and Venice is attacked by the Moor (or merely by sea): retroactive quatrain [C] / **Napoleon**ic campaigns, 1797 [F] / **Muslim invasion** of Italy, 2000 [L].

Peuple infiny paroistra à Vicence
Sans force feu brusler la Basilique
Pres de Lunage[9] deffait grand de Valence,
Lors que Venise par more[10] prendra pique.

VIII.12

A high-born one from Milan appears near Buffalora, while Benedictines commit sabotage: Napoleon III in Italy, 1859 [F] / clergy debates in France [R].

Apparoistra aupres de Buffalorre
L'hault procere[11] entré dedans Milan
L'Abbé de Foix avec ceux de saint Morre
Feront la forbe abillez[12] en vilan.

VIII.13

A love-crossed brother has "Bellerophon" killed by "Proteus," and both lovers are poisoned while the army is at Milan.

Le croisé frere par amour effrenee
Fera par Praytus Bellerophon mourir,
Classe à mil ans[13] la femme forcenee
Beu le breuvage, tous deux apres perir.

VIII.14

Affluence and greed are put before honor, until a crime unmasks a criminal: C16 New World gold imports [C] / stock market crash, 1929 [H] / period of World War III [F] / C20 [R].

Le grand credit d'or, d'argent l'abondance
Fera aveugler par libide l'honneur
Sera cogneu d'adultere l'offence,
Qui parviendra à son grand deshonneur.

VIII.15

A mannish northern woman vexes all creation, hounds failed leaders, and faces Hungary and northern Yugoslavia with a choice between life and death: Nazi Germany [C] / World War III [F] / Margaret Thatcher [L] / Catherine the Great [R].

Vers Aquilon grand efforts par hommasse
Presque l'Europe & l'univers vexer,
Les deux[14] eclipses mettra en telle chasse,
Et aux Pannons vie & mort renforcer.

VIII.16

Greece undergoes severe flooding, even affecting the slopes of Mount Olympus (see **I.69**, **V.31**): asteroid impact and end of world, 3797 [H] / Mediterranean tsunamis, 2004 [L] / future revolution [R] in Italy [F].

Au lieu que HIERON[15] feit sa nef fabriquer,
Si grand deluge sera & si subite,
Qu'on n'aura lieu ne terres s'atacquer
L'onde monter Fesulan Olympique.

VIII.17

[**Summary verse**] "Three brothers" shake the world and put down the affluent, as unprecedented disaster strikes and a maritime city is captured: Kennedy brothers, Hong Kong (?) and Last Times [C] / World War III [F], or **Muslim invasion of Europe** [L], by a triple confederacy [F,L], and capture of **Marseille** [L].

Les bien aisez subit seront desmis
Par les trois freres le monde mis en trouble,
Cité marine saisiront ennemis,
Faim, feu, sang, peste, & de to'[16] maux le double.

VIII.18

Florence causes the death of one previously balked by France, but saved by the birth of late offspring: **Catherine de Médicis** [C] / end of **Russian Revolution** [F] / World War II occupation and liberation of France [R].

De Flora issue de sa mort sera cause,
Un temps devant par jeusne & vieille bueyre[17]
Par les trois lys luy feront telle pause,
Par son fruit sauve comme chair crue mueyre.

VIII.19

The "reds" march to the "support and enlightenment" of the Pope, overwhelming his intimates and killing a cardinal (?): **French Revolution** and French royal family [C] / Robespierre [F] / **Muslim invasion**, 2000–2 [L], and interference with the papacy [L,R].

A soustenir la grand cappe troublee,
Pour l'esclaircir les rouges marcheront,
De mort famille sera presque accablee.
Les rouges rouges le rouge assomeront:[18]

VIII.20

Papal [L] elections are falsified, hostilities break out, and Christendom is sold out to foreigners (see **VIII.19**): failed quatrain [C] / **Muslim invasion**, 2000–2 [L], and interference with papacy [L] / bloody struggle within Church [R].

Le faux messaige par election fainte
Courir par urben, rompue pache arreste,
Voix acheptees, de sang chapelle tainte,
Et à un autre l'empire contraicte.

VIII.21

Three shallow-draft vessels enter **Agde**, spreading a plague of a million invaders who break out at the third attempt: World War III [F] / **Muslim invasion** of France, 2017 [L] / foreign propaganda [R].

Au port de Agde trois fustes entreront
Portant l'infect non foy & pestilence
Passant le pont mil milles embleront,
Et le pont rompre à tierce resistance.

VIII.22

Rebellious Coursan and Narbonne are warned of aerial attacks by "red" Perpignan: World War III and civil war in southwest France [F] / **Muslim invasion** of France, 2017 [L] / Roman help to French cities [R].

Gorsan,[19] Narbonne, par le sel advertir
Tucham, la grace Parpignan trahye,
La ville rouge n'y vouldra consentir,
Par haulte vol drap gris vie faillie.

VIII.23

Anonymous love letters, found in a queen's baggage, are concealed by the police to protect those concerned: **Mary Queen of Scots**' "Casket Letters" [C] / trial of Louis XVI, 1793 [F] / Affair of Diamond Necklace, 1785 [R].

Lettres trouvees de la royne les coffres,
Point de subscrit sans aucun nom d'hauteur
Par la police seront cachez les offres.
Qu'on ne scaura qui sera l'amateur.

VIII.24

The commander of Perpignan is killed by an underling, and the bastard of Lusignan is denied a safe haven.

Le lieutenant à l'entree de l'huys,
Assomera le grand de Parpignan,
En se cuidant saulver à Montpertuis.
Sera deceu bastard de Lusignan.

VIII.25

The father of a lady raped by a secret lover executes both of them.

Cœur de l'amant ouvert d'amour fertive
Dans le ruysseau fera ravyr la Dame,
Le demy mal contrefera lassive,[20]
Le pere à deux privera corps de l'ame.

VIII.26

Cannons are discovered on Barcelonan wasteland as its defeated lord heads for Pamplona (see **VIII.51**) and drizzle shrouds Montserrat abbey: Louis XIII's Spanish campaign, 1640 [F] / **Muslim invasion** of Spain, 2007–13 [L] / new food source [R].

De Caron es[21] trouves en Barcellonne,
Mys descouvers lieu terroeurs & ruyne,
Le grand qui tient ne tient vouldra Pamplonne.
Par l'abbage[22] de Monserrat bruyne.

---

[9] Anagram for *Lugane*.

[10] Probably either *par Maure* or (Latin) *per mare* (by sea): some later editions have *par mort(e)*.

[11] Probable misprint for *procree*.

[12] *habillez*.

[13] Disguised version of *à Milan*.

[14] Here from Latin *dux*, *duces*, "leader/s."

[15] Presumed misprint for *Hieson*, "normal" C16 spelling for *Jieson* (Jason).

[16] *tous*.

[17] Presumably *bure*.

[18] Deliberate "conceit," or play on words.

[19] Misprint for *Corsan*.

[20] Some late editions not unreasonably have *lascive*.

[21] Some later editions have *de Carones* or *de Catones*, others *de Caton os*.

[22] Misprint for *l'abbaye*.

VIII.27

A brave cavalier is ejected from Le Muy when a "phoenix-emperor" has exclusive sight of a secret document: Nazi Liebensborn [F] / **Napoleon**'s return from Elba, 1815 [R].

La voye auxelle[23] l'une sur l'autre fornix[24]
De muy deser[25] hor mis brave & genest,
L'escript [trouvé][26] d'empereur le fenix
Veu en celuy ce qu'à nul autre n'est.

VIII.28

The inscriptions on ostentatious gold and silver images, retrieved from a lake after a town's sacking, have to be edited after public criticism: C20 monetary inflation [C,F] / stock-market crash, 1929 [H] / ancient history [R].

Les simulachres d'or & d'argent enflez,
Qu'apres le rapt au lac furent gettez
Au descouvert estaincts[27] tous & troublez.
Au marbre escript presciptz intergetez.

VIII.29

The buried treasure of Caepio is found under a pillar in St.-Saturnin, **Toulouse** [C,L] after it has been split by an earthquake and a flood: events after 2034 [L].

Au quart pillier lon[28] sacre à Saturne.
Par tremblant terre & deluge fendu
Soubz l'edifice Saturnin trouvee urne,
D'or Capion[29] ravy & puis rendu.

VIII.30

During excavations for a *palais de spectacles* in **Toulouse** [C,L], two treasure-hoards (or a "Pandora's box" [R]) are discovered (see **VIII.29**): events after 2034 [L].

Dedans Tholoze non loing de Beluezer
Faisant un puy loing, palais d'espectacle
Tresor trouvé un chacun ira vexer,
Et en deux locz tout & pres del vasacle.

VIII.31

The first great leader of Peschiera is followed by a tyrant who is humbled in Venice by a triumphant Muslim: Prince Victor Emmanuel and Mussolini [C].

Premier grand fruit le prince de Pesquiere
Mais puis viendra bien & cruel malin,
Dedans Venise perdra sa gloire fiere
Et mys à mal par plus joyue[30] Celin.[31]

---

[23] Possible misprint for *Auxerre.*

[24] Possibly *fournies.*

[25] *desert.*

[26] Suggested replacement for missing word.

[27] Probable misprint for *estonnés.*

[28] *long.*

[29] *Caepion.*

[30] Possible misprint for *jeune.*

[31] Most commentators read this as *Selin.*

VIII.32

A French king is warned to beware his nephew or grandson, who aims to replace his son but will be murdered: failed quatrain [C] / loss of **Napoleon**ic prestige under **Napoleon** III [R].

Garde toy roy Gaulois de ton nepveu
Qui fera tant que ton unique filz.
Sera meurtry à Venus faisant vœu,
Accompaigné de nuict que trois & six.

VIII.33

An unworthily named leader, born near Verona and Vicenza, tries to avenge himself on Venice but is then captured: Mussolini [C,H,R] / massacres of Verona and Venice, 1797, and capture of **Napoleon**, 1815 [F].

Le grand naistra de Veronne & Vincence,
Qui portera un surnom bien indigne.
Qui à Venise vouldra faire vengeance
Luy mesme prins homme du guet & signe

VIII.34

When a "lion" is victorious at **Lyon**, 143,000 "swarthy easterners" are slaughtered in the Jura, and the Pope then dies near **Lyon**: East African floods, 1988 [C] / death of John Paul II [F], 2000 [L] / world wars [R].

Apres victoire du Lyon au Lyon
Sur la montaigne de JURA Secatombe[32]
Delues & brodes septieme million
Lyon, Ulme à Mausol mort & tombe.

VIII.35

Severe weather is forecast for southwest France.

Dedans l'entree de Garone & Bayse
Et la forest non loing de Damazan
Du marsaves[33] gelees, puis gresle & bize
Dordonnois gelle par erreur de mezan.[34]

VIII.36

When its ruler decides to install marble pavements from Tours, **Béziers** does not object: unintelligible quatrain [R].

Sera commis conte oingdre aduché
De Saulne & sainct Aulbin & Bell'œuvre
Paver de marbre de tours loing espluché
Non Bleteram resister & chef d'œuvre.

VIII.37

A fortress by the Thames falls and the King, imprisoned there, is seen in shirtsleeves near a bridge: fall of Windsor Castle to Parliamentarians and execution of Charles I, 1649 [C,H,R] / World War III siege of London [F].

La forteresse aupres de la Tamise
Cherra par lors le Roy dedans serré,
Aupres du pont sera veu en chemise
Un devant mort, puis dans le fort barré.

---

[32] *hecatombe.*

[33] Probable misprint for *marecages.*

[34] Either from Latin *mensis,* "month" or misprint for *Mezin.*

VIII.38

A king from **Blois** reestablishes democratic rule in **Avignon**, building residences from the **Rhône** to Naples [L]: **Henri V** [F] / "Hercules," 2026 [L] / ruler disposes of five opponents [R].

Le Roy de Bloys dans Avignon regner
Une autre foys le peuple emonopolle,[35]
Dedans' le Rosne par murs fera baigner
Jusques à cinq le dernier pres de Nolle.

VIII.39

A ruler of **Toulouse** accepts the former Muslim dispensation, but his marriage fails to convince Foix: aftermath of **Muslim invasion** of France, 2036 (?) [L] / French occupation of Middle East [R].

Qu'aura esté par prince Bizantin,
Sera tollu par prince de Tholoze.
La foy de Foix par le chief Tholentin,[36]
Luy faillira ne refusant l'espouse.

VIII.40

Bloody disputes rack **Toulouse** and extend into Spain: aftermath of **Muslim invasion** of France, 2026 [L] / Charles de Gaulle and Franco-Algerian War 1954–62 [R].

Le sang du Juste par Taurer la daurade,[37]
Pour se venger contre les Saturnins
Au nouveau lac plongeront la maynade,
Puis marcheront contre les Albanins.

VIII.41

An apparently saintly "fox" is elected, then becomes a tyrant: Napoleon III [C,R] / Antichrist [F] / Robespierre [H,R] / future Pope, 2001 [L] / Premier Paul Reynaud, 1940 [R].

Esleu sera Renad[38] ne sonnant mot,
Faisant le saint public vivant pain d'orge,
Tyrannizer apres tant a un cop,[39]
Mettant à pied des plus grans sus la gorge.

VIII.42

A leader from Orleans upsets his followers and dies in his tent at "St.-Memire," though claimed to be merely asleep: Louis-Philippe d'Orléans in rue St.-Merri, 1832 [C,F,H].

Par avarice, par force & violence
Viendra vexer les siens chiefz d'Orleans,
Pres saint Memire assault & resistance,
Mort dans sa tante diront qu'il dort leans.

VIII.43

A royal nephew or grandson seizes power, but lowers his colors after fighting in Lectoure: Louis-Napoleon [C] / Napoleon III [R].

Par le decide de deux choses bastars
Nepveu du sang occupera le regne
Dedans lectoyre seront les coups de dars
Nepveu par peur pleira[40] l'enseigne.

---

[35] Possibly *en monopole.*

[36] Likely misprint for *Tholousin.*

[37] Read as *par Taur et la Daurade.*

[38] Late editions give *Renard.*

[39] *coup.*

[40] Misprint for *pliera.*

VIII.44

A son of **Ogmion** goes astray, making bad alliances and surrendering Pau to Navarre: abandonment of Communism, and future **Henri V** [F] / attempted regicide [R].

Le procrée naturel dogmion,[41]
De sept à neuf du chemin destorner
A roy de longue & amy aumi hom,[42]
Doit à Navarre fort de PAU prosterner.

VIII.45

"Louis" rescues a bandaged older son from Calais with the help of the watch, but is wounded in church at Easter: Louis XVII [F,H,R].

La main escharpe & la jambe bandee,
Longs[43] puis nay de Calais portera[44]
Au mot du guet la mort sera tardee,
Puis dans le temple à Pasques saignera.

VIII.46

"Paul Manus Solis" dies near the **Rhône** at **Tarascon** as three eaglelike brothers attack France: death of Pope Paul VI, 1978 [C,H] / death of John Paul II [F], 2000 [L].

Pol mensolee mourra trois lieuës du rosne,
Fuis les deux prochains tarasc destrois:
Car Mars fera le plus horrible trosne,
De coq & d'aigle de France freres trois.

VIII.47

A witness from Lake Trasimeno uncovers conspirators in Perugia when a despot plays the sage and kills a German: reference to Hannibal [R].

Lac Tresmenien portera tesmoignage,
Des conjurez sarez[45] dedans Perouse,
Un despolle[46] contrefera le sage,
Tuant tedesq de sterne & minuse.

VIII.48

A seer saves Salvatierra in February, while on the Sierra Morena a war of words becomes one of brutal deeds: World War III [F] / counterinvasion of Muslim-occupied Spain, 2034 [L].

Saturne en Cancer, Jupiter avec Mars,
Dedans Fevrier Chaldondon salvaterre.
Sault Castallon assailly de trois pars,
Pres de Verbiesque conflit mortelle guerre.

VIII.49

An assault in Belgium brings about the death of a Muslim leader on the Red Sea: World War III [F] / death of Pope Urban VIII, 1644 [R].

Satur.[47] au beuf jove en l'eau, Mars en fleiche,
Six de Fevrier mortalité donra,
Ceux de Tardaigne[48] à Bruge si grand breche,
Qu'à Ponteroso chef Barbarin mourra.

VIII.50

When plague and famine afflict Capellades and Sagunto, a bastard knight splits a Tunisian ruler's head: Don John of Austria's recapture of Tunis, 1573 [C] / death of President Bourgiba of Tunisia [R].

La pestilence l'entour de Capadille,
Un autre faim pres de Sagont s'appreste:
Le chevalier bastard de bon senille,
Au grand de Thunes fera trancher la teste.

VIII.51

While a Muslim leader is rejoicing over his capture of Cordoba, his opponent retreats to Pamplona to recover (see **VIII.26**), and a prize is taken in the Straits of Gibraltar: retroactive quatrain [C] / **Muslim invasion** of Spain [F], 2007 [L] / abdication of Emperor **Charles V**, 1556 [R].

Le Bizantin faisant oblation,
Apres avoir Cordube à soy reprinse:
Son chemin long repos pamplation,
Mer passant proy par la Colongna prinse.

VIII.52

(Incomplete) A king from Blois sets up his capital in **Avignon** (see **VIII.38**) after his army has been savaged on the Indre River (and has then recovered?): future **Henri V** and World War III [F] / "Hercules" and counterinvasion of Muslim-occupied France, 2022–6 [L] / Pope's journey to crown **Napoleon** [R].

Le roy de Bloys dans Avignon regner,
D'amboise & seme[49] viendra le long de Lyndre[50]
Ongle à Poitiers sainctes aeles ruiner
Devant Boni.[51]

VIII.53

Unable to cross to England, an unprecedentedly high-flying leader meets his Waterloo at Boulogne: **Napoleon** [C] / Pope Pius IX, 1846–78 [F] / **Muslim invasion of Europe**, 2022 (?) [L] / Cardinal Richelieu [R].

Dedans Bolongne vouldra laver ses fautes,
Il ne pourra au temple du soleil,[52]
Il volera faisant choses si haultes
En hierarchie n'en fut oncq un pareil.

VIII.54

By generously making a "wedding-pact" with the Muslims, "**Chyren**" recovers Arras and St.-Quentin, but relegates Spain to the second rank[53]: counterinvasion of Muslim-occupied lands [F], 2034 (?) [L] / later war in Spain [R].

Soubz la colleur du traicte mariage,
Fait magnanime par grand Chyren selin,
Quintin,[54] Arras, recouvrez au voyage
D'espaignolz fait second banc macelin.

VIII.55

A leader trapped between two rivers tries to escape using crude rafts or a pontoon bridge, but he and his followers are slaughtered: **Napoleon** in Russia, 1812 [F].

Entre deux fleuves se verra enserré,
Tonneaux & caques[55] unis à passer outre,
Huict pontz rompus chef à tant enferré
Enfans parfaictz sont jugutez[56] en coultre.

VIII.56

Near the Ebro a weakened force, taking refuge on a mound, is overwhelmed from the right flank: Battle of Dunbar, 1650 [C] / political battles between left and right [R].

La bande foible le tertre occupera
Ceux du hault lieu feront horribles crys,
Le gros troppeau d'estre[57] coin troublera,
Tombe pres D. nebro[58] descouvers les escris.[59]

VIII.57

A simple soldier, gaining power, proves valiant in war but a scourge to the Church: **Napoleon** [C,H,F] / Oliver Cromwell [R].

De souldat simple parviendra en empire,
De robe courte parviendra à la longue
Vaillant aux armes en eglise ou plus pyre,
Vexer les pretres comme l'eau fait l'esponge.

VIII.58

As two brothers dispute the rulership of Britain, one is belatedly advised to call himself Anglican, though revealed to have French connections: James II and William of Orange [C] / abdication of Edward VIII [R].

Regne en querelle aux freres divisé,
Prendre les armes & le nom Britannique
Tiltre Anglican sera tard advisé,
Surprins de nuict mener à l'air Gallique.

VIII.59

Both East and West are twice raised, then dashed, as they are defeated and their fleets pursued: Third Antichrist [C] / World Wars I, II [F,L,R] and/or III [F].

Par deux fois hault, par deux fois mis à bas
L'orient aussi l'occident foyblira
Son adversaire apres plusieurs combats
Par mer chassé au besoing faillira.

---

[48] Possibly *Sardaigne.*

[49] Probable misprint for *Seine.*

[50] *de l'Indre.*

[51] *Bonny.* The rest of the line is missing: possibly *ne aura nul à craindre.*

[52] Various commentators take this as a reference either to Stonehenge or to London's Westminster Abbey, claimed site of a former temple of Apollo.

[53] The events are remarkably reminiscent of the Treaty of Cateau-Cambrésis, 1559.

---

[41] Later editions have *d'Ogmion.*

[42] Read as *ami au mi-homme.*

[43] Some late editions have *Louis.*

[44] Some late editions have *partira.*

[45] Presumably *serrez.*

[46] Probable misprint for *despote.*

[47] Abbreviation for *Saturne.*

---

[54] (St.-)*Quentin.*

[55] *casques.*

[56] Misprint for *jugulez.*

[57] Read as *destre* (*dextre*).

[58] Probably either *du Hebro* or *de l'Ebro.*

[59] Read as *escriptz.*

VIII.60

On behalf of England and **Paris**, the armies of a Lorrainian supreme ruler of France and Italy destroy a violent monster: **Napoleon** and/or Napoleon III [C] / future **Henri V** [F] / "**Hercules**," 2022–8 [L] / World War II Nazi Blitzkrieg [R].

Premier en Gaule, premier en Romanie,
Par mer & terre aux Angloys & Parys
Merveilleux faitz par celle grand mesnie
Violant terax perdra le NORLARIS.

VIII.61

A would-be ruler attains power only when he has lifted all his sieges and recalled his armed forces to France: Napoleon III [C] / liberation of Muslim-occupied France [F] / Nazi aggression [R].

Jamais par le decouvrement du jour
Ne parviendra au signe sceptrifere
Que tous ses sieges ne soyent en sejour,
Portant au coq don du TAG amifere.[60]

VIII.62

With the Vatican sacked, the churches desecrated, and the Pope beside the **Rhône** (see **VII.22**), pestilence is spread by invaders, but a fleeing monarch forgives them: World War III [F] or **Muslim invasion** of Italy, 2000 [L], and flight of John Paul II [F.L].

Lors qu'on verra expiler le saint temple,
Plus grand du rosne leurs sacrez prophaner
Par eux naistra pestilence si ample,
Roy fuit injuste ne fera condamner.

VIII.63

When a wounded criminal kills a woman and child, eight prisoners suffocate themselves.

Quant l'adultere blessé sans coup aura
Meurtry la femme & le filz par despit,
Femme assoumee l'enfant estranglera:
Huit captifz prins, s'estouffer sans respit.

VIII.64

Children are transported to the Islands as southern France falls, and seven countries' leaders despair even while doing their best to support their citizens: World War II [C] / **Muslim invasion of Europe**, 2017–22 [L] / British wartime evacuation [R].

Dedans les Isles les enfans transportez,
Les deux de sept seront en desespoir,
Ceux du terrouer en seront supportez,
Nom pelle[61] *prins des ligues fuy l'espoir.*

VIII.65

To the frustration of an older man, a rival gains power and rules for twenty months as the second-worst tyrant ever: Marshal Pétain, 1940–2 [C] and Hitler [F] / Ayatollah Khomeini [R].

Le vieux frustré du principal espoir
Il parviendra au chef de son empire:
Vingt mois tiendra le regne à grand pouvoir,
Tiran, cruel en delaissant un pire.

VIII.66

When an ancient inscription reading "D.M."[62] is discovered underground (see **IX.84**), a new Roman dispensation is inaugurated under the aegis of a leader and his wife: new "classical" era under "**Hercules**," 2026–34 [L] / new interpretation of Nostradamus [R].

Quand l'escriture D.M. trouvee,
Et cave antique à lampe descouverte,
Loy, Roy, & Prince Ulpian esprouvee,
Pavillon Royne & Duc sous la couverte.

VIII.67

Despite an indecisive civil war, France eventually achieves civil concord and Italy protection: wars, 1557 (?) [C] / Duke of Parma and Don Carlos, 1732–3 [F] / European civil war, 2032 (?) [L] / papal election, 1978 [R].

PAR. CAR. NERSAF,[63] *à ruine grand discorde*
Ne l'un ne l'autre n'aura election,
Nersaf du peuple aura amour & concorde,
Ferrare, Collonne grande protection.

VIII.68

When an older cardinal is deposed by a younger man and a double omen is seen at **Arles**, he travels by water and his prince is embalmed: Richelieu and Cinq-Mars, 1642 [C.R].

Vieux Cardinal par le jeusne deceu,
Hors de sa charge se verra desarmé,
Arles ne monstres double soit aperceu,
Et Liquiduct[64] *& le Prince embausmé.*

VIII.69

One of three archangels overcomes a young man in the form of the "eighth seraph" and for ten years renders him quasi-geriatric.

Aupres du jeune le vieux ange baisser,
Et le viendra surmonter à la fin:
Dis ans esgaux au plus vieux rabaisser,
De trois deux[65] *l'un l'huitiesme seraphin.*

VIII.70

An infamous, villainous tyrant of Iraq, in league with the Great Whore, moves in, leaving the land horrid and black: papal legate in former **Avignon** [C] / Ayatollah Khomeini, 1963–78 [F] / Saddam Hussein and Gulf War, 1981 [H.L].

Il entrera vilain, meschant, infame
Tyrannisant la Mesopotamie,
Tous amys fait d'adulterine d'ame[66]
Tertre[67] *horrible, noir de phisonomie.*[68]

VIII.71

As the number of astrologers increases, their books are banned in "1607" (by liturgical count – see **IV.18**): failed quatrain [C] / Copernicus, Galileo and persecution of astronomers, C16–17 [F] / ditto in 1999 [L] / Hitler, 1933, and the Nazi burning of books [R].

Croistra le nombre si grand des astronomes
Chassez, bannis & livres censurez,
L'an mil six cens & sept par sacre glomes
Que nul aux sacres ne seront asseurez.

VIII.72

A huge defeat takes place at Perugia and Ravenna at festivaltime, and the victors ravage the crops: Gaston de Foix, 1512 [C] / World War III [F] / **Muslim invasion** of Italy, 2000 [L].

Champ Perusin o l'enorme deffaite
Et le conflit tout au pres de Ravenne,
Passage sacre lors qu'on fera la feste,
Vainqueur vaincu cheval manger la venne.[69]

VIII.73

A Muslim soldier kills an already-dying ruler at the behest of an ambitious mother, to both his and the regime's subsequent regret: **Muslim invasion** of France [F] / death of Muslim overlord, 2026 [L] / death of Mussolini [R].

Soldat Barbare le grand Roy frappera,
Injustement non eslongné de mort,
L'avare mere du fait cause sera
Conjurateur & regne en grand remort.

VIII.74

Before a new ruler enters a new land, due punishment for his perfidy causes as much public joy as any welcome he might have had: USA [C].

En terre neufve bien avant Roy entré
Pendant subges[70] *luy viendront faire acueil,*
Sa perfidie aura tel rencontré[71]
Qu'aux citadins lieu de feste & recueil.

VIII.75

When a father and son are murdered, the pregnant mother hides in the bushes at Tours.

Le pere & filz seront meurdris ensemble
Le prefecteur dedans son pavillon
La mere à Tours du filz ventre aura enfle
Caiche verdure de feuilles papillon.

VIII.76

More cudgeler than English king, a lawless and irreligious wretch is destined shortly to rise from obscurity, seize power, and bleed the land: Oliver Cromwell, 1599–1656 [C.H.L].

---

[62] See the *Orus Apollo's* final section, on the Egyptian gods of the underworld.

[63] Presumably *Paris, Carcassonne, France* (anagram).

[64] Possibly *l'aqueduct.*

[65] *d'eux.*

[66] Standard Nostradamian version of *dame.*

[67] Generally read as *terre.*

[68] Read as *physiognomie.*

[69] *la venne* (*l'avoine*).

[70] Read as *subjects.*

[71] *rencontré.*

[72] Possible abbreviation for *sanglants.*

[73] Missing word inserted in late editions.

[74] *enfant.*

---

[60] *armifere.*

[61] Some commentators interpret this as *Montpelle* (*Montpellier*).

Plus Macelin que roy en Angleterre
Lieu obscur nay par force aura l'empire:
Lasche sans foy, sans loy saignera terre,
Son temps s'approche si pres que je souspire.

VIII.77

The Antichrist is destroyed after twenty-seven years of war, persecution, massacre, and bloodshed: the Antichrist [C,H,F], the Kennedy brothers, [C] and nuclear war [H] or **Muslim invasion of Europe** [L], 1999–2026 [F,L]/ Germany, 1918 and 1945 [R].

L'antechrist trois bien tost annichilez,
Vingt & sept ans sang[72] durera sa guerre,
Les heretiques mortz, captifs, exilez,
Sang corps humain eau rogie gresler terre.

VIII.78

A foreign mercenary breaks open the sanctuary, opening its doors to heretics and reinstigating the Church Militant: **Wars of Religion**, 1542–98 or Thirty Years' War, 1618–48 [C] / liberation of Muslim-occupied Italy, 2028 [L].

Un Bragamas avec la langue torte
Viendra des dieux [rompre][73] le sanctuaire,
Aux heretiques il ouvrira la porte
En suscitant l'eglise militaire.

VIII.79

One born in a nunnery, his father killed, fathers a child by a "Gorgon," concealing the fact by burning himself and his child abroad: Adolf Hitler [R].

Qui par fer pere perdra nay de Nonnaire,
De Gorgon sur la [ ] fera sang perfetant
En terre estrange fera si tout de taire,
Qui bruslera luy mesme & son entant.[74]

VIII.80

The "Great Red" persecutes the innocent, burns sacred images, and paralyzes everyone with fear: **Russian Revolution** [C,H] / Robespierre, 1794 [F].

Des innocens le sang de vefue & vierge.
Tant de maulx faitz par moyen se[75] grand Roge
Saintz simulachres trempez en ardant cierge
De frayeur crainte ne verra nul que boge.

VIII.81

An upstart empire is destroyed by the North, while forces from Sicily attack the vassals of Macedonia: Hapsburg civil war [C] / fall of Third Reich, 1943–5 [F,R] / counterinvasion of Muslim-occupied Europe, 2022–37 [L].

Le neuf empire en desolation,
Sera changé du pole aquilonaire.
De la Sicile viendra l'esmotion
Troubler l'emprise[76] à Philip tributaire.

VIII.82

A servant who tries to poison his master is arrested while trying to escape.

Ronge long, sec faisant du bon valet,
A la parfin n'aura que son congie,[77]
Poignant poyson & lettres au collet
Sera saisi eschappé en dangie.[78]

VIII.83

A huge fleet sets sail from Croatia for Istanbul, causing great enemy losses and seizing massive booty: Fourth Crusade, 1204 [C] / counterinvasion of Middle East, 2034–7 [L].

Le plus grand voile hors du port de Zara,
Pres de Bisance fera son entreprinse,
D'ennemy perte & l'amy ne sera
Le tiers à deux fera grand pille & prinse.

VIII.84

Screams are heard throughout Sicily as a veritable plague of ships descends on the Gulf of Trieste: Hapsburg Civil War [C] / **Muslim invasion** of Italy, 2000 [L].

Paterne[79] orra de la Sicile crie,
Tous les aprests du goulphre de Trieste,
Qui s'entenda jusque à la trinacrie.
De tant de voiles fuy, fuy l'horrible peste.

VIII.85

As war rages in the Pays Basque, Northern efforts are frustrated and unsupported: Napoleon III [C] / Wellington, and **Napoleon** [F] / **Muslim invasion of Europe**, 2013–17 (?) [L] / end of Franco-Spanish wars [R].

Entre Bayonne & à saint Jean de Lux
Sera posé de Mars le promottoire[80]
Aux Hanix d'Aquillon Nanar[81] hostera lux
Puis suffocqué au lict sans adjutoire.

VIII.86

Hordes of invaders cross the Pyrenees into France via the Pays Basque and Navarre (see **VIII.85**): World War III [F] / **Muslim invasion** of France, 2013–17 [L].

Par Arnani tholoser ville franque,[82]
Bande infinie par le mont Adrian,[83]
Passe riviere, Hurin[84] par pont la planque
Bayonne entrer tous Bihoro[85] criant.

VIII.87

A death-plot leads to trial and execution for a defeated, elected leader who is responsible for bloodshed: the dethronement and execution of Louis XVI [C].

Mort conspiree viendra en plein effect,
Charge donnee & voiage de mort,
Esleu, crée, receu par siens deffait.
Sang d'innocence devant foy[86] par remort.

VIII.88

A noble king reigns in Sardinia for only three years, uniting various parties after his marriage: Charles Emmanuel IV [C].

Dans la Sardeigne un noble Roy viendra.
Que ne tiendra que trois ans le royaume,
Plusieurs coulleurs avec soy conjondra,[87]
Luy mesmes apres soin someil marrit scome.[88]

VIII.89

Having avoided the clutches of an uncle who slaughtered his children in order to reign, a ruler is dismembered.

Pour ne tumber entre mains de son oncle,
Qui ses enfans par regner trucidez,
Orant au peuple mettant pied sur Peloncle[89]
Mort & traisné entre chevaulx bardez.

VIII.90

When a demented Christian sees an ox in the sanctuary and a pig replacing the virgin, it is an omen that royal authority is about to break down: Hitler [R].

Quand des croisez un trouvé de sens trouble
En lieu du sacre verra un bœuf cornu
Par vierge porc son lieu lors sera comble,[90]
Par roy plus ordre ne sera soustenu.

VIII.91

With Venus in Pisces and a gathering of Christians by the **Rhône**, many suffer from floods.

Frymy[91] les champs des Rodanes entrees
Ou les croysez seront presque unys,
Les deux brassieres en pisces rencontrees
Et un grand nombre par deluge punis.

VIII.92

A commander who leads a great army on a hazardous foreign campaign pillages and imprisons his people on his return: Mao Tse-tung [C,H].

Loin hors du regne mis en hazard voiage
Grand ost duyra pour soy l'occupera,
Le roy tiendra les siens captif ostrage[92]
A son retour tout pays pillera.

---

[79] Could conceivably stand for Palermo.

[80] *promontoire.*

[81] Possible misprint for *Namur.*

[82] Read as *Hernani Tholose et Villefranche.*

[83] *Montdarrain.*

[84] *Hutin.*

[85] *Bigorre.*

---

[75] Misprint for *de* or *du.*

[76] Abbreviation of *entrepri(n)se* for purposes of scansion.

[77] *congé.*

[78] *dang(i)er.*

---

[86] More likely *soy.*

[87] *conjoindra.*

[88] Presumably *son someil matriscome*, the last word being a not untypical Nostradamian mangling of *matrimonial* for purposes of rhyme.

[89] Possibly another Nostradamian mangling, this time of *Pelion.*

[90] Read as *comblé.*

[91] Misprint for *parmi.*

[92] Probable misprint for *ostage.*

VIII.93

After the death of a would-be bishop has caused a schism, another obtains the see for seven months, and reunion is achieved near Venice: schism during World War III [F] / events following death of the Pope [R].

Sept moys sans plus obtiendra prelature
Par son deces grand scisme fera naistre:
Sept moys tiendra un autre la preture
Pres de Venise paix union renaistre.

VIII.94

Because of delay in giving battle, Spain is laid waste by "Albanians": English attack on Cadiz, 1596 [C] / English attack on Spanish treasure ships, 1590 [H] / **Muslim invasion** of Spain, 2007+ [L] / League of Nations [R].

Devant le lac ou plus cher fut getté
De sept mois, & son host desconfit
Seront Hyspans par Albannois gastez
Par delay perte en donnant le conflict.

VIII.95

When a seducer is staked out, a right-wing bishop-commander gains followers: President Ronald Reagan [H].

Le seducteur sera mis en la fosse
Et estaché jusque à quelques temps,
Le clerc uny le chef avec sa crosse
Pycante droite attraira les contens.

VIII.96

Traditional synagogues are taken over by infidels, while "Babylon's daughter" clips refugees' wings: Ottoman mercy to persecuted Jews, 1550–66 [C] / foundation of Israel, 1948, and Golda Meir, 1974 [F] / **Muslim invasion** of Israel, 1998–9 [L].

La synagogue sterile sans nul fruit
Sera receu entre les infideles
De Babylon la fille[93] du porsuit
Misere & triste luy trenchera les aisles.

VIII.97

England's fortunes decline with the birth near Nice of three step[94]-children destined to grow up to ruin their nation: Kennedy brothers [C,R] / **Napoleon** and his two brothers, 1799 [F].

Au fin du VAR changer le pompotans,[95]
Pres du rivage les trois beaux enfans naistre.
Ruyne au peuple par aage competans
Regne au pays changer plus voir croistre.

VIII.98

The Church is ruined and oppressed and its clergy's blood copiously shed for a long time (see ***Lettre à Henri II***): persecution of clergy, 1792 [C] / **Muslim invasion** of France and persecution of Church, 2007–22 [L] / ditto in Soviet countries [R].

Des gens d'eglise sang sera espanché,
Comme de l'eau en si grande abondance:
Et d'un long temps ne sera restanché
Ve Ve au clerc ruyne & doleance.

---

[93] Possibly *file.*

[94] Or "beautiful."

[95] Elsewhere printed *pempotans.*

VIII.99

The power of three secular rulers causes the papacy to shift its headquarters to a Christian country: World War III and Third Antichrist [C,F] / **Muslim invasion** of Italy and flight of Pope, possibly to Chalon-sur-Saône[96] (see **II.97**), 2000+ [L].

Par la puissance des trois rois temporelz
En autre lieu sera mis le saint siege:
Où la substance de l'esprit corporel,
Sera remys & receu pour vray siege.

VIII.100

A surfeit of arms at all levels of society causes much loss of life through religious overzealousness: world revolt against arms race [R].

Pour l'abondance de larme[97] respandue
Du hault en bas par le bas au plus hault
Trop grande foy par ieu[98] vie perdue,
De soif mourir par habondant deffault.

CENTURY IX

Transliterated from **Benoist Rigaud**'s 1568 edition.

IX.1

When a traitor is revealed by documents, the former policy continues until the advent of a new High Constable: Etienne de la Boétie and **Anne de Montmorency** [C].

Dans la maison du traducteur de Bourc[1]
Seront les lettres trouvees sus la table,
Bourgne,[2] roux, blanc, chanu[3] tiendra de cours,
Qui changera au nouveau connestable.

IX.2

A voice is heard in Rome urging flight while "reds" are expelled from Italy and Greece amid bloody conflict: feuds between Papal States and Italian families [C] / Mussolini [C] / counterinvasion of Muslim-occupied Europe, 2027–8 [L].

Du hault du mont Aventin voix ouye,
Vuydez vuydez de tous les deux costez,
Du sang des rouges sera l'ire assomye,
D'Arimin[4] Prato, Columna[5] debotez.

IX.3

Trouble in northeast Italy is stirred up by fifteen captives, while the births of two monsters in Rome presage bloody disasters: failed quatrain [C] / World War II Rome-Berlin Axis [R].

La magna vaqua[6] à Ravenne grand trouble,
Conduitz par quinze enserrez à Fornase[7]
A Romme naistre deux monstres à teste double
Sang, feu, deluge, les plus grands à l'espase.

---

[96] Possible recapitulation of removal of Roman capital to Constantinople in A.D. 330 (see **Sequence of Selected Horographs**).

[97] *larme* or *l'arme:* possibly a deliberate (and carefully constructed) Nostradamian pun – which would not have worked had he used the more natural plural, for example.

[98] Should presumably read *Dieu,* the *D* having fallen out of its setting-stick.

[1] Possibly *Bourg.*

[2] *borgne.*

IX.4

The year after floods reveal ancient artifacts (see **IX.9, VI.66, VIII.29,** and **IX.9**), one of two elected leaders flees, his headquarters ransacked: failed quatrain [C] / flight of Mussolini to Germany [R].

L'an ensuyvant descouvertz par deluge,
Deux chefs esleuz le premier ne tiendra
De fuyr umbre à l'un d'eux le refuge,
Saccagee case qui premier maintiendra.

IX.5

A new, diminutive tyrant occupies Pisa and Lucca to put right his predecessor's failings: Louis Napoleon and Third Estate [C] / **Napoleon** [F].

Tiers doibt du pied au premier semblera.
A un nouveau monarque de bas hault
Qui Pyse & Lucques Tyran occupera
Du precedant corriger le deffault.

IX.6

From Guyenne, vast numbers of British occupy Bordeaux and the Languedoc, calling the area "Anglaquitaine" and later "Western Barbary": World War III liberation of southwest France [F] / counterinvasion of Muslim-occupied France, 2022–6 [L].

Par la Guyenne infinité d'Anglois
Occuperont par nom d'Anglaquitaine
De Languedoc Ispalme Bourdeloys.
Qu'ilz nommeront apres Barboxitaine.

IX.7

Evil befalls whoever opens a monument and fails to close it at once, whoever the ruler may be at the time: opening of Nostradamus's tomb [H,(?)C] / ditto of Tutankhamun [R].

Qui ouvrira le monument trouvé,
Et ne viendra le serrer promptement.
Mal lui viendra & ne pourra prouvé,[8]
Si mieux doit estre roy Breton ou Normand.

IX.8

On attaining power, a younger prince has his father put to death on doubtful evidence, to his later regret.

Puisnay Roy fait son pere mettre à mort,
Apres conflit de mort tres inhoneste:
Escrit trouvé soubson donra remort,
Quand loup chassé pose sus la couchette.

IX.9

An everlasting lamp is discovered by a foraging child in a Vestal temple, and **Nîmes** and **Toulouse** are destroyed by floods (see **X.6**): failed quatrain [C] / World War III crushing of rebels [F] / archeological discovery, C21 [L].

---

[3] *chenu.*

[4] Presumably Rimini.

[5] Possibly *Colonna.*

[6] *Magna Valca,* former port between Ravenna and Ferrara [C].

[7] Possibly either Forni or Forno.

[8] *prouver,* adapted so as to rhyme with line 1.

Quand lampe ardente de feu inextinguible
Sera trouvé au temple des Vestales,
Enfant trouvé feu, eau passant par trible:9
Perir eau Nymes, Tholose cheoir les halles.

IX.10

When the child of a monk and nun is exposed to wild beasts, armies attack cities in southwest France: World War III [F] / **Muslim invasion** of France, 2017 [L] / neglect of spirituality [R].

Moyne moynesse d'enfant mort exposé,
Mourir par ourse & ravy par verrier:10
Par Fois & Pamyes11 le camp sera posé.
Contre Tholose Carcas dresser forrier.

IX.11

When innocents are put to death, so great a plague arises that those who condemned them are forced to flee: execution of Charles I, 1649, and Great Plague of London, 1655 [C,R] / execution of Louis XVI, 1792 [F].

Le juste à tort à mort lon12 viendra mettre
Publiquement & du millieu estaint:
Si grande peste en ce lieu viendra naistre,
Que les jugeans fouyr seront constraint.

IX.12

Silver images of Diana and Mercury are discovered (see **VIII.28**) by a potter gathering clay, to the enrichment of his family: future world religion [H] / archeological discovery at **Nîmes**, C21 [L] / treacherous demagogue [R].

Le tant d'argent de Diane & Mercure
Les simulachres au lac seront trouvez,
Le figulier cherchant argille neufve
Luy & les siens d'or seront abbrevez.13

IX.13

While exiles are being transferred at night, an attack by leaders from Modena against Bologna is discovered by torchlight.

Les exilez autour de la Soulongne
Conduis de nuit pour marcher à Lauxois,
Deux de Modene truculent de Bologne,
Mys descouvers par feu de Burançoys.14

IX.14

Some victims are boiled to death, while seven are either gassed or shot.

Mys en planure chaulderons d'infecteurs,
Vin, miel & huyle, & bastis sur forneaulx
Seront plongez sans mal dit mal facteurs15
Sept, fum.16 extaint au canon des borneaux.17

---

9 Probable misprint for *crible*.

10 Modern French *verrat*.

11 Pamiers.

12 *l'on*.

13 *abbreuvez*.

14 Probably either *Buzançoys* or *Bisançoys*.

15 *malfacteurs*.

16 Abbreviation for *fumee*.

IX.15

Of "reds" detained near Perpignan, most are deported elsewhere, while three are dismembered and five starved: Franco-Spanish struggle around Pyrenees [C] / civil war in southwest France, 2026 [L] / Church feuds [R].

Pres de Parpan18 les rouges detenus,
Ceux du milieu parfondrez menez loing:
Trois mis en pieces & cinq mal soustenus,
Pour le Seigneur & Prelat de Bourgoing.

IX.16

Franco walks out of a meeting in Castile and creates a split, while Ribiere's supporters stop him from crossing the sea: General Francisco Franco [C,H,L,R] appointed Head of Government at Burgos, 1936 [F] and Primo de Rivera [C,F,H,L].

De castel Franco sortira l'assemblee,
L'ambassadeur non plaisant fera scisme:
Ceux de Ribiere seront en la meslee,
Et au grand goulphre desnieront l'entree.

IX.17

A third tyrant worse than Nero spills blood, rebuilds furnaces, then dies, as scandal surrounds the ruler of a new golden age: **French Revolution** [C] / Hitler and the gas chambers [F,R] / Asiatic Antichrist and "**Hercules**," 1999–2034 [L].

Le tiers premier pys que ne feit Neron,
Vuidez vaillant que sang humain respandre:
R'edifier sera le forneron,
Siecle d'or, mort, nouveau roy esclandre.

IX.18

The Elector of the empire carries the lily of the Dauphin from Nancy to Flanders, while Montmorency is burned after erecting a new barrier: Louis XIII, 1633, and execution of Montmorency, 1632 [C,F,R].

Le lys Dauffois portera dans Nansy
Jusques en Flandres electeur de l'empire,
Neufve obturee au grand Montmorency,
Hors lieux prouvez delivre a clere peyne.19

IX.19

When a thunderbolt falls in the forest of Mayenne, the bastard of the ruler of Maine attacks Fougères.

Dans le millieu de la forest Mayenne,
Sol au lyon la fouldre tombera,
Le grand bastard yssu du gran du Maine,
Ce jour Fougeres pointe en sang entrera.

---

17 Misprint for *boureaux*.

18 Abbreviation of *Perpignan*.

19 The rhyme suggests *pyre*: thus "bright fire."

20 Probably *Reims*, respelled to rhyme with *Varennes* in line 3: compare **I.26**.

21 See **Nostradamus Dictionary**.

22 Possibly *pieride*.

23 Version of *Sologne* to rhyme with line 3.

24 *l'Olonne*.

25 *d'où*.

IX.20

A "white butterfly" queen passes through woods near Reims at night, and an elected ruler, a "black monk in gray," causes a storm of fire, blood and dismemberment: flight of Louis XVI and Marie Antoinette to Varennes, 1791 [C,F,H,L,R].

De nuict viendra par la forest de Reines,20
Deux pars vaultorté21 Herne la pierre22 blanche,
Le moine noir en gris dedans Varennes
Esleu cap. cause tempeste feu, sang tranche.

IX.21

A bishop defeats and kills a king (or vice versa) on the bridge at **Blois**, and a messenger carries the news to Olonne: **French Revolution** and Nantes massacres, 1793 [F].

Au temple hault de Bloys sacre Solonne,23
Nuict pont de Loyre, prelat, roy pernicant
Curseur victoire aux maretz de la lone24
Dou25 prelature de blancs à bormeant.26

IX.22

The Dukes of Mantua and Alba confront each other in a church opposite a palace:

Roy & sa court au lieu de langue halbe,27
Dedans le temple vis à vis du palais
Dans le jardin Duc de Mantor & d'Albe,
Albe & Mantor poignard langue & palais.

IX.23

A young prince, playing outside, falls on his head from a roof while his royal father is attending a religious ceremony: second son of Louis XVI [C].

Puisnay jouant au fresch dessouz la tonne,
Le hault du toict du milieu sur la teste,
Le pere roy au temple saint Solonne,
Sacrifiant sacrera fum28 de feste.

IX.24

Two young princes, abducted through the windows of a palace on a rock, are taken via Orléans, **Paris** and St.-Denis, while a nun eats green nut-kernels: escape of Louis XVII from the Temple, 1793 [F].

Sur le palais au rochier des fenestres
Seront ravis les deux petits royaux
Passer aurelle29 Luthece Denis cloistres,
Nonain, mallods30 avaller verts noyaulx.

IX.25

Even though a commander arrives at Rozier (?) early, Spaniards arrive in **Béziers** in time to scupper his efforts: hunting expedition [R].

Passant les pontz venir pres des rosiers,
Tard arrivé plustost qu'il cuydera,
Viendront les noves31 espaignolz à Besiers,
Qui icelle chasse emprinse cassera.

---

26 Probably *abhorreant*.

27 Possible misprint for (or mangling of) *l'antique halle*, despite poor rhyme that results.

28 Abbreviation for *fumee*.

28 Latin *Aurelianum*, Orléans.

30 *molosses* (?).

31 *nouveaux* (?).

IX.26

Attacked in writing, the Pope makes an unwitting gift to his enemies by leaving Nice for Voltri, but then spreads a deliberate rumor beyond Piombino.

Nice sortie sur nom des letres aspres,
La grande cappe fera present non sien[32]
Proche de vultry[33] aux murs de vertes capres
Apres plombin[34] le vent à bon essien.[35]

IX.27

After a Dauphin is attacked by a forest guard on a bridge, an old gamesman passes far beyond both forest and ducal domains: escape of young Louis XVII, 1795 (?) [C].

De bois la garde vent cloz rond pont sera,
Hault le receu frappera le Daulphin,
Le vieux teccon bois unis passera,
Passant plus oultre du duc le droit confin.

IX.28

[**Summary verse**] With confederate fleets landing at Marseille, armies set out from the Adriatic to March on Hungary, Sicily is under gunfire: World War III [F] / **Muslim invasion of Europe**, 2002–5 [L].

Voille Symacle port Massiliolique,
Dans Venise port marcher aux Pannons:
Partir du goulfre & sinus Illirique
Vast à Socile,[36] Ligurs coups de canons.

IX.29

When a weak leader tries to abandon a half-taken town, ships are fired, Charlieu attacked with pitch and St.-Quentin and Calais retaken: fall of Calais, 1558, and restoration of St.-Quentin to French, 1559 [C] under Treaty of **Cateau-Cambrésis** [F].

Lors qu celuy qu'à nul ne donne lieu,
Abandonner vouldra lieu prins non prins:
Feu nef par saignes, bitument à Charlieu,
Seront Quintin Balez[37] reprins.

IX.30

While "Northerners" are dying on the northeast Adriatic coast, the Turkish leader is dismayed by Spanish counterattacks: failed quatrain [C] / World War III [F] / **Muslim invasion of Europe**, 2000 [L] / attack by **Philip II** on Malta [R].

Au port de POULA[38] et de saint Nicolas,
Perir Normande au goulfre Phanaticque,
Cap. de Bisance raues[39] crier helas,
Secors de Gaddes & du grand Philipique.

IX.31

An earthquake rocks northern Italy, while a sleepy Britain is roused to war by its own semidestruction and the Church is split: future events [C] / flooding of UK during planetary alignment of Easter 2000 [F] / **Muslim invasion of Europe**, 2022 (?) [L] / World War II bombing of Coventry [R].

Le tremblement de terre à Mortara,
Cassich saint George à demy perfondrez,
Paix assoupie, la guerre esveillera,
Dans temple à Pasques absysmes enfondrez.

IX.32

When Roman inscriptions are found beneath an unearthed porphyry column and human remains witness to Roman violence, a fleet is active at Mitilini, Lesbos: **Muslim invasion of Europe**, 2000 [L] / discovery of Rosetta stone, 1799 [R].

De fin porphire profond collon trouvee
Dessoubz la laze escriptz capitolin.
Os poil retors[40] Romain force prouvee,
Classe agiter au port de Methelin.

IX.33

"Hercules," standard-bearer of tripartite Gaul, rules supreme over western Europe: Charles de Gaulle [C,H] / future **Henri V** [F] / liberation of Muslim-occupied Europe, 2028 [L] / **Napoleon** [R].

Hercule Roy de Romme & d'Annemarc,[41]
De Gaule trois Guion surnommé,
Trembler l'Itale[42] & l'unde de sainct Marc
Premier sur tous monarque renommé.

IX.34

When a noble husband wears a miter, conflict spreads across the tiles, while another is accused of betraying 500 and oil arrives thanks to county officials at **Narbonne** and la Saulce: Louis XVI and Marie Antoinette at Varennes, 1791 [C,H,R], and return to Tuileries, 1792 [C,H,F,R].

Le part[43] soluz mary sera mittré,
Retour conflict passera sur la thuille:
Par cinq cens un trahyr sera tiltré,
Narbon & Saulce par coutaux[44] avons d'huille.

IX.35

A "blond Ferdinand" goes along with abandoning "the flower" in favor of "Macedon," then gives up the idea and marches against the latter's soldiery instead: World War II and Ferdinand of Bulgaria [C,R] / Charles-Ferdinand of Bourbon's alliance with Condé, and assassination, 1820 [F].

Et Ferdinand blonde sera descorte,[45]
Quitter la fleur suyvre le Macedon.
Au grand besoing defaillira sa routte,
Et marchera contre le Myrmidon.

IX.36

A king captured by a younger man is mistakenly stabbed at Easter and three brothers among life-prisoners kill each other: Kennedy brothers [C,H] and/or attempted assassination of Ronald Reagan, 1981 [H] / execution of Louis XVI, 1793 [R].

Un grand Roy prins entre les mains d'un Joyne[46]
Non loing de Pasque confusion coup cultre:[47]
Perpet. captifs temps que fouldre en la husne,
Lors que trois freres se blesseront & murtre.

IX.37

Garonne floods in December devastate **Toulouse** and render it unrecognizable: rebellion during World War III [F] / events during C21 [L].

Pont & molins en Decembre versez,
En si haut lieu montera la Garonne:
Murs, edifices, Tholose renversez,
Qu'on ne sçaura son lieu autant matronne.

IX.38

British forces landing at Blaye and la Rochelle outflank "the great Macedonian," while a French commander awaits near **Agen** to rescue a Narbonne seduced by negotiations: counterinvasion of Muslim-occupied France, 2022–6 [L].

L'entree de Blaye par Rochelle & l'Anglois,
Passera outre le grand Aemathien,
Non loing d'Agen attendra le Gaulois,
Secours Narbonne deceu par entretien.

IX.39

A long distance night assault is mounted on a fortified palace at Savona: C16 events.

En Arbissel[48] à Veront[49] & Carcari,[50]
De nuict conduitz pour Savonne atrapper,
Le vif Gascon Turbi,[51] & la Scerry[52]
Derrier mur vieux & neuf palais gripper.

IX.40

Near St.-Quentin, in Bourlis Wood, Dutch troops are cut down, and the followers of two stunned younger brothers are tortured and killed: Battle of St.-Quentin, 1557 (?) [C] / World War I (?) [L].

Pres de Quintin dans la forest bourlis,
Dans l'abbaye seront Flamens ranches,[53]
Les deux puisnais de coups my estourdis
Suitte oppressee & garde tous aches.[54]

---

[32] Possibly *nonscient*, i.e. "unwittingly": compare its opposite at the end of line 4.

[33] Voltri, Italy.

[34] Piombino, Italy.

[35] *escient.*

[36] *Sicille.*

[37] Possibly *Seront St Quentin & Calais reprins*: the 1605 edition has *Guines, Calais, Oye.*

[38] Pula, Croatia

[39] *rues* in later editions.

---

[40] *retordu.*

[41] Dannemarc.

[42] Italie.

[43] Presumably either *pars* ("equal," or "peer") or abbreviation for *partenaire.*

[44] Probable misprint for *comtaux.*

[45] *d'escorte.*

---

[46] *jeune.*

[47] Presumably *coutre.*

[48] Albissola Marina, Italy.

[49] Verona (?).

[50] Carcare, Italy.

[51] Turbe, Bosnia?

[52] Serre, Italy?

[53] Preumably *tranchés.*

[54] Presumably *hachés.*

IX.41

"**Chyren**" takes control of **Avignon** despite diplomatic protests from Rome, while **Carpentras** is captured by a black leader with a red plume: **Henri II** [C] / **Henri V** [F], 2034 [L].

Le grand Chyren soy saisir d'Avignon,
De Romme letres en miel plein d'amertume
Letre ambasse partir de Chanignon,
Carpentra pris par duc noir rouge plume.

IX.42

Mediterranean ports combine to send warships against a North African fleet and chase it back to Tunis: Battle of Lepanto, 1571 [C,H] / World War III defeat of Muslims [F] / **Muslim invasion of Europe**, 2002–5 [L].

De Barsellonne, de Gennes & Venise,
De la Secille peste Monet[55] unis,
Contre Barbare classe prendront la vise,
Barbar, poulsé bien loing jusqu'à Thunis.

IX.43

A Christian army lands under the eyes of Muslim troops and defeats them: Battle of Lepanto, 1571 [C] / counterinvasion of Middle East, 2036–7 [L].

Proche à descendre l'armee Crucigere
Sera guettee par les Ismaëlites
De tous cottez batus par nef Raviere,
Prompt assaillis de dix galeres eslites.

IX.44

The people of Geneva are warned to flee extermination by troops from a "land of the rose" when signs appear in the sky: Calvinist purge or attack by **Philip II** (?) [C] / Iraqi invasion of Europe, 1996 [H] / World War III [F] / **Muslim invasion** of Switzerland by Iranians, 2000–2 [L] / nuclear power [R].

Migres, migre de Genesve trestous,
Saturne d'or en fer se changera,
Le contre[56] RAYPOZ exterminera tous,
Avant l'a ruent[57] le ciel signes fera,

IX.45

[**Summary verse**] The insatiable "Mendosus," the worst of tyrants, seizes an empire stretching all the way to Italy and northern France: **Henri IV** [C] / Antichrist and **Muslim invasion of Europe**, 2000–22 [L] / Nazi regime, 1933–45 [R].

Ne sera soul jamais de demander,
Grand Mendosus obtiendra son empire
Loing de la cour fera contremander,
Pymond, Picard, Paris, Tyron[58] le pire.

IX.46

When their leader is strangled by way of example, the people of **Toulouse** are warned to see it as a sign to flee the "reds": World War III defeat of Communists [F] / French civil war, 2026 [L] / Church dispute [R].

Vuydez, fuyez de Tholose les rouges
Du sacrifice faire expiation,
Le chef du mal dessouz l'umbre des courges
Mort estrangler[59] carne omination.

IX.47

Signatories to an unworthy surrender are opposed and imprisoned by the people, along with a suspect new leader: François II [C] / Iranian revolution, 1979 [R].

Les soulz signes[60] d'indigne delivrance,
Et de la multe[61] auront contre advis,
Change monarque mis en perille pence,[62]
Serrez en caige se verront vis à vis.

IX.48

A maritime city is iced-in and blasted by strong winds in winter and spring: Nagasaki and Hiroshima, 1945 [C] / effects of planetary alignment, 2000 [H] / London [R].

La grand cité d'occean maritime,
Environee de maretz en cristal:
Dans le solstice hiemal & la prime,
Sera temptee de vent espouvantal.

IX.49

As Ghent and Brussels march on Antwerp, the English Parliament puts its king to death, and political confusion results: execution of Charles I, 1649 [C,F,L,R].

Gand & Bruceles marcheront contre Envers[63]
Senat de Londres mettront à mort leur roy
Le sel & vin luy seront à l'envers,
Pour eux avoir le regne en desarroy.

IX.50

At his apogee, "Mendosus" overruns part of Lorraine, then his "redness" fades and an uncertain interim leader takes over: **Henri IV**, "Charles X," Mayenne and Guise, 1589 [C] / Antichrist [F,L,R] and future **Henri V** [F] / **Muslim invasion of Europe**, 2022–6 [L].

Mandosus[64] tost viendra a son hault regne
Mettant arriere un peu de Norlaris:
Le rouge blaisme, le masle à l'interregne,
Le jeune crainte & frayeur Barbaris.

IX.51

Despite deaths and betrayals, religious groups oppose the "reds" until persecution gives way to peace: Communism and Fascism [C,F,R] / Muslim-occupied France, 2017–26 [L].

Contre les rouges sectes se banderont,
Feu, eau, fer, corde par paix se minera,[65]
Au pont mourir ceux qui machineront,
Fors un que monde sur tout ruynera.

IX.52

As peace approaches from one side and war from the other, unprecedented persecution afflicts France: Peace of **Cateau-Cambrésis**, 1559 [C] / runup to World War III [F] / **Muslim invasion** of France, 2013–22 [L] / Franco-Algerian war, 1954–62 [R].

La paix s'approche d'un costé, & la guerre
Oncques ne feut la poursuitte si grande,
Plaindre homme, femme, sang innocent par terre
Et ce sera de France a toute bande.

IX.53

A "young Nero" burns pages alive, but eventually three of his own family have him killed: Hitler's holocaust and the July plot, 1944 [F].

Le Neron jeune dans les trois cheminees
Fera de paiges vifz pour ardoir getter
Heureux qui loing sera de telz menees,
Trois de son sang le feront mort guetter.

IX.54

An envoy from Lisbon arrives by sea at Corcubion, northwest Spain, but seventy are ambushed: liberation of Corsica, 1943 [F] / birth of **Napoleon** in Corsica [R].

Arrivera au port de Corsibonne
Pres de Ravenne qui pillera la dame,
En mer profonde legat de la Vlisbonne[66]
Souz roc cachez raviront septante ames.

IX.55

The year after a terrible war in the West, with Mercury, Mars, and Jupiter in Aries, pestilence wipes out both man and beast: World War I and Spanish flu epidemic [C,F], or AIDS [C,H] / **Muslim invasion of Europe**, 2011 or 2012 [L] / future war and plague [R].

L'horrible guerre qu'en l'occident s'apreste
L'an ensuivant viendra la pestilence
Si fort horrible que jeune, vieulx, ne beste,
Sang, feu,[67] Mercure, Mars, Jupiter en France.[68]

IX.56

To the west of **Paris** an army surrenders to the "Scythians," who instantly convert over a thousand and imprison their generals: **Muslim invasion** of France, 2020–1 [L].

Camp pres de Noudam passera Goussan ville
Et a Maiotes laissera son enseigne,
Convertira en instant plus de mille,
Cherchant les deux[69] remettre en chaine legne.

---

[55] *Monech* (Monaco).

[56] Possible error for *la contrée*.

[57] Misprint for *l'advent*, as per later editions.

[58] *tyran*.

---

[59] *estranglé*.

[60] *soussignés*.

[61] *multitude*.

[62] *pense*.

[63] *Anvers* (Antwerp).

[64] *Mendosus*.

[65] Standard version of *terminera*.

---

[66] *Lisbonne*.

[67] Word play on *s'enfuit*.

[68] In contemporary astrology France corresponded to Aries.

[69] Here from Latin *dux, duces*, "leader(s), general(s)."

IX.57

At Dreux a king seeks legitimacy, but kills himself when thunder sounds from on high.

Au lieu de DRUX un Roy reposera
Et cherchera loy[70] changeant d'Anatheme
Pendant le ciel si tres fort tonnera,
Portee neufve Roy tuera soymesme.

IX.58

Three French "reds" are ambushed and killed at Vitry, while a "black" is brought to safety by Bretons: **French Revolution** [C] and battle of Valmy, 1792 [F] / liberation of Muslim-occupied France, 2022+ [L] / British government in France [R].

Au costé gauche a l'endroit de Vitry
Seront guettez les trois rouges de France,
Tous assoumez rouge, noir non murdry,
Par les Bretons remis en asseurance.

IX.59

When a life-giving, red-clothed "Nicol" captures la Ferté-Vidame, a "Louise" is born who will maliciously give Burgundy to the Bretons.

A la Ferté prendra la Vidame[71]
Nicol tenu rouge qu'avoit produit la vie.
La grand Loyse naistra que fera clame.
Donnant Bourgongne à Bretons par envie.

IX.60

Muslims in black headdresses shed blood across a terrified Dalmatia as Islam invades, but are themselves worried by Portuguese intervention: C20 rising Arab power [C] / **Muslim invasion** of Balkans [F], 2000 [L] / Muslim feuds [R].

Conflict Barbar en la Cornere[72] noire.
Sang espandu trembler la d'Almatie,[73]
Grand Ismaël mettra son promontoire
Ranes trembler secours Lusitanie.

IX.61

A "new city" and its neighbors are ransacked and ethnically cleansed, while Maltese are imprisoned by Messinans for their pains: Turkish siege of Malta, 1565, and Christian fleet at Messina, 1571 [C,H] / **Muslim invasion of Europe** and raid on Villeneuve-lès-Maguelonne, 2000–5 [L].

La pille faite à la coste marine,
La cita nova[74] & parentz amenez
Plusieurs de Malte par le fait de Messine,
Estroit serrez seront mal guerdonnez.

IX.62

Christians are held by rank, drugged, in Turkey, until a third are ransomed in October.

Au grand de Cheramon agora
Seront croisez par ranc tous attachez,
Le pertinax Oppi, & Mandragora,
Raugon[75] d'Octobre le tiers seront laschez.

IX.63

Groans and screams are heard in southwest France as war brings untold disasters for six years or more: World War III [F] / **Muslim invasion** of France, 2013–22 [L].

Plainctes & pleurs crys & grands urlemens[76]
Pres de Narbon à Bayonne & en Foix
O quel horrible calamitez changemens,
Avant que Mars revolue quelques foys.

IX.64

A "Macedonian" crosses the Pyrenees and attacks Narbonne, completely overwhelming the defenders: C16 failed quatrain [C] / World War III [F] / **Muslim invasion** of France, 2017 [L].

L'Aemathion passer montz Pyrenees,
En Mars Narbon ne fera resistance,
Par mer & terre fera si grand menee.
Cap. n'ayant terre seure pour demeurance.

IX.65

A prisoner surrenders by moonlight and is deported, while "unripe fruit" becomes a cause both of vilification and of praise: American moon landing, 1969 [C,H,R].

Dedans le coing de luna viendra rendre
Ou sera prins & mys en terre estrange,
Les fruitz immeurs seront à grand esclandre
Grand vitupere à l'un grande louange.

IX.66

With peace and unity, the social order is reversed, communications are reestablished and law suits settled: new World Order [H,R] / reconstruction after liberation of Muslim-occupied Europe, 2022–8 [L].

Paix, union sera & changement,
Estatz, offices bas hault, & hault bien bas,
Dresser voiage le fruict premier torment,
Guerre cesser, civil proces debatz.

IX.67

Papal forces face a **Muslim invasion** via the Alps: failed quatrain [C] / **Muslim invasion of Europe**, 2000 [L].

Du hault des montz à l'entour de Lizer[77]
Port à la roche Valen,[78] cent assemblez
De chasteau neuf pierre late[79] en donzere,
Contre le crest Romans soy assemblez.

IX.68

A "noble" from Montélimar is ambushed and brutally erased from the scene near Lyon on December 13th[80]: sack of Lyon, 1793 [C] / death of John Paul II [F], 2000 [L].

Du mont Aymar[81] sera noble obscurcie,
Le mal viendra au joinct de sonne[82] & rosne
Dans bois caichez soldatz jour de Lucie,
Qui ne fut onc un si horrible throsne.

IX.69

Fugitive leaders hide in the hills to the northwest of Grenoble, while beyond Lyon and Vienne bombardments go on and only a third of the "locusts" are left: liberation of Muslim-occupied France, 2025–6 [L] / bombardment of Italy and Austria [R].

Sur le mont de Bailly & la Bresle[83]
Seront caichez de Grenoble les fiers,
Oultre Lyon, Vien. eulx si grande gresle,
Languou't[84] en terre n'en restera un tiers.

IX.70

Attackers from Vienne hide arms inside torches at **Lyon** on Corpus Christi, but are cut down: future incendiary weapons [R].

Harnois trenchant dans les flambeaux cachez
Dedans Lyon le jour du Sacrement
Ceux de Vienne seront trestout hachez
Par les cantons Latins Mascon[85] ne ment.

IX.71

A fugitive hides among sheep, but is then brought in disgrace to **Carcassonne**: World War III Russian occupation [F] / sacrilege by temporary invaders of France [R].

Aux lieux sacrez animaux veu à trixe,
Avec celuy qui n'osera le jour:
A Carcassonne pour disgrace propice,
Sera posé pour plus ample sejour.

IX.72

About sixty to ninety years after the parliament of **Toulouse** desecrates the churches, a new breed of person arrives: Calvinists [C] / rebellions during World War III [F] / civil war, 2026, and the first extraterrestrial "Messiahs" [L] / new World Order, 2150 [R].

Encor seront les saincts temples pollus,
Et expillez par Senat Tholassain,
Saturne deux trois cicles revollus,
Dans Avril, May, gens de nouveau levain.

IX.73

A blue-turbaned invader reigns in Foix for less than twenty-nine years, until a white-turbaned leader forcibly restrains him: **Muslim invasion of Europe** [C], 2013–32 [L] / liberation of France by future **Henri V** [F].

---

70 Possible misprint for *soy.*

71 *La Ferté-Vidame.*

72 Misprint for *cornete.*

73 Usual Nostradamian transmogrification of *Dalmatie.*

74 **Erickstad** suggests *Naples* (Greek *Neapolis*, "New City").

75 Probable misprint for *rançon*: otherwise *ouragan.*

76 *hurlemens.*

77 *l'Isère.*

78 *Valence.*

79 *Châteauneuf, Pierrelatte.*

80 Julian calendar: for Gregorian equivalent, add 12½ days to **Lemesurier**'s dating.

81 *Montélimar.*

82 *Saône.*

83 Read as *Bully & l'Arbresle.*

84 *langoust.*

85 *Mâcon.*

Dans Foix entrez Roy ceiulee Turbao,[86]
Et regnera moins revolu Saturne
Roy Turban blanc Bizance cœur ban,[87]
Sol Mars, Mercure pres la hurne.

IX.74

In Castile (?) oxen are used for plowing rather than slaughter, until a new cult brings a return to animal sacrifice (see **III.76**): C21 semipagan cults [L] / Artemidorus (100 BC) [R].

Dans la cité de Fertsod[88] *homicide,*
Fait & fait multe beuf arant ne macter,
Retour encores aux honneurs d'Artemide,
Et à Vulcan corps morts sepulturer.

IX.75

Humanitarian aid comes to the ailing people of Greece from France, just as the reverse once happened to **Provence**: Battle of Navarino, 1827 [F] / liberation of Muslim-occupied Europe, 2036–7 [L].

Del l'Ambraxie & du pays de Thrace
Peuple par mer mal & secours Gaulois,
Perpetuelle en Provence la trace
Avec vestiges de leur coustume & loix.

IX.76

Along with a "black," the bloody, rapacious offspring of "Nero" is murdered between two rivers in a covert military operation: attempted assassination of Hitler, 1944 [F].

Avec le noir Rapax & sanguinaire
Yssue du peaultre de l'inhumain Neron
Emmy deux fleuves main gauche militaire,
Sera murtry par Joyne[89] *chaulveron.*

IX.77

A new king invites guests to a wedding, but others plot the lady's death, as well as that of his son and mistress: execution of Marie Antoinette, 1793, and Madame du Barry [C,H] / **French Revolution** [R].

Le regne prins le Roy conviera,
La dame prinse à mort jurez a sort,
La vie à Royne fils on desniera
Et la pellix au sort de la consort.

IX.78

A beautiful Greek lady enjoys many companions, but then is taken captive to Spain and dies wretchedly: Greek democratic ideals [C] / Marie de Medici, 1642 [F] / **Élisabeth de Valois** [R].

La dame Greque de beauté laydique,
Heureuse faicte de procs[90] *innumerable,*
Hors translatee au regne Hispanique,
Captive prinse mourir mort miserable.

IX.79

An admiral who has renounced the throne murders naval mutineers enticed to surrender, then is in turn ambushed: Mutiny on the Bounty, 1789 [R].

Le chef de classe par fraude stratageme,
Fera timides sortir de leurs galleres,
Sortis murtris chef renieur de cresme
Puis par l'embusche luy rendront les saleres.[91]

IX.80

After a tyrant who tries to exterminate his own people by sending the strongest abroad has ruined Pisa and Lucca, the grape-harvest is gathered by teetotal Muslims: **Muslim invasion** of Italy, 2000 [L].

Le Duc voudra les siens exterminer
Envoyera les plus forts lieux estranges
Par tyrannie Pize & Luc ruiner,
Puis les Barbares sans vin feront vendanges.

IX.81

A cunning king tries to ambush his traitorous enemies by arming monks.

Le Roy rusé entendra ses embusches
De trois quartiers ennemis assaillir
Un nombre estrange larmes[92] *de coqueluches*
Viendra Lemprin[93] *du traducteur faillir.*

IX.82

A city long beset by floods and disease is captured when the watch is killed, but is not sacked: dams destroyed by earthquake in Los Angeles or Teheran (?) [R].

Par le deluge & pestilence forte
La cité grande de long temps assiegee,
La sentinelle & garde de main morte,
Subite prinse, mais de nul oultragee.

IX.83

When a May earthquake ruins a crowded theater, even unbelievers call on God and saints: Apocalypse [C,R], 2020s [L]/ Muslim *jihad* [F] / results of May 2000 planetary alignment [H].

Sol vingt de taurus si fort terre trembler,
Le grand theatre rempli ruinera,
L'air, ciel & terre obscurcir & troubler,
Lors l'infidelle Dieu & sainctz voguera.

IX.84

When a flood reveals an ancient Roman tomb, a newly proclaimed king who has discovered his ancestry carries out a massacre: discovery of St. Peter's tomb [C] / "**Hercules**," 2027–8 [L].

Roy exposé parfaira l'hecatombe,
Apres avoir trouvé son origine,
Torrent ouvrir de marbre & plomb la tombe
D'un grand Romain d'enseigne Medusine.

IX.85

A king advances through southwest France to restore **Marseille**, with fighting around **St.-Paul-de-Mausole**: World War III [F] / liberation of Muslim-occupied France, 2025–6 [L].

Passer Guienne, Langedoc & le Rosne,
D'Agen tenens de Marmande & la Roole[94]
D'ouvrir [par foy][95] *par roy*[96] *Phocen tiendra son trosne*
Conflit aupres saint Pol de Mauseole.

IX.86

An army moves to Chartres by way of Bourg-la-Reine, while a sevenfold alliance sends troops into a closed **Paris**: defeat of **Napoleon**, 1815 [C] / coronation of **Henri IV** at Chartres and entry into **Paris**, 1594 [F].

Du bourg Lareyne[97] *parviendront droit à Chartres*
Et feront pres du pont Authoni[98] *panse,*[99]
Sept pour la paix cautelleux comme martres
Feront entree d'armee à Paris clause.[100]

IX.87

The Duc d'Étampes makes an example of the Bishop of Montlhéri in grubbed-up woods near Torfou.

Par la forest du Touphon[101] *essartee,*
Par hermitage sera posé le temple,
Le duc d'Estampes par sa ruse inventee,
Du Mont Lehori[102] *prelat donra exemple.*

IX.88

As northeast France is deceived into hoping for peace and rescue, troops from Savoy descend on Roanne, despite efforts to block their route: fall of Calais to French, 1558 [C].

Calais, Arras secours à Theroanne,
Paix & semblant simulera lescoutte,[103]
Soulde[104] *d'Alabrox descendre par Roanne*
Destornay peuple qui deffera la route.

IX.89

After seven years of success in repulsing the Arabs, "Philip" is attacked again from the south and weakened by a "young **Ogmion**": Louis-Philippe [C,H], and Algerian campaign, 1840–7 [F] / **Philip II** of Spain [R].

Sept ans sera Philip. fortune prospere,
Rabaissera des Arabes l'effaict,[105]
Puis son mydi perplex rebors affaire
Jeusne ognyon[106] *abysmera son fort.*

---

86 Read as *cerulee Turban*, to rhyme with line 3.

87 Probable Nostradamian respelling of *courbant*.

88 Problematic: see **Nostradamus Dictionary**.

89 *jeune.*

90 Presumably either *prochains* or *proces.*

---

91 *salaires.*

92 Possibly *d'armes.*

93 *l'entreprinse.*

94 *la Réole.*

95 Redundant expression, presumably inserted by a typesetter unable to decipher the manuscript.

96 *parroy.*

97 *Bourg-la-Reine.*

---

98 *Anthoni.*

99 *pause*: see line 4.

100 *close.*

101 *Torfou.*

102 *Montlhéri.*

103 *l'écoute.*

104 *souldartz.*

105 *l'effort.*

106 *Ogmyon.*

IX.90

A leader of Greater Germany conducts a bloody invasion of Hungary under the guise of bringing aid: Hitler's eastward expansion [C,H,R] / Wallenstein and Thirty Years' War, 1618–34 [F].

Un capitaine de la grand Germanie
Se viendra rendre par simulé secours
Un Roy des roys ayde de Pannonie,
Que sa revolte fera de sang grand cours.

IX.91

An unknown pestilence sweeps Greece, bringing all social life to a stop: aftermath of **Muslim invasion** of Greece, 2000+ [L].

L'horrible peste Perynte & Nicopolle,
Le Chersonnez tiendra & Marceloyne,[107]
La Thessalie vastera l'Amphipolle,
Mal incogneu & le refus d'Anthoine.

IX.92

Following false intelligence, a liberating king stays clear of a "new city": future attack on New York [C] / liberation of Muslim-occupied Villeneuve-sur-Lot by **"Hercules,"** 2024–6 [L].

Le Roy vouldra dans cité neufve entrer
Par ennemys expunger lon[108] viendra
Captif libere faulx dire & perpetrer,
Roy dehors estre, loin d'ennemys tiendra.

IX.93

With **"Hercules"** attacking the "Macedonian," a rampart is erected to replace the crumbling walls of Bourges before the enemy arrives: Louis XIV and Languedoc Canal, 1681 [C] / World War III liberation of France [F] / tank-battle during counterinvasion of Muslim-occupied France, 2022–4 [L].

Les ennemis du fort bien eslongnez,
Par chariots conduict le bastion,
Par sur les murs de Bourges esgrongnez,
Quand Hercules battra l'Haemathion.

IX.94

While weak nations forge alliances, treacherous enemies scale the strongest wall, as Bratislava is threatened and parts of eastern Germany side with the Muslims: failed quatrain [C] / Nazi annexation of Czechoslovakia, 1939 [F,R] / **Muslim invasion of Europe**, 2000–2 [L].

Faibles galleres seront unies ensemble
Ennemis faux le plus fort en rampart:
Faible assaillies Vratislave[109] tremble,
Lubecq & Mysne[110] tiendront barbare part.

IX.95

A new commander leads an army to a river bank near Parma in expectation of reinforcements from a Milan whose leader has just been imprisoned and blinded: failed quatrain [C] / allied invasion of Calabria, 1943 [F] / **Muslim invasion** of Italy, 2000 [L] / death of Mussolini, 1945 [R].

---

[107] *Macedoyne.*

[108] *l'on.*

[109] Bratislava.

[110] Meissen.

[111] See **Nostradamus Dictionary**.

Le nouveau faict conduyra l'exercite,
Proche apamé[111] jusques au pres du rivage,
Tendant secour de Milannoile[112] eslite,
Duc yeux privé à Milan fer de cage.

IX.96

Denied entry to a city, a general talks his way in, then lets in his army to sack it.

Dans cité entrer exercit desniee,
Duc entrera par persuasion,
Aux foibles portes clam armee amenee,
Mettront feu, mort de sang effusion.

IX.97

Although the second wave of a triple sea-borne force runs out of provisions while desperately seeking its promised land, the first wave succeeds: **Muslim invasion of Europe**, 2000–2 [L] / World War II Nazi invasion of France, 1940 [R].

De mer copies en trois parts divisees,
A la seconde de vivres failleront,
Desesperez cherchant champs Helisees,[113]
Premiers en breche entrez victoire auront.

IX.98

The defection of a defender forces those at Lyon to surrender the commander of Malta: **Muslim invasion of Europe**, 2000–5 [L] / Laval's betrayal of France, 1940 [R].

Les affligez par faute d'un seul taint,
Contremenant à partie opposite,
Aux Lygonnois[114] mandera que contraint
Seront de rendre le grand chef de Molite.[115]

IX.99

After a north (or northward-blowing) wind carrying ashes, lime and dust over the walls causes the abandonment of a siege (or of a see), those involved are forced to withdraw by "rain": **Napoleon**'s retreat from Moscow, 1812 [C] / flight of John Paul II [F], 2000, [L] or eruption of Vesuvius affecting Rome in 2005.[116]

Vent Aquilon fera partir le siege,
Par murs geter centres, chauls, & pousiere,
Par pluye apres qui leur fera bien piege,
Dernier secours encontre leur frontiere.

IX.100

As night and "drizzle" fall, a Western fleet is destroyed by fire, its flagship stained with blood: Pearl Harbor, 1941 [C] / World War III [F] / Mediterranean sea-battle with Muslims, 2005 [L].

Navalle pugne nuit sera superee,
Le feu aux naves à l'occident ruine:
Rubriche neufve la grand nef coloree,
Ire a vaincu, & victoire en bruine.

---

[112] *Milannoise.*

[113] *Elysées.*

[114] *Lyonnois.*

[115] *Melite.*

[116] Astrological extrapolation from major eruption of Vesuvius in A.D. 472: see **Sequence of Selected Horographs**.

CENTURY X

Transliterated from **Benoist Rigaud**'s 1568 edition.

X.1

When a treaty for the exchange of prisoners breaks down, they are either maltreated or killed: World War II Vichy collaboration [C] / US hostages in Iran, 1979–80 [R].

[A][1] L'ennemy l'ennemy foy promise
Ne se tiendra, les captifs retenus:
Prins preme mort & le reste en chemise,
Damné le reste pour estre soustenus

X.2

A large fleet is defeated by a smaller one: World War II [C] / Mediterranean sea-battle against Muslims, 2005 [L] / Spanish Armada, 1588 [R].

Voille gallere voil de nef cachera,
La grande classe viendra sortir la moindre
Dix naves proches le torneront poulser,
Grande vaincue unie à foy[2] joindre.

X.3

A Pope ceases to feed his flock after five years, inadvisedly frees a Polish refugee, and leaves the Vatican: flight of John Paul II [F], 2000 [L].

En[3] apres cinq troupeau ne mettra hors
Un Fuytif pour Penelon[4] l'ashera,[5]
Faulx murmurer secours venir par lors,
Le chef le siege lors habandonnera.

X.4

When a vanished commander-in-chief reappears seven years later, his wife denies all knowledge of it and is cleared: Charles II [C] / General Douglas MacArthur [R].

Sus la munuict conducteur de l'armee
Se saulvera, subit esvanouy,
Sept ans apres la fame non blasmee,
A son retour ne dira oncqu ouy.

X.5

Albi and Castres ally with a Portuguese commander, but are defeated by **Carcassonne** and **Toulouse**, as presaged by an omen: Albigensian Crusade, 1208–13 [C] / World War III and southwest France [F] / **Muslim invasion** of France, 2013–17 [L] / Hitlerian Aryanism [R].

Albi & Castres feront nouvelle ligue,
Neuf Arriens Lisbon & Portugues,
Carcas, Tholosse consumeront leur brigue
Quand chief neuf [ ][6] monstre de Lauragues.

---

[1] Word omitted in earlier editions.

[2] Possibly *soy*.

[3] *an[s]*.

[4] Polone.

[5] *laschera.*

[6] *verra* (?).

X.6

When the river **Gard** floods, the people of **Nîmes** take refuge in the Roman amphitheater and a lamp relights in a buried temple (see **V.66, X.9**): repetition of events of 1577 [R] and 1988 [C] / C21 events [L].

Sardon[7] Nemans si hault desborderont,
Qu'on cuidera Deucalion renaistre,
Dans le colosse[8] la plus part fuyront,
Vesta sepulchre feu estaint apparoistre.

X.7

With a gloating "Macedonian" threatening Nancy, Britain is disturbed and Metz about to fall: **Philip II** [C] / Franco-German War, 1870 [F] / **Muslim invasion of Europe**, 2021–2 [L].

Le grand conflit qu'on appreste à Nancy.
L'aemathien dira tout je soubmetz,
L'Isle Britanne par vin, sel ensolcy,[9]
Hem. mi deux Phi.[10] long temps ne tiendra Metz.

X.8

After a Count of Senegallia has baptized his son, hordes of attackers from Greece cause casualties: son of Napoleon III, 1856 [C] / **Muslim invasion of Europe**, 2000 [L] / death of Admiral Darlan during World War II [R].

Index & poulse parfondera le front
De Senegalia le Conte a son filz propre
La Myrnarmee[11] par plusieurs de prinfront[12]
Trois dans sept jours blesses mors.

X.9

A bad Portuguese ruler earns himself the post-humous name of "Pantsdown."

De Castillon figuieres jour de brune,[13]
De feme infame naistra sowerain prince
Surnom de chausses perhume luy posthume,
Onc Roy ne feut si pire en sa province.

X.10

A murderous criminal, the enemy of all humanity, inflicts worse atrocities than all his predecessors: **Napoleon** [C] / Antichrist [F,L].

Tasche de murdre enormes adulteres,
Grand ennemy de tout le genre humain
Que sera pires qu'ayeux, oncles, ne peres
En fer, feu, eau, sanguin & inhumain.

X.11

A commander advances from Perpignan through the Pyrenees to await his leader: World War III liberation of Europe [F] / liberation of Muslim-occupied Spain, 2034 [L].

---

[7] *Gardon.*

---

[8] i.e. the Colosseum or *Colisée*, now known as the *Arènes.*

---

[9] *en solcy.*

---

[10] *en mi-défi (?).*

---

[11] *Minamee* in some editions: read as *l'armee des Myrmidons.*

---

[12] *de plain front.*

---

[13] *brume.*

X.12

A Pope, criticized as soon as he is elected for being too good-hearted, soon dies: Gregory XIV, 1591 [C] / John Paul I, 1978 [H] / death of John Paul II [F] / Cardinal Santa Severina, 1592 [R].

Esleu en Pape, d'esleu sera mocqué,
Subit soudain esmeu prompt & timide,
Par trop bon doulx à mourir provocqué,
Crainte estainte la nuit de sa mort guide.

X.13

Soldiers enter Antibes hidden under the bellies of sheep, but their attack fails when their weapons are heard: **Napoleon**, 1806 and 1815 [F] / Falklands War [R].

Soulz la pasture d'animaux ruminant
Par eux conduicts au ventre herbipolique
Soldatz caichez les armes bruit menant,
Non loing temptez de cite Antipolique.[14]

X.14

The uncertain defenders of the country east of the **Rhône** are defeated and captured, along with their whores, and converted at Barcelona by Benedictines: personal horoscope [F].

Urnel Vaucile[15] sans conseil de soy mesmes
Hardit timide par crainte prins vaincu,
Accompaigné de plusieurs putains blesmes
A Barcelonne aux chartreux convaincu.

X.15

The old, thirsty father of a duke, denied water by his son even as he dies, is thrown alive into a well, but the son suffers a long but easy death.

Pere duc vieux d'ans & de soif chargé,
Au jour extreme filz desniant les guiere[16]
Dedans le puis vif mort viendra plongé,
Senat au fil[17] la mort longue & legiere.

X.16

A French ruler enjoys power, ignorant of the crimes committed in his name, until told the truth and poisoned: Louis XVIII [C,R].

Heureux au regne de France, heureux de vie
Ignorant sang mort fureur & rapine,
Par non flateurs sera mys en envie,
Roy desrobé trop de foy en cuisine.

X.17

When an imprisoned queen sees her daughter sick with sorrow, screams are heard in Angoulême and a wedding is called off: Marie Antoinette [R], 1793 [C,F].

La royne Ergaste voiant sa fille blesme,
Par un regret dans l'estomach encloz,
Crys lamentables seront lors d'Angolesme,
Et au germain mariage fort clos.

---

[14] Antibes.

---

[15] Drôme et Vaucluse (?).

---

[16] *l'aiguière.*

---

[17] *filz.*

X.18

The Lorraines give way to the Bourbons, while a Pope from Fano is elected and two existing rulers are disempowered: accession of **Henri IV**, 1589 [C,F] and election of Clement VIII, 1592 [L].

Le ranc Lorrain fera place à Vendosme,
Le hault mys bas & le bas mys en hault,
Le filz d'Hamon[18] sera esleu dans Rome
Et les deux grands seront mys en deffault.

X.19

A proud woman saluted by a queen is saved by prayer and rehabilitated once she becomes more humble: **Elizabeth I** [C] / Maharani of Sikkim and Queen Noor of Jordan [R].

Jour que sera par royne saluee,
Le jour apres le salut, la priere,
Le compte fait raison & valbuee,[19]
Par avant humble oncques ne feut si fiere.

X.20

The supporters of a great illiterate are persecuted, and once his assets are made known he is destroyed, to the indignation of the Romans: post-Fascist Italy [C].

Tous les amys qu'auront tenu party,
Pour rude en lettres mys mort & sacagé,
Biens publiez par fixe[20] grand neanty,[21]
Onc Romain peuple ne feut tant outragé.

X.21

A father who honors his minority-supporting son with gifts is scorned and killed: fall of Shah, 1979 [F].

Par le despit du Roy soustenant moindre,
Sera meurdry luy presentant les bagues,
Le pere au filz voulant noblesse poindre
Fait comme à Perse jadis feirent[22] les Magues.

X.22

For not supporting a subsequently scorned divorce, a king of the Isles is hounded out and replaced by one who shows no sign of kingship: abdication of Edward VIII, 1936 [C,H,L,R] / Charles I and Oliver Cromwell, 1649 [F].

Pour ne vouloir consentir au divorce,
Qui puis apres sera cogneu indigne,
Le roy des Isles sera chassé par force
Mis à son lieu que de roy n'aura signe.

---

[18] Some editions have *Mamon*, but *Fanon* is also possible.

---

[19] *valuee.*

---

[20] *six.*

---

[21] *aneanty.*

---

[22] *firent.*

X.23

Despite popular opposition, an army invades Antibes, while Monaco and Fréjus dispute the seashore: Louis XVIII and **Napoleon** C / World War II liberation of Provence, 1944 F / liberation of Muslim-occupied France, 2025–6 L.

Au peuple ingrat faictes les remonstrances,
Par lors l'armee se saisira d'Antibe,
Dans l'arc Monech feront les doleances,
Et à Frejus l'un l'autre prendra ribe.

X.24

A captive prince defeated in Italy sails to **Marseille** unharmed, except for a barrel of honey hit by gunfire: **Napoleon's** escape from Elba, 1815 C,F,R.

Le captif prince aux Italles vaincu
Passera Gennes par mer jusqu'à Marseille,
Par grand effort des forens survaincu
Sauf coup de feu barril liqueur d'abeille.

X.25

A way is opened from the Ebro to Brittany via Portugal, while a great lady commits an outrage in Pellegrue.

Par Nebro[23] ouvrir de Brisanne[24] passage,
Bien eslongnez el tago[25] fara muestra,
Dans Pelligouxe[26] sera commis l'outrage,
De la grand dame assise sur l'orchestra.

X.26

A successor to the leadership avenges his brother-in-law, killing a hostage, while Brittany (or Britain) stays loyal to France: assassination of Robert Kennedy, 1968 C / **Henri IV**, 1589 F / future **Henri V**, 2034 L.

Le successeur vengera son beau frere,
Occuper regne souz umbre de vengeance,
Occis ostacle[27] son sang mort vitupere,
Long temps Bretaigne tiendra avec la France.

X.27

After St. Peter's, Rome, is reopened by force of arms for **'Hercules'** and the future **Henri V**, three papal candidates decline office and a furious dispute ensues: liberation of Vatican F, 2027–8 L / schisms caused by **Charles V** and **Henri II** R.

Par le cinquieme & un grand Hercules
Viendront le temple ouvrir de main bellique,
Un Clement, Jule & Ascans recules,
Lespe,[28] clef, aigle, n'eurent onc si grand picque.

X.28

The most vocal representatives of the lords and commons are elevated by a king, but damaged by untrue sexual allegations: Louis XVI and **French Revolution** R.

---

[23] *Hebro.*

[24] Probable misprint for *Britanne.*

[25] *Tagus:* for *fara muestra* see **Nostradamus Dictionary.**

[26] *Pellegrue* (?).

[27] Possible misprint for *ostaige.*

[28] *l'espee.*

Second & tiers qui font prime musicque
Sera par Roy en honneur sublimee,
Par grasse & maigre presque demy eticque,
Raport de Venus faulx randra deprimee.

X.29

A prisoner caught in a goat-cave at **St.-Paul-de-Mausole** is taken to Tarbes by Bigorrans: arrest of supporters of John Paul II F / incident in former Roman quarry at **Glanum** L.

De Pol MANSOL dans caverne caprine
Caché & prins extrait hors par la barbe,
Captif mené comme beste mastine
Par Begourdans amenee pres de Tarbe.

X.30

The "green" family of a saintly newcomer, though protected by his name, are driven out and changed to red and black: European totalitarianism "changes colors" R.

Nepveu & sang du sainct nouveau venu,
Par le surnom soustient arcs & couvert,
Seront chassez mis a mort chassez nu,
En rouge & noir convertiront leur vert.

X.31

While the Holy Roman Empire rises to power in Germany, Muslims advance across open country, even though their pack-animals would rather be back at home in shelter: Holy Roman Empire and Ottomans C / Russian invasion of Afghanistan F,H / German world conquest R.

Le saint empire viendra en Germanie,
Ismaelites trouveront lieux ouverts.
Anes vouldront aussi la Carmanie,
Les soustenens de terre tous couverts.

X.32

The winner of a scramble for imperial power lasts only two years with naval support: World War III Soviet occupation F.

Le grand empire chacun an[29] devoir estre
Un sur les autres le viendra obtenir,
Mais peu de temps sera son regne & estre,
Deux ans aux naves se pourra soustenir.

X.33

Cruel zealots with daggers under long robes seize the leader of Florence and Firenzuola, thanks to betrayal by immature flatterers: C16 or 17 C / **Muslim invasion** of Italy F, 2000 L.

La faction cruelle à robbe longue,
Viendra cacher souz les pointus poignars
Saisir Florence le duc & lieu diphlongue[30]
Sa descouverte par immeurs & flangnards.

X.34

When a Frenchman away at the wars is betrayed by his younger brother-in-law and, falling, is dragged by his horse, the latter is blamed: King of Naples, Joachim Murat C,R.

Gauloys qu'empire par guerre occupera
Par son beau frere mineur sera trahy,
Par cheval rude voltigeant traynera,
Du fait le frere long temps sera hay.

---

[29] *en.*

[30] *diphtongue.*

X.35

A younger prince burning with desire for his first cousin is murdered while visiting a mausoleum in woman's clothing: failed quatrain C.

Pusnay royal flagrand d'ardant libide,
Pour se jouyr de cousine germaine,
Habit de femme au temple d'Arthemide:
Allant murdry par incogneu du Maine.

X.36

A "United Island" scorns the threats of a "king of the souk" until years of pillage and tyranny force it to think again (see **Sixain 54**): failed quatrain C / **Muslim invasion** of northern Europe, 2017–22 and counterinvasion L / **Philip II**, **Elizabeth I** and Spanish Armada R.

Apres le Roy du soucq[31] guerres parlant,
L'isle Harmotique le tiendra à mepris,
Quelques ans bons rongeant un & pillant
Par tyrranie à l'isle changeant pris.

X.37

A combined force marches from Montmélian with a view to joining battle further to the north, near Geneva: World War III defeat of Russians F.

L'assemblee[32] grande pres du lac de Borget,
Se ralieront pres de Montmelian,
Marchans plus oultre pensifz feront proget
Chambry,[33] Moriane[34] combat sainct Julian.

X.38

After a brief Algerian siege, garrisons defect to the "Holy Muslim", and despite pledges of support from "bearlike ones" in the Adriatic, some French defenders surrender to forces from Switzerland: **Henri IV** C / World War III and Russia F / **Muslim invasion of Europe**, 2000–4 L.

Amour alegre[35] non loing pose le siege,
Au sainct barbar seront[36] les garnisons,
Ursins Hadrie pour Gaulois feront plaige,
Pour peur rendus de l'armee aux Grisons.

X.39

A first son of a widow presides over an unhappy, childless marriage – as well as islands at loggerheads – before the age of eighteen, but his younger successor patches up the quarrel: **François II, Mary Queen of Scots**, and **Charles IX** C,H,R.

Premier fils vefue malheureux mariage,
Sans nuls enfans deux Isles en discord,
Avant dixhuict incompetent eage,
De l'autre pres plus bas sera l'accord.

---

[31] Possibly *sud*, as in late editions.

[32] *l'assemblee.*

[33] *Chambery.*

[34] Possibly *Myans.*

[35] **Fontbrune** suggests a not-untypical Nostradamian reworking of *Amoura, Algiers,* both of them in Algeria.

[36] Possibly *feront.*

X.40

After the death of a father who recommends his young son as British King, London asks the latter to surrender power: Edward VIII [C,H,R] / Pitt the Younger [F] / Prince Charles and his son William [L].

Le jeune nay au regne Britannique
Qu'aura le pere mourant recommandé,
Iceluy mort LONOLE[37] donra topique,
Et à son fils le regne demandé.

X.41

A public celebration or festival is held in the region of **Agen**.

En la frontiere de Caussade & Charlus,[38]
Non guieres loing du fonds de la vallee,
De ville Franche[39] musique à son de luths,
Environnez combouls & grand myttee.

X.42

The British royal family long rules in peace, but is subsequently "confined to barracks" by war: C19 Pax Britannica [C].

Le regne humain d'Anglique geniture
Fera son regne paix union tenir,
Captive guerre demy de sa closture,
Long temps la paix leur fera maintenir.

X.43

An easy-going king is undermined and killed as a result of his own negligence and his unfounded suspicions of his wife: Louis XVI and Marie Antoinette [C,F].

Le trop bon temps trop de bonté royale:
Fais & deffais prompt subit negligence,
Legier croira faux d'espouse loyalle,
Luy mis à mort par sa benevolence.

X.44

Despite involving himself in a civil war, a "native of **Blois**" conquers northern Italy, leaving Granada and coastal Yugoslavia in Muslim hands, but after "seven New Years" he enters the land of shadows: **Henri III**, one of seven Valois children [C] / World War III liberation of Europe [F] / liberation of Muslim-occupied Italy by **'Hercules'**, 2027–34 [L].

Par lors qu'un Roy sera contre les siens,
Natif de Bloys subjuguera Ligures:
Mammel,[40] Cordube & les Dalmatiens,
Des sept puis l'ombre à Roy estrennes & lemures.

X.45

Navarran propaganda casts doubt on the King's credentials, but dubious promises at Cambrai legitimize him at Orléans: **Henri IV**, and Treaty of Cambrai, 1529 [C] / **Henri III** and **IV** [F].

Lombre[41] du regne de Navarre non vray,
Fera la vie de sort[42] illegitime:
La veu promis incertain de Cambray,
Roy Orleans donra mur legitime.

X.46

A would-be Elector of Saxony attempts to justify his sordid life to the people by demanding support from Brunswick: Maurice of Saxony [C] / Duke of Brunswick, 1792 and 1805 [F] / propaganda by German industrialists [R].

Vie sort mort de L'OR vilaine indigne
Sera de Saxe non nouveau electeur:
De Brunsuic mandra d'amour [le] signe,
Faux le rendant au peuple seducteur.

X.47

A lady of Bourneville is garlanded for her treason, while the Bishop of Leon is mugged: conspiracy against **Paris** [R].

De Bourze ville[43] à la dame Guyrlande,
L'on mettra sus par la trahison faicte,
Le grand prelat de Leon par Formande,
Faux pellerins & ravisseurs defaicte.

X.48

Massed invaders entering Europe via southern Spain have difficulties crossing the St.raits and are defeated by guerrilla forces: Spanish Civil War and World War II [C] / General Francisco Franco [F] / **Muslim invasion of Europe**, 2007 [L] / World War II defeat of Fascist Blue Division by Russia [R].

Du plus profond de l'Espaigne enseigne,
Sortant du bout & des fins de l'Europe,
Troubles passant aupres du pont de Laigne,
Sera deffaicte par bandes sa grand troppe.

X.49

At Plaisance (i.e. "delight" – in Hebrew "Eden") on the road from Villeneuve to the "country of hollowed-out mountains",[44] someone is forced to drink poisoned water: poisoning of New York's water supply [C] / World War III invasion of Switzerland near Neufchâtel [F] / poisonous tidal wave overwhelms Atlantic City, New Jersey [R].

Jardin du monde au pres de cité neufve,
Dans le chemin des montaignes cavees,
Sera saisi & plongé dans la Cuve,
Beuvant par force eaux soulfre envenimees.

X.50

With Saturn and three other planets in Aquarius, Luxembourg, the Meuse valley and Lorraine are flooded and betrayed: world wars [R] / **Muslim invasion of Europe**, 2021 [L].

La Meuse aujour terre de Luxembourg,
Descouvrira Saturne & trois en lurne,[45]
Montaigne & pleine, ville, cité & bourg,
Lorrain deluge trahison par grand hurne.

X.51

Parts of Lorraine are united with lower Germany and Switzerland in being invaded by troops from northern France: results of Franco-Prussian war, 1870–1 [C,F] / **Muslim invasion of Europe**, 2022 [L] / World War II [R].

Des lieux plus bas du pays de Lorraine,
Seront des basses Allemaignes unis,
Par ceux du siege Picards, Normans, du Maisne,
Et aux cantons ce seront reunis.

X.52

Many "marriages" are arranged at Ghent, yet the "brides" remain *intacta* into premature old age: failed quatrain [C] / repeated alliances and treaties of Ghent, 1576–1918 [F] / peace in Belgium [R].

Au lieu où LAYE & Scelde[46] se marient,
Seront les nopces de long temps maniees,
Au lieu d'Anvers où la crappe charient,
Jeune vieillesse consorte intamiee.[47]

X.53

Three quarreling concubines await their master's summons, but the "great Muslim" rejects them as "former white-skinned sex": **Henri IV** and his mistresses [C].

Les trois pellices de loing s'entrebatron,
La plus grand moindre demeurera à l'escoute:
Le grand Selin n'en sera plus patron,
Le nommera feu pelte blanche routte.

X.54

A woman born out of wedlock but elevated by some tragedy is taken captive and abducted to Belgium.

Nee en ce monde par concubine fertive,
A deux[48] hault mise par les tristes nouvelles,
Entre ennemis sera prinse captive,
Et amené à Malings & Bruxelles.

X.55

A joyful wedding ends in tears, with husband and mother-in-law scorning "Helen" (or daughter-in-law) once her "Apollo" is dead: **François II, Mary Queen of Scots**, and **Catherine de Médicis** [C,L] / future end of monarchy and ruin of Church [F] / marriage of **Henri IV** and **Marguerite de Valois** [R].

Les malheureues nopces celebreront,
En grande joye, mais la fin malheureuse:
Mary & mere nore desdeigneront,
Le Phybe mort, & nore plus piteuse.

X.56

When a royal bishop suffers a hemorrhage and retires to a living death in Tunis, England breathes more easily.

Prelat royal son baissant trop tiré,
Grand fleux de sang sortira par sa bouche,
Le regne Anglicque par regne[49] respiré,
Long temps mort vif en Tunys comme souche.

---

37 *Londres* in some late editions.

38 *Caylus.*

39 *Villefranche.*

40 Possibly *Mahomet.*

41 *l'ombre.*

42 Or *fort.*

43 *Bourneville.*

44 Evidently the Dordogne and the village of Aubeterre-sur-Dronne, with its rock-hewn church and tombs.

45 *l'urne.*

46 *Leie & Schelde.*

47 Should read *intaminees*, to rhyme with line 2.

48 Here from Latin *dux, ducis*, "leader".

49 *reyne* (?).

X.57

A new leader ignores his regal responsibilities, and filthily abuses the families of his leading supporters.

Le sublevé ne cognoistra son sceptre,
Les enfans jeunes des plus grands honnira:
Oncques ne fut en plus ord cruel estre,
Pour leurs espouses à mort noir bannira.

X.58

At a time of mourning, when a Muslim overlord is fighting a "young Macedonian", France is tottering and the Vatican in peril as he attacks **Marseille** while negotiating with the West: Louis XIV C / World War III F / **Muslim invasion of Europe**, 2000–5 L / World War II R.

Au temps du deuil que le selin monarque,
Guerroyera le jeune Aemathien:
Gaule bransler pericliter la barque,
Tenter Phossens au Ponant entretien.

X.59

Barking dogs betray twenty-five followers of a noble, of various nationalities: World War II R.

Dedans Lyons vingt cinq d'une alaine,[50]
Cinq citoyens Germains, Bressans, Latins,
Par dessous noble conduiront longue traine,
Et descouvers par abbois de mastins.

X.60

The seer bewails the wars and natural disasters that are to befall Malta and a whole range of cities in France and northern Italy: Last Times C / World War III F / Muslim *jihad*, 1988 H / **Muslim invasion of Europe**, 2000–5 L.

Je pleure Nisse, Mannego,[51] Pize, Gennes,
Savone, Sienne, Capue, Modene, Malte:
Le dessus sang & glaive par estrenes
Feu, trembler terre, eau, malheureuse nolte.

X.61

Conspirators from Budapest to Sopron plot to hand over Hungary to the Muslims, but are exposed by an old woman: **Muslim invasion of Europe**, 2000–2 L.

Betta, Vienne, Emorre, Sacarbance,
Voudront livrer aux Barbares Pannone:
Par picque & feu, enorme violance,
Les conjurez descouvers par matrone.

X.62

Budapest announces the arrival of invaders from Slavonia under a Turkish overlord determined to impose Islamic law: beginning of end of Ottoman Empire, 1686 F / **Muslim invasion** of Hungary, 2000–2 L.

Pres de Sorbin[52] pour assaillir Ongrie,
L'heroult de Bude les viendra advertir:
Chef Bizantin, Sallon de Sclavonie,
A loy D'Arabes les viendra convertir.

X.63

Subsistence relief is brought to Hungary, Turkey, and the former Yugoslavia as a prince dies and two heroes treat the Arabs as they in turn once treated Hungary: European counterinvasion, 2036–7 L / Hungarian plague R.

Cydron,[53] Raguse,[54] la cité au sainct Hieron,[55]
Reverdira le mendicant secours,
Mort fils de Roy par mort de deux heron,[56]
L'Arabe Ongrie feront un mesme cours.

X.64

The horrors of war threaten Italy as invaders intent on destroying the Vatican approach Venice and the Rome government falls: Napoleon III and Victor Emmanuel C / fall of Italian fascism, 1945 F / **Muslim invasion** of Italy, 2000 L / papal change of residence R.

Pleure Milan, pleure Luqes, Florance,
Que ton grand Duc sur le char montera,
Changer le siege pres de Venise s'advance,
Lors que Colomne à Rome changera.

X.65

Attacked first by propaganda and then by the sword, the Roman Church faces ruin: attempted assassinations of John Paul II C, or AIDS and the Church H / future moral ruin and collapse of Church F / **Muslim invasion of Europe**, 2000–22 L.

O vaste Romme ta ruyne s'approche,
Non de tes murs de ton sang & sustance:
L'aspre par lettres fera si horrible coche,
Fer poinctu mis à tous jusques au manche.

X.66

As a result of American aid, the British premier "lays an icy slab" in Scotland, as a "red" Antichrist draws them both into war: Polaris C and the Antichrist C,F / Pershing II missiles and Ronald Reagan H / Polaris and **Muslim invasion of Europe**, 2000 L.

Le chef de Londres par regne l'Americh,
L'isle d'Escosse tempiera par gellee:
Roy Reb auront un si faux antechrist,
Que les mettra trestous dans la meslee.

X.67

A May earthquake marked by a precise astrological configuration is accompanied by enormous hailstones: future US west-coast earthquakes C / end of the world, 3797 H / future attack by unknown weapons R.

Le tremblement si fort au mois de May,
Saturne, Caper, Jupiter, Mercure au beuf:
Venus aussi Cancer, Mars, en Nonnay,
Tombera gresle lors plus grosse qu'un euf.

X.68

When a sea-borne force briefly besieges a city, the inhabitants massacre them, but the tables are turned when they return.

L'armee de mer devant cité tiendra.
Puis partira sans faire longue alee,
Citoyens grande proye en terre prendra,
Retourner classe reprendre grand emblee.

X.69

A new leader achieves universal renown before being chased and murdered by armies raised by his sister: future Russo-Muslim alliance F / worldwide civil wars from 1860 onward R.

Le fait luysant de neuf vieux eslevé
Seront si grand par midi aquilon,
De sa seur propre grandes alles levé.
Fuyant murdry au buysson d'ambellon.

X.70

When an "object" causes eyes to swell and smart, snow to fall, and rainfall to decrease, a primate is defeated by a king: meteoric impact (?) L / volcanic eruption at Reggio R.

L'œil par object fera telle excroissance,
Tant & ardante que tumbera la neige,
Champ arrousé viendra en descroissance,
Que le primat succumbera à Rege.

X.71

At a freezing Thursday festival (see **I.50**), a thing (or person) of great beauty is universally honored: Third Antichrist C / Pilgrim Fathers' first Thanksgiving R.

La terre & l'air gelleront si grand eau,
Lors qu'on viendra pour jeudi venerer,
Ce qui sera jamais ne feut si beau,
Des quatre pars le viendront honnorer.

X.72

In July 1999, during a brief peace, a heavenly paymaster-leader[57] stirs up a great Mongol overlord, and war then resumes: Third Antichrist C and destruction of civilized world H / air-borne invasion of France F / refinancing of stalled **Muslim invasion** in Middle East, or papal attempt to appease invaders L / world revolution R.

L'an mil neuf cens nonante neuf sept mois
Du ciel viendra un grand Roy deffraieur[58]
Resusciter le grand Roy d'Angolmois.
Avant apres Mars regner par bon heur.

X.73

A man of God pronounces judgment on past and present events, until the world grows tired of him and legalistic clergy betray him: end of Western world, 1999, and theological disputes F / restoration of Christianity, 2037+ L.

Le temps present avecques le passé
Sera jugé par grand Jovialiste,
Le monde tard luy sera lassé,
Et desloial par le clergé juriste.

---

[50] *haleine.*

[51] Either Monaco or, less likely, *Marnegro* (Black Sea).

[52] Sopron (?).

[53] Either Khania, Cyprus, or Tarsus, Turkey.

[54] Dubrovnik (?).

[55] The former Stridon, on the Dalmatian-Pannonian border, birthplace of St. Jerome.

[56] *heros* (?).

[57] See *Présage* 13: comparative horoscopy suggests a rerun of the future Pope Gregory the Great's mission to Constantinople to head off barbarian invaders in A.D. 579, this time directed to Ankara (see **Sequence of Selected Horographs**).

[58] Most editions have *d'effrayeur.*

X.74

At the end of the seventh millennium, just before the Millennium itself, the dead rise from their graves at a time of "Sacrificial Games": Final War and Last Judgment [C] leading, in A.D. 2000, to 1,000 years of peace and spirituality [H] and First Resurrection [F], 2007 [R], or at time of Olympics, 2828 [L].

Au revolu du grand nombre septiesme
Apparoistra au temps Jeux d'Hacatombe,
Non esloigné du grand eage millesme,
Que les entres sortiront de leur tombe.

X.75

For the last time a long-expected Hermes (deceiver, thief, magician [L]) appears in Turkey, increasingly triumphant in the East and set to dominate Europe: Chinese Antichrist [C] / end of **Henri V** and arrival of Antichrist [F] / future world religious leader [H] / Antichrist and **Muslim invasion of Europe**, 1999+ [L] / consolidation of East under notable scientist [R].

Tant attendu ne reviendra jamais
Dedans l'Europe, en Asie apparoistra
Un de la ligue yssu du grand Hermes,
Et sur tous roys des orientz croistra.

X.76

A parliament notes the triumph of one who is afterward defeated and hounded out, along with his supporters: Senator Harrison Williams of New Jersey, 1982 [R].

Le grand senat discernera la pompe,
A l'un qu'apres sera vaincu chassé,
Ses adherans seront à son de trompe,
Biens publiez ennemys deschassez.

X.77

The assets of thirty discredited priest-warriors are given to their enemies, while a fleet is scattered and surrendered to pirates: Russian acquisition of Italian navy, 1945 [C] / followers of Senator Harrison Williams of New Jersey, 1981 [R].

Trente adherans de l'ordre des quyretres
Bannys leurs biens donnez ses adversaires,
Tous leurs bienfais seront pour desmerites
Classe espargie delivrez aux corsaires.

X.78

Sudden joy in Rome turns to sudden terror and distress, and vice versa, as warring factions each gain the upper hand: disaster during wedding celebrations [R].

Subite joye en subite tristesse
Sera à Romme aux graces embrassees
Dueil, cris, pleurs, larm. sang excellant liesse
Contraires bandes surprinses & troussees.

X.79

Ancient roads are decorated all the way to newly defeated Egypt for a visit by the French **'Hercules'** [F,L]: new international communications-links [R].

Les vieux chemins seront tous embelys
Lon[59] passera à Memphis somentrée,
Le grand Mercure d'Hercules fleur de lys
Faisant trembler terre, mer & contree.

X.80

Bronze doors are opened for a king and duke by force of arms, despite the demolition of a port and sinking of a ship (see **VIII.78, X.27**): failed quatrain (?) [C] / reopening of St. Peter's, Rome, for **'Hercules'** and the future **Henri V**, 2027–8 [L].

Au regne grand du grand regne regnant,
Par force d'armes les grands portes d'arain
Fera ouvrir le roy & duc joignant,
Port demoly nef à fons jour serain.

X.81

After hiding themselves and their valuables in a church, citizens in the West are massacred by their own families: run on gold [C] / attempt to storm Fort Knox [R].

Mys tresor temple citadins Hesperiques
Dans iceluy retiré en secret lieu,
Le temple ouvrir les liens fameliques.
Reprens ravys proye horrible au milieu.

X.82

Seeming fugitives turn and fight ferociously, but are repulsed and murdered: failure of the attack on Fort Knox [R].

Cris, pleurs, larmes viendront avec coteaux
Semblant fouyr donront dernier assault
Lentour[60] parques planter profons plateaux,
Vifs repoulsez & meurdrys de prinsault.

X.83

After apparently peaceful people are expelled from a park (see **X.82**?), they see the flag of a lord, who promptly executes those who are his followers: civil war massacre [R].

De batailler ne sera donné signe,
Du parc seront contraint de sortir hors
De Gand[61] lentour[62] sera cogneu l'ensigne,
Qui fera mettre de tous les siens à mors.

X.84

The absence of a prominent "female bastard" pleases a husband, but her return provokes arguments as he realizes that he has been wasting his time: **Elizabeth I** [C] and **Philip II** [L] / birth of Prince William, 1982 [R].

La naturelle à si hault non bas
Le tard retour fera martis[63] contens,
Le Recloing[64] ne sera sans debarz[65]
En empliant & perdant tout son temps.

X.85

An old Tribune, pressurized not to give up a captive, gibbers with terror while delivering him to friends: Marshal Pétain, 1940–3 [C].

Le vieil tribung au point de la trehemide
Sera pressee captif ne deslivrer.
Le vueil[66] non veuil le mal parlant timide
Par legitime à ses amys livrer.

X.86

A Griffon-like ruler of Europe attacks the Iraqi leader with an international northern army: allies against **Napoleon** [C] / World War II: Warsaw Pact: invasion of France [F] / counterinvasion of Middle East, 2034+ / United St.ates of Europe [R].

Comme un gryphon viendra le roy d'Europe
Accompaigné de ceux d'Aquilon,
De rouges & blancz conduira grand troppe
Et yront contre le roy de Babilon.

X.87

A commander-in-chief lands near Nice and sets up his headquarters at Antibes as marine raids cease: future **Henri V** [F] / counterinvasion of Muslim-occupied France, 2025–6 [L] / landings in southern France and defeat of Japan [R].

Grand roy viendra prendre port pres de Nisse
Le grand empire de la mort si en fera
Aux Antipolles[67] posera son genisse,
Par mer la Pille tout esvanoira.

X.88

Marseille is invaded at the second watch by infantry and mounted troops and devastated to horrifying effect: World War III [F] / **Muslim invasion** of France, 2005 [L].

Piedz & Cheval à la seconde veille
Feront entree vastient[68] tout par la mer,
Dedans le poil entera de Marseille,
Pleurs, crys, & sang, onc nul temps si amer.

X.89

As fifty-seven joyful years of peace, health, and prosperity begin, brick buildings are reconstructed in white stone and aqueducts rebuilt: Millennium [C] or Golden Age [R] / age of Louis XIV [F,H] / post-war reconstruction and peace in France, 1945–2002, or 2037+ [L].

De brique en marbre seront les murs reduits
Sept & cinquante annees pacifiques,
Joie aux humains renoué Laqueduict,[69]
Santé, grandz fruict joye & temps melifique[s].

X.90

After a tyrant dies a hundred deaths, he is replaced by a good-natured scholar who has parliament in his pocket but is riled by an audacious enemy: **Napoleon**, Louis XVIII, and the Duc de Berry [C] / Stalin, Krushchev, and Brezhnev [R].

Cent foys mourra le tyran inhumain.
Mys à son lieu scavant & debonnaire,
Tout le senat sera dessoubz sa main,
Faché sera par malin themeraire.

---

[60] *l'entour.*

[61] Probable misprint for *Grand.*

[62] *l'entour.*

[63] Probable misprint for *marris.*

[64] Possibly *rejoinct.*

[65] *debats.*

[66] *vieil.*

[67] Antibes.

[68] *vastant.*

[69] *l'aqueduct.*

---

[59] *l'on.*

X.91

In "1609" the Roman conclave elects a "black and gray" Pope who turns out to be unprecedently evil: Paul V, 1605–21 [C] / election of Gloria Olivae, 2001 [L] / Hitler's accession to power, 1933 [R].

Clergé Romain l'an mil six cens & neuf,
Au chef de l'an feras election
D'un gris & noir de la Compagne yssu,
Qui onc ne feut [ ][70] si maling.

X.92

To the dismay of the people of Geneva, a leader is killed in full view of his father, who is then publicly trussed up: World War III [F] / fate of the League of Nations [R].

Devant le pere l'enfant sera tué:
Le pere apres entre cordes de jonc,
Genevois peuple sera esvertué,
Gisant le chief au milieu comme un tronc.

X.93

A new Pope is taken hostage and constantly shifted, notably to **Arles** and **Beaucaire**, near recent archeological discoveries (see I.43, **IX, 32**): flight of Pope around 2000 [C] / flight of John Paul II, 2000, or of successor [L].

La barque neufve recevra les voyages,
Là & aupres transfereront l'empire,
Beaucaire, Arles retiendront les hostages,
Pres deux colonnes trouvees de porphire.

X.94

While parts of southern France reject orders from the West, six torture-victims escape in Franciscan garb: failed quatrain [C] / liberation of Muslim-occupied France, 2025 [L] / anti-Spanish rebellion [R].

De Nismes, d'Arles, & Vienne contemner,
N'obey tout à l'edict Hespericque:
Aux labouriez pour le grand condamner,
Six eschappez en habit seraphicque.

X.95

A mighty king subjugates southern Spain and expels the Muslims: **Philip II**, the Moors, and Battle of Lepanto, 1571 [C] / World War III [F] / **Henri V**'s liberation of Spain, 2034+ [L].

Dans les Espaignes viendra Roy trespuissant,
Par mer & terre subjugant or[71] midy,
Ce mal fera rabaissant le croissant,
Baisser les aesles à ceux du vendredy.

X.96

The Marranos[72] eventually defeat the occupiers of Andalusia(?), despite casualties on both sides on account of their differing alphabets [L]: Muslim Shiites versus Sunnis [R].

Religion du nom des mers vaincra,
Contre la secte fils Adaluncatif,
Secte obstinee deploree craindra,
Des deux blessez par Aleph & Aleph.

X.97

As good times give way to bad, people of all ages, trusting too much to luck, are taken away into slavery by Muslim ships: **Muslim invasion of Europe** [F], 2002-25 [L] / Muslim Shiites versus Sunnis [R].

Triremes pleines tout aage captif,
Temps bon à mal, le doux pour amertume:
Proye à Barbares trop tost seront hastifs,
Cupid de veoir plaindre au vent la plume.

X.98

The light of the "joyous maid" is dimmed as wisdom vanishes and chaos, disorder, and general catastrophe spread: Nazi occupation of France, 1940–4 [C] / Muslim occupation of France, 2002–25 [L] / alliance of France with former enemies [R].

La splendeur claire à pucelle joyeuse,
Ne luyra plus long temps sera sans sel:
Avec marchans, ruffiens loups odieuse,
Tous peste[73] mele monstre universel.

X.99

As food resources dry up during a future golden age, care needs to be taken to rein in aggression [C,L]: fall of future European countries [F] / future era of peace and plenty [R].

La fin le loup, le lyon, beuf, & l'asne,
Timide dama seront avec mastins,
Plus ne cherra à eux la douce manne,
Plus vigilance & custode aux mastins.

X.100

To the irritation of the Portuguese, England will have a great empire lasting over 300 years, sending out armies all over the world: British Empire [H,L,R], **Elizabeth I** to Victoria [C] and occupation of Portugal, 1703 [F].

Le grand empire sera par Angleterre,
Le pempotam des ans plus de trois cens:
Grandes copies passer par mer & terre,
Les Lusitains n'en seront pas contens.

---

[70] Word omitted, possibly *pontife*.

[71] Possibly *au*.

[72] The much-persecuted descendants, possibly including Nostradamus himself, of the Spanish Jews forced to convert to Christianity in the fourteenth and fifteenth centuries, but who secretly preserved their faith: the phrase "religion named after the seas" refers, not untypically, to the Spanish word's accidental similarity to *mer* and *marin*.

[73] *pesle mesle.*

THE *LETTRE À HENRI II*

Full text, based on the 1568 edition, and divided into sections. Possible references are as suggested by **Fontbrune**[F], **Hogue**[H], and **Lemesurier**[L]. For a translation see **Roberts**.

A. INTRODUCTION

1.

The seer formally greets his King.

A L'INVICTISSIME, TRÈS PUISSANT, et Tres Chestien Henry roy de France second, Michel Nostradamus son tres-humble, et tres-obeissant serviteur et subject, victoire et felicité.

2.

Nostradamus, eager to honor the King whose presence has haunted his memory ever since their earlier meeting, makes bold to dedicate to him his newly completed thousand verses, by way of symbolically returning to the light of his presence. Quoting Plutarch and comparing the King favorably with the ancient kings of Persia, the seer explains that his predictions – composed more out of instinctive poetic frenzy than by rule or rote – are the result of astronomical calculations pinpointing to the very year, month, and week future events at all latitudes of Europe and North Africa and in parts of Asia Minor.

POUR icelle souveraine observation que j'ay eu, ô Tres-Chrestien et tres-victorieux Roy, depuis que ma face estant long temps obnubilee se presente au devant de la deité de vostre Majesté immesuree, depuis en ça j'ay esté perpetuellement esblouy, ne desistant d'honorer et dignement venerer iceluy jour que premierement devant icelle je me presentay, comme à une singulière Majesté tant humain. Or cherchant quelque occasion par laquelle je peusse manifester le bon coeur et franc courage, que moyennant iceluy mon pouvoir eusse faict ample extension de cognoissance envers vostre serenissime Majesté. Or voyant que par effets le declarer ne m'estoit possible, joint avec mon singulier desir de ma tant longue obtenebration et obscurité, estre subitement esclarcie et transportee au devant de la face du souverain oeil, et du premier Monarque de l'Univers, tellement que j'ay esté en doute longuement à qui je viendrois consacrer ces trois Centuries du restant de mes Propheties, parachevant la miliade, et après avoir eu longuement cogité d'une temeraire audace, ai prins mon addresse envers vostre Majesté, n'estant pour cela estonné, comme raconte le gravissime aucteur Plutarque en la vie de Lycurgue, que voyant les offres et presens qu'on faisoit par sacrifices aux temples des Dieux immortels d'iceluy temps, et à celle fin que l'on ne s'estonnast par trop souvent desdicts fraiz et mises ne s'osoyent presenter aux temples. Ce nonobstant voyant vostre splendeur Royalle accompagnee d'une incomparable humanité ay prins mon adresse, non comme aux Rois de Perse, qu'il n'estoit nullement permis d'aller à eux, ny moins s'en approcher. Mais à un tresprudent, à un tressage Prince j'ay consacré mes nocturnes et prophetiques supputations, composeees plustost d'un naturel instinct, accompagné d'une fureur poëtique, que par reigle de poësie, et la plus part composé et accordé à la calculation Astronomique, correspondant aux ans, moys et sepmaines des regions, contrees, et de la pluspart des Villes et Citez de toute l'Europe, comprenant de l'Affrique, et une partie de l'Asie par le changement des regions, qui s'approchent la plus part de tous ces climats, et composé d'une naturelle faction:

3.

Stuffy people (he continues) will complain that the verses are far easier to scan than to understand. Too difficult though they may indeed prove to interpret, they nevertheless enshrine precisely timed, bare-bones predictions covering events in a range of named places from March 1557, via those of 1585 and 1606, to the beginning of the seventh millennium (as specially computed), when the enemies of Christ will start to thrive and multiply – a future period almost as long as history itself so far.

. . . respondra quelqu'un qui auroit bien besoin de soy moucher, la rithme estre autant facile, comme l'intelligence du sens est difficile. Et pource, ô tres-humanissime Roy, la plus part des quatrains prophetiques sont tellement scabreux, que l'on n'y sçauroit donner voye ny moins aucuns interpreter, toutesfois esperant de laisser par escrit les ans, villes, citez, regions où la plus part adviendra, mesmes de l'année 1585, et de l'année 1606, accommencenant depuis le temps present, qui est le 14 de Mars 1557, et passant outre loing jusques à l'advenement qui sera apres au commencement du 7. millenaire profondement supputé, tant que mon calcul astronomique et autre sçavoir s'a peu estendre, où les adversaires de Jesus-Christ et de son Eglise, commenceront plus fort de pulluler, le tout a esté composé et calculé en jours et heures d'election et bien disposees, et le plus justement qu'il ma esté possible. Et le tout Minerva libera, et non invita,[1] supputant presque autant des adventures du temps advenir, comme des aages passez, comprenant le present, et de ce que par le cours du temps par toutes regions l'on cognoistra advenir tout ainsi nommement comme il est escrit, n'y meslant rien de superflu . . .

4.

Despite the saying that nothing certain can be said of the future, I thought myself capable (he writes) of combining my natural gift with long calculation in order to foretell the future with the aid of quiet meditation and the traditional brazen tripod. Some will of course falsely attribute to me what is not mine. May God defend me from such calumniators, who would as easily criticize me for such perceived "magical practices" as they might other reputable healers and diviners – or indeed Your Majesty's own ancestors for curing the "King's evil", or scrofula. My writings, certainly, will be more valued after my death than before it.

. . . combien que l'on die: Quod de futuris non est determinata omnino veritas.[2] Il est bien vray, Sire, que pour mon natural instinct qui m'a esté donné par mes aïules ne[3] cuidant presager, et adjoustant et accordant iceluy naturel instinct avec ma longue supputation uny, et vuidant l'ame, l'esprit, et le courage de toute cure, solicitude, et fascherie par repos et tranquillité de l'esprit. Le tout accordé et presagé d'une partie trepode aeneo.[4] Combien qu'ils sont plusieurs qui m'attribue ce qu'est autant à moy, comme de ce que n'en est rien, Dieu seul eternel, qui est prescrutateur des humains courages pie, juste et miséricordieux, en est le vray juge, auquel je prie qu'il me vueille defendre de la calomnie des meschans, qui voudroyent aussi calomnieuse-

ment s'enquerir pour quelle cause tous vos antiquissimes progeniteurs Rois de France ont guery des escrouelles, et des autres nations ont guery de la morsures des serpens, les autres ont eu certain instinct de l'art divinatrice, et d'autres cas qui seroyent long ici à racompter. Ce nonobstant ceux à qui la malignité de l'esprit malin ne sera comprins par le cours du temps apres la terrenne mienne extinction, plus sera mon escrit qu'à mon vivant, . . .

5.

If my predictions themselves should prove to be in error, or not to some people's liking, I crave pardon, protesting that to the best of my knowledge and calculation they contain nothing against the Faith. For the period from Adam, via Noah, Abraham, Moses, and David to Christ totaled 4,757 years (according to some authorities, even if not Eusebius). That from Our Redeemer to Mahomet totaled a further 621 years. On this basis I have prepared my calculations with the aid of my inherited prophetic gift.

. . . cependant si à ma supputation des ages je faillois ou ne pourroit estre selon la volonté d'aucuns, plaira à vostre plus qu'imperiale Majesté me pardonner, protestant devant Dieu et ses Saincts, que je ne pretends de mettre rien quelconque par escrit en la presente epistre, qui soit contre la vraye foy Catholique, conferant les calculations Astronomiques, jouxte mon sçavoir: car l'espace de temps de nos premiers, qui nous ont precedez sont tels, me remettant sous la correction du plus sain jugement, que le premier homme Adam fut devant Noé environ mille deux cens quarante deux ans, ne computant les temps par la supputation des Gentils, comme a mis par escrit Varon: mais tant seulement selon les sacrees Escritures, et selon la foiblesse de mon esprit, en mes calculations Astronomiques. Apres Noé, de luy et de l'universal deluge, vint Abraham environ mille huictante ans, lequel à été souverain Astrologue, selon aucuns, il inventa premier les lettres Chaldaïques; apres vint Moyse environ cinq cens quinze ou seize ans, et entre le temps de David et Moyse, ont esté cinq cens septante ans là environ. Puis après entre le temps de David, et le temps de notre Sauveur et Redempteur Jesus-Christ, nay de l'unique Vierge, ont esté (selon aucuns Cronographes) mille trois cens cinquante ans: pourra objecter quelqu'un ceste supputation n'estre veritable, pource qu'elle differe à celle d'Eusèbe. Et depuis le temps de l'humaine redemption jusque à la seduction detestable des Sarrazins, sont esté six cens vingt et un an, là environ depuis en ça l'on peut facilement colliger quels temps sont passez, si la mienne supputation n'est bonne et valable par toutes nations, pour ce que le tout a été calculé par le cours celeste, par association d'esmotion infuse à certaines heures delaissees par l'esmotion de mes antiques progeniteurs:

6.

But the times require that my prophecies, though exact and specific, be clothed in obscure language similar to that of the ancient prophets. Nevertheless I would not compare myself with them. My prophecies come not from myself, but from Divine revelation as perceived through my astrological calculations and through cloudy visions as in a burning-mirror.[5]

Mais l'injure du temps, ô serenissime Roy, requiert que tels secrets evenemens ne soyent manifestez que par aenigmatique sentence, n'ayant qu'un seul sens, et unique intelligence, sans y avoir rien mis d'ambigue n'amphibologique calculation: mais plustost sous obnubilée obscurité par une naturelle infusion approchant à la sentence d'un des mille et deux Prophetes, qui ont esté depuis la creation du monde, jouxte la supputation et Chronique punique de Joel, Effundam spiritum meum super omnem carnem et prophetabunt filii vestri, et filiae vestrae.[6] Mais telle prophetie procedoit de la bouche du S. Esprit, qui estoit la souveraine puissance eternelle, adjoincte avec la celeste àd'aucuns de ce nombre ont predit de grandes et esmerveillables adventures: Moy en cet endroit je ne m'attribue nullement tel tiltre. Ja à Dieu ne plaise, je confesse bien que le tout vient de Dieu, et luy en rends graces, honneur, et louange immortelle, sans y avoir meslé de la divination que provient à fato:[7] mais à Deo, à natura,[8] et la pluspart acompagnee du mouvement du cours celeste, tellement que voyant comme dans un mirouer ardant, comme par vision obnubilee, les grands evenements tristes, prodigieux, et calamiteuses adventures que s'approchent par les principaux culteurs.

B. SUMMARY OF SELECTED PREDICTIONS

1.

Decadence and calamity threaten both Church and laity. France will produce rulers who will cause Europe to tremble. One will support, then abandon the Church, while driving back the Arabs, amalgamating kingdoms and promulgating new laws (Napoleon I [F]). Another will confront England and with much bloodshed invade Italy, though failing to conquer Spain (Napoleon III [F]). Rome, eastern Europe, and Spain will form separate alliances (distinct from that lying between the 50th and 52nd degrees of latitude), all of them subject to an all-conquering northern European power based on the 48th degree (the Axis powers of World War II [F]).

Premierement des temples de Dieu, secondement par ceux qui sont terrestrement soustenus s'aprocher telle decadence, avec mille autres calamiteuses adventures, que par le cours du temps on cognoistra advenir: car Dieu regardera la longue sterilité de la grand Dame, qui puis après concevra deux enfans principaux: mais elle periclitant, celle qui luy sera adjoustée par la temerité de l'aage de mort periclitant dedans le dixhuictiesme, ne pouvant passer le trestesixieme qu'en delaissera trois masles, et une femelle, et en aura deux, celuy qui n'en eut jamais d'un mesme pere, des trois freres seront telles differences, puis unies et accordees, que les trois et quatre parties de l'Europe trembleront: par le moindre d'aage sera la monarchie Chrestienne soustenue, augmentee, sectes eslevees, et subitement abaissees, Arabes reculez, Royaumes unis, nouvelles Loix promulguees: des autres enfans le premier occupera les Lions furieux couronnez, tenans les pattes dessus les armes intrepidez. Le second se profondera si avant par les Latins acompagné, que sera faicte la seconde voye tremblante et furibonde au mont Jovis descendant pour monter aux Pyrennees, ne sera translatee à l'antique monarchie,

---

[1] "Minerva being free and favourable."

[2] "For concerning future events the truth is not fully determined."

[3] Presumed misprint for *me.*

[4] "by the brazen tripod."

[5] i.e. a concave mirror used for concentrating the sun's rays.

[6] "I will pour out my spirit upon all flesh and your sons and your daughters shall prophesy" (Joel 2:28).

[7] "from the prophet."

[8] "from God, from nature."

sera faicte le troisiesme inondation de sang humain, ne se trouvera de long temps Mars en Caresme. Et sera donnee la fille par la conservation de l'Eglise Chrestienne, tombant son dominateur à la paganisme secte des nouveux infideles, elle aura deux enfans, l'un de fidelité, et l'autre d'infidelité par la confirmation de l'Eglise Catholique. Et l'autre qui à sa grande confusion et tarde repentance la voudra ruiner, seront trois regions par l'extreme difference des ligues, c'est assavoir la Romanie, la Germanie, l'Espaigne, qui seront diverses sectes par main militaire, delaissant le 50 et 52. degrez de hauteur, et feront tous homages des religions loingtaines aux regions de l'Europe et de Septentrion de 48. degrez d'hauteur, qui premier par vaine timidité tremblera, puis les plus occidentaux, meridionaux et orientaux trembleront, telle sera leur puissance, que ce qui se fera par concorde et union insuperable des conquestes belliques. De nature seront esgaux: mais grandement differents de foy.

2.

France will ally herself with two powers, as well as with a third that will have overrun eastern Europe, and will free Sicily from the Germans, while the Arabs are generally persecuted by the Latin nations of Europe (future Soviet invasion F).

Apres cecy la Dame sterile de plus grande puissance que la seconde sera receue par deux peuples, par le premier obstiné par celuy qui a eu puissance sur tous, part le deuxiesme et par le tiers qui estendra ses forces vers le circuit de l'Orient de l'Europe aux pannons l'a profligé et succombé et par voille marine fera ses extensions à la Trinacrie Adriatique par Mirmidons et Germaniques du tout succombé, et sera la secte barbarique du tout des Latins grandement affligee et deschassee.

3.

The empire of the Antichrist will arise in the region of Ardalan:[9] he will descend on Europe like Xerxes with his hosts, and the Muslims will make war on the Pope and his Church (future Mongol **invasion of Europe** F,L).

Puis le grand Empire de l'Antechrist commencera dans la Arda et Zersas descendre en nombre grand et innumerable, tellement que la venue du sainct Esprit procedant du 24 degrez,[10] fera transmigration, deschassant l'abomination de l'Antechrist, faisant guerre contre le royal qui sera le grand Vicaire de Jesus-Christ, et contre son Eglise, et son regne per tempus et in occasione temporis,[11] . . .

4.

First there will be an eclipse of unprecedented darkness.

. . . et procedera devant une eclypse solaire le plus obscur, et le plus tenebreux, que soit esté depuis la creation du monde jusques à la mort et passion de Jesus-Christ, et de là jusques icy, . . .

---

9 The northwestern province of the former Persia, also known as Persian Kurdistan.

10 The latitude of Medina, Saudi Arabia, site of the foundation of Islam and its second holiest city: some later editions substitute the 48th degree, apparently cited at **B.1** as the theoretical dividing-line between European Catholics and Protestants.

11 "For a time, and to the end of time."

5.

Following a disturbance the previous spring, a great October transformation will rock the world, but will last only seventy-three years and seven months (World War II F / shifting of earth's axis, 2000 H / Russian Revolution and Soviet Union 1917–1991 L). Then from the 50th degree of latitude will arise one who will renew the entire Christian Church (future Eastern world religious leader H / Pope John Paul II, former Cardinal Archbishop of Krakow, Poland, at 50°N. L). Harmony will break out between scattered kingdoms. An antireligious military power will be toppled and a violent one united. Peoples who had thought to free themselves, but who will thereby merely have imprisoned themselves all the more firmly, will forsake the left to move towards the right and will readopt their ancient religion (collapse of Soviet Union and reunification of Germany L).

. . . et sera au moys d'Octobre que quelque grande translation sera faicte, et telle que l'on cuidera la pesanteur de la terre avoir perdue son naturel mouvement, et estre abismeee en perpetuelles tenebres, seront precedans au temps vernal, et s'en ensuyant apres d'extremes changemens, permutations de regnes, par grands tremblements de terre, avec pullulation de la neusve Babylonne, fille miserable augmentee par l'abomination du premier holocauste, et ne tiendra tant seulement que septante trois ans, sept moys, puis apres en sortira du tige celle qui avoit demeuré tant long temps sterile, procedant du cinquantiesme degré, qui renouvellera toute l'Eglise Chrestienne. Et sera faicte grande paix, union et concorde entre un des enfans des fronts esgarez, et separez par divers regnes: et sera faicte telle paix que demeurera attaché au plus profond baratre le suscitateur et promoteur de la martiale faction par la diversité des religieux, et sera uny le Royaume du Rabieux, qui contrefera le sage. Et les contrees, villes, citez, regnes, et provinces qui auront laissé les premieres voyes pour se deliver, se captivant plus profondement, seront secrettement faschez de leur liberté, et parfaicte religion perdue, commenceront de frapper dans la partie gauche, pour tourner à la dextre, et remettant la saincteté profligée de long temps, avec leur prestin escrit, . . .

6.

After the Great Dog, the even Greater Mastiff will destroy everything, but eventually the churches will be rebuilt and the priesthood restored, even to the point of overindulgence.

. . . qu'apres le grand chien sortira le plus gros mastin,[12] qui fera destruction de tout, mesmes de ce qu'auparavant sera esté perpetré, seront redressez les temples comme au premier temps, et sera restitué le clerc à son pristin estat, et commencera à meritriquer et luxurier, faire et commettre mille forfaits.

7.

As new disaster approaches, crooked leaders and generals will arise, but they will be disarmed by a skeptical populace.

---

12 This term normally refers in contemporary writings (cf **Ronsard**) to Cerberus, hound of hell and Guardian of the Underworld.

13 Presumably the royal line of France F: the future Gallic **Ogmion** or "**Hercules**" L.

Et estant proche d'une autre desolation, par lors qu'elle sera à sa plus haute et sublime dignité, se dresseront de potentats et mains militaires, et luy seront ostez les deux glaives, et ne luy demeurera que les enseignes, desquelles par moyen de la curvature qui les attire, le peuple le faisant aller droit, et ne voulant se condescendre à eux par le bout opposite de la main argue, touchant terre, voudront stimuler jusques à ce que . . .

8.

A new military and regal savior will emerge from a long-since unproductive line,[13] ruling from another "little Mesopotamia."[14] The former tyranny will be put down by a conspiracy.

. . . naistra d'un rameau de la sterile, de long temps, qui delivrera le peuple univers de celle servitude benigne et volontaire, soy remettant àla protection de Mars, spoliant Jupiter de tous ses honneurs et dignitez, pour la cité libre, constitue et assise dans une autre exigue Mezopotamie. Et sera le chef et gouverneur jecté au milieu, et mis au haut lieu de l'air, ignorant la conspiration des conjurateurs, avec le second Trasibulus,[15] qui de long temps aura manié tout cecy: alors les immundicitez, les abominations seront par grande honte objectees et manifestees aux tenebres de la lumiere obtenebree, cessera devers la fin du changement de son regne: . . .

9.

With Western Christendom in decay and decline, Islam will stage a powerful resurgence, especially among the indignant poor of North Africa. Western leaders will fail to act in time and all hell will be let loose.

. . . et les clefs de l'Eglise seront en arriere de l'amour de Dieu, et plusieurs d'entre eux apostarizeront la vraye foy, et des trois sectes,[16] celle du milieu, par les culteurs d'icelle, sera un peu mis en decadence. La prime totallement par l'Europe, la plus part de l'Affrique exterminee de la tierce, moyennant les pauvres d'esprit, que par insensez eslevez par la luxure libidineuse adulteront. La plebe se levera soustenant, dechassera les adherans de legislateurs, et semblera que les regnes affoiblis par les Orientaux que Dieu le Createur aye deslié Satan des prisons infernalles, pour faire naistre le grand Dog et Doham,[17] lesquels feront si grande fraction abominable aux Eglises, que les rouges ne les blancs sans yeux ne sans mains plus n'en jugeront, et leur sera ostee leur puissance

10.

The Church will be persecuted as never before, and two-thirds of the population will be wiped out by pestilence. The owners of fields and houses will be untraceable and grass will grow knee-high and more in the city streets. The clergy will be desolat-

---

14 i.e. a "land between two rivers": possibly **Lyon** F: alternatively **Avignon**, situated between the **Rhône** and **Durance** rivers L.

15 Athenian general who not only staged a successful coup against the ruling oligarchy in 404 B.C. to reestablish democracy, but nine years later brought about a similar democratic revolution in Byzantium, too (now Istanbul): General de Gaulle and the Gaullist era F.

16 From north to south: Protestant, Catholic, and Muslim.

17 Presumably Gog and Magog, the symbolic names given by the Revelation of John to Satan's forces at his last battle with the "people of God".

ed and the invading military will take over Malta, Mediterranean France, and the offshore islands (Russo-American nuclear Armageddon [H] / future **Muslim invasion of Europe** [L]).

Alors sera faicte plus de persecutions aux Eglises, que ne fut jamais. Et sur ces entrefaictes naistra la pestilence si grande, que, des trois parts du monde plus que les deux defaudront. Tellement qu'on ne se sçaura ne cognoistre les appartenans des champs et maisons, et croistra l'herbe par les rues des citez plus haute que les genoulx. Et au clergé sera faicte toute desolation, et usurperont les martiaulx ce que sera retourné de la cité du Soleil[18] de Melite, et des isles St.echades, et sera ouverte la grand chaisne du port qui prend sa denomination au bœuf marin.[19]

11.

A Western counterinvasion will rescue Spain from the invaders and eventually pursue the Arabs back to the Middle East (future Muslim **invasion of Europe** [L]).

Et sera faicte nouvelle incursion par les maritimes plages, volant le sault Castulum[20] deburer de la premiere reprinse Mahumetane. Et ne seront du tout faillement vains, et au lieu que jadis fut l'habitation d'Abraham, sera assaillie par personnes qui auront en veneration les Jovialistes. Et icelle cité de Achem[21] sera environnee et assaillie de toutes parts en tresgrande puissance de gens d'armes. Seront affoiblies leurs forces maritimes par les Occidentaux.

12.

Israel will be depopulated, and the Holy Sepulcher will be turned into farm buildings (future Muslim **invasion** [L]).

Et à ce regne sera faicte grande desolation, et les plus grandes citez seront depeuplees, et ceux qui entreront dedans, seront comprins à la vengeance de l'ire de Dieu. Et demeurera le sepulcre de tant grande veneration par l'espace de longtemps soubs le serain à l'universelle vision des yeux du Ciel, du Soleil, et de la Lune. Et sera converty le lieu sacré en hebergement de troupeau menu et grand, et adapté en substances prophanes.

13.

The Northerners[22] will eventually inflict terrible retribution on the Orientals and free the oppressed peoples, whose native tongues will by now have acquired an Arabic admixture (Russia and China [F] / future Muslim **invasion of Europe** [L]).

O quelle calamiteuse affliction sera par lors aux femmes enceintes! et sera par lors du principal chef Oriental, la plus part esmeu par les Septentrionaux et Occidentaux vaincu, et mis àmort, profligez, et le reste en fuite et ses enfans de plusieurs femmes emprisonnez, et par lors sera accomplie la prophetie du Royal Prophete:[23] Ut audiret gemitus compeditorum, ut solveret filios interemptorum.[24] Quelle grande opression que par lors sera faicte sur les Princes et gouverneurs des Royaumes, mesmes de ceux qui seront mar-

itimes et Orientaux, et leurs langues entremeslees à grande societé: la langue des Latins et des Arabes, par la communication Punique, . . .

14.

The Eastern leaders will be defeated and put to flight, largely as a result of internal quarrels, and for seven years the triumphant Northern Christians, led by two brothers who are yet not brothers, will strike fear into Eastern hearts (counterinvasion following future Muslim **invasion of Europe** [L]).

. . . et seront tous ces Roys Orientaux chassez, profligez, exterminez, non du tout par le moyen des forces des Roys d'Aquilon, et par la proximité de nostre siecle par moyen des trois unis secretement cerchant la mort, et insidies par embusches l'un de l'autre, et durera le renouvellement de Triumvirat sept ans, que la renommee de telle secte fera son estendue par l'univers, et sera soustenu le sacrifice de la saincte et immaculee hostie: et seront lors les Seigneurs deux en nombre d'Aquilon, victorieux sur les Orientaux, et sera en iceux faict si grand bruit et tumulte bellique, que tout iceluy Orient tremblera de la frayeur d'iceux freres, non freres Aquilonaires.

15.

Confused though these predictions and their timings may seem, I could put a date on each of them, but will refrain from doing so unless and until Your Majesty commands it and offers me protection from those who would object and attack me.

Et pource, Sire, que par ce discours je mets presque confusement ces predictions, et quand ce pourra estre et l'advenement d'iceux, pour le denombrement du temps que s'enfuit, qu'il n'est nullement, ou bien peu conforme au superieur: lequel, tant par voye Astronomique, que par autre, mesmes des sacrees Escriptures, qui ne peuvent faillir nullement, que si je voulois à un chacun quatrain mettre le denombrement du temps, se pourroit faire: mais à tous ne seroit aggreable, ne moins les interpreter, jusques à ce, Sire, que vostre Majesté m'aye octroyé ample puissance pour ce faire, pour ne donner cause aux calomniateurs de me mordre.

16.

The seer explains his calculations of the age of the earth, now placing the birth of Adam at 4173 and eight months B.C., and adding a list of astrological data.[25]

Toutesfois, contans les ans depuis la creation du monde, jusques à la naissance de Noé, sont passez mil cinq cens et six ans, et depuis la naissance de Noé jusques à la parfaicte fabrication de l'Arche, approchant d'universelle inondation, passèrent six cens ans (si les dons estoyent Solaires ou Lunaires, ou de dix mixtions) je tiens ce que les sacres

Escriptures tiennent qu'estoyent Solaires. Et à la fin d'iceux six [cens][26] ans, Noé entra dans l'Arche pour estre sauvé du deluge: et fuit iceluy deluge universel sur la terre, et dura un an et deux mois. Et depuis la fin du deluge jusques à la nativité d'Abraham, passa le nombre des ans de deux cens nonante cinq. Et depuis la nativité d'Abraham jusques à la nativité d'Isaac, passerent cent ans. Et depuis Isaac jusques à Jacob, soixante ans, dès l'heure qu'il entra en Egypte jusques à l'yssue d'iceluy, passerent cent trente ans. Et depuis l'entree de Jacob en Egypte jusques à l'yssue[27] d'iceluy passerent quatre cens trente ans. Et depuis l'yssue d'Egypte jusques à l'edification du Temple faicte par Salomon au quatriesme an de son regne, passerent quatre cens octante, ou quatre vingts ans. Et depuis l'edification du Temple jusques à Jesus-Christ, selon la supputation des hierographes, passerent quatre cens nonante ans.[28] Et ainsi par ceste supputation que j'ay faicte colligee par les sacrees lettres, sont environ quatre mille cent septante trois ans et huict mois, peu ou moins. Or de Jesus-Christ en ça, par la diversité des sectes, je le laisse, et ayant supputé et calculé les presentes propheties, le tout selon l'ordre de la chaisne qui contient sa revolution, le tout par doctrine Astronomique, et selon mon naturel instinct, et apres quelque temps et dans iceluy comprenant depuis le temps que Saturne qui tournera entrer à sept du mois d'Avril, jusques au 25 d'Aoust, Jupiter à 14 de Juin jusques au 7 Octobre, Mars depuis le 17 Avril jusques au 22 de Juin, Venus depuis le 9 d'Avril, jusques au 22 de May, Mercure depuis le 3 de Fevrier, jusques au 24 dudit. En apres du premier de Juin, jusques au 24 dudit, et du 25 de Septembre, jusques au 16 d'Octobre. Saturne en Capricorne, Jupiter en Aquarius, Mars en Scorpio, Venus en Pisces, Mercure dans un mois en Capricorne, Aquarius et Pisces, la Lune en Aquarius, la teste du Dragon en Libra: la queue àson signe opposite suyvant une conjonction de Jupiter à Mercure, avec un quadrin aspect de Mars à Mercure, et la teste du Dragon sera avec une conjonction du Soleil à Jupiter, l'annee sera pacifique sans eclipse, et non du tout, et sera le commencement comprenant ce de ce que durera . . .

17.

A persecution of Christians greater than ever occurred in North Africa will last until 1792, when a totally new era will begin (**French Revolution** [F,L,R]). Thereafter the Romans[29] will recover ground somewhat.

. . . et commençant icelle annee sera faicte plus grande persecution à l'Eglise Chrestienne, que n'a esté faicte en Affrique, et durera ceste ici jusques à l'an mil sept cens nonante deux que l'on cuidera estre une renovation du siecle: apres commencera le peuple Romain de se redresser, et dechasser quesques obscures tenebres recevant quelque peu de leur pristine clarté, non sans grande division et continuels changemens.

---

[18] By astrological and zoological association the "solar city" is probably **Lyon**.

[19] Latin *phoca* = seal: *Phocaea* = **Marseille**.

[20] The Sierra Morena, a high plateau stretching across southern Spain.

[21] Presumably "Hashem", family name of the prophet Muhammad: hence presumably Medina, which is known specifically as the "city of the Prophet."

[22] The powers of northern Europe – i.e. what we should probably nowadays call the West.

[23] King David.

[24] "In order that he may hear the sighing of the prisoners and save the children of the dead" (corrupt version of Psalm 102:20).

[25] The calculations as printed seem confused to say the least, and do not in any case fit either the total suggested or the earlier computations under section **A.5**. The concluding details correspond to the year 1783.

[26] Word omitted.

[27] i.e. by his descendants.

[28] This period seems extraordinarily short – indeed, it is some 480 years less than the likely true figure: one has the distinct impression that the seer is (despite all his religious protestations) willfully shuffling his figures to fit his prior astrological conclusions.

[29] i.e. Roman Catholics.

18.

Venice will become extremely powerful (future Muslim **invasion of Europe** L).

Venise en apres en grande force et puissance levera ses aisles si treshaut, ne distant gueres aux forces de l'antique Rome.

19.

Great ships from Turkey, acquired from former military powers to the north (Russia and the Ukraine? L), will sail to Italy, provoking vast naval battles in the Adriatic. Many cities (including the former all-powerful "Babylon" of Europe[30]) will be destroyed utterly on the 45th, 41st, 42nd, and 37th parallels (Turin, Naples, Rome, and Syracuse), and the Church and Pope will be persecuted by maniacal political leaders (World War I F / Second World War H / future Muslim **invasion of Europe** L).

Et en iceluy temps grandes voilles Bisantines associees aux Ligustiques par l'appuy et puissance Aquilonaire, donnera quelque empeschement que des deux Cretenses ne leur sera la Foy tenue. Les arcs edifiez par les antiques Martiaux, s'accompagneront aux ondes de Neptune. En l'Adriatique sera faicte discorde grande, ce que sera uny sera separé, approchera de maison ce que paravant estoit et est grande cité, comprenant le Pempotam la Mesopotamie de l'Europe à quarante cinq, et autres de quarante un, quarante deux et trente sept. Et dans iceluy temps, et en icelles contrees la puissance infernalle mettra à l'encontre de l'Eglise de Jesus Christ la puissance des adversaires de sa loy, qui sera le second Antechrist, lequel persecutera icelle Eglise et son vray Vicaire, par moyen de la puissance des Roys temporels, qui seront par leur ignorance seduicts par langues, qui trencheront plus que nul glaive entre les mains de l'insensé.

20.

The Antichrist's reign will be quite brief: the "Gallic **Hercules**" will lead a huge liberating army into Italy (World War II F / counterinvasion following future Muslim **invasion of Europe** L).

Le susdict regne de l'Antechrist ne durera que jusques au definement de ce nay pres de l'aage et de l'autre à la cité de Plancus;[31] accompagnez de l'esleu de Modone Fulcy, par Ferrare maintenue par Liguriens Adriatiques, et de la proximité de la grande Trinacrie. Puis passera le mont Jovis.[32] Le Gallique ogmium,[33] accompagné de si grand nombre que de bien loing l'Empire de la grande loy sera presenté et par lors et quelque temps apres sera espanché profueement de sang des Innocens par les nocens un peu eslevez: . . .

21.

Vast floods will erase former memories and even wipe out the very knowledge of letters until Satan is bound again (the "Last Times" L).

. . . alors par grands deluges la memoire des choses contenus de tels instrumens recevra innumerable perte, mesmes les lettres: qui sera devers les Aquilonaires par la volonté divine, et entre une fois lie Satan.

22.

Universal peace will arise toward the beginning of the seventh millennium after the Creation (above),[34] with the Holy Sepulcher restored. Some great conflagration will then ensue, though time itself will go on for much longer.

Et sera faicte paix universelle entre les humains, et sera delivree l'Eglise de Jesus Christ de toute tribulation, combien que par les Azostains voudroit mesler dedans le miel de fiel, et leur pestifere seduction: et cela sera proche du septiesme millenaire, que plus le sanctuaire de Jesus Christ ne sera conculqué par les infideles qui viendront de l'Aquilon, le monde approchant de quelque grande conflagration, combien que par mes supputations en mes propheties, le cours du temps aille beaucoup loing.

23.

Unlike in my letter to my son César, I have here included many extraordinary prophecies. It is Northern political power, amply aided by the Orientals, that will in fact lead to the eventual destruction of the Church. After eleven years, three years of amazingly severe persecution will be inflicted by the leaders of the South on the Church, and the sea will run red with blood after a huge naval battle. Pestilence, famine, and unprecedented tribulations will follow in Europe (future Muslim attacks in the Middle East F / future Muslim **invasion of Europe** L).

Dedans l'Epistre que ses ans passez ay dediee àmon fils Cesar Nostradamus j'ay assez apertement declaré aucuns poincts sans presage. Mais icy, ô Sire, sont comprins plusieurs grands et merveilleux advenemens, que ceux qui viendront après le verront. Et durant icelle supputation Astrologique, conferee aux sacres lettres, la persecution des gens Ecclesisastiques prendra son origine par la puissance des Roys Aquilonaires, unis avec les Orientaux. Et celle persecution durera onze ans, quelque peu moins, que par lors defaillira le principal Roy Aquilonaire, lesquels ans accomplis surviendra son uny Meridional, qui persecutera encore plus fort par l'espace de trois ans les gens d'Eglise, par la seduction apostastique, d'un qui tiendra toute puissance absolue à l'Eglise militante, et le saint peuple de Dieu observateur de sa loy, et tout ordre de religion sera grandement persecuté et affligé, tellement que le sang des vrays Ecclesiastiques nagera par tout, et un des horribles Roys temporels, par ses adherans luy seront donnees telles louanges, qu'il aura plus respandu de sang humain des innocens Ecclesiastiques, que nul ne sçauroit avoir du vin: et iceluy Roy commettra de forfaicts envers l'Eglise incroyables, coulera le sang humain par les rues publiques et temples, comme l'eau par pluye impetueuse et rougiront de sang les plus prochains fleuves, et par autre guerre navale rougira la mer, que le rapport d'un Roy à l'autre luy sera dit: Bellis rubuit navalibus aequor.[35] Puis dans la mesme annee et les suyvantes s'en ensuyva la plus horrible pestilence, et la plus merveilleuse par la famine precedente, et si grandes tribulations que jamais soit advenue telle depuis la premiere fondation de l'Eglise Chrestienne, et par toutes les regions Latines. Demeurant par les vestiges en aucunes contrees des Espaignes.

24.

The third Northern leader will rescue and restore his country (Soviet Union F / the future **Henri V** of France L).

Par lors le tiers Roy Aquilonaire entendant la plaincte du peuple de son principal tiltre, dressera si grande armee, et passera par les destroits de ses derniers avites et bisayeulx, qui remettra la plus part en son estat, . . .

25.

The papacy will be restored.

. . . et le grand Vicaire de la cappe sera mis en son pristin estat: . . .

26.

The Holy of Holies[36] will be sacked by pagans and the scriptures destroyed (Muslim **invasion of Europe** L).

. . . . mais desolé, et puis du tout abandonné, et tournera estre Sancta sactorum destruicte par Paganisme, et le vieux et nouveau Testament seront dechassez, brulez, . . .

27.

After the Antichrist, the Prince of Hell will reign, spreading terror and universal destruction for twenty-five years (future Muslim **invasion of Europe** F,L / future ethnic world war H).

. . . en[37] apres l'Antechrist sera le prince infernal, encores par le derniere foy trembleront tous les Royaumes de la Chrestienté, et aussi des infideles, par l'espace de vingt cinq ans, et seront plus grieves guerres et batailles, et seront villes, citez, chasteaux, et tous autres edifices bruslez, desolez, destruicts, avec grande effusion de sang vestal, mariees, et vefves violees, enfans de laict contre les murs des villes allidez et brisez, et tant de maux se commettront par le moyen de Satan, prince infernal, que presque le monde universel se trouvera defaict et desolé: . . .

28.

Before all this, unusual birds crying "Oee! Oee!"[38] will be seen in the sky (Apocalypse, or symbols of a future religion H / the premonitory birds of St. John's Revelation, or merely loudspeaker aircraft L).

. . . et avant iceux advenemens aucuns oyseaux insolites crieront par l'air, Huy, huy, et seront apres quelque temps esvanouys.

29.

After the long period of troubles, a new Golden Age of Saturn will commence, God will hear the cries of His people, Satan will be bound for a thousand years, and then universal peace and harmony will be established between God and man, with the Church finally triumphant (the Last Times L).

Et apres que tel temps aura duré longuement, sera presque renouvellé un autre regne de Saturne, et siècle d'or, Dieu le Createur dira entendant l'affliction de son peuple, Satan sera mis et lié dans l'abysme du barathre dans la profonde fosse: et adonc commencera entre Dieu et les hommes une paix universelle, et demeurera lié environ l'espace de mille ans, et tournera en sa plus grande force, la puissance Ecclesisastique, et puis tourne deslié.

---

[30] Presumably Rome, as per St. John's Revelation.

[31] **Lyon,** founded by Lucius Munatius Plancus in 43 B.C.

[32] Presumably the Capitoline Hill in Rome, ancient seat of government and site of the temple of Jupiter Capitolinus.

---

[33] **Ogmion** or Ogmius, Gallic version of the classical **Hercules**.

[34] i.e. in around the year A.D. 2828.

[35] "The sea blushed red with blood of naval fight": unidentified Latin quotation, possibly from Virgil.

---

[36] Here possibly St. Peter's, Rome, rather than the former Jerusalem temple.

[37] Misprint for *et.*

[38] In Hebrew, "Alas! Alas!": in Old French "Today! Today!".

C. VALEDICTION

1.

But for his enemies and critics, the seer could have offered more exact astrological dates, but will now draw to a close his summary of some of the more grisly future prophecies.

Que toutes ces figures sont justement adaptees par les divines lettres aux choses celestes visibles, c'est à sçavoir, par Saturne, Jupiter, et Mars, et les autres conjoinct, comme plus a plain par aucuns quadrins l'on pourra voir, j'eusse calculé plus profondement et adapté les uns avecques les autres. Mais voyant, ô Serenissime Roy, que quelques uns de la censure trouveront difficulté, qui sera cause de retirer ma plume àmon repos nocturne: Multa etiam ô Rex omnium potentissime praeclara et sane in brevi ventura, sed omnia in hac tua epistola innectere non possumus, nec volumus: sed ad intelligenda quaedam facta horrida fata, pauca libanda sunt, quamvis tanta sit in omnes tua amplitudo et humanitas homines, deosque pietas, ut solus amplissimo et Christianissimo Regis nomine, et ad quem summa totius religionis auctoritas deferatur dignus esse videare.[39]

2.

The seer commends his work to the monarch, assures him of his continued loyalty, and signs off . . .

Mais tant seulement je vous requiers, ô Roy tres-clement, par icelle vostre singuliere et prudente humanité, d'entendre plutôt le desir de mon courage, et le souverain estude que j'ay d'obeyr àvostre serenissime Majesté, depuis que mes yeux furent si proches de vostre splendeur solaire, que la grandeur de mon labeur n'attainct ne requiert.

3.

. . . with the usual Latin formula.

De Salon ce 27 Juin, Mil cinq cens cinquante huict. Faciebat Michaël Nostradamus Salonae Petreae Provinciae.[40]

THE *PRESAGES*

Based on **Seve**'s 1605 edition. Summaries are tentative, pending establishment of final context. Possible subject-references are as suggested by **Fontbrune**[(F)], **Hogue**[(H)], and **Lemesurier**[(L)]. For translations of some verses, see **Lemesurier**. References involving Roman numerals are to the *Centuries*. Compare actual **Table of Events** on page 12.

---

[39] "Many remarkable things, O most puissant King of all, are shortly to happen, but we neither can nor will include them all in this your letter: yet in order that you should understand such horrible events as are predicted, it is necessary to divulge some of them, even though your generosity and humanity toward all men are so great, as is your Divine piety, that you alone are seen to be worthy of the full Christian title of King, to whom the highest authority in all religion should be accorded."

[40] "By Michael Nostradamus, of Salon-de-Crau in Provence."

Presage 1

Summary verse for 1555. The seer's soul, inspired by the Holy Spirit, foresees general disasters.

*D'esprit divin l'ame presage atteinte
Trouble, famine, peste, guerre courir,
Eauz, siccitez, terre mer de sang teinte,
Paix, tresve, a naistre Prelats, Princes mourir.*

Presage 2

Further summary verse for 1555. The seas are commanded by Britain, while **Provence** is protected by the Duc de Tende and war is waged at Narbonne by the heroic Duc de Villars: War of League of Augsburg, 1707 [F].

*La mer Tyrrhene, l'Ocean par la garde
Du grand Neptun & ses tridens soldats.
Provence seure par la main du grand Tende.
Plus Mars, Narbon l'heroiq de Vilars.*

Presage 3

For January 1555. A great bell shatters on the death of a tyrant, freezing weather causes famine, and peace returns after an army has passed by.

*Le gros airain qui les heures ordonne,
Sur le trespas du Tyran cassera:
Pleurs, plaintes, & cris. eaux, glace pain ne donne.
V.S.C.*[1] *paix. l'amée*[2] *passera.*

Presage 4

For February 1555. A council spreads fear around Geneva as a new leader raises an army and a young man is forced by fear and hunger to break cover: World War III [F].

*Prés du Leman [la] frayeur sera grande
Par le conseil, cela ne peut faillir.
Le nouveau Roy fait apprester sa bande,
Le jeune meurt, faim, peur fera saillir.*

Presage 5

For March 1555. War threatens as Saturn aligns with the moon, until a truce is arranged.

O Mars cruel, que tu sera[3] *à craindre,
Plus est la Faux avec l'Argent conjoint
Classe, copiee, au,*[4] *vent, l'ombriche, craindre.
Mer, terre tresve, L'amy à L.V.*[5] *s'est joint.*

Presage 6

For April 1555. Watchfulness is needed, even though the weak are stronger and the troublesome quiet, as hunger and oppression spread and a proud criminal stains the sea red (see **II.78** and the *Lettre à Henri II*): **Muslim invasion of Europe**, 2005 [L].

*De n'avoir garde seras plus offensé.
Le foible fort, l'inquiet pacifique.
La fain on crie, le peuple est oppressé.
La mer rougir, le Long fier & inique.*

Presage 7

For May 1555. During the first part of the month cities rise up against a thin-blooded prince, and an envoy returns on the 23rd with good intentions but false information.

Le cinq, six, quinze, tard & tost l'on se journe.[6]
*Le né sang fin: les citez revoltées.
L'heraut de paix vint*[7] *& trois s'en retourne.
L'ouvert cinq serre.*[8] *nouvelles inventées.*

Presage 8

For June 1555. With Saturn going retrograde near Leo and opposite Aquarius, war fizzles out as "proud Florence" opens the door to healing from north to south: World War III victory of West [F] / pause in **Muslim invasion of Europe**, 2005 [L].

*Loin prés de l'Urne le malin tourne arriere.
Qu'au grand Mars feu donra empeschement
Vers l'Aquilon au midy la grand fiere.
FLORA tiendra la porte en pensement.*

Presage 9

For July 1555. Treachery lets in an "evil explorer" during the first part of the month, as "fire from the sky" terrifies the Vatican and the West quakes, unsure of what to do: **Muslim invasion of Europe**, 2000 [L].

*Huit, quinze & cinq quelle desloyauté
Viendra permettre l'explorateur malin.
Feu du Ciel, foudre, peur, frayeur Papauté,
L'occident tremble, trop serre vin Salin.*[9]

Presage 10

For August 1555. Around the middle of the month a Lady speaks; an older prince is seduced, lightning and hail afflict Dijon and Guyenne, and the blood-thirsty are satisfied.

Six, douze, treize, vint[10] *parlera la Dame.
Laisné sera par femme corrompu,
Dijon, Guyenne gresle, foudre l'entame.
L'insatiable de sang & vin repu,*

Presage 11

For September 1555. As the buildup of an invasion force by a "new Hannibal" (see **II.30**) is held up by wet weather, the seer wonders what his ill-informed countrymen are up to: buildup to World War III [F] / **Muslim invasion of Europe**, 2007 [L].

*Pleurer le Ciel, à-t-il cela fait faire?
La mer s'apreste. Annibal fait ses ruses.
Denys moüille. classe tarde, ne taire
N'a sçeu secret, & à quoy tu t'amuses?*

---

[1] Undeciphered abbreviation.

[2] Misprint either for *l'armée* or for *l'année*.

[3] *seras*.

[4] *eau*.

[5] Unidentified abbreviation.

[6] *sejourne*.

[7] *vingt*.

[8] Probable Nostradamian respelling of *sincere*.

[9] Probable modified version of *vin et sel*.

[10] *vingt*.

Presage 12

For October 1555. The war preparations of the British fleet in the Adriatic are reported in London, intellectuals are imprisoned, and surprise night-attacks take place: World War III [F].

Venus Neptune poursuivra l'entreprise,
Serrez pensifs, troublez les opposans.
Classe en Adrie, citez vers la Tamise.
Le quart bruit blesse de nuict les reposans.

Presage 13

For November 1555. The Pope offers aid, while Venice makes an offer to the Turks, everybody flees who is able to and a wounded leader chases after the treasury.

Le grand du Ciel sous la Cape donra
Secours.[11] Adrie à la porte fait offre.
Se sauvera des dangers qui pourra.
La nuit le Grand blessé poursuit le coffre.

Presage 14

For December 1555. The Turks offer fraudulent peace-terms, while the swollen, frozen **Rhône** sweeps away bridges amid wind and rain.

La porte exclame trop frauduleuse & feinte
La gueule ouverte, condition de paix.
Rhosne au cristal, eau, neige, glace teinte.
La mort, mort, vent, par pluye cassé faix.

Presage 15

For January 1557. An unworthily decorated one is threatened with burning and a leading captive fails to return to Le Buy, while Italy is disturbed and Muslims invade Malta and the Danube: end of World War III [F] / World War II Jewish holocaust [H] / **Muslim invasion of Europe**, 2000–2 [L].

L'indigne orné craindra la grand fornaise.
L'esleu premier, des captifs n'en retourne.
Grand bas du monde, l'Itale non a laise[12]
Barb. Ister, Malte. Et le Buy ne retourne.

Presage 16

For May 1557. The end of a conjunction presages uncertainty and drought, and death and capture await one who mistimes his arrival.

Conjoint icy, au Ciel appert dépesche.
Prise, laissé, mortalité non seure.
Peu pluye, entrée, le Ciel la terre seche.
De fait, mort, pris, arrivé à mal heure.

Presage 17

For June 1557: a naval victory, a divorce in Antwerp, the birth of a lord, "fire from the sky" and earthquakes, forest fires on the Mediterranean islands, the death of a bishop and an attack on the Pope: **Napoleon**ic events, 1809–10 [F].

Victor naval, à Houche, Anvers divorce.
Né grand du Ciel feu, tremblement haut brule
Sardaigne bois, Malte Palerme, Corse.
Prelat mourir, l'un frape sur la Mule.

Presage 18

For July 1557. As a roving envoy shuttles between "dog" and "lion", a town is sacked, landing-craft appear, leaders are captured, France is invaded (see **VIII.21**) and a "maid" allies herself with a "lord": **Muslim invasion of Europe**, 2017 [L].

L'heraut errant du chien au Lion tourne.
Feu ville ardra, pille, prise nouvelle.
Decouvrir fustes. Princes pris. on retourne.
Explor. pris Gall. au grand jointe pucelle.

Presage 19

For August 1557. An elected leader, banished from power, is wounded in combat, surrenders and is indicted, a navy mutinies (see **VII.37**), a city is burned, water is poisoned in the Pyrenees (see **X.49**), and Italian naval operations cease: **Muslim invasion of Europe**, 2025 [L].

De la grand Cour banni-conflit, blessé
Esleu, renduë, accusé, mat. mutins.
En feu cité Pyr. eaux venins, pressé
Ne voguer onde, ne facher les latins.

Presage 20

For September 1557. Pacts collapse, ships are sunk, a city sacked, and ambition results in atrocities and persecutions for which a commander is attacked (see **VII.37**): **Muslim invasion of Europe**, 2005 [L].

Mer, terre aller, foy, loyauté rompuë
Pille, naufrage, à la cité tumulte.
Fier, cruel acte, ambition repeuë,
Foible offensé: le chef de fait inulte.[13]

Presage 21

For October 1557. Cold and rain; amid discord and the rejection of a deportee, the besieged leader of a poisoned city flees (see **IV.66**), to return under happier circumstances once a "new sect" has been destroyed (see **VII.15**): end of Russian Communism, followed by Golden Age [F] / **Muslim invasion** of Genoa, 2000–1 and counterinvasion, 2027 [L].

Froid, grand deluge, de regne dechassé
Niez, discord. Trion,[14] Orient mine.
Poison, mis siege, de la Cité chassé.
Retour felice, neuve secte en ruine.

Presage 22

For November 1557. The sea-coast is blockaded, the country opened to the enemy and a city surrendered, as fallen leaders are replaced and pacts are broken: **Muslim invasion of Europe**, 2000–2022 [L].

Mer close, monde ouvert, cité renduë,
Faillir le Grand, esleu nouveau, grand brume
Floram patere entrer camp. foy rompuë.
Effort sera severe à blanche plume.

Presage 23

For December 1557. Nuns are abducted, a sea-battle occurs, a new bishop dies, and an elected leader mistimes his arrival.

Tutelle à Veste, guerre meurt, translatée,
Combat naval, honneur, mort, prelature.
Entrée, decez. France fort augmentée,
Esleu passé, venu à la mal'heure.

Presage 24

For January 1558. After the ritual peacetime celebration of the funeral wedding of a royal younger brother, world treaties are broken and war erupts: British coronation and **Muslim invasion**, 1998 [L].

Puisné Roy fait, funebre epithalame,
Sacrez esmeus, festins, iceux, soupi[15] Mars.
Nuit larme[16] on crie, hors on conduit la Dame,
L'arrest & pache rompu de toutes pars.

Presage 25

For March 1558: untrue rumors in government, Genoa in revolt, attacks, upheavals, and a fatally disputed papal election: events in 2001 (?) [L].

Vaine rumeur dedans la hierarchie.
Rebeller Gennes: courses, insults, tumultes.
Au plus grand Roy sera la monarchie,
Election, conflit, couverts, sepultes.

Presage 26

For April 1558. After disagreements, one leader comes out on top, while conflict rages in the North: World War III militaristic noises in Russia [F].

Par la discorde defaillir au defaut:
Un tout à coup le remettra au sus.
Vers l'Aquilon seront les bruits si haut,
Lesions, pointes à travers, par dessus.

Presage 27

For May 1558. As alien raids come in from the Tyrrhenian Sea and disease and bloodshed spread, preemptive attacks take place, while envoys urgently speed to and fro: **Muslim invasion of Europe**, 2000–5 [L].

La mer thyrrhene, de differente voile.
Par l'Ocean seront divers asaults.
Peste, poison, sang en maison de toile.
Presults, Legate esmeus marcher mer haut.

Presage 28

For June 1558. Faith is undone as sedition reigns, **'fire from the sky'** descends and leaders quarrel: **Muslim invasion of Europe**, 2000+ [L].

Là où la foy estoit sera rompuë:
Les ennemis les ennemis paistront.
Feu Ciel pleuvra, ardra, interrompuë
Nuit entreprise. Chefs querelles mettront.

Presage 29

For July 1558. With a Muslim fleet at sea, war sweeps in, farms are abandoned, leaders fail each other, and Spanish and German exiles are allowed to return: World War III [F] / **Muslim invasion of Europe**, 2007 [L].

Guerre, tonnerre, mains[17] champs depopulez,
Frayeur & bruit, assault à la frontiere.
Grand Grand failli, pardon aux Exilez.
Germains, Hispans, par mer Barba, banniere.

---

[11] Compare **X.72**.

[12] Read as *l'Italie non à l'aise*.

---

[13] Probable misprint for *insulte*.

[14] Either abbreviation for *Septentrion* (Great Bear) or misprint for *Orion*.

---

[15] *assoupi*: compare **Presage 46**.

[16] Presumably *l'arme*.

[17] *maints*.

Presage 30

For August 1558. Absconders are shackled and Protestants imprisoned as a new "all-powerful one" is elected, but when six "reds" are punished he suffers an avoidable "rain": British election and revolution [F] / papal election, 2001 (?) [L].

Bruit sera vain, les defaillans troussez:
Les Razes pris: esleu le Pempotan:
Faillir deux Rouges & quatre bien croisez.
Pluye empeschable au Monarque potent.

Presage 31

For October 1558. Rain and wind; Muslim fleets attack the Danube and Tyrrhenian coast and invade Sicily, while Florence is starved, Siena overrun and two allied leaders die: **Muslim invasion of Europe** [F], 2000–2 [L] / defeat of Hitler [H].

Pluye, vent, classe Barbare Ister. Tyrrhene
Passer holcades Ceres, soldats munies.
Refuis bienfaits par Flor. franchie Siene.
Les deux seront morts, amitiez unies.

Presage 32

For November 1558. Forces from Venice enter Florence as refugees flee, women are widowed, and leaders step down rather than be killed: Western decadence and World War III [F] / **Muslim invasion** of Italy, 2000 [L].

Venus à la belle entera dedans FLORE.
Les Exilez secrets lairront la place.
Vefues beaucoup, mort de Grand on deplore.
Oster du regne, le Grand Grand ne menace.

Presage 33

For December 1558: wedding celebrations, the death of a famous bishop, rumors of a truce undermined by the enemy, noises of battle by land, sea, and air and successful war-propaganda.

Jeux, festins, nopces, mort Prelat de renom.
Bruit, paix de trefue, pendant l'ennemy mine.
Mer, terre & ciel bruit, fait du grand Brennon.[18]
Cris or, argent, l'ennemy l'on ruine.

Presage 34

Summary verse for 1559: fear, frost, looting, foreign expansion, religious conflict, then plague, heat, fire, and a northern victory in "Henri's city": World War III Russian occupation of **Paris** [F].

Peur, glas, grand pille, passer mer, croistre regne.
Sectes, Sacrez outre mer plus polis.
Peste, chaut, feu. Roy d'Aquilon l'enseigne.
Dresser trophée, cité d'HENRIPOLIS.

Presage 35

For January 1559: downfall of a leader, rain, iced-up wagons, upheaval, abundance, religious atrocities, death of an ungrateful elected leader.

Plus le Grand n'estre, pluye au char le cristal.
Tumulte esmeu de tous biens abondance.
Razez, Sacrez, neufs, vieux espouvental.
Esleu ingrat, mort, plaint, joye, alliance.

Presage 36

For February 1559: rotting grain, disease in the air, locusts (!), a sudden fall and a new birth, then prisoners shackled, lightened burdens and arthritis for an unwilling king.

Grain corrompu, air pestilent, locustes.
Subit cherra, noue nouvelle naistre.
Captifs ferrez,[19] *legers, haut bas, onustes,*
Par ses os mal qu'a Roy n'a voulu estre.

Presage 37

For March 1559: religious quarrels and arrests, the abduction of an elected one, a guerrilla campaign, a new League of seventy nobles and their death, to the King's satisfaction.

Saisis au temple, par sectes longue brigue.
Esleu ravi, au bois forme querelle.
Septante pars naistre nouvelle ligue.
De la leur mort, Roy appaisé nouvelle.

Presage 38

For April 1559. Following a breach of trust, the King is saluted as Victor and Emperor by St. Matthew's Day (September 21st), his proud enemy humbled and in tears: World War III [F] victory of future **Henri V** over Muslims [F,L].

Roy salué Victeur, Imperateur.
La foy faussée, le Royal fait cogneu,
Sang Mathien, Roy fait superateur
De gent superbe, humble par pleurs venu.

Presage 39

For May 1559. Despite a "wedding", "reds" and Protestants part company, a "young black" (or king) is revived by fire and "Ogmios"[20] allies with England: Communism versus religion and rejection of Muslim leader [F].

Par le despit nopces, epithalame.
Par les trois parts Rouges, Razez partis,
Au jeune noir remis par flamme l'ame,
Au grand Neptune Ogmius convertis.

Presage 40

For June 1559. Seven of the ruling house are in turn marked out for death as war and plague sweep in and Western forces flee an Eastern conqueror: Chinese invasion of Europe [F] / **Muslim invasion of Europe**, 2000–22 [L].

De maison sept par mort mortelle suite.
Gresle, tempeste, pestilent mal, fureurs.
Roy d'Orient, d'Occident tous en fuite
Subjuguera ses jadis conquereurs.

Presage 41

For July 1559. The familiar looting, heat and drought are accompanied by overadmiration for a new foreign regime:[21] Common Market seduced by China [F].

Predons pillez, chaleur, grand seicheresse:
Par trop non estre, cas non veu, inouy.
A l'estranger la trop grande caresse.
Neuf pays Roy l'Orient esblouy.

Presage 42

For August 1559: an archeological discovery, the subjection of a city, fields divided, a new deception, war, hunger, and plague in Spain and a carping critic confounded.

L'Urne trouvée, la cité tributaire.
Champs divisez, nouvelle tromperie.
L'Hispan blessé, faim, peste militaire.
Moq. obstivé,[22] *confus, mal, resverie.*

Presage 43

For September 1559. Virgins and widows have a good time coming and should take advantage of it.

Vierges & vesves, vostre bon temps s'aproche.
Point ne sera ce que l'on pretendra.
Loin s'en faudra que soit nouvelle approche.
Bien aisez pris, bien remis, pis tiendra.

Presage 44

For October 1559. One out of three non-Bourbon leaders plots against the other two, for reasons that become clear at the end of the month: quarrel between USA, USSR, and China, and end of future **Henri V**'s reign [F].

Icy dedans se parachevera.
Les 3. Grands hors le BON-BOURG[23] *sera loin.*
Encontre deux l'un d'eux conspirera.
Au bout du mois on verra le besoin.

Presage 45

For November 1559. Wedding negotiations are restarted, the Queen leaves France, Roman (or Romanian) voices are raised and a peace is inadvisedly agreed.

Propos tenus nopces recommencées.
La Grande Grande sortira hors de France.
Voix à Romagne de crier uon[24] *lassée.*
Reçoit la paix par trop feinte asseurance.

Presage 46

For December 1559. War turns joy to tears, bishops are upset by a leader, then war subsides again as vines are tended in icy weather.

La joye en larmes viendra captiver Mars.
Devant le Grand seront esmeus Divins:
Sans sonner mot enteront par trois pars.
Mars assoupi, dessus glas troutent vins.

Presage 47

For January 1560. An unsuccessful council, a year of peace, but plague, hunger, religious expulsions, a papal journey, and a revolt of the hierarchy.

Journée, diete, interim, ne concile.
L'an paix prepare, peste, faim, schismatique.
Mis hors dedans changer Ciel, domicile.
Fin du congé, revolte hierarchique.

---

[18] *Breno.*

[19] Possibly *serrez.*

[20] See under **Ogmyon.**

[21] Not a word, note, about the dramatic death of the King on the first of the month, allegedly already predicted by Nostradamus at **I.35** (first published in 1555)!

[22] *moqueur obstiné.*

[23] Presumed Nostradamian reworking of *Bourbon.*

[24] Misprint for *non.*

Presage 48

For February 1560. The council breaks up, papal authority is reestablished, "red" rebels disarmed, peace established by default and the Pope is made a "widower."

Rompre diete, l'antiq sacré ravoir
Dessous les deux, feu par pardon s'ensuivre.
Hors d'armes Sacre long Rouge voudra avoir.
Paix du neglect. l'Esleu le Vefve vivre.

Presage 49

For March 1560. The Pope makes an unaccustomed journey abroad, but when *bonhomie* changes to cruelty a quick exit follows.

Fera paroir esleu de nouveauté
Lieu de journée sortir hors des limites.
La bonté feinte de changer cruautee.
Du lieu suspect sortiront trestous vistes.[25]

Presage 50

For April 1560. Old times return with the scotching of a plot by Genevan Protestants who disapprove of the Pope's actions: Archbishop Lefèvre and the Roman Catholic traditionalists [F].

Du lieu esleu Razes n'estre contens:
Du lac Leman conduite non prouvée,
Renouveller on fera le vieil temps.
Espeüillera la trame tant couvée.

Presage 51

For May 1560. As peace in Haute Savoie breaks down, a new army is raised and a new alliance is forged.

Pache Allobrox sera interrompu.
Derniere main sera[26] *forte levée.*
Grand conjuré ne sera corrompu.
Et la nouvelle alliance approuvée.

Presage 52

For July 1560. A Catholic injures a governor; hunger, fever, fire, and the smell of blood are abroad; the papal states are honored; and Protestants stir up sedition: a comet marks the Lefèvre traditionalist rebellion [F].

Longue crinite leser Gouverneur,
Faim, fiévré ardante, feu & de sang fumée,
A tous estats Joviaux grand honneur.
Sedition par Razes allumée.

Presage 53

For August 1560. Plague, hunger, fire, and heat, thunder, hail, and a lightning-strike on a church; an edict, an arrest, and grave law-breaking; a leading discoverer and his team held.

Peste, faim, feu & ardeur non cessée.
Foudre, grand gresle, temple du ciel frapée.
L'Edict, Arrest, & grieve loy cassée.
Chef inventeur ses gens & luy hapé.[27]

Presage 54

For September 1560. Protestants are disarmed as their dispute grows, while **Calvin** [L] is deceived by a "thunderbolt" from Rome that pierces them to the marrow: suspension of Archbishop Lefèvre [F].

Privez seront Razes de leurs harnois:
Augmentera leur plus grande querelle.
Pere Liber deceu fulg.[28] *Albanois.*
Seront rongees sectes à la moelle.

Presage 55

For October 1560. "Blind and deaf" bearers of a petition are received, then persecuted, then rehabilitated, to the Queen's satisfaction.

Sera receuë la requeste decente.
Seront chassez & puis remis au sus.
La Grande Grande se trouvera contente.
Aveugles, sourds seront mis au dessus.

Presage 56

For November 1560. Protestants are banished at sword-point as the establishment holds firm with support from the lord of Lyon (or an English lord).

Ne sera mis, les Nouveau[29] *dechassez,*
Noir & de LOIN[30] *& le Grand tiendra fort.*
Recourir armes. Exilez plus chassez
Chanter victoire, non libres reconfort.

Presage 57

For December 1560. After a period of mourning for a dead Protestant leader, alliances are forged and an innocent is murdered at a banquet: deaths of Archbishop Lefèvre and the Pope [F].

Les deuls[31] *laissez, supremes alliances.*
Razes Grand mort, refus fait à l'entrée:
De retour estre, bien fait en oubliance
La mort du juste à banquet perpetrée.

Presage 58

For 1561. The King is killed or disempowered by a pernicious leader during a plague-ridden, overcast year when humor is the only antidote to the antics of the leaders: Henri III [F].

Le Roy Roy n'estre, du Doux[32] *la pernicie*
L'an pestilent, les esmeus[33] *nubileux.*
Tien, qui tiendra, des grands non leticie.
Et passera terme de cavilleux.

Presage 59

For March 1561. Under Mars and Saturn, cavalry trample a courtyard where the burning of an excommunicate has taken place.

Au pied du mur le cendré cordigere,
L'enclos livré foulant cavalerie,
Du temple hors Mars & le Falcigere
Hors. mis, demis. & sus la resverie.

Presage 60

For April 1561. Amid filthy weather and pestilential storms Muslims invade, spreading universal disaster, while leaders are mocked: **Muslim invasion of Europe** [F], 2005–17 [L] / Muslim War of Antichrist [H].

Le temps purgé, pestilente tempeste.
Barbare insult. fureur, invasion.
Maux infinis par ce mois nous appreste
Et les plus Grands, deux moins, d'irrison.[34]

Presage 61

For May 1561. During an outbreak of plague, the once joyful King stands alone against his enemies, his Lady dead and most of the harvest ungathered amid cold weather.

Joye non longue, abandonné des siens.
L'an pestilent, le plus Grand assailli.
La Dame bonne aux champs Elysiens,
Et la plus part des biens froid non cueilly.

Presage 62

For June 1561. English pirates attack the unprepared French, as plague fills the air, leaders are infected and civil conflict continues: Russian Revolution [F].

Courses de LOIN,[35] *ne s'apprester conflicts.*
Triste entreprise, l'air pestilent, hideux.
De toutes parts les Grands seront afflicts.
Et dix & sept assaillir vint[36] *& deux.*

Presage 63

For July 1561: surrenders, recaptures, horrors, bloodshed, hideous faces, horrendously illiterate scholars, losses, hatred, and deprivation.

Repris, rendu, espouvanté du mal,
Le sang par bas, & les faces hideuses.
Aux plus sçavans l'ignare espouvental:
Perte, haine, horreur, tomber bas la piteuse.

Presage 64

For August 1561. Amid arrests and killings, a non-committed group becomes more involved, the more it tries to avoid it – yet, shut up in a ruined barn, is astonishingly rescued.

Mort & saisi des nonchalans le change
S'eslogngnera en s'approchant plus fort.
Serrez unis en la ruine, grange.[37]
Par secours long estonné le plus fort.

Presage 65

For October 1561. The various monastic orders are restored and their persecutors mocked, but nuns are still trussed up.

Gris, blancs & noirs, enfumez & froquez,
Seront remis, demis, mis en leurs sieges,
Les ravasseurs[38] *se trouveront mocquez:*
Et les Vestales serrées en fortes rieges.[39]

---

[28] Abbreviation for *fulgure*.

[29] Presumably either le *Nouveau* or les *Nouveaux*.

[30] Presumed anagram for *Lion* (**Lyon**).

[31] *deuils*.

[32] Possibly from Latin *dux*, "leader, general".

[33] Possible misprint for *ennemis*.

[34] Scansion and rhyme demand *d'irrision*.

[35] Anagram for *Lion* (**Lyon**).

[36] *vingt*.

[37] Misprint for *en la ruiné(e) grange*.

[25] Rhyme-influenced spelling of *vi(s)te*.

[26] Possibly *fera*.

[27] *happés*.

Presage 66

For 1562. After a good, healthy winter and spring, summer is bad and fall worse, with drought and poor harvests (except for grapes), eye-diseases, war, rebellion, and sedition.

Saison d'hiver, ver bon, sain, mal esté.
Pernicieux auton, sec, froment rare,
Du vin assez, mal yeux, faits, molesté
Guerre, mutin, seditieuse tare.

Presage 67

For January 1562. A hidden benevolence arises and a religious peace ensues, but when a "wedding" is called off the mighty are put down and hanged.

Desir occulte pour le bon parviendra.
Religion, paix, amour & concorde.
L'epitalame de tout ne s'accordra.
Les haut qui bas & haut mis a la corde.

Presage 68

For February 1562. A Protestant leader is frustrated as new laws free prisoners and the body of a murdered lord is discovered hidden in his lair: failure and death of Archbishop Lefèvre F.

Pour Razes Chef ne parviendra à bout.
Edicts changez, les serrez mis au large.
Mort Grand trouvé, moins de foy, bas debout.
Dissimulé, transi frappé à bauge.

Presage 69

For March 1562. An Englishman (or the lord of **Lyon**) is captured by a woman, but reacts unpredictably and is killed.

Esmeu de LOIN,[40] de LOIN prés minera.
Pris, captivé, pacifié par femme.
Tant ne tiendra comme on barginera.[41]
Mis[42] non passez, oster de rage l'ame.

Presage 70

For April 1562. An Englishman (or lord of **Lyon**) secretly tries to incite trouble among the people, but is found dead in a kitchen.

De LOIN viendra susciter pour mouvoir.
Vain descouvert contre peuple infini.
De nul cogneu le mal pour le devoir.
En la cuisine trouvé mort & fini.

Presage 71

For May 1562. Conflicts continue worse than ever, and even a pause in hostilities is of no significance, merely allowing plots to be hatched.

Rien d'accordé, pire plus fort & trouble.
Comme il estoit, terre & mer tranquiller.
Tout arresté ne vaudra pas un double.[43]
Dira l'iniq, Conseil d'anichiler.

Presage 72

For June 1562. An ominous and unbelievable uprising by firebrands results in their death or exile.

Portenteux fait, horrible & incroyables![44]
Typhon fera esmouvir les meschans:
Qui puis apres soustenus par le cable,
Et la pluspart exilez sur les champs.

Presage 73

For July 1562. A heavenly envoy ascends the French throne, the universe is pacified by virtue, bloodshed ceases, and bird- or fire-oracles soon replace those based on worms (or verse): coronation of Henri V, 2034 (?) L.

Droit mis au throsne du ciel venu en France
Pacifié par Vertu l'Univers.
Plus sang espandre, bien tost tourner chance
Par les oyseaux, par feu, & non par vers.

Presage 74

For August 1562. Clerics seethe, then "joyful androgynes" are spotted, but having mistimed their arrival are maltreated (see **II.45**): homosexuals, or future extraterrestrials (?) L.

Les colorez, les Sacres malcontens:
Puis tout à coup par Androgyns alegres.
De la pluspart voir, non venu le temps,
Plusieurs d'entr'eux feront leurs soupes maigres.

Presage 75

For September 1562. Establishment figures are restored to power, despite disagreements, while many of the distrusted Protestants are jettisoned: Roman Catholic traditionalists rejoin the Church F.

Remis seront en leur pleine puissance,
D'un point d'accord conjoints,[45] non accordez.
Tous defiez, plus aux Razes fiance.
Plusieurs d'entr'eux à bande debordez.

Presage 76

For October 1562. The Vatican accepts the situation, while a skeptical House of Lorraine listens in silence: future **Henri V** puts an end to conflict F.

Par le legat du terrestre & matin.[46]
La grande Cape à tout s'accommoder,
Estre à l'escoute tacite LORVARIN,[47]
Qu'à son advis ne voudra accorder.

Presage 77

For November 1562. Rumors of an enemy impede an advance and wine is poisoned, but plowing is easy.

D'ennemi vent empeschera la troupe.
Le plus grand point mis avant difficil.
Vin de poison se mettra dans la couppe.
Passer sans mal de cheval gros foussil.

Presage 78

For December 1562. Ice puts an end to a Christmas campaign, while English forces cease to attack, but a sudden catarrh contaminates holy water.

Par le cristal l'entreprise rompuë.
Jeux & festins, de LOIN plus reposer.
Plus ne fera prés des Grands sa repuë.
Subit catarrhe l'eau beniste arrouser.

Presage 79

Summary verse for 1563: a healthy spring marred by conflict, then murders, prisoners, deaths, omens, rain, plague, terror, war, refugees, and new leaders.

Le ver sain, sang, mais esmeu, rien d'accord
Infinis meurtres, captifs, morts, prevenus.
Tant d'eau & peste, peur de tout, sonnez cors.
Pris, morts, fuits, grands devenir, venus.

Presage 80

For January 1563. Amid rain, floods, war, death, and conflict, the late recantation in captivity of a mild leader merely produces more conflict.

Tant d'eau, tant morts, tant d'armes émouvoir.
Rien d'accordé, le Grand tenu captif
Que sang humain, rage, fureur n'avoir.
Tard penitent, peste, guerre, motif,

Presage 81

For February 1563. Enemies are silenced as a good-hearted leader works for peace against much opposition that harms both prisoners and suspects.

Des ennemis mort de langue s'approche.
Le Debonnaire en paix voudra reduire.
Les obstinez voudront perdre la proche.
Surpris, captifs, & suspects fureur nuire.

Presage 82

For March 1563. Fathers, mothers, and wives are alike bereaved as a leader's death ruins everything and peace is once again replaced by conflict.

Peres & meres morts de deuls infinis.
Femmes à deul, la pestilente monstre.
Le Grand plus n'estre tout le monde finir.
Soubs paix, repos, & trestous a l'encontre.

Presage 83

For April 1563. Rulers hold talks while Christendom is shaken and aliens attack the Holy See, then things go from bad to worse as plague, hunger, and atrocities sweep in from the East: the Yellow Invasion F / **Muslim invasion of Europe**, 2000+ L.

En debats Princes & Chrestienté esmuë.
Gentils estranges, siege à Christ molesté.
Venu tresmal, prou bien, mortelle veuë.
Mort Orient peste, faim, mal traité.

Presage 84

For May 1563. An earthquake, the death of a monster, a defeat, countless prisoners, a catastrophe at sea, an uncompromising and vengeful confrontation: **Muslim invasion of Europe**, 2000–5 L.

Terre trembler, tué, prodige, monstre:
Captifs sans nombre, faire defaite, faite.
D'aller sur mer adviendra malencontre,
Fier contre fier mal fait[48] de contrefaire.

---

[38] Presumably *ravisseurs*: otherwise possibly *vavasseurs*.

[39] Misprint for *lieges*.

[40] Presumed anagram for *Lion* (**Lyon**).

[41] Presumably *barguignera*.

[42] Possible misprint for *mais*.

[43] *doublon*.

[44] Presumably *incroyable*.

[45] *conjoints*.

[46] Misprint for *marin*.

[47] Anagram of *Lorrain V*.

[48] Possibly *malfait*.

Presage 85

For June 1563: a fallen criminal attacked, hail and floods, archeological discoveries, a fatal palace revolution, and an ax laid to a tree: events during 2026 (?) L.

L'injuste bas fort l'on molestera.
Gresle, inonder, thresor, & gravé marbre.
Chef de suard[49] *peuple à mort tuera.*
Et attachée sera la lame à l'arbre.

Presage 86

For July 1563. An unsuccessful duel leads to unwelcome consequences, as the worst injured is spared, an envoy withdraws in confusion and relations are broken off.

De quel non mal? inexcusable suite.
Le feu non deul,[50] *le Legat hors confus.*
Au plus blessé ne sera faite luite.
La fin de Juin le fil coupé du fus.[51]

Presage 87

For August 1563. Agreements weaken a satisfactory outcome, while army and Church remain divided, and confused lords seize people and property indiscriminately.

Bons finemens affoiblis par accords.
Mars & Prelats unis n'arresteront.
Les Grands confus par dons incidez corps.
Dignes, indignes, biens indeus saisiront.

Presage 88

For September 1563. With the weather changing for the worse, the leaders, in mourning for "another Louis" (i.e. presumably another Duc de **Bourbon**), have high hopes for a southern truce that denies power or recognition to Protestants: mistakes by Archbishop Lefèvre F.

De bien en mal le temps se changera.
Le pache d'Aust, des plus Grands esperance.
Des Grands deul, LVUIS[52] *trop plus, trebuchera.*
Congnus Razez pouvoir ni congnoissance.

Presage 89

For October 1563. A month of dreadful, uncontrollable disasters involving deaths, plague, famine,and conflicts: **Russian Revolution**, October 1917, and massacre of Romanovs F.

Voicy le mois par maux tant à doubter.[53]
Morts, tous, saigner, peste, faim, quereller
Ceux du rebours d'exil viendront noter.
Grands, secrets, morts, non de controroler.[54]

Presage 90

For November 1563. Despite death, looting, plague, floods, and a dearth of young men who are fit enough to fight, **Montmorency** L remains unassailable.

---

[49] Probably *guard.*

[50] Possibly *duel.*

[51] Presumably *fusee.*

[52] Louis.

[53] *redouter.*

[54] *controler.*

Par mort mort mordre, conseil, vol, pestifere,
On n'osera Marius[55] *assaillir.*
Deucalion un dernier trouble faire.
Peu de gens jeunes: demis morts tressaillir.

Presage 91

For December 1563. Death and disaster mark out the truly living, while damaging ideas spread in high places, and a layman is welcomed back into the Church.

Mort par despit fera les autres Juire:[56]
Et en haut lieu de grands maux advenir.
Tristes concepts à chacun viendront nuire,
Temporel digne, la Messe parvenir.

Presage 92

Summary verse for 1564: a sixth year of rain, but abundant harvests; hatreds, public rejoicing, royal divorces, and disagreements, dying flocks, human changes, public follies, and "poison under the skin."

L'an sextil pluyes, froment abonder, haines.
Aux hommes joye. Princes, Rois en divorce,
Troupeau perir, mutations humains.
Peuple affoulé:[57] *& poison sous l'escorce.*

Presage 93

For January 1564. Variable weather, open discord, a change in military policy, the death or deposition of a lady, a drowning of conspirators, a great rivalry, and an alliance against the King.

Temps fort divers, discorde descouverte.
Conseil belliq, changement pris, changé.
La Grande n'estre, conjurez par eau perte.
Grand simulté, tous au plus Grand rangé.

Presage 94

For February 1564. A great flood, a deliberate rumor of death, a new era, a quarrel between three lords, a worsening of relationships by a firebrand, and a plot only foiled by rain.

Deluge grand, bruit de mort conspirée.
Renoüé siecle, trois Grands en grand discord
Par boutefeux la concorde empirée.
Pluye empeschant, conseils malins d'accord.

Presage 95

For March 1564. Hatreds grow between rulers, quarrels and wars begin, and a great change (or a change of lord) outrages the public and then results in a row.

Entre Rois haines on verra apparoistre,
Dissensions & Guerres commencer.
Grand Changement, nouveau tumulte croistre
L'ordre plebée on viendra offenser.

Presage 96

For April 1564. A popular conspiracy against the establishment is unearthed, its leading female plotter put to death or disempowered.

Secret conjur. conspirer populaire.
La decouverte en machine esmouvoir.
Contre les Grands . . .[58]
Puis trucidée & mise sans pouvoir.

· [55] See **Nostradamus Dictionary**.

[56] Probably *luire.*

[57] *affolé.*

Presage 97

For May 1564. Changeable weather, fevers, plague, listlessness, wars, quarrels, desolation, floods, royal cruelties to children, contented rulers, and a possible death.

Temps inconstant, fievres, peste, langueurs,
Guerres debats, temps desolé sans feindre.
Submerrions,[59] *Prince a mineurs rigueurs.*
Felices Rois & Grands, autre mort craindre.

Presage 98

For June 1564. Fire, plague, flight, variable weather, wind, three lordly deaths, lightning-strikes on Protestants, and an old man dying near the edge of a wood: World War III exodus and Vatican criticism of traditionalists F.

Du lieu feu mis la peste & fuite naistre.
Temps variant, vent, la mort de trois Grands:
De ciel grand foudres estat des Razes paistre.
Vieil pres de mort, bois peu dedans vergans.

Presage 99

For July 1564. With society in danger, rulers congratulate themselves, Protestants seethe at the outcome of a council and public anger is stirred up by Church and rulers alike, one of whom shows his true colors only later: traditionalists versus the Vatican F.

En peril monde & Rois feliciter.
Razes esmeu, par conseil ce qu'estoit:
L'Eglise Rois pour eux peuple irriter.
Un monstrera apres ce qu'il n'estoit.

Presage 100

For August 1564. An imminent flood, bovine disease, a new religious sect, misplaced optimism, pre-legislative trial of a new law, a baited ambush, and suicides of deceived victims.

Deluge prés. peste bouive, neuve
Secte fléchir, aux hommes joye vaine.
De loy sans loy, mis au devant pour preuve,
Apast, embusche: & deceus couper veine.

Presage 101

For September 1564. Floods everywhere, Protestant losses, looting, death, abundance, a cloak-and-dagger escape, and a change of fortunes for old and new: end of Roman Catholic traditionalist movement F.

Tout inonder, à la Razée perte.
Vol de mur, mort, de tous biens abondance.
Eschapera par manteau decouverte.
Des neuf & vieux sera tournée chançe.

Presage 102

For October 1564. A distillation causes seven lords to cough, with blisters in the mouth and throat, while it rains so long that bubbles take on a life of their own (?), and a prominent leader dies.

La bouche & gorge en fervides pustules,
De sept Grands cinq. toux distillante nuire.
Pluye si longe, à non mort tournent bulles.
Le Grand mourir, qui trestous faisoit luire.

---

[58] Incomplete line.

[59] *submersions.*

Presage 103

For November 1564. Both old and great perish amid the sound of firing, the plague dies down, a great lady is born, the hay-crop is diseased, the harvest reduced, and foreigners delight in the deaths of fertile flocks and herds.

Par bruit de feu Grands & Vieux defaillir.
Peste assoupie, une plus grande naistre.
Peste de l'Ara, foin caché, peu cueillir.
Mourir troupeau fertil, joye hors prestre.

Presage 104

For December 1564. As 75 percent inflation causes deaths, the clergy, quietly angry, depart in small groups along deteriorating roads (?).

Alegre point, douce fureur au Sacre.
Enflez trois quatre & au costé mourir.[60]
Voye defaillir, n'estre à demy au sacre:
Par sept & trois, & par quinte courir.

Presage 105

Summary verse for 1565. A hundred times worse than the previous year, even for the high and mighty of state and Church, with disasters, deaths, exiles, devastation, ruination, the death of a great lady, plague, afflictions, and cold north winds or Mistrals.

Pire cent fois cest an que l'an passé.
Même au[61] *plus Grands du regne & de l'Eglise*
Maux infinis, mort. exil, ruine, cassé.
A mort Grande estre, peste, playes & bille.[62]

Presage 106

For January 1565. Snow, blights, rains, afflictions, continuing pestilence, yet royal joy, and plenty of seed-grain, as yet more sectarian gangs prepare for action.

Neiges, roüilleures,[63] *pluyes & playës grandes.*
Au plus Grand joye, pestilence insopie.
Semences, grains beaucoup, & plus de bandes,
S'appresteront, simulte n'amortie.

Presage 107

For February 1565. A major quarrel breaks out between leaders, a high-born cleric hatches a plot, and new sects sow hatred and discord, to public indignation.

Entre les Grands naistre grande discorde,
Le Clerc procere un grand cas brassera:
Nouvelles sectes mettre en haine & discorde,
Tout peuple guerre & change offensera.

Presage 108

For March 1565. Secret religious plots, a perilous change, rain, gales, afflictions for the proud, floods and "pestiferous acts."

Secret conjur. changement perilleux.
Secrettement conspirer [les] factions.
Pluyes grands vents, playes par orgueilleux,
Inonder fleuves, pestifere actions.

Presage 109

For April 1565. Growing plague, sectarian warfare, moderate weather after a wintry spell, quarrels between Catholics and Protestants, floods, and fatal disasters everywhere.

Pulluler peste, les Sectes s'entrebatre.
Temps moderé, l'hyver peu de retour.
De messe & presche grievement soy debatre.
Inonder fleuves, maux, mortels tout autour.

Presage 110

For May 1565. Conflicts affecting the man and woman on the street and even the dead, the death of a great lady at a ceremony to cure scrofula, and the banishment of others: death of France in World War III [F].

Au menu peuple par debats & querelles,
Et par les femmes & defunts grande guerre.
Mort d'une Grande, celebrer escroüelles.
Plus grandes Dames expulsées de terre.

Presage 111

For June 1565. Widowings both male and female; threats to the lives of kings; plague, war, famine, extreme dangers everywhere, and emigrations of minor nobility.

Viduité tant masles que femelles.
De grands Monarques la vie periclitér.
Peste, fer, faim, grand peril pesle mesle.
Troubles par changes, petits Grands concitér.

Presage 112

For July 1565. Hail, blight, afflictions, rumored threats to women, deaths, plague, war, famine in the countryside, and a strangely glittering sky.

Gresle, roüilleure, pluyes & grandes playes,
Preserver femmes, seront cause du bruit,
Mort de plusieurs, peste, fer, faim par hayes,
Ciel sera veu quoy dire qu'il reluit.

Presage 113

For August 1565. A poor grain harvest, corpses as white as snow, sterility, rotting grain, wet weather, an injury to a leader and the deaths of several of his close supporters.

Point ne sera le grain à suffisance.
La mort s'approche à neiger plus que blanc
St.erilité, grain pourri, d'eau bondance.[64]
Le grand blessé, plusieurs de mort de flanc.

Presage 114

For September 1565. Amid a dearth of fruit and grain, high-born nobles and prelates alike egg on their young fighters unpredictably until a Toledan (?) wins a victory.

Guere de fruits, ni grain, arbres & arbrisseaux.
Grand volataille,[65] *procere stimuler.*
Tant temporel que prelat leonceaux.
TOLANDAD[66] *vaincre, proceres reculer.*

Presage 115

For October 1565. With disease and death declining, one leader persecutes four others, two of whom give up the struggle and are exiled, ruined, starved, killed, or simply confounded.

Du tout changé, persecuter l'un quatre.
Hors maladie, bien loin mortalité.
Des quatre deux plus ne viendront debatre.
Exil, ruine, mort, faim, perplexité.

Presage 116

For November 1565. While the nobility's numbers are reduced by great changes, upheavals, war, and plague, money is short and the paying of bills difficult in the leadup to a freezing December.

Des grands le nombre plus grands ne sera tant,
Grands changements, commotions, fer, peste,
Le peu devis: pressez, payez contant.
Mois opposite gelée fort moleste.

Presage 117

For December 1565. More frost and ice than harmony, many widowings, fires, mournings, joyful games and contests, military confrontations, and good marriage prospects.

Forte gelée, glace plus que concorde.
Vesves matrones, feu, deploration.
Jeux, esbats. joye. Mars citera discorde.
Par mariages bonne expectation.

Presage 118

Summary verse for 1566.[67] Deaths of high nobles, dishonor, violence, rumors of decadence among Catholics and Protestants alike, disasters, quarreling neighbors, and beheadings of Church officials.

Aux plus grands mort, jacture d'honneur & violence,
Professeurs de la foy, leur estat & leur secte
Aux deux grandes Eglises divers bruit decadence
Maux, voisins querellans, serfs d'Eglise sans teste.

Presage 119

For January 1566. Factional violence caused by Christians of both persuasions brings death, dishonor and loss of property even for the highest nobility.

Perte, jacture grande, & non sans violance.
Tous ceux de la foy, plus à religion.
Les plus Grands perdront vie, leur honneur & chevance
Toutes les deux Eglises, la coulpe à leur faction.

Presage 120

For February 1566. As Catholics and Protestants confront each other, disease epidemics rage and poisonous rumors spread, while a major leader suffers a grievous loss and others are also dishonored or killed.

A deux[68] *fort grande naistre perte pernitieuse.*
Les plus Grands feront perte, biens, d'honneur, & de vie.
Tant grands bruits couriront, l'une trop odieuse
Grands maladies estre, presche, messe en envie.

---

[60] Should possibly read *Enflez trois quarts & au coste mourir.*

[61] *aux.*

[62] Rhyme demands *bise*, "wind", or possibly *bisse* (heraldic term from Italian *biscia*) "snake."

[63] *rouillures.*

[64] *abondance.*

[65] *volatil(e).*

[66] Possibly "Toledan."

[67] The year of Nostradamus's death: unusually, all the *Présages* for this year are in alexandrines (lines of twelve, rather than ten, syllables).

[68] Here from Latin *dux*, "leader."

Presage 121

For March 1566. Church officials betray bishops and vassals betray their lords, as Protestant and Catholic neighbors quarrel and rumors spread, sometimes fatally.

Les servants des Eglises leurs Seigneurs trahiront.
D'autre Seigneurs aussi par l'indivis des champs.
Voisins de preche & messe entre eux querelleront.
Rumeurs, bruits augmenter, à mort plusieurs couchans.

Presage 122

For April 1566. Agricultural plenty is accompanied by an absence of war, though irreligion, sedition, murder, and mugging continue, a violent fever spreads and the people are restless.

De tous biens abondance terre nous produira:
Nul bruit de Guerre en France, ormi[69] seditions:
Homicides, voleurs par voye on trowera:
Peu de foy: fievre ardente: peuple en esmotion.

Presage 123

For May 1566. As international discord and hatred increase, several leading princes are killed, while a general affliction affects much of Italy, especially the west, and fine weather proves too dry.

Entre peuple discorde inimitié brutale
Geurre, mort de grands princes, plusieurs pars d'Italie:
Universelle playe, plus fort occidentale:
Tempore bonne & pleine, mais fort seiche tarie.

Presage 124

For June 1566. Little grain, but plenty of other produce; a wet spring and summer, but a long, icy winter; an eastern war provoking French rearmament; deaths among flocks and herds, but plenty of honey; and the raising of a siege: Chinese invasion [F].

Les bleds trop n'abonder de tous autres fruits force
L'estê printemps humides, hyver long, neige,glace:
L'orient mis en armes: la France se renforce:
Mort de bestail, prou miel: aux assiegés la place.

Presage 125

For July 1566.[70] Disease and fire destroy orchard fruit, but the olive crop looks good; some French leaders are killed, despite few foreign attacks; nevertheless, Muslim coastal raids threaten, as do other border incursions: World War III chemical weapons and oil discoveries [F].

Par pestilence & feu, fruits d'arbres periront:
Signe d'huile abonder: pere Denis[71] non gueres:
Des grands mourir mais peu estrangers sailliront:
Insult marin barbare: & dangers de frontieres.

Presage 126

For August 1566. Torrential rain, abundant crops, good cattle prices, women no longer threatened, hail, thunder, oppression, death threats, and capital punishment.

Pluies fort excessives, & de biens abondance:
De bestail pris[72] just estre: femmes hors de danger:
Gresles, pluyes, tonnerres: peuple abatu en France:
Part mort travailleront: mort peuple corriger.

Presage 127

For September 1566. End of war and general afflictions, the death of a plotter, limits on **Calvin**ist activities, evil men waylaid by even worse ones, and unprecedented French victories: revolt of Archbishop Lefêvre [F].

Armes, plaies cesser: mort de seditieux:
Le pere Liber grand, non trop abonda:
Malins seront saisis par plus malicieux:
France plus que jamais victrix triomphera.

Presage 128

For October 1566. Drought up until this month halves the fruit crop in Italy and **Provence**, while the King's enemies decrease, one of their prisoners is captured by pirates and they themselves are killed.

Jusqu'à ce mois durer la seicheresse grande,
A l'Itale & Provence: des fruits tous à demy:
Le grand moins d'ennemis: prisonnier de leur bande:
Aux escumeurs pyrates, mourir l'ennemy.

Presage 129

For November 1566. A fearful enemy retires to Greece, leaving suffering and desolation behind, while rumors cease, religion is persecuted and Catholics react ferociously: World War III retreat of Red Army [F] / counterinvasion of Muslim-occupied Europe, 2034+ [L].

L'ennemy tant à craindre retirer en Thracie
Laissant cris hurlemens, & pille desolée:
Cesser bruit mer & terre, religion murtrie:[73]
Joviaux unis en route: toute secte affolée.[74]

Presage 130

Summary verse for 1567.[75] A fatal illness affecting young women, headcolds, misfortune for land-agents, coastal raids, grape harvesting in the mist, plenty of oil, too much rain and war affecting the fruit harvest.

Mort, maladie aux jeunes femmes, rhumes
De teste aux yeux, malheur marchands de terre
De mer infault,[76] femmes mal, vin par brumes.
Prou huile, trop de pluye, aux fruits moleste guerre.

Presage 131

For January 1567. Imprisonments, secret upsets, quarreling neighbors, loss of life, fatal catarrhs, poisonings to settle arguments, terrors, and neglected fields.

Prisons, secrets, ennuis, entre proches discorde.
La vie on donnera, par mal divers catarrhes,
La mort s'en ensuivra, poison fera concorde.
Frayeur, peur crainte grande, voyageant laira d'arres.

Presage 132

For February 1567. Enemies both hidden and open imprisoned, a voyage interrupted by mortal hatred, rivalry resulting from a secret love triangle, public rejoicing, and a dispute solved by "water."

Prisons par ennemis occults & manifestes.
Voyage ne tiendra, inimitié mortelle.
L'amour trois, simultez, secret, publiques festes.
Le rompu ruiné, l'eaü rompra la querelle.

Presage 133

For March 1567.[77] Marriages between public enemies lead to "profitable" deaths, noble friendships are made, and Catholics and Protestants talk to each other, but regret it later.

Les ennemis publics, nopces & mariages:
La mort après, l'enrichi par les morts.
Les grands amis se montrer au passage.
Deux sectes jargonner, de surpris tards remords.

Presage 134

For April 1567. Major "diseases" infect the Church from foreign embassies, provoking a new law, while old clergy grow even older and the King is in friendly country.

Par grandes maladies religion fachée,
Par les enfans & legats d'Ambassade
Don donné d'indign. nouvelle loy laschée;
Bien de vieux peres, Roy en bonne contrade.

Presage 135

For May 1567. Father and son draw together, magistrates are strict, enemies misrepresent a marriage, and unknowns are incorrectly promoted, but supported by friends and wives.

Du pere au fils s'approche, Magistrats dits severes.
Les grandes nopces, ennemis garbelans.
De latens mis avant, par la foy d'improperes:
Les bons amis & femmes contre tels groumelans.

Presage 136

For June 1567. A father's inheritance is found, kings and magistrates dispute over a wedding, and amid public ill-will judges and a mayor are killed, as are three nobles.

Par le tresor, trouvé l'heritage du pere.
Les Roys & Magistrats, les nopces, ennemis.
Le public mal vueillant, les Juges & le Maire
La mort, pœur & frayeur, & trois Grands à mort mis.

Presage 137

For July 1567. As death approaches again, thanks to royal and papal policy, older people make the most of things, while their young heirs discover their walled-up treasure.

Encor la mort s'approche, don Royal & Legat.
On dressera ce qu'est, par veillesse en ruine.
Les Jeunes hoirs, de soupçon nul legat.
Thresor trouvé en plastres & cuisine.

Presage 138

For August 1567. Secret enemies are imprisoned, kings and magistrates tighten their grip, lives are threatened by diseases of the nose and eyes, and two nobles mistime their departure.

---

[69] *hors mi.*

[70] The month of Nostradamus's death.

[71] Reference to France's patron saint: his feast day is October 9th.

---

[72] *prix.*

[73] Some editions have *nutrie.*

[74] Possibly *assoulé.*

[75] All the remaining *Présages* are from Nostradamus's posthumous **Almanach** of 1567.

[76] *insult.*

---

[77] From this point onward the verses are more irregular, often consisting of mixed lines of ten or twelve syllables.

Les Ennemis secrets seront emprisonnez:
Les Rois & Magistrats y tiendront la main seure.
La vie de plusieurs, santé, maladie yeux, nez.
Les deux grands s'en iront bien loin à la male heure.

Presage 139

For September 1567. Prolonged headaches, an enemy wedding performed by a traveling bishop, a noble's nightmare, fire, ruin, a noble found in a strange place, and new errors resulting from a discovery made after a flood.

Longues langueurs de teste nopce, ennemy
Par Prelat & voyage, songe du Grand terreur,
Feu & ruine grande trouvé en lieu oblique,
Par torrent descouvert sortir noves erreurs,

Presage 140

For October 1567. Kings and magistrates impose the death penalty, with young girls sick, nobles with bloated bodies, servants hostile to their master at a wedding, public suffering, and inflated interest rates.

Les Rois & Magistrats par les morts la main mettre,
Jeunes filles malades, & des Grands corps enflé
Tout par langueurs & nopces, ennemis serfs au maistre,
Les publiques douleurs, le composent tout enflé.

Presage 141

For November 1567. A man returning from an embassy stashes away a royal gift, then is found dead by his bed and bench by his closest family and friends: death of Nostradamus [C,F,H,L(?)]

Du retour d'Ambassade, don de Roy, mis au lieu,
Plus n'en fera, Sera allé à Dieu,
Parens plus proches, amis, freres du sang,
Trouvé tout mort prez du lict & du banc.

THE *SIXAINS*

Based on **Seve**'s 1605 edition. Summaries are tentative, pending establishment of context. Possible subject-references are as suggested by **Fontbrune**([F]), **Hogue**([H]), and **Lemesurier**([L]). Dates appear to be liturgical (see **Dating and Sequencing the Prophecies**). For translations of some verses, see **Lemesurier**. References involving Roman numerals are to the ***Centuries***.

Sixain 1

At the dawn of a new era a new alliance is made and aristocracy thrown overboard, while a struggle for power goes on, a ship from Italy docks in **Marseille** bringing the Virgin (or a new Joan of Arc [L]) to France and "Catherine" goes Protestant or is beheaded: Garibaldi and the Third Republic, 1870 [F] / **French Revolution**, **Napoleon**, 1799, and the execution of Queen Marie Antoinette, 1793 (?) [L].

Siecle nouveau, alliance nouvelle,
Un Marquisat mis dedans la nacelle,
A qui plus fort des deux l'emportera:
D'un Duc, d'n[1] Roy, gallere de Florence,
Port à Marseille, Pucelle dans la France,
De Catherine fort[2] chef on rasera.

Sixain 2

Aided by "Leeches,"[3] a "Pigmy" of a leader spends huge amounts and squanders thousands upon thousands of soldiers' lives for nothing, in his efforts to take a town from a stronger country: World War I French and British trench-warfare [L].

Qu d'or, d'argent fera despendre,
Quand Comte voudra ville prendre,
Tant de mille & mille soldats,
Tuez, noyez, sans y rien faire,
Dans plus forte mettra pied terre,
Pigmée ayde des Censuarts.

Sixain 3

After five years of enduring bombardment in underground emplacements, a besieged city is handed over to its enemies, then deluged with water: **Paris**, 1940–5, and World War III [F] / Sarajevo, 1992–7 (?) [L].

La ville sans[4] dessus dessous,
Renversee de mille coups
De canons: & forts dessous terre:
Cinq ans tiendra: le tout remis,
Et laschee a[5] ses ennemis,
L'eau leur sera apres la guerre.

Sixain 4

A newborn prince, feminine by affectation but inwardly masculine, regains his rightful Bourbon inheritance: birth of **Henri V** [F,L].

D'un rond, d'un lis, naistra un si grand Prince,
Bien tost & tard venu dans sa Province,
Saturne en Libra en exaltation:
Maison de Venus en descroissante force,
Dame en apres[6] masculin soubs l'escorse,
Pour maintenir l'heureux sang de Bourbon.

Sixain 5

The cruel ruler of a principality, eventually threatened by a great army, would do well to seek allies, unless he wishes to drink "Orange juice": House of Orange [L].

Celuy qui la Principauté
Tiendra par grande cruauté,
A la fin verra grand phalange:
Par coup de feu tres-dangereux,
Par accord pourroit faire mieux,
Autrement boira suc d'Orange.

Sixain 6

Letters from a Spanish girlfriend trap a dangerous traitor by the name of "Robin" and he is beheaded, while the writer drowns herself: Spanish treason by Duke Biron, 1599, and execution, 1602 [F].

Quand de Robin la traitreuse entreprinse
Mettra Seigneurs & en peine un grand Prince,
Sceu par la Fin, chef on lui trenchera:
La plume au vent, amye dans Espaigne,
Poste attrappé estant en la campagne,
Et l'escrivain dans l'eaüe se jettera.

Sixain 7

When "Leech" joins battle with "Wolf," a great leader makes good the former's food-shortage by sea (see IV.15): German wheat-shortage and Russo-German Pact, 1939 [F] / World War I, II and/or III Atlantic convoys from USA to Britain [L].

La sangsue au loup se joindra,
Lors qu'en mer le bled defaudra,
Mais le grand Prince sans envie,
Par ambassade luy donra
De son bled, pour luy donner vie,
Pour un besoin s'en pourvoira.

Sixain 8

Shortly before "business" commences, an Iranian envoy is rejected by France when he pretends to renounce his religion: preparations for World War III [F] / runup to **Muslim invasion of Europe**, 1999–2000 [L].

Un peu devant l'ouvert commerce
Ambassadeur viendra de Perse,
Nouvelle au franc pays porter:
Mais non receu, vaine esperance,
A son grand Dieu sera l'offense,
Feignant de le vouloir quitter.

Sixain 9

After a war in the Auvergne, a "Lady" tries to deliver her children to the "Leech" but is discovered, while fear of death stalks the land and brothers and sisters are held in the Bastille or some similar prison: revolts, 1792, with royal family held in the Temple [F].

Deux estendars du costé d'Auvergne,
Senestre pris, pour un temps prison regne,
Et une Dame enfans voudra mener:
Au Censuart, mais descouvert l'affaire
Danger de mort murmure sur la terre,
Germain Bastille frere & sœur prissonier.

Sixain 10

The representative of a "Lady" sails abroad to seek help from a "Physician," but is opposed by a "Queen": France seeks aid from USA or Britain, 1940 or 2002+ [L].

Ambassadeur pour une Dame,
A son vaisseau mettra la rame,
Pour prier le grand medecin:
Que de l'oster de telle peine,
Mais en ce s'opposera Royne
Grand peine avant qu'en voir la fin.

Sixain 11

An era is marked by floods in the valley of the **Gard** or Gardon River (compare **X.6**, **IX.9**, **IX.37**): late C21 [L].

Durant ce siecle on verra deux ruisseaux,
Tout un terroir inonder de leurs eaux,
Et submerger par ruisseaux et fontaines:
Coups[7] & Moufrin[8] Beccoyran,[9] & ales[10]
Par le gardon bien souvent travaillez,
Sis cens & quatre alez, & trente moines.

---

[3] See the list of symbolic beasts under **Nostradamus the Poet**.

[4] *sens.*

[5] *à.*

[6] *apprest.*

[7] Comps.

[8] Montfrin.

[9] Now Boucoiran-et-Nozières.

[10] Alès.

---

[1] *d'un.*

[2] Possible misprint for *son.*

Sixain 12

In "1605" a dispute between two leaders makes the news when murder is committed during Mass: events in 1997 [L].[11]

Six cens & cinq tresgrand' nouuelle,
De deux Seigneurs la grand querelle,
Proche de Genaudan sera,
A une Eglise apres l'offrande
Meurtre commis, prestre demande
Tremblant de peur se sauuera.

Sixain 13

An "adventurer" or "future one" is poisoned at the behest of a pre-eminent world ruler in "1606" or "1609": events in 1998 or 2001 [L].

L'aventurier six cens & six ou neuf,
Sera surpris par fiel mis dans un œuf,
Et peu apres sera hors de puissance
Par le puissant Empereur general,
Qu'au monde n'est un pareil ny esgal,
Dont un chascun luy rend obeissance.

Sixain 14

In "1605" a siege recommences in the spring after subsiding, as usual, with the onset of winter: World War II, 1939–40 [F] / siege of Sarajevo, 1992–7 (?) [L].

Au grand siege encor grands forfaits,
Recommençant plus que jamais
Six cens & cinq sur la verdure,
La prise & reprise sera,
Soldats és champs jusqu'en froidure
Puis apres recommencera.

Sixain 15

A new Pope sees the beginning of the long reign of a renowned Bourbon prince with whose forces his own are to be allied: successor of John Paul II [F] or final Pope [L], and future **Henri V** of France [F,L].

Nouveau esleu patron du grand vaisseau,
Verra long temps briller le clere flambeau
Qui sert de lampe à ce grand territoire,
Et auquel temps [les][12] armez[13] sous son nom.
Joinctes à celles de l'heureux de Bourbon
Levant, Ponant, & Couchant sa memoire.

Sixain 16

Either in October "1605" or in June "1606" a new "sea-monster's steward" is ritually crowned: British accession and coronation, or US presidential inauguration, 1997 and/or 1998 [L].

En Octobre six cens & cinq,
Pourvoyeur du monstre marin,
Prendra du souverain le cresme
Ou en six cens & six, en Juin,
Grand'joye aux grands & au commun
Grands faits apres ce grand baptesme.

Sixain 17

When an ailing but cheerful leader fails to live out the year, those assembled to celebrate his name-day are disappointed, and shortly afterward two of them confront each other: death of "Hercules," 2034 (?) [L].

Au mesme temps un grand endurera,
Joyeux mal sain, l'an complet ne verra,
Et quelques uns qui seront de la feste,
Feste pour un seulement, à ce jour,
Mais peu après sans faire long sejour,
Deux se donront, l'un l'autre de la teste.

Sixain 18

Thanks to a sinister expedient, the Greek "Nightingale" sees an end to her troubles in "1605": end of Greek border-troubles with Turkey, 1997 [L].

Considerant la triste Philomelle
Qu'en pleurs & cris sa peine renouvelle,
Racourcissant par tel moyen ses jours,
Six cens & cinq, elle en verra l'issue,
De son tourment, ja la toile tissue,
Par son moyen senestre aura secours.

Sixain 19

The hateful anger of a "firebrand" grows more intense between "1605" and "1617," as the long-dormant **"Crocodile"** stirs to life again: rise of North African anti-European Muslim militancy, 1997–2009 [L].

Six cens & cinq, six cens & six & sept,
Nous monstrera jusques [à] l'an dixsept,
Du boutefeu lire,[14] hayne & envie,
Soubs l'olivier d'assez long temps caché,
Le Crocodil sur la terre a caché,[15]
Ce qui estoit mort, sera pour lors en vie.

Sixain 20

One who has repeatedly known prison and freedom, now unsure of his true identity, seeks a cause to die for.

Celuy qui a par plusieurs fois
Tenu la cage & puis les bois,
R'entre à son premier estre
Vie sauve peu apres sortir,
Ne se sçachant encor cognoistre,
Cherchera subject pour mourir.

Sixain 21

[**Summary verse**] The "author of all ills" starts his reign in "1607," oppresses the subjects of the "Leech," makes his way to France to gather his forces, but fails to invade the Leech's homeland: Adolf Hitler [F] / **Antichrist**, Britain, and **Muslim invasion of Europe**, 1999–2022 [L].

L'Autheur des maux commencera regner
En l'an six cens & sept sans espargner
Tous les suject qui sont à la sangsue,
Et puis apres s'en viendra peu à peu,
Au franc pays r'allumer son feu,
S'en retournant d'où elle est yssue.

Sixain 22

An instigator of assassinations eventually suffers worse himself when he is captured and constantly shifted from place to place while under day-and-night guard.

Cil[16] qui dira, descouvrissant l'affaire,
Comme du mort, la mort pourra bien faire
Coups de poignard par un qu'auront induit,
Sa fin sera pis qu'il n'aura fait faire
La fin conduit les hommes sur la terre,
Gueté partout, tant le jour que la nuit.

Sixain 23

When the ship of state is shaken from stem to stern by waves and rocks from "1607" to "1610," and the sea is strewn with corpses, the experience actually renews its life and vigor: **Muslim invasion** of France between 1999 and 2003 [L].

Quand la grand nef, la proüe & gouvernail,
Du franc pays & son esprit vital,
D'escueils & flots par la mer secoüee,
Six cens & sept, & dix cœur assiegé
Et des reflus de son corps affligé,
Sa vie estant sur[17] ce mal renoüee.

Sixain 24

In "1608" and "1620" (or in "1628") a "Mercurial one" does not have much longer to live, as dangers threaten from disease, fire, and water – all of them avoidable – but war proves the final nail in the coffin: "death of France" at hands of **Muslim invasion**, 2000–12 [L].

Le Mercurial non de trop longue vie,
Six cens & huict & vingt, grand maladie,
Et encor pis danger de feu & d'eau,
Son grand amy lors luy sera contraire,
De tels hazards se pourroit bien distraire,
Mais bref, le fer luy fera son tombeau.

Sixain 25

In "1606" and/or "1609" an aged chancellor as big as an ox makes his last visit to France before retiring into oblivion: Hitler on Champs Élysées, 1940 [H] / Chancellor Kohl's last visit to **Paris** at end of final term, 1998 or 2001 [L].

Six cens & six, six cens & neuf,
Un Chancelier gros comme un bœuf,
Vieux comme le Phœnix du monde,
En ce terroir plus ne luyra,
De la nef d'oubly passera
Aux champs Elisiens faire ronde.

Sixain 26

Of two religious brothers, one stands up for France and, failing serious illness in "1606," defends it until "1610," dying shortly thereafter: events in 1998 and 2002 [L].

Deux freres sont de l'ordre Ecclesiastique,
Dont l'un prendra pour la France la pique,
Encor un coup, si l'an six cens & six
N'est affligé d'une grand'maladie,
Les armes en main jusques six cens & dix,
Guieres plus loing ne s'estendant sa vie.

---

[11] See **Dating and Sequencing the Prophecies.**

[12] One-syllable word omitted.

[13] *armees.*

[14] *l'ire.*

[15] *attaché.*

[16] Old form of *celui.*

[17] *par.*

Sixain 27

During the Third Age (that of Mars[18]) "fire from the sky" spreads from the west and south toward the east, sterilizing the soil and leaving behind a country littered with glowing "carbuncles" and laid waste by famine: World War III F / far future calamities, shortly before final Apocalypse of 3797 L.

Celeste feu du costé d'Occident,
Et du Midy, courir jusques au Levant,
Vers demy morts sans point trouver racine.
Troisiesme aage, à Mars le Belliqueux,
Des Escarboucles on verra briller feux,
Aage Escarboucle, & à la fin famine.

Sixain 28

In "1609" or "1614," "old Charon" celebrates Easter during Lent, making it official in "1610," to the astonishment of a "Physician" who is taken to court over it: echo in 2001 or 2006 of the 1582 introduction of the Gregorian calendar by Pope Gregory XIII and Aloysius Lilius – possibly some kind of "new order" introduced by Germany and resisted by Britain L.

L'an mil six cens & neuf ou quatorziesme,
Le vieux Charon fera Pasques en Caresme,
Six cens & six, par escrit le mettra
Le Medecin, de tout cecy s'estonne,
A mesme temps assigné en personne
Mais pour certain l'un d'eux comparoistra.

Sixain 29

The "Griffon" (or *Gryphon*) is urged to rearm, lest the "**Elephant**" suddenly attack him amid fiery seas in "1608": World War III F / Mediterranean naval battle and **Muslim invasion of Europe** from Africa, 2000+ L.

Le Griffon se peut apprester
Pour à l'ennemy resister
Et renforcer bien son armee,
Autrement l'Elephant viendra
Qui d'un abord le surprendra,
Six cens & huict, mer enflammee.

Sixain 30

The "Leech" and the "Doctor of the falling sickness" tear up their peaceful intentions and set fire to the "Empire," so freeing France from its "epilepsy": future counterinvasion against Muslims F, by Britain and USA, 2022–6 L.

Dans peu de temps Medecin du grand mal,
Et la sangsuë d'ordre & rang inegal,
Mettront le feu à la branche d'Olive,
Poste courir, d'un & d'autre costé,
Et par tel feu leur Empire accosté,
Se r'alumant du franc finy salive.

Sixain 31

A war-hero from **Toulouse** is suddenly slain in strange wise by the "**Crocodile**," to huge public curiosity and amazement: Yom Kippur War, 1973 F,H / pivotal event (see **IX.19**, **I.26**, and *Sixain 45*) during **Muslim invasion of Europe**, 2020–2 L.

Sixain 32

During a grape harvest beneficial to the army, thunder, fire, water, and blood descend in unprecedented manner.

Celuy qui a les hazards surmonté,
Qui fer, feu, eauë n'a jamais redouté,
Et du pays bien proche du Basacle.
D'un coup de fer tout le monde estonné,
Par Crocodil estrangement donné,
Peuple ravi de veoir un tel spectacle.

Sixain 32

During a grape harvest beneficial to the army, thunder, fire, water, and blood descend in unprecedented manner.

Vin à foison, tres-bon pour les gendarmes,
Pleurs & soupirs, plainctes cris & alarmes
Le Ciel fera ses tonnerres pleuvoir
Feu, eau & sang, le tout meslé ensemble,
Le Ciel de sol, en fremit & en tremble,
Vivant n'a veu ce qu'il pourra bien veoir.

Sixain 33

Severe famine hits the south of France, with people eating roots and wild acorns, and even cannibalism in Viverois: Muslim-occupied France, 2026+ L.

Bien peu apres sera tres-grand misere,
Du peu de bled, qui sera sur la terre,
Du Dauphiné, Provence & Viverois,
Au Viverois est un pauvre presage,
Pere de fils, sera antropophage,
Et mangeront racine & gland du bois.

Sixain 34

Fratricidal war rages until a Bourbon puts an end to the Arab empire, but Israel is ruined: World War III F / counterattack against Middle Eastern Muslims by future **Henri V**, 2034–7 L.

Princes & Seigneurs tous se feront la guerre,
Cousin germain, le frere avec le frere,
Finy l'Arby[19] de l'heureux de Bourbon,
De Hierusalem les Princes tant aymables,
Du fait commis enorme & execrable,
Se ressentiront sur la bourse sans fond.

Sixain 35

A "Lady" mourns a death (see Sixain 31) as leaders flee, abandoning their children to a powerful invasion by "Snakes" and "**Crocodile**s": Yom Kippur War, 1973 F / **Muslim invasion of Europe**, 2017–22 L.

Dame par mort grandement attristee,
Mere & tutrice au sang qui l'a quittee,
Dame & Seigneurs, faits enfans orphelins,
Par les aspics & par les Crocodilles,
Seront surpris forts Bourgs, Chasteaux & Villes
Dieu tout puissant les garde des malins.

Sixain 36

Word of popular revolution is spread throughout France by mealy-mouthed rumor-mongers whose incendiary pronouncements are like scorpion-stings: C16 revolts and civil wars, or runup to **French Revolution** L.

La grand rumeur qui sera par la France,
Les impuissant[20] voudront avoir puissance,
Langue emmiellee & vrays Cameleons,
De boute-feux, allumeurs de chandelles,
Pyes & geys, rapporteurs de nouvelles
Sont[21] la morsure semblera Scorpions.

Sixain 37

After a murderous struggle, an old, strong order is defeated by a new, initially weak one when one of them invades an empire: Anglo-French relations during and after counterinvasion of Muslim-occupied Europe, 2023+ L.

Foible & puissant seront en grand discord,
Plusieurs mourront avant faire l'accord
Foible au puissant vainqueur se fera dire,
Le plus puissant au jeune cedera,
Et le plus vieux des deux decedera,
Lors que l'un d'eux envahira l'Empire.

Sixain 38

Amid floods, war, and disease, a "Great St.eward" shows his worth, and in "1615" or "1619" a "Great Prince" enters the annals of Christendom: US (or British) intervention in Europe, and future **Henri V**, 2007 or 2011 L.

Par eau, & par fer, & par grande maladie,
Le pourvoyeur à l'hazard de sa vie
Sçaura combien vaut le quintal du bois,
Six cens & quinze, ou le dixneufiesme,
On gravera d'un grand Prince cinquiesme
L'immortel nom, sur le pied de la Croix.

Sixain 39

A "super-monster's steward" shines with unparalleled brilliance as he routs "**Elephant**" and "**Wolf**": World War III F / US or British-led counterinvasion of Muslim-occupied Europe, 2023–34 L.

Le pourvoyeur du monstre sans pareil,
Se fera veoir ainsi que le Soleil,
Montant le long la ligne Meridienne,
En poursuivant l'Elephant & le loup,
Nul Empereur ne fit jamais tel coup,
Et rien plus pis à ce Prince n'advienne.

Sixain 40

A disinherited prince wins back his homeland from the irritable "Leech": future **Henri V** L wrests **Provence** F from British control L.

Ce qu'en vivant le pere n'avoit sceu,
Il acquerra ou par guerre, ou par feu,
Et combattra la sangsue irritée,
Ou jouyra de son bien paternel
Et favory du grand Dieu Eternel,
Aura bien tost sa Province heritée.

Sixain 41

After a sea-battle off Gibraltar, atrocities are committed as Pamplona is attacked and overrun: Battle of Trafalgar, 1805, and sieges of Pamplona, 1808–42 F/ **Muslim invasion of Europe**, 2007+ L.

Vaisseaux, galleres avec leur estendar,
S'entrebattront pres du mont Gilbattar,
Et lors sera fors fait[22] à Pampelonne,
Qui pour son bien souffrira mille maux,
Par plusieurs fois soustiendra des assaux,
Mais à la fin unie à la Couronne.

---

[18] Apparently from around 2975 to 3335, if the system of "ages" mooted in the *Lettre à Henri II* is to be followed – unless the reference is simply to a World War III.

[19] *l'Araby.*

[20] *impuissants.*

[21] *dont.*

[22] Probably *forfaits.*

Sixain 42

From "1610," Rome is beset by attacking troops, fire, and flood, until eventually liberated by the French: **Muslim invasion** of Italy, 2000+, and liberation, 2027–8 [L].

La grand'Cité où est le premier homme,[23]
Bien amplement la Ville je vous nomme,
Tout en allarme, & le soldat és champs
Par fer & eaue, grandement affligee,
Et à la fin, des François soulage,
Mais ré[24] sera des six cens & dix ans.

Sixain 43

After local revolts, **Provence** is forcibly reoccupied until relieved by a great leader via **Beaucaire**: revolt against Richelieu, 1632 [F] / liberation of Muslim-occupied **Provence**, 2036 [L].

Le petit coing, Provinces mutinees,
Par forts Chasteaux se verront dominees,
Encor un coup par la gent militaire,
Dans bref seront fortement assiegez,
Mais ils seront d'un tres grand soulagez,
Qui aura fait entree dans Beaucaire.

Sixain 44

In "1610" a great Prince becomes enamored of France, and in "1615" wounds it with his love-dart, ensnaring it with heavenly aid in "1625": Socialism and François Mitterrand [F] / **Muslim invasion** of France and aerial attacks, 2007–17 [L].

La belle roze en la France admiree,
D'un tres-grand Prince à la fin desiree,
Six cens & dix, lors naistront ses amours
Cinq ans apres, sera d'un grand blessee
Du trait d'Amour, elle sera enlassee,
Si à quinze ans du Ciel reçoit secours.

Sixain 45

[**Summary verse**] After a surprise attack by the "Crocodile" on a leading relative of the "Leech," another attack is made on the "Wolf," with then-unknown results: World War III [F] / **Muslim invasion of Europe** and counterinvasion, 1999–2023 [L].

Par Crocodil estrangement donné,
A un bien grand, parent de la sangsuë,
Et peu apres sera un autre coup
De guet à pend,[25] commis contre le loup,
Et de tels faits on en verra l'issuë.

Sixain 46

After a "Steward" has routed "Leech" and "Wolf," France experiences its greatest disaster: World War III defeat of West F / huge numbers of deaths from disease (see **IX.55**) following liberation of Muslim-occupied France, 2026+ [L].

Le pourvoyeur mettra tout en desroute,
Sangsuë et loup, en mon dire n'escoutte
Quand Mars sera su signe du Mouton
Joint à Saturne, & Saturne à la Lune,
Alors sera ta plus grande infortune,
Le Soleil lors en exaltation.

Sixain 47

A new, "swarthy" leader of Hungary advances to Rome and wages a three-year war on his neighbor, which only overwhelming force can possibly repress: **Muslim invasion** of Italy, 2000 [L].

Le grand d'Hongrie, ira dans la nacelle,
Le nouveau né, fera guerre nouvelle
A son voisin qu'il tiendra assiegé,
Et le noireau[26] avec[27] son altesse,
Ne souffrira, que par trop on le presse,
Durant trois ans ses gens tiendra rangé.

Sixain 48

The "Phoenix," best and last son of "old Charon," reappears in France (see **Sixain 25**) and reigns long and happily in the best tradition of his predecessors: Chancellor Helmut Kohl (?) [L].

Du vieux Charon on verra le Phænix,
Estre premier & dernier de ses fils,
Reluire en France, & d'un chacun aymable,
Regner long temps, avec tous les honneurs
Qu'auront jamais eu ses predecesseurs
Dont il rendra sa[28] gloire memorable.

Sixain 49

A great alliance with France, aided by the "Leech" in the south, "puts out the fire" and founds a lasting peace: liberation of France, 2022–6 [L].

Venus & Sol, Jupiter & Mercure
Augmenteront le genre de nature
Grande alliance en France se fera,
Et du Midy la sangsue de mesme,
Le feu esteint par ce remede extreme,
En terre ferme Olivier plantera.

Sixain 50

A prostrate England, hungry but well-armed, manages to generate superhuman "fire" to resist a great "flood": World War III [F] / start of counterinvasion of Muslim-occupied Europe, 2022–3 [L].

Un peu devant ou apres l'Angleterre
Par mort de loup, mise aussi bas que terre,
Verra le feu resister contre l'eaue,
Le r'alumant avecques telle force
Du sang humain, dessus l'humaine escorce
Faite[29] de pain, bondance de cousteau.

Sixain 51

An old city taken over and sustained by a conqueror is retaken by the French, but reduced in the process: liberation of Muslim-occupied Rome, 2027–8 (?) [L].

La ville qu'avoit en ses ans
Combatu l'injure du temps,
Qui de son vainqueur tient la vie,
Celuy qui premer l'a surprist,
Que peu apres François réprist,
Par combats encor affoiblie.

Sixain 52

A half-starved city has cause to recall St. Bartholomew's Day, as fighting erupts countrywide at the behest of a Lady: St. Bartholomew's Day massacre, 1572 [F,L].

La grand Cité qui n'a pain à demy,
Encor un coup la sainct Berthelemy
Engravera au profond de son ame,
Nismes, Rochelle Geneve & Montpellier,
Castre, Lyon, Mars entrant au Belier,
S'entrebattront le tout pour une Dame.

Sixain 53

The "Phoenix" does not die until "1670," after three others have died – one from illness after fifteen years, another violently after twenty-one, and a third by drowning after thirty-nine: life of Hitler, 1889–1945 [F] / 2062 (?) [L].

Plusieurs mourront avant que Phænix meure,
Jusques six cens septante est sa demeure,
Passé quinze ans, vingt & un, trente neuf,
Le premier est subjet à maladie,
Et le second au fer, danger de vie,
Au feu à l'eau, est subjet trente neuf.

Sixain 54

Shortly after a "Great Lady" dies (between "1615" and "1620"), a rain of fire and iron falls on Flanders and England, which after a long siege is forced to take the war to its neighbors: fall of Third Republic, 1940 [F] / **Muslim invasion of Europe**, 2007–12 and 2022–3 [L].

Six cens & quinze, vingt, Grand Dame mourra
Et peu apres un fort long temps plouvra,
Plusieurs pays, Flandres & l'Angleterre
Seront par feu & par fer affligez,
De leurs voisins longuement assiegez,
Contraints seront de leur faire la guerre.

Sixain 55

Great distress is felt at the execution or murder of a great Lady: execution of Marie Antoinette, 1793 [F] / fall of France, 2007–22 [L].

Un peu devant ou apres tres grand'Dame
Son ame au Ciel, & son corps soubs la lame,
De plusieurs gens regrettee sera,
Tous ses parens seront en grand'tristesse,
Pleurs & soupirs d'une Dame en jeunesse,
Et à deux[32] grands, le dueil[31] delaissera.

Sixain 56

[**Summary verse**] With the "Elephant" everywhere, "St.eward" joins "Griffon" to destroy it, doing great deeds near the Holy Land once two "brothers" have worked their will on the Church: South Africa and World War III [F] / counterinvasion of Middle East by USA and allies after European civil war, 2032+ [L].

Tost l'Elephan de toutes parts verra
Quand pourvoyeur au Griffon se joindra,
Sa ruine proche & Mars qui tousjours gronde
Fera grand faits aupres de terre saincte
Grands estendars sur la terre & sur l'onde,
Si la nef a esté de deux freres enceinte.

---

[23] Note the hidden word "Rome" – one of Nostradamus's more outrageous puns.

[24] Misprint for *ce*.

[25] *guet-apens*.

[26] *noiraud*.

[27] Scansion demand *avecques*.

[28] *la*.

[29] Misprint for *faute*.

[30] Possibly from Latin *dux, ducis*, "leader".

[31] *deuil*.

Sixain 57

An emperor is troubled even before an engagement turns into a wedding, but France's new bride dies soon afterward: **Napoleon**'s marriages, 1796 and 1809 [F] / Anglo-French relations before or after counterinvasion of Muslim-occupied Europe, 2022–3 (?) [L].

Peu apres l'aliance faite,
Avant solemniser la feste,
L'Empereur le tout troublera
Et la nouvelle mariee
Au franc pays par sort liee,
Dans peu de temps apres mourra.

Sixain 58

The death of the "Leech" (see **Sixain 57** above) bodes well for France, as an alliance allows her to dominate Britain: World War III collapse of Soviet empire [F] / decline of Britain following liberation of Muslim-occupied France, 2026 [L].

Sangsüe en peu de temps mourra,
Sa mort bon signe nous donra,
Pour l'accroissement de la France,
Alliances se trouveront
Deux grand Royaumes se joindront,
François aura sur eux puissance.

THE 'EXTRA' QUATRAINS

Based mainly on **Garencières**' 1672 version. Roman numerals denote **Centuries**. Summaries are tentative, pending establishment of sequence and thus context. Possible subject-references are as suggested by **Fontbrune**(F), **Hogue**(H), **Lemesurier**(L), and **Roberts**(R). For translations see all except **Fontbrune**.

VII.43

When two unicorns are seen, one yawning, the other bowing, with people in the middle surrounded by pillars, a laughing nephew or grandson flees.

Lorsqu'on verra les deux licornes,
L'une baislant,[32] l'autre abaislant,[33]
Monde au milieu, pilier aux bornes,
S'enfuyra le neveu riant.[34]

VII.44

A rightful Bourbon suffers unjust flight and persecution: **French Revolution** (?) [H,L].

Alors qu'un bour sera fort bon,
Portant en soy les marques de justice,
De son sang lors portant son nom
Par fuite injuste recevra son supplice[35]

---

[32] Possible misprint for *baillant*.

[33] Possible misprint for *abaissant*.

[34] This quatrain seems technically too poor to be by Nostradamus: nowhere else, either, does he mention unicorns.

[35] If by Nostradamus, this quatrain is distinctly unusual in having alternate lines of eight and ten syllables.

VII.43a

With **Paris** at war and senators in credit, France is suddenly troubled and a rich king exiled: parliamentary inquiry into the Marquis d'Ancre, 1617 (see **VII.1**) [R].

Lutece en Mars, Senateurs en credit,
Par une nuit Gaule sera troublee,
Du grand Cræsus l'Horoscope predit,
Par Saturnus, sa puissance exilee.

VII.44a

Two newcomers are caught red-handed by a scullion while poisoning a Prince's food, then arrested and tortured.

Deux de poison saisis nouveaux Venus,
Dans la cuisine du grand Prince venus;
Par le souillard tous deux au faict cogneus,
Prins qui cuidoit de mort l'aisne vexer.

VII.73

Sieges are intensified, booty seized, churches taken over, prisoners captured, inflation endured, and an upstart (or schoolboy) put on the throne: C16 events [L] / **French Revolution** and **Napoleon** [R].

Renfort de sieges manubis & maniples,[36]
Changez le sacre & passe sur le Pronsne,[37]
Prins captifs n'arreste les priz triples,
Plus par fonds mis, esleve, mis au trosne.

VII.80

In the west of "free Britain," lowlands and highlands are reconnoitred, then a Scottish rebellion occurs on a warm, rainy night: future Scottish war of independence, 2020+ [L] / John Paul Jones [R].

L'Occident libres les Isles Britanniques,
Le recogneu passer le bas, puis haut,
Ne content trist Rebel, corff,[38] Escotiques,
Puis rebeller par plui & par nuict chaud.

VII.82

Although few countermeasures are taken against widespread banditry and rebel activity, the return of a Protestant from a journey to a Muslim land is celebrated.

La stratageme simulte sera rare,
La mort en voye rebelle par contree,
Par le retour du voyage Barbare,
Exalteront la protestante entree.

VII.83

Amid hot winds, advice, and fears, a defenseless, newly married man is attacked in bed at night and joy turned to tears.

Vent chaud, conseil, peurs, [&][39] timidite,
De nuict au lit assailly sans les armes,
D'oppression grand[40] calamite,
L'Epithalame converty pleurs & larmes.

---

[36] *manipules*.

[37] Misprint for *prosne*.

[38] *Corfou* (?), or version of *corsaires*.

[39] Extra syllable needed.

[40] Scansion demands *grande*.

VIII.1a

Would-be rebels are punished and their opportunity denied.

Seront confus plusieurs de leurs attente,
Aux habitants ne sera pardonne,
Qui bien pensoient persevere l'attente,
Mais grand loisir ne leur sera donne.

VIII.2a

Those who attempt to persuade leaders to make peace are unlikely to succeed unless and until they themselves become models of legality: C16 Wars of Religion [L].

Plusieurs viendront, & parleront de paix,
Entre Monarques & Seigneurs bien puissans,
Mais ne sera accorde de si pres,
Que ne se rendent, plus qu'autres obeissans.

VIII.3a

Unprecedented madness is matched by unprecedented wretchedness as wolves combine to go on the prowl: C16 Wars of Religion [L].

Las quelle fureur, helas quelle pitie,
Il y aura entre beaucoup de gens!
On ne vit onc une telle amitie,
Qu'auront les loups a courir diligens.

VIII.4a

With attempts to negotiate merely met with violence and closed ears (see **VIII.2a**), God alone can bring peace: C16 Wars of Religion [L].

Beaucoup de gens viendront parlementer,
Aux grands seigneurs qui leur feront la guerre,
On ne voudra en rien les escouter,
Helas! si Dieu n'envoye paix en terre.

VIII.5a

Although rescuers hurriedly set out from distant lands, they are too late to help: **Muslim invasion of Europe**, 2020+ [L].

Plusieurs secours viendront de tous costez,
De gens loingtains qui voudront resister;
Ils seront tout a coup bien hastez,
Mais ne pourront pour celte heure assister.

VIII.6a

France is threatened by invading countries, including Austria: World War II (?) [L].

Las quel plaisir ont Princes estrangers!
Garde toy bien qu'en ton pays ne vienne,
Il y auroit de terribles dangers,
En maints contrees, mesme en la Vienne.

XI.91

A "Hacker," a "Prophet" and a third figure bring invasion and pestilence to **Aix**, made twice as bad by the occupiers of **Marseille**: **Muslim invasion of Europe**, 2000+ (?) [L].

Mesnier, Manthis & le tiers qui viendra,
Peste & nouveau insult, enclos troubler,
Aix & les lieux fureur dedans mordra,
Puis les Phocens viendront leur mal doubler.

XI.97

With soldiers hidden in wood-piles near the disputed Villefranche and Mâcon, the King's fortunes change in spring when forces from Chalon-sur-Saône and Moulins cut them down.

Par Ville-Franche, Mascon en desarroy,
Dans les fagots, seront soldats cachez,
Changer de temps enprime[41] *pour le Roy,*
Par de chalon & moulins tous hachez.

XII.5

Fire and famine sweep **Provence** and destroy the Church, while a frustrated leader is driven out: C16 events or **Muslim invasion** of France, 2000+ (?) [L].

Feu, flamme, faim, furt,[42] *farouche, fumee,*
Fera faillir, froissant fort, foy faucher;
Fils de Deite! toute Provence humee,
Chasse de Regne, enrage sans crocher.[43]

XII.24

With a massive rescue-force from Guyenne stalled near Poitiers, **Lyon** surrenders to forces from Montleul and Vienne and is sacked and looted: **Muslim invasion** of France, 2000–2 [L].

Le grand secours venu de la Guenne,
S'arrestera tout aupres de Poitiers,
Lyon rendu par Montluel & Vienne,
Et saccagez par tout gens de mestiers.

XII.36

[**Summary verse**] A ferocious Turkish invasion-force destined to ruin France builds up in Cyprus, and this and another fleet from North Africa then go on to wreak havoc, especially that crossing via Gibraltar: **Muslim invasion of Europe**, 2000+ [L].

Assault farouche en Cypre se prepare,
Larme a l'œil, de ta ruine proche;
Bizance classe, Morisque, si grand tare,
Deux differente, le grand vast par la roche.

XII.52

After a leader divides his forces into two and listens to four advisers, a weak force fails to defend a gap, while lightning strikes **Aigues Mortes** and the Mediterranean coast.

Deux corps un chef, champs divisez en deux,
Et puis respondre a quatre ouys,
Petits pour grands, a pertuis mal pour eux,
Tour d'Aigues foudre, pire pour Eussouis.[44]

XII.55

Amid bad advice, worse ideas, disloyalty, fighting and lawbreaking, townspeople, and their defenders alike become wild, fretful, and addicted to war: C16 developments [L].

Tristes conseils, desloyaux, cauteleux
Advis meschant, la loy sera trahie,
Le peuple esmeu, farouche, querelleux,
Tant bourg que ville, toute la paix haye.

XII.56

With leaders at each other's throats and violent hatred and dissent everywhere, madness and anger sweep the country, bringing war and disaster: C16 Wars of Religion [L,R].

Roy contre Roy & le Duc contre Prince,
Haine entre iceux, dissension horrible,
Rage & fureur sera tout province,
France grande guerre & changement terrible.

XII.59

Agreements and pacts are broken, friendships undermined by quarrels, hatreds endemic, religion corrupted, and **Marseille** torn apart: C16 Wars of Religion [H,L].

L'accord & pache sera du tout rompue;
Les amitiez polues par discorde,
L'haine envieillie, tout foy corrompue,
Et l'esperance, Marseille sans concorde.

XII.62

Blois sees wars, disputes, upheavals, contradictory reports, and an attack: C16 Wars of Religion (?) [H,L].

Guerres, debats, a Blois guerre & tumulte,
Divers aguets, adveux inopinables,
Entrer dedans Chasteau Trompette, insulte,
Chasteau du Ha,[45] *qui en seront coulpables.*

XII.65

A leader angrily insists that his forces hold firm as all hearts quake, disaster overwhelms Langon and huge forces attack the southwest: salt-tax revolt, 1548, **Muslim invasion of Europe**, 2007–18, or civil war 2032 [L] / League of Nations [R].

A tenir fort par fureur contraindra,
Tout cœur trembler, Langon advent terrible,
Le coup de pied mille pied se rendra,
Guiront,[46] *Garon, ne furent plus horribles.*

XII.69

As the Swiss in Spain (?) flee the successors of Suleiman the Magnificent, warlords make ready and chaos returns: **Muslim invasion of Europe**, 2007+ [L] / future French leader [R].

Ejovas[47] *proche, esloigner Lac Leman,*
Fort grands appreste, retour confusion,
Loin des neveux, du feu grand Supelman,[48]
Tous de leur suyte.[49]

XII.71

Rivers and streams may slow the tide of evil, but anger's flame cannot be quenched, spreading faster than rumor to wreck religious foundations (or "as Protestants wreck . . ."), houses, manors, and palaces alike: C16 Wars of Religion, or **Muslim invasion of Europe**, 2000+ [L].

Fleuves, rivieres de mal seront obstacles,
La vieille flame d'ire non appaisee,
Courir en France, cecy comme d'oracles,
Masons, manoirs, palais, secte rasee.

---

[41] *en prime*, "in spring".

[42] Presumably *furet*.

[43] This absurdly alliterative verse is by far the worst of its kind in the ***Propheties***. If indeed by Nostradamus, it probably represents a failed and – fortunately – abandoned attempt at the genre.

[44] Misprint for *Enssouis*: probably Ensuès-la-Redonne, west of Marseille.

[45] *Haut* (?).

[46] Possibly *Gironde*.

[47] Possibly Ejulve in Spain.

[48] Presumably *Suleiman*.

[49] Incomplete line.

CONCORDANCE TO THE *PROPHETIES*

BASED ON THE 1555, 1557, 1568, AND 1605 EDITIONS

(excluding small particles, and subject to variations of spelling from edition to edition)

Roman figures refer to numbers of *Centuries*:
Pr. = *Presage*. S. = *Sixain*

Aage III.14, III.46, IV.14, V.50, V.56, VII.35, VIII.97, X.97, S.27
Abandonera IV.13
Abandonné IV.65, Pr.61
Abandonner IX.29
Abandonnera IV.45
Abas III.63
Abatre V.10
Abatu Pr.126
Abayeront IV.93
Abbage VIII.26
Abbatre I.33
Abbaye VIII.26, IX.40
Abbé II.56, VIII.12
Abbés I.44
Abbois X.59
Abbreuvez IX.12
Abbrevez IX.12
Abeille X.24
Abelhos IV.26
Abhominable VI.90
Abhorreant IX.21
Abillez VIII.12
Abismant I.69
Abisme I.21, IV.40
Abismes VII.7
Abolira V.76
Abondance VIII.14, VIII.98, VIII.100, Pr.35, Pr.101, Pr.113, Pr.122, Pr.126
Abondant V.32
Abonder Pr.92, Pr.124-5
Abondera Pr.127
Abord S.29
Abourdera I.30
Absence VII.9
Absent V.15
Absolution III.60
Absumes IX.31
Abysmera IX.89
Ac VII.1
Accablee VIII.19
Accablés VI.47
Accommoder Pr.76
Accompaigné VI.48, VII.4, VIII.32, X.14, X.86
Accompa(i)gnés III.83
Accomplie III.52
Accomplit I.48
Accomply IV.5
Accord I.57, III.38, V.3, V.37, X.39, Pr.75, Pr.79, Pr.94, S.5, S.37
Accordé Pr.71, Pr.80
Accorder Pr.76
Accordez Pr.75
Accordra Pr.67
Accords Pr.87
Accosté S.30
Accroissement S.58
Accusé IV.10, IV.91, Pr.19
Accusera VI.37
Ache VII.18
Acheptees VIII.20
Aches IX.40
Acheve I.25, I.38
Achiles VII.1
Acité I.24
Acompaigné I.9
Aconile IV.71

Aconite IV.71
Acord I.11
Acquerra S.40
Acre III.26
Acte V.44, Pr.20
Actions Pr.108
Acueil VIII.74
Acueil(l)ir II.64
Adaluncatif X.96
Adeerant IV.87
Adherans III.80, X.76-7
Adherant IV.87, VII.21
Adorée II.87
Adjoignant II.22
Adjutoire VIII.85
Admet II.80
Admiree S.44
Adresser IV.70
Adrian VIII.86
Adric V.27, Pr.12-13
Aduché VIII.36
Adultere VI.59, VIII.14, VIII.63
Adulteres X.10
Adulterine VIII.70
Adust IV.67
Aduste II.81, VI.92
Advance V.32, X.64
A(d)venir I.14, Pr.91
Advent IX.44
Adversaire I.36, III.1, III.15, IV.65, VI.75, IV.92, VIII.59
Adversaires X.77
Advertir V.83, VIII.22, X.62
Advertira V.57
Adverty VII.37
A(d)viendra I.43, I.46, II.35, Pr.84
A(d)vienne I.43, S.39
Advis IX.47, Pr.76
Advisé VIII.58
Aeles VIII.52
Aelles I.6
Aemathien IX.38, X.7, X.58
Aemathion IX.64
Aemulateur V.79
Aenigmatique V.7
Aenobarbe V.45, V.59
Aër VI.27
(A)erain I.1, I.74, II.15, V.19, V.41, VII.25
Aesle III.52
Aesles V.79, X.95
Affaire II.76, V.65, IX.89, S.9, S.22
Affamez VI.69
Affliction I.91, V.48
Afflicts Pr.62
Affligé V.19, S.23, S.26
Affligee S.42
Affligez IX.98, S.54
Afflit I.91
Affoiblie S.51
Affoiblis Pr.87
Affolé Pr.92
Affolée Pr.129
Affollee VI.10
Affoulé Pr.92
Affrique IV.68, V.11, V.23, V.48, V.69
Affublés IV.98
Agassas VIII.1
Agath IV.94
Agde IV.94, VIII.21
Agen IV.72, IX.38, IX.85
Agennois VII.12
Agine I.79
Agiter IX.32
Agora IX.62
Ag(g)ripine III.53, VI.4
Agrippe VI.91
Agur V.6
Aide III.7, III.87
Aidera I.93
Aigle I.23, I.31, I.38, II.44, II.85, III.37, III.52, IV.70, V.42, VI.46, VI.78, VIII.4, VIII.8-9, VIII.46, X.27

Aigles VI.71
Aigre III.99
Aiguière X.15
Ainés VI.11
Ains I.10, I.25
Ainsi S.39
Air I.55, II.86, III.44, IV.67, VIII.58, IX.83, X.71, Pr.36, Pr.62
Airain Pr.3
Aise Pr.15
Aisez VIII.17, Pr.43
Aisles VIII.96
Aisnay VI.95
Aisné IV.87, IV.94, IV.99, V.45, VI.91, VII.38, VII.42
Aisnee IV.96
Aistra I.78
Ait VI.71
Aix I.71, II.88, IV.86, IV.76
Alabrox IX.88
Alaine X.59
Alane V.54
Al(l)arme S.42
Alarmes S.32
Albanins VIII.40
Albannois VIII.94
Albanois IV.98, V.46, V.91, Pr.54
Albe VI.68, VII.29, IX.22
Albi X.5
Albinge VI.62
Albissola IX.39
Albois V.82
Alee X.68
Alegre X.38, Pr.104
Alegres Pr.74
Alegro V.27
Alein III.99
Alema(i)gne III.78, IV.94
Alentour III.43, V.7
Aleph X.96
Ales S.11
Alez S.11
Aliance S.57
Aliter VI.100
Al(l)ant I.65, X.35
Allé Pr.141
Allegués II.47
Allemaignes X.51
Aller Pr.20, Pr.84
Alles X.69
Alliance V.4, Pr.35, Pr.51, S.1, S.49
Alliances Pr.57, S.58
Allobroges VII.31
Allobrox IV.42, Pr.51
Allumée Pr.52
Allumelle IV.35
Allumer S.21
Allumeurs S.36
Almatie IX.60
Alors II.62, V.16, VI.22, S.46
Aloy X.72
Aloys I.40
Alpes III.33, III.39, V.20, V.68, VI.28, VII.20, VII.31
Altesse S.47
Alumant S.30, S.50
Alus VI.33
Amant I.42, VIII.25
Amas I.61, IV.82, VI.1, VI.28
Amassés III.8
Amateur VIII.23
Ambassade IX.41, Pr.134, Pr.141, S.7
Ambassadeur II.21, IX.16, S.8, S.10
Ambassadeurs I.85, VII.20
Ambellon X.69
Ambigue I.34
Ambition VI.62, VI.93, Pr.20
Amboise VIII.52
Ambraxie IX.75
Ame II.13, III.2, IV.24, V.22, VI.71, VI.80, VIII.25, VIII.70, Pr.1, Pr.39, Pr.69, S.52, S.55

Amecon III.21
Amée Pr.3
Amender IV.17
Amené X.54
Amenee IX.96, X.29
Amenez IX.61
Amer X.88
Amere VII.11
Americh X.66
Amertume IX.41, X.97
Ames IX.54
Ami VIII.44
Amifere VIII.61
Amis II.89, III.33, III.69, VII.22, Pr.133, Pr.135, Pr.141
Amitié I.99
Amitiez Pr.31
Amortie Pr.106
Amortis II.35
Amour VI.89, VIII.13, VIII.25, VIII.67, X.38, X.46, Pr.67, Pr.132, S.44
Amours VII.9, S.44
Amphipolle IX.91
Ample VIII.62, IX.71
Amplement S.42
Amuses Pr.11
Amy III.55, V.9, VI.52, VIII.44, VIII.83, Pr.5, S.24
Amye S.6
Amys VII.33, VIII.70, X.20, X.85
An I.47, I.49, II.39, III.55, III.77, IV.43, IV.67-8, IV.84, IV.86, IV.97, V.50, V.87, VI.2, VI.26, VI.54, VIII.71, IX.4, IX.55, X.3, X.32, X.72, X.91, 2047, Pr.58, Pr.61, Pr.92, Pr.105, S.17, S.19, S.21, S.26, S.28
Anatheme IX.57
Ancienne III.37
Ancone I.75, VIII.9
Ancon(n)e II.74, III.43
Anconnois VII.4
Androgyn II.45
Androgyns Pr.74
Andronne VI.17
Aneanty X.20
Aneau VII.23
Anes X.31
Ang. III.51
Ange I.56, VIII.69
Ang(i)ers III.51
Angiers I.20
Anglaquitaine IX.6
Angleterre III.70, V.51, VIII.76, X.100, S.50, S.54
Anglican VIII.58
Anglicque X.56
Anglique X.42
Anglois III.9, III.16, III.80, IV.54, V.34, V.59, V.93, VI.12, IX.6, IX.38
Angloise V.35
Anglois VIII.60
Angolesme X.17
Angolmois X.72
Angon I.90
Anichiler Pr.71
Animal II.44
Animaux II.40, IX.71, X.13
Année Pr.3
Annees X.89
Annemarc IX.33
Annibal II.30, Pr.11
Annibalique III.93
Annichilez VIII.77
Anninite II.15
Ans I.17, I.31, I.48, I.58, II.9, III.42, III.57, III.94, IV.7, IV.95-6, V.78, V.92, VI.63, VI.75, VII.13, VII.15, VIII.13, VIII.69, VIII.77, VIII.88, IX.89, X.4, X.15, X.32, X.36, X.100, S.3, S.42, S.44, S.47, S.51, S.53
Antechrist VIII.77, X.66

Ant(h)enne II.2, IV.92
Antenoree VI.76
Anthoine IX.91
Anthoni IX.86
Antibe X.23
Antibes X.13, X.87
Antibol III.82
Anticipé V.9
Antioche I.74
Antiopolique X.13
Antipolles X.87
Antiq Pr.48
Antique I.45, II.12, II.50-51, III.37, V.39, V.41, V.47, V.49, VI.76, VIII.66, IX.22
Antiques I.69, V.66, VI.99, VII.14
Antoine IV.88
Antropophage II.75, S.33
Anvers IX.49, X.52, Pr.17
(A)ornement III.94
Apaiser IV.10
Apamé IX.95
Aparoistra I.17
Apast Pr.100
Apennines III.39, III.43
Apennis II.29, V.61
Apens S.45
Aperceu I.17, I.64, II.6, VIII.68
Apopletique III.36
Apouvrie VI.8
Appaisé Pr.37
Appaiser II.29
Apparante VII.6
Apparence I.91, VI.30
Apparente II.43
Apparoir II.41
Apparoissant II.5, IV.33
Apparoistra III.21, VI.6, VI.44, VI.61, VI.66, VIII.4-5, VIII.12, X.74-5
Apparoistre X.6, Pr.95
Appenins II.29
Ap(p)erceu III.41
Appert Pr.16
Apportera IV.20
Appraroistra III.21
Apprest S.4
Ap(p)reste III.10, VIII.50, X.7, Pr.60
Apprester Pr.4, Pr.62, S.29
Appresteront Pr.106
Approchans III.76
Ap(p)rochant III.76, Pr.64
Ap(p)roche I.16, I.56, III.87, IV.82, V.32, VI.96, VIII.76, IX.52, X.65, Pr.43, Pr.81, Pr.113, Pr.135, Pr.137
Ap(p)rocher I.67, II.97, III.18
Ap(p)rochera III.32
Appropriant V.53
Approucher VI.97
Approuchera X.80
Approuvée Pr.51
Ap(p)uy III.67, VI.8
Apres I.24, I.28, I.30, I.46, I.66, I.69, I.74, II.23, II.31, II.40, II.46, II.54, II.80-81, II.87, III.1, III.18, III.42, III.44, III.54, III.65, III.86, III.95, IV.1, IV.6, IV.30, IV.36, IV.56, IV.65, IV.77, IV.84, IV.86, V.4, V.37, V.48, V.92, VI.17, VI.24, VI.38, VI.70, VI.75, VII.82-3, VI.86, VI.90, VII.3, VII.18, VII.30, VIII.13, VIII.28, VIII.34, VIII.41, VIII.51, VIII.59, VIII.88, IX.6, IX.8, IX.26, IX.84, IX.99, X.3-4, X.19, X.22, X.36, X.72, X.76, X.92, Pr.72, Pr.99, Pr.133, S.3-4, S.12-14, S.16-17, S.20-21, S.33, S.44-5, S.50-51, S.54-5, S.57
Apreste II.46, III.18, IX.55, Pr.11
Aprests VIII.84
Apretz V.15

Aprins IV.87
Aproche I.8, III.46, VII.30, Pr.43
Aprochera IV.91
Aproches III.87
Apuy II.59, III.57
Apvril I.80
Aquatique I.29, I.50, III.21
Aqueduct V.58, V.66, VIII.68, X.89
Aquilee V.99
Aquillee IV.69
Aquillon VIII.85
Aquilloye I.58, V.99
Aquilon II.68, I.91, VIII.15, IX.99, X.69, X.86, Pr.8, Pr.26, Pr.34
Aquilonaire I.49, VIII.81
Aquin VII.31
Aquitaine II.1, IV.74
Aquitanique III.32, III.83
Ara Pr.103
Arabe III.27, III.31, IV.39, V.25, V.27, V.47, X.63
Arabes V.73, VI.54, IX.89, X.62
Arabesque VI.55
Arabie V.55
Arabiq VI.44
Arabique V.74
Araby S.34
Araigner VI.84
Arain X.80
Arant IX.74
Araxes III.31
Arbissel IX.39
Arbois V.82
Arbon VI.56
Arbre II.70, III.11, III.91, Pr.85
Arbres II.7, II.31, Pr.114, Pr.125
Arbresle IX.69
Arbrisseaux Pr.114
Arby S.34
Arc II.65, II.77, IV.27, VII.1, X.23
Arche III.13
Archeduc V.58
Arcs II.77, X.30
Arcz III.40, IV.47
Ardant II.96, VI.58, VIII.80, X.35
Ardante IV.59, V.66, X.70, Pr.52
Ardente IX.9, Pr.122
Ardeur IV.67, Pr.53
Ardoir IX.53
Ardoise VII.39
Ardra VI.35, Pr.18, Pr.28
Ards VIII.3
Arduenne V.45
Arduer V.45
Are I.19
Arethusa I.87
Aretin II.12
Argel I.73
Argent I.53, III.3, III.13, VI.9, VII.25, VIII.14, VIII.28, IX.12, Pr.5, Pr.33, S.2
Argille I.21, IX.12
Argilleuse I.21
Aride I.17
Aries I.51, III.57, III.77, VI.35
Arimin IX.2
Aripine VI.4
Aristocratique V.67
Arles I.71, VII.2, VIII.68, X.93-4
Arme II.85, VIII.100
Armée II.72, III.81, III.88, IV.62-3, IV.78, IV.91, V.20, V.22, V.44, V.57, VI.56, VI.75, VII.16, VII.39, VIII.79, IX.43, IX.86, IX.96, X.4, X.8, X.23, X.38, X.68, Pr.3, S.29
Armées I.75, S.15
Armenie III.31, V.50, V.54, V.94
Armes I.78, II.85, III.6, III.11, IV.43, V.27, VIII.57-8, IX.81,

Bresle IX.69
Bressans X.59
Bresse I.6, V.82, VII.31
Bretagne III.70
Bretaigne VI.53, X.26
Breteuil VIII.5
Breton IX.7
Bretons III.9, IX.58-9
Breuvage VIII.13
Brigue II.100, V.51, V.80, X.5, Pr.37
Briller S.15, S.27
Brindis V.99
Brique II.100, IV.55, X.89
Brisanne X.25
Brises I.65
Britanique V.99, VI.7
Britaniques II.1
Britanne X.7, X.25
Britannique III.57, IV.96, V.34, VI.41, VIII.58, X.40
Broche I.74, VII.28
Brodde III.92
Brodes IV.3, VIII.34
Bru II.50
Bruceles IX.49
Brucelles II.15, II.50, IV.81, VI.47
Bruge VIII.49
Bruges V.94
Bruict I.64
Bruine IV.46, V.35, IX.100
Bruit I.76, I.95, II.44, II.70, II.85, II.91, III.35, IV.28, V.1, VI.50, VI.70, VII.41, X.13, Pr.12, Pr.29-30, Pr.33, Pr.94, Pr.103, Pr.112, Pr.118, Pr.122, Pr.129
Bruits Pr.26, Pr.120-21
Brule Pr.17
Brume X.9, Pr.22
Brumes Pr.130
Brundis V.99, VII.31
Brune X.9
Brunsuic X.46
Brusler III.17, VIII.11
Bruslera II.41, IV.23, VI.97, VIII.79
Bruslés II.51
Bruslez VI.17
Brutale Pr.123
Brute I.12
Brutes I.64
Bruxelles X.54
Bruyne II.83, VII.37, VIII.26
Bruynes VI.27
Bruyneux VI.25
Bruyt VII.41
Bude X.62
Bueyre VIII.18
Buffalorre VIII.12
Bugie VI.54
Bulles Pr.102
Bully IX.69
Burançoys IX.13
Bureau VI.65
Buriné V.66
Butin III.12, V.21, V.57
Butins I.83
Buy Pr.15
Buysson X.69
Buzançoys IX.13

Cable IV.84, Pr.72
Caché I.19, I.25, I.27, I.84, II.17, IV.29, V.8, V.28, V.34, X.29, Pr.103, S.19
Cachée IV.33
Cachées I.41
Cacher X.33
Cachera X.2
Cachés II.47-8, V.65, VI.27, VI.35
Cachez VIII.23, IX.54, IX.70
Caepion III.29
Cage IX.95, S.20
Caiché VI.37, VII.75
Caichez IX.68-9, X.13
Caige I.10, I.35, II.24, III.10, IX.47
Cailhau IV.44
Cainct VII.27
Caindra VI.1
Caindre VI.33, VI.75
Calais VIII.45, IX.29, IX.88

Calamité II.65, III.10, VI.96
Calamiteuse VI.24
Calamitez IX.63
Calcine IV.23
Calpre I.77, III.78
Calumnié VII.95
Cambray X.45
Cameleons S.36
Camp II.17, II.22, II.24, II.26, III.99, IV.9-10, IV.12-13, IV.41, V.85, VI.99, IX.10, IX.56, Pr.22
Campa(i)gne II.84, S.6
Campane I.90
Campanie II.31
Campano IV.44
Camps V.4
Cancer V.98, VI.4, VI.6, VI.24, VI.35, VIII.48, X.67
Canine IV.15
Canon II.75, III.84, IX.14
Canons III.37, IX.28, S.3
CANTIO VI.100
Canton VIII.5
Cantons IX.70, X.51
Cap VII.37, IX.20, IX.30, IX.64
Capadille VIII.50
Cape Pr.13, Pr.76
Caper II.35, X.67
Capion VIII.29
Capitaine IV.83, IV.92, VII.9, VII.28, IX.90
Capitole VI.13
Capitolin IX.32
Capne I.99
Cappe II.69, IV.11, V.78, VIII.19, IX.26
Capres IX.26
Capricorne VI.15
Caprine X.29
Captif II.66, III.66, III.76, III.78, III.83, IV.34, IV.38, V.9, V.15, V.70, VI.32, VI.54, VI.91, VII.29, VII.34, VIII.92, IX.92, X.24, X.29, X.85, X.97, Pr.80
Captifs/z VIII.77, IX.36, X.1, Pr.15, Pr.36, Pr.79, Pr.81, Pr.84
Captive IV.41, V.14
Captifz I.14, I.24, I.72, I.92, II.20, II.79, III.13, III.48, III.78, III.87, IV.42, V.97, VI.49, VI.85, VIII.63
Capti(f)ve VI.58, VII.18, IX.78, X.42, X.54, Pr.69
Captiver Pr.46
Captivité I.65, III.10
Capua V.99
Capue V.99, V.60
Caques VIII.55
Carcare IX.39
Carcari IX.39
Carcas I.5, IX.100, IX.10, X.5
Carcassonne III.62, VIII.67, IX.71
Cardinal IV.4, VIII.68
Caresme S.28
Caresse Pr.41
Caresses VI.83
Carmanie X.31
Carne IX.46
Caron VIII.26
Carpen V.76
Carpentra IX.41
Carpentras V.76
Carte I.39
Cas I.43, II.55, II.76, II.92, IV.11, VII.16, Pr.41, Pr.107
Casane VII.32
Case IX.4
Caspre VII.10
Casques VIII.55
Cassé VIII.8, Pr.14, Pr.105
Cassée Pr.53
Cassera IX.25, Pr.3
Cassés II.77
Cassich IX.31
Cassilin II.31
Castallon VIII.48
Caste V.52
Castel IX.16
Castillon X.9
Castor II.15, II.90
Castre S.52
Castres IV.44, X.5
Castulon I.31, I.93
Catarrhe Pr.78
Catarrhes Pr.131

Catherine S.1
Caton VIII.26
Cause I.46, IV.39, V.85, VI.73, VIII.18, VIII.73, IX.20, Pr.112
Caussade X.41
Cautelleux IX.86
Cavaillon V.76
Cavalerie VII.27, Pr.59
Cave V.10, VI.73, VII.32, VIII.66
Cavees X.49
Caverne V.10
Cavilleux Pr.58
Caylus X.41
Cecile II.71
Cecy S.28
Cedera S.37
Ceiulee IX.73
Cela IV.1, Pr.4, Pr.11
Celé II.78
Celebrer Pr.110
Celebrera I.58, V.18
Celebreront X.55
Celeste I.80, IV.100, S.27
Celestes II.16, IV.18
Celin VIII.31
Celique III.2, VI.22
Celiques III.7
Celle VII.5, VIII.60
Celles S.15
Celtes I.93, II.71
Celtique II.69, II.72, II.85, II.99, III.83, IV.63, V.1, V.10, V.99, VI.3-4, VI.28, VI.53, VI.60
Celtiques IV.4, VI.99
Celuy I.66, I.96, II.98, III.30, III.94, IV.11, IV.43, V.17, V.82, VI.57, VI.71, VII.2, VII.54, VII.11, VII.36, VIII.71, IX.34, X.72, X.91, X.100, S.11-14, S.16, S.18-19, S.21, S.23-6, S.28-9, S.38, S.42, S.44, S.53-4
Censuart S.9
Censuarts S.2
Censunto VI.100
Censurez VIII.71
Cent II.62, III.56, III.57, IV.16, VI.5, VI.41, VI.49, IX.67, X.90, Pr.105
Centre I.87
Centres IX.99
Cents III.77
Cercueil VIII.5
Ceres Pr.31
Cerf V.4
Certain S.28
Cerulee IX.73
Cerveau I.11, IV.31
Cervoise VII.34
Ces IV.25
Cesarées I.33
Cessée I.70, Pr.53
Cesser IX.66, Pr.127, Pr.129
Cessera II.53
Cest IV.90, Pr.105
Ceucalion II.81
Cévennes I.64
Cha(a)lon III.69
Chacun VIII.30, X.32, Pr.91, S.48
Chaine I.27, III.79, IX.56
Chaines I.65, II.21, VII.24
Chair VI.32, VI.56, IV.90, V.16, VIII.18
Chaisne III.79
Chaisnes IV.84
Chaldondon VIII.48
Chaleur II.3, Pr.41
Chalmé VI.55
Chalon I.22
Chalons IV.17
Chambery X.37
Chambry X.37
Chameau IV.85, V.68
Champ I.23, I.35, I.43, V.5, V.91, VIII.72, X.70
Champagne II.84
C(h)ampaigne II.84, III.52, IV.36
Champs I.78, II.19, II.31, II.95, III.31, III.99, V.30, V.64,

VIII.91, IX.97, Pr.29, Pr.42, Pr.61, Pr.72, Pr.121, S.14, S.25, S.42
Chance Pr.73, Pr.101
Chancelier S.25
Chandelles S.36
Change I.56, I.96, II.10, II.83, II.90, III.46, III.49, III.93, IV.14, IV.16, IV.21, VI.2, VI.8, VI.50, VIII.81, IX.47, IX.64, Pr.93, Pr.107, Pr.115
Changeant I.8, I.40, IX.57, X.36
Changée I.72, II.66
Changees III.36
Changemens IX.63
Changement I.20, I.40, I.43, I.59, III.19, IV.21, IX.66, Pr.93, Pr.95, Pr.108
Changements Pr.116
Changer III.57, IV.17, V.6, VI.17, VII.17, VIII.97, X.64, Pr.47, Pr.49
Changera II.41, III.15, IV.21, V.11, VI.4, IX.1, VI.44, X.64, Pr.88
Changeront II.60, V.26, V.92
Changés I.96, VI.20, Pr.111
Changez V.77, Pr.68
Chanignon IX.41
Chansons I.14
Chant I.64, VI.54
Chanter Pr.56
Chantz I.14
Chanu IX.1
Chapeaux V.46
Chapelle VIII.20
Char X.64, Pr.35
Charbon IV.85
Charge I.96, V.60, V.71, VI.13, VIII.68, VIII.87, X.15
Charient X.52
Chariots IX.93
Charlieu III.29
Charlus X.41
Charon S.28, S.48
Charpin I.80
Chartres III.49, IV.61, IX.86
Chartreux X.14
Chascun II.11, II.29, III.98, VI.61, S.13
Chassant II.8, IV.4
Chassé IV.12, IV.21, IV.77, IV.84-5, V.4, V.80, VI.61, VIII.8, VIII.15, VIII.59, IX.8, IX.25, X.22, X.76, Pr.21
Chassée II.44
Chasser IV.70, VI.49, VII.13
Chassera II.67, III.17, V.13, V.74, VI.87, VII.21
Chasseront III.9
Chassés I.5, IV.18, IV.69, IV.94
Chassez IV.52, VIII.71, X.30, Pr.55-6
Chasteau II.93, VIII.3, IX.67
Chasteaux S.35, S.43
Chastier II.12
Chastiera II.12
Châteauneuf IX.67
Chatres IV.61
Chatz II.42
Chau IV.52
Chaulderons IX.14
Chauls X.99
Chault IV.67
Chaulveron X.76
Chausses X.9
Chaut Pr.34
Chaux IV.52

Chefs III.12, IX.4, Pr.28
Cheirenesse III.68
Chemin I.7, II.21, III.72, VIII.44, VIII.51, X.49
Cheminees IX.53
Chemins X.79
Chemise V.73, VIII.37, X.1
Chenu IX.1
Cheoir IX.9
Cher I.44, I.60, VIII.94
Cheramon IX.62
Cherchant I.42, V.7, IX.12, IX.56, IX.97
Cherchera IV.57, S.20
Chere V.22
Cherra II.9, II.39, II.51, V.81, VI.37, VIII.37, X.99, Pr.36
Cherron(n)esse III.68, V.90
Cherrouesse V.90
Chersonnez IX.91
Cherté III.5, III.34
Cheval I.77, I.86, VIII.72, X.34, X.88, Pr.77
Chevalier III.53, VIII.6
Chevance VII.64, Pr.119
Chevau(l)x IX.23, V.91, VII.7, VIII.89
Chevaux III.6
Chevelue II.43, V.9, VI.6
Cheveu(l)x III.83
Chief I.58, II.54, VII.39, X.5, X.92
Chiefz VIII.42
Chien Pr.18
Chiens II.42, IV.93
Chio VI.55
Chivaz VIII.8
Choina IV.32
Choir VIII.7
Choses VIII.43, VIII.53
Chrestien IV.77
Chrestienté I.53, Pr.83
Christ VI.18, Pr.83
Chyren II.79, IV.34, VI.70, VIII.54, IX.41
Ciclades III.64
Cicle I.62
Cicles IX.72
Ciel I.23-4, I.27, I.46, I.55-7, I.63-4, I.91, I.98, I.100, II.18, II.27, II.29, II.43, II.45-6, II.56, II.70, II.81, II.85, II.92, II.96, III.2, III.7, III.11, III.16-18, III.46, IV.29, IV.43, IV.49-50, IV.93, V.32, V.98, V.100, V.97, VII.36, VIII.2, VIII.10, IX.44, IX.57, IX.83, X.72, Pr.9, Pr.11, Pr.13, Pr.16-17, Pr.28, Pr.33, Pr.47, Pr.53, Pr.73, Pr.98, Pr.112, S.32, S.44, S.55
Cierge VI.33, VIII.5, VIII.80
Cieulx VI.2, VI.70
Cil S.22
Cimbes VIII.89
Cimbres II.44, III.8
Cinq I.73, I.98, III.45, III.94, IV.26, V.92, VI.2, VII.27, VII.97, VII.11, VII.26, VIII.38, IX.15, IX.34, X.3, X.59, Pr.7, Pr.9, Pr.102, S.3, S.12, S.14, S.16, S.18-19, S.44
Cinquante X.89
Cinquieme X.27
Cinquiesme VIII.88, S.38
Cipres V.17, VI.53
Circonder V.87
Circonvoisins V.85
Circuir I.19
Circuit II.88
Circundé V.87
Cire I.44
Cita IX.61
Citadins III.6, IV.69, VII.19, VIII.74, X.81
Cité I.5, I.8, I.24, I.33, I.41, I.87, II.4, II.26, II.53-4, I.66, II.81, II.90, II.97, III.11, III.13, III.22, III.33, III.36, III.46, III.50, III.79, III.81, III.84-5, IV.1, IV.8, IV.16, IV.21, IV.52, IV.69, IV.80, IV.82, V.4-5, V.8, V.12, V.30, V.33, V.35, V.81, V.84, V.86, V.97, VI.4, VI.48, VI.55, VI.73, VI.76, VI.80, VI.85, VI.92, VI.96-8, VII.13, VII.15, VII.22, VIII.17, IX.48,

IX.74, IX.82, IX.92, IX.96, X.13, X.49-50, X.63, X.68, Pr.19-22, Pr.34, Pr.42, S.42, S.52
Citera Pr.117
Cités I.20, II.6, III.12, V.76, VI.35
Citez Pr.7, Pr.12
Citoyens VII.22, X.59, X.68
Ciutad IV.26
Civil IX.66
Civiles III.63
Civille IV.78
Clade IV.5
Clair VI.58
Claire I.80, X.98
Clairs III.46
Clam IX.96
Clamé VI.78, IX.59
Clamée I.92
Clarté II.91, III.94, IV.48, VIII.6
Classe I.9, I.73, I.75, I.77, I.90, II.5, II.22, II.59-60, II.64, II.86, II.99, III.13, III.64, III.87, III.90, IV.2, IV.5, IV.23, IV.37, IV.92, V.8, V.23, V.34-5, V.48, VI.44-5, VI.64, VI.75, VII.33, VII.37, VIII.13, IX.32, IX.42, IX.79, X.2, X.68, X.77, Pr.5, Pr.11-12, Pr.31
Classes I.35, V.2, VI.77
Claude VII.84
Clause IX.86
Clef X.27
Clemence VII.17
Clement X.27
Clerc VIII.95, VIII.98, Pr.107
Clercz V.15
Clere IX.18, S.15
Clergé X.73, X.91
Clers III.46
Climat I.55, III.77
Climaterique V.98
Cloistres IX.24
Clos II.12, III.6, X.17
Close III.62, V.96, IX.86, Pr.22
Closture X.42
Cloz IX.27
Coche X.65
Coeur/cueur I.9, I.11, III.15-16, III.76, IV.5, V.21, V.73, V.1, V.74, VI.81, VII.34, VIII.25, IX.73, S.23
Coeurs I.5
Coffre Pr.13
Coffres VIII.23
Congneu VI.59, VIII.14, X.22, X.83, Pr.38, Pr.70
Congnoissace VII.17
Congnoissance VII.17
Congnoistra X.57
Congnoistre S.20
Coin VII.56
Coing I.49, III.32, IX.65, S.43
Col IV.47
Coleur II.92
Colier V.67
Colisée X.6
Coller IV.58
Collet VIII.82
Colleur VIII.54
Collisse VII.80
Collon IX.32
Collonne VIII.67
Cologne V.94, VI.40
Colomne X.64
Colomnes X.93
Colonge V.43
Colongna VIII.51
Colonna IX.2
Colonne V.51
Colonnes I.82
Coloree IX.100
Colorez Pr.74
Colosse X.6
Columna IX.2
Combat I.14, II.34, III.1, IV.5, IX.83, VII.7, X.37, Pr.23
Combatans III.7
Combatre I.23, IV.75
Combats VIII.59, S.51
Combattra S.40
Combatu VII.19, S.51
Combien I.8, II.2, I.23, VII.99, S.38

VIII.29, VIII.91, IX.3-4, IX.82, X.50, Pr.21, Pr.94, Pr.100
Deluges I.17
Demandé X.40, S.12
Demander IX.45
Demanderont IV.39
Demeurance IX.64
Demeure II.71, S.53
Demeurera X.53
Demi III.80
Demie VI.65
Demipler IV.98
Demiples IV.98
Demis II.3, II.89, Pr.59, Pr.65, Pr.90
Demolue V.9
Demoly X.80
Démon I.42
Demoura VI.88
Demoureee VI.63
Demourer VII.35
Demourra II.4, III.84
Demouura V.75
Demy I.25, I.64, III.69, vI.61, VIII.25, IX.31, X.28, X.42, Pr.104, Pr.128, S.27, S.52
Dend II.58
Denier V.2
Denis IX.24, Pr.125
Den(t)s II.7, III.42
Denys Pr.11
Depart I.81
Dépesche Pr.16
Deplaisant II.20
Deploration Pr.117
Deplore Pr.32
Deplore X.96
Depopuler III.8
Depopulez Pr.29
Deportés I.59, II.7
Deprimee X.28
Depuis II.4, III.56
Dernier II.55, II.82, III.92, III.100, IV.88, V.2, VIII.38, IX.99, X.82, Pr.90, S.48
Derniere IV.64, VI.33, Pr.51
Derrier II.50, II.61, IX.39
Desarmé VIII.68
Desarroy IV.22, IV.49
Desborderont X.6
Descassé V.4
Descend II.33
Descendre IX.43, IX.88
Descendu VII.5
Deschassé V.4
Deschassee V.22, VI.74
Deschassera VI.80
Deschassez X.76
Desconfit VIII.94
Desconfiture V.93
Descorte IX.35
Descourant VII.99
Descouvers VIII.26, VIII.56, IX.13, X.59, X.61
Descouvert VII.28, IV.30, IV.62, VIII.28, Pr.70, Pr.139, S.9
Descouverte II.68, VI.55, VIII.66, X.33, Pr.93
Descouvertz IX.4
Descouvrant VI.96
Descouvrira X.50
Descouvriront II.14
Descouvrissant S.22
Descries VI.23
Descroissance X.70
Descroissante S.4
Desdeigneront X.55
Deser VII.27
Desers VI.82
Desert VII.20, VIII.27
Deserte VI.55
Desertes VI.48
Deserteur VII.65
Desesperez IX.97
Desespoir VI.82, VI.34, VIII.64
Desflotez V.95
Deshonneur VIII.14
Deshonore I.25
Desir Pr.67
Desiree S.44
Desiroit VI.31
Desjoinct V.23
Deslie I.40
Deslivrer X.85
Desloial X.73
Desloyal II.58, VI.45

Desloyale I.12
Desloyauté Pr.9
Desmerites X.77
Desmis VIII.17
Desniant X.15
Desniee IX.86
Desniera IX.77
Desnieront IX.16
Desnuees V.85
Desolation VIII.81
Desolé III.93, V.45, VI.88, Pr.97
Desolée II.4, III.84, IV.82, Pr.129
Desordre VI.32
Despartir II.34
Despendre VI.41, S.2
Despit VIII.63, X.21, Pr.39, Pr.91
Despolle VIII.47
Despote VIII.47
Despuis V.13
Desrobé X.16
Desroutte S.46
Dessoubz I.27, IV.26, VI.15, VI.24, IX.32, X.11, X.90
Dessous X.59, Pr.48, S.3
Dessouz IX.23, IX.46
Dessus II.27, II.85, II.87, IV.18, VI.15, X.60, Pr.26, Pr.46, Pr.55, S.3, S.50
Destitué I.6
Destornay IX.88
Destorné VIII.5
Destorner VIII.44
Destranchés VII.45
Destre VIII.56
Destresse II.82
Destrois VIII.46
Destruicte VI.85
Destruire I.96, IV.24, V.84
Desvoyé VI.46
Detenus IX.15
Determine III.97
Deterrés VII.41
Detrencher V.33
Detrenchés IV.81
Detresse IV.9, V.98
Detriment I.4
Deu V.70
Deucalion II.81, X.6, Pr.90
Deuil X.58, S.55
Deuils Pr.57
Deul Pr.82, Pr.86, Pr.88
Deuls Pr.57, Pr.82
Deux I.6, I.15, I.22, I.28, I.35, I.37, I.52, I.54, I.58-9, I.75, I.77, I.85, I.87, I.99, Pr.6-7, II.18, II.35, II.41, II.52, II.89, II.97, III.5, III.12-13, III.16, III.29, III.31, III.42, III.57, III.98-9, IV.44, IV.57, IV.59-60, IV.68, IV.90, IV.94-5, V.1-2, V.22-3, V.45, V.48, V.57, V.78, V.80, V.86, VI.10-11, VI.33, VI.47, VI.58, VI.62, VI.65, VI.77, VII.89, VII.98, VII.5, VII.26, VII.33, VII.36, VII.42, VIII.13, VIII.15, VIII.25, VIII.30, VIII.43, VIII.46, VIII.55, VIII.59, VIII.64, VIII.69, VIII.83, VIII.91, IX.2-4, IX.13, IX.20, IX.24, IX.40, IX.56, IX.72, IX.76, X.7, X.18, X.32, X.39, X.54, X.63, X.93, X.96, Pr.30-31, Pr.44, Pr.48, Pr.60, Pr.62, Pr.115, Pr.118-20, Pr.133, Pr.138, S.1, S.9, S.11-12, S.17, S.26, S.37, S.55-6, S.58
Devastant III.54
Devenir Pr.79
Devenu III.58
Devenuz IV.16
Devers III.92, V.25, V.59, VI.32
Deviendra IV.48, IV.74, VI.22
Deviendront II.36, VI.8
Deviendu V.22
Devis Pr.116
Devoir X.32, Pr.70
Devorateurs VI.66
Devorera II.37
Dextre IX.69, V.75
Dez III.40
Diabolique I.42
Dial V.77

Diane II.28, IX.12
Dict III.68, V.56
Diete Pr.47-8
Dieu I.25, I.51, I.6, V.73, VII.36, VIII.100, IX.83, Pr.141, S.8, S.35, S.40
Dieux I.91, II.30, IV.55, VII.12, VIII.78
Different II.54, IV.87
Differente Pr.27
Difficil Pr.77
Difficile IV.21
Difforme V.97
Digne Pr.91
Dignes Pr.87
Dignité VI.40
Dijon IV.17, Pr.10
Diminuant IV.25
Diminue I.63
Diphlongue X.33
Diphtongue X.33
Dira I.12, I.76, I.95, II.2, III.3, IV.68, X.4, X.7, Pr.71, S.22
Dire II.30, III.24, V.60, V.96, VI.59, IX.92, Pr.112, S.37, S.46
Diront I.60, VIII.42
Dis VIII.15
Disant VI.73, VI.94
Disat VI.94
Discernera X.76
Disciples IV.31
Discord I.57, X.39, Pr.21, Pr.94, S.37
Discorde I.18, I.69, VI.3, VIII.67, Pr.26, Pr.93, Pr.107, Pr.117, Pr.123, Pr.131
Diserte VI.48
Disgrace IX.71
Disme III.76
Disperue VI.6
Dissensions Pr.95
Dissention II.95
Dissimulant I.40
Dissimulé Pr.68
Dissimulee VII.21
Dissimulés VII.2
Distant III.4, VI.67
Distillante Pr.102
Distraire S.24
Dit V.91, IX.14
Dits Pr.135
Diurne I.26
Divers II.20, III.29, IV.66, VI.17, Pr.27, Pr.93, Pr.118, Pr.131
Diverses III.76, V.63
Divin I.2, I.88, II.13, II.27, III.2, IV.5, VII.36, Pr.1
Divine I.2, IV.24, VI.72
Divins I.14, IV.43, Pr.46
Divisé I.81, V.21, VIII.58
Divisee V.80
Divisees IX.97
Divisera I.83
Divisés I.78
Divisez Pr.42
Division II.95
Divorce X.22, Pr.17, Pr.92
Dix I.42, V.71, VII.31, VII.37, IX.43, X.2, Pr.62, S.23, S.26, S.42, S.44
Dixhuict X.39
Dixneufiesme S.38
Dixsept V.92, VI.59, S.19
Docte VI.99
Doctrine VI.72
Dogmion VIII.44
Doibt IX.5
Dois III.24
Doit VIII.44, IX.7
Dole I.100, IV.42
Doleance VIII.98
Doleances X.23
Dolle IV.42, V.82, VI.47, VII.4
Domaine II.54
Domestique III.44
Domicile Pr.47
Dominateur V.93
Dominees S.43
Don III.90, IV.26, VIII.61, Pr.134, Pr.137, Pr.141
Donnant VIII.94, IX.59
Donné II.32, III.22, III.48, III.85, IV.1, V.36, VI.79, VII.8, IX.29, X.83, Pr.3, Pr.134, S.31, S.45

Donnee VI.18, VIII.87
Donner V.30, S.7
Donnera V.38, Pr.131
Donnez X.77
Donnoient VI.69
Donra III.94, IV.15, IV.32, VI.56, VII.2, VIII.7, VIII.49, IX.8, IX.87, X.40, X.45, Pr.8, Pr.13, S.7, S.58
Donront V.4, X.82, S.17
Donrra III.2, III.94
Dons III.95, IV.19, Pr.87
Dont S.13, S.26, S.36, S.48
Donzere IX.67
Dor VI.9
Dordonnois VIII.35
Doré II.87
Doree III.26, VI.14
Dormant VI.11
Dormir VI.30
Dort VIII.42
Dou IX.21
Double I.85, III.55, IV.13, IV.57, V.44, VIII.17, VIII.68, IX.3, Pr.71
Doublon Pr.71
Dou(b)te III.55, III.57
Doubter Pr.89
Douce X.99, Pr.104
Douera V.52
Doulce I.97
Douleur VI.63
Douleurs Pr.140
Doulx X.12
Dourra V.52
Doutance IV.90
Doux X.97, Pr.58
Douze VI.11, Pr.10
Drap VIII.22
Dressé I.45, VII.29
Dressent I.57
Dresser III.43, V.51, V.69, VI.12, VII.32, IX.10, IX.66, Pr.34
Dressera I.77, II.63, III.61, Pr.137
Dresseront III.26, VI.79
Dreux IX.57
Droit V.45, IX.27, IX.86, Pr.73
Droite VIII.95
Drôme X.14
DRUX IX.57
Dubieuse VI.95
Dubieux I.37, VI.13
Dubrovnik X.63
Duc IV.17, VI.38, VII.51, IV.73, IV.91, IV.98, V.9, V.94, VI.31, VI.53, VI.55, VII.4, VII.29, VIII.66, IX.22, IX.27, IX.41, IX.80, IX.87, IX.95-6, X.11, X.15, X.33, X.64, X.80, S.1
Duché V.3
Ducteur III.96
Due IX.11
Dueil II.47, IV.7, V.18, VIII.3, X.78, S.55
Duel Pr.85
Duelle I.35, II.34, II.67, IV.91
Duelles III.16
Duero III.62
Duict III.68, VI.29
Duira I.76
Dun I.21, IV.9
Dur II.75, III.45, V.16
Durance III.99, VIII.1
Durant II.43, IV.55, S.11, S.47
Duré II.87
Duree VI.20
Durement VII.38
Durer Pr.128
Durera VIII.77
Dureront I.31
Duumvirat V.23
Duyra VIII.92

Eage X.39, X.74
éans III.51
Eau IV.20, IV.98, VI.1, VIII.7, VIII.49, VIII.57, VIII.77, VIII.98, IX.9, IX.51, X.10, X.60, X.71, Pr.5, Pr.14, Pr.78-80, Pr.93, Pr.113, Pr.132, S.3, S.24, S.32, S.38, S.53
Eaue I.54, IV.58, IV.80, IV.86, V.71, V.87, VI.10, VI.38, VII.32, VII.34, S.6, S.31, S.42, S.45

S.50
Eaues III.70, V.86
Eaux I.11, II.29, II.31, II.87, III.70, VI.94, X.49, Pr.3, Pr.19, S.11
Eauz Pr.1
Ebrieu VI.18
Ebro VIII.56
Ecclesiastique I.15, V.77, VI.3, S.26
Eclipse IV.29
Eclypses VIII.15
Ecosse III.78
écoute IX.88
Edict I.40, II.7, IV.18, V.18, V.72, V.97, X.94, Pr.53
Edicts Pr.68
Edifice VIII.100, VIII.29
Edifices VI.66, IX.37
Edifier IX.17
Effacer VII.20
Effaict IX.89
Effaieur I.75
Effet III.51
Efforrs II.52, II.68
Effort IX.89, X.24, Pr.22
Efforts VIII.15
Effraié VI.47
Effraiera VI.56
Effrayeur II.30, V.22, V.65, X.72
Effréné VII.91
Effrenee VIII.13
Effroy I.33, III.1, I.42
Effusion I.55, IX.96
Egaux I.54
Egee III.89, V.95
Egeste IV.80
Egipte II.86, III.77, V.25
Eglise I.52, III.17, V.25, V.73-4, VIII.57, VIII.78, VIII.98, Pr.99, Pr.105, Pr.118, S.12
Eglises Pr.118-19, Pr.121
Eguillon IV.79
Eguillons IV.79
Egypte I.40
El X.25
Electeur IX.18, X.46
Election VIII.20, VIII.67, X.91, Pr.25
Elephan S.56
Elephant S.29, S.39
Elisiens IX.97
Elysées IX.97
Elysiens Pr.61
Emanuel IV.10, VIII.21
Embasmé VIII.68
Embelys X.79
Emblee X.68
Embleront VII.10, VIII.21
Embosque IV.26
Embrassees X.78
Embuche V.22, IX.79, Pr.100
Embusches III.37, VI.91, IX.81
E(s)meut II.52
Emmené II.58
Emmenee VIII.8
Emmenees I.49, IV.2
Emmiellee S.36
Emmy V.58, IX.76
Emonopolle VIII.38
Emorre X.61
émouvoir Pr.80
Empereur I.60, IV.65, V.6, VIII.27, S.13, S.39, S.57
Empeschable Pr.30
Empeschant IV.51, V.95, Pr.94
Empeschee VII.27
Empeschement Pr.8
Empeschera II.18, Pr.77
Empire I.32, I.39, I.43, I.60, I.74, III.28, III.49, III.59, III.92-3, III.97, IV.39, V.24, V.45, V.95, VI.3, VII.12, VII.67, VIII.20, VIII.57, VIII.65, VIII.76, VIII.81, IX.18, IX.45, X.31-2, X.34, X.87, X.93, X.100, S.30, S.37
Empirée Pr.94
Empirees VI.23
Empliant X.84
Empoisoné VIII.65
Emportera III.53, S.1
Empoysoné VII.24
Emprinse IX.25

Emprise V.63, VIII.81
Emprisonnez Pr.138
Emulente II.43
Enceinte S.56
Enchainé IV.34
Enclin S.15
Enclos III.23, Pr.59
Encloz X.17
Enclume VII.3
Encombres V.95
Encontre I.24, IV.13, IV.52, VII.22, IX.99, Pr.44, Pr.82
Encor I.42, VI.81, VIII.92, IV.27, IV.74, IX.72, Pr.137, S.14, S.20, S.24, S.26, S.43, S.51-2
Encore III.24
Encores V.35, IX.74
Encunder IV.60
Endormie VII.22
Endormir VII.4
Endroict I.54
Endroit IX.58
Endurera V.24, S.17
Endymion II.73
Enfance III.15
Enfans I.10, I.99, II.11, IV.60, VIII.55, VIII.64, VIII.89, VIII.97, X.39, X.57, Pr.134, S.9, S.35
Enfant I.65, I.67, I.95, II.24, III.35, III.42, VI.60, V.61, V.73, VI.39, VII.11, VIII.63, VIII.79, IX.9-10, X.92
Enfer I.10
Enfermée II.5
Enfermés VII.19
Enfermez VIII.8
Enferré VIII.55
Enflamme VI.19
Enflammee II.27, S.29
Enflammer III.27
Enfle VIII.75, Pr.140
Enflez VIII.28, Pr.104
Enfoncee III.37
Enfondrez IX.31
Enfouetz VI.66
Enfumez Pr.65
Engaigé VII.23
Engin II.76, II.79
Engloutira VI.19
Engravera S.52
Enguerris III.29
Enlassee S.44
Ennem V.81
Ennemi Pr.77
Ennemie III.61
Ennemis I.13, I.29, II.23, II.43, II.50, II.76, II.80, II.90, III.29, III.33, III.69, III.71, III.91, IV.43, IV.52, V.10, V.48, V.81-2, VI.30, VII.38, VII.74, VII.15, VII.28, VIII.17, IX.81, IX.93-4, X.54, Pr.28, Pr.58, Pr.81, Pr.128, Pr.132-3, Pr.135-6, Pr.138, Pr.140, S.3
Ennemy I.97, II.47, III.79, III.100, IV.51, V.8, V.49, VI.14, VI.56, VI.68, VI.99, VIII.83, X.1, X.10, Pr.33, Pr.128-9, Pr.139, S.29
Ennemys IX.92, X.76
Ennobly I.45, III.72
Ennosigée I.87
Ennuis Pr.131
Enorme VIII.72, X.61, S.34
Enormes VI.95, X.10
Enrichi Pr.133
Enseigne III.47, V.52, VI.42, VIII.43, IX.56, IX.84, X.48, Pr.34
Enseignes IV.3
Ensemble III.8, III.5, III.22-3, VII.21, VIII.75, IX.94, S.32
Enserré VIII.55
Enserrés VII.41
Enserrez VIII.1, IX.3
Ensevelis IV.20
Ensigne X.83
Ensolcy X.7
Ensuivant IX.55
Ensuivra Pr.131
Ensuivre III.67, Pr.48
Ensuyvant IX.4
Ensuyvre IV.51

Fertsod IX.74
Ferveur IV.59
Fervides Pr.102
Feste I.50, VIII.72, VIII.74, IX.23, S.17, S.57
Festes I.58, II.16, Pr.132
Festins Pr.24, Pr.33, Pr.78
Fesulan VII.8, VIII.16
Feu I.42, I.46, I.62, I.71, I.87, I.97, II.34-5, II.46, II.61, II.65, II.81, II.91-2, III.7, III.22, III.37, III.80, III.84, IV.23, IV.28, IV.31, IV.34-5, V.40, IV.47, IV.80, IV.98, IV.100, V.8, V.21, V.27, V.60, V.98, V.100, VI.10, VI.16, VI.19, VI.34, VI.38, VI.80, VI.97, VII.18, VII.28, VII.30, VIII.1-2, VIII.7, VIII.10-11, VIII.17, IX.3, IX.9, IX.13, IX.20, IX.29, IX.51, IX.55, IX.96, IX.100, X.6, X.10, X.24, X.53, X.60-61, Pr.8-9, Pr.17-19, Pr.28, Pr.34, Pr.48, Pr.52-3, Pr.73, Pr.86, Pr.98, Pr.103, Pr.117, Pr.125, Pr.139, S.5, S.21, S.24, S.27, S.30-32, S.40, S.49-50, S.53-4
feu du ciel I.46, II.81, III.7, V.98, V.100, VIII.2, Pr.9, Pr.17, Pr.28
Feuilles VIII.75
Feus I.11, II.40
Feut IX.52, X.9, X.19-20, X.71, X.91
Feux II.18, II.26, II.77, IV.67, V.61, S.27, S.36
Feuz/z II.16, V.34
Fevrier III.96, VIII.48-9
Fez VI.54, V.80
Fiance V.49, Pr.75
Fiancee II.98
Fidel(l)e III.41
Fiel III.16, S.13
Fier II.34, V.29, Pr.6, Pr.20, Pr.84
Fiere II.70, II.79, VIII.31, X.19, Pr.8
Fiers IX.69
Fiévré Pr.52, Pr.122
Fievres Pr.97
Figuieres X.9
Figulier IX.12
Fil II.48, IV.63, X.15, Pr.86
File VIII.96
Filera IV.85
Filet V.58
Fille II.54, IV.99, VIII.96, X.17
Filles IV.71, Pr.140
Fils IX.77, X.39-40, X.63, X.96, Pr.135, S.33, S.48
Fils/z I.41, II.11, III.18, IV.7, IV.53, IV.60-61, IV.83, IV.87, IV.91, IV.67, IV.77, VI.91, VIII.32, VIII.63, VIII.75, X.8, X.15, X.18, X.21
Fin II.96, III.21, III.56, IV.25, V.98, VI.9, VII.6, VII.12, VIII.69, VIII.97, IX.32, X.55, X.99, Pr.7, Pr.47, Pr.86, S.5-6, S.10, S.22, S.27, S.41-2, S.44
Finements Pr.87
Finera I.100
Fini Pr.70
Finie I.70
Finir Pr.82
Finira I.100
Fins X.48
Finy I.98, S.30, S.34
Firent X.21
Fitine VI.89
Fixe X.20
Fixes III.46
Fiz IV.58
Flagrand X.35
Flamans III.9, III.53, VI.12
Flambe I.1
Flambeau II.96, S.15
Flambeaux IX.70
Flamens IX.40
Flaminique V.77
Flamme I.97, IV.24, IV.82, VI.19, VI.97, Pr.39
Flanc Pr.113
Flancz II.50
Flandres III.17, III.19, V.94, IX.18, S.54

Flangnards X.33
Flateurs X.16
Fléaux I.20, I.63, II.6
Fleche IV.9
Fléchir Pr.100
Fleiche VIII.49
Flesche II.61
Fleues I.20
Fleur IV.20, V.39, VI.83, IX.35, X.79
Fleurir II.69
Fleurira II.97
Fleurs V.89, VI.62
Fl(e)uve I.86-7, II.23, II.57, II.61, III.20, III.61, III.72, IV.17, IV.80, V.98, VI.3-4
Fl(e)uves I.20, II.17, II.24, II.35, II.97, VI.27, VI.33, VI.98, VIII.55, IX.76, Pr.108-9
Fleux X.56
Flor Pr.31
Flora II.84, VII.8, VIII.18, Pr.8
Floram Pr.22
Florance X.64
FLORE Pr.32
Florence III.74, IV.60, V.3, V.39, VI.36, VII.48, VII.77, VII.32, VII.7, X.33, S.1
Florir V.39
Florira V.52
Floter V.95
Flots S.23
Fluve V.80, VI.99
Fluves VI.33, VI.52, VII.30
Foible III.28, VIII.56, Pr.6, Pr.20, S.37
Foibles III.6, IX.96
Foiblesse VIII.4
Foin Pr.103
Fois I.71, III.10, III.31, III.57, IV.30, VII.5, VIII.59, IX.10, Pr.105, S.20, S.41
Foison S.32
Foix III.25, V.100, VIII.12, VIII.39, IX.63, IX.73
Foldre IV.43
Folie I.40, III.68
Folies III.63
Folliges III.63
Fond I.21, III.3, S.34
Fondation I.69
Fondement VI.66
Fondements II.8
Fonds X.41
Fondu III.13
Fondz V.9
Fons X.80
Font X.28
Fontaines IV.66, S.11
Forbe VIII.12
Force I.15, I.33, I.94, II.16, III.71, III.100, VIII.4, VIII.11, VIII.42, VIII.76, IX.32, X.22, X.49, X.80, Pr.124, S.4, S.50
Forcenee VIII.13
Forces IV.50, VI.70, IV.73, VI.62, VII.33
Forché II.67
Forens X.24
Forest V.58, VIII.35, IX.19-20, IX.40, IX.87
Forestz VI.7
Forfait III.51
Forfaits S.14, S.41
Forge II.7, VI.76
Formande X.47
Forme I.29, VII.28, Pr.37
Fornaise Pr.15
Fornase IX.3
Forneaulx IX.14
Forneron IX.17
Fornese IX.3
Fornix VIII.27
Forrier IX.10
Fors II.11, III.6, VI.61, VI.96, IX.51, S.41
Fort I.5, I.74-5, I.80, I.95, II.25, II.37, II.39, II.54, II.58, II.61, II.67, III.6, III.73, III.76, III.82, III.98, IV.21, IV.32, IV.52, IV.57, IV.59, IV.66-7, IV.82, IV.86, IV.90, IV.97, V.33, V.50, V.68, V.96, VI.39-40, VI.56, VI.70, VI.72, VI.87, VI.98, VII.19, VII.24, VII.27, VIII.3, VIII.37, VIII.44, IX.55, IX.57,

IX.83, IX.89, IX.93-4, X.17, X.45, X.67, Pr.6, Pr.23, Pr.56, Pr.64, Pr.71, Pr.85, Pr.93, Pr.116, Pr.120, Pr.123, Pr.126, S.1, S.54
Forte I.29, II.58, III.22, IX.82, Pr.51, Pr.117, S.2
Fortement S.43
Forteresse II.25, IV.65, V.82, VIII.37
Forteresses IV.40
Fortes II.1, III.98, Pr.65
Forts II.67, III.6, IX.80, S.3, S.35, S.43
Fortune I.66, III.16, V.32, IX.89
Fossan III.96
Fosse IV.80, VII.7, VIII.95
Fossen I.58
Foudre I.26, I.65, II.76, III.6, Pr.9-10, Pr.53
Foudres Pr.98
Fougeres IX.19
Foulant Pr.59
Fouleront I.6
Fournies VIII.27
Foussan III.96, VII.30
Fouyr IX.11, X.82
Foy I.70, I.86, II.9, II.60, II.86, IV.22, VI.69, VIII.21, VIII.39, VIII.76, VIII.87, VIII.100, IX.85, X.1, X.2, X.16, Pr.20, Pr.22, Pr.28, Pr.38, Pr.68, Pr.118-19, Pr.122, Pr.135
Foyble I.34
Foyblira VIII.59
Foys I.8, I.15, VIII.38, IX.63, X.90
Fragile I.12
Fragues VI.94
Fraieur III.1
Franc V.18, V.87, S.8, S.21, S.23, S.30, S.57
franc pays S.8, S.21, S.23, S.57
France I.73, I.78, II.2, II.34, III.14-15, III.23-4, III.55, III.57, III.99, IV.2, IV.93, V.42, V.49, V.77, VI.12, VI.16, VII.3, VIII.4, VIII.46, VIII.67, IX.52, IX.55, IX.58, X.16, X.26, Pr.23, Pr.45, Pr.73, Pr.122, Pr.124, Pr.126-7, S.1, S.26, S.36, S.44, S.48-9, S.58
Franche IV.16, V.35, V.80, X.41
Franchie Pr.31
Franco IX.16
Francois III.27, S.42, S.51, S.58
Francoise VII.39
Francoys I.34
Frand VI.3
Frankfort III.53, VI.87
Franque VIII.86
Frapé III.59, Pr.17
Frapee Pr.53
Frap(p)é I.27, II.27, II.56, II.92, V.14, Pr.68
Frappée IV.33
Frapper I.83
Frap(p)era II.29, VIII.73, IX.27
Frappés II.43
Fratricider VI.11
Fraud VII.3
Fraude III.85, V.83, IX.79
Frauder II.36
Fraudulente IV.42, VI.77
Frauduleuse Pr.14
Fraulde VII.33
Fraulx V.5
Frayeur I.94, III.88, VIII.80, IX.50, Pr.4, Pr.9, Pr.29, Pr.131, Pr.136
Freins III.82
Fréjus III.82, X.23
Fremit S.32
Frena(i)sie II.12
Frenetique II.28
Frere I.84, IV.61, VI.96, V.36, VIII.13, X.26, X.34, S.9, S.34
Freres I.85, II.20, II.34, II.95, III.98, IV.94, V.50, VI.7, VIII.17, VIII.46, VIII.58, IX.36, Pr.141, S.26, S.56

Fresch IX.23
Fresz IV.63
Frise VI.41
Frivole VI.32
Frize IV.89
Frofaim VI.81
Froid III.4, Pr.21, Pr.61
Froidure S.14
Froit III.4, V.63, VI.69, VI.81, VII.34
Froment II.75, IV.15, Pr.66, Pr.92
Front II.20, IV.25, V.2, V.9, X.8
Frontiere IX.99, X.41, Pr.29
Frontieres III.4, Pr.125
Froquez Pr.65
Fruict I.10, IX.66, X.89
Fruit VIII.18, VIII.31, VIII.96
Fruits Pr.114, Pr.124-5, Pr.128, Pr.130
Fruitz IX.65
Frustré VIII.65
Frustree III.89
Frustres III.87
Frymy VIII.91
Fucin II.73
Fugitifs II.7
Fugitif IV.53
Fuict V.17
Fuicte I.10
Fuir VIII.1
Fuira III.54, IV.83, IV.92
Fuis II.26, II.72, II.77, IV.79, VII.8, VIII.46
Fuit I.19, VIII.62
Fuite II.49, IV.12, IV.40, Pr.98
Fuitifs III.7
Fuits Pr.79
Fuitte V.12
Fulg Pr.54
Fulgure VIII.6, Pr.54
Fulgures I.65, II.16
Fum IX.14, IX.23
Fumee IX.14, IX.23, Pr.52
Funebre Pr.24
Furent VIII.28
Fureur V.13, V.60, V.71, VI.27, VII.32, VI.59, VI.68, VI.72, X.16, Pr.60, Pr.80-81, Pr.104
Fureurs Pr.40
Furieuse VI.68
Furieux I.83, II.34
Fus Pr.86
Fusee Pr.86
Fuste I.28, II.81
Fustes VIII.16, VIII.21, Pr.18
Fuy VIII.64, VIII.84
Fuyant I.98, X.69
Fuyez IX.46
Fuyr IX.4
Fuyra I.58
Fuyront X.6
Fuytif X.3

Gach IV.26
Gaddes IX.97, IX.30
Gaigné I.75
Gaigner VII.40
Gain IV.21
Galees VII.26
Galeres IX.43
Gall Pr.18
Galle III.53
Gallere X.2, S.1
Galleres IX.79, IX.94, S.41
Gallique VI.7, VIII.58
Gallotz V.63, VI.62, VII.10
Gand II.16, II.50, IV.19, V.94, IX.49, X.83
Gandole IV.97
Gang II.60
Gange II.60, IV.51
Gar II.25
Garbelans Pr.135
Garda II.73
Gardé I.68, II.14, II.25, II.59, II.97, III.34, IV.46, IV.75, VIII.32, IX.27, IX.40, IX.82, Pr.2, Pr.6, S.35
Garderont IV.35
Gardés III.43, IV.8, VI.43
Gardoing S.58
Gardon VIII.6, X.6, S.11
Garnisons X.38
Garnissant IV.53
Garone VIII.35

Garonne II.25, II.33, III.12, III.43, VI.1, VI.79, VIII.2, IX.37
Garse V.12
Gascogne VI.86
Gascon IX.39
Gascons IX.3, IV.76
Gastant II.84
Gastera III.33
Gastez VIII.94
Gauche I.91, V.6, IX.58, IX.76
Gaule I.31, I.51, I.70, II.29, II.72, II.83, IV.5, V.36, V.54, VI.83, VIII.60, IX.33, X.58
Gaules IV.12
Gaulois I.6, I.90, II.39, II.63, II.69, II.78, II.94, III.49, III.100, IV.37, IV.54, IV.91, V.40, VI.85, VII.25, VIII.32, IX.38, IX.75, X.38
Gauloise I.18, I.59, III.38, III.87, V.3, VII.20, VII.34
Gaulois X.34
Gauloyse II.99
Gaulsier V.57
Gebenoise II.64
Gelée Pr.116-17
Gelées II.1, VIII.35
Gelés II.17
Gelle VIII.35
Gellee X.66
Gelleront X.71
Gên II.33
Genaudan S.12
Gendarmes S.32
Gene VII.4
Genest VI.27
Genesve IX.44
Geneve IV.9, IV.42, VII.4, VIII.6, S.52
Genevois IV.59, X.92
Genevoise II.64
Genisse S.87
Geniture X.42
Gennes II.37, IV.60, VI.66, V.28, V.64, VI.78, VI.81, VII.30, VII.39, IX.42, X.24, X.60, Pr.25
Genoilles III.32
Genre VI.18, X.10, S.49
Gens I.3, I.28, I.42, I.60, II.6, II.62, III.8, III.17, III.20, III.24, III.35, III.58, III.78, IV.83, VI.32, VIII.8, VIII.98, IX.72, Pr.53, Pr.90, S.47, S.55
Gensdarmes I.78, IV.52
Gent I.14, I.83, II.54, I.64, II.70-71, II.74, II.78-9, II.99, III.32, III.38, III.57, III.64, III.83, IV.2, IV.41, IV.100, V.13, V.26, V.42, V.51-2, V.55, V.74, V.99, VI.1, VI.3, VI.18, VI.20, VII.22, VII.34, VII.39, VIII.10, Pr.38, S.43
gent militaire IV.2, S.43
Gentils Pr.83
Gents III.43, III.58, VII.32
George IX.31
Georges IV.17
Germain II.24, II.39, II.87, X.17, S.9, S.34
Germaine VI.77, X.35
Germains II.39, III.67, IV.74, X.59, Pr.29
Germanie III.76, III.90, V.43, V.94, IX.90, X.31
Germanique III.32, III.57, V.74
Geter IX.99
Get(t)é III.40, IV.92, VI.40, VIII.94
Getter IX.53
Get(t)és II.11, II.17
Gettez VIII.28
Geux IV.36, VII.22
Geys S.36
Ghent IV.19
Gien II.14
Gienne II.14
Gilbattar S.41
Giron V.3
Gironde II.61, VI.79
Gisant X.92
Glace I.22, I.52, Pr.3, Pr.14, Pr.117, Pr.124
Glaifue VI.92
Glaifues I.11

Glaive II.56, II.91, II.96, III.11, X.60
Glaives III.75
Gland S.33
Glandes IV.79
Glas Pr.34, Pr.46
Glaz III.40
Globe I.58, V.93
Globes V.8
Gloire II.11, III.15, VIII.31, S.48
Glomes VIII.71
Gloze III.62
Goff(r)es II.8
Gorge II.7, III.42, III.96, IV.35, VI.76, VIII.41, Pr.102
Gorgon III.79
Gorsan VIII.22
Gosier IV.58
Gotique I.42
Gouffre V.84, VI.44
Goulfre IX.28, IX.30
Goulphre VIII.84, IX.16
Goussan IX.56
Gousse III.75
Goustant V.36
Goute II.84
Gouvernail S.23
Gouvernement II.2
Gouverneur III.81, VI.45, Pr.52
Gouvert IV.11
Grace VII.18, VIII.22
Graces X.78
Grain Pr.36, Pr.113-14
Grains Pr.106
Gran IX.19
Granci VI.79
Granée VI.33
Grange I.98, Pr.64
Grans I.17, I.69, I.87, II.66, II.74, II.80, II.89, III.12, III.44, III.54, III.62, IV.3, IV.44, IV.70, V.15, V.46, V.65, V.86, VI.8, VII.8, VII.29, VII.31, VIII.41
Grant I.28, II.46-7, II.85, S.-301, V.35
Grappé I.27
Grapper II.56
Grasse X.28
Grave VI.9, Pr.85
Gravée V.33
Gravera S.38
Gravier I.29
Grecs I.83
Gregue III.87
Grenade III.20, V.55
Grenoble IV.42, IX.69
Grenouilles II.33
Greque IX.78
Gresle I.22, I.66, III.56, V.97, VII.7, VIII.35, IX.69, X.67, Pr.10, Pr.40, Pr.53, Pr.85, Pr.112
Gresler VIII.77
Gresles Pr.126
Gresse I.22, VII.40
Grevés I.5, II.6
Grieve Pr.53
Grievement Pr.109
Griffon S.29, S.56
Grillés IX.65
Grinsant V.13
Grippe VI.91
Gripper IX.39
Gris I.100, VI.65, VIII.22, IX.20, X.91, Pr.65
Grisons X.38
Grogne III.87
Gronde S.56
Groppe VI.40
Gros II.41, I.83, IV.44, V.4, VIII.56, Pr.3, Pr.77, S.25
Grosse X.67
Groumelans Pr.135
Groupe VI.40
Gryphon X.86
Gtand VI.13
Guaires VI.12
Guarantir VI.33
Guarantira II.88
Guard Pr.85
Guer IV.100
Guerdonnez IX.61
Guere Pr.114
Gueres Pr.125
Guerir IV.10
Guerisse III.73

VIII.48-9, VIII.85, IX.55,
IX.63-4, IX.73, X.67, X.72,
Pr.2, Pr.5, Pr.8, Pr.24, Pr.46,
Pr.59, Pr.87, Pr.117, S.27, S.46,
S.52, S.56
Marsan IV.72
Marsaves VIII.35
Marseille I.71-2, III.86, III.88,
IX.24, X.88, S.1
Martial V.26, V.77
Martiaulx VI.43, VI.95
Martire I.44, VI.59, VI.62
Martis X.84
Martres III.86
Mary IX.34, X.55
Mas IV.79, VI.1
Mascon III.69, IX.70
Masculin I.86, S.4
Masle IX.50
Masles III.89, Pr.111
Masques II.10
Masses V.33
Massiliolique IX.28
Mastin II.41, V.4
Mastine X.29
Mastinées II.17
Mastins X.59, X.99
Mat Pr.19
Mathien Pr.38
Matiere V.29
Matin Pr.76
Matrimonial VIII.88
Matriscome VIII.88
Matrone X.61
Matrones Pr.117
Matronne III.37
Mature VI.100
Mau(l)x I.24, VII.6, VIII.80
Maures VIII.6
Mauris VIII.6
Mauseole IX.85
Mausol VIII.34
Mausole IV.27
Maux VIII.17, Pr.60, Pr.89,
Pr.91, Pr.105, Pr.109, Pr.118,
S.21, S.44
Maye VIII.7
Mayenne IX.19
Maynade VIII.40
Mazeres V.100
Medalles VI.9
Mede III.31, III.64
Medecin S.10, S.28, S.30
Medusine IX.84
Meffait III.51
Meissen IX.94
Mele X.98
Melifique X.89
Melite II.49, IX.98
Mellie VI.45
Mellite VI.45
Mellites I.9
Même Pr.105
Memire VIII.42
Memoire V.40, S.15
Memorable S.48
Memphis X.79
Menace Pr.32
Menant VI.28, X.13
Menasse I.15, II.81
Mende IV.44
Mendicant X.63
Mendosus IX.45, IX.50
Mené III.10, IV.34, IV.85,
VII.29, X.29
Menee VI.92, VIII.8, IX.64
Menées I.49, III.62, VII.26,
IX.53
Mener IV.58, VIII.58, S.9
Menez IX.15
Mensolee VIII.46
Mensongers V.91
Ment IX.70
Menton II.20
Menu Pr.110
Mepris X.36
Meprisant III.67
Mer I.18, I.20, I.29, I.41, I.50,
I.55, I.63, I.92, II.3, II.5, II.15,
II.18, II.40, II.74, II.78, II.85,
II.94, III.5, III.9, III.21, III.23,
III.62, III.78, III.82, III.86,
III.88-9, IV.2, IV.4, IV.14-15,
IV.19, IV.21, IV.94, V.3, V.11,
V.25-6, V.35, V.44, V.48, V.55,
V.64, V.95, V.98, VI.33, VI.56,

VI.64, VI.80, VI.85, VII.10,
VII.20, VIII.9, VIII.51,
VIII.59-60, IX.54, IX.64, IX.75,
IX.97, X.24, X.68, X.79,
X.87-8, X.95, X.100, Pr.1-2,
Pr.5-6, Pr.11, Pr.20, Pr.22,
Pr.27, Pr.29, Pr.33-4, Pr.71,
Pr.84, Pr.129-30, S.7, S.23, S.29
mer & terre II.40, IV.21, V.48,
VII.10, VIII.60, IX.64, X.95,
X.100, Pr.5, Pr.20, Pr.33, Pr.129
Mercure II.65, III.3, IV.28-9,
IV.97, V.93, IX.12, X.55,
IX.73, X.67, X.79, S.49
Mercurial S.24
Mercy III.37, VI.81
Mere III.16, IV.7, V.73, VII.11,
VIII.73, VIII.75, X.55, S.35
Meres Pr.82
Meridienne S.39
Merite III.66
Merveille III.86
Merveilleux I.43, II.55, II.92,
VIII.60
Meschans Pr.72
Meschant VIII.70
Meselle IV.91
Mes(g)nie I.99, III.31
Meslé II.78, X.98, Pr.111, S.32
Meslee V.28, V.33, VI.10, VI.16,
X.66
Mesler V.36
Meslera V.72
Mesme II.51, IV.43, V.5, V.32,
V.92, VIII.33, VIII.79, X.63,
S.17, S.28, S.49
Mesmes I.69, II.1, III.4, III.60,
VI.78, VIII.88, X.14
Mesnie I.80
Mesopotamie III.61, III.99,
VII.22, VIII.70
Mespriseront I.85
Messagier V.71
Messagiers VI.93
Messaige VIII.20
Messe Pr.91, Pr.109, Pr.120-21
Messie V.53
Messine IX.61
Mestre IV.80
Metal VII.19
Metalique V.7
Metaulx V.66
Methelin V.27, IX.32
Met(t)ant III.1, VIII.41, VIII.89,
IX.50
Met(t)ants I.89
Met(t)ra I.39, I.79, III.59, VI.10,
IV.99, V.73, V.93, VI.28,
VIII.10, VIII.15, IX.60, X.3,
X.47, X.66, Pr.77, S.2, S.6,
S.10, S.28, S.46
Mettre V.80, V.6, V.16-17,
VI.19, VII.31, VII.21, VII.37,
IX.8, IX.11, X.83, Pr.107,
Pr.140
Met(t)ront I.13, III.83, VII.36,
IX.49, IX.96, Pr.28, S.30
Metz X.7
Meubles I.28
Meurdris VIII.75
Meurdry X.21
Meurdrys X.82
Meure S.53
Meurs I.98
Meusniers VII.17
Meurte II.47, V.36, Pr.4, Pr.23
Meurtre II.61, II.92, VI.92, S.12
Meurtres Pr.79
Meurtris VI.94
Meurtry I.52, IV.10, V.22,
VIII.32, VIII.63
Meurtrys I.59
Meuse V.50
Mezan VII.35
Mezin VIII.35
Mi VIII.44, X.7, Pr.122
Midi X.69
Midy III.3, IV.31, V.75, X.95,
Pr.8, S.27, S.49
Miel I.44, I.57, VI.89, IX.14,
IX.41, Pr.124
Mieux IX.7, S.5
Migre IX.44
Migres IX.44

Mil I.48-9, I.98, III.77, VI.54,
VIII.13, VIII.21, VIII.71, X.72,
X.91, S.28
Mil(l)an III.37, IV.34, IV.90,
V.99, VI.31, VI.78, VII.87,
VIII.7, VIII.12, IX.95, X.64
Milannoile IX.95
Milannoise IX.95
Milhau IV.44
Milieu I.32, IX.15, IX.23, X.81,
X.92
Militaire I.16, I.97, IV.2, VI.33,
VIII.78, IX.76, Pr.42, S.43
Millane VII.32
Mille IV.16, VI.41, VI.49,
VII.31, IX.56, S.2-3, S.41
Milles VIII.21
Millesme X.74
Mil(l)ieu I.2, I.65, I.82, III.11,
IV.9, IV.32, V.96, IX.11, IX.19
Mil(l)ion I.72, I.92, II.94, V.25,
VIII.34
Milve V.45, VI.16
Minamee X.8
Mince I.88, IV.7, VI.15
Mine I.13, I.48, I.53, Pr.21,
Pr33, 214
Minera IX.51, Pr.69
Mineur IV.7, X.34
Mineurs Pr.97
Minui(c)t II.77
Minuse VIII.47
Miples IV.58
Miracle VI.51
Mirande I.46, VIII.2
Mirandole VII.4
Mis I.29, I.36, I.43-4, I.59, I.68,
I.81, I.94, II.12, II.37, II.39,
II.43, II.50, II.86, II.93, II.98,
III.55, III.66, III.71, III.80,
IV.12, IV.14, IV.18-19, IV.21,
IV.28-30, IV.32, IV.34, IV.43,
IV.84, V.39, VI.29, VI.51,
VI.59, VII.15, VII.18, VII.28,
VIII.17, VIII.27, VIII.59,
VIII.92, VIII.95, VIII.99, IX.15,
IX.47, X.22, X.30, X.43, X.65,
Pr.21, Pr.47, Pr.55-6, Pr.59,
Pr.65, Pr.67-9, Pr.73, Pr.77,
Pr.98, Pr.100, Pr.124, Pr.135-6,
Pr.141, S.1, S.13
Mise I.2, II.61, III.52, X.54,
Pr.96, S.50
Miserable I.61, IV.84, IX.78
Misere VIII.96, S.33
Mitilene III.47
Mittré IX.34
Mobil I.54
Mocqué IV.61, X.12
Mocquez IX.65
Modene VI.73, IX.13, X.60
Moderé Pr.109
Moderés I.93
Moelle Pr.54
Moeurs III.49
Moindre II.63, IV.88, IV.95,
X.2, X.21, X.53
Moine I.95, VI.60, IX.20
Moines I.44, S.11
Moins I.60, II.33, III.87, IV.2,
VI.71, IX.73, Pr.60, Pr.68,
Pr.128
Mois I.23, II.84, IV.95, IV.100,
VIII.65, VIII.94, X.67, X.72,
Pr.44, Pr.60, Pr.89, Pr.116,
Pr.128
Moissac VII.12
Moitié III.48
Molesté Pr.66, Pr.83, Pr.116,
Pr.130
Molestera Pr.85
Molins IX.37
Molite VI.98
Molosses X.24
Moment III.100, IV.22
Monaco IX.42, X.60
Monarchie I.48, II.69, IV.50,
VI.25, VII.57, Pr.25
Monarq I.12
Monarque I.4, I.31, I.36, I.59,
I.70, I.99, II.12, II.69, III.20,
III.11, III.17, III.47, IV.77,
IV.97, V.21, V.38, IX.5, IX.33,
IX.47, X.58, Pr.30
Monarques II.38, II.58, Pr.111
Monde I.45, I.63, II.22, III.92,

IV.77, V.31, V.96, VI.70,
VIII.17, IX.51, X.49, X.54,
X.73, Pr.15, Pr.22, Pr.82, Pr.99,
S.13, S.25, S.31, S.45
Monech II.4, III.10, IV.37,
IV.91, VI.62, VIII.4, IX.42,
X.23
Monet IX.42
Monge VI.86
Monnoyes I.40
Monopole I.79, II.49, VIII.38
Mons IV.2
Monserrat VIII.26
Monstier I.95
Monstra IV.59
Monstre I.80, I.90, II.32, II.70,
III.34, III.61, IV.20, V.88, VI.19,
VI.44, X.5, X.98, Pr.82, Pr.84,
S.16, S.39
Monstrer IV.69
Monstrera VI.61, Pr.99, S.19
Monstres I.90, VIII.68, IX.3
Mont II.83, III.17, III.96, III.99,
IV.3, IV.31, V.57-8, V.61, V.76,
VII.32, VIII.86, IX.2, IX.68-9,
IX.87, S.41
Montaige I.69
Montaignars IV.63
Montaigne I.69, VII.28, VIII.34,
X.50
Montaignes III.54, III.58, X.49
Montant S.39
Montauban III.56
Montdarrain VIII.86
Monté V.1
Montélimar IX.68
Monter VI.12, VIII.16
Montera V.75, IX.37, X.64
Monthurt IV.79
Montlhéri IX.87
Montlimart IV.42
Montmelian X.37
Montmorency IX.18
Monton II.88
Montpelle VIII.64
Montpellier III.56, VIII.64, S.52
Montpertuis III.24
Montrer Pr.133
Montserrant I.66
Montz II.48, V.26, VI.99, IX.64,
IX.67
Monument VII.29, IX.7
Monuments VII.14
Moq Pr.42
Moquerie III.74
Moqueur Pr.42
Morbile IV.98
Morbilles IV.98
Mord III.37
Mordre VI.32, Pr.90
Mords I.77
Moriane X.37
Moricque III.95
Morra II.9, III.100, IV.7
Morre VIII.12
Morrez III.87
Morveu V.59
Mor(t)s I.81, I.92, II.26, II.39,
II.70, II.92, III.12, III.68,
III.82, III.85, IV.20, IV.45,
IV.52, IV.69, IV.75, IV.67, VI.94,
X.8, X.83
Morsure S.36
Mort I.10, I.16, I.22, I.30,
I.35-6, I.38-9, I.89, I.94, II.2,
II.13, II.18, II.25, II.34, II.42,
II.45, II.47, II.53, II.56-7,
II.90-91, II.95, II.98, III.15,
III.36, III.48, III.59, III.66-7,
III.71, III.77, III.86, III.91, IV.2,
IV.14, IV.18, IV.43, IV.55,
IV.65, IV.75, IV.89, IV.91,
IV.100, V.8-10, V.15-17, V.21,
V.38, V.43, VI.11, VI.28,
VI.31-2, VI.37, VI.52, VI.74,
VI.76, VI.80, VII.17, VII.21,
VII.37, VII.40, VII.42, VIII.15,
VIII.18-19, VIII.34, VIII.37,
VIII.42, VIII.45, VIII.73,
VIII.87, VIII.89, IX.8, IX.10-11,

IX.17, IX.46, IX.49, IX.53,
IX.77-8, IX.96, X.1, X.12,
X.15-16, X.20, X.26, X.30,
X.40, X.43, X.46, X.55-7, X.63,
X.87, Pr.14, Pr.16, Pr.23,
Pr.32-3, Pr.35, Pr.37, Pr.40,
Pr.57, Pr.64, Pr.68, Pr.70, Pr.81,
Pr.83, Pr.85, Pr.90-91, Pr.94,
Pr.97-8, Pr.101-2, Pr.105,
Pr.110, Pr.112-13, Pr.115,
Pr.118, Pr.121, Pr.123-4,
Pr.126-7, Pr.130-31, Pr.133,
Pr.136-7, Pr.141, S.9, S.19, S.22,
S.35, S.50, S.58
Mortalité VIII.49, Pr.16, Pr.115
Mortara IX.31
Morte VIII.11, IX.82
Mortel VIII.11
Mortelle I.28, III.98, VII.26,
VIII.48, Pr.40, Pr.83, Pr.132
Mortels Pr.109
Morts I.11, III.68, III.71, III.74,
Pr.31, Pr.79-80, Pr.82, Pr.89-90,
Pr.133, Pr.140, S.27
Mortz VIII.77
Moselle I.89
Mot VIII.41, VIII.45, Pr.46
Motif Pr.80
Mots III.67
Mouches VI.89
Moufrin S.11
Mouille Pr.11
Mouldre I.65
Moulle I.2
Mourant IV.77, X.40
Mourir I.10, I.35, III.42, VIII.38,
VIII.13, VIII.100, IX.10, IX.51,
IX.78, X.12, Pr.1, Pr.17,
Pr.102-4, Pr.125, Pr.128, S.20
Mo(u)rra I.27, I.77, I.88, I.100,
II.9, II.56, II.62, III.19, III.66,
III.84, IV.6-7, IV.84, V.18, VI.6,
VIII.46, VIII.49, X.90, S.54,
S.57-8
Mourront I.85, II.7, S.37, S.53
Mouteur II.46
Mouton I.88, S.46
Mouvoir Pr.70
Movement I.11
Moyen III.85, V.44, VIII.80,
S.18   •
Moyennant VII.96, IV.98
Moyne VI.73, IX.10
Moynesse IX.10
Moys I.47, III.38-9, V.37, V.81,
V.90, VI.52, VIII.93
Mué II.65
Muestra X.25
Mueyre VIII.18
Mule Pr.17
Mulet II.60, VI.36
Multe IX.47, IX.74
Multitude IX.47
Munies Pr.31
Munismes V.23
Munuict X.4
Mur II.57, I.63, III.50, III.56,
III.84, V.18, V.81, VIII.2, IX.39,
X.45, Pr.59, Pr.101
Muraille III.37
Murailles VI.73
Murdre X.10
Murdry IX.58, X.35, X.69
Murmure S.9
Murmurer X.3
Murs I.29, III.7, III.33, III.56,
IV.52, IV.90, VII.51, VIII.38,
IX.26, IX.37, IX.93, IX.99,
X.65, X.89
Murte II.92
Murtie Pr.129
M(e)urtre III.51, VII.11, IV.71,
V.12, IX.36
M(e)urtrir III.48
Murtrira IV.86
Murtris VI.69, IV.78, IX.79
Murtry IV.55, VI.77, IV.76
Musicque X.28, S.41
Musniers VI.17
Mutations I.51, Pr.92
Mutin Pr.66
Mutinees S.43
Mutins Pr.19
Muy VIII.27
Myans X.37
Mydi IX.89

Myneral V.36
Myrmidon IX.35
Myrmidons X.8
Myrnarmee X.8
Mys II.13, I.77, V.82, VIII.26,
VIII.31, IX.13-14, IX.65, X.16,
X.18, X.20, X.81, X.90
Mysich III.60
Mysne IX.94
Mystique III.2
Myttee X.41

Nacelle V.49, S.1, S.47
Nacelles IV.81
Nacre III.24
Nager III.68, V.52, VIII.1
Nagera I.57, III.52, II.57, VIII.13,
III.87-8
Nageront II.60
Naissance IV.96, V.61
Naistra I.50, I.58, I.60, I.78,
I.80, I.90, II.32, III.35, III.42,
III.58, IV.93, V.9, V.20, V.55,
V.74, V.79, V.84, VI.44, VI.91,
VII.32, VIII.4, VIII.33, VIII.62,
IX.59, X.9, S.4
Naistre V.26, V.48, VIII.93,
VIII.97, IX.3, IX.11, Pr.1,
Pr.36-7, Pr.98, Pr.103, Pr.107,
Pr.120
Naistront III.76, S.44
Namront VIII.85
Nanar VIII.85
Nancy III.3, X.7
Nansol IV.27
Nansy IX.18
Nantes I.20, IV.46, V.33, VI.74,
Naples I.11, II.16, III.25, III.74,
V.43, VII.6, VIII.9
Nappe IV.11
Narbon I.72, I.99, II.59, III.92,
IV.94, VI.56, IX.34, IX.63-4,
Pr.2
Narbonne I.5, VIII.22, IX.38
Natif IV.89, X.44
Nation II.99, III.38, III.92
Nations III.83
Nativité II.13
Nature S.49
Naturel VII.44
Naturelle X.84
Naufrage III.33, II.56, V.31,
Pr.20
Naufraige II.33, II.86
Nautique V.3, V.95
Navale III.1, III.29, VII.3
navale pugne III.29
Naval(l)e I.40, VI.91, IX.100
Navarre IV.79, V.89, VIII.44,
X.45
Navarrois III.25
Naves IX.100, X.2, X.32
Navigant V.15
Navire V.2
Navires VII.26
Nay II.7, II.57-8, II.73, II.82,
II.92, III.69, IV.95, V.41, V.45,
V.84, V.97, VI.3, VI.52, VI.95,
VIII.1, VIII.45, VIII.76,
VIII.79, X.40
Neant II.12
Neanty X.20
Nebro VIII.56, X.25
Necessité VII.34
Nee X.54
Nef I.30, II.15, II.65, II.93,
IV.91, VII.37, VIII.16, IX.29,
IX.43, IX.100, X.2, X.80, X.23,
S.25, S.56
Nefz I.18, V.62, VII.37
Neglect I.73, Pr.48
Neglet V.39
Negligence I.18, X.43
Negresilve I.16
Neige II.29, V.70, Pr.14, Pr.124,
Neiger Pr.113
Neiges Pr.106
Nemans V.58, X.6
Neptun Pr.2
Neptune I.77, II.59, II.78, III.1,
IV.33, VI.90, Pr.12, Pr.39
Nepveu IX.92, VII.73, VI.22,
VI.82, VIII.32, VIII.43, X.30
Neron IX.17, IX.53, IX.76

NERSAF VIII.67
Nerte VII.37
Neuf I.81, II.7, II.9, II.84, IV.78, V.90, VIII.44, VIII.81, IX.39, IX.67, X.5, X.69, X.72, X.91, Pr.41, Pr.101, S.13, S.25, S.28, S.53
Neufs Pr.35
Neufve I.24, I.87, II.89, III.70, III.97, VI.97, VIII.74, IX.12, IX.18, IX.57, IX.92, IX.100, X.49, X.93
Neuve Pr.21, Pr.100
Ne(p)veu III.17
Ne(p)veux III.29
Nez II.20, II.67, V.45, VI.32, Pr.138
Ni Pr.88, Pr.114
Nice III.14, III.82, V.64, VII.30, IX.26
Nicene VII.19
Nicol IX.59
Nicolas IX.30
Nicopolle IX.91
Nictobriges IV.76
Niez Pr.21
Nira IV.59
Nismes III.56, X.94, S.52
Nisse X.60, X.87
Noble VIII.88, IX.68, X.59
Nobles I.11, V.71
Noblesse X.21
Nocent VI.37
Nocturne I.26, IV.83, V.41, V.81
Noilleux I.43
Noir I.74, III.43, III.60, IV.47, IV.85, V.29, VI.10, VI.25, VI.33, VI.38, VI.81, VII.2, VII.5, VIII.70, IX.20, IX.41, IX.58, IX.76, X.30, X.57, X.91, Pr.39, Pr.56
Noire I.77, II.79, VI.36, IX.60
Noireau S.47
Noires VII.14
Noirs VI.16, Pr.65
Nolle III.74, VIII.38
Nolte X.60
Nom I.76, II.88, IV.54, VIII.23, VIII.58, VIII.64, IX.6, IX.26, X.96, S.15, S.38
Nombre I.19, II.37-8, II.89, IV.3, V.64, VIII.71, VIII.91, IX.81, X.74, Pr.84, Pr.116
Nombril II.22
Nomme S.42
Nommera X.53
Nommeront IX.6
Nompariel V.83
Nonain IX.24
Nonante III.57, X.72
Nonchalans Pr.64
Nonchalence V.38
Nonnaire VIII.79
Nonnay X.67
Nonobstant I.30
Nonseggle VI.46
Nopce Pr.139
Nopces X.52, X.55, Pr.33, Pr.39, Pr.45, Pr.133, Pr.135-6, Pr.140
Nore X.55
Noriques III.58
NORLARIS VIII.60, IX.50
Normand IX.7
Normande IX.30
Normans VI.16, VI.97, VII.10, X.51
Norneigre VI.7
North II.17
Norveige VI.7
Noter Pr.89
Noudam IX.56
Noue Pr.36
Nourir I.21
Nourris III.29
Nouveau I.52, I.61, I.63, I.87, I.94, III.72, III.78, IV.31, V.3, VI.20-21, VI.23-4, VI.51, VII.42, VIII.40, IX.1, IX.5, IX.17, IX.72, IX.95, X.30, X.46, Pr.4, Pr.22, Pr.56, Pr.95, S.1, S.15, S.47
Nouveauté Pr.49
Nouveaux I.3, II.16, II.19, VI.6, IV.36, V.46, V.96, IX.25, Pr.56
Nouvel(l)e I.53, II.18, III.67,

III.97, IV.35, V.51, VI.66, VII.11, X.5, Pr.18, Pr.36-7, Pr.42-3, Pr.51, Pr.134, S.1, S.8, S.12, S.47, S.57
Nouvelles IV.13, VI.29, X.54, Pr.7, Pr.107, S.36
Nova IX.61
Noveau VI.1
Novel I.7
Novelles I.66
Noves IX.25, Pr.139
Novices I.44
Noyaulx IX.24
Noyes II.26, III.12
Noyez S.2
Nu X.30
Nubileuse VI.48
Nubileux Pr.58
Nud III.30, IV.22, V.67, V.73
Nudos IX.26
Nudz VI.69
Nue I.86
Nuech IV.26, IV.44
Nuees V.85
Nueh IV.44
Nui(c)t I.1, I.39, I.41, I.64, II.35, II.41, III.17, III.30, III.91, IV.8, IV.35, IV.41, IV.78, IV.93, V.8, V.17, VI.6, VI.30, VI.36, VI.44, VI.53, VI.65, VI.68, VII.2, VII.7, VII.32, VIII.58, IX.20-21, IX.39, Pr.12
Nuictz I.46, V.83
Nuira I.78
Nuire I.96, II.34, Pr.81, Pr.91, Pr.102
Nuit IX.13, IX.100, X.12, Pr.13, Pr.24, Pr.28, S.22
Nuits IV.17
Nuitz II.52
Nul I.76, III.34, IV.50, V.49, VI.81, VI.87, VIII.27, VIII.71, VIII.80, VIII.96, IX.29, IX.82, X.88, Pr.70, Pr.122, Pr.137, S.39
Nuls X.39
Numismes VI.23
Nuremberg III.53, VI.15
Nutrie Pr.129
Nuy IV.17
Nuyt IV.31
Ny II.4, VI.96, S.13
Nymes V.59, IX.9

Obeissance S.13
Obey X.94
Obfusquera V.72
Object X.70
Oblation VIII.51
Oblique Pr.139
Obnubiler IV.25
Obscur III.17, VIII.76
Obscurcie I.84, IX.68
Obscurcir IX.83
Obscurs V.84
Observera II.24
Obsesse IV.52, VII.33
Obstiné Pr.42
Obstinee X.96
Obstinez Pr.81
Obstivé Pr.42
Obtenir X.32
Obtiendra IV.75, VIII.93, IX.45
Obturee IX.18
Occean IX.48
Occident III.27, III.35, V.34, VIII.59, IX.55, IX.100, Pr.9, Pr.40, S.27
Occidental V.62
Occidentale Pr.123
Occis II.51, X.26
Occult II.78, III.2
Occulte IV.28, Pr.67
Occultes III.63
Occults Pr.132
Occuper II.19, III.97, V.27, X.26
Occupera I.75, IV.37-8, V.11, V.29, VIII.43, VIII.56, VIII.92, IX.5, X.34
Occuperont III.98, VI.82, IX.6
Ocean II.68, III.1, III.90, Pr.2, Pr.27
Oceane III.9
Octante VI.2
Octobre III.77, IX.62, S.16
Odieuse X.98, Pr.120

Oeil I.6, I.23, I.27, III.41, III.55, III.92, IV.15, IV.25, VII.11, X.70
Oesteuf I.65
Oeuf VII.24, S.13
Oeuvre VI.37, VIII.36
Offence IV.64, VI.96, VIII.14
Offensé Pr.6, Pr.20, S.8
Offenser Pr.95
Offensera Pr.107
Offert IV.34
Offices IX.66
Offrande S.12
Offre Pr.13
Offres VIII.23
Offrir I.24
Ogmion V.80, VIII.4, VIII.44
Ogmius Pr.39
Ogmyon VI.42, IX.89
Ognyon IX.89
Oingdre VIII.36
Oingt VI.86, VI.24, VI.89
Oingz VII.36, VII.40
Ointe I.57
Oiseau I.100, V.81
Oisel I.24
Olchade III.64
Olestant III.82
Olive S.30
Olivier S.19, S.49
Olonne IX.21
Olympique VIII.16
Ombre V.64, X.44, X.45
Ombriche Pr.5
Omination IX.46
Omnesq VI.100
Onc(q) II.30, III.28, IV.40, VI.23, IX.68, X.9, X.20, X.27, X.88, X.91
Oncle VIII.89
Oncles X.10
Oncq VIII.53
Oncqu X.4
Oncques II.76, IX.52, X.19, X.57
Onde I.2, I.63, II.86, III.6, IV.77, V.95, VI.79, VIII.16, Pr.19, S.56
Ongle VIII.52
Ongrie II.90, VIII.9, X.62-3
Onques II.6, IV.54, VI.96
Onustes Pr.36
Onze IV.30
Oppi IX.7
Opposans Pr.12
Opposera V.87, S.10
Opposite I.55, V.52, IX.98, Pr.116
Oppressé Pr.6
Oppressee IX.40
Opprobre III.77
Or/os I.35, I.42, I.53, II.92, III.2, III.13, III.67, III.72, IV.30, IV.34, IV.42, V.19, V.41, V.66, V.69, VI.8-9, VI.49, VI.3, VII.25, VII.28, VII.32, VIII.14, VIII.28-9, IX.12, IX.17, IX.4, 1046, X.95, Pr.33, S.2
Oracle III.4
Oraison III.37
Oraisons I.14, IV.25
Orange S.5
Orant VIII.89
Orchestra X.25
Ord X.57
Ordonne Pr.3
Ordre III.79, VIII.90, X.77, Pr.95, S.26, S.30
Oreilles I.96
Orge VII.42, VIII.41
Orgeilleux II.55
Orgon I.90, V.62
Orgueilleux Pr.108
Orgueilleux II.92
Orguion II.73
Oriens I.50
Orient I.9, I.49, I.60, III.35, V.62, V.81, VI.21, VII.80, VII.21, Pr.40-41, Pr.83, Pr.124
Oriental II.29
Orientau(l)x III.78
Orients III.47
Orientz X.75
Origine VIII.10, IX.84
Orion VI.35, Pr.21
Orl III.51, IV.61

Orleans I.20, III.51, III.66, IV.61, V.89, VIII.42, X.45
Ormi Pr.122
Ormis VI.4
Orné VIII.5, Pr.15
Ornée I.96
Ornement III.76
Oron III.25
Orphelins S.35
Orra I.64, II.91, II.100, VIII.84
Oruches VI.99
Os I.42, III.23, VIII.26, IX.32, Pr.36
Oscueil I.56
Oseaux II.23
Osera V.67, IX.71, Pr.90
Oseront I.21, III.18
Ospbre III.77
Ost IV.12, IV.34, IV.37, VIII.92
Ostacle IX.12
Ostage VIII.92
Ostaige X.26
Osté X.32
Oster V.5, Pr.32, Pr.69, S.10
Ostera II.79, VI.3
Ostrage VIII.92
Ostun II.74, VII.4
Oubliance Pr.57
Oubly S.25
Ou(l)trage I.86
Ou(l)tragée I.72, II.89, IX.82
Oultre I.31, II.85, III.23, III.38, IV.12, IV.46, IV.81, V.3, V.51, VI.70, VI.79, VII.87, IX.27, IX.69, X.10
Ouragan IX.62
Ours V.4, VI.44
Ourse IX.10
Outrage II.25, X.20, X.25
Outragee II.53
Outre IV.74, VIII.55, IX.38, Pr.34
Ouvers II.12
Ouvert I.18, V.50, V.59, VII.2, VIII.25, Pr.7, Pr.22, S.8
Ouverte II.68, V.19, VI.65, VII.37, Pr.14
Ouvertes IV.70, VII.14
Ouverts II.12, X.31
Ouvraige V.56
Ouvree V.29
Ouvrir IX.84-5, X.25, X.27, X.80-81
Ouvrira I.89, VIII.78, IX.7
Ouy IV.24, X.4
Ouye II.75, IX.2
Ouys II.77
Overt VI.65
Overte V.35
Oyes IV.43
Oyseau I.34, II.23, II.75
Oyseaux II.44, Pr.73
Oz IV.56, V.7, V.69, VI.50, VI.66, VII.41

Pache IV.73, V.19, V.50, V.82, X.64, VIII.20, Pr.24, Pr.51, Pr.88
Paches VII.18
Pacifie Pr.69, Pr.73
Pacifiera VI.24
Pacifique Pr.77, V.6, Pr.6
Pacifiques X.89
Pacquet I.39
Paganisme III.76
Paiges IX.53
Pain V.90, VII.34, VIII.41, Pr.3, S.50, S.52
Paistre Pr.98
Paistront Pr.28
Paix I.4, I.38, I.63, I.69, I.92, II.9, II.43, III.28, III.54, IV.5, IV.20, IV.97, V.4, V.44, VI.22-3, VI.38, VI.64, VI.90, VII.18, VIII.93, IX.31, IX.51-2, IX.66, IX.86, IX.88, X.42, Pr.1, Pr.3, Pr.7, Pr.14, Pr.33, Pr.45, Pr.47-8, Pr.67, Pr.81-2
Palais I.23, II.66, II.93, VIII.30, IX.22, IX.24, IX.39
Palaix II.93
Palays VII.23
Palerme II.16, VII.6, VIII.9, Pr.17
Palerne VIII.9
Palestine III.97

Palme VI.48
Palmerin I.30
Palonne V.51
Pamiers IX.10
Pampelonne S.41
Pamphylie VII.60
Pamplation VIII.51
Pamplonne VIII.26
Pampon VIII.1
Pamyes IX.10
Pannone X.61
Pannonie IX.90
Pannoniques III.58
Pannonois V.47
Pannons V.48, VIII.15, IX.28
Panons V.13
Panse III.86
Pánta IV.32
Pantamime VII.73
Papauté Pr.9
Pape VI.26, X.12
Papillon VIII.75
Parachever I.97
Parachevera VI.37, Pr.44
Parc I.65, X.83
Pardon Pr.29, Pr.48
Pardonné VI.8
Pardonnee VI.96
Pardonner I.24, IV.98
Pardonnés III.22
Pareil VIII.53, S.13, S.39
Parens V.84, Pr.141, S.55
Parent S.45
Parentele III.28
Parenter VI.71
Parentz IX.61
Pareure I.34
Parfaict I.62
Parfaictz VIII.55
Parfaira IX.84
Parfin V.38, VIII.82
Parfondera X.8
Parfondra VI.44
Parfondrees V.62
Parfondrez IX.15
Paris III.51, III.56, III.93, V.30, VIII.67, IX.45, IX.86
Parlamenteront V.1
Parlant II.70, X.36, X.85
Parlement IV.72
Parler I.59, I.64, III.44
Parlera Pr.10
Parme IV.69, VI.78, V.22, VII.5
Parmy VII.91
Paroir Pr.49
Paroistra I.89, VIII.11
Paroistront I.38
Parpan IX.15
Parpignam X.11
Parpignan VI.56, VIII.22, VIII.24
Parque I.70
Parques I.59, X.82
Parroy IX.85
Par(t)s I.73, II.69, II.72, III.5, III.56, IV.80, VIII.48, IX.20, X.71, Pr.24, Pr.37, Pr.46, Pr.123
Part II.24
Partenaire II.34
Partiaulx VI.95
Partie I.34, VI.49, IX.98
Partir VII.12, IX.28, IX.41, IX.99
Partira II.22, VIII.45, X.68
Partis Pr.39
Partout S.22
Parts III.99, IX.97, Pr.39, Pr.62, S.56
Party X.20
Parvenir Pr.91
Parviendra II.11, II.25, III.28, III.73, VI.36, VI.67, VI.80, VIII.14, VIII.57, VIII.61, VIII.65, Pr.67-8
Parviendront IX.86
Parys VIII.60
Pas X.100, Pr.71
Pasées I.63
Pasle III.1, V.28
Pasmee III.81
Pasque IX.36
Pasques VIII.45, IX.31, S.28
Passage VIII.72, X.11, X.25, Pr.133
Passa(i)ge I.18, V.50
Passa(i)ges IV.19, VII.33

Passant III.54, IV.88, V.17, VIII.21, VIII.51, IX.9, IX.25, IX.27, X.48
Passe I.84, III.1, III.23, V.28, VIII.86, X.73, Pr.23, Pr.105, S.53
Passées I.63
Passer II.20, II.29, II.74, III.43, IV.81, V.26, V.51, VI.69, VII.4, VII.10, VII.20, VIII.55, IX.24, IX.64, IX.85, X.11, X.100, Pr.31, Pr.34, Pr.77
Passera I.86, II.48, II.94, V.11, V.20, V.60, VI.65, IX.27, IX.34, IX.38, IX.56, X.24, X.79, Pr.34, Pr.58, S.25
Passeront III.33, III.98
Passés I.48, IV.46, IV.81, IV.95
Passez IV.78, Pr.69
Pasteur I.25, VI.28
Pasture IV.29, X.13
Patere Pr.22
Paterne VIII.84
Paternel S.40
Paternelle VI.39
Patré III.96
Patrer IV.11
Patron X.53, S.15
Pau/Po I.26, I.33, II.43, II.63, II.94, III.75, IV.70, VI.79, VIII.1, VIII.44
Pause VIII.18, IX.86
Pauvre S.33
Pauvres III.28, III.35
Pavé III.9
Paver VIII.36
Pavillon V.76, VIII.66, VIII.75
Pavillons II.44
Paye VIII.7
Payer III.76
Payez Pr.116
Pays I.5, I.82, III.33, V.89, VIII.92, VIII.97, IX.75, X.51, Pr.41, S.8, S.21, S.23, S.31, S.54, S.57
Paysans IV.63
Pdues VI.62
Peaultre VI.67, IX.76
Pecune VII.25
Peine I.45, S.6, S.10, S.18
Peines III.44
Pelion VIII.89
Pelle VIII.64
Pellegrue X.25
Pellerins X.47
Pellices S.53
Pelligouxe X.25
Pellix IX.77
Pelloponnese V.90
Peloncle VIII.89
Pelte X.53
Pempotam X.100
Pempotan Pr.30
Pempotans VIII.97
Pence IX.47
Pend S.45
Pendant II.55, IV.38, VIII.9, VIII.74, IX.57, Pr.33
Pendu I.2, II.48, II.92, V.28, VII.1
Pendus IV.47
Penelon X.3
Penetran(t)s II.14
Penetrer IV.37
Penitent Pr.80
Pense IX.47
Pensement Pr.8
Pensera IV.15
Penserent I.64
Pensif I.24
Pensifs Pr.12
Pensifz X.37
Penulti(es)me II.28
Per IV.26
Percee II.62
Percer III.62
Percera III.16
Percés IV.70
Perdant X.84
Perdement V.78
Perdra I.4, II.26, I.63, IV.34, VI.14, VIII.31, VIII.60, VIII.79
Perdre VII.39, Pr.81
Perdront Pr.119
Perdu I.25
Perdue VI.58, VIII.100

NOSTRADAMUS DICTIONARY
OF UNUSUAL TERMS FOUND IN THE *PROPHETIES*

For use in conjunction with a large, conventional French-English dictionary. References are to the earliest available editions.

ECCL. LAT. = Ecclesiastical Latin
ENG. = English
GERM. = German
GRK. = Greek
HEB. = Hebrew
IT. = Italian
LAT. = Latin
MED. FR. = Medieval French
O. FR. = Old French
PROV. = Provençal
SPAN. = Spanish
TURK. = Turkish
VULG. LAT. = Vulgar Latin
< = "derives from"
* = hypothetical form

& = et, ou (or almost any other small particle)
& seme = essaim

A

abelhos (PROV.) = abeilles
a caché: either *accaché* or (more likely) *attaché*
Acité = A cité
Aconile: misprint for *Aconite*
acre < GRK. *akros*, "tip"
Adaluncatif: meaning unknown, possibly (via misprint and modified ending) < *Andalusia*, or < *adamantin*, "hard as iron" (?)
adjutoire < LAT. *adjutorium*, "help, succor"
Adrian, mont = Montdarrain, plaine de, near Spanish border south of Bayonne
Adrie = Adria (Etruscan *Hatria*), classical precursor of (a) Venice, about 16 miles/26 kms to northeast, as chief port of the (b) Adriatic (LAT. *Mare Adriaticum*), to which it gave its name
aduché < O.PR. *aducha.* "bought"
adulteres < LAT. *adulterium*, "corruption, crime"
adust(e) < LAT. *adustus*, "burned to ashes"
adventure < LAT. *'adventura*, "things to come"
a(d)vertir < LAT. *advertere*, "to turn toward"
Aemathien / Aemathion (< LAT. *Emathius*), "Macedonian": probable ref. to Alexander the Great
ærain < LAT. *aeramen*, "bronze"; or < LAT. *aerarium*, "treasury, exchequer"
agassas = agaces, "magpies"
Agath (< GRK. *Agatha*, "good") = Agde
Agine = Agen
Agripine < LAT. *Colonia Agrippina* = Cologne
ail = Aie!, "Ouch!"

ains, "but" (with negative)
Alabrox: see Allobrox
Alane, "Alania," territory of former Sarmati, northeast of Black Sea
Alban(n)ois: either Albanians or (more often) people from Alba Longa (mother city of Rome), or from the Alban mountains
Albe: Alba Longa, mother city of Rome, lying about 15 miles/24 kms southeast
Albinge = Albenga, Italy
Alein = **Alleins** (village near Nostradamus's hometown of **Salon**)
ales = Alès
alles < O.FR. "crowds": or misprint for *aesles*, "wings"
Allobroges: ancient rebellious mountain tribe of the Savoy region
Allobrox < LAT. *Allobroges* (q.v.)
allumelle = à lamelle, "blade"
aloys, "standards" (of metals, coins, etc.)
Ambellon = Ambès, or Ambierle (?)
Ambraxie = Ambracia (now Arta, western Greece)
amecon = hameçon, "fish-hook"
amifere / armifere, "arms-bearing"
Amphipolle: Amphipolis, town of ancient Macedonia (now Neokhori)
an = (1) "year," (2) en
anagaronique < GRK. *anagnorisis*, "recognition leading to dénouement": thus, in the original sense of the term, "apocalyptic"
Anatheme < GRK. *anathema*, "something dedicated or accursed"
Anconne, la Marque d': the Marches of Ancona, a long strip of land on the east coast of Italy
Androgyn, "androgyne" (< GRK., "man-woman")
Androne, "narrow lane or path"
aneau, "(Papal) ring"
Angolmois: pun on *Angoulême / Angoumois*, possibly used as anagram for *Mongolois* or partial anagram of *Langobardi*
Angon, l' = Langon
aninite: misprint for *crinite* (*astre crinite* = "bearded star, comet")
Annibalique, "of Hannibal," thus "of the invaders from Africa"
an(n)ichilez (past participle) < LAT. *annihilatus*, "reduced to nothing"
ans sang durera = (1) *ans sans durer a*, (2) *ans endurera* = endurer, "to withstand"
ant(h)ene = antenne, "yardarm"
antenoree = d'Antenor (legendary founder of Padua)
Antibol (< LAT. *Antipolis*) = Antibes
Antipolles < LAT. *Antipolis*, "Antibes," treated as false plural
Antropophage < GRK. *anthropophagos*, "man-eater, cannibal"
apamé = à Parme or Apameste, or <

GRK. *apamao*, "to cut off"
apast = appât, "bait"
appert < LAT. *apertus*, "open"
apprest, "affectation"
aprins = appris
Aquillee: classical Aquileia near Venice
Aquilloye = *loi d'Aquila*, "law of the eagle"; or *loi d'Aquillon*, "law of the North"; or Aquileia, near Venice (see **Aquillee**)
Aquilon (< LAT. *aquilo*), "the north"
aquilonaire < LAT. *aquilo*, "the north"
Ara (cognate with LAT. *arare* "to plow"), "arable land, grainfields"
arant < O.FR. *arer*, "to plow"
Araxes = Araks, river forming border between Iran on the one hand and Armenia and Azerbaijan on the other
arche < LAT. *arca*, "ark": thus, "ship"
Arda, la: Ardalan or Persian Kurdistan, the northwestern province of former Persia; otherwise Ardahan in northeast Turkey
ardra, ard < O.FR. *ardoir / ardre* < LAT. *ardere*, "to burn"
arduenne silve (< LAT. *silva*, "wood, forest"), "the forest of the Ardennes"
are (< LAT. *ara*), "altar, hearth, refuge" or (< LAT. *area*) "open space in town"
Aretin < LAT. *Arentius*, "Arezzo"
Argel = Algiers
Arimin < LAT. *Ariminum*, "Rimini"
Armonique: misprint for *Armorique*, "of Armorica" (Brittany and western Normandy)
Armoriq: Armorica (Brittany)
Arnani = Hernani, Spain
arpen (O.FR.), "acre"
arq = arche (< LAT. *arcus*, but as though < LAT. *arca*: hence, presumably, the feminine in V.9)
arres < LAT. *arrha*, "signs, tokens, pledged or pawned articles"
Arriens = Arrianus (*c.* AD 100–180), native of Nicopolis, Greek soldier, statesman, and historian of Alexander's campaigns
Artamide/Arthemide, temple d', "mausoleum," after the original temple to the dead King Mausolus of Caria, erected in 353 B.C. by his widow Artemisia and thereafter accounted one of the Seven Wonders of the ancient world
Artemide, "Artemis," Greek moon-goddess and hunting deity, equivalent of Roman Diana
Arton < GRK. *arktos*, "(Great) Bear": hence "northern"
Artoniques < GRK. *arktos*, "(Great) bear": hence, "northerners"
aruspices < LAT. *haruspex*, "seer, prophet"
à sang . . . ramer, "to swim in blood"
Ascans = Ascanus

Asie = Asia Minor, i.e. Anatolia, Turkey
asinier = ânier, "ass-driver": or = asiniens, "asinine ones"
asnier, "donkey-driver"; or possible pun on *aîné*
Asonne < LAT. *Ausonia*, "(lower) Italy"
Asop (later editions have *Ascop*) < GRK. *askopos*, "unseen, unheard of, inconceivable, incredible"
aspre < LAT. *asper*, "harsh"
assallie = assaillie
assomye, "assuaged"
astre aninite, misprint for *astre crinite* (< LAT. *crinis*, "hair") as in later editions, "bearded star": thus, "comet"
astre crinite, "bearded star" (comet)
atacquer = attacher: normally it was *attaquer* (< IT.) that was Frenchified into *attacher*, rather than vice versa, but in VIII.16 it was presumably the rhyme that was decisive.
à Tende = attendre: possible word-play on the title of Nostradamus's friend the Duc de Tende
aubereau < *aubert* (MED. FR. slang), "silver, money"
au chef de l'an (lit. "at the head of the year"), "at New Year"
auge (astr.), "apsis, aphelion, high point" (< LAT. *augere*, "to increase, augment")
augment = augmentation
au puy brises: "broken at the well": ref. to Ecclesiastes 12:6
Aurelle < LAT. *Aurelianum*, "Orleans"
Ausone, Ausonne < LAT. *Ausonia*, "(lower) Italy"
Aust / Auster (LAT.), "south wind"
austre < LAT. *austerus*, "austere"
au toc de la campano (PROV.) = au son du tocsin
Aux = Auch
auxelle, either = Auxerre, or < LAT. *auxilium*, "aid, succor"
avaigne = avoine
avent < LAT. *adventus*, "advent, arrival"
Aventin, one of Rome's seven hills
avint = advint: read *Qu'avint aux Romains viendra par Babel*
avistard = avis tard
Azostains, "hedonists"

B

balance: "(lands subject to) Gemini"; or (literally) 'trading nations (of the West)'; or pun on LAT. *libra/libera*, "scales"/"free"
ban = bannira (?)
Barb' / Barb / Barba = Barbare
Barbare = Berber (reference to the original North African invaders of Spain): thus, "Muslim" and, by Christian extension, "infidel, heathen"
Barbaris < GRK. *barbaros*, "babbling, stammering"; or genitive of *Barbare*

Barboxitaine: either "Western Barbary" or compression of LAT. *(Aheno)barbus occitan(us)*

Barchinons < LAT. *Barcino*, "Barcelonans"

Barcins < LAT. *Barcino*, Carthaginian Barcelona

barg(u)inera, "will bargain"

Barré, la (< O.FR. *barré*, "motley"), the Carmelite Order (**Cheetham**)

barril, LAT. *barriculus* = baril, "cask, barrel"

Barrois, "of Bar-le-Duc"

Basacle: celebrated water-mill at **Toulouse**, also mentioned by François **Rabelais** in *Pantagruel*

Basil < GRK. *basileus*, "king"

Bastarnan < LAT. *Bastarnes*, ancient tribe of eastern Europe resident between Vistula and Danube

bauge, "muddy place, swamp, pigsty"

Becoyran: Boucoiran (on river Gard)

beffroy = beffroi, "belfry" (originally "defense-works, fortifications")

Begich: possibly < TURK. *beg*, "Bey," or misprint for *Berich*. < LAT. *Bituriges*, Berry (Cher-et-Indre), as in later editions

Begorn = Bigorre (confirmed by near-rhyme with *Perigort* in line 1)

Begourdans, "people of Bigorre"

bellique (< LAT. *bellum*), "of war"

beluezer = baluchon, "miner's bucket" (?)

Benac < LAT. *Benacus* = Lake Garda, Italy

bender = bander

besson (Dial.), "twin"

Betique < LAT. *Baetis*, the Guadalquivir River

Betta: possible misreading of Buda (western Budapest)

blaime = O.FR. *bleime*, "wounded"

Blaue = Blaye

bled = blé

blenni (< GRK *blennos*), "snotty"

blesiq = blésoise, "of Blois"

Bleterram: see Bliterre

Bliterre < LAT. *Julia Baeterrae*, "**Béziers**": the local inhabitants are called *Biterrois* to this day.

bocin, = PROV. *boucin*, "scrap" (originally meat of old he-goat, hare, or rabbit)

boge = bouge

Bohesme = Czechoslovakia

bondance = abondance

Boristhenes: classical name for Dnieper River in Russia

bouive < LAT. *bos, bovis*, "of cattle"

bourlis, la, forest: possibly Bourlon Wood, just west of Cambrai and not far from the Canal de St.-Quentin, scene of a bloody battle in World War I

bouscade (PROV. < IT. *bosco*, "wood") = embuscade, "ambush"

bout, O.FR. "blow, violence"

bragamas < O.PROV. *briamonso*, "soldier of fortune" (**Cheetham**)

Branches, au milieu de: literally *au mi-lieu de*, "in the inner shrine of" + *Branchis* (Latinized form of *Branchidai*, Didym, Turkey), site of celebrated ancient oracle of Apollo Didymaeus

Brannonices (LAT.), tribe from the

Eure and Sarthe region

brassieres, les deux, "the two burnes": probable ref. to Saturn or Jupiter

Bresse: either La Bresse, France, or Breschia, Italy

brique: misprint for *brigue*

Brodde: see Brodes

Brodes: Prov. term for inhabitants of Alpine country around Isère River (< LAT. *Allobroges*); also = O.FR. *brode*, "unworthy, dark, swarthy." See III.92, VIII.34

Brudis = Brindisi, Italy

bueyre: presumably = bure, "rough homespun"

Buffalorre = Buffalora, small village near Milan

Bugie = Bougie (Bejaia), Algeria

Burançoys: possibly Buzançais

bureau: originally "russet fabric"

Buy, le = Le-Buis-les-Baronnies, Drôme

C

cailhau (PROV.), "insult" (**Cheetham**); or = caillou, "fool, dupe"

cainct < LAT. *cinctum*, "precinct, area around"

caindra = craindra

calcine < LAT. *calcina*, "lime"

Calpre (< LAT. *Calpe*), "Gibraltar"

camp < LAT. *campus*, "(battle)field" and thus "battle, army"

campane < LAT. *campana*, "bell"

campano (PROV.): see *campane*

candentes < LAT. *cadere*, "falling"

Cap., "head, cape," but also (< LAT. *caput*, "head"), "captain"

Capadille = Capellades, Spain

Caper: abbr. for *Capricorne*

Capion = Caepio, Roman consul who sacked **Toulouse** in 106 B.C., but failed to return its (even now undiscovered) treasures to Rome

Capitolin, "of the Roman Capitol, or government"

cappe (= *cape*) < LAT. *cappa*, "sleeveless cape, cloak" and thus possibly "cassock"; but also "trysail, storm-sail"

capres, "caper-bushes"

caprine, "of goats"

car, (1) "for": (2) misprint for *cuir* (as in later editions) < LAT. *corium* < GRK. *chorion*, "skin, leather" (VII.25)

Car Bourd. = Carcassonne, Bordeaux

Carcas = Carcassonne

carne omination < LAT. *carne ominatum*, "entrail-reading"

Caron es: later editions have *Carones*, possibly "carronades" (short, large-bore cannons)

Carpen = Carpentras

casane: probably < IT. *casa*, "cottage"

case, "cottage"

Caspre (printed *Caſpre*): error for LAT. *Calpe*), "Gibraltar"

Cassich < GRK. *Cassiterides*, "tin islands" (Cornwall and the Scillies)

Cassilin (printed *Caſsilin*): unusual spelling suggests that the "si" is a misreading of some other single letter: possibly Casoli, near Naples

caste < LAT. *castus*, "chaste, pure"

castel (SOUTHERN FRENCH "castle") = Castile (?)

Castor & Polux: the Heavenly Twins: presumed reference at II.90 to Hungary's twin capital cities of Buda and Pest; otherwise to the zodiacal sign of Gemini

Castulon < LAT. *Castulonensis*, "of the city of Castulo" (now Cazorla in southeastern Spain)

cause < LAT. *causa*, (1) "cause," (2) "legal process, situation, condition"

cave (normally "cellar, vault"), possibly (< LAT. *cavea*) "theater, den"

cavilleux < O.FR. *caviller*, "jesting"

ceiulee = cérulé, < LAT. "dark blue or green"

celestes: misprint for *scelestes* < LAT. *scelestus*, "criminal"

celiq(s). = céleste(s)

celiques = célestes

Censuart (< *sangsue*, "leech"), "leechlike one, extortioner"; alternatively < *Sang-ſuant*, "sweater of blood," and thus "toiler, worker."

cent, main = sang humain

Ceres = Persephone, goddess of the isle of Sicily and deity of the crops, esp. grain (cf. English "cereals")

Cesarés, "Caesarean," thus "Imperial"

Ceucalion = "Deucalion" in later editions: Greek equivalent of biblical Noah, thus "flood"

chaine, "chain," or = chêne

Chaldondon < LAT. *Chaldeus*, "Chaldean, soothsayer, astrologer"

chalmé < IT. *calma* < LAT. *cauma*, GRK. *kauma*, "noonday heat"

Champagne (*Campaigne* in later editions) = "Campania"

champs Helisees = champs Élysées, "Elysian fields"

change(r): normally used by Nostradamus to indicate some kind of astrologically linked disaster

changée: possible misprint for chargée

Chanignon = Canino (Italy)

charient = charrient, "carry, wash down"

charpin = charpie, "mincemeat"

chassé = chasse, "batten of loom"

chau = chaux

chauls (< LAT. *calidus*) = chauds

chaulveron: either = chaulier, "lime-burner," or dim. of chauve, "bald"

chausses perhume (< LAT. *per* + *humus*), "pants-down"

chaut < LAT. *calere*, "heat" in the sense of hot temper, raised emotions, etc.

chef < LAT. *caput*, "head": with *Aries*, "first point of"

cheirenesse < GRK. *chersonesos*, ATTIC *chersonesos*, "peninsula"

Cheramon agora: former name of Usak, in Turkey (**Cheetham**)

cherra: future of ch(e)oir, "to fall"

cherronesse < GRK. *chersonesos*, ATTIC *chersonesos*, "peninsula": thus, the Peloponnese

Chersonnez: see **cherronesse**

chevance, "real estate"

Chio: either Chios (Greek island) or

anagram for Sochi, on the Black Sea

Chivaz = Chivasso, Italy

choir, "fall"

Chyren, anagram for *Henryc(us)*, "Henry"

Cimbres, "Cimbri" (German tribe from Jutland that invaded Spain in 105 B.C.)

Cinq changeront en tel reuolu terme: read *Tel terme révolu, (ils le) changeront en cinq (ans)*. The mutilated rhyme-scheme suggests that the original may have read something like: *Changeront en cinq (ans) du terme la forme*.

circonder < LAT. *circumdare*, "to surround, encircle"

circuir (< LAT. *circuire*), "to go around"

cita nova (O. PROV.) = cité nouvelle: thus, either "Villeneuve" or "Naples" (< GRK. *Neapolis*, "New City")

cité neufve: usually transliteration of Villeneuve in France, but possibly Villanova d'Asti or Naples in Italy (see **cita nova**)

cité solaire: normal Nostradamian code for **Lyon**, by zoological and astrological analogy

citez < LAT. *citare*, "put into motion"

ciutad (PROV. < LAT. *civitas*) = cité

chevance, O.FR., "real estate, landed property"

clade < LAT. *clades*, "disaster, defeat"

clam, LAT., "secretly, in private"

clame < LAT. *clamor*, "clamor, outcry"

classe < LAT. *classis*, "summons" > "body of men summoned" > "fleet, army," used in its original sense at I.35

claude < LAT. *claudus*, "lame"

clistre = clystere, "washer-out, syringe, injection"

coche, "notch, score-mark"

coeur hault, prudet mis: read as *coeur prudent, haut mis*

collisee = Colisée

Colongna = Colonnes d'Hercule, "Gibraltar" (?)

Columna / Colomne: Cape Colonna, southernmost point of Greece; otherwise apparent reference to the Colonnas, ancient aristocratic family long regarded as virtually synonymous with Rome itself, and famous in Nostradamus's day for the poetess Vittoria Colonna, close friend of Michelangelo.

combien que = bien que, "although"

combouls < GRK. *kymbalon*, "cymbals"

commettra < LAT. *committere*, "to put together, join"

Compagne: either "countryside" or "Campania" (origin of the term)

concaver, "to hollow out, excavate"

conciter < LAT. *concitare*, "to set sail"

coniure va; misprint for *conjurera*

connisse < LAT. *connissus*, "brought forth"

contens, possible contraction of *continens*

contrade < O.PROV. *contrada* (< late LAT.), "country"

contree < O.PROV. *contrada*, "country"

copie(s) < LAT. *copia*, "army, forces, troops"

coprins = compris

cordigere < LAT. *chorda* + *gerens*, "cord-

bearer": thus, probably = *cordelier*, "Franciscan friar," or "bound hand and foot"

Corduba, LAT., "Cordoba"

corff: either *Corfou* or misprinted version of *corsaires*

cornere, misprint for *coronete* (as per later editions), "ornamental headdress," dim. of O.FR. *corone* < LAT. *corona*, "crown"

Corsibonne = possibly Corcubión, northwest Spain

coulpe < LAT. *culpa*, "blame"

courges < LAT. *cohourde* < Lat. *cucurbita*, "gourds"

crappe = crape, "filth, effluent, chaff"

crest = créscent

criant, "crying"; otherwise misprint for *craint(e)*

crinite < LAT. *crinitus*, "hairy"

croc = croqué, "hooked"; or abbr. for *crocodilles*

croisez, literally "thwarted"

croix, "crosses" and thus by extension "Crusaders, Christians"

cron roy, version of GERM. *Kronprinz* (see second half of line)

crucigere (< LAT. *crux*, "cross" + *gerere*, "to bear, manage, rule"), either "cross-bearing" or "Christian-ruling" – i.e. "set to overcome and dominate Christianity" – or even (< LAT. *crucifigere*) "crucifying"

crustamin < LAT. *Crustuminus*: of former Sabine town of Crustumeria; river Conca (**Cheetham**)

cultre = *coutre*, "large knife"

cunicules < LAT. *cuniculus*, rabbit: thus "rabbit-holes, underground galleries" by association with *cunette*, "fortification ditch"

curieux < LAT. *curiosus*, "full of care" or "having care or charge of"

cuser < LAT. *cudere*, "to mint"

Cydron = Cydonia, modern Khania (Cyprus) or *Kydnos*, the river of Tarsus, Turkey

cymbe < GRK *kymbe*, "hollow or inside of vessel"

D

Dace: region of Romania

d'Almatie, "Dalmatia"

d'Amant & Pselin: read *du Démon Psellin* (i.e. *de* **Psellus**)

dame, "lady," or < LAT. *dama*, "deer"

d'ame = dame

d'Annemarc = de Danemark

darbon = d'Arbon (on Lake Constance, Switzerland), or compression of *de Narbo(nne)*

dars = dards

Dauffois: either = Dauphinois, or "of the Dauphin"

daurade: Notre Dame la Daurade, church in **Toulouse**

debatre < LAT. *debatuere*, "to beat down"

debeller < LAT. *debellare*, "to conquer, put down"

deboutez = déboutés, "dismissed"

deceuz = déçus

decide (< LAT. *decidere*, "cutting away"

defaite < O.FR. *desfaire*, "undoing, defeat"

deffendra < LAT. *defendere*, "to ward off"

deffraieur: < O.FR. *desfrayer*, "to defray, settle, pay up, appease"

definer = définir, in the sense of "to put an end to"

de fouldre à vierge = à verge de foudre: the words have been reordered à la Virgil

delues < LAT. *deludere*, "to play false"

De maison sept, "seven of the (ruling) house"

de miples < GRK. *demiopleres*, "abounding in public"

demis: p.p. of O.FR. *desmettre*, "to lay or send down": later editions have *(seront) amis*

de nueh l'intrado (PROV.) = de nuit l'entrée

de route = déroute

desnier ont = dénieront

destranché < LAT. *detruncare*, "to cut or hew apart, mutilate, behead"

destre < LAT. *dexter*, "right (hand)"

destrois (< LAT. *districtus*, "drawn tight") = détroit, "strait, narrows"

detrenchés (< LAT. *detruncare*), "mutilated, beheaded"

Deucalion: Greek equivalent of the biblical Noah

deul = deuil

deux, "two," or = d'eux, or (more often) ducs < LAT. *dux, duces* "leader(s), general(s)"

Deux pars vaultorte, "two parts deviously" (?)

devers, usually "toward," but in V.25 probably = de vers

dextre < LAT. *dexter*, "right"

d'Humaine = Nosradamian word-play on "de Maine"

dial < LAT. *Dialis*, "of Dis / Jupiter"

diete, O.FR., "assembly, council, parliament, conference"

diphlongue, lieu: "diphthongal, or double-sounding place" – possibly either Firenzuola or Fiesole

divisé = devisé, "ordained"

D.M.: LAT. *Ditis Manibus*, "in the hands of Dis, or Pluto"; on the other hand, the final section of Nostradamus's *Orus Apollo* is itself entitled *Comment ilz appelloient les dieux infernaulx qu'ilz appelloient manes D.M.*

doit = doigt

dole = dol, "fraud"

doleance = douleur, but also "complaint, whining"

don = "gift," but also misprint for *d'où*

double < SPAN. *doble*, "doubloon"

drap = drapeau (?)

du bout (possible misprint for *tout*, as in later editions) **Torrent & champ**, "of every rushing stream and field"

duc / dui(c)t < LAT. *dux*, "general, leader"

duira (< LAT. *ducere*, "to lead") = conduira

du maling falcigere, "of the scythe-bearing evil one": Nostradamus habitually uses both terms for the Planet

Saturn which, as the slowest-moving of the known planets until Nostradamus's day, was always associated with Old Father Time

du polle artiq: writers of the time often used the word "pole" where we would use "hemisphere," a word that they tended to reserve for the earth itself (compare Marlowe, for example)

du rosne: occasionally = de Rome

duyra: see **duira**

E

eage = age

eaue, "water"; also Nostradamian code for Aquarius

eclypses < LAT. *eclipsis* < GRK. *ekleipsis*, "failure, eclipse"

effaieur: misprint for *effraieur* (< effrayer), "fear" (effroi)

Egee, "Aegean"

egeste (< LAT. *egestum*, "carried out"), "dug out"

emblee < O.FR. *embler*, "to take, seize, carry off": hence "looting, theft, robbery"

embler, O.FR. < LAT. *involare*, "to seize, capture, attack, sack, strip"

embosque (PROV.) = embuscade

emmy = en mi, "in between"

emonopolle = en monopole, "exclusively"

Emorre: some later editions have *Comorre*, probable misreading of *Comarne*, "Komarno"

emprinse = entreprinse

en = (1) "in", (2) ans

enclin < LAT. *inclinare*, "to decline, lower, draw toward setting"

encunder < LAT. *incondere*, "to jerry-build," or "to unbuild, demolish, take apart"

Endymion: sleepy, mythical Greek youth beloved of Selene, the moon

enfant de Germain: later editions have *enfant Germain*

enferré, "placed in irons"

enfouetz (< VULG. LAT. *infodictus* < LAT. *infodere*) = enfoui

engin, par (< LAT. *ingenium*), "by skill"

en marque = en marche, or possibly "taking reprisals"

ennosigée < GRK. *ennosigaios*, "earth-shaker" (normally applied to Poseidon)

ensolcy = en souci

ententifs = attentifs

entres = enterrés, "buried"

entreprinse = entreprise

enyurés = enivrés

epithalame < LAT. *epithalamium*, "wedding-chant"

erain < LAT. *aerarium*, "treasury, exchequer"

Eretrion = Eretria, Greece

Ergaste < LAT. *Ergastulum*, "workshop, penitentiary"

es = en les

esbrotés = ébroussés, "stripped"

escient, à bon escient, "knowingly, deliberately"

esclave, O.FR. "slave" < MED. LAT. *sclavus*, "Slav" < LATE GRK *sklabos* <

SLAVONIC *slovo*, "word"; *sloviti*, "speak": thus either "slave" or "Slav"

escoudre (O.PROV. < LAT. *excutere*), "to flail, or thresh"

esgrongnez = O.FR. *esgruignier*, "to reduce to pieces, cut apart" (**Fontbrune**)

eslites = élus, "chosen"

esmotion < LAT. *emotio, -nis*, "stirring-up"

espargie < O.FR. *espargier*, "to sprinkle, scatter"

espeüillera < O.FR. *espoiller* < LAT. *spoliare*, "will spoil, ruin"

esponce = éponge

estache(z) O.FR. (< O.GERM. *stakka*), "staked out"

estinique < N.T. GRK. *ethnikos*, "foreign, heathen, gentile"

estoille en barbe, "bearded star," thus "comet, meteor"

estoupé = étoupé, "stuffed up" (of ears)

estraine / estrennes = étrenne, "New Year's gift"

estres = astres, "stars"; or êtres, "beings"

estrillés = étrillés

estude < LAT. *studium*, "zeal, application"

Ethne: presumably not "Etna" but "Elne"

Euge (LAT.), "Bravo!"

Euxine, pont < LAT. *Pontus Euxinus*, the Black Sea

exancle (< LAT. *exanclatus* or *exantlus*), "suffered, endured": thus, "worn out, exhausted" (**Fontbrune**)

excubies < LAT. *excubans*, "on guard"

exercite < LAT. *exercitus*, "army"

exil < LAT. *exilis*, "thin, meager, poor"; *exilitas*, "poverty"

expiler < LAT. *expilare*, "to plunder"

expiration: possible misprint for *expiation*, as per later editions

expugner < LAT. *expugnare*, "to storm"

expuise = épuise

extispices < LAT. *extispex*, "soothsayer"

eyssame (PROV.) = essaim

F

face = visage

faict < LAT. *factum*, "fact, fate," in absence of French word < LAT. *fatum*, "fate"

faillir, "to fail," but more anciently "to deceive"

fain = faim

faisant maye, "in the midst of (May) celebrations"

faix, load-bearing part of bridge

falcigere (< LAT. *falx, falcem*, "sickle"), "sickle or scythe bearer": thus, Saturn

fara muestra, SPAN.: probable misprint for *faro muestra*, "a lighthouse shines"

fato (ablative of LAT. *fatum*), "from Fate"

faugnards = fangeux, "muddy, filthy"

faulce = fausse

faulx, faux < LAT. *falsus*, "false ones," but also < LAT. *falx*, "scythe/sickle": hence "followers of the (false) Muslim lunar crescent"

Favene = Faenza, Italy

feit (< LAT. *fecit*) = made

felice < LAT. *felix*, "happy, fortunate"

felin: misprint for *ſelin* (selin), "of Selene the moon-goddess": hence, "lunar, of the Muslim crescent"

fenera < feindre, "to limp, halt"

fenestre, "window," or misprint for *senestre*, "left-hand, sinister"

fer, "iron" and thus "sword"; or misprint for *feu*

fera Perme, "will grant leave"

ferrugine (< LAT. *ferrugo, -inis*), "rust-colored" and thus "red"

Fertsod: unidentified city – possibly *Fer* + *tso* (HEB. "filthy") + suggestive final *d* – Nostradamian portmanteau code-name for Ferdinand V of Castile, who expelled the Jews (possibly including Nostradamus's ancestors) from Spain in 1492; otherwise possibly Fermo in Italy, or (less likely) Fertöszentmiklós, in western Hungary

Fesulan = fessan, "broad of bottom," incorporating pseudo-geographical reference to Fiesole, Italy < LAT. *Faesulae*

fiance < O.FR. "engagement, promise, trust"

figuieres, Castillon: probably Figueira de Gastello Rodrigo, Portugal

figulier < LAT. *figulus*, "potter"

finements = *finiments*, "finishings, conclusions"

finera (O.FR.), "will pay for"; or = finira

fitine: see **sitine**

flambe (O.FR.) = flamme

flaminique < LAT. *flamen*, cult-priest, "priestly"

flangnards < PROV. *flaougnard*, "flatterer"

fleues = fléaux

fleur de lys, "lily-of-the-valley," thus, "French"

fleurs, "flowers"; also misprint for *fléaux*

Flor., Flora = Florence

Floram patere, LAT. (literally) "to open the flower"

fluve = fleuve

folliges (< LAT. *folliculus*, "bladder, ball") = folies

forbe, "trickery" (**Fontbrune**)

forché = fourché (?)

forens / forrier < LAT. *foranus*, "foreign," or < *foris*, "outside"

forge < LAT. *fabrica*, "workshop"

Formande: possible corruption of Benavente or Bernesga (River)

fors = forts

Foussan = Fossano, Italy

foussil, version of *fossoir*, "viticulteur's plow"

foy = fidèles

foy Punique (< LAT.), "bad faith"

fragues < VULG. LAT. *fraga* = fraises

fraulx < LAT. *fraus*, "fraud, trickery, error"

Freins: error for *Freius*, "Fréjus"

fresch, au = au frais, "in the cool"

fresz < LAT. *frendere, fressus*, "crushed"

frofaim = froid, faim

froit = froid

froquez < *froc*, "befrocked, arrayed in monk's frock"

Fucin = the former Lake Fucino, Italy

Fuis le rang: misprint for *Puis le sang* (as per much later editions)

fulgure, "(lightning) flash"

furet, O.FR., "thief"

fuste, originally a shallow-draft galley, thus possibly "landing craft"

G

gach (PROV.) = guet

Gad = Gand, "Ghent"

Gaddes < LAT. *Gades*, "Cadiz"

gaindra (IT. *guadagnare*) = gagnera

Gallotz = Gaulois, "Frenchmen"

Gand = Ghent

Gandole: possible misprint for Candosa, Portugal, though rhyme and scansion (IV.97) suggest *Gades* (LAT., "Cadiz")

Ganges: small town to the north of Montpellier

Gang. Iud. = *Gange judaïque*, "Jewish Ganges" (i.e. holy river) and thus "Jordan"

garbelans < IT. *garbellare*, "to misrepresent, mangle, mutilate"

Gardoing = "by the Gard(on) River"

gastant = gâtant < LAT. *vastare*, "to lay waste"

gastera = gâtera (< LAT. *vastare*), "will lay waste"

Gaulsier: see **mont Gaulsier**

Gebenoise, "of Cévennes (south of France)"

genisse (here m., therefore not "heifer"!) = genêt ("broom"), < masculinized form of LAT. *genista / genesta* (the more normal modern word *balai* comes originally from the Breton word for the same plant)

Gennes = Genoa

genoilles, O.FR. = genoux

gent < LAT. *gens, gentis*, "people, tribe": often used by Nostradamus to mean "army"

gentils < ECCL. LAT. *gentilis*, "gentiles, heathen"

gent Punique = "Carthaginian race or army": thus, "North Africans"

Germain, "full brother/sister/cousin," but also < LAT. *Germanus*, Roman name for eastern Europe generally, to east of Rhine and north of Danube

Germanie, see **Germain** at III.90 possible misprint for *Cermanie*. "Kerman" (as in 1568 ed.), city and province of southeastern Persia

germanique, "pertaining to Germanus" (see **Germain**)

gettéz = jetés: or misprint for *gelez*, "frozen"

geux = jeux

glaifves, glaive < LAT. *gladius*, "sword": standard Nostradamian term for "war"

glas, glaz, "death-knell"

globe < LAT. *globus*, "troop, crowd, body or mass of people"

glomes < LAT. *glomus*, "ball of yarn" and thus "conglomeration, assembly, congregation": some commentators assume that the reference is to the councils of the early Church

gloze (< GRK. *glossa*, "word requiring explanation"), "glossed, noted"

goffes, O.FR. "heavy, crude"

Gorsan = Coursan

Gotique, "medieval," and thus "uncivilized"

Goussan ville = Goussonville (rather than Goussainville in northeast **Paris**)

gousse, "shell, husk, pod"

gouvert: abbr. for *gouvernement*

granci = garanti

grand: often used for *grande* before noun, as in modern grand'mère, grand'chose, etc.

Grande Grande, la: possibly Queen Catherine de Médicis

grand Hadrie, la: Nostradamian code for Venice, the Adriatic's chief city: see **Adrie**

granée: misprint for *gravée*

greffe: misprint for *greſle* = grêle, "hail"

grenoilles: possible misprint for second edition's **genoilles** (q.v.)

grippe, "quarrel, caprice"

Grisons: "gray (headed) ones," or "people of the Swiss canton of Grisons"

grogne: misprint in III.87 (as rhyme reveals) for *gregue* (PROV.) = grecque

groppe < IT. *gruppa / groppa* = groupe

groumelans: possibly < GERM. *grummeln*, DUTCH. *grommelen*, "to grumble, mutter"

guerdonnez < O.FR. *gueredon*, "rewarded"

guerres, "wars": or = guère, "hardly"

Guien, either "of Guyenne" or (< *gui*) "mistled"

Guin = Guyenne

Guion (O.FR.), "standard-bearer," contraction of *guidon*, "guide, leader"

H

hacatombe (< GRK. *hekatombe*, "a hundred oxen"), "ritual sacrifice": hence "slaughter"

Hadrie, Adria (ETRUSCAN *Hatria*), classical precursor of (a) Venice, some 16 miles/26kms northeast, as chief port of the (b) Adriatic (LAT. *Mare Adriaticum*), to which it gave its name

Hadrie, la grande: Venice, chief city of the Adriatic

Haemathion < LAT. *Emathius*, "Macedonian" (possible reference to Alexander the Great)

halbe < O.FR. *hâbler* < SPAN. *hablar*, "to speak, talk" (gen. pejorative)

Hamon: another name for the biblical Issachar: also the father of Shechem, who was done to death, along with his followers, for defiling Jacob's daughter Dinah

Hanix < LAT. *annixus*, "effort"

hare < O.FR. *harer*, to harry, set a dog on someone: thus, "hunt, chase"

Harmotique < GRK. *harmos*, "joint"

Hasse = Hesse

hausse < LAT. *haustum*, "drink, draft"

Hebro = Ebro

hecatombe / heccatombe (< GRK.), "ritual slaughter"

Hem. mi deux Phi = probable reworking of *en mi-défi*, "in mid-defiance"

HENRIPOLIS: invented term ("Henry's City"), presumably for **Paris**

herbipolique, au ventre: "to the heart of Grassville" – almost certainly Cannes (= "reeds")

Hercules, either the "Gallic Hercules" (see Ogmyon) or occasionally "Gibraltar"

Heredde < LAT. *heres, heredis*, "heir"

Herne = *Ierne*, anagram for *reine*

Hespaigne = Espagne

Hesperie (< GRK. *Hesperides*), "the west"

Hesperique < GRK. *hesperios*, "western"

Hetrurie, "Etruria": thus "Italy"

hiemal < LAT. *hiemalis*, "of winter"

HIERON, GRK. *hieros*, "sacred"; but normally taken as misprint for *Hieson*, "Jason"

Hieron, la cité du sainct: St. Jerome's city – presumably either his birthplace of Stridon on the northern Dalmatian frontier, or Rome, or Antioch (where he was ordained), or Constantinople (where he studied)

hilter: misprint, not for *Hitler* (tempting as the assumption may be), but for *Hiſter*, classical name for lower Danube (< GRK. *Histros*), here confirmed by its listing alongside *Ryn*, "Rhine"

Hister: Latin name for lower Danube < GRK. *Histros*

hoirs (O.FR., "heirs") **Romulides, les**, "the heirs of Romulus": thus, "the Italians"

holcades < GRK. *holkas, -ados*, "transport vessel, barge" (cf. ENG. "hulk")

Houche = district of Antwerp (**Fontbrune**)

hurne, la (= urne), "the water-pot" (ancient Babylonian designation of Aquarius)

huys, O.FR. "doors"

hyppolite (< GRK.), "of (Saint) Hippolytus": thus, "chaste, austere, religious"

Hyrcanie = Hyrcania, former province of northeastern Persia

Hyspans: Hispanics, & thus Spaniards

hystra < O.FR. *issir*, "to go or come out"

I

ia = déjà

Ibere (< GRK.), the Iberian peninsula

ieulx = yeux

Ilerde = *Lerida* (eastern Spain)

Illirique, "Illyrian, Dalmatian"

Imperateur, LAT. *Imperator*, "Emperor"

inbitables, misprint for *inhabitables*

incidez < LAT. *incidere*, "fallen"

incoruz < LAT. *incorruptos*, "uncorrupted"

infecteurs (< LAT. *infector*), "dyers"

insopie, "unsleeping"

instans < LAT., "(those) present"

Insubre(s) < LAT. *Insubria*, Milan region of Italy.

insult(e) < LAT. *insultare*, "to leap at"), "attack"

intaminee < LAT. *intaminatus*, "non-contaminated, undefiled"

intepree = *interpretee*, or possible misprint for *intemptee* < LAT. *intentatus*, "stretched out"

internitions, < LAT. *internecare*, "mutual killings"; later editions have *intentions*

intestin, "internal, domestic, civil (war, disorder)"

intrado (PROV.) = entrée

invercunde < LAT. *inverecundus*, "immodest"

Ionchere = Jonchères, possibly St.-Maurice; or Jonquères; or Junquera

Iovaliste, "man of Jupiter": hence, "man of God"

Iris (< GRK.), "rainbow"

irrision < LAT. *irrisio*, "mockery"

isle volce, l': L'Isle-sur-Sorgue, main town of Vaucluse

Ismaël, "Ishmael": thus, "Arab"

Ismaëlites, "sons of Ishmael": thus, "Arabs"

Ispalme: anagram of LAT. *mel*, "honey" + *apis*, "bee"

Ister, classical name for lower Danube < GRK. *Histros*: see **Hister**

istra < O.FR. *issir* < LAT. *exire*, "to issue, leave, go out, come forth"

Iud < LAT. *Judaei* = "Jewish"

J

ja = déjà

jacture < LAT. *jactura*, "loss, abandonment"

jou (O.FR.) = joug, "yoke"

Joviaux (< LAT. *Jovis*, "Jupiter"), "men of God, papal"

Julian, sainct: April 12th

K

Kappa, Theta, Lambda = the Greek letters k, θ and λ (K, TH and L)

L

labouriez, O.FR. < LAT. *labor*, "to slip, slide, waver, err, perish, be ruined, deteriorate, disintegrate"

lacticineuse (< LAT. *lac, lactis*) "milky"

laenées < LAT. *lanatus*, "woolly"; or (more likely) misprint for *laevé(e)s* < LAT. *laevus*, "left-handed, sinister"

Laigne < LAT. *lagena*, "narrow-necked bottle"

lainé = l'aîné

lairra = laissera

lame = "blade," and thus "sword"; but also = l'âme

Langoult: misprint for *Langouſt* (langoust) < O.PROV. *langosta* < LAT. *locusta*, "grasshopper" (ref. to the "locusts" of St. John's Revelation)

l'aquilon < LAT. *aquilo*, "the north"

l'a ruent = la ruée, though later editions have *l'advent*

lasche: literally "coward," but formerly used simply to mean "wretch" or "dishonorable person"

l'aschera = lâchera

lassotie (*la sottie* O.FR.) = la sottise

latebre < LAT. *latebra*, "den, hiding place"

Latona (LAT.) = GRK *Leto*, mother of Apollo (the sun) and Artemis (the moon): thus "sun and moon"

Lauragues: region of southwestern France extending into the Pyrenean foothills around the upper Garonne and Aude

Lauxois: possibly Auxerre, or even Auch (< LAT. *Ausci*)

laydique, "of Laïs," Corinthian courtesan of the fifth century B.C., famed as the most beautiful woman of her time

laze < GRK. *laas*, "stone"

leans, O.FR., "inside"

Lebron = Lubéron

lectoyre = Lectoure

legne < O.PROV. *legna* < LAT. *lignum*, "wood"

lemā = Leman (Geneva)

lemures < LAT., "ghosts"

lengos (PROV.) = langues

lerme sabee, "Sabean tear": according to **Roberts**, a term formerly used to describe frankincense

les = lésé

les côter: apparent total misprint in II.62: rhyme suggests *la comete*, as per later editions

les deux malins: astrologically, Mars and Saturn

Lespe = l'épée

Lestore = Lectoure

leticie < LAT. *letum*, "death"

Liber (< LAT.) "the Book"

libere < LAT. *liber*, "free, open": **le Pere libere**, possibly **Calvin**

libinique = libyen

Libitine = Libitina, Roman goddess of death

ligne, "line, naval battle formation"

ligur, Ligurs, Ligurins: "Ligurian, Italian" < *Liguri*, former tribe of northern Italy and Provence

ligustique < LAT. *Ligusticus*, "Ligurian"

limbe (< LAT. *limbus*, "border"), "hem"

limé < O.FR. *liem*, "leash"), "bound"

l'imitrophe du Mans, "from near le Mans"

linterne: now village of Patria in Campania (Italy)

Liquiduct: either misprint for *l'aqueduct* or < LAT. *liquidus* + *ductus*, "conveyed by liquid"

livaigne (*l'avaigne* in later editions) = l'avoine, "oats"

Lizer = l'Isère

locz < LAT. *locus* = lieux

lôde = l'onde (q.v.)

Logarion: probable misprint for

Logmion: later editions have *Legation*

Logmion / logmyon = l'Ogmion: Ogmios, the Gallic version of Heracles/Hercules, as reported by the second-century Greek orator Lucian

loisel = l'oiseau

lon = dès longtemps

lone, la = lône, "pond"; or contraction of *l'Olonne*

longin < O.PROV. *longinc*, "afar"

lon orra = l'on ouïra = ouïr, "to hear" (cf. ENG. "Oyez! Oyez!")

lou (PROV.) = le

louera (< LAT. *locare*), "will hire, borrow"; or misprint for *jouira* (< LAT. *gaudere*) "will enjoy"

loy, "law": thus "authority, dominion, tradition"

loz < LAT. *laus, laudes*, "praise"

Lozan = Lausanne

loz de beurre: misprint (III.82) for *loz de guerre*, probably "war-honors or eulogy"

luite = lutte

lume < LAT. *lumen*, "light"

Luna, "moon, month"

Lunage: anagram for Lugano

lunaires = luminaires (cf. III.5)

lurne = l'Urne (Aquarius)

Lusitains, "inhabitants of Lusitania, Portuguese"

Lusitanie: classical name for Portugal

l'usitant = Lusitan, "Portuguese or western Iberian"

Lut[h]ece < LAT. *Lutetia*, "**Paris**"

lu ye: misprint for *luyre* in V.2 (cf. rhyme in line 3)

L.V.: unknown abbreviation

l'vrie: misprint for Ivry

Lygonnois (< LAT. *Lugdunum*, "**Lyon**"), "Lyonnais"

Lygustiq., lygustique < LAT. *Ligusticus*, "Ligurian": thus, "Italian"

lyman = Léman

lymbe: see **limbe**

lyphres < GRK. *lypros*, "persistent, indefatigable"

Lyris = L'iris, "the rainbow"

lys = fleur de lys: thus, "France"

M

Macedon: see **Aemathien**

macelin < LAT. *macellum*, "covered market": or < O.FR. **macelenc*, "maceling, mace-man"

macter < LAT. *mactare*, "to slaughter"

magna vaqua: either "great nothing" or *Magna Valca*, former port between Ravenna and Ferrara (**Cheetham**)

Magnes (LAT. "magnetic stone"), "magnesium oxide or peroxide"

Magonce < LAT. *Magontiacum*, "Mainz"

main < LAT. *manus*, "force," generally military

Maiotes < GRK. *Maiotai*, "Scythians"

malefice, "evil spell": thus "harm"

malencombre < O.FR. *malencontre*, "misfortune"

malfait < LAT. *malefacere*, "crime, malefaction"

malo sepmano (PROV.) = mauvaise semaine

Mandosus: see **Mendosus**

Mandragora: LAT., "mandrake"

manger: often used to mean "attack, snap at, devour"

maniples = manipules, "companies of soldiers"

mansol < LAT. *manus solis* (see **Mausol**)

Manthis < GRK. *mantis*, "prophet"

manubis: probably < LAT. *manibus*: thus "by forces" or "by armies"

Marc, l'unde de sainct: presumably the "sea of Venice," i.e. the Adriatic

Marceloyne = Macedoine, "Macedonia"

marestz = marais

Marius, Gaius: great Roman consul (elected seven times) and less-than-

brilliant general, most famed for defeating the German tribes: probable reference to Anne de **Montmorency**, High Constable of France between 1538 and 1567

marnegro < LAT. *mare nigrum*, "Black Sea"

Marquis du Pont = le Marquis du Pont à Mousson, perpetual title of the younger son of the House of Lorraine (**Cheetham**)

Mas, le = le Mas d'Agenais, near Agen

masles: misprint for *masses*, "sledge-hammers"

Massiliolique < LAT. *massilioticus*, "of **Marseille**"

mastin, le gros, "the Great Mastiff": conventional C16 term (see **Ronsard**) for Cerberus, classical "hound of hell" and two- or three-headed Guardian of the Underworld

mastine, beste, "mastiff": see **mastin**

mastinées < O.FR. "damaged, destroyed"

Mauris = mauresques, "Moors"

Mausol: reference to **St.-Paul-de-Mausole**, just south of **St.-Rémy**; but also apparently used by Nostradamus at V.57 and VIII.46 to refer to the Pope known as *Paul Manus Solis*, or "Paul-Handiwork-of-the-Sun" (generally supposed to be the present one), an evident reference to **St. Malachy**'s papal prophecies

maye < LAT. *Maia*, "May, maypole, May festival"

maynade, O.PR. *marinada* = ménage

Mede = Media (ancient kingdom of northern Iran)

Medusine, "of Medusa"

Mel(l)ite(s) < GRK. *Melite*, "Malta"

Memire, saint = St.-Merri (?)

Mendosus (LAT.), "full of errors or faults," in association with LAT. *mendax, -acis*, "lie, falsehood": thus the "Great Liar"

Meselle (*Mellele* or *Mole* in later editions): probable error for *Mellites*

mesgnie/mesnie < LAT. *mansionem*, "house(hold)"

mestre (< PROV. = maître), "colonel, first regimental company"

Methelin = Mitilini (Lesbos)

Meysinier/Mesnier: pseudo-anagram for *menuisier* (< LAT. *minutiare*, "to reduce, make small"), originally "hewer, carver, cutter, planer"

Migres, migre < LAT. *migrare*, "to go, leave"

Milannoile (misprint for *Milannoiſe*) "Milanese"

mil(l)ieu = mi-lieu, "central place": thus, "holy of holies"

milve < LAT. *miluus*, "kite"

miner = terminer

mittée < GRK. *mitos*, "string, thread" (?); or = **mittrée**

mittré, "mitered"; or slang "in prison"

Molite = Melite

monde = "people, population"

Monech < LAT. *Moneceus*, "Monaco"

Monet = *Monech*

monge < LAT. *monachus*, "monk"

monstre < LAT. *monstrum*, "omen"

mont Aymar = Montélimar (?)

mont Gaulsier (printed *mont Gaulsier* – not, note, *mont Gaulfier* if subsequent editions are to be believed), despite much hot air to the contrary on the part of some recent commentators): possibly = Gaule Cimonts, "Cisalpine Gaul" (i.e. Northern Italy)[F]. **Leroy** admittedly adduces an outcrop of the Alpilles close to **St.-Paul-de-Mausole** (compare V.57, line 4) known locally as *le Mont Gaussier* (formerly *Gausserius* or *Galserius*), but geographical puns (especially on this, his home area) are not unknown in Nostradamus.

Montpertuis: possibly Perthus Pass, Pyrenees (**Cheetham**); otherwise a possible reference to Pertuis, by the **Durance**, just south of the **Lubéron** and northeast of **Salon**

morbile < O.FR. "smallpox"

more = Maure, or misprint for LAT. *mare* or French *mort(e)*

Morre, saint = Saint-Maur, or St. Maur himself, founder of the French Benedictines

morrere = moudre, "to grind, mill"

Moufrin: misprint for Montfrin on Gard River

moulle = mouille

mueyre = mûr

Mule, "papal slipper"

mulet: "mule"; also possible ref. to Philip of Macedon's proverbial "mule laden with gold"

munismes < LAT. *munimenta*, "fortifications"; or misprint for *numismes* < LAT. *numisma*, coinage

murte: *meurtre* in later editions

murtri = meurtri

muy = Le Muy, southeast France

Myrmidon: code for Achilles or one of his followers: thus, "unquestioning, pitiless ruffian"

Myrnarmee = *Mimnermia*, a title of Venus (**Cheetham**); or portmanteau version of *armee des Myrmidons*

N

n'a garde = lit. "far be (it) from him"

nager, "to swim, be awash," but also "to navigate, sail" (< LAT. *navigare*)

Nanar: unidentified player in the drama, but possibly Namur

Nansol: misprint for Mausol; ref. to **St.-Paul-de-Mausole**, just north of **St.-Rémy-de-Provence**

naves = LAT. *naves*, "ships"

nay = né

ne: self-sufficient negative in sixteenth-century French

nef < LAT. *navis*, "ship"; also "vessel, nave (of church)," hence, "church"

nef d'oubly, "the boat of forgetting," i.e. that of the mythical Charon, ferry to the underworld

nefz < LAT. *naves*, "ships"

Negrepont < LAT. *niger*, "black" + GRK. *pontos*, "sea"

Negresilve < LAT. *Silva Nigra*, "Black Forest"

Nemans (LAT. *Nemausus*) = **Nîmes**

Neptune: *not* the planet (first discovered in 1846), but the Roman god of the sea, normally denoting England

nepveu < LAT. *nepotem*, "grandchild" or "descendant" (as in Rabelais)

nerte, la = La Nerthe, northwest of **Marseille**

ne tient: possible respelling of Nettuno (Italy) or Netanya (Israel)

neuf Arriens, "a new Arrian" (Greek soldier, statesman and historian)

neufve = neuve

nice (< LAT. *nescius*, "unknowing") "simple-minded"

Nicene, "of Nice"

Nicopolle: either Nikopol, Bulgaria, or the former Nicopolis, just north of Preveza, Greece: the latter seems more likely

Nictobriges, inhabitants of the Agen area

Nira: nonexistent place name, but anagram of Iran

Nisse = Nice

nocent (< LAT. *nocere*, "to hurt"), "villain, guilty" (opp. of *innocent*)

noir: may occasionally serve as pseudo-anagram for *roi*, but probably much less often than some commentators would suggest

noirs: Nostradamian code for Benedictines (**Cheetham**)

Nolle, "Nola" (near Naples)

nolte < LAT. *nolitus*, "unwanted"

nom pelle: often taken as anagram for *Montpelle* (Montpellier)

Nonnay = nonnain, "young nun," and thus "virgin" = the constellation Virgo

Nonseggle: possibly Nonza (Corsica), with improvized ending to rhyme with line 4

nore = Nora / Eleanor / Helen: or (< LAT. *nurus*) "daughter-in-law"

Noriques, montaignes: Noric Alps (< LAT. *Noricum* = Austria), stretching across much of Austria and Bavaria

NORLARIS: pseudo-anagram for *Lorraine*, signaled by usual capitals in first edition

Normans, "northerners"

norneigre = Norvège

north < ENG. (unusually)

notice, "knowledge"

Noudam = Houdan

noves < LAT. *novus*, "new"

nuech (PROV.) = nuit

O

obnubiler < LAT *obnubilare*, "to cloud over"

obsesse < LAT. *obsidere, obsessum*, "to besiege"

occis: p.p. of O.FR. *occire* < LAT. *occidere*, "to kill"

occult < LAT. *occultus*, "secret"

oesteuf: former name for tennis-ball

Ogmion, Ogmios, Ogmius: the mythical Gallic version of the classical Hercules

oingt = oint

olchade < GRK. *holkas, -ados*, "cargo-ship"; error for *olchades* (as

printed in later editions), to rhyme with *Ciclades* in line 3 of III.64

Olestant < GRK. *olesthos*, "destruction," *oleter*, "destroyer, murderer"

ombriche: possibly = Ombrie, "Umbria"

oncq/onqs/oncques = jamais

onde = eau, mer

onuste: corrupt der. from LAT. *onus*, "burden"

Oppi: abbrev. for *opium*(?)

opposite < LAT. *oppositus*, "facing, adjacent, next"

or: (1) "gold," (2) misprint for au

orant < LAT. *orare*, "to pray"; or (more likely) = oyant < *ouïr*, "to hear"

orchestra: area of theater in front of stage

ord (O.FR.) < LAT. *horridus*, "filthy, disgusting": cf. modern *ordure*

Orguion, l' = l'Orgueilleux (?): Nostradamus never hesitates to mangle his endings in order to make a rhyme

oron, l' = Oloran

orra < *ouïr*, "to hear"

os: "bones," but also misprint for *or(d)*

oscueil = écueil, "reef, rocks"

ospbre: misprint for *opprobre*, "opprobrium, disgrace"

ost < O.FR. *host*, "army"

Ostun = Autun

outre, "beyond"

ouy = ouïr, "to hear"

ouye = ouïe, "heard"

oyes = ouïes

P

pache < LAT. *pax*, "peace, truce, pact"

palmerin, "of the (ceremonial or triumphal) palm-tree"

pamplation: fake adjective < *Pampelune*, "Pamplona" to rhyme with *oblation*

Pannon(i)e < LAT. *Pannonia*, region centred on Hungary, and including northern Croatia and western Romania

Pannons: inhabitants of **Pannonia**: in classical times the region, centered on Hungary, was largely Slav and partially Celtic, but not yet racially Ugric

Panos = **Pannons**

Pánta choina philòn: misspelling of GRK. *Pánta chiona philòm*, "all things held in common among friends" (**Cheetham**)

par: often used for *pour*

parc, "park"; but also < LAT. *parcus*, "economical, frugal, sparing"

PAR. CAR. NERSAF: presumably **Paris, Carcassonne** and (by anagram) France

Par dons lænees (possibly *Pardons laenées*): meaning unclear, but see **laenées**

parenter: dubious, but possibly < *par + enterrer*, "to bury finally"

pareure (O.FR.) "preparation," and thus eventually "ornament"

parfond[e]ra < LAT. *perfundere*, "to fill, imbue, sprinkle, moisten"; also "to fill with apprehension," and thus "to disturb, disquiet, alarm"

par foy par roy = *parfois parroi* (as per

later editions), or an unintended repetition by printer

par more < LAT. *per mare*, "by sea"; later editions have *par morte*, "through death" (?)

par mort articles = à l'article de la mort, "on the point of death"

par paix se minera = par le pays se (dissé)minera

Parpan = Perpignan

parque: see **parc**: in pl., "the Fates"

pars = parts: thus, "portions," or (O.FR.) "confinements, births"; also < LAT., "equal," and thus "peer"

partiaulx, "partisan"

passe: pres. tense of passer; or misprint for *pasle*

patrer < LAT. *patrare*, "to achieve, commit, perform"

Pau = generally not Pau in the Basses Pyrénées, but the Po River in northern Italy

paye: later editions have playe

peaultre < LAT. *paluster, -ris*, "foul, dirty, unclean, vicious"

pecune < LAT. *pecunia*, "money"

Pelligouxe: either Pellegrue, northeast of La Réole, or **Pélissanne**, just east of **Salon**

pellix < LAT. *pellex*, "concubine"

Peloncle: possible Nostradamian version of Mt. Pelion, Greece, typically mangled to rhyme and scan

Pempotan < GRK. *pan*, "all" + LAT. *potens*, "powerful": favorite Nostradamian invented word

percee, "way in"

perecliter, "to imperil"

pere Denis: probably St. Denis, patron saint of France (feastday October 9th)

Pere Liber, "Free Father": possibly John **Calvin**

perfetant < LAT. *per + fetere*, "to stink utterly"

perhume < LAT. *per humum*, "on the ground": see **chausses**

perinthe: modern Eski Eregli (**Cheetham**), but some later editions have *Corinthe*

Perme = Parme, "Parma"

pernicant < LAT. *pernecare*, "to kill"

pernicie < LAT. *per + nex, necis*, "death by violence"

Perouse: either Pérouges in the **Rhône** valley east of **Lyon**, or (more normally) Perugia in Italy

perse, "Iranian"; or "blue" (cf. Rabelais)

pertinax, LAT., "holding fast"

Perusin, "of Perugia"

Perynte: probable misreading for *Corynthe* (cf. V.90)

pesche < LAT. *piscis*, "fish"

Pesquiere = Peschiera, Italy

pestifere: "plague-bearing"

Phanaticque < LAT. *Sinus Flanaticus*: Gulf of Kvarner, Croatia

Pharos: in most cases probably stands for the Greek island of Paros rather than Alexandria's ancient lighthouse-island

phintriase = phthiriasis (infestation with lice)

Phoce, Phocen, Phocean (< LAT. *Phocaea*), "(of) **Marseille**"

Phocens, "people from **Marseille**" (< LAT. *Phocaea*)

Phossens: see **Phocens**

piege < LAT. *pedica*, "foot-bindings, shackles": hence modern "snare, trap"

pierre, (1) "rock, stone," (2) = piéride, "Muse, butterfly" (esp. cabbage white), (3) possibly "ax" (**Cheetham**)

pique? = pique! (? is often printed for ! in the 2nd edition)

piques, "arms": thus, by extension, "armies" (cf. *piquet*)

piramide: local term for pillar of stone left by Romans in middle of ancient stone quarry at **Glanum**, **St.-Paul-de-Mausole**, just north of **St.-Rémy-de-Provence**

piscature (< LAT. *piscator*), "fisherman," notably St. Peter, and thus "the Pope"

pitié < LAT. *pietas*, "pity, piteousness," but originally < LAT. *pietas, pietatem*, "piety"

Pize & Luc: Pisa and Lucca

plancente / placente < Lat *placenta*, "flat cake"

Plancus: Lucius Munatius Plancus, founder of **Lyon** in 43 B.C.

plaige < O.FR. *pleige*, "pledge"

pleigant: presumed misprint for *piegeant*

plic (< LAT. *plicare*, to fold) = pli, "envelope"

ploiera = pliera

plume au vent, "trusting to luck"

Plus oultre, "further away": epithet historically applied to himself by the Emperor **Charles V**

poccilateur < LAT., "cupbearer"

pœn' / Peonus < LAT. *(Alpes) Poeninae*, "Pennine Alps"

pole < GRK. *polis*, "town, city"

polemars = O. PROV. "twine, cord" (**Cheetham**)

Pol mensolee = St.-Paul-de-Mausole, but also < LAT. *Paulus Manus Solis*, "Paul-Handiwork-of-the-Sun": see **Mausol**

Ponant (< LAT. *ponere*), "occident, west" (= couchant)

pong(n)ale < O.FR. *poignal*, "dagger"

pont: usually < GRK. *pontos*, "sea"; but also "bridge" or (as abbrev. for *tête de pont*) "bridgehead"

Ponteroso = "Red Sea"

pont Euxine, "Black Sea"

porc: "pig," or misprint for *port*

porceau, demi: possible reference to Milan, via mythical discovery of sheep-pig hybrid at city's foundation

port: misprint for *pont* < GRK. *pontos*, "sea"

porte, normally "door," but also "Sublime Porte," chief office of Ottoman Empire

porteur = porteur de nouvelles

posthume, "posthumous," thus "last-born"

postulaire (printed *poſtulaire*): later editions have *populaire*

Pouille, la = l'*Apulie*, Apulia (Puglia), southeastern Italy

poulse (< LAT. *pulsus*) = poussé

pour: often used for *par*

Praytus = Proteus

prediteurs = prédateurs (as in later editions); or = prédicateurs

predons < LAT. *praeda*, "booty"

preme (< LAT. *premere*, "press, arrest"), "pressure, aggression, pursuit"

presults < LAT., "preemptive attacks"

preteur < LAT. *praetor*, "governor, ruler"

preture, "Praetorship": thus, rulership, governorship or some other high position

prime, "springtime"

prins (< LAT. *prehensus*) = pris

prinsault, de, "at the first attack"

prinse (< LAT. *prehensa*) = prise, "taken": note careful noun/adjective agreement throughout, except where necessary to make rhyme

print: misprint for *prins(e)*

procere < LAT. *proceres*, "high-born first citizen"; or misprint for *procree*

prodigés < LAT. *prodigere* < *prod* + *agere*, "to drive forth" sometimes misprint for *profligés*

proditeur < LAT. *proditor*, "traitor"

profligeant < LAT. *profligare*, "to dash forward, overthrow"

profligés/proffligez < LAT. *profligati*, "dashed forward, overthrown, defeated"

promontoire, dresser, "to stand forth"

propin, abbrev. of LAT. *propinquus*, "near"

proterve < LAT. *protervus*, "wanton, perverse, peevish"

prou, "much, very"

Ptolon: disguised and "Hellenized" form of *Toulon*

pugne < LAT. *pugna*, "battle"

puids < LAT. *podium*, "parapet"

pui nay / puis nay = puîné, "younger" (of two brothers)

puits, "well," but also "hole, shaft, cockpit"

punique (< LAT. *Punicus*, "Carthaginian"), "North African"

Punique fuste, "African shallow-draft galley"

purgé, "purged," thus (literally), "having had its bowels emptied"

puy = appui

Pymond = Piedmont, northern Italy

Pyr. = Pyrenees

pyre < GRK./LAT. *pyra*, "fire": thus, *clere pyre* = "bright fire"

Q

quant & quant < LAT. *quantum*, "how many"

quarree = (place) carrée; unless intended to mean "apartment"

que: vague function in sixteenth-century French; often used for *qui*

querre = querir, quérir

Quintin = St.-Quentin

quirinal, "of Quirinus" (Romulan version of Mars)

qui tient ne tient = qui tient Netanya (or possibly Nettuno in Italy) (?)

quyretes = *Curetes*, priest-warriors who protected the infant Zeus on Crete

R

rabieuse = rabique, "rabid"

raffe ne riffe, probably < *rafler*, "to sack, carry off" + *riffe*, "fire"

Raguse = Ragusa, either the town in southern Sicily or modern Dubrovnik, Croatia

rameau, literally "branch": thus often "relation, offspring, descendant"

ramee = rameau

ramer, "to row," and thus, "to swim"; or = *raméaire/ramaire*, "consequently"

ranc = rang

rane = < LAT. *rana*, "frog"; but also = ranula (MED.: cyst under tongue)

Rapis: anagram for **Paris**

raugon: possibly misprint for *rançon*, or version of *ouragan*, "hurricane"

ravasseurs, see **vavasseurs**

raves = ravages; later editions have *rues*

raviere < *ravir*, "to ravish, snatch"

RAYPOZ: anagram of *PAY. ROZ* = pays (de la) rose (q.v.)

Razes, "shaven": often abbrev. for *tetes razes*, "shaven heads," normal sixteenth-century term for Protestants

Reb < LAT. *ruber*, "red"

Recloing: possible corruption of *rejoinct* < LAT. *rejunctio*, "reunion"

recordz (< LAT. *recordari*, "to recall"), "remembrance, witness"

recteur < LAT. *rector*, "ruler"; but see also LAT. *rectus*, "right"

reduire < LAT. *reducere*, "to lead back"

referer < LAT. *referre*, "to reproduce, represent"

reflux = reflux, "ebb tide"

refus d'Anthoine, le: possible ref. to St. Anthony's celebrated withdrawal from society

Rege: either < LAT. *rex, regis*, "king," or one of the two Reggios in Italy

regne = "kingdom, government, power"

Reims: may occasionally stand for Rennes

Rein(e)s = version of Rheims

remort = re + mordre

reperse < LAT. *respergere*, "to sprinkle, spatter"

reposé / repousé < LAT. *repausare*, "to stop or cease again"

reprinse = reprise

repu: p.p. of *repaître*, "to feed"

resdonce: misprint for *response*

reserant = reserrant, "keeper, locker-up"

reseré = re + serrer

reserer = resserrer, "to put by, lock away"

resneurs: misprint for *resveurs* = rêveurs

ressasies = rassasiés, "satisfied, placated"

resver = rêver

resverie, normally "dreaming," but also < LAT. *(r)aestuare*, "to boil, seethe" or *exvagare*, "to prowl"

Resviers: possible misprint for *Besiers* (**Béziers**)

revaler = ravaler

revolue < LAT. *revolutus*, "having achieved its circuit or course": thus (of astrological prophecy) "fulfilled"

revolution < LAT. *revolutio*, "return or revolution of stars": thus "prophetic fulfillment" (see **revolue**)

ribe < LAT. *ripa*, "shore" (hence "Riviera")

Ribiere = Rivière, "Riviera"; or "Rivera" (?)

riblée, "trued up, dressed" (generally of millstone)

rieges: probable misprint for *lieges*, Nostradamian coinage for *bindings* (< LAT. *ligare*, "to bind")

roche (V.32) (rhyme-imposed substitution) read "pierre": the book of Revelation here apparently referred to contains no "seventh rock"; also = Gibraltar

Rodanes < LAT. *Rhodanus*, "**Rhône**"

roge = rouge

Romanie: either Romania or Roman domains in general

Rome = occasional misprint for **Rhône**

Ro(u)an = Rouen

Roane = Roanne

rose: national Iranian emblem signifying the blood of Islamic (Shia) martyrs

Roubine = Robine (River), tributary of Aude River

rouges: normally "reds," but occasionally short for *chapeaux rouges*, "Roman Catholic cardinals"

route, "road," but also (< LAT. *rupta*, "broken") "rout"

routte (< LAT. *rugitus*, "reddening"), "rut, sexual excitement"

rubre < LAT. *ruber*, "red"

rubriche (< LAT. *rubrica*), "red" (originally chalk)

S

s. = saint(s)

sabee: "Sabean," or "Mandaean": see under **lerme sabee**

Sacarbance < LAT. *Scarbantia*, "Sopron" (**Cheetham**)

Sagont = Sagunto, Spain

saigne = saignée, "drainage-ditch"

Saillinons: possible variant of *Salonois*, "inhabitants of **Salon**"; or < IT. *Savigliano*

Salin, "salt-marsh," but possible play on **Salon**, itself originally surrounded by salt-marshes

sallon < O.FR. *saillant*, "sallying forth": play on the name of Nostradamus's hometown

salvaterre < LAT. *salvat terram*, "saves the land"; or one of the various Salvatieras in Spain

Samarobryn (pl.) < *Samarobriva*, Celtic name for Amiens, possibly used as geographical pun-cum-portmanteau-word referring to *Samaritain(s)*

sang, feu, "blood and fire," or = s'enfuit

sang Mathien = Saint Matthieu (?)

sang Troyen, lit. "Trojan blood": reference to alleged Trojan origin of French royal line, as celebrated by **Ronsard** in his abortive and uncompleted *Franciade*

sanguin, "bloody"

saouler < soûler, "to satisfy, quench"

sapience < LAT. *sapientia*, "wisdom"

saran (PROV.) = sauront

Sardon: misprint for *Gardon*, another name for the **Gard** River at **Nîmes**

sarrés: possibly < Sarra, town of Phoenicia

s'atacquer = s'attacher

Saturne = Saturn, but also = Saint Saturnin (St.-Sernin), esp. at **Toulouse**

Saturnins: parishioners of St.-Sernin

Sault Castallon < LAT. *Saltus Castulonensis*: Sierra Morena (**Cheetham**)

saults = assauts

Saurome < LAT. *Sauromates*, "Sarmathia," vague area between Baltic and Caspian seas

Savillan = Savigliano, Italy

Saxe, "Saxony" (?)

sceptes = scepters

sceptre, le = scepter, thus also the celestial ruler, Jupiter

sceptrifere, "scepter-bearing"

scyphe < GRK. *skyphos*, "cup, chalice"

se (printed *ſe*): occasionally misprint for *le* and *si*

Secatombe: misprint for *hecatombe*, "ritual sacrifice"

second banc macelin (< LAT. *macellum*, "market"), "on the back stall of the market"

secte, "sect," but also possibly "cut off": in Nostradamus's eyes, any sect other than the Roman Catholic mainstream was by definition heretical and "cut off"

sedifrages < LAT. "seat-breakers": thus, possibly "destroyers of the Vatican"

seez & Ponce = Sées et Pons

seille < LAT. *situla* = seau, "bucket"

Seisset: misprint for Seissel = Seyssel

sel, literally "salt," but more often "wisdom, counsel"

se leur sembloit = ainsi leur sembloit-il, "so it seemed to them"

selin, selline < GRK. *Selene*, goddess of the moon: thus "(he/they of the lunar) Crescent, the Muslims"

semond < LAT. *submonere*, "to advise secretly"

senestre (< LAT. *sinister*), "left, of left-hand path, sinister"

Senis = Cenis

Senoise = misprint for *Genoise*, "of Genoa"

sentine, "bilges"

sentu, "perfumed, scented" (?)

sepmano (PROV.) = semaine

Septentrionale, "of the Septentrion, or Great Bear": thus, "northern"

sepulchre = sépulture

sepulturer < LAT., "to bury"

seraphicque < *Seraphims*, *l'Ordre des*, original title of the Franciscans

serve, "in bondage"

seul = "alone": at I.1 possibly < O.FR. *seel* (MOD. FR. *seau*), "bucket," or contraction of *s[on] oeil*; elsewhere "solitary one," apparent Nostradamian term for monk or priest

seur = sûr

Sex = abbrev. for LAT. *Sextus*: part of inscription on civic arch at **St.-Paul-de-Mausole**, just north of **St.-Rémy-de-Provence**

sexe, "sex," but more often homonym of *sectes*

SEXT., "Sextus," erector of the Roman mausoleum at **Glanum** (**St.-Rémy**); also possible geographical pun and Nostradamian blind for (LAT.) *(per)secutus*: capitals often signal some kind of "special" treatment in Nostradamus

siecle (< LAT. *saeculum*, "generation") = cycle, order, age, era

siegen (PROV.): read as *seront*

signe < LAT. *signum*, "trace, mark"

si ingere = s'y ingère

silene = Selin (see above)

sillera = filera (?)

silve < LAT. *silva*, "wood, forest"

simulte < LAT. *simultas*, "rivalry"

sinus < LAT., "bay"

sitant = (si) tant

sitine: problematical, but possibly = *sistine*, "of Sextus," ref. to Raphael's celebrated depiction of Sixtus II with the Madonna, signifying divine approval of the Vatican

Socile = Sicile, "Sicily"

soiller = souiller

solaires: opposite of *lunaires* – thus, "those who oppose the Muslims"

sol alegro, "in bright sunlight"

Soliman: more correct spelling of "Suleiman" (the Magnificent): thus, by extension, any comparable eastern Muslim leader

Sologne / Soulongne = Sologne, flat marshy area of swamps and lakes in central France between the Loire and Cher rivers, just east of Blois

soluz = LAT. *solus*, "sole, solitary, alone"

somentrée = misprint for *surmontée*

son(n)és, "found out"

sophe < GRK. *sophos*, "sage"

Sorbin: Serbia (< SERBIAN *srb*)

so sag: misprint for *sõ sã* = son sang

soubmets = "[I] subjugate, put down"

soucq < ARABIC *suq* ("market place"); some later editions have *sud*

soucsue < LAT. *succulentus*, "sweet"

souldars = soldats

souspir < LAT. *suspicere*, "to look askance"

soustenement = soutenance, "support"

soy = se

spches: later editions have *proches*

sperants < LAT. *sperantes* = espérant(s)

stecades < LAT. *Stoechades* = les Isles d'Hyères

subdite < LAT. *subducta*, "dragged under"

subjourner (< LAT. *subdiurnare*) = séjourner

subrogé < LAT. *subrogatus*, "surrogate, substituted"

Sueves < LAT. *Suevi* = Swabians (inhabitants of the area comprising southeast Germany and Switzerland)

superateur < LAT. *superator*, "victor"

superbe < LAT. *superbus*, "proud, haughty"

superee < LAT. *superatus*, "overcome"

superstie: misprint for *supersite* (as rhyme reveals) = sursise, "stayed, delayed"

supperee (< LAT. *superare*, "to overcome, defeat"), "defeated"

sur < LAT. *super*, "above"

Sur le canon du respiral estaige = *Sur le canon dur et spiral étage*, "Both on the battlefield and in academic circles" (?). The seer's own house has a particularly fine stone spiral staircase.

surrez: possibly *surets*, "young apple-trees"

symacle < GRK. *symmachis*, "allied"

T

TAG < GRK. *tagma*, "body of soldiers or ordinance"

Tag. = Tagus

Tamins = Tamise, "Thames": thus, "England"

Tamise, "Thames": thus, "England"

tant à un cop = tout à coup

taras = **Tarascon** on the **Rhône**

tare, "loss, damage"

Tarpee, mont, "Tarpeian rock," ancient Rome's place of execution

Tarracon(n)e: either **Tarascon** or Tarragona, but possibly a double Nostradamian pun standing for Catalonia and thus (via a secondary twist) for the *Catalaunian Fields*, near Troyes, where Attila the Hun was defeated on June 24th, 451, by an alliance of Romans (Italians) and Visigoths (French) – who would then be the *amis de Tarracone* of VII.22.

Tartarie, la grande, "Greater Tartary," i.e. Turkestan, comprising most of central Asia including much of western China.

tasché = attaché

Taur: Notre Dame de Taur, **Toulouse**

tauropole < GRK. *taurobolos*, "bull sacrifice, slaughter"

teccon < *teck*, a former game for academics

tedesqu (< IT.), "German"

tempiera = *(t')empierrera*, "will pave (you)" (?)

tempter = tenter, "to touch, feel, try"

Tenant: misprint for *Ton(n)ant* (see below)

tension < LAT. *tensio, -nis*, O.FR. *tenson*, "struggle, quarrel"

terax < GRK. *teras*, "omen, sign, wonder, monster"

terre: occasionally = terreur

terrouer: old form of *terroir*

tertre ("mound, knoll") = terre, "land" (as per later editions), partly disguised so as to resemble *tefte* (teste), "head"; or possibly the waking Nostradamus had the typical Babylonian "tell," or city-mound in mind

Tesin / Thesin = (river) Ticino

Tholo Bay. = **Toulouse**, Bayonne

Tholose / Tholoze / Tholosse < Pre-Roman *Tolosa* = **Toulouse**

Tholossain, "of **Toulouse**"

throsne, "throne"; but possibly = *thrène*

< GRK. *threnos*, "lament"

Thunes = Tunis

Ticin = Ticino: thus, "Pavia"

tiedera = tiendra

Timbre = Tiber

toc: *au toc de la campano* (PROV.), "at the sound of the alarm-bell"

tollu < LAT. *tollere*, "to lift up"

ton = taon

Tonant, "Thunderer": thus, Jupiter

torte / tortu (O.FR.) = tordu

tournera = retournera

tourt = tourtre (< LAT. *turtur*), "dove"

tout sexe deu = de tout sexe (?)

tradiment (O. FR.), "betrayal"

traducteur, "translator," but also "betrayer"

trailler < LAT. *trahere*, "to drag, haul": *tranche & traille* = "draw and quarter" (?)

trammer, se = se tramer, "to be hatched, plotted"

tramontane < IT. *tramontana*, "north wind," originally from over the Alps into northern Italy

tranner < LAT. *tranare*, "to cross over, swim across"

translat(é) < LAT. *transferre, -latum*, "carried across, transferred"

Trapesonce: see **trebisonde**

trassés = tracés

trebisonde = Trebizond (modern Trabzon in Turkey)

trehemide: probable Nostradamian invention for *tremblement*

treilhos (PROV.) = treilles

Tresmenien = Lake Trasimeno, Italy

treuve (< FRANKISH *'triuwa*: cf. GERM. *Treue*) = trève, "truce"

trible = later editions have *crible*, "sieve, screen"

Tricastin: area covering parts of the départements of Drôme and Vaucluse in southeastern France

Tridental = the area around Trento (< LAT. *Tridentium*)

trinacrie < GRK. *Trinakria* ("three points"), "Sicily"

Tripolis, Chio: possibly Tripolis and Chios in Greece, but more likely disguise-words for the Turkish fishing-port of Tirebolu, to the west of Trabzon (*Trapesonce*), and Sochi, on the Russian Black Sea coast

trixe < GRK. *thrix*, "hair, wool, fleece"

troche < GRK. *trochos*, "wheel": thus, "cycle"

trois = très, via LAT. *tres* (?)

trombe, "water-spout"; or *trompe*, "trumpeting"

trophee, "victory-memorial"

troutent: possibly either *troussent* ("they bundle up") or *tronquent*, "they truncate, cut back")

trucidé < LAT. *trucidare*, "to slaughter"

Tucham: reference to the Revolt of the Tuchins of 1382–4, a peasant rebellion against the Church and aristocracy of **Toulouse** and elsewhere in southwestern France

tumbe (< LAT. *tumbare*) = tombe

Turinge = Thuringia

Tustie, "Tuscany"

Tycin = Ticino River

tyfon: see **Typhon**
Tymbre = Tiber
Typhon = Typhon, fire-breathing giant of Greek mythology, cognate with Mount Etna, and thus also with volcanos and earthquakes
Tyrren = Tyrrhenian *and/or* tyrant, "dictator, ruler" (in early Greek the sense was not necessarily pejorative)
Tyrrene = the Tyrrhenian Sea to the west of Italy
tyson = tison, "firebrand, half-burned log"; but see *tyfon*

U

uberté < LAT. *ubertas*, "abundance, plenty"; or misprint for *liberté*
Ulme = *mule* (anagram), "papal slipper"
Ulpian: *Ulpius* was one of the names of the Emperor Trajan
umbre = omber
un / un': sometimes used for *une*
undans (< LAT. *undo*, "to wave, be agitated"), "waving, rolling, agitated"
unde = onde
unde de sainct Marc, l', "the waters of Venice"
un versie: (should read *versien* to rhyme with *Athenien* in line 2, as in later editions): corruption of *en Verseau*, "in Aquarius"
urben < LAT. *urbem* (acc.), "town, city"
urne / urna (LAT.), "water-jar," presumably the celestial one of Aquarius: hence, January or February
Urnel Vaucile: possible misprint for "Drôme et Vaucluse"

Ustagois < LAT. *usus*, "exercisers of ancient rights, tenants"
Uticense (LAT. *Castrum Uteciense*) = Uzès, north of **Nîmes**

V

vaisseaux, "naves": thus, "churches"
Valen. cent = *Valence sont*
vapin, "from Vapincuum" (= Gap, present-day capital of Hautes Alpes)
vasacle = Basacle
vast < LAT. *vastare*, "to lay waste"; or < LAT. *vastum*, "devastation"; or < LAT. *vastus*, "devastated"
Vast = Vasto, Italy
vastée < LAT. *vastare*, "to lay waste, devastate"
vavasseurs < LAT. *vassis vassorum*, "vassal of vassals" – i.e. lowest of the low
vefue = veuve
velle < LAT. *velum, -a* = voile
venguddos (PROV.) = venus
venin, "poison *or* medicine," by analogy with Grk *pharmakon*: thus, "drugs"
Venitiens, "Venetians": thus, "Italians"
venne, la = *l'aveine* (< LAT. *avena*), former spelling of l'avoine, "oats"
Vent Aquilon, "the north wind"
Venus = Venus; but sometimes = Venise; the city of Venice was formerly known as *Stella Maris*, the "star of the sea" (i.e. Venus again)
venuste < LAT. *venustus*, "charming, agreeable"
ver, LAT., "spring"
Verbiesque (< MED. FR. *verbier*, "to

chatter"), "of words," disguised as fake place name in familiar Nostradamian fashion
Verceil = Vercelli
Vermine, rogne = Vermine ronge
Vernai (Varneigne in later editions) = **Vernègues** (though neither version rhymes properly with *aigre* in line 4 of III.99)
verrier < LAT. *verres*, "boar"
Verseil = Vercelli
ver. serp < LAT. *versus serpens*, "snake coiled back on itself, coiled serpent"
versien < verseau: thus, "Aquarian"
vestales, LAT. *Vestales*, originally virgins sacred to the state goddess Vesta, Roman equivalent of the Greek Hestia: in Nostradamus, standard code for Roman Catholic nuns
Veste, "Vesta," Roman goddess of hearth and fire: probable ref. to her temple servants, the Vestal Virgins
vestutisque, "decaying, decrepit, rusty"
veu = vu
veutz: misprint for *veulx*; or = voeux (< LAT. *votum*)
Ve ve < LAT. *vae*, "woe"
viendra = se vendra (?)
vierge: possible misprint for *verge* (III.44)
Viglanne & Resviers: difficult to identify: the former could be either Le Vigan in France, or Vigliano or Viggiano in Italy; the latter Revere in Italy
vindication, "revenge"

vindicte (< LAT. *vindicta*), "vengeance"
vin (et) sel: literally "wine, wit"
vire, crossbow-bolt designed to twist (**Fontbrune**)
vitrix < LAT. *victrix*, "female conqueror"
Vitry: possibly Vitry-le-François, south of Châlons-sur-Marne, founded by François I in Nostradamus's own lifetime to replace Vitry-en-Perthois, destroyed by Imperial troops
vitupere, "vituperator, abuser, reviler"
vobisque = (*Dominus*) *vobiscum* (LAT.), "The Lord be with you"
voguera < LAT. *vocare*, "to call"
voil(l)e, ("sail") = "ship, fleet"
volataille = volatile, "light, winged"
Volsicque / volsques / volsqs < LAT. *Vocae*, "people of the Languedoc"
vopisque = **vobisque**
vorer = dévorer
vrie, l': misprint for *Ivry*, either a suburb of **Paris** or one of at least two other northern French towns of the same name
V.S.C. / U.S.C.: unknown abbreviation
vuyder = vider

Y

Yrés, "irate," < LAT. *ira*, "anger"
yssu < O.FR. *issir*, "to issue forth"

Z

Zara = the port of Zadar (Croatia)
Zersas: generally assumed to be a transcription of *Xerxes*

INDEX TO INTERPRETATIONS

SUBJECT INDEX